THE
CARAVAN
& CAMPING
GUIDE
2019

Published by AA Publishing, a trading name of AA Media Limited, whose registered office is Fanum House, Basing View, Basingstoke, Hampshire RG21 4EA. Registered number 06112600

© AA Media Limited 2018

51st edition 2018

The contents of this publication are believed correct at the time of printing. Nevertheless, the publishers cannot be held responsible for any errors or omissions or for any changes in the details given in this guide or for the consequences of any reliance on the information provided by the same. This does not affect your statutory rights.

Assessments of the AA campsites are based on the experience of the AA Caravan & Camping Inspectors on the occasion(s) of their visit(s) and therefore descriptions given in this guide necessarily contain an element of subjective opinion which may not reflect or dictate a reader's own opinion on another occasion. See pages 10–11 for a clear explanation of how, based on our Inspectors' inspection experiences, campsites are graded.

AA Media Limited strives to ensure accuracy of the information in this guide at the time of printing. Due to the constantly evolving nature of the subject matter the information is subject to change. AA Media Limited will gratefully receive any advice from our readers of any necessary updated information.

For any enquiries relating to this guide, please contact lifestyleguides@theAA.com

Website addresses are included in some entries as specified by the respective establishment. Such websites are not under the control of AA Media Limited and as such AA Media Limited has no control over them and will not accept any responsibility or liability in respect of any and all matters whatsoever relating to such websites including access, content, material and functionality. By including the addresses of third party websites the AA does not intend to solicit business or offer any security to any person in any country, directly or indirectly.

Photographs in the gazetteer are provided by the establishments. The acknowledgements for all other images are on page 463.

This guide was compiled by the AA Lifestyle Guides team and Servis Filmsetting Ltd, Stockport.

Country and county opening page descriptions: Nick Channer.

Cover design: Austin Taylor

A version of Pitch Perfect on pages 20–26 first appeared in issue 1 of *Quality Matters*, an AA Publication.

Maps prepared by the Mapping Services Department of AA Publishing.

Maps © AA Media Limited 2018.

Contains Ordnance Survey data © Crown copyright and database right 2018.

Ireland map contains data available from openstreetmap.org © under the Open Database License found at opendatacommons.org

A CIP catalogue record for this book is available from the British Library.

Printed in Italy by Printer Trento.

ISBN: 978-0-7495-7985-2

A05632

Visit www.theaa.com/camping

Contents

Welcome to the AA Caravan & Camping Guide 2019

Last year, the AA Caravan and Camping Guide turned 50. As we look ahead to the next half century, there's much to be excited about. More and more people are spending their holidays in the UK and a trip outdoors – in a tent, caravan, glamping site or motorhome – is how they're choosing to go about it.

Keep innovating

Today's campers, often newcomers to the scene, are seeking new and interesting ways to spend a night under the stars. Glamping options are now a common feature at many sites and you can expect to see wooden pods, tipis, yurts, bell tents, safari tents, shepherd's huts, vintage caravans and the like across the UK. This guide lists more than 200 places where you can choose to camp in luxury – check out our list on pages 44–47.

And it's not just about new forms of camping. More sites than ever before are expanding and upgrading their offering and facilities. Last year's Campsite of the Year, The Old Oaks Touring Park in Glastonbury, Somerset, speaks of the need to keep innovating in our main feature (see pages 20–26).

Award-winning sites

Following nominations by our inspectors, we award an overall Campsite of the Year winner (page 14) from four national finalists; five regional winners, a Glamping winner and a Holiday Centre winner. All are selected for their outstanding overall quality and high levels of customer care and all of them have not stopped in their pursuit of the perfect park. Two special awards recognise the best small campsite, and the most improved campsite.

Platinum Pennants

To recognise this push for ever higher standards, we have introduced a Platinum award, given to parks with a quality score of 95% and above with a 5-Pennant grading. There are 36 'Platinum Parks' in this year's guide – see page 32 for a full list.

The best sites

There are so many ways to recognise a quality site. In addition to the Pennant ratings and quality scores, we also provide quick reference lists (pages 28–32) that detail the AA inspectors' favourite campsites. For example, it might be because the park has stunning views or a good restaurant on site.

There are so many different ways to choose a place to stay and we hope you find this guide invaluable in helping you plan your next foray into the great outdoors.

How to use the
AA Caravan & Camping Guide

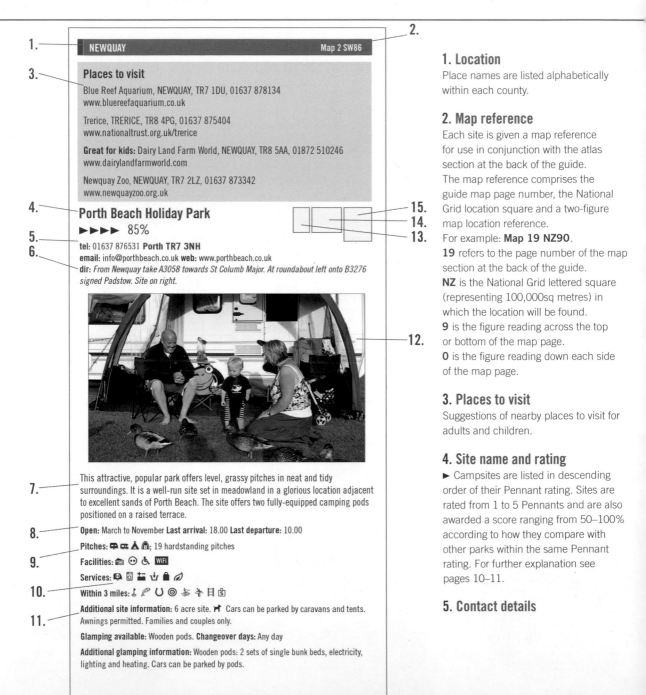

1. NEWQUAY   Map 2 SW86

2.

3. **Places to visit**

Blue Reef Aquarium, NEWQUAY, TR7 1DU, 01637 878134
www.bluereefaquarium.co.uk

Trerice, TRERICE, TR8 4PG, 01637 875404
www.nationaltrust.org.uk/trerice

Great for kids: Dairy Land Farm World, NEWQUAY, TR8 5AA, 01872 510246
www.dairylandfarmworld.com

Newquay Zoo, NEWQUAY, TR7 2LZ, 01637 873342
www.newquayzoo.org.uk

4. **Porth Beach Holiday Park**

▶▶▶▶ 85%

15.
14.
13.

5. **tel:** 01637 876531 **Porth TR7 3NH**

6. **email:** info@porthbeach.co.uk **web:** www.porthbeach.co.uk
dir: *From Newquay take A3058 towards St Columb Major. At roundabout left onto B3276 signed Padstow. Site on right.*

12.

7. This attractive, popular park offers level, grassy pitches in neat and tidy surroundings. It is a well-run site set in meadowland in a glorious location adjacent to excellent sands of Porth Beach. The site offers two fully-equipped camping pods positioned on a raised terrace.

8. **Open:** March to November **Last arrival:** 18.00 **Last departure:** 10.00

9. **Pitches:** 🚐 🚙 ⛺ 🏠; 19 hardstanding pitches

Facilities: 🏪 ⊙ ♿ WiFi

Services: 🚽 🚿 🧺 ♨ 🔒 🌀

10. **Within 3 miles:** 🚶 🎣 ∪ ◎ 🏇 🚴 🎯 💲

11. **Additional site information:** 6 acre site. 🚗 Cars can be parked by caravans and tents. Awnings permitted. Families and couples only.

Glamping available: Wooden pods. **Changeover days:** Any day

Additional glamping information: Wooden pods: 2 sets of single bunk beds, electricity, lighting and heating. Cars can be parked by pods.

1. Location
Place names are listed alphabetically within each county.

2. Map reference
Each site is given a map reference for use in conjunction with the atlas section at the back of the guide. The map reference comprises the guide map page number, the National Grid location square and a two-figure map location reference.
For example: **Map 19 NZ90.**
19 refers to the page number of the map section at the back of the guide.
NZ is the National Grid lettered square (representing 100,000sq metres) in which the location will be found.
9 is the figure reading across the top or bottom of the map page.
0 is the figure reading down each side of the map page.

3. Places to visit
Suggestions of nearby places to visit for adults and children.

4. Site name and rating
▶ Campsites are listed in descending order of their Pennant rating. Sites are rated from 1 to 5 Pennants and are also awarded a score ranging from 50–100% according to how they compare with other parks within the same Pennant rating. For further explanation see pages 10–11.

5. Contact details

6. Directions

Brief directions from a recognisable point, such as a main road, are included in each entry. Please contact the individual site for more detailed directions or use the AA Route Planner at **theAA.com**, and enter the site's postcode.

7. Description

Descriptions are based on information supplied by the AA inspector at the time of the last visit.

Please note: The AA Pennant classification is based on the touring pitches and the facilities only. AA inspectors do not visit or report on statics or chalets for hire under the AA Caravan & Camping quality standards scheme. However, the AA has a category of **HOLIDAY HOME PARK** and these static caravan, chalet or lodge-only parks are inspected.

8. Opening, arrival and departure times

Parks are not necessarily open all year and while most sites permit arrivals at any time, checking beforehand is advised (see page 12).

9. Pitches

Rates given after each appropriate symbol ⌗ (caravan), ⌗ (motorhome), ⅄ (tent) are the minimum overnight cost for one unit. The prices can vary according to the number of people in the party, but some parks have a fixed fee per pitch regardless of the number of people. Please note that some sites charge separately for certain facilities, including showers; and some sites charge a different rate for pitches with or without electricity. Prices are supplied to us in good faith by the site operators and are as accurate as possible. They are, however, only a guide and are subject to change during the currency of this publication. ⌗ indicates that the campsite offers one or more types of glamping accommodation (see point 13, below).
* If this symbol appears before the prices, it indicates that the prices are for 2019.

10. Symbols

These are divided into Pitches, Leisure, Facilities, Services and Within 3 miles sections. A guide to the symbols can be found on page 9 and on pages throughout the guide.

11. Additional site information

This includes information about the size of the site, whether dogs are accepted or not, whether cars can be parked by a caravan or tent, and whether awnings are permitted. We also include any restrictions and any additional facilities the site would like their visitors to be made aware of. If the site offers glamping, further information is shown at the end of the entry. As most sites now accept credit and debit cards, we only indicate those that don't accept cards ⌗.

12. Photograph

Optional photograph(s) supplied by the campsite.

13. Glamping

⌗ The campsite offers one or more types of 'glamorous camping' accommodation, i.e. wooden pods, tipis, yurts, bell tents, safari tents, shepherd's huts, vintage caravans etc. Details are shown at the bottom of the entry.

14. Best of British

A group of around 50 parks, both large and small, which focus on high quality facilities and amenities. **www.bob.org.uk**

15. David Bellamy Awards

Many AA recognised sites are also recipients of a David Bellamy Award for Conservation. The awards are graded Gold, Silver and Bronze.

The symbols we show indicate the 2017/18 winners as this was the most up-to-date information at the time of going to press. For the 2018/19 winners please see **www.bellamyparks.co.uk**

Facilities for disabled guests

The Equality Act 2010 provides legal rights for disabled people including access to goods, services and facilities, and means that service providers may have to consider making adjustments to their premises. For more information about the Act see: **www.gov.uk/ definition-of-disability-under-equality-act-2010**

If a site has told us that they provide facilities for disabled visitors their entry in the guide will include the following symbol: ♿

The sites in this guide should be aware of their responsibilities under the Act. However, we recommend that you always phone in advance to ensure the site you have chosen has facilities to suit your needs.

Guide to symbols

Pitches

Caravan

Motorhome

Tent

Glamping accommodation

Leisure

Indoor swimming pool

Outdoor swimming pool

Tennis court

Games room

Children's playground

Kids' club

Stables & horse riding

Golf course

Boat hire

Cycle hire

Cinema

Entertainment

Fishing

Mini golf

Watersports

Gym

Sports field

Pitch n putt

Facilities

Baths/showers

Electric shaver sockets

Hairdryer

Ice packs facility

Baby facilities

Disabled facilities

Shop or supermarket on site or within 200 yards

BBQ area

Picnic area

WiFi available

Car hire can be arranged

Services

Café or restaurant

Fast food/Takeaway

Electric hook-up

Motorhome service point

Launderette

Licensed bar

Calor Gas

Campingaz

Battery charging

Toilet fluid

Other

Dogs accepted

No dogs permitted

No credit or debit cards

2019 prices

rating not confirmed

The AA classification scheme

AA parks are classified on a 5-point scale according to their style and the range of facilities they offer. As the number of Pennants increases, so the quality and variety of facilities is generally greater.

What can you expect at an AA-rated park?

All AA parks must meet a minimum standard: they should be clean, well maintained and welcoming. In addition they must have a local authority site licence (unless specially exempt), and satisfy local authority fire regulations.

The AA inspection

Each campsite that applies for AA recognition receives an unannounced visit each year by one of the AA's highly qualified team of inspectors. They make a thorough check of the site's touring pitches, facilities and hospitality. The sites pay an annual fee for the inspection, recognition and rating, and receive a text entry in the *AA Caravan & Camping Guide*.

AA inspectors pay when they stay overnight on a site. The criteria used by the inspectors in awarding the AA Pennant rating is shown on this and the opposite page.

AA Quality percentage score

AA rated Campsites, Caravan Parks, Holiday Centres, Holiday Home Parks and Glamping-only sites are awarded a percentage score alongside their Pennant rating. This is a qualitative assessment of various factors including customer care and hospitality, toilet facilities and park landscaping. The % score runs from 50% to 100% and indicates the relative quality of parks with the same number of Pennants. For example, one 3-Pennant park may score 70%, while another 3-Pennant park may achieve 90%. Like the Pennant rating, the percentage is reassessed annually.

The Pennant criteria

One Pennant parks

These parks offer a fairly simple standard of facilities including:
- No more than 30 pitches per acre
- At least 5% of the total pitches allocated to touring caravans
- An adequate drinking water supply and reasonable drainage
- Washroom with flush toilets and toilet paper provided, unless no sanitary facilities are provided in which case this should be clearly stated
- Chemical disposal arrangements, ideally with running water, unless tents only
- Adequate refuse disposal that is clearly signed
- Well-drained ground and some level pitches
- Entrance and access roads of adequate width and surface
- Location of emergency phone clearly signed
- Emergency phone numbers fully displayed

Two Pennant parks

Parks in this category should meet all of the above requirements, but offer an increased level of facilities, services, customer care, security and ground maintenance. They should include the following:
- Separate washrooms, including at least two male and two female toilets and washbasins per 30 pitches
- Hot and cold water direct to each basin
- Externally lit toilet blocks
- Warden available during day, times to be indicated
- Whereabouts of shop/chemist is clearly signed
- Dish-washing facilities, covered and lit
- Basic security (i.e. lockable gate and/or CCTV)
- Reception area

Three Pennant parks

Many parks come within this rating and the range of facilities is wide. All parks will be of a very good standard and will meet the following minimum criteria:
- Facilities, services and park grounds are clean and well maintained, with buildings in good repair and attention paid to customer care and park security

- Evenly surfaced roads and paths
- Clean modern toilet blocks with all-night lighting and containing toilet seats in good condition, soap and hand dryers or paper towels, mirrors, shelves and hooks, shaver and hairdryer points, and lidded waste bins in female toilets
- Modern shower cubicles with sufficient hot water and attached, private changing space
- Electric hook-ups
- Some hardstanding/wheel runs/firm, level ground
- Laundry with automatic washing and drying facilities, separate from toilets
- Children's playground with safe equipment
- 24-hour public phone on site or nearby where mobile reception is poor
- Warden availability and 24-hour contact number clearly signed

Four Pennant parks

These parks have achieved an excellent standard in all areas, including landscaping of grounds, natural screening and attractive park buildings, and customer care and park security. Toilets are smart, modern and immaculately maintained, and generally offer the following facilities:

- Spacious vanity unit style washbasins, at least two male and two female per 25 pitches
- Fully-tiled shower cubicles with doors, dry areas, shelves and hooks, at least one male and one female per 30 pitches
- Availability of washbasins in lockable cubicles, or combined toilet/washing cubicles, or a private/family room with shower/toilet/washbasin

Other requirements are:
- Baby changing facilities
- A shop on site, or within reasonable distance
- Warden available 24 hours
- Reception area open during the day, with tourist information available
- Internal roads, paths and toilet blocks lit at night
- Maximum 25 pitches per campable acre
- Toilet blocks heated October to Easter
- Approximately 50% of pitches with electric hook-ups
- Approximately 10% of pitches have hardstandings
- Late arrivals enclosure
- Security barrier and/or CCTV

Five Pennant Premier parks

Premier parks are of an extremely high standard, set in attractive surroundings with superb mature landscaping. Facilities, security and customer care are of an exceptional quality. As well as the above they will also offer:

- First-class toilet facilities including several designated self-contained cubicles, ideally with toilet, washbasin and shower
- Toilet block(s) should be heated
- Ideally electric hook-ups to 75% of pitches
- Approximately 20% of pitches have hardstandings
- Some fully-serviced 'super' pitches: of larger size, with water and electricity supplies connected
- A motorhome service point
- Excellent security

Many Premier Parks will also provide:
- Heated swimming pool
- Well-equipped shop
- Café or restaurant and bar
- A designated walking area for dogs (if accepted)

HOLIDAY CENTRES

In this category we distinguish parks that cater for all holiday needs including cooked meals and entertainment. They provide:
- A wide range of on-site sports, leisure and recreational facilities
- Supervision and security at a very high level
- A choice of eating outlets
- Facilities for touring caravans that equal those available to rented holiday accommodation
- A maximum density of 25 pitches per acre
- Clubhouse with entertainment
- Laundry with automatic washing machines

HOLIDAY HOME PARKS

These are static-only parks offering holiday caravans, chalets or lodges for hire and catering for all holiday needs. They provide:
- Quality holiday hire caravans and chalets or luxurious lodges
- A wide range of on-site sports, leisure and recreational facilities
- Supervision and security at a very high level
- A choice of eating outlets
- Clubhouse with entertainment

GLAMPING-ONLY SITES

These sites, offering a different camping experience from touring with caravans, motorhomes and tents, are also inspected and rated from 1 to 5 Pennants. This is an assessment of the quality and variety of facilities a site offers.

Platinum Pennants ►►►►►

Platinum Pennants are awarded to camping sites scoring 95% and above with a 5-Pennant rating.

Gold Pennants ►►►►►

AA Gold Pennants are awarded to camping sites scoring 90% and above within the 1–5 Pennant ratings.

Useful information

Booking information

It is advisable to book in advance during peak holiday seasons and in school or public holidays. It is also wise to check whether or not a reservation entitles you to a particular pitch. It does not necessarily follow that an early booking will secure the best pitch; you may simply have the choice of what is available at the time you check in.

Some parks may require a deposit on booking which may be non-returnable if you have to cancel your holiday. If you do have to cancel, notify the proprietor at once because you may be held legally responsible for partial or full payment unless the pitch can be re-let. Consider taking out insurance such as AA Travel Insurance: visit theAA.com/travel-insurance or call 0808 169 1195 for details to cover a lost deposit or compensation. Some parks will not accept overnight bookings unless payment for the full minimum period (e.g. two or three days) is made.

Last arrival Unless otherwise stated, parks will usually accept arrivals at any time of the day or night, but some have a special 'late arrivals' enclosure where you have to make temporary camp to avoid disturbing other people on the park. Please note that on some parks access to the toilet block is by key or pass card only, so if you know you will be late, do check what arrangements can be made.

Last departure Most parks will specify their latest departure time. Do check with the park if this is not given. If you overstay the departure time you could be charged for an extra day.

Chemical closet disposal point

You will usually find one on every park, except those catering only for tents. It must be a specially constructed unit, or a toilet permanently set aside for the purpose of chemical disposal and with adjacent rinsing and soak-away facilities. However, some local authorities are concerned about the effect of chemicals on bacteria in cesspools etc, and may prohibit or restrict provision of chemical closet disposal points in their areas.

Complaints

If you have any complaints speak to the park proprietor or supervisor immediately, so that the matter can be sorted out on the spot. If this personal approach fails you may decide, if the matter is serious, to approach the local authority or tourist board. AA guide users may also write to:

The Caravan & Camping Scheme Co-ordinator,
AA Lifestyle Guides, 8th floor, Fanum House,
Basing View, Basingstoke, RG21 4EA

The AA may at its sole discretion investigate any complaints received from guide users for the purpose of making any necessary amendments to the guide. The AA will not in any circumstances act as representative or negotiator or undertake to obtain compensation or enter into further correspondence or deal with the matter in any other way whatsoever. The AA will not guarantee to take any specific action.

Dogs

Dogs may or may not be accepted at parks; this is entirely at the owner's or warden's discretion (assistance dogs should be accepted). Even when the park states that they accept dogs, it is still discretionary, and certain breeds may not be considered as suitable, so we strongly advise that you check when you book. Some sites have told us they do not accept dangerous breeds. (The following breeds are included in the Dangerous Dogs Act 1991 – Pit Bull Terrier, Japanese Tosa, Dogo Argentino and Fila Brasileiro). Dogs should always be kept on a lead and under control, and letting them sleep in cars is not encouraged.

Electric hook-up

Many parks have electric hook-ups on some, or all, of their pitches; if you need an electric connection you should request it when making your booking. Generally the voltage is 240v AC, 50 cycles, although this can vary slightly according to the location. The supply can vary considerably from 5 amps to 16 amps although 16 amps is becoming the norm – again you should check with the campsite if this is important to you. Remember, if your consumption is greater than the supply the electricity will trip out and need resetting.

Electric hook-up connections are now standardised in the UK with the blue coloured safety connectors. However, it is good practice to always connect your cable to your caravan, motorhome or tent electric distribution unit **before** connecting to the hook-up supply.

It is also important that tents or trailer tents have a Residual Circuit Device (RCD) for safety reasons and to avoid overloading the circuit. Caravans and motorhomes have RCDs built in. You should remember that if your RCD trips out at 16 amps and the campsite supply is say 10 amps you can easily overload the supply and cause the hook-up to trip out.

It is quite easy to check what demands your appliances can place on the supply at any one time. Details are normally available in the caravan or motorhome handbooks which show the wattage of appliances fitted.

The amperage used is based on the wattage of appliance divided by the supply voltage.

The following table is a quick check of electrical consumption, depending what is switched on.

Average amperage (based on a 240v supply)

Caravan fridge (125 watts)	0.5 amps
Caravan heater set at (500 watts)	2.1 amps
Caravan heater set at (1000 watts)	4.2 amps
Caravan heater set at (2000 watts)	8.4 amps
Caravan water heater (850 watts)	3.5 amps
Kettle (domestic type) (1500 watts)	6.3 amps
Kettle (low wattage type) (750 watts)	3.1 amps
Hairdryer (2100 watts)	8.8 amps
Microwave (750 watts)	3.1 amps
TV (flat-screen LED type) (30 watts)	0.13 amps
Battery charger (built-in type) (200 watts)	0.8 amps

Motorhomes
At some parks motorhomes are only accepted if they remain static throughout the stay. Also check that there are suitable level pitches at the parks where you plan to stay.

Overflow pitches
Campsites are legally entitled to use an overflow field which is not a normal part of their camping area for up to 28 days in any one year as an emergency method of coping with additional numbers at busy periods. When this 28-day rule is being invoked site owners should increase the numbers of sanitary facilities accordingly. In these circumstances the extra facilities are sometimes no more than temporary portacabins.

Parking
Some park operators insist that cars are left in a parking area separate from the pitches; others will not allow more than one car to be parked beside each caravan, tent or glamping unit.

Park restrictions
Many parks in our guide are selective about the categories of people they will accept on their parks. In the caravan and camping world there are many restrictions and some categories of visitor are banned altogether. Where a park has told us of a restriction/s this is included in the notes in their entry.

On many parks in this guide, unaccompanied young people, single-sex groups, single adults, and motorcycle groups will not be accepted. The AA takes no stance in this matter, basing its Pennant classification on facilities, quality and maintenance. On the other hand, some parks cater well for teenagers and offer magnificent sporting and leisure facilities as well as lively entertainment events; others have only very simple amenities. A small number of parks in our guide exclude all children in order to create an environment aimed at holiday makers in search of total peace and quiet (see page 43).

Pets
The importation of animals into the UK is subject to strict controls. Penalties for trying to avoid these controls are severe. However, the Pet Travel Scheme (PETS) allows cats, dogs, ferrets and certain other pets coming from the EU and certain other countries to enter the UK without quarantine provided the appropriate conditions are met.
For more details: www.gov.uk/take-pet-abroad/overview
PETS Helpline: 0370 241 1710

Pets resident in the British Isles (UK, Republic of Ireland, Isle of Man and Channel Islands) are not subject to any quarantine or PETS rules when travelling within the British Isles.

Seasonal touring pitches
Some park operators allocate a number of their hardstanding pitches for long-term seasonal caravans. These pitches can be reserved for the whole period the campsite is open, generally between Easter and September, and a fixed fee is charged for keeping the caravan on the park for the season. These pitches are in great demand, especially in popular tourist areas, so enquire well in advance if you wish to book one.

Shops
The range of provisions in shops is usually in proportion to the park's size. As far as AA Pennant requirements are concerned, a mobile shop calling several times a week, or a general store within easy walking distance of the park is acceptable.

AA Campsites of the Year

CONCIERGE CAMPING ▶▶▶▶▶
CHICHESTER, WEST SUSSEX, page 285

Developing this stunning park has been a labour of love for Tracey and Guy Hodgkin and since opening in 2015 they have added four magnificent safari tents in their own paddock and in 2018 extended the park to accommodate 27 units. It's true to say that the Hodgkin's have raised the quality bar for all campsites to aspire to – it's a first-class small park and the attention to detail throughout is very impressive. Everything is top spec, from the swish reception, replete with local produce shop, coffee and drinks, late arrival and breakfast hampers, to the state-of-the-art amenities block, which are top hotel standard including Ratham Estate toiletries, air-blade hand-driers, eight stunning new shower rooms, an excellent family/disabled room, and smart Concierge Camping branding on glass doors. The heating/boiler system is the best, heating the block in winter and providing air-conditioning in summer. The huge new Emperor pitches boast their own mini-safari tent complete with Smart TV, dishwasher, fridge freezer, coffee machine, wood-fired oven and burner, and decked area. An upmarket stopover close to Chichester, Goodwood and the South Downs for the discerning caravanner/motorhomer looking for a touch of luxury. An exciting park.

GLEN NEVIS CARAVAN & CAMPING PARK ▶▶▶▶ 92%
FORT WILLIAM, HIGHLAND, page 347

Situated in stunning Glen Nevis close to Neptune's Staircase on the Caledonian Canal and just a few miles from Fort William, this large and very well maintained park is set in a beautifully landscaped area of mature trees beside the River Ness, with easy access to the path leading to Ben Nevis. The site is divided into areas by beech hedges to give a sense of seclusion to caravan and motorhome users, who have superb hardstanding pitches and their own quality amenity blocks; tent campers have their own specific areas and large well-kept amenity blocks. There has been significant investment in the park over the past couple of years to cater for the change in customer demand, with extra electric hook ups to pitches, and for those seeking a glamping experience, ten luxury, wooden camping pods have been installed in Deer Park – all have unrivalled views towards Ben Nevis and are perfect for when the weather turns inclement in the mountains. In addition, the park has fishing rights on the River Ness, an excellent café-restaurant, a well-equipped shop, and guests are welcome to explore the 1,000 acres of the Glen Nevis Estate during their stay. A worthy winner for Scotland.

Following nominations by our inspectors, we award an overall winner from three national finalists, five regional winners, a holiday centre winner and a glamping-only site winner — all are selected for their outstanding overall quality and high levels of customer care. Our two special awards recognise the best small campsite and the most improved campsite.

WALES

TRAWSDIR TOURING CARAVANS & CAMPING PARK
►►►►► 93%
BARMOUTH, GWYNEDD, page 374

Trawsdir Park is located a few minutes' drive north from the seaside town of Barmouth and year-on-year investment at this quality coastal park has resulted in a superb holiday destination, where physical standards and levels of customer care are guaranteed to be memorable. The touring and camping areas maximise the stunning coastal views and pitch sizes provide optimum privacy. A wide range of both indigenous and cultivated flora and fauna creates an ambience of peace and tranquillity and even the excellent dish wash facility has picture windows. The excellent amenities block is designed with stylish decor, smart divisional cladding, modern fixtures and fittings and good privacy options. An excellent children's playground and a well-stocked shop are also popular features. Owner Bob Williams leads the way in sustainable tourism and was one of the earlier pioneers, investing in eco-friendly systems to deliver constant hot water and electricity supplies throughout the park. Recently, superfast WiFi has been introduced throughout the park and an all-weather surfaced illuminated walk has been created to the nearby pub, which offers take-away pizza and fish and chips in addition to imaginative meals. A top Welsh park.

SOUTH WEST ENGLAND

TRETHEM MILL TOURING PARK ►►►►►
ST JUST-IN-ROSELAND, CORNWALL, page 104

Owned and run by three generations of the Akeroyd family, this park stands tucked away in a sheltered valley in the heart of the Roseland peninsula, close to St Mawes and Portscatho, and just a mile from the sea and glorious coastal path walks. Since winning the Most Improved Campsite Award in 2012, they have continually looked for ways to improve the facilities, investing year on year in upgrading the park. It is now one of Cornwall's top parks, fully deserving its new Platinum Pennant status. The Akeroyd's really do look after their loyal customers, many of whom return every year to experience the high levels of customer care and the large fully serviced hardstanding pitches that offer excellent privacy through the thoughtful planting of trees and shrubs between pitches. Carefully tended and beautifully landscaped, the park enjoys a lovely rural setting and offers quality in all areas and excellent amenities, including a spacious reception/shop and ultra-modern and spotlessly clean toilets that feature three fully serviced cubicles with underfloor heating. In addition, expect great attention to detail around the park, from well manicured grassy pitches and weed-free hardstandings to expertly trimmed trees and shrubbery, and glorious seasonal flower displays.

AA Campsites of the Year *continued*

SOUTH EAST ENGLAND

BROADHEMBURY CARAVAN & CAMPING PARK
▷▷▷▷▷ **90%** ASHFORD, KENT, page 207

Tucked away in peaceful countryside close to Ashford and well placed as a stopover for the Channel Tunnel and Dover ferry port, this long established (48 years) park continues to impress due to its high standards of maintenance from hands-on family owners and high levels of customer care. Sally Taylor and partner Lee Stone took over the day-to-day running of the park in 2016 and they are doing a grand job, continuing to improve the park to ensure Broadhembury meets guest expectations of a quality 5 Pennant park. The toilet block in the adults-only field is top notch – an eco build with solar heating, air recycling system, underfloor heating, automatic lighting, and a rainwater harvesting system. It is now self-sustaining, feeding electricity back to the grid. The toilet block in the family section of the park was smartly refurbished for the 2018 season. Development of the adults-only section has seen the addition of fully serviced hardstanding pitches, an excellent motorhome service point, and two lovely Lotus Belle tents, the park's first foray into glamping. There's also a very smart reception, excellent provision for families, a well-equipped campers' kitchen, and spacious, well-laid out pitches in both touring areas.

HEART OF ENGLAND

OXON HALL TOURING PARK ▷▷▷▷▷ **90%**
SHREWSBURY, SHROPSHIRE, page 251

Oxon Hall is a popular touring park located a few minutes' walk from Shrewsbury's Park and Ride, providing regular buses to the historic town with its many attractions and excellent facilities. The main strengths of this park are its excellent landscaping, pitch quality and high standards of customer care. The hardworking grounds team create a wonderful display of colour, whatever the season and a balance of indigenous and cultivated planting combines with neat lush grassed areas, results in a feeling of peace and tranquillity. Within the grounds and adjacent to the excellent well-stocked shop is a wildlife pond, with a large variety of wildlife. The shop also displays a wide range of caravan accessories in addition to provisions and the smart reception within has generous opening hours. Level and spacious touring pitches are generously spaced to ensure optimum privacy – many are deeper to facilitate the larger units including RV motorhomes. The modern heated amenities block is tastefully designed with superb flooring, stylish decor, modern fixtures and fittings and good privacy options. This long-established leisure destination thoroughly deserves its success and year on year investment ensures that customer expectations are always exceeded.

NORTH WEST ENGLAND

OLD HALL CARAVAN PARK ►►►► 91%
CAPERNWRAY, LANCASHIRE, page 213

A meandering drive along a mature tree lined road creates a wonderful feeling of anticipation, passing sensitively placed holiday homes and on arrival at the first plateau, a warm welcome is assured at the reception and information room. Long established and with year on year investment, this park is close to the pretty village of Over Kellet, but also has the benefit of being in easy reach of both the Fylde Coast and the Southern Lake District. Many very contented holiday home owners appreciate the generously spaced allocated pitches, creating excellent privacy and the newest development is at the top end, with stunning views of the surrounding countryside. In addition to a dramatic background of woodland to an arboretum standard, many thousands of new saplings, hedging and shrubs have been planted and coupled with superb displays of pretty seasonal flowers, create a wonderful backdrop to aid peace and relaxation. The touring area is also excellent, with all level hardstanding and fully serviced pitches being generously spaced. The heated amenity block for touring customers has recently been refurbished to a very high standard, with excellent flooring, stylish decor, top-notch modern fixtures and fittings and very good privacy options for all.

NORTH EAST ENGLAND

ORD HOUSE COUNTRY PARK ►►►► 92%
BERWICK-UPON-TWEED, NORTHUMBERLAND, page 242

Ord House Country Park is a high quality destination close to the glorious Northumberland coastline. Set in the grounds of an 18th-century country house, the beautifully landscaped touring park is well managed and this shows in all aspects of the park, for example, in the time and effort taken to create the tasteful floral displays to the spotlessly clean and well maintained amenity blocks. The latter have recently been refurbished with hotel standard fixtures and fittings and contain family bath and shower suites and first-class rooms for disabled guests. All in all, the attention to detail in the presentation of this park is very impressive as is the ongoing investment to maintain quality in all areas, notably the excellent provision for children with a fantastic adventure playground, mini-golf and a football field, and well tended and screened pitches that offer good privacy. The impressive new entertainment building mirrors the physical quality of the park, with a family friendly section with soft play area, and a space for adults to relax in which has log burners and a softer feel. Environmental initiatives (woodland walks, bird houses, wild flower planting, hedghog hotels) are to be commended and add to the overall ethos of the park.

AA Campsites of the Year *continued*

HOLIDAY CENTRE OF THE YEAR

SEARLES LEISURE RESORT ▷▷▷▷▷ 92%
HUNSTANTON, NORFOLK, page 237

What started as a simple caravan field some 83 years ago is now an award-winning holiday destination providing first class entertainment, attractions and facilities for all ages. All thanks to the vision, passion and hard work of four generations of the Searle family, who continue to invest in and manage this large seaside holiday complex. Their philosophy for the park is 'one of continuous improvement and enhancing the guest experience'. This is a business that never stands still and every year they offer something new to delight the visitors with improvements. Tourers have their own areas, including two excellent toilet blocks, both fully refurbished in 2017, and pitches are individually marked by small maturing shrubs. A new barbecue area, upgraded water points and re-landscaping around the amenity blocks were among the improvements to the touring area in 2018, and six very smart lodges were added to the park. At inspection this year, all facilities were spotlessly clean and a general feeling of pride for the park was noted from the friendly and hard working staff. There is an abundance of facilities and activities are available within the park to keep the whole family entertained. A top quality family-owned holiday centre, worthy winners of this award.

GLAMPING SITE OF THE YEAR

PENHEIN GLAMPING ▷▷▷▷▷ 91%
LLANVAIR DISCOED, MONMOUTHSHIRE, page 381

The words 'in an idyllic location' can often be over used but with this stunning leisure destination the description is accurate. Penhein Glamping is the brainchild of Helen and James Hearn and the site's Persian influence honours James's mother who was born in Iran. The long-established farm estate is situated in a superb elevated position and guests arrive via a long and undulating drive, passing livestock, whilst admiring the amazing display of mature trees. The elegant period estate house is the reception for the Glamping experience and after crossing a field, guests arrive at the edge of woodland, where they find imported Alachigh tents, all well spaced to create optimum privacy. Each tent is equipped to provide a balance between quality and comfort, with antique furnishings and many thoughtful extras that exceed expectations, with an en suite toilet and washbasin just one example. A communal yurt containing oak furnishings is an additional benefit and after a long day of fresh air and exercise, a luxurious shower block with stone floors, underfloor heating, hot monsoon showers and a Victorian roll-up bath is particularly welcome. James and Helen also created outdoor furnishings from recycled timber and the displays of wild flowers and herbs are a magnet for wildlife.

SMALL CAMPSITE OF THE YEAR

KETTLEWELL CAMPING ▶▶▶▶ 80%
KETTLEWELL, NORTH YORKSHIRE, page 309

On the edge of the beautiful village of Kettlewell, Nigel Lambert is certainly living his dream with the creation of this superb leisure destination, situated just a few minutes' walk from a wide range of pubs, restaurants and both craft and general shops. The campsite is set in the beautiful Yorkshire Dales and the Lake District is an easy drive away. The main camping area has been developed from original farmland and adjacent fields and properties still farm in the traditional manner, with lambing at springtime always a memorable experience. Local stone walls surround the level camping area and small campervans are also welcome. Camping at Kettlewell has a great additional benefit with the top-notch amenity block containing underfloor heating, a stylish and imaginative decor and modern fixtures and fittings with power showers, which are especially welcome after a long day's trek. Nigel has also created a super group field, a few minutes away from the main field and this is popular with family groups. This very peaceful location also contains a smaller toilet and shower block of a similar standard to the main one and at the edge of this large undulating area is a large play area and trickling brook, with the only welcome distractions being the sounds of running water and birdsong.

MOST IMPROVED CAMPSITE

SUMMER VALLEY TOURING PARK ▶▶▶▶ 90%
TRURO, CORNWALL, page 108

Summer Valley is a very attractive and secluded site in a rural setting midway between the A30 and the cathedral city of Truro, which is just a five-minute drive and can easily be reached by bus, cycle or on foot. The fabulous surfing and swimming beach at Perranporth, one of Cornwall's finest beaches, is just five miles away. Since taking over the park in 2016, hard-working owners Kate and Phil Hockey have invested time and money and worked wonders in improving the facilities on the park for guests enjoyment over the past year, which has seen the Quality Score for the park rise to 90%, Gold Award standard. In addition to major drainage work across the site, improvements include moving, redesigning and upgrading the children's play area; installing free WiFi across the park; upgrading the toilets and showers in both the Ladies and Gents facilities; creating five fully serviced hardstanding pitches and some super grass pitches with electricity for large tents; removal of trees across the park; revamping the dishwashing area; and adding a new shop, campers' kitchen, and a security barrier at the entrance. There is also a gleaming new glamping pod with decking tucked away in a quiet corner of the park.

PITCH PERFECT

Winner of last year's overall AA Campsite of the Year award, The Old Oaks Touring Park is among the best in the industry. **Kate Jenkinson** asks the owners how they got to the top — and how they intend to stay there too.

This year, The Old Oaks Touring Park in Somerset has become one of the first parks in the UK to receive a 5-Pennant platinum award from the AA.

It follows hot on the heels of their 5 Star Gold rating from VisitEngland and winning the prestigious AA Campsite of the Year Award last year. For managers James and Tara White, it was simply further validation that the couple were continuing to lead the family business in the right direction.

Established by James' parents, Sally and Jim, the White family has run the 15-acre camping and touring park near Glastonbury for more than 30 years. The business has evolved from just five pitches and a bed and breakfast to 100 pitches over six paddocks and glamping options including shepherd's huts, wooden pods and luxury cedar lodges.

Tara says the recognition from the AA and VisitEngland 'means the world to us' and recognises all their hard work growing the park. But being at the top brings its own challenges, and Tara and James are constantly working to maintain their good reputation and award-winning status. 'You have to constantly work to live up to your reputation as a five-star park and one of the very best,' says Tara. 'Also, we're not ones for standing still. So if somebody says we're the best park, we need to be the best plus!'

For Tara, the key is to continually strive to exceed customers' expectations, which in an era of online review sites and social media is a tough task. As the industry changes and customers become more sophisticated and travel-savvy, they expect more for their money. Listening to the wants of their customers, Tara says, goes a long way to helping them satisfy guests and win awards. 'We constantly review what we are doing and how we can make changes,' says Tara. 'We research other parks of a similar nature, looking at their websites and reviews. If they're one of the best, then we want to know why and what we can learn from that.'

Looking for new trends

Where once holiday-makers would take off on a camping trip for a few weeks at a time, today people are often opting to take shorter breaks. Trying to adapt to this change in customer behaviour led Tara and James to introduce glamping. 'Having a mix of camping, glamping and caravanning allows a wider demographic,' says Tara. 'Owning a caravan and a towing vehicle, and having somewhere to store it, is out of reach financially for many young people. By encouraging them to come glamping and being on the park with the caravanners and seeing their lifestyle, it might plant the seed for the future and perhaps contribute to sustaining the lifecycle of caravanning.'

The park is also adults-only – excluding children and discouraging groups – which has served the business well. Initially the change to adults-only lost the park some business, but finding a niche, as well as attracting younger adults through glamping, eventually paid off. For Old Oaks, high and low seasons that coincide with school holidays don't exist, and business is steady from May through to mid October.

'It makes it easier for us as a business because we don't have all the health and safety implications that you have to think about with children. It is also very quiet and tranquil – sometimes we will have a full park and I'll be out in the garden at night and you cannot hear a thing, which is perfect for people wanting to escape and get away from it all. So it works for us.'

As well as being listed and rated with the AA and VisitEngland, Old Oaks is a member of both Tranquil Parks, a group of independently owned adult-only parks, and the Best of British group of independent parks. These affiliations are crucial to the success of their business, Tara says, enabling them to market directly to their target audience. With the bigger funds and resources at their disposal, these organisations are able to put member businesses in front of prospective customers in a way an individual park would not be able to, making them an excellent return on investment.

Offering add-on services

As well as partnerships with tourism organisations, the Whites see great value in teaming up with local businesses. Says Tara, 'We are about three miles out of town in our own little bubble, so it is important to know that there are other businesses who we can form relationships with to the benefit of all.'

Consequently, Old Oaks offers a range of add-on services from nearby providers to complement its own facilities. These add

Shepherd's huts feature washing and cooking facilities

An adults-only policy has proved a great success

A CUSTOMER-FIRST APPROACH

We asked Tara White from Old Oaks to pick out her number-one tip for running a successful campsite.

Tara says, 'It's all about the customers – you must put their needs first. Everybody says this, but not everybody necessarily does it. If your customer is happy then you're doing it right, but without your customer, you haven't got a business. You can find out what people really want by researching the industry, including your competitors.

Be aware of current trends and what others are offering, to remain competitive and set yourself apart. And you should always seek to exceed expectations. Don't just satisfy your customers' expectations: be better than that. Make them say "wow".'

'You've got to think about what might be of interest to your customers. It's about the extra things that they weren't expecting, and the things they didn't know they wanted'

value for customers, set the business apart from competitors and introduce customers to businesses in the nearby town. Six nights a week the park offers meals to park guests from nearby restaurants, from fish and chips and pizza, to Indian, Chinese and kebabs. The business has also established a unique relationship with the Abbey Tea Rooms in Glastonbury, providing discounts that encourage repeat patronage and an exclusive meal offering during the Glastonbury Carnival each year. 'You've got to think about what might be of interest to your customers,' Tara says.

Caravan cleaning is another service offered at The Old Oaks, and one that the Whites hope will be the decider for holiday-makers weighing up their business against another. 'It's about the other extra things that they weren't expecting, and the things they didn't know they wanted. Whenever I go anywhere, I always try to stop and ask, "Wouldn't it be nice if…"'

Six steps to touring park success

1. Examine the competition. What are they doing well that you could be doing too? Constantly evaluating the competition helps you adapt for success.
2. Future proof your business. Contemporary trends such as glamping help draw in younger visitors, who could also become your middle aged or older visitors of the future!
3. Find a unique selling point. The Old Oaks is an adults-only site, but perhaps you're the opposite – child friendly. Find your niche appeal and use it in your marketing.
4. Join industry organisations. They have the marketing oomph to spread the word about your business.
5. Provide add-on services. Teaming up with local businesses – for instance restaurants – can benefit your guests.
6. Be a 21st century marketer. To survive, embrace digital marketing – or find someone who will embrace it for you!

The AA's overall Campsite of the Year winner last year

Marketing: a modern approach

Looking at what other parks do helps Tara set competitive prices, and judge how much to increase those prices each year. 'We are constantly improving our park,' she says, 'and we need to finance those improvements. People keep coming back, so we believe that we offer value for money.'

Getting the word out about that value for money is another matter. No longer are marketing and advertising budgets spent on magazine and print – the advent of social media has changed the game. Facebook is the main marketing platform for Old Oaks, allowing, says Tara, more targeted communication with the right audience. Twitter and Instagram are also on the business's marketing radar along with e-marketing and the dispatch of emails on mass. 'That works very well,' says Tara, 'and the listings on websites such as Best of British, UK Campsite, Tranquil Parks and glamping-related websites.'

Tara is also exploring opportunities with Airbnb and booking.com, with some early success already. Generally, she is keen to embrace all social and digital avenues, saying it is vital to keep abreast of trends and ahead of the competition.

It's this willingness to adapt and explore new opportunities that is helping Old Oaks thrive. In fact, as well as the AA and VisitEngland accolades, Tara herself recently received two best student awards in a foundation degree in tourism parks management from Bournemouth University and Kingston Maurward College, Dorchester. She says the biggest skills she gained from her studies were improved managerial acumen and the ability to better research business decisions. She says, 'I became a manager before I had any managerial experience, so the course taught me a lot. Now, if I have an idea, I'm more confident to try it and if it doesn't work then it doesn't work. But that's how you become successful – by trying things.'

First-time campers: a checklist of Dos, and a couple of Don'ts

Key: C = caravans M = motorhomes T = tents

Before you leave home or the site (hitching)

► Before you go away for the first time practise putting up your tent; hitching and unhitching your caravan; reversing your motorhome or towed van into an enclosed space. **(CMT)**

► Make a list of all the essentials you need to take with you. Mains lead, gas cylinder, levelling ramps and/or chocks... all the way through to small essentials like a box of matches, spare fuses, and a torch (check batteries). **(CMT)**

► Check all interior items are safely stored, cupboards closed, all interior electrics are set correctly, turn off gas bottles, make sure roof lights and windows are closed and the external door is locked. **(CM)**

► Empty fresh and waste water containers and toilet casseltes. **(CM)**

► Check that corner steadies are raised tightly, and chocks and steps stowed. **(C)**

► Connect tow bracket electric plugs, check that the breakaway safety cable is connected and, if used, that the anti-snake device is fitted correctly. **(C)**

► Check the caravan's noseweight. **(C)**

► Adjust the hitch height – i.e. above the car's towball. **(C)**

► Secure the hitch on the towball. **(C)**

► Use the jockey wheel to raise the car about 2.5cm to ensure the caravan and car are properly coupled. If fitted, also check the tow hitch indicator (green = correctly coupled). **(C)**

► Raise the jockey wheel and lock in position. **(C)**

► Check that the caravan number plate is secure (and that it replicates the towing vehicle's number plate). **(C)**

► Ask another person to stand behind the caravan or motorhome to check all the lights and indicators work. **(CM)**

► On leaving a site disconnect the hook-ups and make that final check of the empty pitch. **(CM)**

Arriving at your destination (unhitching)

► Tell the site this is your first time. They're more likely to go out of their way to help. **(CMT)**

► Listen to what the site staff tell you when you arrive (if you're a family, it's a good idea for you all to step into reception – that way you all understand the same message). **(CMT)**

► Check caravan handbrake is on, chocks are in place and corner steadies are lowered. **(C)**

► Lower jockey wheel and level the caravan and then lock in place. **(C)**

► Give everyone in the family designated tasks when you arrive on site (finding the way to the toilet block, locating the nearest fresh water point etc). **(CMT)**

► Get to know your surroundings. An early-evening stroll around any campsite is a great opportunity to check out the facilities. **(CMT)**

► Say hello to your neighbours. They might just come in handy, and who knows you might a make a lot of new friends. **(CMT)**

DON'T churn up the grass. You're only ruining things for subsequent visitors. If you have a bit of a mishap, let the staff know so they can rectify things as soon as possible.

And finally **DON'T** be afraid to ask. All the campsites in this guide are adept at helping first-timers – most will happily guide you to your pitch if you ask. Although you'll soon find your fellow campers are happy to chip in and help out, too.

There's even more useful information on how to safely tow a caravan or trailer at:
www.theaa.com/motoring_advice/general-advice/towing-advice-what-you-need-to-know.html

The best sites for...

If you're looking for a site with a specific quality or recommended facilities, the following lists will help.

WATERSIDE PITCHES

ENGLAND

Low Wray National Trust Campsite,
Ambleside, Cumbria
South End Caravan Park,
Barrow-in-Furness, Cumbria
Hill of Oaks & Blakeholme,
Windermere, Cumbria
River Dart Country Park,
Ashburton, Devon
Riverside C&C Park,
South Molton, Devon
Sleningford Watermill Caravan Camping Park,
North Stainley, North Yorkshire

SCOTLAND

Banff Links Caravan Park,
Banff, Aberdeenshire
Inver Mill Farm Caravan Park,
Dunkeld, Perth & Kinross
Skye C&C Club Site,
Edinbane, Isle of Skye

WALES

Riverside Camping,
Caernarfon, Gwynedd

NORTHERN IRELAND

Rushin House Caravan Park,
Belcoo, County Fermanagh

STUNNING VIEWS

ENGLAND

Tristram C&C Park,
Polzeath, Cornwall
Sykeside Camping Park,
Patterdale, Cumbria
Warcombe Farm C&C Park,
Woolacombe, Devon
Highlands End Holiday Park,
Bridport, Dorset

East Fleet Farm Touring Park,
Weymouth, Dorset
Sea Barn Farm,
Weymouth, Dorset
New Hall Farm Touring Park,
Southwell, Nottinghamshire
Wimbleball Lake,
Dulverton, Somerset
Howgill Lodge,
Bolton Abbey, North Yorkshire
Wolds Way Caravan and Camping,
West Knapton, North Yorkshire

CHANNEL ISLANDS

Rozel Camping Park,
St Martin, Jersey

SCOTLAND

Carradale Bay Caravan Park,
Carradale, Argyll & Bute
Oban C&C Park,
Oban, Argyll & Bute
Resipole Farm Holiday Park,
Acharacle, Highland
Invercoe C&C Park,
Glencoe, Highland
John O'Groats Caravan Site,
John O'Groats, Highland
Strathfillan Wigwam Village,
Tyndrum, Stirling

WALES

Bron-Y-Wendon Caravan Park,
Llanddulas, Conwy
Bodnant Caravan Park,
Llanrwst, Conwy
Beach View Caravan Park,
Abersoch, Gwynedd
Tyn-y-Mur Touring & Camping,
Abersoch, Gwynedd
Trawsdir Touring C&C Park,
Barmouth, Gwynedd
Eisteddfa,
Criccieth, Gwynedd

Fishguard Bay Resort,
Fishguard, Pembrokeshire
Skysea C&C Park,
Port Eynon, Swansea

GOOD ON-SITE RESTAURANTS

ENGLAND

Stroud Hill Park,
St Ives, Cambridgeshire
Tristram C&C Park,
Polzeath, Cornwall
Park Cliffe Camping & Caravan Estate,
Windermere, Cumbria
Hidden Valley Park,
Braunton, Devon
Cofton Holidays,
Dawlish, Devont
Highlands End Holiday Park,
Bridport, Dorset
Bay View Holiday Park,
Bolton le Sands, Lancashire
The Old Brick Kilns,
Barney, Norfolk
Beaconsfield Farm Caravan Park,
Shrewsbury, Shropshire

CHANNEL ISLANDS

Durrell Wildlife Camp,
Trinity, Jersey

SCOTLAND

Sands of Luce Holiday Park,
Sandhead, Dumfries & Galloway
Glen Nevis C&C Park,
Fort William, Highland

Tristram Caravan & Camping Park, Cornwall

TOP TOILETS

ENGLAND

Carnon Downs C&C Park,
  Truro, Cornwall
Skelwith Fold Caravan Park,
  Ambleside, Cumbria
Beech Croft Farm,
  Buxton, Derbyshire
Crealy Adventure Park and Resort,
  Clyst St Mary, Devon
Riverside C&C Park,
  South Molton, Devon
Meadowbank Holidays,
  Christchurch, Dorset
Shamba Holidays,
  St Leonards, Dorset
Ord House Country Park,
  Berwick-upon-Tweed, Northumberland
Teversal C&C Club Site,
  Teversal, Nottinghamshire
The Old Oaks Touring Park,
  Glastonbury, Somerset
Moon & Sixpence,
  Woodbridge, Suffolk
Riverside Caravan Park,
  High Bentham, North Yorkshire
Wayside Holiday Park,
  Pickering, North Yorkshire
Moor Lodge Park,
  Leeds, West Yorkshire

SCOTLAND

Beecraigs C&C Site,
  Linlithgow, West Lothian
Skye C&C Club Site,
  Edinbane, Isle of Skye

ON-SITE FISHING

ENGLAND

Fields End Water Caravan Park & Fishery,
  Doddington, Cambridgeshire
Upper Tamar Lake,
  Kilkhampton, Cornwall
Back of Beyond Touring Park,
  St Leonards, Dorset
Woodland Waters,
  Ancaster, Lincolnshire

Lakeside Caravan Park & Fisheries,
  Downham Market, Norfolk
Northam Farm Caravan & Touring Park,
  Brean, Somerset
Marsh Farm Caravan Site,
  Saxmundham, Suffolk
Sumners Ponds Fishery & Campsite,
  Barns Green, West Sussex

SCOTLAND

Hoddom Castle Caravan Park,
  Ecclefechan, Dumfries & Galloway
Resipole Farm Holiday Park,
  Acharacle, Highland
Milton of Fonab Caravan Park,
  Pitlochry, Perth & Kinross

WALES

Afon Teifi C&C Park,
  Newcastle Emlyn, Carmarthenshire
Ynysymaengwyn Caravan Park,
  Tywyn, Gwynedd

THE KIDS

ENGLAND

Trevornick,
  Holywell Bay, Cornwall
Eden Valley Holiday Park,
  Lostwithiel, Cornwall
Golden Valley C&C Park,
  Ripley, Derbyshire
Freshwater Beach Holiday Park,
  Bridport, Dorset
Sandy Balls Holiday Village,
  Fordingbridge, Hampshire
Brokerswood Country Park,
  Westbury, Wiltshire
Golden Square C&C Park,
  Helmsley, North Yorkshire
Goosewood Holiday Park,
  Sutton-on-the-Forest, North Yorkshire

SCOTLAND

Beecraigs C&C Site,
  Linlithgow, West Lothian
Blair Castle Caravan Park,
  Blair Atholl, Perth & Kinross

WALES

Home Farm Caravan Park,
  Marian-Glas, Isle of Anglesey
Trawsdir Touring C&C Park,
  Barmouth, Gwynedd
Kiln Park Holiday Centre,
  Tenby, Pembrokeshire

BEING ECO-FRIENDLY

ENGLAND

South Penquite Farm,
  Blisland, Cornwall
Camping Caradon Touring Park,
  Looe, Cornwall
River Dart Country Park,
  Ashburton, Devon
Brook Lodge Farm C&C Park,
  Cowslip Green, Somerset

SCOTLAND

Carradale Bay Caravan Park,
  Carradale, Argyll & Bute
Shieling Holidays Mull,
  Craignure, Isle of Mull

WALES

Caerfai Bay Caravan & Tent Park,
  St Davids, Pembrokeshire

►►►►► Platinum Parks

Platinum Parks are the very best sites in the UK, having achieved a 5-Pennant rating with a quality score of 95% and over.

ENGLAND

CORNWALL

BUDE
Wooda Farm Holiday Park

CARLYON BAY
Carlyon Bay Caravan & Camping Park

CRANTOCK (NEAR NEWQUAY)
Trevella Park

MEVAGISSEY
Seaview International Holiday Park

NEWQUAY
Hendra Holiday Park

PADSTOW
Padstow Touring Park

REDRUTH
Globe Vale Holiday Park

ST IVES
Polmanter Touring Park

ST JUST-IN-ROSELAND
Trethem Mill Touring Park

TRURO
Carnon Downs Caravan & Camping Park

WHITE CROSS
Piran Meadows Resort and Spa

CUMBRIA

AMBLESIDE
Skelwith Fold Caravan Park

DEVON

AXMINSTER
Hawkchurch Resort & Spa

NEWTON ABBOT
Dornafield
Ross Park

SIDMOUTH
Oakdown Country Holiday Park

DORSET

BRIDPORT
Highlands End Holiday Park

POOLE
South Lytchett Manor Caravan & Camping Park

WAREHAM
Wareham Forest Tourist Park

ISLE OF WIGHT

NEWBRIDGE
The Orchards Holiday Caravan Park

RYDE
Whitefield Forest Touring Park

WOOTTON BRIDGE
Woodside Bay Lodge Retreat

LANCASHIRE

SILVERDALE
Silverdale Caravan Park

LINCOLNSHIRE

CAISTOR
Caistor Lakes Leisure Park

NORTHUMBERLAND

BELFORD
South Meadows Caravan Park

OXFORDSHIRE

STANDLAKE
Lincoln Farm Park Oxfordshire

SOMERSET

BISHOP SUTTON
Bath Chew Valley Caravan Park

BREAN
Warren Farm Holiday Centre

CHEDDAR
Cheddar Woods Resort & Spa

GLASTONBURY
The Old Oaks Touring Park

SUSSEX, WEST

CHICHESTER
Concierge Camping

CHANNEL ISLANDS

JERSEY

TRINITY
Durrell Wildlife Camp

SCOTLAND

FIFE

ST ANDREWS
Cairnsmill Holiday Park
Craigtoun Meadows Holiday Park

WALES

ANGLESEY, ISLE OF

MARIAN-GLAS
Home Farm Caravan Park

WREXHAM

EYTON
Plassey Holiday Park

▶▶▶▶▶ Premier Parks

Premier Parks are among the top sites in the UK, having achieved either a 5 gold (pages 31–32) or 5 black (pages 33–35) Pennant rating.

ENGLAND

CAMBRIDGESHIRE

DODDINGTON
Fields End Water Caravan Park & Fishery

ST IVES
Stroud Hill Park

CHESHIRE

CODDINGTON
Manor Wood Country Caravan Park

WHITEGATE
Lamb Cottage Caravan Park

CORNWALL

HAYLE
St Ives Bay Holiday Park

HOLYWELL BAY
Trevornick

LANDRAKE
Dolbeare Park Caravan and Camping

NEWQUAY
Treloy Touring Park

PERRANPORTH
Perran Sands Holiday Park

POLZEATH
Gunvenna Holiday Park

PORTHTOWAN
Porthtowan Tourist Park

REJERRAH
Newperran Holiday Park

ST IVES
Trevalgan Touring Park

ST MERRYN (NEAR PADSTOW)
Atlantic Bays Holiday Park

WATERGATE BAY
Watergate Bay Touring Park

CUMBRIA

BEWALDETH
Keswick Reach Lodge Retreat

KESWICK
Castlerigg Hall Caravan & Camping Park

SILLOTH
Stanwix Park Holiday Centre

WINDERMERE
Park Cliffe Camping & Caravan Estate

DEVON

BRAUNTON
Hidden Valley Park

CLYST ST MARY
Crealy Adventure Park and Resort

COMBE MARTIN
Stowford Farm Meadows

DARTMOUTH
Woodlands Grove Caravan & Camping Park

DAWLISH
Cofton Holidays

DREWSTEIGNTON
Woodland Springs Adult Touring Park

SOUTH MOLTON
Riverside Caravan & Camping Park

TAVISTOCK
Woodovis Park

WOOLACOMBE
Twitchen House Holiday Village
Warcombe Farm Caravan & Camping Park

DORSET

BRIDPORT
Freshwater Beach Holiday Park

CHARMOUTH
Wood Farm Caravan & Camping Park

POOLE
Rockley Park

Treloy Touring Park, Cornwall

WEYMOUTH
East Fleet Farm Touring Park
Weymouth Bay Holiday Park

WIMBORNE MINSTER
Wilksworth Caravan Park

HAMPSHIRE
FORDINGBRIDGE
Sandy Balls Holiday Village

KENT
ASHFORD
Broadhembury Caravan & Camping Park

MARDEN
Tanner Farm Touring Caravan & Camping
    Park

LANCASHIRE
CAPERNWRAY
Old Hall Caravan Park

LEICESTERSHIRE
MELTON MOWBRAY
Eye Kettleby Lakes

LINCOLNSHIRE
WOODHALL SPA
Woodhall Country Park

NORFOLK
BARNEY
The Old Brick Kilns

CLIPPESBY
Clippesby Hall

HOPTON ON SEA
Hopton Holiday Village

HUNSTANTON
Searles Leisure Resort

NORTHUMBERLAND
BELLINGHAM
Bellingham Camping & Caravanning
    Club Site

BERWICK-UPON-TWEED
Ord House Country Park

NOTTINGHAMSHIRE
TEVERSAL
Teversal Camping & Caravanning Club
    Site

OXFORDSHIRE
HENLEY-ON-THAMES
Swiss Farm Touring & Camping

SHROPSHIRE
SHREWSBURY
Beaconsfield Farm Caravan Park
Oxon Hall Touring Park

WHEATHILL
Wheathill Touring Park

SOMERSET
BATH
Bath Mill Lodge Retreat

BREAN
Holiday Resort Unity

BURNHAM-ON-SEA
Burnham-on-Sea Holiday Village

WATCHET
Doniford Bay Holiday Park

WELLS
Wells Touring Park

WIVELISCOMBE
Waterrow Touring Park

STAFFORDSHIRE
LONGNOR
Longnor Wood Holiday Park

SUFFOLK
DUNWICH
Haw Wood Farm Caravan Park

LEISTON
Cakes & Ale

WOODBRIDGE
Moon & Sixpence

SUSSEX, WEST
CHICHESTER
Concierge Glamping

PAGHAM
Church Farm Holiday Park

YORKSHIRE, NORTH
ALLERSTON
Vale of Pickering Caravan Park

FILEY
Flower of May Holiday Park

HIGH BENTHAM
Riverside Caravan Park

SCOTLAND
ABERDEENSHIRE
HUNTLY
Huntly Castle Caravan Park

DUMFRIES & GALLOWAY
BRIGHOUSE BAY
Brighouse Bay Holiday Park

GATEHOUSE OF FLEET
Auchenlarie Holiday Park

LOTHIAN, EAST
DUNBAR
Thurston Manor Leisure Park

PERTH & KINROSS
BLAIR ATHOLL
Blair Castle Caravan Park

STIRLING
ABERFOYLE
Trossachs Holiday Park

SCOTTISH ISLANDS
ARRAN, ISLE OF
KILMORY
Runach Arainn

WALES
ANGLESEY, ISLE OF
DULAS
Tyddyn Isaf Caravan Park

GWYNEDD
BARMOUTH
Trawsdir Touring Caravans & Camping
    Park

PWLLHELI
Hafan y Môr Holiday Park

TAL-Y-BONT
Islawrffordd Caravan Park

MONMOUTHSHIRE
LLANVAIR DISCOED
Penhein Glamping

PEMBROKESHIRE
ST DAVIDS
Caerfai Bay Caravan & Tent Park

POWYS
BRECON
Pencelli Castle Caravan & Camping Park

NORTHERN IRELAND
COUNTY ANTRIM
BUSHMILLS
Ballyness Caravan Park

►►►►► Premier Parks

ENGLAND

CORNWALL

HAYLE
Riviere Sands Holiday Park

LEEDSTOWN (NEAR HAYLE)
Calloose Caravan & Camping Park

LOOE
Camping Caradon Touring Park
Tencreek Holiday Park
Tregoad Park

LOSTWITHIEL
Eden Valley Holiday Park

NEWQUAY
Monkey Tree Holiday Park

PADSTOW
Padstow Holiday Park

ST AGNES
Beacon Cottage Farm Touring Park

ST AUSTELL
River Valley Holiday Park

ST IVES
Ayr Holiday Park

TRURO
Cosawes Park
Truro Caravan and Camping Park

CUMBRIA

APPLEBY-IN-WESTMORLAND
Wild Rose Park

FLOOKBURGH
Lakeland Leisure Park

KIRKBY LONSDALE
Woodclose Caravan Park

PENRITH
Lowther Holiday Park

POOLEY BRIDGE
Park Foot Caravan & Camping Park

ULVERSTON
Bardsea Leisure Park

WATERMILLOCK
The Quiet Site

WINDERMERE
Hill of Oaks & Blakeholme

DERBYSHIRE

BIRCHOVER
Barn Farm Campsite

DEVON

COMBE MARTIN
Newberry Valley Park

DAWLISH
Lady's Mile Holiday Park

ILFRACOMBE
Hele Valley Holiday Park

KENNFORD
Kennford International Holiday Park

KINGSBRIDGE
Island Lodge Caravan & Camping Site
Parkland Caravan and Camping Site

PAIGNTON
Beverley Park Caravan & Camping Park

SAMPFORD PEVERELL
Minnows Touring Park

SIDMOUTH
Salcombe Regis Caravan & Camping
  Park

TAVISTOCK
Harford Bridge Holiday Park
Langstone Manor Camping & Caravan
  Park

WOOLACOMBE
Golden Coast Holiday Village
Woolacombe Bay Holiday Village & Spa

DORSET

ALDERHOLT
Hill Cottage Farm Camping and Caravan
  Park

CHARMOUTH
Newlands Holidays

CHIDEOCK
Golden Cap Holiday Park

CHRISTCHURCH
Meadowbank Holidays

HOLDITCH
Crafty Camping

ST LEONARDS
Shamba Holidays

SHAFTESBURY
Dorset Country Holidays

SWANAGE
Ulwell Cottage Caravan Park

Bron Derw Touring Caravan Park, Conwy

WEYMOUTH
Littlesea Holiday Park
Seaview Holiday Park

ESSEX
MERSEA ISLAND
Waldegraves Holiday Park

ISLE OF WIGHT
NEWPORT
Wight Glamping Holidays

KENT
AYLESFORD
Kits Coty Glamping

LANCASHIRE
BLACKPOOL
Marton Mere Holiday Village

FAR ARNSIDE
Hollins Farm Camping & Caravanning

FLEETWOOD
Cala Gran Holiday Park

THORNTON
Kneps Farm Holiday Caravan Park

LINCOLNSHIRE
CLEETHORPES
Thorpe Park Holiday Centre

MABLETHORPE
Golden Sands Holiday Park

MERSEYSIDE
SOUTHPORT
Riverside Holiday Park

NORFOLK
BELTON
Rose Farm Touring & Camping Park

CAISTER-ON-SEA
Caister-on-Sea Holiday Park

GREAT YARMOUTH
Seashore Holiday Park

KING'S LYNN
King's Lynn Caravan and Camping Park

NORTH WALSHAM
Two Mills Touring Park

NORTHAMPTONSHIRE
BULWICK
New Lodge Farm Caravan & Camping
    Site

NORTHUMBERLAND
BERWICK-UPON-TWEED
Berwick Holiday Park
Haggerston Castle Holiday Park

RUTLAND
GREETHAM
Rutland Caravan & Camping

SHROPSHIRE
BRIDGNORTH
Stanmore Hall Touring Park

TELFORD
Severn Gorge Park

SOMERSET
BRIDGETOWN
Exe Valley Caravan Site

CROWCOMBE
Quantock Orchard Caravan Park

GLASTONBURY
Middlewick Farm

SUSSEX, EAST
BEXHILL
Kloofs Caravan Park

HASTINGS & ST LEONARDS
Combe Haven Holiday Park

WARWICKSHIRE
HARBURY
Harbury Fields

WILTSHIRE
LANDFORD
Greenhill Farm Caravan & Camping Park

WORCESTERSHIRE
HONEYBOURNE
Ranch Caravan Park

YORKSHIRE, EAST RIDING OF
FLAMBOROUGH
Thornwick Bay Holiday Village

SKIPSEA
Skirlington Leisure Park

TUNSTALL
Sand le Mere Holiday Village

YORKSHIRE, NORTH
ALNE
Alders Caravan Park

HARROGATE
Ripley Caravan Park
Rudding Holiday Park

HELMSLEY
Golden Square Caravan & Camping Park

OSMOTHERLEY
Cote Ghyll Caravan & Camping Park

RIPON
Riverside Meadows Country Caravan Park

SNAINTON
Jasmine Caravan Park

SUTTON-ON-THE-FOREST
Goosewood Holiday Park

THIRSK
Hillside Caravan Park

WYKEHAM
St Helens in the Park

CHANNEL ISLANDS

GUERNSEY
CASTEL
Fauxquets Valley Campsite

JERSEY
ST MARTIN
Rozel Camping Park

SCOTLAND

AYRSHIRE, SOUTH
AYR
Craig Tara Holiday Park

DUMFRIES & GALLOWAY
ECCLEFECHAN
Hoddom Castle Caravan Park

KIRKCUDBRIGHT
Seaward Holiday Park

DUNBARTONSHIRE, WEST
BALLOCH
Lomond Woods Holiday Park

LOTHIAN, EAST
LONGNIDDRY
Seton Sands Holiday Village

MORAY
LOSSIEMOUTH
Silver Sands Holiday Park

PERTH & KINROSS
BLAIR ATHOLL
River Tilt Caravan Park

STIRLING
TYNDRUM
Strathfillan Wigwam Village

WALES

ANGLESEY, ISLE OF
DWYRAN
LLanfair Hall

CARMARTHENSHIRE
NEWCASTLE EMLYN
Cenarth Falls Holiday Park

CEREDIGION
NEW QUAY
Quay West Holiday Park

CONWY
LLANDDULAS
Bron-Y-Wendon Caravan Park

LLANRWST
Bron Derw Touring Caravan Park

DENBIGHSHIRE
PRESTATYN
Presthaven Sands Holiday Park

GWYNEDD
BARMOUTH
Hendre Mynach Touring Caravan
  & Camping Park

BETWS GARMON
Bryn Gloch Caravan & Camping Park

DINAS DINLLE
Dinlle Caravan Park

PORTHMADOG
Greenacres Holiday Park

MONMOUTHSHIRE
USK
Pont Kemys Caravan & Camping Park

PEMBROKESHIRE
TENBY
Kiln Park Holiday Centre

POWYS
BUILTH WELLS
Fforest Fields Caravan & Camping Park

CHURCHSTOKE
Daisy Bank Caravan Park

LLANIDLOES
Red Kite Touring Park

SWANSEA
PONTARDDULAIS
River View Touring Park

WREXHAM
OVERTON
The Trotting Mare Caravan Park

NORTHERN IRELAND

COUNTY FERMANAGH
BELCOO
Rushin House Caravan Park

River Valley Holiday Park, Cornwall

► Gold Pennant parks

Gold Pennants are awarded to sites with a quality score of 90% and above within the 1–5 Pennant ratings.

ENGLAND

CAMBRIDGESHIRE

COMBERTON
►►►► Highfield Farm Touring Park

DODDINGTON
►►►►► Fields End Water Caravan Park & Fishery

ST IVES
►►►► Stroud Hill Park

CHESHIRE

CODDINGTON
►►►►► Manor Wood Country Caravan Park

WHITEGATE
►►►►► Lamb Cottage Caravan Park

CORNWALL

BUDE
►►► Budemeadows Touring Park

HAYLE
►►►►► St Ives Bay Holiday Park

HELSTON
►►►► Lower Polladras Touring Park

HOLYWELL BAY
►►►►► Trevornick

KENNACK SANDS
►►►► Chy Carne Holiday Park

LANDRAKE
►►►►► Dolbeare Park Caravan and Camping

MARAZION
►►►► Wayfarers Caravan & Camping Park

NEWQUAY
►►►►► Treloy Touring Park
►►►► Trencreek Holiday Park

PERRANPORTH
►►►►► Perran Sands Holiday Park

POLZEATH
►►►►► Gunvenna Holiday Park
►►► Tristram Caravan & Camping Park

PORTHTOWAN
►►►►► Porthtowan Tourist Park

PORTREATH
►►►► Tehidy Holiday Park

REDRUTH
►►►► Lanyon Holiday Park

REJERRAH
►►►► Newperran Holiday Park

ROSUDGEON
►►►► Kenneggy Cove Holiday Park

ST IVES
►►►►► Trevalgan Touring Park

ST JUST [NEAR LAND'S END]
►►► Roselands Caravan and Camping Park

ST MERRYN (NEAR PADSTOW)
►►►►► Atlantic Bays Holiday Park

SENNEN
►►►► Trevedra Farm Caravan & Camping Site

SUMMERCOURT
►►►► Carvynick Holiday Park

TRURO
►►►► Summer Valley Touring Park

WADEBRIDGE
►►►► The Laurels Holiday Park

WATERGATE BAY
►►►►► Watergate Bay Touring Park

CUMBRIA

BEWALDETH
►►►► Keswick Reach Lodge Retreat

KESWICK
►►►► Castlerigg Hall Caravan & Camping Park

SILLOTH
►►►► Stanwix Park Holiday Centre

WINDERMERE
►►►► Park Cliffe Camping & Caravan Estate

DERBYSHIRE

BUXTON
►►►► Beech Croft Farm
►►►► Lime Tree Park

MATLOCK
►►►► Lickpenny Caravan Site

DEVON

BRAUNTON
►►►►► Hidden Valley Park

BUCKFASTLEIGH
►► Churchill Farm Campsite

CLYST ST MARY
►►►► Crealy Adventure Park and Resort

COMBE MARTIN
►►►►► Stowford Farm Meadows

DARTMOUTH
►►►►► Woodlands Grove Caravan & Camping Park

DAWLISH
►►►►► Cofton Holidays

DREWSTEIGNTON
►►►►► Woodland Springs Adult Touring Park

MORTEHOE
►►►► North Morte Farm Caravan & Camping Park

SOUTH MOLTON
►►►►► Riverside Caravan & Camping Park

TAVISTOCK
►►►►► Woodovis Park

TORQUAY
►►►► Widdicombe Farm Touring Park

WOOLACOMBE
►►►►► Twitchen House Holiday Village
►►►►► Warcombe Farm Caravan & Camping Park

DORSET

BRIDPORT
►►►►► Freshwater Beach Holiday Park
►►► Graston Copse Holiday Park

CHARMOUTH
►►►►► Wood Farm Caravan & Camping Park

CORFE CASTLE
▶▶▶▶ Corfe Castle Camping & Caravanning Club Site

LYME REGIS
▶▶▶▶ Shrubbery Touring Park

POOLE
▶▶▶▶▶ Rockley Park

ST LEONARDS
▶▶▶▶ Back of Beyond Touring Park

WEYMOUTH
▶▶▶▶▶ East Fleet Farm Touring Park
▶▶▶ Rosewall Camping
▶▶▶ West Fleet Holiday Farm
▶▶▶▶▶ Weymouth Bay Holiday Park

WIMBORNE MINSTER
▶▶▶▶ Charris Camping & Caravan Park
▶▶▶▶▶ Wilksworth Caravan Park

GLOUCESTERSHIRE

CHELTENHAM
▶▶▶▶ Briarfields Motel & Touring Park

CIRENCESTER
▶▶▶▶ Mayfield Park

HAMPSHIRE

FORDINGBRIDGE
▶▶▶▶▶ Sandy Balls Holiday Village

KENT

ASHFORD
▶▶▶▶▶ Broadhembury Caravan & Camping Park

MARDEN
▶▶▶▶▶ Tanner Farm Touring Caravan & Camping Park

LANCASHIRE

CAPERNWRAY
▶▶▶▶▶ Old Hall Caravan Park

LEICESTERSHIRE

MELTON MOWBRAY
▶▶▶▶▶ Eye Kettleby Lakes

LINCOLNSHIRE

BOSTON
▶▶▶▶ Long Acres Touring Park

MARSTON
▶▶▶▶ Wagtail Country Park

TATTERSHALL
▶▶▶▶ Tattershall Lakes Country Park

THORPE ST PETER
▶▶▶▶ Grooby's Pit

WOODHALL SPA
▶▶▶▶ Petwood Caravan Park
▶▶▶▶▶ Woodhall Country Park

NORFOLK

BARNEY
▶▶▶▶▶ The Old Brick Kilns

CLIPPESBY
▶▶▶▶▶ Clippesby Hall

HOPTON ON SEA
▶▶▶▶ Hopton Holiday Village

HUNSTANTON
▶▶▶▶▶ Searles Leisure Resort

NORTHUMBERLAND

BAMBURGH
▶▶▶ Waren Caravan & Camping Park

BELLINGHAM
▶▶▶▶▶ Bellingham Camping & Caravanning Club Site

BERWICK-UPON-TWEED
▶▶▶▶▶ Ord House Country Park

NOTTINGHAMSHIRE

TEVERSAL
▶▶▶▶▶ Teversal Camping & Caravanning Club Site

OXFORDSHIRE

BLETCHINGDON
▶▶▶▶ Greenhill Leisure Park

HENLEY-ON-THAMES
▶▶▶▶▶ Swiss Farm Touring & Camping

SHROPSHIRE

SHREWSBURY
▶▶▶▶ Beaconsfield Farm Caravan Park
▶▶▶▶ Cartref Caravan & Camping
▶▶▶▶▶ Oxon Hall Touring Park

WHEATHILL
▶▶▶▶▶ Wheathill Touring Park

SOMERSET

BATH
▶▶▶▶ Bath Mill Lodge Retreat

BREAN
▶▶▶▶▶ Holiday Resort Unity
▶▶▶▶ Northam Farm Caravan & Touring Park

BURNHAM-ON-SEA
▶▶▶▶▶ Burnham-on-Sea Holiday Village

COWSLIP GREEN
▶▶▶ Brook Lodge Farm Camping & Caravan Park

PORLOCK
▶▶▶▶ Burrowhayes Farm Caravan & Camping Site & Riding Stables

SHEPTON MALLET
▶▶ Greenacres Camping

WATCHET
▶▶▶▶▶ Doniford Bay Holiday Park

WELLS
▶▶▶▶▶ Wells Touring Park

WIVELISCOMBE
▶▶▶▶ Waterrow Touring Park

STAFFORDSHIRE

LONGNOR
▶▶▶▶▶ Longnor Wood Holiday Park

SUFFOLK

DUNWICH
▶▶▶▶▶ Haw Wood Farm Caravan Park

KESSINGLAND
▶▶▶▶ Heathland Beach Holiday Park

LEISTON
▶▶▶▶▶ Cakes & Ale

SAXMUNDHAM
▶▶ Marsh Farm Caravan Site

WOODBRIDGE
▶▶▶▶▶ Moon & Sixpence

SUSSEX, WEST

BARNS GREEN
▶▶▶▶▶ Sumners Ponds Fishery & Campsite

CHICHESTER
▶▶▶▶▶ Concierge Glamping

PAGHAM
▶▶▶▶▶ Church Farm Holiday Park

WEST MIDLANDS

MERIDEN
▶▶▶▶ Somers Wood Caravan Park

WILTSHIRE

AMESBURY
▶▶▶ Stonehenge Touring Park

SALISBURY
▶▶▶▶ Coombe Touring Park

YORKSHIRE, EAST RIDING OF

BRANDESBURTON
▶▶▶▶ Blue Rose Caravan Country Park

SPROATLEY
▶▶▶▶ Burton Constable Holiday Park & Arboretum

▶ Gold Pennant parks *continued*

YORKSHIRE, NORTH

ALLERSTON
▶▶▶▶▶ Vale of Pickering Caravan Park

FILEY
▶▶▶▶ Crows Nest Caravan Park
▶▶▶▶ Flower of May Holiday Park
▶▶▶▶ Lebberston Touring Park

HARROGATE
▶▶▶▶ Harrogate Caravan Park

HIGH BENTHAM
▶▶▶▶▶ Riverside Caravan Park

NABURN
▶▶▶▶ Naburn Lock Caravan Park

ROBIN HOOD'S BAY
▶▶▶▶ Grouse Hill Caravan Park
▶▶▶▶ Middlewood Farm Holiday Park

SCARBOROUGH
▶▶▶ Arosa Caravan & Camping Park

STAINFORTH
▶▶▶▶ Knight Stainforth Hall Caravan & Campsite

WHITBY
▶▶▶▶ Ladycross Plantation Caravan Park

CHANNEL ISLANDS

GUERNSEY

ST SAMPSON
▶▶▶ Le Vaugrat Camp Site

SCOTLAND

ABERDEENSHIRE

HUNTLY
▶▶▶▶▶ Huntly Castle Caravan Park

ARGYLL & BUTE

CARRADALE
▶▶▶ Carradale Bay Caravan Park

DUMFRIES & GALLOWAY

BRIGHOUSE BAY
▶▶▶▶▶ Brighouse Bay Holiday Park

GATEHOUSE OF FLEET
▶▶▶▶▶ Auchenlarie Holiday Park

SANDHEAD
▶▶▶▶ Sands of Luce Holiday Park

WIGTOWN
▶▶▶ Drumroamin Farm Camping & Touring Site

HIGHLAND

AVIEMORE
▶▶▶▶ Aviemore Glamping

FORT WILLIAM
▶▶▶▶ Glen Nevis Caravan & Camping Park

LOTHIAN, EAST

DUNBAR
▶▶▶▶▶ Thurston Manor Leisure Park

LOTHIAN, WEST

LINLITHGOW
▶▶▶▶▶ Beecraigs Caravan & Camping Site

PERTH & KINROSS

BLAIR ATHOLL
▶▶▶▶▶ Blair Castle Caravan Park

PITLOCHRY
▶▶▶▶ Milton of Fonab Caravan Park

STIRLING

ABERFOYLE
▶▶▶▶▶ Trossachs Holiday Park

BLAIRLOGIE
▶▶▶▶ Witches Craig Caravan & Camping Park

SCOTTISH ISLANDS

ARRAN, ISLE OF

KILMORY
▶▶▶▶ Runach Arainn

SKYE, ISLE OF

EDINBANE
▶▶▶▶ Skye Camping & Caravanning Club Site

WALES

ANGLESEY, ISLE OF

DULAS
▶▶▶▶▶ Tyddyn Isaf Caravan Park

CEREDIGION

ABERAERON
▶▶▶ Aeron Coast Caravan Park

DENBIGHSHIRE

RHUALLT
▶▶▶▶ Penisar Mynydd Caravan Park

GWYNEDD

BARMOUTH
▶▶▶▶ Trawsdir Touring Caravans & Camping Park

CRICCIETH
▶▶▶▶ Eisteddfa

PWLLHELI
▶▶▶▶▶ Hafan y Môr Holiday Park

TAL-Y-BONT
▶▶▶▶▶ Islawrffordd Caravan Park

MONMOUTHSHIRE

LLANVAIR DISCOED
▶▶▶▶ Penhein Glamping

PEMBROKESHIRE

FISHGUARD
▶▶▶▶ Fishguard Bay Resort

ST DAVIDS
▶▶▶▶ Caerfai Bay Caravan & Tent Park

POWYS

BRECON
▶▶▶▶▶ Pencelli Castle Caravan & Camping Park

SWANSEA

RHOSSILI
▶▶▶ Pitton Cross Caravan & Camping Park

NORTHERN IRELAND

COUNTY ANTRIM

BUSHMILLS
▶▶▶▶▶ Ballyness Caravan Park

AA WALKING GUIDES

The 50 Best Walks of 2–10 Miles by Region and City

- Easy-to-follow directions with clear waypointed maps
- Colour-coded routes – pick from easy strolls through to more challenging walks
- Fascinating background reading for every walk
- Advice for dog owners
- Great for a full day out with recommended sights and attractions plus places to eat and drink

Follow @TheAA_Lifestyle

AA Holiday Centres

These parks cater for all holiday needs. See page 11 for further information.

ENGLAND

CORNWALL
HAYLE
►►►►► St Ives Bay Holiday Park

LOOE
►►►►► Tencreek Holiday Park

NEWQUAY
►►►►► Hendra Holiday Park

PERRANPORTH
►►►►► Perran Sands Holiday Park

WATERGATE BAY
►►►►► Watergate Bay Touring Park

CUMBRIA
FLOOKBURGH
►►►►► Lakeland Leisure Park

POOLEY BRIDGE
►►►►► Park Foot Caravan & Camping Park

SILLOTH
►►►►► Stanwix Park Holiday Centre

DEVON
WOOLACOMBE
►►►►► Golden Coast Holiday Village
►►►►► Twitchen House Holiday Village

DORSET
BRIDPORT
►►►►► Freshwater Beach Holiday Park

WEYMOUTH
►►►►► Littlesea Holiday Park
►►►►► Seaview Holiday Park

ESSEX
MERSEA ISLAND
►►►►► Waldegraves Holiday Park

ST OSYTH
►►►► The Orchards Holiday Park

LANCASHIRE
BLACKPOOL
►►►►► Marton Mere Holiday Village

LONGRIDGE
►►►► Beacon Fell View Holiday Park

LINCOLNSHIRE
CLEETHORPES
►►►►► Thorpe Park Holiday Centre

MABLETHORPE
►►►►► Golden Sands Holiday Park

MERSEYSIDE
SOUTHPORT
►►►►► Riverside Holiday Park

NORFOLK
BELTON
►►►► Wild Duck Holiday Park

CAISTER-ON-SEA
►►►►► Caister-on-Sea Holiday Park

HUNSTANTON
►►►►► Searles Leisure Resort

NORTHUMBERLAND
BERWICK-UPON-TWEED
►►►►► Haggerston Castle Holiday Park

SOMERSET
BREAN
►►►►► Holiday Resort Unity
►►►►► Warren Farm Holiday Centre

BURNHAM-ON-SEA
►►►► Burnham-on-Sea Holiday Village

SUSSEX, WEST
SELSEY
►►►► Warner Farm

YORKSHIRE, EAST RIDING OF
FLAMBOROUGH
►►►►► Thornwick Bay Holiday Village

SKIPSEA
►►►►► Skirlington Leisure Park

TUNSTALL
►►►►► Sand le Mere Holiday Village

YORKSHIRE, NORTH
FILEY
►►►► Blue Dolphin Holiday Park
►►►►► Flower of May Holiday Park
►►►► Primrose Valley Holiday Park
►►►► Reighton Sands Holiday Park

SCOTLAND

AYRSHIRE, SOUTH
AYR
►►►►► Craig Tara Holiday Park

DUMFRIES & GALLOWAY
GATEHOUSE OF FLEET
►►►►► Auchenlarie Holiday Park

LOTHIAN, EAST
LONGNIDDRY
►►►►► Seton Sands Holiday Village

WALES

DENBIGHSHIRE
PRESTATYN
►►►►► Presthaven Sands Holiday Park

GWYNEDD
PORTHMADOG
►►►►► Greenacres Holiday Park

PWLLHELI
►►►►► Hafan y Môr Holiday Park

PEMBROKESHIRE
TENBY
►►►►► Kiln Park Holiday Centre

SWANSEA
SWANSEA
►►►► Riverside Caravan Park

NORTHERN IRELAND

COUNTY ANTRIM
BALLYCASTLE
►►►► Causeway Coast Holiday Park

Adults only – no children parks

The following parks are children-free sites with facilities just for adults.

ENGLAND

CAMBRIDGESHIRE
DODDINGTON
Fields End Water Caravan Park & Fishery

ST IVES
Stroud Hill Park

CHESHIRE
LOWER WITHINGTON
Welltrough Hall Farm Caravan Site

WETTENHALL
New Farm Caravan Park

WHITEGATE
Lamb Cottage Caravan Park

CORNWALL
CHACEWATER
Killiwerris Touring Park

MARAZION
Wayfarers Caravan & Camping Park

ROSE
Higher Hendra Park

CUMBRIA
CARLISLE
Green Acres Caravan Park

MEALSGATE
Larches Caravan Park

DEVON
DREWSTEIGNTON
Woodland Springs Adult Touring Park

TORQUAY
Widdicombe Farm Touring Park

DORSET
HOLDITCH
Crafty Camping

HURN
Fillybrook Farm Touring Park

ST LEONARDS
Back of Beyond Touring Park

SHAFTESBURY
Lower Liston Farm Touring Park

GLOUCESTERSHIRE
CHELTENHAM
Briarfields Motel & Touring Park

LANCASHIRE
BLACKPOOL
Manor House Caravan Park

ESPRICK
Charoland Farm

LEICESTERSHIRE
MELTON MOWBRAY
Eye Kettleby Lakes

LINCOLNSHIRE
BOSTON
Long Acres Touring Park
Orchard Park

CAISTOR
Caistor Lakes Leisure Park
Wolds View Touring Park

THORPE ST PETER
Grooby's Pit

NORFOLK
NORTH WALSHAM
Two Mills Touring Park

STANHOE
The Rickels Caravan & Camping Park

SWAFFHAM
Breckland Meadows Touring Park

NORTHAMPTONSHIRE
BULWICK
New Lodge Farm Caravan & Camping
   Site

NOTTINGHAMSHIRE
SOUTHWELL
New Hall Farm Touring Park

OXFORDSHIRE
BURFORD
Wysdom Touring Park

SHROPSHIRE
SHREWSBURY
Beaconsfield Farm Caravan Park

TELFORD
Severn Gorge Park

WHEATHILL
Wheathill Touring Park

SOMERSET
BISHOP SUTTON
Bath Chew Valley Caravan Park

BRIDGETOWN
Exe Valley Caravan Site

GLASTONBURY
The Old Oaks Touring Park

HIGHBRIDGE
Greenacre Place Touring Caravan Park

SPARKFORD
Long Hazel Park

WELLS
Wells Touring Park

WIVELISCOMBE
Waterrow Touring Park

STAFFORDSHIRE
LONGNOR
Longnor Wood Holiday Park

SUFFOLK
HOLLESLEY
Run Cottage Touring Park

THEBERTON
Sycamore Park

WOODBRIDGE
Moat Barn Touring Caravan Park

WEST MIDLANDS
MERIDEN
Somers Wood Caravan Park

YORKSHIRE, EAST RIDING OF
BRANDESBURTON
Blue Rose Caravan Country Park

YORKSHIRE, NORTH
HARROGATE
Shaws Trailer Park

HELMSLEY
Foxholme Caravan Park

YORK
Rawcliffe Manor Caravan Park

YORKSHIRE, WEST
LEEDS
Moor Lodge Park

WALES

MONMOUTHSHIRE
ABERGAVENNY
Wernddu Caravan Park

POWYS
CHURCHSTOKE
Daisy Bank Caravan Park

CRICKHOWELL
Riverside Caravan & Camping Park

LLANDRINDOD WELLS
Dalmore Camping & Caravanning Park

LLANIDLOES
Red Kite Touring Park

WREXHAM
OVERTON
The Trotting Mare Caravan Park

Glamping sites

These campsites offer one or more types of glamping accommodation, i.e. wooden pods, tipis, yurts, bell tents, safari tents, shepherd's huts, geo domes and vintage caravans.

ENGLAND

BERKSHIRE

FINCHAMPSTEAD
California Chalet & Touring Park

CHESHIRE

DELAMERE
Fishpool Farm Caravan Park

LOWER WITHINGTON
Welltrough Hall Farm Caravan Site

CORNWALL & ISLES OF SCILLY

BLISLAND
South Penquite Farm

BODMIN
Mena Farm

BRYHER (ISLES OF SCILLY)
Bryher Camp Site

BUDE
Wooda Farm Holiday Park

CARLYON BAY
East Crinnis Camping & Caravan Park

CRANTOCK (NEAR NEWQUAY)
Trevella Park

HAYLE
Atlantic Coast Holiday Park
Higher Trevaskis Caravan & Camping
    Park
St Ives Bay Holiday Park

HOLYWELL BAY
Trevornick

KILKHAMPTON
Upper Tamar Lake

LANDRAKE
Dolbeare Park Caravan and Camping

LOOE
Tregoad Park

NEWQUAY
Hendra Holiday Park
Porth Beach Holiday Park
Trenance Holiday Park

PERRANPORTH
Perran Sands Holiday Park
Tollgate Farm Caravan & Camping Park

POLZEATH
Gunvenna Holiday Park

PORTREATH
Tehidy Holiday Park

PORTSCATHO
Trewince Farm Touring Park

RUTHERNBRIDGE
Ruthern Valley Holidays

ST AUSTELL
Meadow Lakes Holiday Park

ST MARY'S (ISLES OF SCILLY)
Garrison Campsite

ST MERRYN
Tregavone Touring Park

TRURO
Summer Valley Touring Park

WADEBRIDGE
Lowarth Glamping

CUMBRIA

AMBLESIDE
Low Wray National Trust Campsite
Skelwith Fold Caravan Park

APPLEBY-IN-WESTMORLAND
Wild Rose Park

GREAT LANGDALE
Great Langdale National Trust Campsite

KESWICK
Castlerigg Hall Caravan & Camping Park

KIRKBY LONSDALE
Woodclose Caravan Park

MILNTHORPE
Hall More Caravan Park

NETHER WASDALE
Church Stile Farm & Holiday Park

PATTERDALE
Sykeside Camping & Caravan Park

PENRITH
Lowther Holiday Park

PENTON
Twin Willows

POOLEY BRIDGE
Waterfoot Caravan Park

SILLOTH
Stanwix Park Holiday Centre

WASDALE HEAD
Wasdale Head National Trust Campsite

WATERMILLOCK
The Quiet Site
Ullswater Holiday Park

WINDERMERE
Hill of Oaks & Blakeholme
Park Cliffe Camping & Caravan Estate

DERBYSHIRE

RIPLEY
Golden Valley Caravan & Camping Park

ROSLISTON
Beehive Woodland Lakes

DEVON

ASHILL
Leafy Fields Glamping

AXMINSTER
Andrewshayes Holiday Park

BERRYNARBOR
Mill Park Touring Caravan & Camping
    Park

CLAYHIDON
Kingsmead Centre Camping

CLYST ST MARY
Crealy Adventure Park and Resort

COMBE MARTIN
Newberry Valley Park

CROYDE
Bay View Farm Caravan & Camping Park

DAWLISH
Lady's Mile Holiday Park

DREWSTEIGNTON
Woodland Springs Adult Touring Park

ILFRACOMBE
Hele Valley Holiday Park

KENTISBEARE
Forest Glade Holiday Park

OTTERY ST MARY
Cuckoo Down Farm Glamping

PAIGNTON
Whitehill Country Park

SIDMOUTH
Oakdown Country Holiday Park

SOURTON CROSS
Bundu Camping & Caravan Park

TAVISTOCK
Harford Bridge Holiday Park
Langstone Manor Camping & Caravan
Park
Woodovis Park

WOOLACOMBE
Europa Park
Woolacombe Bay Holiday Village & Spa

DORSET
ALDERHOLT
Hill Cottage Farm Camping and Caravan
Park

BERE REGIS
Rowlands Wait Touring Park

BRIDPORT
Graston Copse Holiday Park
Highlands End Holiday Park

CHARMOUTH
Newlands Holidays

CHIDEOCK
Golden Cap Holiday Park

CORFE CASTLE
Woodyhyde Camp Site

FERNDOWN
St Leonards Farm Caravan & Camping
Park

HOLDITCH
Crafty Camping

LYME REGIS
Hook Farm Caravan & Camping Park
Shrubbery Touring Park

OWERMOIGNE
Sandyholme Holiday Park

POOLE
South Lytchett Manor Caravan &
Camping Park

ST LEONARDS
Back of Beyond Touring Park

SHAFTESBURY
Dorset Country Holidays

SWANAGE
Ulwell Cottage Caravan Park

WEYMOUTH
Littlesea Holiday Park
Seaview Holiday Park

WIMBORNE MINSTER
Charris Camping & Caravan Park

HAMPSHIRE
FORDINGBRIDGE
Sandy Balls Holiday Village

HERTFORDSHIRE
HODDESDON
Lee Valley Caravan Park Dobbs Weir

ISLE OF WIGHT
BRIGHSTONE
Grange Farm

NEWPORT
Wight Glamping Holidays

KENT
ASHFORD
Broadhembury Caravan & Camping Park

AYLESFORD
Kits Coty Glamping

MARDEN
Tanner Farm Touring Caravan & Camping
Park

WHITSTABLE
Homing Park

LANCASHIRE
BOLTON LE SANDS
Bay View Holiday Park

CROSTON
Royal Umpire Caravan Park

FAR ARNSIDE
Hollins Farm Camping & Caravanning

SILVERDALE
Silverdale Caravan Park

THORNTON
Kneps Farm Holiday Caravan Park

LEICESTERSHIRE
MELTON MOWBRAY
Eye Kettleby Lakes

LINCOLNSHIRE
CAISTOR
Wolds View Touring Park

LANGWORTH
Barlings Country Holiday Park

TATTERSHALL
Tattershall Lakes Country Park

THORPE ST PETER
Grooby's Pit

WOODHALL SPA
Woodhall Country Park

LONDON
E4 CHINGFORD
Lee Valley Campsite

N9 EDMONTON
Lee Valley Camping & Caravan Park

NORFOLK
BELTON
Rose Farm Touring & Camping Park
Wild Duck Holiday Park

CROMER
Forest Park

HUNSTANTON
Searles Leisure Resort

KING'S LYNN
King's Lynn Caravan and Camping Park

NORTHUMBERLAND
BAMBURGH
Waren Caravan & Camping Park

BELLINGHAM
Bellingham Camping & Caravanning
Club Site

BERWICK-UPON-TWEED
Ord House Country Park

WOOLER
Riverside Leisure Park

NOTTINGHAMSHIRE
TEVERSAL
Teversal Camping & Caravanning Club
Site

OXFORDSHIRE
FRINGFORD
Glebe Leisure

HENLEY-ON-THAMES
Swiss Farm Touring & Camping

SHROPSHIRE
WEM
Lower Lacon Caravan Park

SOMERSET
BREAN
Holiday Resort Unity

BURNHAM-ON-SEA
Burnham-on-Sea Holiday Village

COWSLIP GREEN
Brook Lodge Farm Camping & Caravan
Park

DULVERTON
Wimbleball Lake

GLASTONBURY
Middlewick Farm
The Old Oaks Touring Park

MARTOCK
Southfork Caravan Park

SPARKFORD
Woodland Escape

Glamping sites *continued*

STAFFORDSHIRE

LONGNOR
Longnor Wood Holiday Park

SUFFOLK

HOLLESLEY
Run Cottage Touring Park

SUSSEX, WEST

BARNS GREEN
Sumners Ponds Fishery & Campsite

CHICHESTER
Concierge Glamping

WILTSHIRE

BERWICK ST JAMES
Stonehenge Campsite & Glamping Pods

LANDFORD
Greenhill Farm Caravan & Camping Park

YORKSHIRE, EAST RIDING OF

BRANDESBURTON
Dacre Lakeside Park

SPROATLEY
Burton Constable Holiday Park &
  Arboretum

YORKSHIRE, NORTH

ALLERSTON
Vale of Pickering Caravan Park

ALNE
Alders Caravan Park

CHOP GATE
Lordstones Country Park

FILEY
Flower of May Holiday Park

KIRKLINGTON
Camp Kátur

MASHAM
Old Station Holiday Park

ROBIN HOOD'S BAY
Grouse Hill Caravan Park
Middlewood Farm Holiday Park

ROSEDALE ABBEY
Rosedale Abbey Caravan Park

THIRSK
Hillside Caravan Park

WYKEHAM
St Helens in the Park

CHANNEL ISLANDS

GUERNSEY

ST SAMPSON
Le Vaugrat Camp Site

VALE
La Bailloterie Camping

JERSEY

ST MARTIN
Rozel Camping Park

ST OUEN
Daisy Cottage Campsite

TRINITY
Durrell Wildlife Camp

ISLE OF MAN

KIRK MICHAEL
Glen Wyllin Campsite

SCOTLAND

ABERDEENSHIRE

MINTLAW
Aden Caravan and Camping Park

ARGYLL & BUTE

OBAN
Oban Caravan & Camping Park

AYRSHIRE, SOUTH

BARRHILL
Barrhill Holiday Park

DUMFRIES & GALLOWAY

BRIGHOUSE BAY
Brighouse Bay Holiday Park

ECCLEFECHAN
Hoddom Castle Caravan Park

GATEHOUSE OF FLEET
Auchenlarie Holiday Park

KIRKCUDBRIGHT
Seaward Holiday Park

PALNACKIE
Barlochan Caravan Park

SANDYHILLS
Sandyhills Bay Holiday Park

DUNBARTONSHIRE, WEST

BALLOCH
Lomond Woods Holiday Park

FIFE

ST ANDREWS
Cairnsmill Holiday Park
Craigtoun Meadows Holiday Park

HIGHLAND

ACHARACLE
Resipole Farm Holiday Park

AVIEMORE
Aviemore Glamping

DUROR
Achindarroch Touring Park

EVANTON
Black Rock Caravan Park

FORT WILLIAM
Glen Nevis Caravan & Camping Park

GLENCOE
Invercoe Caravan & Camping Park

LOTHIAN, EAST

DUNBAR
Belhaven Bay Caravan & Camping Park

LOTHIAN, WEST

EAST CALDER
Linwater Caravan Park

LINLITHGOW
Beecraigs Caravan & Camping Site

MORAY

ELGIN
Woodlands Rest

PERTH & KINROSS

BLAIR ATHOLL
Blair Castle Caravan Park

SCOTTISH BORDERS

PAXTON
Paxton House Caravan Park

PEEBLES
Crossburn Caravan Park

STIRLING

TYNDRUM
Strathfillan Wigwam Village

SCOTTISH ISLANDS

ARRAN, ISLE OF

KILDONAN
Seal Shore Camping and Touring Site

KILMORY
Runach Arainn

MULL, ISLE OF
CRAIGNURE
Shieling Holidays Mull

SKYE, ISLE OF
EDINBANE
Skye Camping & Caravanning Club Site

WALES

ANGLESEY, ISLE OF
DWYRAN
LLanfair Hall

GWYNEDD
ABERSOCH
Bryn Bach Caravan & Camping Site

BARMOUTH
Trawsdir Touring Caravans & Camping
   Park

CAERNARFON
Plas Gwyn Caravan & Camping Park
Riverside Camping

CRICCIETH
Eisteddfa

DINAS DINLLE
Dinlle Caravan Park

MONMOUTHSHIRE
LLANVAIR DISCOED
Penhein Glamping

PEMBROKESHIRE
FISHGUARD
Fishguard Bay Resort

HAVERFORDWEST
Nolton Cross Caravan Park

TENBY
Kiln Park Holiday Centre

POWYS
BUILTH WELLS
Fforest Fields Caravan & Camping Park

CHURCHSTOKE
Daisy Bank Caravan Park

LLANDRINDOD WELLS
Disserth Caravan & Camping Park

SWANSEA
PONTARDDULAIS
River View Touring Park

RHOSSILI
Pitton Cross Caravan & Camping Park

WREXHAM
BRONINGTON
The Little Yurt Meadow

EYTON
Plassey Holiday Park

Woodhall Country Spa, Lincolnshire

Island camping

The island locations listed in this guide may have different rules and regulations for caravanning and camping. If unsure, always call ahead of your trip to check.

CHANNEL ISLANDS
Tight controls are operated because of the narrow width of the mainly rural roads. On all of the islands tents can be hired on recognised campsites and some sites offer luxury glamping units. Early booking is strongly recommended during July and August.

Alderney
Neither caravans nor motorhomes are allowed, and campers must have a confirmed booking on the one official campsite before they arrive on the island.

Guernsey
Only islanders may own and use towed caravans, but a limited number of motorhomes are permitted on the island. The motorhome, used for overnight accommodation, must be not more than 9.45 metres long and 2.3 metres wide, must be booked into an authorised site (Fauxquets Valley Campsite, La Bailloterie or Le Vaugrat Camp Site) and a permit must be obtained from the site operator before embarking on a ferry for Guernsey – Condor Ferries will not accept motorhomes without this permit.

The permit must be displayed in the window at all times, motorhomes must return to the site each night, and permits are valid for a maximum of one month. Permission is not required to bring a trailer tent to the island. (See www.visitguernsey.com).

Herm and Sark
These two small islands are traffic free. Herm has a small campsite for tents, and these can also be hired. Sark has two campsites. New arrivals are met from the boat by a tractor which carries people and luggage up the steep hill from the harbour. All travel is on foot, by bike, or by horse and cart.

Jersey
Visiting caravans and motorhomes (size restrictions apply) require a permit (maximum one month) that must be displayed at all times and they are restricted to one journey to, and one journey from, the campsite and the port. Bookings should be made through the chosen campsite and they will also arrange a permit. Caravans must remain on the designated campsites for the period of the permit. Motorhomes can travel around the island on a daily basis but must return to the designated campsite each night. For more details: www.gov.je/travel/informationadvice/travellers/pages/caravan.aspx

ISLE OF MAN
A permit maybe required, and obtained in advance. For details see www.gov.im/categories/leisure-and-entertainment/camping/

ISLES OF SCILLY
Caravans and motorhomes are not allowed on the islands, and campers must stay at official sites. Booking is advisable on all sites, especially during school holidays.

SCOTLAND
For advice on wild camping in Scotland see the Scottish Outdoor Access Code website (www.outdooraccess-scotland.scot)

Arran, Coll, Islay and Mull
All have official campsites and welcome caravans, motorhomes and tents; wild camping is also permitted but access rights apply (check each island's website for details).

Skye
Caravans, motorhomes and tents are permitted and there are official campsites.

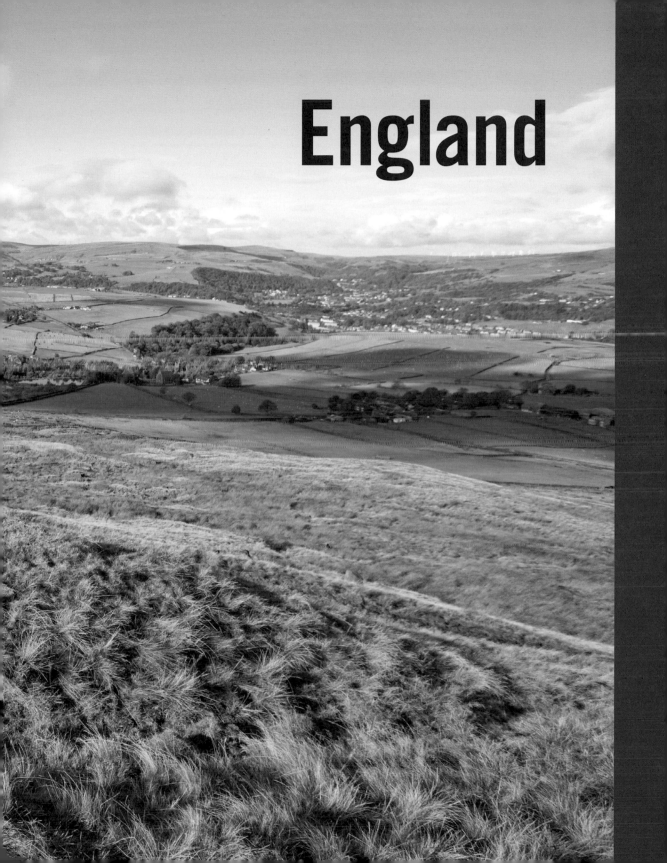

England

BERKSHIRE

FINCHAMPSTEAD — Map 5 SU76

Places to visit

West Green House Gardens, HARTLEY WINTNEY, RG27 8JB, 01252 844611
www.westgreenhouse.co.uk

Museum of English Rural Life, READING, RG1 5EX, 0118 378 8660
www.merl.org.uk

Great for kids: The Look Out Discovery Centre, BRACKNELL, RG12 7QW,
01344 354400, www.bracknell-forest.gov.uk/be

California Chalet & Touring Park

►►► 83%

tel: 0118 973 3928 & 07917 055444 **Nine Mile Ride RG40 4HU**
email: enquiries@californiapark.co.uk **web:** www.californiapark.co.uk
dir: From A321 (south of Wokingham), right onto B3016 to Finchampstead. Follow Country
Park signs on Nine Mile Ride.

A simple, peaceful and well located woodland site with secluded pitches among the
trees, adjacent to the country park. Several pitches occupy a prime position beside
the lake with their own fishing area. The site has large hardstandings and the toilet
block has quality vanity units and fully tiled showers. The sparsely planted trees
allow sunshine onto pitches. Future investment plans remain very positive for this
well located park.

Open: All year **Last arrival:** flexible **Last departure:** noon

Pitches: 🚐 🚍 ▲ 🏠; 44 hardstanding pitches

Leisure: ⚠ ✐

Facilities: 🏠 ☺ 🅿 🅱 ⓢ 🍴 WiFi

Services: 🔁 🗓 🚽 ⚓ 🔒 🆃

Within 3 miles: ⅃ ∪ ◎ 🎒

Additional site information: 5.5 acre site. 🐕 Cars can be parked by caravans and tents.
Awnings permitted. No ground fires, no washing of caravans.

Glamping available: Wooden pods.

Additional glamping information: Cars can be parked by pods.

NEWBURY

Places to visit

Highclere Castle & Gardens, HIGHCLERE, RG20 9RN, 01635 253210
www.highclerecastle.co.uk

Great for kids: The Living Rainforest, HAMPSTEAD NORREYS, RG18 0TN,
01635 202444, www.livingrainforest.org

NEWBURY — Map 5 SU46

Bishops Green Farm Camp Site

►►► 85%

tel: 01635 268365 **Bishops Green RG20 4JP**
dir: Exit A339 (opposite New Greenham Park) towards Bishops Green and Ecchinswell.
Site on left, approximately 0.5 mile by barn.

A sheltered and secluded meadowland park close to the Hampshire–Berkshire
border, offering very clean and well-maintained facilities, including a toilet block
with a disabled/family room. There are woodland and riverside walks to be enjoyed
around the farm, and coarse fishing is also available. The site is very convenient for
visiting the nearby market town of Newbury with an attractive canal in the town
centre.

Open: April to October **Last arrival:** 21.00 **Last departure:** 11.30

Pitches: * 🚐 from £20; 🚍 from £20; ▲ from £20; 10 hardstanding pitches

Leisure: ✐

Facilities: 🏠 ✻ ⓢ

Services: 🔁 🗓

Additional site information: 1.5 acre site. 🐕 Cars can be parked by caravans and tents.
Only 1 car can be parked by caravan. Awnings permitted. Quiet after 21.00. Visitors'
charge applicable.

RISELEY — Map 5 SU76

Places to visit

Basildon Park, LOWER BASILDON, RG8 9NR, 01491 672382
www.nationaltrust.org.uk/basildonpark

Great for kids: Beale Park, LOWER BASILDON, RG8 9NW, 0118 976 7480
www.bealepark.org.uk

Wellington Country Park

►►► 86%

tel: 0118 932 6444 **Odiham Road RG7 1SP**
email: info@wellington-country-park.co.uk **web:** www.wellington-country-park.co.uk
dir: M4 junction 11, A33 south towards Basingstoke. Or M3 junction 5, B3349 north
towards Reading.

A peaceful woodland site, popular with families, set within an extensive country
park, which comes complete with lakes and nature trails, accessible to campers
after the country park closes. The park offers good facilities that include a laundry.
There's also a herd of Red and Fallow deer that roam the meadow area. This site is
ideal for those travelling on the M4 but it is advised not to follow sat nav as it takes
you to a central point of the post code, which is not the entrance.

Open: March to November **Last arrival:** 17.30 (16.30 in low season) **Last departure:** noon

Pitches: 🚐 🚍 ▲; 18 hardstanding pitches

Leisure: 🎵

Facilities: 🏠 ☺ 🅿 ✻ 🅱 🎍 WiFi

Services: 🔁 🗓 🍴 🛒 🚽 🔒

Within 3 miles: ⅃ ∪ ◎ 🎣 ⓢ

Additional site information: 80 acre site. 🐕 Cars can be parked by caravans and tents.
Awnings permitted. No open fires. Miniature railway, crazy golf, animal farm, Splash Zone,
access to Wellington Country Park.

LEISURE: 🏊 Indoor swimming pool 🏊 Outdoor swimming pool ⚠ Children's playground 👶 Kids' club 🎾 Tennis court 🎱 Games room ▭ Separate TV room
⅃ golf course ⚑ Pitch n putt 🚣 Boats for hire 🚲 Bikes for hire ▤ Cinema 🎵 Entertainment ✐ Fishing ◎ Mini golf 🏄 Watersports 💪 Gym ⚽ Sports field ∪ Stables
FACILITIES: 🏠 Baths/Shower ☺ Electric shaver sockets 🅿 Hairdryer ✻ Ice Pack Facility 🍼 Baby facilities 🅱 Disabled facilities ⓢ Shop on site or within 200yds
🍴 BBQ area 🅿 Picnic area WiFi WiFi

BRISTOL

See Cowslip Green (Somerset)

CAMBRIDGESHIRE

COMBERTON   Map 12 TL35

Places to visit

IWM Duxford, DUXFORD, CB22 4QR,
www.iwm.org.uk/visits/iwm-duxford

Chilford Hall Vineyard, LINTON, CB21 4LE, 01223 895600
www.chilfordhall.co.uk

Great for kids: Linton Zoological Gardens, LINTON, CB21 4NT, 01223 891308
www.lintonzoo.com

Highfield Farm Touring Park
▶▶▶▶ 92%

tel: 01223 262308 **Long Road CB23 7DG**
email: enquiries@highfieldfarmtouringpark.co.uk
web: www.highfieldfarmtouringpark.co.uk
dir: M11 junction 12, A603 (Sandy). 0.5 mile, right onto B1046 to Comberton.

Run by a very efficient and friendly family, the park is on a well-sheltered hilltop, with spacious pitches including a cosy backpackers' and cyclists' area, and separate sections for couples and families. Around the family farm there is a one and a half mile marked walk that has stunning views.

Open: April to October **Last arrival:** 20.00 **Last departure:** 14.00

Pitches: 🚐 from £18; 🚌 from £18; ⚠ from £18; 52 hardstanding pitches

Facilities: 🏠 ⊙ ℉ ✳ Ⓢ

Services: 🔌 🗓 ⬇ 🔋 ⌀ Ⓣ

Within 3 miles: ⚓ 🎣 ↻

Additional site information: 8 acre site. Maximum 2 dogs per pitch. Cars can be parked by caravans and tents. Awnings permitted. Postbox.

DODDINGTON   Map 12 TL49

Places to visit

WWT Welney Wetland Centre, WELNEY, PE14 9TN, 01353 860711
www.wwt.org.uk/welney

Flag Fen Archaeology Park, PETERBOROUGH, PE6 7QJ, 01733 864468
www.vivacity-peterborough.com/museums-and-heritage/flag-fen

Premier Park

Fields End Water Caravan Park & Fishery
▶▶▶▶▶ 92%

tel: 01354 740199 **Benwick Road PE15 0TY**
email: info@fieldsendfishing.co.uk **web:** www.fieldsendcaravans.co.uk
dir: Exit A141, follow signs to Doddington. At clock tower in Doddington turn right into Benwick Road. Site 1.5 miles on right after sharp bends.

This meticulously planned and executed park makes excellent use of its slightly elevated position in The Fens. The 33 fully serviced pitches, all with very generous hardstandings, are on smart terraces with sweeping views of the countryside. The two upgraded toilet blocks contain several combined cubicle spaces, and there are shady walks through mature deciduous woodland adjacent to two large and appealingly landscaped fishing lakes. High quality pine lodges are available as holiday lets.

Open: All year (restricted service: seasonal café) **Last arrival:** 20.00
Last departure: noon

Pitches: 🚐 from £21; 🚌 from £21; ⚠ from £20; 26 hardstanding pitches

Leisure: 🎣

Facilities: 🏠 ⊙ ℉ ✳ ♿ Ⓢ 🔋 WiFi

Services: 🔌 🗓 🍴 Ⓣ

Within 3 miles: ⚓ ◎

Additional site information: 20 acre site. Adults only. Cars can be parked by caravans and tents. Awnings permitted. No large groups.

PITCHES: 🚐 Caravans 🚌 Motorhomes ⚠ Tents 🏠 Glamping accommodation **SERVICES:** 🔌 Electric hook-up 🗓 Launderette 🍺 Licensed bar
🔋 Calor Gas ⌀ Campingaz Ⓣ Toilet fluid 🍴 Café/Restaurant 🍔 Fast Food/Takeaway 🔋 Battery charging ⬇ Motorhome service point
* 2019 prices ⊗ No credit or debit cards 🐕 Dogs permitted ⊗ No dogs

GUYHIRN
Map 12 TF40

Places to visit

Peckover House & Garden, WISBECH, PE13 1JR, 01945 583463
www.nationaltrust.org.uk/peckover

WWT Welney Wetland Centre, WELNEY, PE14 9TN, 01353 860711
www.wwt.org.uk/welney

Tall Trees Leisure Park
►►►► 77%

tel: 01945 450952 & 450131 **Gull Road PE13 4ER**
email: enquiries@talltreesleisurepark.co.uk **web:** www.talltreesleisurepark.co.uk
dir: *A47 from Peterborough towards Wisbech. Left onto B1187 signed Guyhirn.*

Tall Trees Leisure Park is a family-run caravan site set in 35 acres of a former commercial fruit farm. There are 59 electric pitches, each with its own water tap, set out in two perfectly level and maturely landscaped fields. There is also a separate, large rally field. Toilets are provided in well-maintained raised buildings and include a toilet and shower block; the reception also houses a small shop. Security is given high priority with an entrance barrier and CCTV. Please note, no tents are allowed on the park.

Open: All year **Last arrival:** 17.00 **Last departure:** noon

Pitches: 🚐 from £16; 🚙 from £16; 6 seasonal pitches

Facilities: 🖼 ✳ ♿ ⑤

Services: 🔌 🔼 🛄 🌀 Ⓣ

Within 3 miles: ✎ 月

Additional site information: 35 acre site. 🐕 Cars can be parked by caravans. Awnings permitted.

HEMINGFORD ABBOTS
Map 12 TL27

Places to visit

RSPB - Fen Drayton Lakes, SWAVESEY, CB24 4RB, 01954 233260
www.rspb.org.uk/discoverandenjoynature/seenature/reserves/guide/f/fendraytonlakes/index.aspx

Houghton Mill, HOUGHTON, PE28 2AZ, 01480 301494
www.nationaltrust.org.uk/houghton-mill-and-watercloses-meadows

Great for kids: The Raptor Foundation, WOODHURST, PE28 3BT, 01487 741140
www.raptorfoundation.org.uk

Quiet Waters Caravan Park
►►► 83%

tel: 01480 463405 **PE28 9AJ**
email: quietwaters.park@btopenworld.com **web:** www.quietwaterscaravanpark.co.uk
dir: *From A14 junction 25 (east of Huntingdon) follow Hemingford Abbots signs. Site in village centre.*

This is an attractive little site on the banks of the Great Ouse that has been in the same family ownership for over 80 years. It is located in a really charming village just a mile from the A14, making an ideal centre from which to tour the

---

Stroud Hill Park
Touring Caravans & Camping

A superb, exclusively adult, quiet, landscaped rural site designed to a very high specification in a secluded and sheltered spot in Pidley, near St Ives, Cambridgeshire, for touring caravans, motor homes and tents. Well behaved dogs are welcome. This premier site has been awarded many industry accolades in recognition of the high standard of the on-site facilities. At the heart of the site is a green oak framed building which houses reception, bar and restaurant (The Barn Restaurant) along with excellent toilets and showers. The facilities are built to be accessible to all. There are 60 pitches (44 hard standing and 16 grass pitches) all with 16 amp electric hook up, fresh water connection and grey water disposal. Large motor homes can be accommodated. Course fishing, pay-as-you-go golf courses and ten-pin bowling are among the attractions nearby.

- Early arrival (after 9.00am)
- 365 day opening
- No late stay fees
- Free Wifi

AA ►►►►►
Caravan & Camping 2016
Gold Award

AA
CAMPSITE OF THE YEAR 2008

TRANQUIL TOURING PARKS

TOP 100 SITES 2016

LEISURE: 🏊 Indoor swimming pool 🏊 Outdoor swimming pool 🎢 Children's playground 🛶 Kids' club 🎾 Tennis court 🎱 Games room 📺 Separate TV room
⛳ golf course 🏌 Pitch n putt ⛵ Boats for hire 🚲 Bikes for hire 🎦 Cinema 🎵 Entertainment 🎣 Fishing ⛳ Mini golf 🏄 Watersports 🏋 Gym ⚽ Sports field ♺ Stables
FACILITIES: 🛁 Baths/Shower ⊙ Electric shaver sockets 💈 Hairdryer ✳ Ice Pack Facility 🍼 Baby facilities ♿ Disabled facilities ⑤ Shop on site or within 200yds
🍖 BBQ area 🎋 Picnic area 📶 WiFi

Cambridgeshire area. There are fishing opportunities, rowing boats for hire and many walks and cycling routes directly from the park. There are holiday statics for hire.

Open: April to October **Last arrival:** 20.00 **Last departure:** noon

Pitches: from £24; from £24; from £24; 18 hardstanding pitches

Leisure: **Facilities:** WiFi

Services: **Within 3 miles:**

Additional site information: 1 acre site. Dogs must be kept on leads at all times. Cars can be parked by caravans and tents. Awnings permitted. Boat mooring.

HUNTINGDON   Map 12 TL27

Places to visit

Ramsey Abbey Gatehouse, RAMSEY, PE26 1DH, 01284 747500
www.nationaltrust.org.uk/ramsey-abbey-gatehouse

RSPB - Fen Drayton Lakes, SWAVESEY, CB24 4RB, 01954 233260
www.rspb.org.uk/discoverandenjoynature/seenature/reserves/guide/f/fendraytonlakes/index.aspx

Great for kids: The Raptor Foundation, WOODHURST, PE28 3BT, 01487 741140
www.raptorfoundation.org.uk

Huntingdon Boathaven & Caravan Park
▶▶▶ 80%

tel: 01480 411977 & 07952 414750 **The Avenue, Godmanchester PE29 2AF**
email: info@huntingdonboathaven.co.uk **web:** www.huntingdonboathaven.co.uk
dir: A14 junction 24, follow Godmanchester and Huntingdon signs onto B1044. Under A14, at mini roundabout 2nd exit into Post Street. Just before A14 flyover bridge, left into site.

A small, well laid out site overlooking a boat marina and the River Ouse, set close to the A14 and within walking distance of Huntingdon town centre. The toilets are clean and well kept. A pretty area beside the marina has been created for tents, with wide views across the Ouse Valley. Weekend family activities are organised throughout the season.

Open: All year (restricted service: Winter — open subject to weather conditions)
Last arrival: 21.00 **Last departure:** variable

Pitches: from £19; from £19; from £12; 18 hardstanding pitches;
12 seasonal pitches

Leisure: **Facilities:** WiFi

Services: **Within 3 miles:**

Additional site information: 2 acre site. Dogs must be kept on leads at all times and owners must clear up after their dogs. Cars can be parked by caravans. Awnings permitted. Boat mooring and boat hire available.

ST IVES

Places to visit

The Farmland Museum and Denny Abbey, WATERBEACH, CB25 9PQ,
01223 860988
www.english-heritage.org.uk/daysout/properties/denny-abbey-and-the-farm-land-museum

Oliver Cromwell's House, ELY, CB7 4HF, 01353 662062
www.olivercromwellshouse.co.uk

ST IVES   Map 12 TL37

Premier Park

Stroud Hill Park
▶▶▶▶▶ 93%

tel: 01487 741333 & 07831 119302 **Fen Road, Pidley PE28 3DE**
email: stroudhillpark@gmail.com **web:** www.stroudhillpark.co.uk
dir: Exit B1040 in Pidley, follow signs for Lakeside Lodge Complex, into Fen Road, site on right in 0.75 mile.

Stroud Hill Park is a superb, adults-only landscaped touring caravan site designed to a very high specification in Pidley. This premier site has been awarded many industry accolades in recognition of the high standard of the on-site facilities. At the heart of the site is a green oak-framed building which houses the reception, bar and restaurant (The Barn Restaurant) along with excellent toilets and showers. The facilities are built to be accessible to all. There are 60 pitches (44 hardstanding and 16 grass pitches), all with 16 amp electric hook-up, fresh water connection and grey water disposal, and large motorhomes can be accommodated. Pay-as-you-go golf courses and ten-pin bowling are among the attractions nearby. Well-behaved dogs are welcome.

Open: All year **Last arrival:** 22.00 (arrival from 09.00) **Last departure:** 17.00
Pitches: ; 44 hardstanding pitches; 10 seasonal pitches **Leisure:**
Facilities: WiFi **Services:**
Within 3 miles:

Additional site information: 6 acre site. Adults only. Cars can be parked by caravans and tents. Awnings permitted. No late-stay fee. Car hire can be arranged.
See advert opposite

PITCHES: Caravans Motorhomes Tents Glamping accommodation **SERVICES:** Electric hook-up Launderette Licensed bar
Calor Gas Campingaz Toilet fluid Café/Restaurant Fast Food/Takeaway Battery charging Motorhome service point
* 2019 prices No credit or debit cards Dogs permitted No dogs

WISBECH
Map 12 TF40

Places to visit
Peckover House & Garden, WISBECH, PE13 1JR, 01945 583463
www.nationaltrust.org.uk/peckover

Great for kids: WWT Welney Wetland Centre, WELNEY, PE14 9TN, 01353 860711
www.wwt.org.uk/welney

Little Ranch Leisure
▶▶▶ 87%

tel: 01945 860066 **Begdale, Elm PE14 0AZ**
web: www.littleranchleisure.co.uk
dir: *From roundabout on A47 (southwest of Wisbech), take Redmoor Lane to Begdale.*

A friendly family site set in an apple orchard, with 25 fully serviced pitches and a beautifully designed, spacious toilet block. The site overlooks two fishing lakes and pitches are available by the water; the famous horticultural auctions at Wisbech are nearby.

Open: All year

Pitches: ⊞ ⊞ ▲; 40 hardstanding pitches

Facilities: ☺ ☌ ✳ ♿

Services: ⊞ ⊙ ♨

Within 3 miles: ✎ ⊟ ⓢ

Additional site information: 10 acre site. ⌖ ⊚ Cars can be parked by caravans and tents. Awnings permitted.

CHESHIRE

CODDINGTON
Map 15 SJ45

Places to visit
Cholmondeley Castle Gardens, CHOLMONDELEY, SY14 8AH, 01829 720383
www.cholmondeleycastle.com

Hack Green Secret Nuclear Bunker, NANTWICH, CW5 8AP, 01270 629219
www.hackgreen.co.uk

Great for kids: Dewa Roman Experience, CHESTER, CH1 1NL, 01244 343407
www.dewaromanexperience.co.uk

Chester Zoo, CHESTER, CH2 1LH, 01244 380280
www.chesterzoo.org

Premier Park

Manor Wood Country Caravan Park
▶▶▶▶▶ 91%

tel: 01829 782990 & 07762 817827 **Manor Wood CH3 9EN**
email: info@manorwoodcaravans.co.uk **web:** www.cheshire-caravan-sites.co.uk
dir: *From A534 at Barton, turn opposite Cock O'Barton pub signed Coddington. Left in 100 yards. Site 0.5 mile on left.*

A secluded landscaped park in a tranquil country setting with extensive views towards the Welsh Hills across the Cheshire Plain. The park offers fully serviced pitches, a heated outdoor swimming pool and all-weather tennis courts. The generous pitch density provides optimum privacy and the superb amenity block has excellent decor, underfloor heating and smart modern facilities with very good privacy options. Wildlife is encouraged and there is a fishing lake; country walks and nearby pubs are added attractions. A new reception, café and shop is planned for 2019 season.

Open: All year (restricted service: October to March — swimming pool closed)
Last arrival: 19.00 **Last departure:** 11.00

Pitches: ⊞ from £22; ⊞ from £22; ▲ from £20; 38 hardstanding pitches; 30 seasonal pitches

Leisure: ⊛ ⋀ ◷ ◉ ⌀ ⚽

Facilities: ⊟ ☺ ☌ ✳ ♿ ⊞ WiFi

Services: ⊞ ⊙ ♨

Within 3 miles: ⚓ ⓢ

Additional site information: 8 acre site. ⌖ Awnings permitted. No noise after 23.00. Table tennis, pool table.

DELAMERE
Map 15 SJ56

Places to visit

Jodrell Bank Discovery Centre, JODRELL BANK, SK11 9DL, 01477 571766
www.jodrellbank.net

Little Moreton Hall, CONGLETON, CW12 4SD, 01260 272018
www.nationaltrust.org.uk/little-moreton-hall

Great for kids: Chester Zoo, CHESTER, CH2 1LH, 01244 380280
www.chesterzoo.org

Fishpool Farm Caravan Park

▶▶▶▶ 85%

tel: 01606 883970 & 07501 506583 **Fishpool Road CW8 2HP**
email: enquiries@fishpoolfarmcaravanpark.co.uk
web: www.fishpoolfarmcaravanpark.co.uk
dir: From A49 (Tarporley to Cuddington road), onto A54 signed Chester. At Fishpool Inn left onto B5152 (Fishpool Road). Site on right.

The staff at this site are friendly, helpful and really know the area well so you can get the most out of your visit. This is a lovely site with hardstanding touring pitches (with electric hook-up) and 20 tent pitches plus static vans, two smaller Shieling vans and lodges for hire. There are several good walks nearby.

Open: 15 February to 15 January **Last arrival:** 19.00 **Last departure:** noon

Pitches: 🚐 from £25; 🚙 from £25; ▲ from £25; 🏠 see prices below; 14 hardstanding pitches

Leisure: ◆ ⊔ ◉

Facilities: 🏠 ⊙ ☺ ✳ ఈ 🗄 ⌴ WiFi

Services: 🔌 🗑 🖳

Within 3 miles: 🎣 🐾 U ◉ ≋

Additional site information: 5.5 acre site. 🐕 Cars can be parked by caravans and tents. Awnings permitted. No noise after 23.00. Dog walks, play area.

Glamping available: Wooden pods from £80.

Additional glamping information: Jacuzzi available.

KNUTSFORD

Places to visit

The Tabley House Collection, KNUTSFORD, WA16 0HB, 01565 750151
www.tableyhouse.co.uk

Great for kids: Jodrell Bank Discovery Centre, JODRELL BANK, SK11 9DL, 01477 571766, www.jodrellbank.net

KNUTSFORD
Map 15 SJ77

Woodlands Park
▶▶▶ 78%

tel: 01565 723429 & 01332 810818 **Wash Lane, Allostock WA16 9LG**
dir: M6 junction 18, A50 north towards Holmes Chapel. 3 miles, into Wash Lane by Boundary Water Park. Site 0.25 mile on left.

A very tranquil and attractive park in the heart of rural Cheshire, and set in 16 acres of mature woodland where in spring the rhododendrons look stunning. Tourers are located in three separate wooded areas that teem with wildlife and you will wake up to the sound of birdsong. This park is just five miles from Jodrell Bank.

Open: March to 6 January **Last arrival:** 21.00 **Last departure:** 11.00

Pitches: 🚐 🚙 ▲

Facilities: ⊙ ఈ

Services: 🔌 🗑

Within 3 miles: 🎣 🐾 🎣

Additional site information: 16 acre site. 🐕 ⊗ Cars can be parked by caravans and tents. Awnings permitted. No skateboards or rollerblades.

LOWER WITHINGTON
Map 15 SJ86

Places to visit

Capesthorne Hall, CAPESTHORNE, SK11 9JY, 01625 861221
www.capesthorne.com

Welltrough Hall Farm Caravan Site

▶▶▶ 79%

tel: 07734 605965 **SK11 9EF**
email: welltroughnick@gmail.com **web:** www.welltroughcaravansite.co.uk
dir: Entrance on junction with Trap Street.

Located in a stunning, elevated and lush grassed area on an arable and beef cattle farm on the outskirts of the peaceful hamlet of Lower Withington, this newly developed park offers lovely views of the countryside and nearby Jodrell Bank from the spacious, fully serviced pitches. Shower and toilet facilities are housed in purpose built blocks or portacabins and future plans include additional modern facilities. Although an adults-only site, a 3-acre dog walk and a hot and cold doggie wash are available, in addition to an on-site farm shop.

Open: All year **Last arrival:** 21.00 **Last departure:** noon

Pitches: * 🚐 from £20; 🚙 from £20; 🏠 see prices below; 17 hardstanding pitches

Facilities: 🏠 WiFi

Services: 🔌 🗑 🖳 ⚒ 🛢 ⊘

Within 3 miles: 🎣 🐾 U 🎣

Additional site information: 1.5 acre site. Adults only. 🐕 Cars can be parked by caravans. Awnings permitted. Site owner to be informed if friends or relatives are to visit. Home-produced beef for sale.

Glamping available: 1 wooden pod from £60; 1 shepherd's hut from £70.

Additional glamping information: 2 night minimum stay. Wooden pod has en suite facility. Cars can be parked by pod and hut.

PITCHES: 🚐 Caravans 🚙 Motorhomes ▲ Tents 🏠 Glamping accommodation **SERVICES:** 🔌 Electric hook-up 🗑 Launderette 🍻 Licensed bar
🛢 Calor Gas ⊘ Campingaz 🅣 Toilet fluid 🍽 Café/Restaurant 🖳 Fast Food/Takeaway 🔋 Battery charging ⚒ Motorhome service point
* 2019 prices 🚫 No credit or debit cards 🐕 Dogs permitted ⊗ No dogs

NORTHWICH

Map 15 SJ67

Places to visit

Arley Hall & Gardens, NORTHWICH, CW9 6NA, 01565 777353
www.arleyhallandgardens.com

Lion Salt Works, MARSTON, CW9 6ES, 01606 275066
www.lionsaltworks.westcheshiremuseums.co.uk

Belmont Camping

▶▶▶ 85%

tel: 01606 891235 & 07530 450019 **Belmont Hall, Great Budworth CW9 6HN**
email: belmontcamping@aol.com web: www.belmontcamping.co.uk
dir: *M56 junction 10, take A559 to Northwich. After 3 miles entrance at junction of A559 and Pole Lane (Note: for sat nav use postcode CW9 6JA)*

Part of a former, small country estate in Great Budworth, under five miles from Northwich. A long meandering drive with a fine display of mature trees and fishing lakes is the approach to the peaceful touring and camping areas. Pitch density is generous to enhance privacy, and all caravan and motorhomes have either hardstandings and electric hook-ups or full services that include waste water disposal. Well-equipped toilet and shower facilities are located within a former indoor horse training arena.

Open: All year **Last arrival:** by prior arrangement **Last departure:** by prior arrangement
Pitches: * 🚐 from £18; 🚐 from £18; ▲ from £18; 15 hardstanding pitches
Leisure: 🎣
Facilities: 🛁 ✳ ⚕ 🚻 WiFi
Services: 🔌 🔲 🛒 ⬇
Within 3 miles: ⅃ ∪ ⚓ 🎯 🛒
Additional site information: 1 acre site. 🐾 🐕 Cars can be parked by caravans and tents. Awnings permitted. No noise after 23.00, children must be supervised, no campfires. Nature walk.

SIDDINGTON

Places to visit

Capesthorne Hall, CAPESTHORNE, SK11 9JY, 01625 861221
www.capesthorne.com

Gawsworth Hall, GAWSWORTH, SK11 9RN, 01260 223456
www.gawsworthhall.com

Great for kids: Jodrell Bank Discovery Centre, JODRELL BANK, SK11 9DL, 01477 571766, www.jodrellbank.net

SIDDINGTON

Map 15 SJ87

Capesthorne Hall

▶▶▶▶ 88%

tel: 01625 861221 **Congleton Road SK11 9JY**
email: info@capesthorne.com web: www.capesthorne.com
dir: *Access to site from A34 between Congleton to Wilmslow. Phone site for detailed directions.*

Located within the grounds of the notable Jacobean Capesthorne Hall, this lush, all level site provides generously sized pitches, all with electricity and most with hardstandings. The Scandanavian-style amenity block has a smart, quality, modern interior and very good privacy levels. Guests also have the opportunity to visit the award-winning gardens on certain days and there are many extensive walking opportunities leading directly from the camping areas.

Open: March to October **Last arrival:** 22.00 **Last departure:** noon
Pitches: * 🚐 from £25; 🚐 from £25; 30 hardstanding pitches
Facilities: 🛁 ⚕ 🚻 WiFi
Services: 🔌 🔲 🍽
Within 3 miles: ⅃ ◎ 🛒
Additional site information: 5 acre site. 🐾 Cars can be parked by caravans. Awnings permitted. Minimum stay 3 nights on bank holiday weekends. No motorised scooters or skateboards. Gas BBQs only. Touring area may close if large events take place (contact site for details). Access to Capesthorne Hall and Gardens – additional cost for hall only.

WETTENHALL

Map 15 SJ66

Places to visit

Cholmondeley Castle Gardens, CHOLMONDELEY, SY14 8AH, 01829 720383
www.cholmondeleycastle.com

New Farm Caravan Park

▶▶▶ 88%

tel: 01270 528213 & 07970 221112 **Long Lane CW7 4DW**
email: info@newfarmcheshire.com web: www.newfarmcheshire.co.uk
dir: *M6 junction 16, A500 towards Nantwich, right onto Nantwich bypass (A51). At lights turn right, follow A51, Caster and Tarporely signs. After Calveley right into Long Lane, follow site sign. Site in 2 miles.*

Diversification at New Farm led to the development of four fishing lakes and the creation of a peaceful small touring park. The proprietors provide a very welcome touring destination within this peaceful part of Cheshire. Expect good landscaping, generous hardstanding pitches, a spotless toilet block, and good attention to detail throughout. Nearly all pitches are very spacious and fully serviced. Please note, there is no laundry.

Open: All year **Last arrival:** 20.00 (earliest arrival from 13.30) **Last departure:** 11.30
Pitches: 🚐 from £24; 🚐 from £24; 23 hardstanding pitches; 10 seasonal pitches
Leisure: 🎣
Facilities: 🛁 📠 🚻 WiFi
Services: 🔌 🛒 ⬇
Within 3 miles: ⅃ ∪ ⚓ 🛒
Additional site information: 40 acre site. Adults only. 🐾 Maximum 2 dogs per pitch. Cars can be parked by caravans. Awnings permitted. No noise after 22.00.

WHITEGATE

Map 15 SJ66

Places to visit

Beeston Castle, BEESTON, CW6 9TX, 01829 260464
www.english-heritage.org.uk/daysout/properties/beeston-castle-and-woodland-park

Chester Cathedral, CHESTER, CH1 2HU, 01244 500958
www.chestercathedral.com

Premier Park

Lamb Cottage Caravan Park

►►►►► 92%

tel: 01606 882302 **Dalefords Lane CW8 2BN**
email: info@lambcottage.co.uk **web:** www.lambcottage.co.uk
dir: *From A556 turn at Sandiway lights into Dalefords Lane, signed Winsford. Site 1 mile on right.*

A secluded and attractively landscaped adults-only park in a glorious location where the emphasis is on peace and relaxation. The serviced pitches are spacious with wide grass borders for sitting out and the high quality toilet block is spotlessly clean and immaculately maintained. A good central base for exploring this area, with access to nearby woodland walks and cycle trails.

Open: All year **Last arrival:** 20.00 **Last departure:** noon

Pitches: 🚐 🚐; 45 hardstanding pitches; 14 seasonal pitches

Facilities: 🏠 ⊙ 🇫 ♿ WiFi

Services: 🔌 🗑 ⚓

Within 3 miles: ⚓ ✏ ∪ ⒮

Additional site information: 6 acre site. Adults only. 🐾 Cars can be parked by caravans. Awnings permitted. No tents (except trailer tents), no commercial vehicles.

Cornwall

It's not hard to see why thousands of tourists and holidaymakers flock to Cornwall every year. It has just about everything — wild moorland landscapes, glorious river valley scenery, picturesque villages and miles of breathtaking coastline. It has long been acknowledged as one of Britain's top holiday destinations.

Cornwall's southerly latitude and the influence of the Gulf Stream make the county the mildest and sunniest climate in Britain. It's not surprising therefore that one of its greatest and most popular pursuits is surfing. With more than 80 surfing spots, and plenty of sporting enthusiasts who make their way here to enjoy other similar coastal activities, such as wave-surfing, kite surfing and blokarting, the county is an internationally famous surfing hot spot. Blessed with wonderful surf beaches, Newquay is Cornwall's surfing capital. Nearby Watergate Bay is renowned for its glassy waves and Sennen, near Land's End, is where you might even get to surf with dolphins. Certainly the sea is strikingly blue here and the sands dazzlingly white.

A long-running TV series, filmed in a scenic location, is often a guaranteed way to boost tourism and that is certainly the case at Port Isaac on the north Cornwall coast. The village doubles as Portwenn in the drama *Doc Martin*, starring Martin Clunes as the irascible local GP. Much of Port Isaac has been used for location shooting over the years and it's quite common to bump into actors from the series at different points in the village when filming is taking place. Many films and TV series have been shot in Cornwall – including productions of Daphne du Maurier's *Jamaica Inn* and *Rebecca*, though the original version of the latter, made in 1940, was Alfred Hitchcock's first film in Hollywood and shot entirely in California.

In the book, the setting is a large house on the Cornish coast where the atmosphere is decidedly gothic. Daphne du Maurier modelled the house – which she called Manderley – and its location on the Menabilly estate, near Fowey. *Rebecca* was published in 1938 and five years later the writer made Menabilly her home. The house is not open to the public, but it is possible to explore the setting for the story on foot, following a leafy path from the car park at Menabilly Barton Farm to Polridmouth Bay where there are two secluded and remote coves. A bird's eye view of the entire area is possible from the path to Gribben Head, though Menabilly, at the heart of the story, is hidden by trees, thus preserving the mystery of the book.

The Cornish coastline offers breathtakingly beautiful scenery. The north coast is open and exposed; the 735-ft High Cliff, between Boscastle and St Gennys, represents the highest sheer drop cliff in the county. The Lizard, at Cornwall's most southerly point, is a geological masterpiece of awesome cliffs, stacks and arches.

In recent years new or restored visitor attractions have helped to increase tourism in the region – Tim Smit has been the inspiration and driving force behind two of the county's most visited attractions. The Eden Project is famous for its giant geodesic domes housing exotic plants from different parts of the globe, while nearby the Lost Gardens of Heligan at Pentewan has impressive kitchen gardens and a wildlife hide.

Perhaps the last word on this magical corner of Britain should go to Daphne du Maurier. In her book *Vanishing Cornwall*, published in 1967, she wrote: 'A county known and loved in all its moods becomes woven into the pattern of life, something to be shared. As one who sought to know it long ago…in a quest for freedom, and later put down roots and found content, I have come a small way up the path. The beauty and the mystery beckon still.'

◁ Shipwreck near Land's End

CORNWALL & ISLES OF SCILLY

ASHTON
Map 2 SW62

Places to visit

Godolphin House, GODOLPHIN CROSS, TR13 9RE, 01736 763194
www.nationaltrust.org.uk/godolphin

Poldark Tin Mine and Gardens, TRENEAR, TR13 0ES, 01326 573173
www.poldarkmine.org.uk

Great for kids: Flambards, HELSTON, TR13 0QA, 01326 573404
www.flambards.co.uk

Boscrege Caravan & Camping Park
▶▶▶ 80%

tel: 01736 762231 **TR13 9TG**

email: enquiries@caravanparkcornwall.com **web:** www.caravanparkcornwall.com
dir: A394 from Helston signed Penzance. In Ashton (Lion and Lamb pub on right) right
into Higher Lane, approximately 1.5 miles (thatched cottage on right) left at site sign.
(Note: for recommended towing route contact the park).

A quiet and bright little touring park divided into small paddocks with hedges, that
offers plenty of open spaces for children to play in. This family-owned park has
clean, well-painted toilet facilities and neatly trimmed grass. By an Area of
Outstanding Natural Beauty at the foot of Tregonning Hill, this site makes an ideal
base for touring the southern tip of Cornwall; Penzance, Land's End, St Ives and the
beaches in between are all within easy reach.

Open: All year (restricted service: November to Easter – no caravans, motorhomes or
tents) **Last arrival:** 22.00 **Last departure:** 11.00

Pitches: 🚐 � 🏕; 10 seasonal pitches

Leisure: 🎠 ⚽

Facilities: 🛁 ⊙ 🏷 ☀ 🪑 🎪 WiFi

Services: 🔌 🗑 🧺 🔒 🥚 T

Within 3 miles: 🎣 ⛳ ∪ ◎ 🚣 ≋ 🛍

Additional site information: 14 acre site. 🚗 Cars can be parked by caravans and tents.
Awnings permitted. No fires, no noise after 23.00, no groups. Microwave and freezer
available; fresh eggs available. Car hire can be arranged.

BLACKWATER
Map 2 SW74

Places to visit

Royal Cornwall Museum, TRURO, TR1 2SJ, 01872 272205
www.royalcornwallmuseum.org.uk

East Pool Mine, POOL, TR15 3NP, 01209 315027
www.nationaltrust.org.uk/east-pool-mine

Great for kids: National Maritime Museum Cornwall, FALMOUTH, TR11 3QY,
01326 313388, www.nmmc.co.uk

Trevarth Holiday Park
▶▶▶▶ 87%

tel: 01872 560266 **TR4 8HR**
email: trevarth@btconnect.com **web:** www.trevarth.co.uk
dir: Exit A30 at Chiverton roundabout onto B3277 signed St Agnes. At next roundabout
follow Blackwater signs. Site on right in 200 metres.

A neat and compact park with touring pitches laid out on attractive, well-screened
high ground adjacent to the A30 and A39 junction. This pleasant little park is
centrally located for touring, and is maintained to a very good standard. There is a
large grassed area for children to play on which is away from all tents.

Open: April to October **Last arrival:** 21.30 **Last departure:** 11.30

Pitches: 🚐 from £14; � from £14; 🏕 from £14; 14 hardstanding pitches;
6 seasonal pitches

Leisure: 🎠 🎱

Facilities: 🛁 ⊙ 🏷 ☀ WiFi

Services: 🔌 🗑 🧺 ⚰ 🔒 🥚

Within 3 miles: ⛳ ∪ 🚣 🛍

Additional site information: 4 acre site. 🚗 Cars can be parked by caravans and tents.
Awnings permitted. No gazebos, no noise after 22.30.

BLISLAND

Places to visit

Lanhydrock, LANHYDROCK, PL30 5AD, 01208 265950
www.nationaltrust.org.uk/lanhydrock

Tintagel Old Post Office, TINTAGEL, PL34 0DB, 01840 770024
www.nationaltrust.org.uk/tintagel-old-post-office

LEISURE: 🏊 Indoor swimming pool 🏊 Outdoor swimming pool 🎠 Children's playground 👦 Kids' club 🎾 Tennis court 🎱 Games room 📺 Separate TV room
🏌 golf course ⛳ Pitch n putt 🚣 Boats for hire 🚲 Bikes for hire 🎬 Cinema 🎵 Entertainment 🎣 Fishing ◎ Mini golf 🚣 Watersports 🏋 Gym ⚽ Sports field ∪ Stables
FACILITIES: 🛁 Baths/Shower ⊙ Electric shaver sockets 🏷 Hairdryer ☀ Ice Pack Facility 🍼 Baby facilities ♿ Disabled facilities 🛍 Shop on site or within 200yds
🎪 BBQ area 🪑 Picnic area WiFi WiFi

BLISLAND
Map 2 SX17

South Penquite Farm
▶▶▶ 87%

tel: 01208 850491 & 07494 864246 **South Penquite PL30 4LH**
email: camping@southpenquite.co.uk **web:** www.southpenquite.co.uk
dir: *From Exeter on A30 exit at 1st sign to St Breward on right, (from Bodmin 2nd sign on left). Follow narrow road across Bodmin Moor. Ignore left and right turns until South Penquite Farm Lane on right in 2 miles.*

This genuine 'back to nature' site is situated high on Bodmin Moor on a farm committed to organic agriculture. As well as camping there are facilities for adults and children to learn about conservation, organic farming and the local environment, including a fascinating and informative farm trail (pick up a leaflet); there is also a Geocaching trail. Toilet facilities are enhanced by a timber building with quality showers and a good disabled facility. The site has designated areas where fires may be lit. Organic home-reared lamb burgers and sausages are for sale, and one field contains four Mongolian yurts, available for holiday let. In addition, there is bunkhouse accommodation and one wooden pod adjoining.

Open: April to October **Last arrival:** dusk **Last departure:** 14.30

Pitches: * 🚐 from £20; 🛖 from £20; 🏠 see prices below

Leisure: /⚊ 🔍 ♟

Facilities: 🗄 ☺ ✳ 🎴

Services: 🔲

Within 3 miles: ⌔ ∪ 🅢

Additional site information: 4 acre site. ⊗ Cars can be parked by tents. Awnings permitted. No caravans, no pets. Camp fires permitted.

Glamping available: Wooden pod from £30; yurts from £50. **Changeover days:** Any day

Additional glamping information: Yurts. 2 night minimum stay. Cars can be parked by pod and yurts.

BODMIN

Places to visit
Restormel Castle, RESTORMEL, PL22 0EE, 01208 872687 www.english-heritage.org.uk/daysout/properties/restormel-castle

Lanhydrock, LANHYDROCK, PL30 5AD, 01208 265950 www.nationaltrust.org.uk/lanhydrock

Great for kids: Eden Project, ST AUSTELL, PL24 2SG, 01726 811911 www.edenproject.com

BODMIN
Map 2 SX06

Mena Farm
▶▶▶▶ 82%

tel: 01208 831845 **PL30 5HW**
email: enquiries@menafarm.co.uk **web:** www.menafarm.co.uk
dir: *Exit A30 onto A389 (north) signed Lanivet and Wadebridge. In 0.5 mile 1st right, pass under A30. 1st left signed Lostwithiel and Fowey. In 0.25 mile right at top of hill. 0.5 mile, 1st right. Entrance 100 yards on right.*

This grassy site is about four miles from the Eden Project and midway between the north and south Cornish coasts. Set in a secluded, elevated position with high hedges for shelter, it offers plenty of peace and quiet. There is a small coarse fishing lake on site, hardstanding pitches, a shop, and three bell tents are available for hire. The site is on the Saint's Way, and nearby is the neolithic hill fort of Helman Tor, the highest point on Bodmin Moor. Approximately one mile away is a fish and chip restaurant in Lanivet – and from this village, there is a bus service to Bodmin.

Open: All year **Last arrival:** 22.00 **Last departure:** noon

Pitches: 🚐 from £20; 🛖 from £21; 🛖 from £15; 🏠 see prices below; 3 hardstanding pitches

Leisure: /⚊ 🔍 ▢ 🎱 ♟ ⚽

Facilities: 🗄 ☺ 🎴 ✳ ♿ 🛁 🍴 🎴 [WiFi]

Services: 🔌 🔲 🎴 🛒 ⚓ 🔋 ✉ ⛽ 🚰 [T]

Within 3 miles: ⌔ ∪ 🛼 🚴

Additional site information: 4 acre site. 🐕 No dangerous dogs. Cars can be parked by caravans and tents. Awnings permitted. No noise after 22.00. No generators. Nature trails, bike service. Car hire can be arranged.

Glamping available: 3 bell tents from £65. **Changeover days:** Any day

Additional glamping information: Bell tents are fully equipped including bedding (sleep 4). No dogs or pets. Cars can be parked by bell tents.

BRYHER (ISLES OF SCILLY)
Map 2 SV81

Bryher Camp Site
▶▶▶ 85%

tel: 01720 422068 **TR23 0PR**
email: relax@bryhercampsite.co.uk **web:** www.bryhercampsite.co.uk
dir: *Accessed from the mainland by ferry, plane or by boat from main island of St Mary's.*

Set on the smallest inhabited Scilly Isle with spectacular scenery and white beaches, this tent-only and glamping site is in a sheltered valley surrounded by hedges. Pitches are located in paddocks at the northern end of the island which is only a short walk from the quay. There is a good, modern toilet block, and plenty of peace and quiet. Although located in a very quiet area, the Fraggle Rock Bar and a well-equipped shop are within easy reach. There is easy boat access to all the other islands.

Open: April to October

Pitches: 🛖 from £21.50; 🏠 see prices below

Leisure: ⚽

Facilities: 🗄 ☺ 🎴 ✳ 🍴 🎴

Services: 🔲 🛒 🔋 ⚓

Within 3 miles: ⌔ ♟ ∪ ◎ 🛼 🚴 🅢

Additional site information: 2.25 acre site. Awnings permitted. No pets.

Glamping available: Bell tents from £50. **Changeover days:** Saturdays (July and August); any day April to June and September to October

---

BUDE

Map 2 SS20

See also Bridgerule (Devon) and Holsworthy (Devon)

Places to visit

Penhallam Manor, WEEK ST MARY, EX22 6XW,
www.english-heritage.org.uk/daysout/properties/penhallam-manor

Platinum Park

Wooda Farm Holiday Park

▶▶▶▶▶

tel: 01288 352069 **Poughill EX23 9HJ**
email: stay@wooda.co.uk web: www.wooda.co.uk
dir: *From A39 at Stratton follow Poughill and brown site signs into Stamford Hill. Approximately 1 mile to site on right.*

An attractive park set on raised ground overlooking Bude Bay, with lovely sea views. The park is divided into paddocks by hedges and mature trees, and offers high quality facilities in extensive colourful gardens. A variety of activities is provided by way of the large sports hall and hard tennis court, and there's a super children's playground. There are holiday static caravans for hire. An interactive information screen in the reception area is for customer use.

Open: April to early November (restricted service: April to May and mid September to early November – bar, takeaway and cocktail bar; shop reduced opening hours)
Last arrival: 20.00 **Last departure:** 10.30

Pitches: 🚐 from £21; 🚙 from £21; ▲ from £14; 🏠 see prices below; 80 hardstanding pitches; 10 seasonal pitches

Leisure: 🎣 ♣ 🔍 ⬜ ↓ 🎣 🎯 🐎 🍽 ⚽
Facilities: 🛁 ⊙ 📺 ✳ ♿ 🛒 🎪 🚿 WiFi
Services: 🔌 🔲 🍺 🍴 🛒 🛍 🕁 🔒 🌱 🚽
Within 3 miles: ∪ ◎ 🛥 🎣 🗓

Additional site information: 50 acre site. 🐕 Restrictions on certain dog breeds. Cars can be parked by caravans and tents. Awnings permitted. No skateboards, rollerblades or scooters. Woodland walks, farmyard animals, beauty salon, cocktail bar, cycle trail, sports facilities.

Glamping available: Vintage caravan from £200 for 3 nights.

Changeover days: Friday and Monday

Additional glamping information: Vintage caravan: sleeps 2. Short breaks available (Friday to Monday; Monday to Friday; Friday to Friday) Cars can be parked by caravan.

See advert opposite

Budemeadows Touring Park

▶▶▶▶ 92%

tel: 01288 361646 **Widemouth Bay EX23 0NA**
email: holiday@budemeadows.com web: www.budemeadows.com
dir: *3 miles south of Bude on A39. Follow signs after turn to Widemouth Bay. Site accessed via layby from A39.*

This is a very well-kept site of distinction, with good quality facilities, hardstandings and eight fully serviced pitches. Budemeadows is set on a gentle sheltered slope in nine acres of naturally landscaped parkland, surrounded by mature hedges. The internal doors in the facility block have all been painted in pastel colours to resemble beach huts. The site is just one mile from Widemouth Bay, and three miles from the unspoilt resort of Bude.

Open: All year (restricted service: September to late May – shop, bar and pool closed; takeaway in summer only) **Last arrival:** 21.00 **Last departure:** 11.00

Pitches: 🚐 🚙 ▲; 34 hardstanding pitches; 4 seasonal pitches

Leisure: 🛥 🔍 ⬜
Facilities: 🛁 ⊙ 📺 ✳ ♿ 🛒 🚿 🎪 WiFi
Services: 🔌 🔲 🍺 🛍 🕁 🔒 🌱 🚽
Within 3 miles: ↓ 🎣 ∪ ◎ 🛥 🎣 🗓

Additional site information: 9 acre site. 🐕 Cars can be parked by caravans and tents. Awnings permitted. No noise after 23.00, breathable groundsheets only, no open fires or firepits. Table tennis, giant chess, baby changing facility.

Upper Lynstone Caravan Park

▶▶▶▶ 87%

tel: 01288 352017 **Lynstone EX23 0LP**
email: reception@upperlynstone.co.uk web: www.upperlynstone.co.uk
dir: *From Bude follow Widemouth Bay signs. Site 0.75 mile south of Bude on coastal road (Vicarage Road becomes Lynstone Road) on right.*

There are extensive views over Bude to be enjoyed from this quiet, sheltered family-run park, a terraced grass site suitable for all units. There's a spotlessly clean and top quality toilet block, plus a children's playground and a reception with a shop that sells basic food supplies and camping spares. Static caravans are available for holiday hire. A path leads directly to the coastal footpath with its stunning sea views, and the old Bude Canal is just a stroll away.

Open: April to October **Last arrival:** 21.00 **Last departure:** 10.00

Pitches: 🚐 from £20; 🚍 from £20; 🔺 from £16; 8 hardstanding pitches

Leisure: ⚠

Facilities: 🛢 ☺ 🐾 ✳ ♿ 🖾 🚽 WiFi

Services: 🔌 🖾 🔋 🔒 ⊘ T

Within 3 miles: 🎣 🔗 ∪ ◎ ⛳ ⛷ 🎠

Additional site information: 6 acre site. 🐕 Cars can be parked by caravans and tents. Awnings permitted. No groups. Family bathroom.

Willow Valley Holiday Park
▶▶▶▶ 85%

tel: 01288 353104 **Bush EX23 9LB**
email: willowvalley@talk21.com **web:** www.willowvalley.co.uk
dir: On A39, 0.5 mile north of junction with A3072 at Stratton.

A small sheltered park in the Strat Valley with level grassy pitches and a stream running through it. All areas of this attractive park have been improved, including a smart toilet block and an excellent reception and shop. The park has direct access from the A39, and is only two miles from the sandy beaches at Bude. There are four pine lodges for holiday hire.

Open: March to end October **Last arrival:** 21.00 **Last departure:** 11.00

Pitches: 🚐 🚍 🔺, 0 hardstanding pitches

Leisure: ⚠

Facilities: ☺ 🐾 ✳ ♿ 🚽 🚽 🖾

Services: 🔌 🖾 🔋 🔒 ⊘ T

Within 3 miles: 🎣 🔗 ∪ ◎ ⛷

Additional site information: 4 acre site. 🐕 ⊕ Cars can be parked by caravans and tents. Awnings permitted.

CAMELFORD	Map 2 SX18

Places to visit

Tintagel Castle, TINTAGEL, PL34 0HE, 01840 770328
www.english-heritage.org.uk/daysout/properties/tintagel-castle

Tintagel Old Post Office, TINTAGEL, PL34 0DB, 01840 770024
www.nationaltrust.org.uk/tintagel-old-post-office

Juliots Well Holiday Park
▶▶▶▶ 85% HOLIDAY HOME PARK

tel: 01840 213302 & 07874 001606 **PL32 9RF**
email: brennan.gissing@swholidayparks.co.uk
web: www.southwestholidayparks.co.uk/holiday-homes/juliots-well/Juliots-Well-Times
dir: A39 to Camelford, 0.25 mile beyond town (just after the sign for Valley Truckle) turn right onto B3266, then 2nd left on sharp bend, signed Juliots Well. 500 yards on right.

Set in the wooded grounds of an old manor house, this quiet site enjoys lovely, extensive views across the countryside. A rustic inn on site occasionally offers entertainment, and there is plenty to do, both on the park and in the vicinity. Transformed into a holiday home park in 2017, this well-laid-out and managed park offers four grades of holiday homes to suit all budgets, including luxury lodges. Added attractions include a games room, a good outdoor play area, an 18-hole golf course and excellent surrounding walks.

Open: 31 March to November **Last departure:** 10.00

Leisure: ⚠

Facilities: 🛢 🖾 WiFi

Within 3 miles: 🎣 ∪ ⛷ 🎠 🚽

Additional site information: 🐕 BBQs permitted.

CAMELFORD *continued*

Lakefield Caravan Park

►►► 82%

tel: 01840 213279 **Lower Pendavey Farm PL32 9TX**
email: lakefieldcaravanpark@btconnect.com **web:** www.lakefieldcaravanpark.co.uk
dir: *From A39 in Camelford onto B3266, right at T-junction, site 1.5 miles on left.*

Set in a rural location, this friendly park is part of a specialist equestrian centre, and offers good quality services. All the facilities are immaculate and spotlessly clean. Riding lessons and hacks are always available, with a BHS qualified instructor. Newquay, Padstow and Bude are all easily accessed from this site.

Open: Easter or April to October **Last arrival:** 22.00 **Last departure:** 11.00

Pitches: 🚐 🚍 ▲

Leisure: ⚽

Facilities: ⊙ ⌂ ❄

Services: 🔌 🍴 📦 🔒 🧺 🆃

Within 3 miles: 🎣 ⛳ ↻ 🎿 🛒

Additional site information: 5 acre site. 🐾 Cars can be parked by caravans and tents. Awnings permitted. On-site lake.

CARLYON BAY

Places to visit

The Shipwreck and Heritage Centre, ST AUSTELL, PL25 3NX, 01726 69897
www.shipwreckcharlestown.com

The Lost Gardens of Heligan, PENTEWAN, PL26 6EN, 01726 845100
www.heligan.com

Great for kids: Wheal Martyn, ST AUSTELL, PL26 8XG, 01726 850362
www.wheal-martyn.com

Eden Project, ST AUSTELL, PL24 2SG, 01726 811911
www.edenproject.com

CARLYON BAY   Map 2 SX05

Platinum Park

Carlyon Bay Caravan & Camping Park

►►►►►

tel: 01726 812735 **Bethesda, Cypress Avenue PL25 3RE**
email: holidays@carlyonbay.net **web:** www.carlyonbay.net
dir: *Exit A390 west of St Blazey, left onto A3092 for Par, right in 0.5 mile. Cypress Avenue to Carlyon Bay.*

An attractive, secluded site set amongst a belt of trees with background woodland. The spacious grassy park is beautifully landscaped and offers quality toilet and shower facilities and plenty of on-site attractions, including a well-equipped games room, TV room, café, an inviting swimming pool, and occasional family entertainment. It is less than half a mile from a sandy beach and the Eden Project is approximately two miles away.

Open: Easter to late September (restricted service: Easter to mid May and mid to end September – swimming pool, takeaway and shop closed) **Last arrival:** 21.00 **Last departure:** 11.00

Pitches: 🚐 🚍 ▲; 12 hardstanding pitches   **Leisure:** 🏊 Λ 🔍 ⬚ 🎵 ⚽
Facilities: ⊙ ⌂ ❄ ♿ 🆂 🍖 📶   **Services:** 🔌 🗑 🍴 🚿 📦 ⬆ 🔒 🧺 🆃
Within 3 miles: 🎣 ⛳ ↻ ◎ 🎿 🛶 🎯

Additional site information: 35 acre site. 🐾 Cars can be parked by caravans and tents. Awnings permitted. No noise after 23.00, no hoverboards or motorised scooters (except invalid mobility scooters). Crazy golf. Children's entertainment July to August only.

See advert opposite

East Crinnis Camping & Caravan Park

▶▶▶▶ 86%

tel: 01726 813023 & 07435 974961 **Lantyan, East Crinnis PL24 2SQ**
email: info@eastcrinnis.com **web:** www.eastcrinnis.com
dir: *From A390 (Lostwithiel to St Austell), take A3082 signed Fowey at roundabout by Britannia Inn, site on left.*

A small rural park with spacious pitches set in individual bays, about one mile from the beaches at Carlyon Bay, and just two miles from the Eden Project. The friendly owners keep the site very clean and well maintained, and also offer three self-catering holiday lodges, two yurts and one geo dome for hire. The park offers a takeaway food facility but it's only a short walk to Par where restaurants can be found.

Open: March to October **Last arrival:** 20.00 **Last departure:** noon

Pitches: ⌂ ⌂ ▲ ⌂; 9 hardstanding pitches; 18 seasonal pitches

Leisure: ⌂ ✎ ⚽

Facilities: ☺ ☞ ✳ ♿ ⓢ ⊟ ☴ [WiFi]

Services: ⌂ ⌂ ♨ [T]

Within 3 miles: ⌂ ∪ ◎ ≋ ≛ ⊟

Additional site information: 2 acre site ⌖ Cars can be parked by caravans and tents. Awnings permitted. No noise after 23.00. Wildlife and pond area with dog walk.

Glamping available: Yurts; geo dome.

Additional glamping information: Cars can be parked by yurts.

Lavender Fields Touring Park

▶▶▶▶ 83%

tel: 01209 832188 & 07855 227773 **Penhale Road TR14 0LU**
email: info@lavenderfieldstouring.co.uk **web:** www.lavenderfieldstouring.co.uk
dir: *Exit A30 at Camborne West junction. At top of slip road left at roundabout, 2nd exit, through Roseworthy, left after Roseworthy signed Carnhell Green, over level crossing to T-junction, turn left. Site 750 yards on right.*

A family owned and run park in the heart of the Cornish countryside on the outskirts of the idyllic village of Carnhell Green, yet only a short car or bus ride to towns and glorious golden beaches. Developed on an old mine waste site, the park is maturing well, with lush grass and neat and tidy pitches, and has a smart toilet block and some good hardstandings for larger units. There are wonderful countryside views to the south which gives this site a pleasant open feel. A kettle in the dishwashing area is provided for campers' use. Dogs are very welcome to accompany their owners and can stay free of charge.

Open: All year **Last arrival:** 20.00 **Last departure:** 10.00

Pitches: ⌂ from £12.50; ⌂ from £12.50; ▲ from £10, £1 hardstanding pitches; 5 seasonal pitches

Leisure: ⌂ **Facilities:** ⌂ ☺ ☞ ✳ ♿ ⓢ

Services: ⌂ ⌂ ♨ **Within 3 miles:** ⌂ ✎ ∪ ◎ ≋ ≛ ⊟

Additional site information: 6 acre site. ⌖ Cars can be parked by caravans and tents. Awnings permitted.

PITCHES: ⌂ Caravans ⌂ Motorhomes ▲ Tents ⌂ Glamping accommodation **SERVICES:** ⌂ Electric hook-up ⌂ Launderette ⌂ Licensed bar ⌂ Calor Gas ✎ Campingaz [T] Toilet fluid ⌂ Café/Restaurant ⌂ Fast Food/Takeaway ♨ Battery charging ♨ Motorhome service point
* 2019 prices ⌂ No credit or debit cards ⌖ Dogs permitted ⊗ No dogs

CHACEWATER — Map 2 SW74

Places to visit

Royal Cornwall Museum, TRURO, TR1 2SJ, 01872 272205
www.royalcornwallmuseum.org.uk

Trelissick, TRELISSICK, TR3 6QL, 01872 862090
www.nationaltrust.org.uk/trelissick

Killiwerris Touring Park

►►►► 85%

tel: 01872 561356 & 07734 053593 **Penstraze TR4 8PF**
email: killiwerris@aol.com **web:** www.killiwerris.co.uk
dir: *Take A30 towards Penzance, at Chiverton Cross roundabout take 3rd exit signed St Agnes. At next mini roundabout take Blackwater exit, in 500 yards left into Kea Downs Road, park 1 mile on right.*

A small, adults-only, family-run touring park, just five miles from Truro and four miles from the coastal village of St Agnes, making it an ideal base for exploring west Cornwall. The site has a sunny aspect yet is sheltered by mature trees giving it a very private feel. The facilities are of an exceptionally high standard and include a modern and smart amenity block. It is a peaceful spot in which to relax and get away from the crowds.

Open: All year **Last arrival:** 21.00 **Last departure:** 11.00

Pitches: * 🚐 from £22; 🚌 from £22; 17 hardstanding pitches

Facilities: 🛁 🔌 💨 ❄ ♿ [S]

Services: 🔧 🌀

Within 3 miles: ⛳ 🎣 🐎 🎬

Additional site information: 2.2 acre site. Adults only. 🐕 Cars can be parked by caravans. Awnings permitted. Car hire can be arranged. Internet access available.

COVERACK — Map 2 SW71

Places to visit

Great for kids: Cornish Seal Sanctuary, GWEEK, TR12 6UG, 01326 221361
www.visitsealife.com/gweek

Flambards, HELSTON, TR13 0QA, 01326 573404
www.flambards.co.uk

Little Trevothan Caravan & Camping Park

►►►► 82%

tel: 01326 280260 **Trevothan TR12 6SD**
email: holidays@littletrevothan.co.uk **web:** www.littletrevothan.co.uk
dir: *A3083 onto B3293 signed Coverack, approximately 2 miles after Goonhilly Earth Station, right at petrol station onto unclassified road. Approximately 1 mile, turn 3rd left. Site 0.5 mile on left.*

A secluded site, with excellent facilities, near the unspoilt fishing village of Coverack, with a large recreation area and good play equipment for children. An excellent new toilet block opened for the 2018 season. The nearby sandy beach has lots of rock pools for children to play in, and the many walks starting from both the park and the village offer stunning scenery.

Open: March to October **Last arrival:** 21.00 **Last departure:** noon

Pitches: * 🚐 from £14.50; 🚌 from £14.50; ⛺ from £14.50; 14 hardstanding pitches; 18 seasonal pitches

Leisure: 🛝 ♟ 📺 ⚽

Facilities: 🛁 🔌 💨 ❄ [S] 🍖

Services: 🔧 🌀 🛒 🛍 🍃 [T]

Within 3 miles: 🎣 🌊

Additional site information: 10.5 acre site. 🐕 Cars can be parked by caravans and tents. Awnings permitted. Quiet time between 22.00–08.00. Large playing field with children's play area.

CRANTOCK (NEAR NEWQUAY) — Map 2 SW76

Places to visit

Trerice, TRERICE, TR8 4PG, 01637 875404
www.nationaltrust.org.uk/trerice

Platinum Park

Trevella Park

►►►►►

tel: 01637 830308 **TR8 5EW**
email: holidays@trevella.co.uk **web:** www.trevella.co.uk
dir: *Between Crantock and A3075.*

A well-established and very well-run family site, with outstanding floral displays. Set in a rural area close to Newquay, this stunning park boasts three teeming fishing lakes for both the experienced and novice angler, and a superb outdoor swimming pool and paddling area. The spotlessly clean toilet facilities include excellent en suite wet rooms. All areas are neat and clean and the whole park looks stunning. Canvas geo domes, fully equipped ready-erected tents and safari tents are available for hire.

Open: 23 March to 29 October (restricted service: Easter to mid May and mid September to October – pool closed) **Last arrival:** 21.00 **Last departure:** 10.00

Pitches: 🚐 from £21; 🚌 from £21; ⛺ from £17; 🛖 see prices below; 60 hardstanding pitches; 12 seasonal pitches

Leisure: 🏖 🛝 ♟ 🎣

Facilities: 🛁 🔌 💨 ❄ ♿ [S] 🍖 🧺 🍼 [WiFi]

Services: 🔧 🌀 🍽 🎂 🛒 ⚓ 🛍 🍃 [T]

Within 3 miles: ⛳ 🐎 ◎ 🌊 ⛵ 🎬

Additional site information: 60 acre site. 🐕 Cars can be parked by caravans and tents. Awnings permitted. Families and couples only, under 21s conditions apply, please check with site. Crazy golf, children's ranger activities, 3 children's play areas, nature trail. Fresh croissants and pasties available.

Glamping available: Safari tents from £57; ready-erected tents from £44; geo domes from £69; safari lodges from £88; safari en suite tents from £81.

Changeover days: Monday, Friday and Saturday

Additional glamping information: Geo domes have hot tubs. Cars can be parked by glamping units.

LEISURE: 🏊 Indoor swimming pool 🏖 Outdoor swimming pool 🛝 Children's playground 👋 Kids' club 🎾 Tennis court ♟ Games room 📺 Separate TV room ⛳ golf course 🏌 Pitch n putt ⛵ Boats for hire 🚲 Bikes for hire 🎬 Cinema 🎵 Entertainment 🎣 Fishing ◎ Mini golf 🌊 Watersports 🏋 Gym ⚽ Sports field 🐎 Stables
FACILITIES: 🛁 Baths/Shower 🔌 Electric shaver sockets 💨 Hairdryer ❄ Ice Pack Facility 🍼 Baby facilities ♿ Disabled facilities [S] Shop on site or within 200yds 🍖 BBQ area 🧺 Picnic area [WiFi] WiFi

Treago Farm Caravan Site

▶▶▶▶ 89%

tel: 01637 830277 **TR8 5QS**
email: info@treagofarm.co.uk **web:** www.treagofarm.co.uk
dir: *From A3075 (west of Newquay) follow Crantock signs. Site signed beyond village.*

A grass site in open farmland in a south-facing sheltered valley with a fishing lake. This friendly family park has spotless toilet facilities, which include three excellent heated family rooms, plus a good shop and bar with takeaway food, and it has direct access to Crantock and Polly Joke beaches, National Trust land and many natural beauty spots.

Open: April to early October (restricted service: mid May, mid September to October – reduced hours in shop and bar) **Last arrival:** 22.00 **Last departure:** 18.00

Pitches: 🚐 🚐 ⚊

Leisure: 🎣 ⬜

Facilities: 🏪 ☺ 🍳 ✳ 🛁 🍴 🪑

Services: 🔌 🔄 🍽 🎮 🔋 🔒 🧴 🆃

Within 3 miles: 🛝 🚲 ∪ ◎ ⛳ 🎣

Additional site information: 5 acre site. 🐾 Cars can be parked by caravans and tents. Awnings permitted.

Quarryfield Holiday Park

▶▶▶ 85%

tel: 01637 872792 & 830338 **TR8 5RJ**
email: info@quarryfield.co.uk **web:** www.quarryfield.co.uk
dir: *From A3075 (Newquay to Redruth road) follow Crantock signs. Site signed.*

This park has a private path down to the dunes and golden sands of Crantock Beach, about 10 minutes away, and it is within easy reach of all that Newquay has to offer, particularly for families. The park has very modern facilities, and provides plenty of amenities including a great swimming pool.

Open: Easter to October **Last arrival:** 23.00 **Last departure:** 10.00

Pitches: 🚐 🚐 ⚊; 33 seasonal pitches

Leisure: 🏊 🎠 🎣 **Facilities:** 🏪 ☺ 🍳 ✳ ♿ 🛁 🍴 🪑 WiFi

Services: 🔌 🔄 🍽 🍴 🔋 ⛽ 🔒 🧴

Within 3 miles: 🛝 🚲 ∪ ◎ 🎣 ⬜

Additional site information: 10 acre site. 🐾 Cars can be parked by caravans and tents. Awnings permitted. No campfires, quiet after 22.30.

CUBERT	Map 2 SW75

Places to visit

Trerice, TRERICE, TR8 4PG, 01637 875404
www.nationaltrust.org.uk/trerice

Great for kids: Dairy Land Farm World, NEWQUAY, TR8 5AA, 01872 510246
www.dairylandfarmworld.com

Cottage Farm Touring Park

▶▶▶▶ 84%

tel: 01637 831083 **Treworgans TR8 5HH**
email: contact@cottagefarmpark.co.uk **web:** www.cottagefarmpark.co.uk
dir: *From A392 towards Newquay, left onto A3075 towards Redruth. In 2 miles right signed Cubert, right again in 1.5 miles signed Crantock, left in 0.5 mile.*

A small grassy touring park situated in the tiny hamlet of Treworgans, in sheltered open countryside close to a lovely beach at Holywell Bay. This quiet family-run park boasts very good quality facilities including a fenced playground for children, with a climbing frame, swings, slides etc.

Open: April to September **Last arrival:** 22.30 **Last departure:** noon

Pitches: 🚐 from £13; 🚐 from £13; ⚊ from £13; 2 hardstanding pitches

Leisure: 🎠 **Facilities:** 🏪 ☺ 🍳 ✳ **Services:** 🔌 🔄 🔋

Within 3 miles: 🛝 🚲 ∪ ◎ ⛳ 🎣 🎣 📅 💲

Additional site information: 2 acre site. 🐾 Cars can be parked by caravans and tents. Awnings permitted. No noise after 23.00.

FALMOUTH	Map 2 SW83

Places to visit

Pendennis Castle, FALMOUTH, TR11 4LP, 01326 316594
www.english-heritage.org.uk/daysout/properties/pendennis-castle

Trebah Garden, MAWNAN SMITH, TR11 5JZ, 01326 252200
www.trebah-garden.co.uk

Great for kids: National Maritime Museum Cornwall, FALMOUTH, TR11 3QY, 01326 313388, www.nmmc.co.uk

Tregedna Farm Touring Caravan & Tent Park

▶▶▶ 82%

tel: 01326 250529 **Maenporth TR11 5HL**
email: enquiries@tregednafarmholidays.co.uk **web:** www.tregednafarmholidays.co.uk
dir: *Take A39 from Truro to Falmouth. Turn right at Hill Head roundabout. Site 2.5 miles on right.*

Set in the picturesque Maen Valley, this gently-sloping, south-facing park is part of a 100-acre farm. It is surrounded by beautiful wooded countryside just minutes from the beach, and has spacious pitches and well-kept facilities.

Open: April to September **Last arrival:** 22.00 **Last departure:** 13.00

Pitches: 🚐 from £17; 🚐 ⚊; 6 hardstanding pitches **Leisure:** 🎠

Facilities: 🏪 ☺ ✳ **Services:** 🔌 🔄 **Within 3 miles:** 🛝 🚲 ◎ 🎣 🎣 📅 💲

Additional site information: 12 acre site. 🐾 1 dog only per pitch. 🐕 Cars can be parked by caravans and tents. Awnings permitted. No open fires. Boat storage.

GOONHAVERN
Map 2 SW75

See also Rejerrah

Places to visit

Trerice, TRERICE, TR8 4PG, 01637 875404
www.nationaltrust.org.uk/trerice

Blue Reef Aquarium, NEWQUAY, TR7 1DU, 01637 878134
www.bluereefaquarium.co.uk

Great for kids: Newquay Zoo, NEWQUAY, TR7 2LZ, 01637 873342
www.newquayzoo.org.uk

Dairy Land Farm World, NEWQUAY, TR8 5AA, 01872 510246
www.dairylandfarmworld.com

Little Treamble Farm Touring Park
▶▶▶▶ 85%

tel: 01872 573823 & 07971 070760 **Rose TR4 9PR**
email: info@treambleholidays.co.uk **web:** www.treambleholidays.co.uk
dir: *A30 onto B3285 signed Perranporth. Approximately 0.5 mile right into Scotland Road signed Newquay. In approximately 2 miles to T-junction, right onto A3075 signed Newquay. 0.25 mile left at Rejerrah sign. Site signed 0.75 mile on right.*

This site, within easy reach of Padstow, Newquay and St Ives, is set in a quiet rural location with extensive countryside views across an undulating valley. There is a small toilet block with a disabled facility and a well-stocked shop. This working farm is adjacent to a Caravan Club site.

Open: All year **Last departure:** noon

Pitches: 🚐 🚕 Å

Facilities: 🅿 ✳ Ⓢ

Services: 🔌 🗑 🎣 Ⓣ

Within 3 miles: ↓ 🏌 ∪ ◎

Additional site information: 1.5 acre site. 🐾 Cars can be parked by caravans and tents. Awnings permitted.

GORRAN

Places to visit

The Lost Gardens of Heligan, PENTEWAN, PL26 6EN, 01726 845100
www.heligan.com

Caerhays Castle Gardens, GORRAN, PL26 6LY, 01872 501310
www.caerhays.co.uk

Great for kids: Wheal Martyn, ST AUSTELL, PL26 8XG, 01726 850362
www.wheal-martyn.com

Eden Project, ST AUSTELL, PL24 2SG, 01726 811911
www.edenproject.com

GORRAN
Map 2 SW94

Treveor Farm Campsite
▶▶▶ 86%

tel: 01726 842387 **PL26 6LW**
email: info@treveorfarm.co.uk **web:** www.treveorfarm.co.uk
dir: *From St Austell bypass left onto B3273 for Mevagissey. On hilltop before descent to village turn right onto unclassified road for Gorran. Right in 5 miles, site on right.*

A small family-run camping park set on a working farm, with grassy pitches backing onto mature hedging. This quiet site, with good facilities, is close to beaches and offers a large coarse fishing lake.

Open: April to October **Last arrival:** 21.00 **Last departure:** 11.00

Pitches: 🚐 🚕 Å; 12 hardstanding pitches

Leisure: 🅰

Facilities: 🛁 ☉ 🅿 ✳ WiFi

Services: 🔌 🗑

Within 3 miles: 🎣 Ⓢ

Additional site information: 4 acre site. 🐾 Cars can be parked by caravans and tents. Awnings permitted.

Treveague Farm Caravan & Camping Site
▶▶▶ 83%

tel: 01726 842295 **PL26 6NY**
email: treveaguefarmcampsite@outlook.com **web:** www.treveaguefarm.co.uk
dir: *B3273 from St Austell towards Mevagissey, pass Pentewan at top of hill, right signed Gorran. Past Heligan Gardens towards Gorran Churchtown. Follow brown tourist signs from fork in road. (Note: roads to site are single lane and very narrow. It is advisable to follow these directions and not sat nav).*

Spectacular panoramic coastal views can be enjoyed from this rural park, which is set on an organic farm and well equipped with modern facilities. A stone-clad toilet block with a Cornish slate roof is an attractive feature, as is the building that houses the smart reception, café and shop, which sells meat produced on the farm. There is an aviary with exotic birds, and also chinchillas are kept. A footpath leads to the fishing village of Gorran Haven in one direction, and the secluded sandy Vault Beach in the other. The site is close to a bus route.

Open: April to September **Last arrival:** 21.00 **Last departure:** noon

Pitches: 🚐 🚕 Å

Leisure: 🅰 ⚽

Facilities: 🛁 ☉ 🅿 ✳ ♿ Ⓢ 🎪 WiFi

Services: 🔌 🗑 🍴 🍽 🛒 🧺

Within 3 miles: 🏌 🎣 ⚓

Additional site information: 4 acre site. 🐾 Cars can be parked by caravans and tents. Awnings permitted. No fires. Bird and animal hide available.

LEISURE: 🏊 Indoor swimming pool 🏊 Outdoor swimming pool 🅰 Children's playground 🖐 Kids' club 🎾 Tennis court 🎱 Games room ⬛ Separate TV room ↓ golf course 🏌 Pitch n putt 🚣 Boats for hire 🚲 Bikes for hire 🎬 Cinema 🎵 Entertainment 🎣 Fishing ◎ Mini golf 🏄 Watersports 🏋 Gym ⚽ Sports field ∪ Stables **FACILITIES:** 🛁 Baths/Shower ☉ Electric shaver sockets 🅿 Hairdryer ✳ Ice Pack Facility 🍼 Baby facilities ♿ Disabled facilities Ⓢ Shop on site or within 200yds 🍴 BBQ area 🎪 Picnic area WiFi WiFi

GORRAN HAVEN
Map 2 SX04

Places to visit
Caerhays Castle Gardens, GORRAN, PL26 6LY, 01872 501310
www.caerhays.co.uk

The Lost Gardens of Heligan, PENTEWAN, PL26 6EN, 01726 845100
www.heligan.com

Great for kids: Wheal Martyn, ST AUSTELL, PL26 8XG, 01726 850362
www.wheal-martyn.com

Eden Project, ST AUSTELL, PL24 2SG, 01726 811911
www.edenproject.com

Trelispen Caravan & Camping Park
▶ 74%

tel: 01726 843501 **PL26 6NT**
email: trelispen@care4free.net **web:** www.trelispen.co.uk
dir: *B3273 from St Austell towards Mevagissey, on hilltop at crossroads before descent into Mevagissey turn right onto unclassified road to Gorran. Through village, 2nd right towards Gorran Haven, site signed on left in 250 metres. (Note: it is advisable to follow these directions not sat nav).*

A quiet rural site set in three paddocks, and sheltered by mature trees and hedges. The simple toilets have plenty of hot water, and there is a small laundry. Sandy beaches, pubs and shops are nearby, and Mevagissey is two miles away. There is a bus stop 100 yards from the site with a regular service to Mevagissey and St Austell.

Open: Easter and April to October **Last arrival:** 22.00 **Last departure:** noon

Pitches:

Facilities: 🏠 ☺ ☀

Services: ⊡ 🔲

Within 3 miles: ✐ ≋ ≉ 🛉

Additional site information: 2 acre site. 🐕 ⊛ Cars can be parked by caravans and tents. Awnings permitted. 30-acre nature reserve.

HAYLE

Places to visit
Tate St Ives, ST IVES, TR26 1TG, 01736 796226
www.tate.org.uk/stives

Barbara Hepworth Museum & Sculpture Garden, ST IVES, TR26 1AD, 01736 796226, www.tate.org.uk/stives

HAYLE
Map 2 SW53

St Ives Bay Holiday Park

▶▶▶▶▶ 93% HOLIDAY CENTRE

tel: 01736 752274 **73 Loggans Road, Upton Towans TR27 5BH**
email: enquiries@stivesbay.co.uk **web:** www.stivesbay.co.uk
dir: *Exit A30 at Hayle then immediately right onto B3301 at mini roundabouts. Site entrance 0.5 mile on left.*

An extremely well-maintained holiday park with a relaxed atmosphere situated adjacent to a three mile beach. The various camping fields are set in hollows amongst the sand dunes and are very tastefully laid out, with the high camping fields enjoying stunning views over St Ives Bay. The touring sections are in a number of separate locations around the extensive site. The park is specially geared for families and couples, and as well as the large indoor swimming pool there are two pubs with seasonal entertainment. There are 17 camping pods for hire.

Open: Easter to 30 October **Last arrival:** anytime **Last departure:** 09.00

Pitches: 🚐 from £10; 🚍 from £10; ⛺ from £10; 🏠 see prices below

Leisure: ≋ ⋔ ♨ 🎣 ☐ 🎵 ✐

Facilities: 🏠 ☺ 🅿 ☀ � 🛉 Ⅱ 📶 **WiFi**

Services: ⊡ 🔲 🍷 🍽 🍔 🔋 ↯ 🔋 ⊘ Ⅰ **Within 3 miles:** 🏃 ⛳ ⊛ ≋

Additional site information: 90 acre site. No pets. Crazy golf.

Glamping available: Wooden pods from £165 per week. **Changeover days:** Saturday

Additional glamping information: Cars can be parked by pods.

See advert on page 72

PITCHES: 🚐 Caravans 🚍 Motorhomes ⛺ Tents 🏠 Glamping accommodation **SERVICES:** ⊡ Electric hook-up 🔲 Launderette 🍷 Licensed bar 🔋 Calor Gas ⊘ Campingaz Ⅰ Toilet fluid 🍽 Café/Restaurant 🍔 Fast Food/Takeaway 🔋 Battery charging ↯ Motorhome service point * 2019 prices ⊛ No credit or debit cards 🐕 Dogs permitted 🚫 No dogs

HAYLE continued

Premier Park

Riviere Sands Holiday Park

▶▶▶▶▶ 88% HOLIDAY HOME PARK

tel: 01736 752132 **Riviere Towans TR27 5AX**

email: rivieresands@haven.com **web:** www.haven.com/rivieresands

dir: A30 towards Redruth. Follow signs into Hayle, straight on at double mini-roundabout. Turn right opposite petrol station signed Towans and beaches. Park 1 mile on right.

Close to St Ives and with direct access to a safe, white-sand beach, Riviere Sands is an exciting holiday park with much to offer families. Children can enjoy the crazy golf, amusements, swimming pool complex, and the beach of course; the evening entertainment for adults is extensive and lively. There is a good range of holiday caravans and apartments.

Open: 24 March to 30 October

Holiday Homes: Sleep 8 Bedrooms 2 Bathrooms 1 Toilets 1 Microwave Freezer TV Sky/Freeview

Leisure: 🏊 🏖 ⚿ 👋 🎯

Additional site information: 🚫

Atlantic Coast Holiday Park

▶▶▶▶ 85%

tel: 01736 752071 **53 Upton Towans, Gwithian TR27 5BL**

email: enquiries@atlanticcoastpark.co.uk **web:** www.atlanticcoastpark.co.uk

dir: From A30 into Hayle, right at double roundabout. Site 1.5 miles on left.

Fringed by the sand dunes of St Ives Bay and close to the golden sands of Gwithian Beach, the small, friendly touring area continues to improve year on year and offers fully serviced pitches. There's freshly baked bread, a takeaway and a bar next door. This park is ideally situated for visitors to enjoy the natural coastal beauty and attractions of southwest Cornwall. There is superb landscaping and planting, and

campers have the use of facilities such as a kettle and microwave. Static caravans are available for holiday hire.

Open: March to early January **Last arrival:** 20.00 **Last departure:** 11.00

Pitches: 🚐 from £27; 🚏 from £27; ▲ from £27; 🏕 see prices below; 4 hardstanding pitches

Leisure: ⚿ 🔍

Facilities: 🛁 ☺ ⚿ ✳ ♿ Ⓢ 🚼 🛒 WiFi

Services: 🖤 🔟 Ⓣ

Within 3 miles: ↧ ⚲ ∪ ◎ 🚣

Additional site information: 4.5 acre site. 🐕 Cars can be parked by caravans and tents. Awnings permitted. No commercial vehicles, gazebos or day tents. Freshly baked bread, croissants, pasties, newspapers available.

Glamping available: Shepherd's hut from £100. **Changeover days:** Any day

Additional glamping information: Own private hot tub and decking area. Cars can be parked by hut.

Higher Trevaskis Caravan & Camping Park

▶▶▶ 86%

tel: 01209 831736 **Gwinear Road, Connor Downs TR27 5JQ**

email: info@highertrevaskiscaravanpark.co.uk

web: www.highertrevaskiscaravanpark.co.uk

dir: On A30 at Hayle roundabout take exit signed Connor Downs, in 1 mile right signed Carnhell Green. Site 0.75 mile just after level crossing.

An attractive paddocked and terraced park in a sheltered rural position on a valley side with views towards St Ives. The terrace areas are divided by hedges. This secluded park is personally run by welcoming owners who ensure it remains a peaceful location.

Open: mid April to September **Last arrival:** 20.00 **Last departure:** 10.30

Pitches: 🚐 🚏 ▲; 🏕 see prices below; 4 hardstanding pitches

Leisure: ⚽

Facilities: 🏠 ⊙ 🗜 ✳ $ WiFi

Services: 🔌 🗑 🛒 🔒 🌿 T

Within 3 miles: ⚓ 🌙 ◎ 🏄

Additional site information: 6.5 acre site. 🐕 Maximum 2 dogs per pitch, certain dog breeds not accepted (contact site for details). 🚗 Cars can be parked by caravans and tents. Awnings permitted. 5mph speed limit on site, balls games permitted on designated field only.

Glamping available: Pods from £45.

Additional glamping information: Minimum 7 day booking in July and August. Cars can be parked by pods.

Treglisson Touring Park
▶▶▶ 83%

tel: 01736 753141 **Wheal Alfred Road TR27 5JT**
email: treglisson@hotmail.co.uk **web:** www.treglisson.co.uk
dir: *From A30 (Camborne towards Penzance) take 4th exit at roundabout signed Hayle. Left at next mini roundabout, follow site signs. Approximately 1.5 miles past golf course, site sign on left.*

A small secluded site in a peaceful wooded meadow and a former apple and pear orchard. This quiet rural site has level grass pitches and a well-planned modern toilet block, and is just two miles from the glorious beach at Hayle with its vast stretch of golden sand

Open: Spring Bank Holiday to end of September **Last arrival:** 20.00 **Last departure:** 11.00

Pitches: 🚐 from £12; 🚕 from £12; ▲ from £12; 6 hardstanding pitches

Leisure: ⚙

Facilities: 🏠 ⊙ 🗜 ✳ ♿ 🛋 WiFi

Services: 🔌 🗑 🛒

Within 3 miles: ⚓ 🌙 ∪ ◎ 🏄 $

Additional site information: 3 acre site. 🐕 Cars can be parked by caravans and tents. Awnings permitted. Maximum 6 people per pitch, maximum tent size of 7 metres.

| HELSTON | Map 2 SW62 |

See also Ashton

Places to visit
Great for kids: Flambards, HELSTON, TR13 0QA, 01326 573404
www.flambards.co.uk

Cornish Seal Sanctuary, GWEEK, TR12 6UG, 01326 221361
www.visitsealife.com/gweek

Lower Polladras Touring Park
▶▶▶▶ 90%

tel: 01736 762220 **Carleen, Breage TR13 9NX**
email: lowerpolladras@btinternet.com **web:** www.lower-polladras.co.uk
dir: *From Helston take A394 then B3302 (Hayle road) at Ward Garage, 2nd left to Carleen, site 2 miles on right.*

An attractive rural park with extensive views of surrounding fields, appealing to families who enjoy the countryside. The planted trees and shrubs are maturing, and

help to divide the area into paddocks with spacious grassy pitches. The site has a dish-washing area, a games room, a dog and nature walk, two fully serviced family rooms and WiFi.

Open: April to January **Last arrival:** 22.00 **Last departure:** noon

Pitches: 🚐 from £15; 🚕 from £15; ▲ from £15; 28 hardstanding pitches; 17 seasonal pitches

Leisure: ⚙ 🎱 ⚽

Facilities: 🏠 ⊙ 🗜 ✳ ♿ $ 🛋 🛋 WiFi

Services: 🔌 🗑 🛒 ⚡ 🔒 🌿 T

Within 3 miles: ⚓ 🌙 ∪ ◎ 🏄 🎣 🎯

Additional site information: 4 acre site. 🐕 Cars can be parked by caravans and tents. Awnings permitted. No drones, hoverboards or camp fires. Caravan storage.

Skyburriowe Farm
▶▶▶ 83%

tel: 01326 221646 **Garras TR12 6LR**
email: bkbenney@hotmail.co.uk **web:** www.skyburriowefarm.co.uk
dir: *From Helston take A3083 to The Lizard. After Culdrose Naval Airbase continue straight on at roundabout, in 1 mile left at Skyburriowe Lane sign. In 0.5 mile right at Skyburriowe B&B/Campsite sign. Pass bungalow to farmhouse. Site on left.*

A leafy no-through road leads to this picturesque farm park in a rural location on the Lizard Peninsula. The toilet block offers excellent quality facilities, and most pitches have electric hook-ups. There are some beautiful coves and beaches nearby, and for a great day out, Flambards theme park is also close by. Under the supervision of the owner, children are permitted to watch his herd of Friesian cows being milked.

Open: April to October **Last arrival:** 22.00 **Last departure:** 11.00

Pitches: 🚐 from £24; 🚕 from £24; ▲ from £24; 4 hardstanding pitches

Facilities: 🏠 ⊙ ✳ ♿ WiFi

Services: 🔌 🛒

Within 3 miles: ⚓ 🌙 ∪ 🏄 🎣 🎯 🎯

Additional site information: 4 acre site. 🐕 Cars can be parked by caravans and tents. Awnings permitted. Quiet after 23.00. Fresh seasonal vegetables available.

PITCHES: 🚐 Caravans 🚕 Motorhomes ▲ Tents ⚙ Glamping accommodation **SERVICES:** 🔌 Electric hook-up 🗑 Launderette 🛋 Licensed bar
🔒 Calor Gas 🌿 Campingaz T Toilet fluid 🍴 Café/Restaurant 🛒 Fast Food/Takeaway 🛒 Battery charging ⚡ Motorhome service point
* 2019 prices 🚫 No credit or debit cards 🐕 Dogs permitted 🚫 No dogs

HOLYWELL BAY | Map 2 SW75

Places to visit

Trerice, TRERICE, TR8 4PG, 01637 875404
www.nationaltrust.org.uk/trerice

Premier Park

Trevornick

▶▶▶▶▶ 94%

tel: 01637 830531 & 832905 **TR8 5PW**
email: bookings@trevornick.co.uk **web:** www.trevornick.co.uk
dir: *3 miles from Newquay exit A3075 towards Redruth. Follow Cubert and Holywell Bay signs.*

A large seaside holiday complex with excellent facilities and amenities. There is plenty of entertainment including a children's club and an evening cabaret, adding up to a full holiday experience for all the family. A sandy beach is just a 15-minute footpath walk away. The park has 55 Euro tents for hire.

Open: Easter and mid May to September **Last arrival:** 21.00 **Last departure:** 10.00

Pitches: * 🚐 from £25; 🚐 from £25; ⛺ from £22; 🏠 see prices below; 53 hardstanding pitches; 8 seasonal pitches

Leisure: 🏊 🏕 ✋ 🔍 ⌨ ♪ 🎣 ⚽ Spa

Facilities: 🚿 ☉ 🔞 ✳ ♿ 🏧 🚮 WiFi

Services: 🚰 🔲 🚽 🍴 🏪 🛒 🔒 🧺 🚽

Within 3 miles: ∪ ◎ 🚣 🚴 ⛳

Additional site information: 20 acre site. 🚗 Cars can be parked by caravans and tents. Awnings permitted. Families and couples only. Arcade, dog walking field.

Glamping available: Ready-erected tents from £46. **Changeover days:** Saturday

Additional glamping information: Ready-erected tents are fully equipped; some are dog friendly. Cars can be parked by tents.

INDIAN QUEENS

Places to visit

Wheal Martyn, ST AUSTELL, PL26 8XG, 01726 850362
www.wheal-martyn.com

Trerice, TRERICE, TR8 4PG, 01637 875404
www.nationaltrust.org.uk/trerice

INDIAN QUEENS | Map 2 SW95

Gnome World Caravan & Camping Park

▶▶▶▶ 82%

tel: 01726 860812 & 860101 **Moorland Road, Indian Queens TR9 6HN**
email: gnomesworld@btconnect.com
dir: *Signed from slip road at A30 and A39 roundabout in village of Indian Queens – site on old A30, now an unclassified road.*

Set in open countryside, this spacious park is set on level grassy land only half a mile from the A30 (Cornwall's main arterial route) and in a central holiday location for touring the county, and accessing the sandy beaches on the north Cornwall coast. Ablaze with summer flowering plants, it offers spotless facilities, an exciting children's playground and a shop. Please note that there are no narrow lanes to negotiate.

Open: March to December **Last arrival:** 22.00 **Last departure:** noon

Pitches: 🚐 🚐 ⛺; 25 hardstanding pitches

Facilities: 🚿 ☉ 🔞 ✳ ♿ 🛋 WiFi

Services: 🚰 🔲 🔒

Within 3 miles: 🚴 ∪ 🏪

Additional site information: 4.5 acre site. 🚗 Cars can be parked by caravans and tents. Awnings permitted.

See advert opposite

ISLES OF SCILLY

See Bryher and St Mary's

LEISURE: 🏊 Indoor swimming pool 🏊 Outdoor swimming pool 🏕 Children's playground ✋ Kids' club 🎾 Tennis court 🔍 Games room 🖵 Separate TV room ⛳ golf course 🏌 Pitch n putt 🚣 Boats for hire 🚲 Bikes for hire 🎬 Cinema ♪ Entertainment 🎣 Fishing ◎ Mini golf 🏄 Watersports 🏋 Gym 🏐 Sports field ∪ Stables **FACILITIES:** 🚿 Baths/Shower ☉ Electric shaver sockets 🔞 Hairdryer ✳ Ice Pack Facility 🚼 Baby facilities ♿ Disabled facilities 🏪 Shop on site or within 200yds 🍖 BBQ area 🧺 Picnic area WiFi WiFi

KENNACK SANDS
Map 2 SW71

Places to visit

Cornish Seal Sanctuary, GWEEK, TR12 6UG, 01326 221361
www.visitsealife.com/gweek

Great for kids: Flambards, HELSTON, TR13 0QA, 01326 573404
www.flambards.co.uk

Chy Carne Holiday Park
▶▶▶▶ 92%

tel: 01326 290200 **Kuggar, Ruan Minor TR12 7LX**
email: enquiries@chycarne.co.uk **web:** www.chycarne.co.uk
dir: From A3083 onto B3293 after Culdrose Naval Air Station. At Goonhilly ESS right onto unclassified road signed Kennack Sands. Left in 3 miles at junction.

This spacious, beautifully maintained, 12-acre park is in a quiet rural location and has excellent family facilities and a stunning toilet block. There are extensive sea and coastal views over the sand at Kennack Sands, less than half a mile away. Food is available from the site's takeaway, and the local pub is not far away in the village.

Open: Easter to October **Last arrival:** dusk **Pitches:** ➡ ➡ ▲; 7 hardstanding pitches
Leisure: ⚓ ⚲ **Facilities:** 🏠 ☺ 🄿 ✳ 🔥 🖁 🚿 🚽 WiFi
Services: 🔌 🔘 🍽 🍴 🍺 🛒 🏕 🔋 ⌀ 🔲 **Within 3 miles:** 🗘 🌊 ∪ ◎ ♒
Additional site information: 12 acre site. ⚲ Cars can be parked by caravans and tents. Awnings permitted. Table tennis, football table, pool table.

Silver Sands Holiday Park
▶▶▶ 88%

tel: 01326 290631 **Gwendreath TR12 7LZ**
email: info@silversandsholidaypark.co.uk **web:** www.silversandsholidaypark.co.uk
dir: From Helston follow signs to St Keverne. After Goonhilly Satellite Station turn right at crossroads signed Kennack Sands, 1.5 miles, left at Gwendreath sign, site 1 mile. (Note: it is advisable to follow these directions not sat nav).

A small, family-owned park in a remote location, with individually screened pitches providing sheltered suntraps. The owners continue to upgrade the park, improving

the landscaping, access roads and toilets; lovely floral displays greet you on arrival. A footpath through the woods leads to the beach and the local pub. One of the nearby beaches is the historic Mullion Cove, and for the children, a short car ride will ensure a great day out at the Flambards theme park.

Open: 21 March to 2 November **Last arrival:** 18.00 **Last departure:** 11.00
Pitches: * ➡ from £16; ➡ from £16; ▲ from £14 **Leisure:** ⚲ ❀
Facilities: 🏠 ☺ 🄿 ✳ 🖁 🚿 🚽 WiFi **Services:** 🔌 🔘 🔋 ⌀
Within 3 miles: 🗘 🌊 ∪ ♒
Additional site information: 9 acre site. ⚲ Cars can be parked by caravans and tents except when ground is saturated. Awnings permitted. No noise after 22.00. Woodland walk to the beach. Car hire can be arranged.

KILKHAMPTON
Map 2 SS21

Upper Tamar Lake
▶▶ 75%

tel: 01288 321712 **Upper Tamar Lake EX23 9SB**
email: info@swlakestrust.org.uk **web:** www.southwestlakes.co.uk
dir: From A39 at Kilkhampton onto B3254, left in 0.5 mile onto unclassified road, follow signs approximately 4 miles to site.

A well-trimmed, slightly sloping site overlooking the lake and surrounding countryside, with several signed walks. The site benefits from the excellent facilities provided for the watersports centre and coarse anglers, with a rescue launch on the lake when the flags are flying. A good family site, with Bude's beaches and the surfing waves only eight miles away.

Open: April to October **Last departure:** 11.00
Pitches: ➡ ➡ ▲ 🏠; 2 hardstanding pitches **Leisure:** ⚲ 🌊
Facilities: 🏠 🄿 ✳ 🖁 🚿 **Services:** 🔌 🍴 🛒
Within 3 miles: 🗘 ∪ ♒ 🗘 🐟
Additional site information: 1 acre site. ⚲ Cars can be parked by caravans and tents. Awnings permitted. No open fires, off-ground BBQs only. No swimming in lake. Canoeing, sailing, windsurfing.
Glamping available: Wooden pods.
Additional glamping information: Cars can be parked by pods.

PITCHES: ➡ Caravans ➡ Motorhomes ▲ Tents 🏠 Glamping accommodation **SERVICES:** 🔌 Electric hook-up 🔘 Launderette 🍺 Licensed bar
🔋 Calor Gas ⌀ Campingaz 🔲 Toilet fluid 🍽 Café/Restaurant 🍴 Fast Food/Takeaway 🔋 Battery charging ⚡ Motorhome service point
* 2019 prices ⊗ No credit or debit cards ⚲ Dogs permitted ⊗ No dogs

LANDRAKE   Map 3 SX36

Places to visit

Cotehele, CALSTOCK, PL12 6TA, 01579 351346
www.nationaltrust.org.uk/cotehele

Mount Edgcumbe House & Country Park, TORPOINT, PL10 1HZ, 01752 822236
www.mountedgcumbe.gov.uk

Great for kids: Wild Futures' Monkey Sanctuary, LOOE, PL13 1NZ, 01503 262532
www.monkeysanctuary.org

Premier Park

Dolbeare Park Caravan and Camping

►►►►► 91%

tel: 01752 851332 **St Ive Road PL12 5AF**
email: reception@dolbeare.co.uk **web:** www.dolbeare.co.uk
dir: *A38 to Landrake, 4 miles west of Saltash. At footbridge over A38 turn right, follow signs to site (0.75 mile from A38).*

Set in meadowland close to the A38 and the Devon–Cornwall border, this attractive touring park is run by innovative, forward-thinking owners who have adopted a very 'green' approach to running the park. The smart toilet block is very eco-friendly – electronic sensor showers, an on-demand boiler system, flow control valves on the taps, and low-energy lighting, as well as an impressive family room. The park is extremely well presented, with excellent hardstanding pitches, a good tenting field that offers spacious pitches, and good provision for children with a separate ball games paddock and nature trail. Expect high levels of customer care and cleanliness. The on-site shop sells fresh bread and local produce. One pre-erected, fully-equipped Eurotent and two Lotus Belle tents are available for hire.

Open: All year **Last arrival:** 18.00 (fee payable for arrivals after 18.00)
Last departure: 11.00

Pitches: 🚐 from £20; 🚎 from £20; ▲ from £16.50; 🏠 see prices below;
54 hardstanding pitches; 12 seasonal pitches

Leisure: /ᐱ\ ❁

Facilities: 🛁 ⊙ 🗲 ✳ 🕭 ⑤ 🛱 📶

Services: 🔌 🗑 ♨ 🛒 ⚒ 🛢 🌿 Ⓣ

Within 3 miles: 🎣 ⌕ ∪ ⚓

Additional site information: 9 acre site. 🐾 Cars can be parked by caravans and tents. Awnings permitted. No cycling, no kite flying. Off licence, free use of fridge and freezer, freshly baked bread and croissants available.

Glamping available: Lotus Belle tents from £210; ready-erected tent from £280.

Changeover days: Friday and Saturday

Additional glamping information: Lotus Belle tent prices are seasonally variable. Cars can be parked by tents.

LEEDSTOWN (NEAR HAYLE)   Map 2 SW63

Places to visit

East Pool Mine, POOL, TR15 3NP, 01209 315027
www.nationaltrust.org.uk/east-pool-mine

Godolphin House, GODOLPHIN CROSS, TR13 9RE, 01736 763194
www.nationaltrust.org.uk/godolphin

Premier Park

Calloose Caravan & Camping Park
►►►►► 86%

tel: 01736 850431 & 0800 328 7589 **TR27 5ET**
email: sales@calloose.co.uk **web:** www.calloose.co.uk
dir: *From Hayle take B3302 to Leedstown, turn left opposite village hall before entering village. Site 0.5 mile on left at bottom of hill.*

A comprehensively equipped leisure park in a remote rural setting in a small river valley. This very good park is busy and bustling, and offers bright, clean toilet facilities, an excellent games room, an inviting pool, a good children's play area, and log cabins and static caravans for holiday hire.

Open: All year **Last arrival:** 22.00 **Last departure:** 11.00

Pitches: 🚐 🚎 ▲; 29 hardstanding pitches

Leisure: 🏊 /ᐱ\ ⌕ ✎ ▭

Facilities: ⊙ 🗲 ✳ 🕭 ⑤ 🛱

Services: 🔌 🗑 ♨ 🍽 ♨ 🛒 🛢 🌿 Ⓣ

Within 3 miles: ⌕

Additional site information: 12.5 acre site. 🐾 Cars can be parked by caravans and tents. Awnings permitted. No noise after midnight, no pets in statics or log cabins. Crazy golf, skittle alley.

LOOE   Map 2 SX25

Places to visit

Antony House, TORPOINT, PL11 2QA, 01752 812191
www.nationaltrust.org.uk/antony

Mount Edgcumbe House & Country Park, TORPOINT, PL10 1HZ, 01752 822236
www.mountedgcumbe.gov.uk

Great for kids: Wild Futures' Monkey Sanctuary, LOOE, PL13 1NZ, 01503 262532
www.monkeysanctuary.org

Premier Park

Tregoad Park

►►►►► 85%

tel: 01503 262718 **St Martin PL13 1PB**
email: info@tregoadpark.co.uk **web:** www.tregoadpark.co.uk
dir: *Signed with direct access from B3253, or from east on A387 follow B3253 for 1.75 miles towards Looe. Site on left at bottom of cliff.*

Investment continues at this smart, terraced park with extensive sea and rural views, about a mile and a half from Looe. All pitches are level. The facilities are well maintained and spotlessly clean, and there is a swimming pool with

LEISURE: 🏊 Indoor swimming pool 🏊 Outdoor swimming pool /ᐱ\ Children's playground 🖐 Kids' club 🎾 Tennis court 🎱 Games room ▭ Separate TV room
🏌 golf course ⛳ Pitch n putt ⛵ Boats for hire 🚲 Bikes for hire 🎬 Cinema 🎵 Entertainment 🎣 Fishing ◎ Mini golf 🏄 Watersports 🏋 Gym ⚽ Sports field ∪ Stables
FACILITIES: 🛁 Baths/Shower ⊙ Electric shaver sockets 🗲 Hairdryer ✳ Ice Pack Facility 🛒 Baby facilities 🕭 Disabled facilities ⑤ Shop on site or within 200yds
🛒 BBQ area 🛱 Picnic area 📶 WiFi

adjacent jacuzzi and sun patio, and a licensed bar where bar meals are served in the conservatory. The site has fishing lakes stocked with carp, tench and roach. There is a bus stop at the bottom of the drive for the Plymouth and Truro routes. Static caravans, holiday cottages and camping pods are available for holiday hire.

Open: All year (restricted service: low season – bistro closed) **Last arrival:** 20.00 **Last departure:** 11.00

Pitches: 🚐 🚌 ⛺ 🛖; 60 hardstanding pitches

Leisure: 🏊 🛝 ✋ 🏓 📺 🎵 🎾 ⛳ ⚽ 🏊 Spa

Facilities: 🛁 ☺ 🚿 ✲ ♿ 🛒 🍖 🪑 WiFi

Services: 🔌 🧺 🍷 🍴 🍔 🔋 🚰 🛢 🔥 [T]

Within 3 miles: 🎣 🐎 🎯 🌊 ⛵ 🏬

Additional site information: 55 acre site. 🐕 Cars can be parked by caravans and tents. Awnings permitted. Crazy golf, ball sports area.

Glamping available: Wooden pods. **Changeover days:** Any day

Additional glamping information: 2 and 4 berth wooden pods are available. Minimum stay 1 night. Cars can be parked by pods.

Premier Park

Camping Caradon Touring Park

►►►►► 84%

tel: 01503 272388 **Trelawne PL13 2NA**
email: enquiries@campingcaradon.co.uk **web:** www.campingcaradon.co.uk
dir: *Site signed from junction of A387 and B3359, between Looe and Polperro. Take B3359 towards Pelynt then 1st right. Site 250 metres on left.*

Set in a quiet rural location between the popular coastal resorts of Looe and Polperro, this family-run and developing eco-friendly park is just one and half miles from the beach at Talland Bay. The site caters for both families and couples. The owners take great pride in the site and offer quality facilities and service to their campers throughout their stay; their constant aim is to provide a carefree and relaxing holiday. The local bus stops inside the park entrance.

Open: All year (restricted service: November to March – prior bookings only) **Last arrival:** 20.00 **Last departure:** 11.00

Pitches: 🚐 from £16; 🚌 from £16; ⛺ from £13; 23 hardstanding pitches

Leisure: 🛝 🏓

Facilities: 🛁 ☺ 🚿 ✲ ♿ 🛒 🪑 WiFi

Services: 🔌 🧺 🍷 🍴 🍔 🔋 🚰 🛢 🔥 [T]

Within 3 miles: 🎾 🎯 🌊 ⛵

Additional site information: 3.5 acre site. 🐕 Cars can be parked by caravans and tents. Awnings permitted. Quiet from 23.00–07.00 and barrier not operational. Family room with TV, undercover washing-up area, RCD lead hire, rallies welcome.

Premier Park

Tencreek Holiday Park

►►►►► 83% HOLIDAY CENTRE

tel: 01503 262447 **Polperro Road PL13 2JR**
email: reception@tencreek.co.uk **web:** www.dolphinholidays.co.uk
dir: *Take A387, 1.25 miles from Looe. Site on left.*

Occupying a lovely position with extensive countryside and sea views, this holiday centre is in a rural spot but close to Looe and Polperro. There is a full family entertainment programme, with an indoor swimming pool, an adventure playground and an exciting children's club. The superb amenity blocks include several private family shower rooms with toilet and washbasin.

Open: All year **Last arrival:** 22.00 **Last departure:** 10.00

Pitches: 🚐 from £15.25; 🚌 from £15.25; ⛺ from £15.25; 12 hardstanding pitches; 120 seasonal pitches

Leisure: 🏊 🛝 ✋ 🧒 🏓 🎵 ⚽

Facilities: 🛁 ☺ 🚿 ✲ ♿ 🛒 🚼 WiFi

Services: 🔌 🧺 🍷 🍴 🍔 🔋 🚰 🛢 🔥 [T]

Within 3 miles: 🎣 🎾 🐎 🎯 🌊 ⛵ 🏬

Additional site information: 24 acre site. 🐕 Families and couples only. Multi-sports pitch.

See advert on page 78

LOSTWITHIEL
Map 2 SX15

Places to visit

Restormel Castle, RESTORMEL, PL22 0EE, 01208 872687
www.english-heritage.org.uk/daysout/properties/restormel-castle

Lanhydrock, LANHYDROCK, PL30 5AD, 01208 265950
www.nationaltrust.org.uk/lanhydrock

Great for kids: Eden Project, ST AUSTELL, PL24 2SG, 01726 811911
www.edenproject.com

Premier Park

Eden Valley Holiday Park

▶▶▶▶▶ 87%

tel: 01208 872277 **PL30 5BU**
email: edenvalleyholidaypark@btconnect.com **web:** www.edenvalleyholidaypark.co.uk
dir: 1.5 miles southwest of Lostwithiel on A390 turn right at brown/white sign in 400 metres. (Note: it is advisable to follow these directions not sat nav).

A grassy park set in attractive paddocks with mature trees. The gradual upgrading of facilities continues, and both buildings and grounds are carefully maintained and include an impressive children's play area. This park is ideally located for visiting the Eden Project, the nearby golden beaches and sailing at Fowey. There are also two self-catering lodges.

Open: Easter or April to October **Last arrival:** 22.00 **Last departure:** 11.30
Pitches: 🚐 from £15.50; 🚌 from £15.50; ⛺ from £15.50; 40 hardstanding pitches; 25 seasonal pitches
Leisure: 🅰 🔍 ⚽
Facilities: 🛁 ⊙ 🗡 ✳ ♿ 🅂 🎍 WiFi
Services: 🔌 🔲 🛒 ⬆ 🛢 ∅
Within 3 miles: 🎣 🗡 ∪ 🛶 ⛴
Additional site information: 12 acre site. 🐕 No large dogs. Cars can be parked by caravans and tents. Awnings permitted. Table football, pool, table tennis, football. Walks, wildlife conservation information room.

LUXULYAN

Places to visit

Restormel Castle, RESTORMEL, PL22 0EE, 01208 872687
www.english-heritage.org.uk/daysout/properties/restormel-castle

Eden Project, ST AUSTELL, PL24 2SG, 01726 811911
www.edenproject.com

Great for kids: Wheal Martyn, ST AUSTELL, PL26 8XG, 01726 850362
www.wheal-martyn.com

LEISURE: 🏊 Indoor swimming pool 🏊 Outdoor swimming pool 🅰 Children's playground 🪁 Kids' club 🎾 Tennis court 🎱 Games room 📺 Separate TV room 🏌 golf course ⛳ Pitch n putt ⛵ Boats for hire 🚲 Bikes for hire 🎬 Cinema 🎵 Entertainment 🎣 Fishing ⛳ Mini golf 🏄 Watersports 🏋 Gym ⚽ Sports field ∪ Stables
FACILITIES: 🛁 Baths/Shower ⊙ Electric shaver sockets 🗡 Hairdryer ✳ Ice Pack Facility 👶 Baby facilities ♿ Disabled facilities 🅂 Shop on site or within 200yds 🍖 BBQ area 🎍 Picnic area WiFi WiFi

LUXULYAN
Map 2 SX05

Croft Farm Holiday Park
►►► 80%

tel: 01726 850228 **PL30 5EQ**
email: enquiries@croftfarm.co.uk **web:** www.croftfarm.co.uk
dir: Exit A30 at Bodmin onto A391 towards St Austell. In 7 miles left at double roundabout onto unclassified road towards Luxulyan/Eden Project, continue to roundabout at Eden, left signed Luxulyan. Site 1 mile on left. (Note: do not approach any other way as roads are very narrow).

A peaceful, picturesque setting at the edge of a wooded valley, and only one mile from The Eden Project. Facilities include a well-maintained toilet block, a well-equipped dishwashing area, replete with freezer and microwave, and a revamped children's play area reached via an attractive woodland trail. There is a good bus service to St Austell and Luxulyan (the bus stop is at the site's entrance) and trains run to Newquay.

Open: 21 March to 21 January **Last arrival:** 18.00 **Last departure:** 11.00
Pitches: 🚐 🚏 ▲; 18 hardstanding pitches; 10 seasonal pitches
Leisure: 🎱
Facilities: 🏠 ☉ 🍴 ⚒ 🆂 🛒 WiFi
Services: 🔌 🔲 🛒 🔋 🧺 Ⓣ
Within 3 miles: ↨ 🚵 🚴 🏄 🎏
Additional site information: 10.5 acre site. 🐕 Cars can be parked by caravans and tents. Awnings permitted. No skateboarding, ball games only in playing field, quiet between 23.00-07.00. Woodland walk, information room.

MARAZION
Map 2 SW53

Places to visit
St Michael's Mount, MARAZION, TR17 0HS, 01736 710507
www.stmichaelsmount.co.uk

Trengwainton Garden, PENZANCE, TR20 8RZ, 01736 363148
www.nationaltrust.org.uk/trengwainton

Wayfarers Caravan & Camping Park
►►►► 91%

tel: 01736 763326 **Relubbus Lane, St Hilary TR20 9EF**
email: elaine@wayfarerspark.co.uk **web:** www.wayfarerspark.co.uk
dir: Exit A30 onto A394 signed Helston. 2 miles, left at roundabout onto B3280 signed Goldsithney. Through Goldsithney. Site 1 mile on left on bend (Note: slow down at 1st brown sign; it is advisable to ignore sat nav as directions are not suitable if towing a caravan).

Located in the centre of St Hilary, two and half miles from St Michael's Mount, this is a quiet, sheltered park in a peaceful rural setting. It offers spacious, well-drained pitches and very well maintained facilities, including a chill-out barbecue area. It has a separate car park for campers which makes their area a safer environment.

Open: May to September **Last arrival:** 18.00 **Last departure:** 11.00
Pitches: 🚐 🚏 ▲; 25 hardstanding pitches
Facilities: 🏠 ☉ 🍴 ⚒ ♿ 🆂 🛒 🍴
Services: 🔌 🔲 🛒 ⚓ 🔋 🧺 Ⓣ

Within 3 miles: ↨ 🚵 ♨ ◎ 🏄 🎏

Additional site information: 4.8 acre site. Adults only. 🐕 Cars can be parked by caravans and tents. Awnings permitted. No pets. Car hire can be arranged.

Wheal Rodney Holiday Park
►►► 86%

tel: 01736 710605 **Gwallon Lane TR17 0HL**
email: reception@whealrodney.co.uk **web:** www.whealrodney.co.uk
dir: Exit A30 at Crowlas, signed Rospeath. Site 1.5 miles on right. From Marazion centre turn opposite Fire Engine Inn, site 500 metres on left.

Set in a quiet rural location surrounded by farmland, with level grass pitches and well-kept facilities. Within half a mile are the beach at Marazion, the causeway and the ferry boat to St Michael's Mount. A cycle route is within 400 yards; Penzance is only a short car or cycle ride away.

Open: Easter to October **Last arrival:** 20.00 **Last departure:** 11.00
Pitches: 🚐 🚏 ▲ **Leisure:** 🎱 **Facilities:** 🏠 ☉ 🍴 ⚒ 🆂 WiFi
Services: 🔌 🔲 🛒 **Within 3 miles:** ↨ 🚵 🚴 ◎ 🏄
Additional site information: 2.5 acre site. 🐕 Cars can be parked by caravans and tents. Awnings permitted. Quiet after 22.00. Car hire can be arranged.

MAWGAN PORTH
Map 2 SW86

Places to visit
Prideaux Place, PADSTOW, PL28 8RP, 01841 532411
www.prideauxplace.co.uk

Goss Moor National Nature Reserve, CARNE, 01726 891096
www.gov.uk/government/publications/cornwalls-national-nature-reserves/cornwalls-nature-reserves

Sun Haven Valley Country Holiday Park
►►►► 86%

tel: 01637 860373 & 0800 634 6744 **TR8 4BQ**
email: sunhaven@sunhavenvalley.com **web:** www.sunhavenvalley.com
dir: Exit A30 at Highgate Hill junction for Newquay; follow signs for airport. At T-junction turn right. At beach level in Mawgan Porth take only road inland, then 0.25 mile. Site 0.5 mile beyond 'S' bend.

An attractive site with level pitches on the side of a river valley; being just off the B3276, this makes an ideal base for touring the Padstow and Newquay areas. The very high quality facilities include a TV lounge and a games room in a Swedish-style chalet, and a well-kept adventure playground. Trees and hedges fringe the park, and the ground is well drained.

Open: Easter to October **Last arrival:** 22.00 **Last departure:** 10.30
Pitches: 🚐 from £14.50; 🚏 from £14.50; ▲ from £14.50; 11 hardstanding pitches
Leisure: 🎮 🎱 🖥 **Facilities:** 🏠 🍴 ⚒ 🆂 🛒 🍴 WiFi
Services: 🔌 🔲 🔋 🧺 Ⓣ **Within 3 miles:** ↨ 🚵 ◎ 🏄
Additional site information: 5 acre site. 🐕 Cars can be parked by caravans and tents. Awnings permitted. Families and couples only, no noise after 22.30. Microwave available, table tennis, woodland walk, dog exercise field.

PITCHES: 🚐 Caravans 🚏 Motorhomes ▲ Tents 🏕 Glamping accommodation **SERVICES:** 🔌 Electric hook-up 🔲 Launderette 🍸 Licensed bar 🔋 Calor Gas ⚓ Campingaz Ⓣ Toilet fluid 🍴 Café/Restaurant 🍔 Fast Food/Takeaway 🔋 Battery charging ⚙ Motorhome service point * 2019 prices ⊗ No credit or debit cards 🐕 Dogs permitted ⊗ No dogs

MAWGAN PORTH *continued*

Trevarrian Holiday Park

▶▶▶ 86%

tel: 01637 860381 & 0845 225 5910 (*Calls cost 7p per minute plus your phone company's access charge*) **TR8 4AQ**
email: holiday@trevarrian.co.uk **web:** www.trevarrian.co.uk
dir: *From A39 at St Columb roundabout turn right onto A3059 towards Newquay. Fork right in approximately 2 miles for St Mawgan onto B3276. Turn right, site on left.*

A well-established and well-run holiday park overlooking Mawgan Porth beach. This park has a wide range of attractions including a free entertainment programme in peak season and a 10-pin bowling alley with licensed bar. It is only a short drive to Newquay and approximately 20 minutes to Padstow.

Open: All year **Last arrival:** 22.00 **Last departure:** 11.00

Pitches: ⊡ ⊡ ▲; 10 hardstanding pitches

Leisure: ⚜ ◖ ▢ ♫ ☺

Facilities: ⊙ ▱ ☀ ⟐ ⑤ WiFi

Services: ▣ ⊡ ☏ ◈ ⚐ ☷ ⬆ ▯ ⊘ ⓣ

Within 3 miles: ⌇ ⚲ ∪ ◎ ⛾ 目

Additional site information: 7 acre site. ☡ Cars can be parked by caravans and tents. Awnings permitted. No noise after midnight. Crazy golf.

MEVAGISSEY   Map 2 SX04

See also Gorran and Pentewan

Places to visit

The Lost Gardens of Heligan, PENTEWAN, PL26 6EN, 01726 845100
www.heligan.com

The Shipwreck and Heritage Centre, ST AUSTELL, PL25 3NX, 01726 69897
www.shipwreckcharlestown.com

Platinum Park

Seaview International Holiday Park

▶▶▶▶▶

tel: 01726 843425 & 01626 818350 **Boswinger PL26 6LL**
email: seaview@swholidayparks.co.uk **web:** www.seaviewinternational.com
dir: *From St Austell take B3273 signed Mevagissey. Turn right before entering village. Follow brown tourist signs to site. (Note: very narrow lanes to this site; it is advisable to follow these directions not sat nav).*

An attractive holiday park set in a beautiful environment overlooking Veryan Bay, with colourful landscaping, including attractive flowers and shrubs. It continues to offer an outstanding holiday experience, with its luxury family pitches, super toilet facilities, takeaway, shop and an alfresco eating area complete with a TV screen. The beach is just half a mile away. There is also an 'off the lead' dog walk, and a 'ring and ride' bus service to Truro, St Austell and Plymouth stops at the park gate. Static caravans are available for holiday hire.

Open: April to end September **Last arrival:** 22.00 **Last departure:** 10.00

Pitches: ⊡ ⊡ ▲; 27 hardstanding pitches; 31 seasonal pitches

Leisure: ⚜ ⚟ ⌂ ☺

Facilities: ▤ ⊙ ▱ ☀ ⟐ ⑤ ☷ ▯ 尺 ⬆ ▮ ⊘ ⓣ WiFi
Services: ▣ ⊡ ☏ ◈ ⬆ ▯ ▮ ⊘ ⓣ
Within 3 miles: ⌇ ⚲ ∪ ◎ ⛾ ⛾

Additional site information: 28 acre site. ☡ Restrictions on certain dog breeds. Cars can be parked by caravans and tents. Awnings permitted. Crazy golf, volleyball, badminton, scuba diving, boules, tennis, football pitch, dog walking area.

MULLION   Map 2 SW61

Places to visit

Great for kids: Cornish Seal Sanctuary, GWEEK, TR12 6UG, 01326 221361
www.visitsealife.com/gweek

Flambards, HELSTON, TR13 0QA, 01326 573404
www.flambards.co.uk

Franchis Holiday Park

▶▶▶ 80%

tel: 01326 240301 **Cury Cross Lanes TR12 7AZ**
email: enquiries@franchis.co.uk **web:** www.franchis.co.uk
dir: *Exit A3083 on left 0.5 mile past Wheel Inn, between Helston and The Lizard.*

A mainly grassy site surrounded by hedges and trees, located on Goonhilly Downs and in an ideal position for exploring the Lizard Peninsula. The site is divided into two paddocks for tourers, and the pitches are a mix of level ones and those that are slightly sloping. There are good facilities for families, and for a fun-filled family day out Flambards Theme Park is less than 20 minutes' drive away in Helston.

Open: 6 April to 30 September **Last arrival:** 20.00 **Last departure:** 10.30

Pitches: * ⊡ from £16; ⊡ from £16; ▲ from £12; 19 seasonal pitches

Facilities: ▤ ⊙ ☀ WiFi

Services: ▣ ⊡

Within 3 miles: ⌇ ⚲ ∪ ⛾ ⑤

Additional site information: 16 acre site. ☡ Cars can be parked by caravans and tents. Awnings permitted.

NEWQUAY

See also Rejerrah

Places to visit

Blue Reef Aquarium, NEWQUAY, TR7 1DU, 01637 878134
www.bluereefaquarium.co.uk

Trerice, TRERICE, TR8 4PG, 01637 875404
www.nationaltrust.org.uk/trerice

Great for kids: Dairy Land Farm World, NEWQUAY, TR8 5AA, 01872 510246
www.dairylandfarmworld.com

Newquay Zoo, NEWQUAY, TR7 2LZ, 01637 873342
www.newquayzoo.org.uk

LEISURE: ⚜ Indoor swimming pool ⚟ Outdoor swimming pool ⌂ Children's playground ⚐ Kids' club ☺ Tennis court ◖ Games room ▢ Separate TV room
⌇ golf course ⚲ Pitch n putt ⛾ Boats for hire ☷ Bikes for hire 目 Cinema ♫ Entertainment ⚲ Fishing ◎ Mini golf ⚟ Watersports ☜ Gym ☺ Sports field ∪ Stables
FACILITIES: ▤ Baths/Shower ⊙ Electric shaver sockets ▱ Hairdryer ☀ Ice Pack Facility ▯ Baby facilities ⟐ Disabled facilities ⑤ Shop on site or within 200yds
尺 BBQ area 尺 Picnic area WiFi WiFi

NEWQUAY
Map 2 SW86

Platinum Park

Hendra Holiday Park
▶▶▶▶▶ HOLIDAY CENTRE

tel: 01637 875778 **TR8 4NY**
email: enquiries@hendra-holidays.com **web:** www.hendra-holidays.com
dir: *A30 onto A392 signed Newquay. At Quintrell Downs over roundabout, signed Lane, site 0.5 mile on left.*

A large complex with holiday statics and superb facilities including an indoor fun pool and an outdoor pool. There is a children's club for the over 6s, evening entertainment during high season, a skateboard park, fish and chip shop and a fantastic coffee shop. The touring pitches, occupying 12 fields, are set amid mature trees and shrubs, and some have fully serviced facilities. All amenities are open to the public. This site generates most of its own electricity from a 1.5 megawatt solar farm. The Hendra Pod Village area has 10 smart wooden pods for hire. This park offers the complete holiday package for all, including children of all ages. As well as the beaches at Newquay, there are plenty of attractions in the area.

Open: 23 March to 5 November (restricted service: April to Spring bank holiday and September to October – outdoor pool closed) **Last arrival:** dusk **Last departure:** 10.00
Pitches: ⊡ from £14.45; ⊡ from £14.45; ⚊ from £14.45; ⚊ see prices below; 35 hardstanding pitches
Leisure: ≋ ⚐ ⚑ 🏊 ❀ ▢ ♫ ⛳ ⚽
Facilities: ▥ ⊙ ⌗ ✳ ♿ ⛁ ▤ ⟂ ⚒ WiFi

Services: ⚡ ⊡ ⟂ ⚑ 🍴 ⚒ ⚓ ⚒ ⚒ ⌀ T
Within 3 miles: ⌁ ⚲ ∪ ◎ ⚑ ⚑ ⚑ ⊟

Additional site information: 80 acre site. ⚑ Families and couples only. Land train rides, skate and scooter park, indoor play.

Glamping available: Wooden pods (unfurnished) from £40; premium pods (equipped) from £80. **Changeover days:** Any day

Additional glamping information: Wooden pods have heating, lighting, outside tables and chairs, outside storage chest and BBQ stand. Premium pods have in addition, 1 double bed and 2 single beds, fridge, kettle, crockery and cutlery, washing-up bowl. Minimum stay 3 nights. Cars can be parked by pods.

See advert on page 82

PITCHES: ⊡ Caravans ⊡ Motorhomes ⚊ Tents ⚊ Glamping accommodation **SERVICES:** ⚡ Electric hook-up ⊡ Launderette ⟂ Licensed bar ▤ Calor Gas ⌀ Campingaz T Toilet fluid 🍴 Café/Restaurant ⚒ Fast Food/Takeaway ⚓ Battery charging ⟂ Motorhome service point
* 2019 prices ⊘ No credit or debit cards ⚑ Dogs permitted ⊗ No dogs

NEWQUAY *continued*

Premier Park

Treloy Touring Park

▶▶▶▶▶ 91%

tel: 01637 872063 **TR8 4JN**
email: stay@treloy.co.uk **web:** www.treloy.co.uk
dir: *On A3059 (St Columb Major to Newquay road).*

An attractive site with fine countryside views, that is within easy reach of resorts and beaches. The pitches are set in four paddocks with mainly level but some slightly sloping grassy areas. Maintenance and cleanliness are very high. There is a heated swimming pool and separate paddling pool surrounded by a paved patio area with tables, an excellent reception, shop and first aid room. Three dedicated family shower rooms are available.

Treloy Touring Park

Open: 24 May to 10 September **Last arrival:** 20.00 **Last departure:** 10.00

Pitches: * 🚐 from £18; 🚌 from £18; ⛺ from £18; 30 hardstanding pitches; 15 seasonal pitches **Leisure:** 🌊 🛝 🎱 🎵 ⚽

Facilities: 🛁 🔌 💨 ❄ ♿ 🛒 🍖 🪑 👶 📶 **Services:** 🥡 🧼 🍷 🍽 🧺 🔋 🚰 👜 🌿 [T] **Within 3 miles:** ⛳ 🎣 🐎 ◎ 🏄 ⛵ 🎬

Additional site information: 23 acre site. 🐕 Cars can be parked by caravans and tents. Awnings permitted. No noise after 23.00. Concessionary green fees at Treloy Golf Club. Car hire can be arranged.

See advert opposite

LEISURE: 🏊 Indoor swimming pool 🌊 Outdoor swimming pool 🛝 Children's playground 👋 Kids' club 🎾 Tennis court 🎱 Games room 📺 Separate TV room ⛳ golf course 🏌 Pitch n putt ⛵ Boats for hire 🚲 Bikes for hire 🎬 Cinema 🎵 Entertainment 🎣 Fishing ◎ Mini golf 🏄 Watersports 🏋 Gym ⚽ Sports field 🐎 Stables
FACILITIES: 🛁 Baths/Shower 🔌 Electric shaver sockets 💨 Hairdryer ❄ Ice Pack Facility 👶 Baby facilities ♿ Disabled facilities 🛒 Shop on site or within 200yds 🍖 BBQ area 🪑 Picnic area 📶 WiFi

PITCHES: Caravans Motorhomes Tents Glamping accommodation SERVICES: Electric hook-up Launderette Licensed bar
Calor Gas Campingaz Toilet fluid Café/Restaurant Fast Food/Takeaway Battery charging Motorhome service point
* 2019 prices No credit or debit cards Dogs permitted No dogs

NEWQUAY *continued*

Premier Park

Monkey Tree Holiday Park
►►►►► 88%

tel: 01872 572032 **Hendra Croft, Scotland Road TR8 5QR**
email: enquiries@monkeytreeholidaypark.co.uk
web: www.monkeytreeholidaypark.co.uk
dir: *From M5 at Exeter take A30 to Redruth (ignore all signs for Newquay). At Carland Cross roundabout (with windmills to right) continue and follow signs for Perranporth. After 1 mile turn right at Boxheater junction onto the B3285 signposted Perranporth. After 0.5 mile turn right at crossroads into Scotland Road. After 1 mile, park on left.*

A large, well-managed holiday park situated on Cornwall's north coast close to Newquay and just minutes from Fistral Beach and Perranporth Beach – perfectly placed for surfing and great family days out. There's something for everyone here and the whole park is impressive, very neat and tidy, and the 700 pitches include standard, serviced, premium, super, super-deluxe and ultra-deluxe pitches, the latter having en suite facilities on the pitch. There are also five dedicated pitches for RVs and motorhomes over 24ft long, and 64 holiday homes for hire. Facilities include eight well-maintained toilet blocks, an outdoor heated pool, a fishing lake, and a clubhouse with nightly entertainment in season.

Open: from 24 March **Last arrival:** 18.00 **Last departure:** 10.00

Pitches: 🚐 🚗 ▲

Leisure: 🏊 ⚡ 🖐 🔍 ⭤ 🎵 ✎

Facilities: 🛁 ⊙ 🚻 🚹 🍴 🎪 ⬅ WiFi

Services: 🔌 🟦 🍴 🍽 🍺 📦 🖊 🔒 ⊘

Within 3 miles: ⚓ ∪

Additional site information: 52 acre site. 🐾 Cars can be parked by caravans and tents. Awnings permitted.

Trencreek Holiday Park
►►►► 90%

tel: 01637 874210 **Hillcrest, Higher Trencreek TR8 4NS**
email: trencreek@btconnect.com **web:** www.trencreekholidaypark.co.uk
dir: *A392 to Quintrell Downs, right towards Newquay, left at 2 mini roundabouts into Trevenson Road to site.*

An attractively landscaped park in the village of Trencreek, with modern toilet facilities of a very high standard. Two well-stocked fishing lakes, and evening entertainment in the licensed clubhouse, are extra attractions. Located about two miles from Newquay with its beaches and surfing opportunities.

Open: Spring Bank Holiday to mid September **Last arrival:** 22.00 **Last departure:** noon

Pitches: 🚐 from £12.30; 🚗 from £12.30; ▲ from £12.30; 8 hardstanding pitches

Leisure: 🏊 🔍 ⭤ ✎

Facilities: 🛁 ⊙ 🗝 ✳ 🚻 🍴 🎪 WiFi

Services: 🔌 🟦 🍴 🍽 🎪 ⬅ 🖊 🔒 ⊘ T

Within 3 miles: ⚓ ∪ ◎ 🎿 🍴 📅

Additional site information: 10 acre site. ⊗ Cars can be parked by caravans and tents. Awnings permitted. Families and couples only.

Porth Beach Holiday Park
►►►► 85%

tel: 01637 876531 **Porth TR7 3NH**
email: info@porthbeach.co.uk **web:** www.porthbeach.co.uk
dir: *From Newquay take A3058 towards St Columb Major. At roundabout left onto B3276 signed Padstow. Site on right.*

This attractive, popular park offers level, grassy pitches in neat and tidy surroundings. It is a well-run site set in meadowland in a glorious location adjacent to excellent sands of Porth Beach. The site offers two fully-equipped camping pods positioned on a raised terrace.

Open: March to November **Last arrival:** 18.00 **Last departure:** 10.00

Pitches: 🚐 🚗 ▲ 🏠; 19 hardstanding pitches

Facilities: 🛁 ⊙ 🚻 WiFi

Services: 🔌 🟦 🎪 🖊 🔒 ⊘

Within 3 miles: ⚓ ✎ ∪ ◎ 🎿 🍴 📅 🛒

Additional site information: 6 acre site. 🐾 Cars can be parked by caravans and tents. Awnings permitted. Families and couples only.

Glamping available: Wooden pods. **Changeover days:** Any day

Additional glamping information: Wooden pods: 2 sets of single bunk beds, electricity, lighting and heating. Cars can be parked by pods.

See advert on page 83

Trethiggey Holiday Park
▶▶▶▶ 85%

tel: 01637 877672 **Quintrell Downs TR8 4QR**
email: enquiries@trethiggey.co.uk **web:** www.trethiggey.co.uk
dir: A30 onto A392 signed Newquay at Quintrell Downs roundabout, left onto A3058, pass Newquay Pearl centre. Site 0.5 mile on left.

A family-owned park in a rural setting that is ideal for touring this part of Cornwall. It is pleasantly divided into paddocks with maturing trees and shrubs, and offers coarse fishing and tackle hire. This site has a car park for campers as the camping fields are set in a car-free zone for children's safety.

Open: March to December **Last arrival:** 21.00 **Last departure:** 10.30
Pitches: 🚐 🚍 ⚊; 35 hardstanding pitches; 12 seasonal pitches
Leisure: ⚒ 🎣 ✎
Facilities: 🏢 ☉ ℙ ✳ ⚓ ⑤ ▥ ☷ 🛒 WiFi
Services: 🔌 ⑤ 🍺 🍴 🍟 ⚡ ⚓ ⛟ ⚓ T
Within 3 miles: ↕ ∪ ◎ ☷ ✳ ⑤

Additional site information: 15 acre site. ➤ Cars can be parked by caravans and tents. Awnings permitted. No noise after midnight. Off licence, recreation field.

See advert on page 83

Trenance Holiday Park
▶▶▶▶ 82%

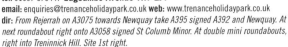

tel: 01637 873447 **Edgcumbe Avenue TR7 2JY**
email: enquiries@trenanceholidaypark.co.uk **web:** www.trenanceholidaypark.co.uk
dir: From Rejerrah on A3075 towards Newquay take A395 signed A392 and Newquay. At next roundabout right onto A3058 signed St Columb Minor. At double mini roundabouts, right into Treninnick Hill. Site 1st right.

A mainly static park popular with tenters, close to Newquay's vibrant nightlife, and with a café serving excellent breakfasts and takeaways. Set on high ground in an urban area of town, with cheerful owners and clean facilities; the site offers a motorhome service point. The local bus stops at the site entrance.

Open: mid April to mid September (restricted service: mid April to mid May – shop closed)
Last arrival: 22.00 **Last departure:** 10.00
Pitches: 🚐 🚍 ⚊ 🏕
Leisure: 🎣
Facilities: 🏢 ☉ ℙ ✳ ⚓ ⑤ WiFi
Services: 🔌 ⑤ 🍴 ⚡ ⛟ ⚓ ⚓ T
Within 3 miles: ↕ ✎ ∪ ◎ ☷ ✳ ⑤

Additional site information: 12 acre site. Cars can be parked by caravans and tents. Awnings permitted. No pets, no noise after midnight.

Glamping available: Wooden pods. **Changeover days:** Any day

Additional glamping information: Wooden pods: electricity supplied. No drainage or water. No en suite toilets. Cars can be parked by pods.

Trebellan Park
▶▶▶ 85%

tel: 01637 830522 **Cubert TR8 5PY**
email: enquiries@trebellan.co.uk **web:** www.trebellan.co.uk
dir: South of Newquay from A392 onto A3075 towards Rejerrah. In approximately 4 miles, turn right signed Cubert. Left in 0.75 mile onto unclassified road.

A terraced grassy rural park within a picturesque valley with views of Cubert Common, and adjacent to the Smuggler's Den, a 16th-century thatched inn. This park has a very inviting swimming pool and three well-stocked coarse fishing lakes.

Open: May to October **Last arrival:** 21.00 **Last departure:** 10.00
Pitches: 🚐 from £22; 🚍 from £22; ⚊ from £16
Leisure: ⚒ ▭ ✎
Facilities: 🏢 ☉ ℙ ✳ ⚓ ☷ WiFi
Services: 🔌 ⑤ ⚡
Within 3 miles: ↕ ∪ ◎ ☷ ⑤

Additional site information: 8 acre site. ➤ Cars can be parked by caravans and tents. Awnings permitted. Families and couples only.

PITCHES: 🚐 Caravans 🚍 Motorhomes ⚊ Tents 🏕 Glamping accommodation **SERVICES:** 🔌 Electric hook-up ⑤ Launderette 🍺 Licensed bar
⚓ Calor Gas ⚡ Campingaz T Toilet fluid 🍴 Café/Restaurant 🍟 Fast Food/Takeaway ⚓ Battery charging ⛟ Motorhome service point
* 2019 prices ⊗ No credit or debit cards ➤ Dogs permitted ⊗ No dogs

NEWQUAY *continued*

Riverside Holiday Park
►►► 82%

tel: 01637 873617 **Gwills Lane TR8 4PE**
email: info@riversideholidaypark.co.uk **web:** www.riversideholidaypark.co.uk
dir: *A30 onto A392 signed Newquay. At Quintrell Downs at roundabout follow Lane sign. 2nd left in 0.5 mile onto unclassified road signed Gwills. Site in 400 yards.*

A sheltered valley beside a river in a quiet location is the idyllic setting for this lightly wooded park that caters for families and couples only; the site is well placed for exploring Newquay and Padstow. There is a lovely swimming pool. The site is close to the wide variety of attractions offered by this major resort. Self-catering lodges, cabins and static vans are for hire.

Open: Easter to end October **Last arrival:** 22.00 **Last departure:** 10.00

Pitches: * ♫ from £15; ♫ from £15; ▲ from £15

Leisure: 🏊 ⚘ 🔍 ☐

Facilities: 🛁 ☺ ℱ ✳ ♿ ⓢ WiFi

Services: 🔌 ☐ ⬆ 🍴 ⬛ 🛒 🔒 ⬡ Ⓣ

Within 3 miles: ⛳ ℘ ∪ ◎ �’ ↯ 🎣

Additional site information: 11 acre site. 🐾 Cars can be parked by caravans and tents. Awnings permitted. Families and couples only.

PADSTOW

See also Rumford

Places to visit

Prideaux Place, PADSTOW, PL28 8RP, 01841 532411
www.prideauxplace.co.uk

The Shipwreck and Heritage Centre, ST AUSTELL, PL25 3NX, 01726 69897
www.shipwreckcharlestown.com

Great for kids: Eden Project, ST AUSTELL, PL24 2SG, 01726 811911
www.edenproject.com

Platinum Park

Padstow Touring Park
►►►►►

tel: 01841 532061 **PL28 8LE**
email: bookings@padstowtouringpark.co.uk **web:** www.padstowtouringpark.co.uk
dir: *1 mile south of Padstow, on east side of A389 (Padstow to Wadebridge road).*

Improvements continue at this top quality park set in open countryside above the quaint fishing town of Padstow, which can be approached via a footpath directly from the park. This site is divided into paddocks by maturing bushes and hedges that create a peaceful and relaxing holiday atmosphere. The main facility blocks have been designed and decorated to a very high standard, plus there is a good children's play area, a well-stocked shop and an excellent coffee lounge with a decked terrace offering country views.

Open: All year **Last arrival:** 21.00 **Last departure:** 11.00

Pitches: ♫ from £21; ♫ from £21; ▲ from £13.50; 77 hardstanding pitches

Leisure: ⚘

Facilities: 🛁 ☺ ℱ ✳ ♿ ⓢ 🅿 🛒 WiFi

Services: 🔌 ☐ ⬆ 🔒 ⬡ Ⓣ

Within 3 miles: ⛳ ℘ ∪ ◎ �’ ↯

Additional site information: 13.5 acre site. 🐾 Cars can be parked by caravans and tents. Awnings permitted. No groups, no noise after 22.00. Freshly baked bread, coffee lounge, camp kitchen, dog wash.

Premier Park

Padstow Holiday Park
►►►►► 85% HOLIDAY HOME PARK

tel: 01841 532289 **Cliffdowne PL28 8LB**
email: mail@padstowholidaypark.co.uk **web:** www.padstowholidaypark.co.uk
dir: *Exit A39 onto either A389 or B3274 to Padstow. Site signed 1.5 miles before Padstow.*

In an Area of Outstanding Natural Beauty and within a mile of the historic fishing village of Padstow (which can be reached via a footpath), this static-only park with 12 well-equipped units for hire has seen huge investment in recent years and provides comfortable relaxing accommodation in a quiet and peaceful atmosphere. A superb, new building housing the reception, coffee lounge and an impressive 20-metre swimming pool opened in 2018. This is a quiet base that is convenient for the many attractions Cornwall has to offer.

Open: early February to early January

Holiday Homes: Sleep 4 Bedrooms 2 Bathrooms 1 Toilets 2 Two-ring burner Microwave Freezer TV Sky/Freeview DVD player WiFi

Leisure: 🏊 ⚘

Within 3 miles: ℘ ∪

Additional site information: 🐾

LEISURE: 🏊 Indoor swimming pool ⚘ Outdoor swimming pool ⚘ Children's playground ✋ Kids' club ⚘ Tennis court 🔍 Games room ☐ Separate TV room ⛳ golf course ⚘ Pitch n putt ⚘ Boats for hire ⚘ Bikes for hire ⬛ Cinema ♫ Entertainment ℘ Fishing ◎ Mini golf ⚘ Watersports ⚘ Gym ⚘ Sports field ∪ Stables
FACILITIES: 🛁 Baths/Shower ☺ Electric shaver sockets ℱ Hairdryer ✳ Ice Pack Facility 🛒 Baby facilities ♿ Disabled facilities ⓢ Shop on site or within 200yds 🍴 BBQ area ⬛ Picnic area WiFi WiFi

PENTEWAN
Map 2 SX04

Places to visit

The Lost Gardens of Heligan, PENTEWAN, PL26 6EN, 01726 845100
www.heligan.com

The Shipwreck and Heritage Centre, ST AUSTELL, PL25 3NX, 01726 69897
www.shipwreckcharlestown.com

Great for kids: Eden Project, ST AUSTELL, PL24 2SG, 01726 811911
www.edenproject.com

Little Winnick Touring Park
▶▶▶▶ 85%

tel: 01726 843687 **PL26 6DL**
email: mail@littlewinnick.co.uk **web:** www.littlewinnick.co.uk
dir: A390 to St Austell, then B3273 towards Mevagissey, site in 3 miles on left.

A small, well maintained rural site within walking distance of Pentewan and its beautiful beach. It has neat level pitches, including some hardstanding pitches, an excellent children's play area, and an ultra-modern toilet block. It borders the River Winnick and also the Pentewan cycle trail from St Austell to Pentewan, and The Lost Gardens of Heligan and Mevagissey are nearby. There is a bus stop outside the park to Mevagissey and Gorran Haven or St Austell (Asda), Charlestown and Fowey.

Open: Easter to early October **Last arrival:** 20.00 **Last departure:** 11.00

Pitches: 🚐 from £10; 🚐 from £10; ▲ from £10; 38 hardstanding pitches; 10 seasonal pitches

Leisure: 🅰 ⚙ **Facilities:** 🚿 ☉ 🕭 ⚒ ♿ 🛅 🎄 🛒 WiFi
Services: 🔌 🛅 🔋 ⚙
Within 3 miles: 🐟 🔗 ⛵ ⛳ 🏕

Additional site information: 14 acre site. ✄ Cars can be parked by caravans and tents. Awnings permitted. No noise 22.00-07.00.

Heligan Caravan & Camping Park
▶▶▶▶ 84%

tel: 01726 842714 & 844414 **PL26 6BT**
email: info@heligancampsite.com **web:** www.heligancampsite.com
dir: From A390 take B3273 for Mevagissey at crossroads signed 'No caravans beyond this point'. Right onto unclassified road towards Gorran, site 0.75 mile on left.

A pleasant peaceful park adjacent to The Lost Gardens of Heligan, with views over St Austell Bay and well-maintained facilities, including a smart disabled/family

room. Guests can also use the extensive amenities at the sister park, Pentewan Sands, and there's a footpath with direct access to The Lost Gardens of Heligan.

Open: 16 January to 26 November (reception opening times: 09.00–11.00 and 17.00–18.00) **Last arrival:** 22.00 **Last departure:** 10.30

Pitches: 🚐 🚐 ▲; 24 hardstanding pitches; 12 seasonal pitches

Facilities: 🚿 ☉ 🕭 ⚒ ♿ 🛅 WiFi

Services: 🔌 🛅 🔋 ⚙ 🔋 🅰 ⚙

Within 3 miles: 🐟 🔗 ⛵ 🏕 🏌 🏕

Additional site information: 12 acre site. ✄ Cars can be parked by caravans and tents. Awnings permitted.

PERRANPORTH
Map 2 SW75

See also Rejerrah

Places to visit

Royal Cornwall Museum, TRURO, TR1 2SJ, 01872 272205
www.royalcornwallmuseum.org.uk

Trerice, TRERICE, TR8 4PG, 01637 875404
www.nationaltrust.org.uk/trerice

Great for kids: Blue Reef Aquarium, NEWQUAY, TR7 1DU, 01637 878134
www.bluereefaquarium.co.uk

Premier Park

Perran Sands Holiday Park
▶▶▶▶▶ 91% HOLIDAY CENTRE

tel: 01872 573551 **TR6 0AQ**
email: perransands@haven.com **web:** www.haven.com/perransands
dir: A30 onto B3285 towards Perranporth. Site on right before descent on hill into Perranporth.

Situated amid 500 acres of protected dune grassland, and with a footpath through to the surf and three miles of golden sandy beach, this lively park is set in a large village-style complex. It offers a complete range of on-site facilities and entertainment for all the family, which makes it an extremely popular park. There are two top-of-the-range facility blocks. Safari tents, super tents, geo domes and yurts are available for hire.

Open: mid March to end October (restricted service: mid March to May and September to end October – some facilities may be reduced) **Last arrival:** 22.00 **Last departure:** 10.00

Pitches: 🚐 🚐 ▲; 🏠 see prices below; 28 hardstanding pitches

Leisure: 🏊 🏊 🅰 🎣 🎵 🏹 ⚽ **Facilities:** 🚿 ☉ 🕭 ⚒ ♿ 🛅 🎄 WiFi
Services: 🔌 🛅 🍴 🍽 🍟 ⚙ 🅰 ⚙ **Within 3 miles:** 🐟 🔗 ⛵ ◎ 🏕
Additional site information: 550 acre site. ✄ Maximum 2 dogs per booking, certain dog breeds banned. No commercial vehicles, no bookings by persons under 21 years unless a family booking.

Glamping available: Safari tents from £129; super tents from £99; yurts from £198; geo domes from £239. **Changeover days:** Mondays, Fridays and Saturdays

Additional glamping information: All glamping units: minimum stay 3 nights. Safari tents and geo domes have own kitchen.

PERRANPORTH *continued*

Tollgate Farm Caravan & Camping Park
►►►► 85%

tel: 01872 572130 **Budnick Hill TR6 0AD**
email: enquiries@tollgatefarm.co.uk **web:** www.tollgatefarm.co.uk
dir: *Exit A30 onto B3285 to Perranporth. Site on right 1.5 miles after Goonhavern.*

A quiet site in a rural location with spectacular coastal views. Pitches are divided into four paddocks sheltered and screened by mature hedges, and there's a fully-equipped campers' kitchen. Children will enjoy the play equipment and pets' corner. The three miles of sand at Perran Bay are just a walk away through the sand dunes, or by car it is a three-quarter mile drive. There are now five fully-serviced premium pitches (three grass and two hardstanding) as well as five camping pods for hire. There are also wardens on site.

Open: Easter to September **Last arrival:** 20.00 **Last departure:** 10.30

Pitches: 🚐 🚍 ▲ ⛺; 10 hardstanding pitches; 12 seasonal pitches

Leisure: 🎢 ⚽

Facilities: 🛁 ☺ 🌡 ☀ 💧 🛒 ▥ 🏖 🚲 WiFi

Services: 🔌 🗑 🛒 ⛽ 🔒 🍴 🅣

Within 3 miles: 🎣 🏌 ⛳ ◎ 🚣 🚤 🎡

Additional site information: 10 acre site. 🐾 Cars can be parked by caravans and tents. Awnings permitted. No large groups. Car hire can be arranged.

Glamping available: Wooden pods

Additional glamping information: Wooden pods: minimum stay 2 nights (off-peak season), 3 nights (peak season). Sleep 4.

Higher Golla Touring & Caravan Park
►►► 87%

tel: 01872 573963 & 07800 558407 **Penhallow TR4 9LZ**
email: trevor.knibb@gmail.com **web:** www.caravanparkincornwall.com
dir: *A30 onto B3284 towards Perranporth (straight on at junction with A3075). Approximately 2 miles. Site signed on right.*

This peacefully located park is just two miles from Perranporth and its stunning beach, and extensive country views can be enjoyed from all pitches. It has high quality and immaculate toilet facilities, and every pitch has electricity and a water tap.

Open: 4 May to 21 September (restricted service: low season (excluding Spring bank holiday) – shop closed) **Last arrival:** 20.00 **Last departure:** 10.30

Pitches: * 🚐 from £16; 🚍 from £16; ▲ from £13; 2 hardstanding pitches; 4 seasonal pitches

Facilities: 🛁 ☺ 🌡 ☀ 💧 🏖 WiFi

Services: 🔌 🗑 ⛽ 🔒 🅣

Within 3 miles: 🎣 🏌 ◎ 🚣

Additional site information: 3 acre site. 🐾 Cars can be parked by caravans and tents. Awnings permitted. No kite flying, quiet between 21.00–08.00. Debit cards accepted (no credit cards). Large dog walk.

Perranporth Camping & Touring Park
►►► 77%

tel: 01872 572174 **Budnick Road TR6 0DB**
email: info@perranporth-camping.co.uk **web:** www.perranporth-camping.co.uk
dir: *At mini roundabout in Perranporth take B3285 towards Newquay. 0.5 mile to site.*

A pleasant site, great for families and just a five-minute, easy walk to Perranporth's beautiful beach and less than 10 minutes to the shops and restaurants in the town centre. There is a clubhouse/bar and heated swimming pool for the sole use of those staying on the site. There is also a takeaway food outlet and small shop. Nine static caravans are available for holiday hire.

Open: Easter to September (restricted service: end September – shop, swimming pool and club facilities closed) **Last arrival:** 23.00 **Last departure:** noon

Pitches: 🚐 🚍 ▲; 4 hardstanding pitches

Leisure: 🏊 🎢 🎱 📺

Facilities: 🛁 ☺ 🌡 ☀ 💧 🛒 ▥ 🏖 WiFi

Services: 🔌 🗑 🍴 🛒 🛒 🔒 🍴 🅣

Within 3 miles: 🎣 🏌 ◎ 🚣 🚤

Additional site information: 6 acre site. 🐾 Cars can be parked by caravans and tents. Awnings permitted. No noise after 23.00.

POLPERRO   Map 2 SX25

Places to visit

Restormel Castle, RESTORMEL, PL22 0EE, 01208 872687
www.english-heritage.org.uk/daysout/properties/restormel-castle

Great for kids: Wild Futures' Monkey Sanctuary, LOOE, PL13 1NZ, 01503 262532
www.monkeysanctuary.org

Great Kellow Farm Caravan & Camping Site
►► 82%

tel: 01503 272387 **Lansallos PL13 2QL**
email: enquiries@greatkellowfarm.co.uk **web:** www.greatkellowfarm.co.uk
dir: *From Looe take A387 towards Polperro, right on B3359 signed Pelynt. In Pelynt left at church follow Lansallos sign. Left at crossroads. 0.75 mile, at staggered crossroads left, follow site signs. (Note: access is via single track lanes. It is advisable to follow these directions not sat nav).*

Set on a high level grassy paddock with extensive views of Polperro Bay, this attractive site is on a working dairy and beef farm, and close to National Trust properties and gardens. It is situated in a very peaceful location close to the fishing village of Polperro.

Open: March to 3 January **Last arrival:** 22.00 **Last departure:** noon

Pitches: 🚐 from £12; 🚍 from £12; ▲ from £12; 20 seasonal pitches

Facilities:

Services: ⊞

Within 3 miles: ⚲ ⛵ ⑤

Additional site information: 3 acre site. 🐕 Cars can be parked by caravans and tents. Awnings permitted. No noise after 23.00.

POLRUAN
Map 2 SX15

Places to visit
Restormel Castle, RESTORMEL, PL22 0EE, 01208 872687
www.english-heritage.org.uk/daysout/properties/restormel-castle

Great for kids: Wild Futures' Monkey Sanctuary, LOOE, PL13 1NZ, 01503 262532
www.monkeysanctuary.org

Polruan Holidays-Camping & Caravanning
▶▶▶▶ 85%

tel: 01726 870263 **Polruan-by-Fowey PL23 1QH**
email: polholiday@aol.com **web:** www.polruanholidays.co.uk
dir: A38 to Dobwalls, left onto A390 to East Taphouse. Left onto B3359. Right in 4.5 miles signed Polruan.

A very rural and quiet site in a lovely elevated position above the village, with immaculate pitches and stunning views of the sea. The River Fowey passenger ferry is close by, and the site has a good shop, a spacious reception area, and barbecues are available to borrow. The bus for Polperro and Looe stops outside the gate, and the foot ferry to Fowey, which runs until 11pm, is only a 10-minute walk away.

Open: Easter to October **Last arrival:** 21.00 **Last departure:** 11.00

Pitches: 🚐 from £17; 🚐 from £17; ▲ from £17; 7 hardstanding pitches

Leisure: ⚑

Facilities: 📶 ⊙ ⚑ ✳ ⑤ 🍴 ⌇ 🛒 WiFi

Services: ⊞ ⑤ 🔋 🛢 ⌀ ⊤

Within 3 miles: ⚲ ⛳ ♨ ⇵ ⚓

Additional site information: 3 acre site. 🐕 Cars can be parked by caravans and tents. Awnings permitted. No skateboards, rollerskates, bikes, water pistols or water bombs. Car hire can be arranged.

POLZEATH
Map 2 SW97

Places to visit
Tintagel Castle, TINTAGEL, PL34 0HE, 01840 770328
www.english-heritage.org.uk/daysout/properties/tintagel-castle

---

Premier Park

Gunvenna Holiday Park
  92%

tel: 01208 862405 **St Minver PL27 6QN**
email: gunvenna.bookings@gmail.com **web:** www.gunvenna.com
dir: From A39 north of Wadebridge take B3314 (Port Isaac road), site 4 miles on right.

An attractive park with extensive rural views in a quiet country location, yet within three miles of Polzeath. This popular park is family owned and run, and provides good facilities in an ideal position for touring north Cornwall. The park has excellent hardstanding pitches, maturing landscaping and a beautiful indoor swimming pool with a glass roof. A mini wooden glamping cabin, a railway carriage, a holiday cottage and static caravans are for hire. The beach at Polzeath is very popular with surfers.

Open: Easter to October **Last arrival:** 20.30 **Last departure:** 11.00

Pitches: 🚐 from £20.50; 🚐 from £20.50; ▲ from £20.50; 🏠 see prices below; 33 hardstanding pitches; 18 seasonal pitches

Leisure: 🏊 ⚑ 🎣 **Facilities:** 📶 ⊙ ⚑ ✳ ♿ ⑤ 🍴 ⌇ WiFi

Services: ⊞ ⑤ 🔋 🛢 ⇵ 🛢 ⌀ ⊤ **Within 3 miles:** ⚲ ⚲ ♨ ⇵ ⚓ 🏇

Additional site information: 10 acre site. 🐕 Cars can be parked by caravans and tents. Awnings permitted. Children under 16 years must be accompanied by an adult in the pool, owners must clear up after their dogs.

Glamping available: Cabin, railway carriage from £55. **Changeover days:** Any day

Additional glamping information: Cars can be parked by cabin and carriage.

Tristram Caravan & Camping Park
▶▶▶ 90%

tel: 01208 862215 **PL27 6TP**
email: info@tristramcampsite.co.uk **web:** www.polzeathcamping.co.uk
dir: From B3314 onto unclassified road signed Polzeath. Through village, up hill, site 2nd right.

An ideal family site, positioned on a gently sloping cliff with grassy pitches and glorious sea views, which are best enjoyed from the terraced premier pitches, or over lunch or dinner at Café India adjacent to the reception overlooking the beach. There is direct, gated access to the beach, where surfing is very popular, and the park has a holiday bungalow for rent. The local amenities of the village are only a few hundred yards away.

Open: March to November (restricted service: mid September – reseeding the site) **Last arrival:** 21.00 **Last departure:** 10.00

Pitches: * 🚐 from £26; 🚐 from £26; ▲ from £13

Facilities: 📶 ⊙ ⚑ ✳ ♿ ⑤ WiFi

Services: ⊞ ⑤ 🍴 🔋 🛢 🛢 ⌀ ⊤

Within 3 miles: ⇵ ⚲ ⚲ ◎ ♨ ⇵ 🏇

Additional site information: 10 acre site. 🐕 Cars can be parked by caravans and tents. Awnings permitted. No ball games, no disposable BBQs, no noise between 23.00-07.00. Surf equipment hire.

See advert on page 90

POLZEATH *continued*

Southwinds Caravan & Camping Park
▶▶▶ 89%

tel: 01208 863267 & 862215 **Polzeath Road PL27 6QU**
email: info@southwindscamping.co.uk **web:** www.polzeathcamping.co.uk
dir: *Exit B3314 onto unclassified road signed Polzeath, site on right just past turn to New Polzeath.*

A peaceful site with beautiful sea and panoramic rural views, within walking distance of a golf complex, and just three quarters of a mile from beach and village. There are three spacious fields that offer plenty of room for cars to be parked by tents or caravans. There's an impressive reception building, replete with tourist information, TV, settees and a range of camping spares. Dogs are welcome.

Open: May to mid September **Last arrival:** 21.00 **Last departure:** 10.30

Pitches: * 🚐 from £20; 🚍 from £20; ⛺ from £10 **Facilities:** 🛁 ⊙ 🏳 ✳ 👥 📶

Services: 🔌 🗑 🍽 🛒 ⚰ 🛢 🥖 Ⓣ **Within 3 miles:** ⅃ 🎣 ∪ 🛶 🛥 ⛵ 🎏 🗒 💲

Additional site information: 16 acre site. 🐾 Cars can be parked by caravans and tents. Awnings permitted. Families and couples only, no disposable BBQs, no noise 23.00–07.00. Restaurant and farm shop adjacent, Stepper Field open mid July to August.

See advert below

Premier Park

Porthtowan Tourist Park
▶▶▶▶▶ 92%

tel: 01209 890256 **Mile Hill TR4 8TY**
email: admin@porthtowantouristpark.co.uk **web:** www.porthtowantouristpark.co.uk
dir: *From A30 at Redruth follow Portreath, B3300 and brown camping signs. On B3300 in approximately 2 miles turn right at T-junction, follow site sign. Site on left at top of hill.*

A neat, level grassy site on high ground above Porthtowan, with plenty of shelter from mature trees and shrubs. The superb toilet facilities considerably enhance the appeal of this peaceful rural park, which is almost midway between the small seaside resorts of Portreath and Porthtowan, with their beaches and surfing. The site has a well-stocked shop and there is a purpose-built games and meeting room with a good library where tourist information leaflets are

---

LEISURE: 🏊 Indoor swimming pool 🏊 Outdoor swimming pool 🛝 Children's playground ✋ Kids' club 🎾 Tennis court 🎱 Games room ▭ Separate TV room ⅃ golf course ⛳ Pitch n putt 🚣 Boats for hire 🚲 Bikes for hire 🎬 Cinema 🎵 Entertainment 🎣 Fishing ◎ Mini golf 🏄 Watersports 🏋 Gym 🏉 Sports field ∪ Stables
FACILITIES: 🛁 Baths/Shower ⊙ Electric shaver sockets 🪮 Hairdryer ✳ Ice Pack Facility 🍼 Baby facilities 👥 Disabled facilities 💲 Shop on site or within 200yds 🍖 BBQ area 🌲 Picnic area 📶 WiFi

available. A tearoom adjacent to the campsite serves takeaway meals during the peak season (limited opening hours at other times of the year).

Porthtowan Tourist Park

Open: April to end October **Last arrival:** 20.00 **Last departure:** 11.00

Pitches: * ⊞ from £20; ⊞ from £20; ⋀ from £20; 14 hardstanding pitches; 8 seasonal pitches

Leisure: ⋀ ⚈ ⚽

Facilities: 🖼 ☉ ⌾ ⚒ ⚳ ⑤ 🚻 WiFi

Services: 🔌 ⑥ ⛟ ⚒ 🔋 ⌀ Ⓣ

Within 3 miles: ⌔ ⚲ ∪ ⛴ ⊟

Additional site information: 5 acre site. 🐕 Cars can be parked by caravans and tents. Awnings permitted. No bikes or skateboards in July and August. Table tennis.

See advert below

Wheal Rose Caravan & Camping Park
▶▶▶▶ **77%**

tel: 01209 891496 **Wheal Rose TR16 5DD**
email: whealrose@aol.com **web:** www.whealrosecaravanpark.co.uk
dir: *Exit A30 at Scorrier sign, follow signs to Wheal Rose, onto A3047 then into Westway, site 0.5 mile on left.*

A quiet, peaceful park in a secluded valley setting, which is well placed for visiting both the lovely countryside and the surfing beaches of Porthtowan (two miles away). The friendly owner works hard to keep this park in immaculate condition, including the bright toilet block and well-trimmed pitches. There is a swimming pool and a games room.

Open: March to December **Last arrival:** 21.00 **Last departure:** 11.00

Pitches: ⊞ ⊞ ⋀; 6 hardstanding pitches

Leisure: ⚈ ⚈ ⚽

Facilities: ☉ ⌾ ⚒ ⚳ ⑤ 🚻 🚻 WiFi

Services: 🔌 ⑥ ⛟ 🔋 ⌀ Ⓣ

Within 3 miles: ⌔ ⚲ ∪ ⛴ ⊟

Additional site information: 6 acre site. 🐕 Cars can be parked by caravans and tents. Awnings permitted. 5mph speed limit, minimum noise after 23.00, gates locked 23.00.

PITCHES: ⊞ Caravans ⊞ Motorhomes ⋀ Tents 🏕 Glamping accommodation **SERVICES:** 🔌 Electric hook-up ⑥ Launderette 🍺 Licensed bar
🔋 Calor Gas ⌀ Campingaz Ⓣ Toilet fluid 🍽 Café/Restaurant 🏭 Fast Food/Takeaway ⛟ Battery charging ⚒ Motorhome service point
* 2019 prices ⊘ No credit or debit cards 🐕 Dogs permitted ⊗ No dogs

PORTREATH
Map 2 SW64

Places to visit
East Pool Mine, POOL, TR15 3NP, 01209 315027
www.nationaltrust.org.uk/east-pool-mine

Tehidy Holiday Park

►►►► 90%

tel: 01209 216489 **Harris Mill, Illogan TR16 4JQ**
email: holiday@tehidy.co.uk **web:** www.tehidy.co.uk
dir: *Exit A30 at Redruth/Portreath junction onto A3047 to 1st roundabout. Left onto B3300. At junction straight over signed Tehidy Holiday Park. Past Cornish Arms pub, site 800 yards at bottom of hill on left.*

An attractive wooded location in a quiet rural area only two and a half miles from popular beaches. The site has mostly level pitches on tiered ground, and the toilet facilities are bright and modern. Holiday static caravans and wooden wigwams are available for hire.

Open: All year (restricted service: November to March – shop and part of shower block closed) **Last arrival:** 20.00 **Last departure:** 10.00

Pitches: * 🚐 from £14; 🚐 from £14; ▲ from £14; 🏠 see prices below; 11 hardstanding pitches; 4 seasonal pitches

Leisure: 🅰 🎣 ▭ ⚽ **Facilities:** 🛁 ☉ 🧴 ✳ ♿ 🅂 🧺 🎍 🚽 WiFi

Services: 🔌 🔋 🛢 ⌀ ⊤ **Within 3 miles:** 🛶 🖊 ∪ ◎ 🏊 ⛷ 🎪

Additional site information: 4.5 acre site. ⊗ Cars can be parked by caravans and tents. Awnings permitted. No pets, no noise after 23.00. Pre-booking required for large motorhomes and caravans. Off licence, cooking shelter, trampoline.

Glamping available: Wooden wigwams from £50. **Changeover days:** Any day

Additional glamping information: Wooden wigwams (sleep maximum of 5) offer cooking shelter, heating, fridge/freezer, microwave, kettle, TV, BBQ and picnic bench. Cars can be parked by wigwams.

PORTSCATHO
Map 2 SW83

Places to visit
St Mawes Castle, ST MAWES, TR2 5DE, 01326 270526
www.english-heritage.org.uk/daysout/properties/st-mawes-castle

Trelissick, TRELISSICK, TR3 6QL, 01872 862090
www.nationaltrust.org.uk/trelissick

Trewince Farm Touring Park

►►► 83%

tel: 01872 580430 **TR2 5ET**
email: info@trewincefarm.co.uk **web:** www.trewincefarm.co.uk
dir: *From St Austell take A390 towards Truro. Left on B3287 to Tregony, follow signs to St Mawes. At Trewithian, turn left to St Anthony. Site 0.75 mile past church.*

A site on a working farm with sea views from its elevated position. There are many quiet golden sandy beaches close by, and boat launching facilities and mooring can be arranged at the nearby Percuil River Boatyard. The village of Portscatho with shops, pubs and attractive harbour is approximately one mile away.

Open: April to September **Last arrival:** 23.00 **Last departure:** 11.00

Pitches: 🚐 from £14; 🚐 from £14; ▲ from £14; 🏠 see prices below

Facilities: 🛁 ☉ 🧴 ✳ 🎍

Services: 🔌 🔋 🛢

Within 3 miles: 🖊 🏊 ⛷ 🅂

Additional site information: 3 acre site. 🐕 🚭 Cars can be parked by caravans and tents. Awnings permitted.

Glamping available: Wooden pods from £45.

Additional glamping information: Cars can be parked by pods.

LEISURE: 🏊 Indoor swimming pool 🏊 Outdoor swimming pool 🅰 Children's playground 👋 Kids' club 🎾 Tennis court 🎱 Games room ▭ Separate TV room 🏌 golf course 🏌 Pitch n putt 🚤 Boats for hire 🚲 Bikes for hire 🎬 Cinema 🎵 Entertainment 🎣 Fishing ◎ Mini golf 🏄 Watersports 💪 Gym 🏟 Sports field ∪ Stables
FACILITIES: 🛁 Baths/Shower ☉ Electric shaver sockets 🧴 Hairdryer ✳ Ice Pack Facility 👶 Baby facilities ♿ Disabled facilities 🅂 Shop on site or within 200yds 🎍 BBQ area 🎍 Picnic area WiFi WiFi

REDRUTH
Map 2 SW64

Places to visit

East Pool Mine, POOL, TR15 3NP, 01209 315027
www.nationaltrust.org.uk/east-pool-mine

Pendennis Castle, FALMOUTH, TR11 4LP, 01326 316594
www.english-heritage.org.uk/daysout/properties/pendennis-castle

Great for kids: National Maritime Museum Cornwall, FALMOUTH, TR11 3QY, 01326 313388, www.nmmc.co.uk

Platinum Park

Globe Vale Holiday Park

▶▶▶▶▶

tel: 01209 891183 **Radnor TR16 4BH**
email: info@globevale.co.uk **web:** www.globevale.co.uk
dir: From A30 at roundabout (northeast of Redruth) follow Portreath and B3300 signs. At next crossroads right into Radnor Road, follow brown site signs. In 0.5 mile turn left at site sign. Site 0.5 mile on left.

A family owned and run park set in a quiet rural location yet close to some stunning beaches and coastline. The park's touring area has a number of full facility hardstanding pitches, a high quality toilet block, a comfortable lounge bar serving bar meals, and holiday static caravans.

Open: All year **Last arrival:** 20.00 **Last departure:** 10.00

Pitches: * 🚐 from £20; 🚍 from £20; ⛺ from £20; 57 hardstanding pitches; 10 seasonal pitches

Leisure: 🎢 🎱 ⚽ **Facilities:** 🏠 ☀ ♿ 🖲 WiFi

Services: 🔌 🗑 🍴 🍽 🍺 🔋 ⬇ 🔒 🌿 **Within 3 miles:** 🚶 🏄 🚲

Additional site information: 18 acre site. 🐕 Cars can be parked by caravans and tents. Awnings permitted. Shower block heated in winter.

See advert opposite

Lanyon Holiday Park

▶▶▶▶ 90%

tel: 01209 313474 **Loscombe Lane, Four Lanes TR16 6LP**
email: info@lanyonholidaypark.co.uk **web:** www.lanyonholidaypark.co.uk
dir: Exit A30 signed Camborne and Pool onto A3047. Straight on at next two lights. Pass Tesco Extra on left. Right signed Four Lanes, over rail bridge. In Four Lanes right at staggered crossroads onto B2397, 2nd right at Pencoys Hall into Loscombe Lane. Site on left in approximately 400 metres.

A small, friendly rural park in an elevated position with fine views to distant St Ives Bay. This family owned and run park continues to be upgraded in all areas; there is a smart toilet block and two family rooms. The park has a very inviting swimming pool and a well-stocked bar and restaurant (open on Fridays and Saturdays from late May until 1st September and each evening during summer school holiday times). Stithians Reservoir for fishing, sailing and windsurfing is two miles away, and the site is close to a cycling trail. Two holiday cottages are available for hire.

Open: March to October (restricted service: March to Spring bank holiday and 1st weekend in September to October – bar and restaurant closed. March and October – pool closed) **Last arrival:** 21.00 **Last departure:** 11.00

Pitches: 🚐 from £21; 🚍 from £21; ⛺ from £17; 5 seasonal pitches

Leisure: 🏊 🎢 🎱 ⛳ 🎵 **Facilities:** 🏠 ☺ 🖲 ☀ 🔥 WiFi

Services: 🔌 🗑 🍴 🍽 🍺 🔋 **Within 3 miles:** 🚶 🎣 ⛳ ◎ 🏄 🚲 🎯

Additional site information: 14 acre site. 🐕 Cars can be parked by caravans and tents. Awnings permitted. Families only, no commercial vehicles. Breakfast catering van during peak season school holidays.

St Day Tourist Park

▶▶▶▶ 81%

tel: 01209 820459 **Church Hill, St Day TR16 5LE**
email: holidays@stday.co.uk
dir: On A30 from Bodmin towards Redruth. 2 miles after Chiverton roundabout, left onto A3047 to Scorrier. Site signed. 2 miles, left at Crossroads Motel onto B3298. Follow campsite signs, site on right.

This rurally located park, run by keen, friendly owners, is situated in a quiet area between Falmouth and Newquay and within close walking distance of the attractive village of St Day. It provides a very good touring area with modern, centrally positioned toilet facilities. The touring pitches are divided by hedging plants to create some privacy. There is a separate small field for tents.

Open: Easter to October **Last arrival:** phone site if arriving after 18.00 **Last departure:** 10.30

Pitches: 🚐 🚍 ⛺ **Facilities:** 🏠 🖲 ☀ ♿ 🖲 🔥 WiFi

Services: 🔌 🗑 🔋 **Within 3 miles:** ⛳ 🎯

Additional site information: 6 acre site. 🐕 Cars can be parked by caravans and tents. Awnings permitted.

PITCHES: 🚐 Caravans 🚍 Motorhomes ⛺ Tents 🏕 Glamping accommodation **SERVICES:** 🔌 Electric hook-up 🗑 Launderette 🍴 Licensed bar 🍺 Calor Gas 🌿 Campingaz Ⓣ Toilet fluid 🍽 Café/Restaurant 🍔 Fast Food/Takeaway 🔋 Battery charging ⬆ Motorhome service point * 2019 prices ⊗ No credit or debit cards 🐕 Dogs permitted ⊗ No dogs

REDRUTH *continued*

Cambrose Touring Park
▶▶▶ 80%

tel: 01209 890747 **Portreath Road TR16 4HT**
email: cambrosetouringpark@gmail.com **web:** www.cambrosetouringpark.co.uk
dir: *A30 onto B3300 towards Portreath. Approximately 0.75 mile at 1st roundabout right onto B3300. Take unclassified road on right signed Porthtowan. Site 200 yards on left.*

Situated in a rural setting surrounded by trees and shrubs, this park is divided into grassy paddocks. It is about two miles from the harbour village of Portreath. The site has an excellent swimming pool with a sunbathing area.

Open: April to October **Last arrival:** 22.00 **Last departure:** 11.30

Pitches: ➡ from £12.50; ⬛ from £12.50; ▲ from £12.50; 6 seasonal pitches

Leisure: ⬥ ⋀ ⬧ ⚽

Facilities: ⬠ ☺ ⌗ ✳ ⬥ ⑤ WiFi

Services: ⬥ ⬤ ⬛ ⬛ ⬛ ⬛ ⟙

Within 3 miles: ⬦ ⬦ ∪ ◎ ⊟

Additional site information: 6 acre site. 🐾 Cars can be parked by caravans and tents. Awnings permitted. No noise after 23.30. Mini football pitch.

Stithians Lake Country Park
▶▶▶ 75%

tel: 01209 860301 **Stithians Lake, Menherion TR16 6NW**
email: stithianswatersports@swlakestrust.org.uk **web:** www.southwestlakes.co.uk
dir: *From Redruth take B3297 towards Helston. Follow brown tourist signs to Stithians Lake, entrance by Golden Lion Inn.*

This basic campsite is a two-acre field situated adjacent to the Watersports Centre, which forms part of a large activity complex beside Stithians Lake. The toilet and shower facilities at the centre were refurbished for the 2018 season and include a new family room; there is an excellent waterside café that also serves breakfasts. This is the perfect campsite for watersport enthusiasts.

Open: 3 April to 31 October **Last arrival:** any time **Last departure:** 11.00

Pitches: ➡ ⬛ ▲

Leisure: ⋀ ⬧

Facilities: ✳ ⬥ ⊟ WiFi

Services: ⬥ ⬤ ⬤

Within 3 miles: ∪ ⬦ ⬦ ⊟ ⑤

Additional site information: 2.1 acre site. 🐾 Cars can be parked by caravans and tents. Awnings permitted. No noise after midnight, no swimming in lake, charges apply for the use of equipment on lake.

REJERRAH

Places to visit

Trerice, TRERICE, TR8 4PG, 01637 875404
www.nationaltrust.org.uk/trerice

Blue Reef Aquarium, NEWQUAY, TR7 1DU, 01637 878134
www.bluereefaquarium.co.uk

Great for kids: Newquay Zoo, NEWQUAY, TR7 2LZ, 01637 873342
www.newquayzoo.org.uk

REJERRAH
Map 2 SW75

Premier Park

Newperran Holiday Park
▶▶▶▶▶ 91%

tel: 01872 572407 & 07967 558252 **TR8 5QJ**
email: holidays@newperran.co.uk **web:** www.newperran.co.uk
dir: *4 miles southeast of Newquay and 1 mile south of Rejerrah on A3075. Or A30 (Redruth), exit B3275 (Perranporth), at 1st T-junction right onto A3075 towards Newquay, site 300 metres on left.*

A family site in a lovely rural position near several beaches and bays. This airy park offers screening on some pitches, which are set in paddocks on level ground. High season entertainment is available in the park's top quality country inn, and the café has an extensive menu. There is also a swimming pool with a separate toddlers' paddling area and a skateboard park.

Open: Easter to October **Last arrival:** 21.00 **Last departure:** 10.00

Pitches: ➡ ⬛ ▲; 34 hardstanding pitches; 15 seasonal pitches

Leisure: ⬥ ⋀ ⬧ ♫ ⚽ **Facilities:** ⬠ ☺ ⌗ ✳ ⬥ ⑤ ⬛ WiFi

Services: ⬥ ⬤ ⬛ ⬛ ⬛ ⬛ ⬥ ⬛ ⬛ ⟙

Within 3 miles: ⬦ ⬦ ∪ ◎ ⬧ ⬧ ⊟

Additional site information: 25 acre site. 🐾 Cars can be parked by caravans and tents. Awnings permitted. Families and couples only. Car hire can be arranged.

ROSE
Map 2 SW75

Places to visit

Trerice, TRERICE, TR8 4PG, 01637 875404
www.nationaltrust.org.uk/trerice

Newquay Zoo, NEWQUAY, TR7 2LZ, 01637 873342
www.newquayzoo.org.uk

Higher Hendra Park
▶▶▶ 80%

tel: 01872 571496 & 07932 572580 **Higher Hendra, Treamble TR4 9PS**
email: cowe43@btinternet.com **web:** www.higherhendraholidays.com
dir: *From A30 between Carland Cross and Zelah Hill take B3285 signed Goonhavern and Perranporth. 0.5 mile turn right into Scotland Road signed Rejerrah. At T-junction right on A3075 signed Newquay. In 300 yards left signed Rejerrah. In approximately 0.75 mile site on right.*

Situated down quiet lanes close to Perranporth, this small adults-only touring park comprises just 10 very spacious pitches (8 hardstandings; 2 grass) set in a neat and well-landscaped semi-circle, all with electricity and stunning views across rolling fields to St Agnes Beacon. Good quality toilet and shower facilities are housed in a smart cabin. This is a very peaceful base – perfect for walking and visiting the nearby beaches.

Open: All year **Last departure:** 10.00

Pitches: ➡ from £20; ⬛ from £20; 8 hardstanding pitches

Facilities: ⬠ ⬥ **Services:** ⬥ ⬤ **Within 3 miles:** ⬦ ⬦ ∪ ⑤

Additional site information: 2 acre site. Adults only. 🐾 ⬤ Cars can be parked by caravans. Awnings permitted.

LEISURE: ⬥ Indoor swimming pool ⬥ Outdoor swimming pool ⋀ Children's playground ⬥ Kids' club ⬥ Tennis court ⬥ Games room ⬜ Separate TV room
⬦ golf course ⬥ Pitch n putt ⬥ Boats for hire ⬥ Bikes for hire ⊟ Cinema ♫ Entertainment ⬧ Fishing ◎ Mini golf ⬥ Watersports ⬥ Gym ⬥ Sports field ∪ Stables
FACILITIES: ⬠ Baths/Shower ☺ Electric shaver sockets ⬥ Hairdryer ✳ Ice Pack Facility ⬛ Baby facilities ⬥ Disabled facilities ⑤ Shop on site or within 200yds
⬛ BBQ area ⬥ Picnic area WiFi WiFi

ROSUDGEON
Map 2 SW52

Places to visit

Trengwainton Garden, PENZANCE, TR20 8RZ, 01736 363148
www.nationaltrust.org.uk/trengwainton

Great for kids: Flambards, HELSTON, TR13 0QA, 01326 573404
www.flambards.co.uk

Kenneggy Cove Holiday Park
▶▶▶▶ 92%

tel: 01736 763453 **Higher Kenneggy TR20 9AU**
email: enquiries@kenneggycove.co.uk **web:** www.kenneggycove.co.uk
dir: *On A394 between Penzance and Helston, turn into unclassified lane opposite sign for site.*

Set in an Area of Outstanding Natural Beauty with spectacular sea views, this family-owned park is quiet and well kept. There is a well-equipped children's play area, superb toilets, and, in addition to a variety of meals available in the excellent site café, takeaway pizzas are baked on site. A short walk along a country footpath leads to the Cornish Coastal Path, and onto the golden sandy beach at Kenneggy Cove. It's a half mile walk to the main road to pick up the local bus which goes to Penzance or Helston, with many pretty Cornish coves en route. There is also a fish and chip shop and Chinese restaurant with takeaway a short drive away.

Open: mid May to September **Last arrival:** 21.00 **Last departure:** 11.00
Pitches: 🚐 🚌 🅰
Leisure: 🎱 ⚽
Facilities: 🚿 🛁 ⊙ 🌄 ☀ 🛒 🍴 📶
Services: 🔌 🔄 ♨ 🧳 🔋 🔒 🗑
Within 3 miles: ⚓ 🎣 ∪ 🚶 🛒

Additional site information: 4 acre site. 🐕 🐕 Cars can be parked by caravans and tents. Awnings permitted. No large groups, no noise after 22.00. Fresh bakery items, breakfasts, home-made evening meals.

RUMFORD
Map 2 SW87

Places to visit

Prideaux Place, PADSTOW, PL28 8RP, 01841 532411
www.prideauxplace.co.uk

Great for kids: Crealy Adventure Park & Resort, CLYST ST MARY, EX5 1DR, 01395 233200, www.crealy.co.uk

Music Water Touring Park
▶▶▶ 81%

tel: 01841 540257 **PL27 7SJ**
email: info@musicwatertouringpark.co.uk **web:** www.musicwatertouringpark.co.uk
dir: *From A39 at Winnards Perch roundabout take B3274 signed Padstow. Left in 2 miles onto unclassified road signed Rumford and St Eval. Site 500 metres on right.*

Set in a peaceful location yet only a short drive to the pretty fishing town of Padstow, and many sandy beaches and coves. This family owned and run park has grassy paddocks, and there is a quiet lounge bar and a separate children's games room.

Open: April to October **Last arrival:** 23.00 **Last departure:** 10.30
Pitches: 🚐 from £13; 🚌 from £13; 🅰 from £13
Leisure: 🎱 🎮 🔍
Facilities: ⊙ 🌄 ☀ 🍴 🪑
Services: 🔌 🔄 ♨ 🧳 🔋 🔒 🗑
Within 3 miles: 🎣 🏇 ∪ 🚶 🛒 📅 🛒

Additional site information: 8 acre site. 🐕 Maximum 2 dogs per pitch (no Pit Bull Terriers). 🚗 Cars can be parked by caravans and tents. Awnings permitted. One tent per pitch. Pets' corner (ponies, chickens).

PITCHES: 🚐 Caravans 🚌 Motorhomes 🅰 Tents 🏠 Glamping accommodation **SERVICES:** 🔌 Electric hook-up 🔄 Launderette 🍸 Licensed bar
🔋 Calor Gas 🔥 Campingaz 🚽 Toilet fluid 🍽 Café/Restaurant 🍔 Fast Food/Takeaway 🔋 Battery charging ⛽ Motorhome service point
* 2019 prices 🚫 No credit or debit cards 🐕 Dogs permitted 🚫 No dogs

RUTHERNBRIDGE Map 2 SX06

Places to visit

Prideaux Place, PADSTOW, PL28 8RP, 01841 532411
www.prideauxplace.co.uk

Cornwall's Regimental Museum, BODMIN, PL31 1EG, 01208 72810
www.cornwalls-regimentalmuseum.org

Great for kids: Pencarrow, BODMIN, PL30 3AG, 01208 841369
www.pencarrow.co.uk

Crealy Adventure Park & Resort, CLYST ST MARY, EX5 1DR, 01395 233200
www.crealy.co.uk

Ruthern Valley Holidays 🛖

►►► 83%

tel: 01208 831395 **PL30 5LU**
email: camping@ruthernvalley.com **web:** www.ruthernvalley.com
dir: *A389 through Bodmin, follow St Austell signs, then Lanivet signs. At top of hill right onto unclassified road signed Ruthernbridge. Follow site signs.*

An attractive woodland site peacefully located in a small river valley west of Bodmin Moor. This away-from-it-all park is ideal for those wanting a quiet holiday, and the informal pitches are spread in four natural areas, with plenty of sheltered space. There are also 12 lodges, heated wooden wigwams, wooden pods, 'mega' pods and static holiday vans for hire.

Open: All year **Last arrival:** 20.30 **Last departure:** noon

Pitches: 🚐 🚌 ⛺ 🛖; 2 hardstanding pitches

Leisure: 🚲

Facilities: ⊙ ✲ [S] 🍖 ⊼ [WiFi]

Services: 🔌 🧺 🧊 🍽 🔒 🍃 [T]

Within 3 miles: ⛳ 🎣 ∪

Additional site information: 7.5 acre site. 🚫🐕 Cars can be parked by caravans and tents. Awnings permitted. No noise 22.30–07.00, no fires. Farm animals, freshly baked bread and croissants.

Glamping available: 4 wooden wigwams; 3 wooden pods; mega pods.

Additional glamping information: Cars can be parked by pods and wigwams.

ST AGNES Map 2 SW75

Places to visit

Royal Cornwall Museum, TRURO, TR1 2SJ, 01872 272205
www.royalcornwallmuseum.org.uk

Trerice, TRERICE, TR8 4PG, 01637 875404
www.nationaltrust.org.uk/trerice

Premier Park

Beacon Cottage Farm Touring Park

►►►►► 84%

tel: 01872 552347 & 07879 413862 **Beacon Drive TR5 0NU**
email: jane@beaconcottagefarmholidays.co.uk
web: www.beaconcottagefarmholidays.co.uk
dir: *From A30 at Threeburrows roundabout take B3277 to St Agnes, left into Goonvrea Road, right into Beacon Drive, follow brown sign to site.*

A neat and compact site on a working farm, utilising a cottage and outhouses, an old orchard and adjoining walled paddock. The location on a headland looking northeast along the coast has stunning views towards St Ives, and the keen friendly family owners keep all areas of their site very well maintained.

Open: April to October **Last arrival:** 20.00 **Last departure:** noon

Pitches: 🚐 from £19; 🚌 from £19; ⛺ from £19; 5 hardstanding pitches; 6 seasonal pitches

Leisure: 🛝 ⚽

Facilities: 🛁 ⊙ 💨 ✲ ⊼ [WiFi]

Services: 🔌 🧺 🍽 ⚓ 🔒 🍃

Within 3 miles: ⛳ 🎣 ∪ ◎ 🌊 ⛵ [S]

Additional site information: 5 acre site. 🐕 Cars can be parked by caravans and tents. Awnings permitted. No large groups, no noise after 22.00. Secure year-round caravan storage, dog exercise field.

Presingoll Farm Caravan & Camping Park
►►►► 85%

tel: 01872 552333 **TR5 0PB**
email: pam@presingollfarm.co.uk **web:** www.presingollfarm.co.uk
dir: From A30 at Chiverton roundabout take B3277 towards St Agnes. Site 3 miles on right.

An attractive rural park adjoining farmland, with extensive views of the coast beyond. Family owned and run, with level grass pitches, and a modernised toilet block in smart converted farm buildings. There is also a camporc' room with microwave, freezer, kettle and free coffee and tea, and a children's play area. This is an ideal base for those touring the Newquay and St Ives areas.

Open: Easter and April to October **Last departure:** 10.00

Pitches: 🚐 from £16; 🚐 from £16; ▲ from £16; 6 hardstanding pitches

Leisure: ⚲

Facilities: 🖼 ☺ ℙ ✳ ⅙ ⑤ 🚻 WiFi

Services: 🔌 🖸 🔋

Within 3 miles: ⌕ ℘ ↻

Additional site information: 5 acre site. 🐕 Cars can be parked by caravans and tents. Awnings permitted. No large groups. Car hire can be arranged.

ST AUSTELL

See also Carlyon Bay

Places to visit

The Shipwreck and Heritage Centre, ST AUSTELL, PL25 3NX, 01726 69897
www.shipwreckcharlestown.com

Eden Project, ST AUSTELL, PL24 2SG, 01726 811911
www.edenproject.com

Great for kids: Wheal Martyn, ST AUSTELL, PL26 8XG, 01726 850362
www.wheal-martyn.com

ST AUSTELL — **Map 2 SX05**

Premier Park

River Valley Holiday Park
►►►►► 89%

tel: 01726 73533 **London Apprentice PL26 7AP**
email: mail@rivervalleyholidaypark.co.uk **web:** www.rivervalleyholidaypark.co.uk
dir: Take B3273 from St Austell to London Apprentice. Site signed, direct access to site from B3273.

A neat, well-maintained family-run park set in a pleasant river valley. The quality toilet block and attractively landscaped grounds make this a delightful base for a holiday. All pitches are hardstanding, mostly divided by low fencing and neatly trimmed hedges, and the park offers a good range of leisure facilities, including an inviting swimming pool, a games room, an internet room, and an excellent children's play area. There is direct access to river walks and an off-road cycle trail to the beach at Pentewan. The site is on the bus route to St Austell.

Open: April to end September **Last arrival:** 21.00 **Last departure:** 11.00

Pitches: 🚐 from £16; 🚐 from £16; ▲ from £16; 45 hardstanding pitches

Leisure: 🏊 ⚲ 🎱 🎯

Facilities: 🖼 ☺ ℙ ✳ ⅙ ⑤ WiFi

Services: 🔌 🖸

Within 3 miles: ⌕ ℘ ↻ 🛶 ⛷ 🎣

Additional site information: 2 acre site. 🐕 Cars can be parked by caravans and tents. Awnings permitted.

ST AUSTELL *continued*

Meadow Lakes Holiday Park
▶▶▶▶ 87%

tel: 01726 882540 & 01934 823288 **Hewas Water PL26 7JG**
email: info@meadow-lakes.co.uk **web:** www.meadow-lakes.co.uk
dir: *From A390 (4 miles southwest of St Austell) onto B3287 signed Tregony. 1 mile, site on left.*

Set in a quiet rural area, this extensive park is divided into paddocks with mature hedges and trees, and has its own coarse fishing lakes. This friendly, family park has enthusiastic and hands-on owners – all facilities are immaculate and spotlessly clean. The park offers organised indoor and outdoor activities for children in the summer holidays (there is a play barn for when the weather is unsuitable for using the two outdoor play areas), and at other times caters for adult breaks. There are animals in pens which children can enter. Self-catering lodges, static caravans, wooden pods and smaller cabins are available for hire. The bus to Truro and St Austell stops within half a mile of the site.

Open: mid March to mid January **Last arrival:** 20.00 **Last departure:** 11.00
Pitches: 🚐 from £13.50; 🚙 from £13.50; ⛺ from £13.50; 🛖 see prices below; 11 hardstanding pitches; 30 seasonal pitches
Leisure: 🏊 🎠 🏓 🎯 🎱 ⚽
Facilities: 🛁 ✂ ✳ ♿ ⑤ 🤱 🚼 WiFi
Services: 🔌 ⑤ 🍴 ⚕ 🍷
Within 3 miles: ⛳ ⌣ 🎣 🎏

Additional site information: 56 acre site. 🐕 Cars can be parked by caravans and tents. Awnings permitted. No commercial vehicles, no noise after 23.00. Table tennis, tots' TV room, zip wire, skittles, hot tub hire.

Glamping available: Wooden pods from £39. **Changeover days:** Any day
Additional glamping information: Wooden pods: check in at 16.00; departure by 10.00. Cars can be parked by pods.

See advert opposite

Court Farm Holidays
▶▶▶ 82%

tel: 01726 823684 & 07973 773681 **St Stephen PL26 7LE**
email: info@courtfarmcornwall.co.uk **web:** www.courtfarmcornwall.co.uk
dir: *Take A3058 towards St Austell, through St Stephen (pass Peugeot garage), right at St Stephen/Coombe Hay/Langreth/Industrial site sign. Site 400 yards on right.*

Set in a peaceful rural location, this large camping field offers plenty of space, and is handy for the Eden Project and the Lost Gardens of Heligan. Star-gazing facilities at the Roseland Observatory (including astronomy lectures) are among the on-site attractions. It is a five-minute walk to a Co-op store, and also to the bus stop on the Newquay to St Austell route.

Open: May to August **Last arrival:** by dark **Last departure:** 11.00
Pitches: * 🚐 from £18.50; 🚙 from £18.50; ⛺ from £15; 5 hardstanding pitches
Facilities: ☉ ✳ 🍴 ⚏ WiFi
Services: 🔌 ⑤ 🍷
Within 3 miles: ⛳ 🎣 ⌣ 📅 ⑤

Additional site information: 4 acre site. 🐕 Cars can be parked by caravans and tents. Awnings permitted. No noise after dark.

ST BLAZEY GATE   Map 2 SX05

Places to visit

Eden Project, ST AUSTELL, PL24 2SG, 01726 811911
www.edenproject.com

St Catherine's Castle, FOWEY, 0370 333 1181
www.english-heritage.org.uk/daysout/properties/st-catherines-castle

Great for kids: Wheal Martyn, ST AUSTELL, PL26 8XG, 01726 850362
www.wheal-martyn.com

Doubletrees Farm
▶▶▶▶ 83%

tel: 01726 812266 **Luxulyan Road PL24 2EH**
email: doubletreesfarm@gmail.com **web:** www.doubletreesfarm.co.uk
dir: *On A390 at Blazey Gate. Turn by Leek Seed Chapel, almost opposite petrol station. After approximately 300 yards turn right by public bench into site.*

A popular park with terraced pitches that offers superb sea and coastal views. It is close to beaches, and the Eden Project is only a 20-minute walk away. This site is very well maintained by the friendly owners and the facilities are spotlessly clean. There is a Chinese restaurant and a fish and chip shop just 300 yards away.

Open: All year **Last arrival:** 20.00 **Last departure:** 11.30
Pitches: 🚐 from £17; 🚙 from £17; ⛺ from £16; 10 hardstanding pitches
Facilities: 🛁 ☉ ✳ ♿ 🍴 WiFi
Services: 🔌 ⑤ 🍴 ⚕ 🍷   **Within 3 miles:** ⛳ 🎣 ⌣ ◎ 📅 ⑤

Additional site information: 1.57 acre site. 🐕 🐾 Cars can be parked by caravans and tents. Awnings permitted. No noise after midnight.

LEISURE: 🏊 Indoor swimming pool 🏊 Outdoor swimming pool 🎠 Children's playground 🙌 Kids' club 🎾 Tennis court 🎱 Games room 📺 Separate TV room ⛳ golf course 🏌 Pitch n putt 🚣 Boats for hire 🚴 Bikes for hire 🎬 Cinema 🎵 Entertainment 🎣 Fishing ◎ Mini golf 🏄 Watersports 🏋 Gym 🏟 Sports field ⌣ Stables
FACILITIES: 🛁 Baths/Shower ☉ Electric shaver sockets ✂ Hairdryer ✳ Ice Pack Facility 🚼 Baby facilities ♿ Disabled facilities ⑤ Shop on site or within 200yds 🍖 BBQ area 🅰 Picnic area WiFi WiFi

ST COLUMB MAJOR
Map 2 SW96

Places to visit

Prideaux Place, PADSTOW, PL28 8RP, 01841 532411
www.prideauxplace.co.uk

Cornwall's Regimental Museum, BODMIN, PL31 1EG, 01208 72810
www.cornwalls-regimentalmuseum.org

Great for kids: Pencarrow, BODMIN, PL30 3AG, 01208 841369
www.pencarrow.co.uk

Crealy Adventure Park & Resort, CLYST ST MARY, EX5 1DR, 01395 233200
www.crealy.co.uk

Trewan Hall
▶▶▶▶ 86%

tel: 01637 880261 & 07900 677397 **TR9 6DB**
email: enquiries@trewan-hall.co.uk **web:** www.trewan-hall.co.uk
dir: From A39 north of St Columb Major (do not enter town) turn left signed Talskiddy and St Eval. Site 1 mile on left.

Trewan Hall lies at the centre of a Cornish estate amid 36 acres of wooded grounds. The site's extensive amenities include good toilet facilities, hook-ups and good security, plus a 25-metre swimming pool, and a free, live theatre in a stone barn throughout July and August. The campsite shop stocks everything from groceries to camping equipment. The site also has fine gardens, four acres of woodland for dog walking and a field available for ball games. St Columb is just a short walk away.

Open: 10 May to 9 September (restricted service: low season – shop opens for shorter hours) **Last arrival:** 20.00 **Last departure:** noon
Pitches: 🚐 from £14; 🚃 from £14; ▲ from £14
Leisure: 🏊 🏊 🎠 🎯 🎵 ☺
Facilities: 🛁 ⊙ ✂ ☀ 🚿 ⑤ 🪑 **WiFi**
Services: 🔌 🗑 🛒 🧺 🔒 🧹 Ⓣ
Within 3 miles: 🎣 ⛳ 🏌 ☺ 🏊 🚴
Additional site information: 14.27 acre site. 🚗 Cars can be parked by caravans and tents. Awnings permitted. Families and couples only, no cycling, no driving on fields from midnight–08.00, no noise after 23.00. Library, billiard room, table tennis, pool table.

ST IVES

Places to visit

Barbara Hepworth Museum & Sculpture Garden, ST IVES, TR26 1AD, 01736 796226, www.tate.org.uk/stives

Tate St Ives, ST IVES, TR26 1TG, 01736 796226
www.tate.org.uk/stives

ST IVES
Map 2 SW54

Platinum Park

Polmanter Touring Park
▶▶▶▶▶

Best of British

tel: 01736 795640 **Halsetown TR26 3LX**
email: reception@polmanter.co.uk **web:** www.polmanter.co.uk
dir: Signed from B3311 at Halsetown.

A well-developed touring park on high ground, Polmanter is an excellent choice for family holidays – high quality is evident everywhere, from the immaculate, modern toilet blocks to the outdoor swimming pool and hard tennis courts. The pitches are individually marked and sited in meadows, and the tastefully landscaped park also offers a field with full-facility hardstanding pitches to accommodate larger caravans and motorhomes. A smart new reception and shop opened in 2018 and this new building has two upstairs apartments available for hire. The fishing port of St Ives and the beaches are just a mile and a half away, and there is a convenient bus service in high season.

Open: 1 April to 28 October **Last arrival:** 21.00 **Last departure:** 10.00
Pitches: 🚐 from £24; 🚃 from £24; ▲ from £24; 60 hardstanding pitches
Leisure: 🏊 🎠 🏊 🎯 ☺ **Facilities:** 🛁 ⊙ ✂ ☀ 🚿 ⑤ **WiFi**
Services: 🔌 🗑 🛒 🍽 🛒 🧺 ⚒ 🧹 Ⓣ
Within 3 miles: 🎣 ⛳ ☺ 🏊 🚴 🚴 🌿
Additional site information: 20 acre site. 🚗 Cars can be parked by caravans and tents. Awnings permitted. Family camping only, no skateboards, rollerblades or heelys. Putting green, treatment rooms, indoor soft play. Pool open mid May to mid September.

See advert on page 99

Premier Park

Trevalgan Touring Park

▶▶▶▶▶ 92%

Best of British

tel: 01736 791892 **Trevalgan TR26 3BJ**
email: reception@trevalgantouringpark.co.uk **web:** www.trevalgantouringpark.co.uk
dir: *From A30 follow holiday route to St Ives. B3311 through Halsetown to B3306. Left towards Land's End. Site signed 0.5 mile on right.*

Serious investment by the hands-on owners has taken place over the last few years at this welcoming park, which is set in a rural area on the coastal road from St Ives to Zennor. The park is surrounded by mature hedges but there are still extensive views over the sea. There is a smart wood-clad reception and shop (daily-baked bread and pastries are available), excellent upmarket toilet facilities which have family rooms and underfloor heating, and extensive landscaping across the park that has resulted in more spacious pitches which offer both privacy and shelter. A regular bus service connects the park with St Ives from late May to September. A good base for motorhomes.

Trevalgan Touring Park

Open: May to 29 September **Last arrival:** 20.00 **Last departure:** 11.00
Pitches: * 🚐 from £18; 🚌 from £18; ▲ from £18; 13 hardstanding pitches
Leisure: 🎠 🎣 ⚽
Facilities: 📷 🚻 🚿 ⚙ 🔥 🚹 🛒 WIFI
Services: 🔌 🔄 🚽 🛢 🐾 T
Within 3 miles: 🐟 🦌 ☕ ◎ 🚴 🛶 🍴 📅

Additional site information: 9 acre site. 🐕 Cars can be parked by caravans and tents. Awnings permitted. Fresh bread, pastries, coffee, local produce available.

See advert below

PITCHES: 🚐 Caravans 🚌 Motorhomes ▲ Tents 🏠 Glamping accommodation **SERVICES:** 🔌 Electric hook-up 🔄 Launderette 🍺 Licensed bar 🛢 Calor Gas ⊘ Campingaz T Toilet fluid 🍽 Café/Restaurant 🍟 Fast Food/Takeaway 🔋 Battery charging 🚐 Motorhome service point * 2019 prices ⊘ No credit or debit cards 🐕 Dogs permitted ⊗ No dogs

ST IVES *continued*

Premier Park

Ayr Holiday Park
▶▶▶▶▶ 89%

tel: 01736 795855 **TR26 1EJ**
email: recept@ayrholidaypark.co.uk **web:** www.ayrholidaypark.co.uk
dir: *From A30 follow St Ives 'large vehicles' route via B3311 through Halsetown onto B3306. Site signed towards St Ives town centre.*

A well-established park on a cliff side overlooking St Ives Bay, with a heated toilet block that makes winter holidaying more attractive. There are stunning views from most pitches, and the town centre, harbour and beach are only half a mile away, with direct access to the coastal footpath. This makes an excellent base for surfing enthusiasts. Please note that it is advisable not to follow sat nav; use these directions and avoid the town centre.

Open: All year **Last arrival:** 22.00 **Last departure:** 11.00
Pitches: ⌖ from £20; ⌖ from £20; ▲ from £20; 31 hardstanding pitches
Leisure: ⛱ ⚐ ◉
Facilities: ▦ ◉ ⚑ ✳ ⛄ ⑤ ⊓ WiFi
Services: ◉ ⓢ ⍓ ⍵ ⛟ ⊞ ⍾ ⚱ ⌀ ⊤
Within 3 miles: ↓ ⚘ ∪ ◎ ⚐ ⚒ ⚑ ⊟

Additional site information: 6 acre site. ⌖ Cars can be parked by caravans and tents. Awnings permitted. No disposable BBQs.

Higher Penderleath Caravan & Camping Park
▶▶▶▶ 82%

tel: 01736 798403 & 07840 208542 **Towednack TR26 3AF**
email: holidays@penderleath.co.uk **web:** www.penderleath.co.uk
dir: *From A30 take A3074 towards St Ives. Left at 2nd mini roundabout, approximately 3 miles to T-junction. Left, then immediately right. Next left.*

Set in a rugged rural location, this tranquil park has extensive views towards St Ives Bay and the north coast. Facilities are all housed in modernised granite barns, and include spotless toilets with fully serviced shower rooms, and there's a quiet licensed bar with beer garden, a food takeaway, breakfast room and bar meals. The owners are welcoming and helpful. There is a bus service to St Ives, available in high season.

Open: All year **Last arrival:** 21.30 **Last departure:** 10.30
Pitches: ⌖ ⌖ ▲; 5 seasonal pitches
Leisure: ⚐ ◉ **Facilities:** ▦ ◉ ⚑ ✳ ⛄ ⑤ ⍾
Services: ◉ ⓢ ⍓ ⍵ ⛟ ⊞ ⚱ ⌀ ⊤
Within 3 miles: ↓ ⚘ ∪ ◎ ⚐ ⚒ ⚑ ⊟

Additional site information: 10 acre site. ⌖ Dogs must be well behaved and on a fixed short lead. Cars can be parked by caravans and tents. Awnings permitted. No campfires, no noise after 23.00.

ST JUST [NEAR LAND'S END]   Map 2 SW33

Places to visit

Geevor Tin Mine, PENDEEN, TR19 7EW, 01736 788662
www.geevor.com

Carn Euny Ancient Village, SANCREED, 0370 333 1181
www.english-heritage.org.uk/daysout/properties/carn-euny-ancient-village

Roselands Caravan and Camping Park
▶▶▶ 90%

tel: 01736 788571 & 07718 745065 **Dowran TR19 7RS**
email: info@roselands.co.uk **web:** www.roselands.co.uk
dir: *From A30 (Penzance bypass) onto A3071 for St Just. 5 miles, left at sign after tin mine chimney, follow signs to site.*

A small, friendly park in a sheltered rural setting, an ideal location for a quiet family holiday. The owners continue to upgrade the park, and in addition to the attractive little bar there is an indoor games room, children's playground and good toilet facilities.

Open: March to October **Last arrival:** 21.00 **Last departure:** 11.00

Pitches: 🚐 from £15; 🚌 from £15; ⛺ from £12.50

Leisure: 🛝 🎱

Facilities: 🛁 ☺ 🚿 ❄ [$] 🍖 🪑 [WiFi]

Services: 🔌 🧺 🍷 🔥 🍃 [T]

Within 3 miles: ⛳ 🎣 🐎 🌊

Additional site information: 4 acre site. 🐕 Cars can be parked by caravans and tents. Awnings permitted. Dog walks on moor adjacent to park.

Trevaylor Caravan & Camping Park

►►► 86%

tel: 01736 787016 & 07816 992519 **Botallack TR19 7PU**
email: trevaylor@cornishcamping.co.uk **web:** www.cornishcamping.co.uk
dir: *On B3306 (St Just to St Ives road), site on right 0.75 mile from St Just.*

A sheltered grassy site located off the beaten track in a peaceful location at the western tip of Cornwall; it makes an ideal base for discovering Penzance and Land's End. The dramatic coastline and the pretty villages nearby are truly unspoilt. Clean, well-maintained facilities, including a good shop, are offered along with a bar serving meals. The enthusiastic owners offer pitches with electric hook-ups and a shower block with heating. An open-top bus stops at the entrance to the site.

Open: All year **Last arrival:** 21.00 **Last departure:** 11.00

Pitches: 🚐 🚌 ⛺; 11 hardstanding pitches

Leisure: 🛝 🎱 📺

Facilities: 🛁 🚿 ❄ [$] [WiFi]

Services: 🔌 🧺 🍷 🍴 🍔 🔋 ⛛ 🔥 🍃 [T]

Within 3 miles: ⛳ 🎣 🐎 🌊

Additional site information: 6 acre site. 🐕 Cars can be parked by caravans and tents. Awnings permitted. Quiet after 22.00.

Secret Garden Caravan & Camping Park

►►► 81%

tel: 01736 788301 **Bosavern House TR19 7RD**
email: mail@bosavern.com **web:** www.secretbosavern.com
dir: *Exit A3071 near St Just onto B3306 (Land's End road). Site 0.5 mile on left.*

A neat little site in a walled garden behind a guest house, where visitors can enjoy breakfast, and snacks in the bar in the evening. This site is in a fairly sheltered location with all grassy pitches. Please note that there is no children's playground.

Open: March to October **Last arrival:** 22.00 **Last departure:** noon

Pitches: 🚐 from £20; 🚌 from £20; ⛺ from £20

Facilities: 🛁 ☺ ❄ [WiFi]

Services: 🔌 🧺 🍷 🔋 ⛛

Within 3 miles: ⛳ 🎣 🌊 [$]

Additional site information: 1.5 acre site. 🐕 Cars can be parked by caravans and tents. Awnings permitted. No open fires or fire pits.

ST JUST-IN-ROSELAND
Map 2 SW83

Places to visit

St Mawes Castle, ST MAWES, TR2 5DE, 01326 270526
www.english-heritage.org.uk/daysout/properties/st-mawes-castle

Trelissick, TRELISSICK, TR3 6QL, 01872 862090
www.nationaltrust.org.uk/trelissick

REGIONAL WINNER – SOUTH WEST ENGLAND
AA CAMPSITE OF THE YEAR 2019

Platinum Park

Trethem Mill Touring Park
►►►►►

tel: 01872 580504 **TR2 5JF**
email: reception@trethem.com **web:** www.trethem.com
dir: *From Tregony on A3078 to St Mawes. 2 miles after Trewithian, follow signs to site.*

A top quality park in all areas, immaculately maintained and with good amenities including a reception, shop, laundry and disabled/family room. This carefully-tended and sheltered park is in a lovely rural setting, with spacious pitches separated by young trees and shrubs. The very keen family who own the site are continually looking for ways to enhance its facilities. A pizza van, serving excellent wood-fired pizzas, visits the site once a week.

Open: April to mid October **Last arrival:** 19.00 **Last departure:** 11.00
Pitches: ⊞ from £22; ⊞ from £22; ▲ from £22; 67 hardstanding pitches

Leisure: ⚐ ✿
Facilities: ⌂ ☉ ⴷ ✳ ⴺ ⑤ WiFi
Services: ⚟ ◎ ⊻ ⌂ ⊘ ⊤
Within 3 miles: ✐ ≩ ⇞

Additional site information: 11 acre site. ⋈ Cars can be parked by caravans and tents. Awnings permitted. No bikes, skateboards or rollerblades. Information centre. Car hire can be arranged.
See advert on page 103

ST MARY'S (ISLES OF SCILLY)
Map 2 SV91

Places to visit

Isles of Scilly Museum, ST MARY'S, TR21 0JT, 01720 422337
www.iosmuseum.org

Bant's Carn Burial Chamber and Halangy Down Ancient Village, ST MARY'S, TR21 0NS, www.english-heritage.org.uk/daysout/properties/bants-carn-burial-chamber-and-halangy-down-ancient-village

Garrison Campsite
►►► 86%

tel: 01720 422670 **Tower Cottage, The Garrison TR21 0LS**
email: info@garrisonholidays.com **web:** www.garrisonholidays.com
dir: *10 minutes' walk from quay to site*

Set on the top of an old fort with superb views, this park offers tent-only pitches in a choice of well-sheltered paddocks, including eight fully-equipped, ready-erected tents which are available for hire. There are modern toilet facilities (with powerful showers), a superb children's play area and a good shop at this attractive site, which is only 10 minutes from the town, the quay and the nearest beaches. There is easy access to the other islands via the direct boat service from the Hugh Town quay; the campsite owners will transport all luggage, camping equipment etc to and from the quay. Good food is available in the many hostelries in the main town.

Open: Easter to October **Last arrival:** 20.00 **Last departure:** 19.00

Pitches: ▲ from £21; ⋒ see prices below

Facilities: ⌂ ☉ ⴷ ✳ ⑤

Services: ⚟ ◎ ⊟ ⌂ ⊘

Within 3 miles: ↧ ✐ ∪ ≩ ⇞

Additional site information: 9.5 acre site. ⋈ Dogs by prior arrangement only. No cars on site, no open fires.

Glamping available: Ready-erected tents from £130. **Changeover days:** Monday to Saturday

Additional glamping information: Ready-erected tents sleep 1-4 people (£220 for 4), minimum stay 3 nights. No dogs allowed.

LEISURE: ≋ Indoor swimming pool ≋ Outdoor swimming pool ⚐ Children's playground ⛹ Kids' club ♞ Tennis court ⚄ Games room ☐ Separate TV room ↧ golf course ⴺ Pitch n putt ≩ Boats for hire ⴻ Bikes for hire ⊟ Cinema ♫ Entertainment ✐ Fishing ◉ Mini golf ≋ Watersports ✦ Gym ✿ Sports field ∪ Stables
FACILITIES: ⌂ Baths/Shower ☉ Electric shaver sockets ⴷ Hairdryer ✳ Ice Pack Facility ⴲ Baby facilities ⴺ Disabled facilities ⑤ Shop on site or within 200yds ⛺ BBQ area ⋒ Picnic area WiFi WiFi

ST MERRYN (NEAR PADSTOW)　　Map 2 SW87

Places to visit

Prideaux Place, PADSTOW, PL28 8RP, 01841 532411
www.prideauxplace.co.uk

Great for kids: Crealy Adventure Park & Resort, CLYST ST MARY, EX5 1DR, 01395 233200, www.crealy.co.uk

Premier Park

Atlantic Bays Holiday Park

▶▶▶▶▶　90%

tel: 01841 520855 **St Merryn PL28 8PY**
email: info@atlanticbaysholidaypark.co.uk **web:** www.atlanticbaysholidaypark.co.uk
dir: *From A30 southwest of Bodmin take exit signed Victoria and Roche, 1st exit at roundabout. At Trekenning roundabout 4th exit signed A39 and Wadebridge. At Winnards Perch roundabout left, B3274 signed Padstow. Left in 3 miles, follow signs.*

Atlantic Bays has a mix of hardstanding and grass pitches, a high quality toilet and shower block and a comfortable bar and restaurant. The park is set in a rural area yet only two miles from the coast and beautiful sandy beaches, and within easy reach of the quaint fishing village of Padstow, and Newquay for fantastic surfing.

Open: March to 2 January **Last arrival:** 21.00 **Last departure:** noon

Pitches: ⛟ ⛟ ▲; 50 hardstanding pitches; 6 seasonal pitches

Leisure: ⚏ ☜ ⚽

Facilities: ☺ ⛿ ☀ ⚒ ⓢ ☷ ⌂ ➴ WiFi

Services: ⚡ ⓞ ⛿ ⏤ ⚓ T

Within 3 miles: ⚲ ⌒ ∪ ⊚ ⥗ ⊱ H

Additional site information: 27 acre site. ⚲ Cars can be parked by caravans and tents. Awnings permitted.

Carnevas Holiday Park

▶▶▶▶　86%

tel: 01841 520230 **Carnevas Farm PL28 8PN**
email: carnevascampsite@aol.com **web:** www.carnevasholidaypark.com
dir: *From St Merryn on B3276 towards Porthcothan Bay. In approximately 2 miles turn right at site sign onto unclassified road opposite Tredrea Inn. Site 0.25 mile on right.*

A family-run park on a working farm, divided into four paddocks on slightly sloping grass. The toilets are central to all areas, and there is a small licensed bar serving bar meals. An ideal base for exploring the fishing town of Padstow or the surfing beach at Newquay.

Open: April to October (restricted service: April to end May and early September to end October – shop, bar and restaurant closed)

Pitches: ⛟ from £13; ⛟ from £13; ▲ from £13

Leisure: ⚏ ☜

Facilities: ⌂ ☺ ⛿ ☀ ⚒ ⓢ WiFi

Services: ⚡ ⓞ ⛿ ⎟○⎜ ⏤ ⚓ ⌂ ⛁ ➴ T

Within 3 miles: ⚲ ⌒ ∪ ⥗

Additional site information: 8 acre site. ⚲ Cars can be parked by caravans and tents. Awnings permitted. No skateboards, no supermarket deliveries.

Tregavone Touring Park

▶▶▶　82%

tel: 01841 520148 & 07812 841024 **Tregavone Farm PL28 8JZ**
email: info@tregavonefarm.co.uk **web:** www.tregavonefarm.co.uk
dir: *From A389 towards Padstow, right after Little Petherick. In 1 mile just after Padstow Holiday Park turn left onto unclassified road signed Tregavone. Site on left in approximately 1 mile.*

Situated on a working farm with unspoilt country views, this spacious grassy park, run by friendly family owners, has seen investment in recent years which includes the addition of a quality, new shower block. Tregavone Touring Park makes the ideal base for exploring the north Cornish coast and the seven local golden beaches with surfing areas, or for enjoying quiet country walks that lead from the park.

Open: March to October

Pitches: ⛟ from £15; ⛟ from £15; ▲ from £15; ⋒ see prices below; 24 seasonal pitches

Leisure: ⚏ ⚽

Facilities: ⌂ ☺ ⛿ ☀ ⓢ ☷ WiFi

Services: ⚡ ⓞ ⚓

Within 3 miles: ⚲ ⌒ ∪ ⊚ ⥗ ⊱

Additional site information: 3 acre site. ⚲ Cars can be parked by caravans and tents. Awnings permitted.

Glamping available: Bell tents from £30. **Changeover days:** Friday

Additional glamping information: Furnished with double beds, fridge, shared kitchen area with BBQ, gas stove, fire pit and picnic table. Cars can be parked by tents.

PITCHES: ⛟ Caravans ⛟ Motorhomes ▲ Tents ⋒ Glamping accommodation **SERVICES:** ⚡ Electric hook-up ⓞ Launderette ⎟○⎜ Licensed bar ⛁ Calor Gas ⌀ Campingaz T Toilet fluid ⎟○⎜ Café/Restaurant ⏤ Fast Food/Takeaway ⚓ Battery charging ➴ Motorhome service point * 2019 prices ⊘ No credit or debit cards ⚲ Dogs permitted ⊗ No dogs

SENNEN Map 2 SW32

Places to visit

Carn Euny Ancient Village, SANCREED, 0370 333 1181
www.english-heritage.org.uk/daysout/properties/carn-euny-ancient-village

Chysauster Ancient Village, GULVAL, TR20 8XA, 07831 757934
www.english-heritage.org.uk/daysout/properties/chysauster-ancient-village

Great for kids: Geevor Tin Mine, PENDEEN, TR19 7EW, 01736 788662
www.geevor.com

Trevedra Farm Caravan & Camping Site

►►►► 90%

tel: 01736 871818 & 871835 **TR19 7BE**
email: trevedra@btconnect.com **web:** www.trevedrafarm.co.uk
dir: *Take A30 towards Land's End. After junction with B3306 turn right into farm lane. (Note sat nav directs beyond site entrance to next lane which is unsuitable for caravans).*

A working farm with dramatic sea views over to the Scilly Isles over Gwynver Beach, just a mile from Land's End. This popular campsite offers an excellent, well-appointed toilet block, a well-stocked shop plus cooked breakfasts, Sunday roasts and evening meals are available from the food bar; takeaway is also available. The heated amenity block includes four separate bathrooms. There is direct access to the coastal footpath, and two beautiful beaches are just a short walk away.

Open: Easter (or April) to October **Last arrival:** 19.00 (later arrivals by prior arrangement) **Last departure:** 10.30

Pitches: * 🚐 from £21.50; 🚌 from £21.50; ⛺ from £18

Facilities: 🛁 ⊙ 💨 ❄ ♿ [S] [WiFi]

Services: 🛠 🧼 🍽 🍟 🛒 ⚓ 🔒 🌿 [T]

Within 3 miles: ⛳ 🎣 🌊

Additional site information: 8 acre site. 🐕 Cars can be parked by caravans and tents. Awnings permitted. No open fires, no noise 22.00–08.00. Fresh produce, newspapers, bread, milk, local meat available. Car hire can be arranged.

SUMMERCOURT Map 2 SW85

Places to visit

Trerice, TRERICE, TR8 4PG, 01637 875404
www.nationaltrust.org.uk/trerice

Blue Reef Aquarium, NEWQUAY, TR7 1DU, 01637 878134
www.bluereefaquarium.co.uk

Great for kids: Dairy Land Farm World, NEWQUAY, TR8 5AA, 01872 510246
www.dairylandfarmworld.com

Carvynick Holiday Park

►►►► 94%

tel: 01872 510716 **TR8 5AF**
email: info@carvynick.co.uk **web:** www.carvynick.co.uk
dir: *Accessed from A3058.*

Set within the gardens of an attractive country estate and under new ownership, this spacious park offers fully serviced pitches suitable for caravans and motorhomes, as well as two new shower blocks, and a washing-up area. The extensive on-site amenities, shared by the high-quality time share village, include an indoor leisure area with swimming pool, fitness suite, badminton court and a bar and restaurant serving good food.

Open: All year **Last arrival:** 18.00 **Last departure:** 11.00

Pitches: * 🚐 from £35; 🚌 from £35; ⛺ from £25; 47 hardstanding pitches

Leisure: 🏊 🛝 🎱 ⛳ 🏋 Spa

Facilities: 🛁 ⊙ 💨 ❄ ♿ [S] 🍖 🧺 [WiFi]

Services: 🛠 🧼 🍺 🍽 🍟 ⚓

Additional site information: 13 acre site. 🐕 Dogs must be exercised off site. Cars can be parked by caravans. Awnings permitted. 5-hole golf course, sauna, badminton court.

TINTAGEL

See also Camelford

Places to visit

Tintagel Castle, TINTAGEL, PL34 0HE, 01840 770328
www.english-heritage.org.uk/daysout/properties/tintagel-castle

Tintagel Old Post Office, TINTAGEL, PL34 0DB, 01840 770024
www.nationaltrust.org.uk/tintagel-old-post-office

Great for kids: Tamar Otter & Wildlife Centre, LAUNCESTON, PL15 8GW, 01566 785646, www.tamarotters.co.uk

TINTAGEL
Map 2 SX08

Headland Caravan & Camping Park
▶▶▶ 77%

tel: 01840 770239 **Atlantic Road PL34 0DE**
email: headland.caravan@btconnect.com **web:** www.headlandcaravanpark.co.uk
dir: From B3263 follow brown tourist signs through village to site.

A peaceful family-run site in the mystical village of Tintagel, close to the ruins of Tintagel Castle, famous for its connection with the legend of King Arthur. There are two well-terraced camping areas with sea and countryside views, immaculately clean toilet facilities, and good, colourful planting across the park. The Cornish coastal path and the spectacular scenery are just two of the attractions here, and there are safe bathing beaches nearby. There are holiday statics for hire.

Open: Easter to October **Last arrival:** 21.00

Pitches: 🚐 from £15; 🚎 from £14; ▲ from £15; 1 hardstanding pitch

Leisure: ⋀ **Facilities:** 🛁 ⊙ 🏳 ⚹ ⑤ WiFi

Services: 🔌 ⑤ 🛒 ⤵ 🔋 ⊘ Ⓣ **Within 3 miles:** 🖋 ∪ 🎿 ⚞

Additional site information: 5 acre site. ⚞ Dogs must be exercised off site. Cars can be parked by caravans and tents. Awnings permitted. Quiet after 23.00. No camp fires.

TORPOINT
Map 3 SX45

Places to visit

Antony House, TORPOINT, PL11 2QA, 01752 812191
www.nationaltrust.org.uk/antony

Mount Edgcumbe House & Country Park, TORPOINT, PL10 1HZ, 01752 822236
www.mountedgcumbe.gov.uk

Great for kids: Wild Futures' Monkey Sanctuary, LOOE, PL13 1NZ, 01503 262532
www.monkeysanctuary.org

Whitsand Bay Lodge & Touring Park
▶▶▶▶ 86%

tel: 01752 822597 **Millbrook PL10 1JZ**
email: enquiries@whitsandbayholidays.co.uk **web:** www.whitsandbayholidays.co.uk
dir: From Torpoint take A374, left at Anthony onto B3247 for 1.25 miles to T-junction. Turn left, 0.25 mile, right into Cliff Road. Site 2 miles on left.

A very well-equipped park with panoramic coastal, sea and countryside views from its terraced pitches. A quality park with upmarket toilet facilities and other amenities. There is a guided historic walk around The Battery most Sundays, and a bus stop close by.

Open: All year (restricted service: September to March — opening hours at bar reduced)
Last arrival: 19.00 **Last departure:** 10.00

Pitches: 🚐 from £12.50; 🚎 from £12.50; ▲ from £12.50; 30 hardstanding pitches; 15 seasonal pitches

Leisure: 🏊 ⋀ 🖐 ⚲ 🎵

Facilities: 🛁 ⊙ ⚹ ⑤ ⑤ 🏳 🛒 WiFi

Services: 🔌 ⑤ 🖾 🍽 🍴 🍔 ⤵

Within 3 miles: ⅃ 🖋 ∪ ◎ 🎿 ⚞

Additional site information: 27 acre site. ⚞ Cars can be parked by caravans and tents. Awnings permitted. Families and couples only. Chapel, library, heritage centre. Car hire can be arranged.

TRURO
Map 2 SW84

See also Portscatho

Places to visit

Royal Cornwall Museum, TRURO, TR1 2SJ, 01872 272205
www.royalcornwallmuseum.org.uk

Trelissick, TRELISSICK, TR3 6QL, 01872 862090
www.nationaltrust.org.uk/trelissick

Platinum Park

Carnon Downs Caravan & Camping Park
▶▶▶▶▶

tel: 01872 862283 **Carnon Downs TR3 6JJ**
email: info@carnon-downs-caravanpark.co.uk
web: www.carnon-downs-caravanpark.co.uk
dir: Take A39 from Truro towards Falmouth. 1st left at Carnon Downs roundabout, site signed.

A beautifully mature park set in meadowland and woodland close to the village amenities of Carnon Downs. The four toilet blocks provide exceptional facilities in bright modern surroundings. An extensive landscaping programme has been carried out to give more spacious pitch sizes, and there is an exciting children's playground with modern equipment, plus a football pitch.

Open: All year **Last arrival:** 22.00 **Last departure:** 11.00

Pitches: 🚐 from £23; 🚎 from £23; ▲ from £23; 80 hardstanding pitches

Leisure: ⋀ 🖵

Facilities: 🛁 ⊙ 🏳 ⚹ ⑤ WiFi

Services: 🔌 ⑤ 🖾 ⤵ 🔋 ⊘ Ⓣ

Within 3 miles: ⅃ 🖋 ∪ ◎ 🎿 ⚞ 🖿 ⑤

Additional site information: 33 acre site. ⚞ Cars can be parked by caravans and tents. Awnings permitted. No children's bikes in July and August. Babies' and children's bathroom. Car hire can be arranged.

PITCHES: 🚐 Caravans 🚎 Motorhomes ▲ Tents ⋔ Glamping accommodation **SERVICES:** 🔌 Electric hook-up ⑤ Launderette 🍽 Licensed bar
🛢 Calor Gas ⊘ Campingaz Ⓣ Toilet fluid 🍴 Café/Restaurant 🍔 Fast Food/Takeaway 🔋 Battery charging ⤵ Motorhome service point
* 2019 prices ⊛ No credit or debit cards ⚞ Dogs permitted ⊗ No dogs

TRURO *continued*

Premier Park

Cosawes Park

►►►►► 85%

tel: 01872 863724 **Perranarworthal TR3 7QS**
email: info@cosawes.com **web:** www.cosawes.co.uk
dir: *Exit A39 midway between Truro and Falmouth. Direct access at site sign after Perranarworthal.*

A small touring park, close to Perranarworthal, in a peaceful wooded valley, midway between Truro and Falmouth, with a two-acre touring area. There are spotless toilet facilities (with underfloor heating) that include two smart family rooms. Its stunning location is ideal for visiting the many nearby hamlets and villages close to the Carrick Roads, a stretch of tidal water, which is a centre for sailing and other boating activities.

Open: All year **Last arrival:** 21.00 **Last departure:** 10.00

Pitches: 🚐 🚌 ⛺; 30 hardstanding pitches; 15 seasonal pitches

Facilities: 🛁 ⊙ 💨 ❄ ♿ 🍖 🧺 📶

Services: 🔧 🫧 🚰 ⬇ ⛽ [T]

Within 3 miles: ⛳ 🎣 🐴 ◎ 🌊 ⛵ 🛒

Additional site information: 2 acre site. 🐕 Cars can be parked by caravans and tents. Awnings permitted. No skates, scooters, bicycles etc. Morning barista in summer peak season. Car hire can be arranged.

Premier Park

Truro Caravan and Camping Park

►►►►► 85%

tel: 01872 560274 **TR4 8QN**
email: info@trurocaravanandcampingpark.co.uk
web: www.trurocaravanandcampingpark.co.uk
dir: *Exit A390 at Threemilestone roundabout onto unclassified road towards Chacewater. Site signed on right in 0.5 mile.*

An attractive south-facing and well-laid out park with spacious pitches, including good hardstandings, and quality modern toilets that are kept spotlessly clean. It is situated on the edge of Truro yet close to many beaches, with St Agnes just 10 minutes away by car; it is equidistant from the rugged north coast and the calmer south coastal areas. There is a good bus service from the gate of the park to Truro.

Open: All year **Last arrival:** 18.00 **Last departure:** 10.30

Pitches: 🚐 🚌 ⛺; 26 hardstanding pitches

Facilities: ⊙ 💨 ❄ ♿ 📶

Services: 🔧 🫧 🚰 ⬇ ⛽ ♻ [T]

Within 3 miles: ⛳ 🎣 🐴 ◎ 🎬 🛒

Additional site information: 8.5 acre site. 🐕 Cars can be parked by caravans and tents. Awnings permitted.

AA MOST IMPROVED CAMPSITE OF THE YEAR 2019

Summer Valley Touring Park

►►►► 90%

tel: 01872 277878 **Shortlanesend TR4 9DW**
email: summervalleytruro@gmail.com **web:** www.summervalley.co.uk
dir: *From Truro take B3284 to Shortlanesend (approximately 3 miles). Through village, site on left.*

A very attractive and secluded site in a rural setting midway between the A30 and the cathedral city of Truro, which is just a five-minute drive away and can easily be reached by bus, cycle or on foot. Since taking over the park just a few years ago, owners Kate and Phil Hockey have invested both time and money to improve the facilities for their guests' enjoyment – to reflect this, the Quality Score for the park has risen to 90% and achieved gold Pennants. In addition to major drainage work across the site, improvements include moving and upgrading the children's play area, installing free WiFi across the park, refurbishing the toilets and showers, creating five fully serviced hardstanding pitches, removing some trees, adding a new shop, campers' kitchen and a security barrier at the entrance. There is also a new glamping pod with decking.

Open: All year **Last arrival:** 20.00 **Last departure:** 11.00

Pitches: 🚐 🚌 ⛺ 🛖; 5 hardstanding pitches; 6 seasonal pitches

Leisure: 🛝

Facilities: 🛁 ⊙ 💨 ❄ 🛒 👶 📶

Services: 🔧 🫧 🍴 🚰 ⛽ ♻ [T]

Within 3 miles: ⛳ 🎣 🐴 ◎ 🌊 🎬

Additional site information: 3 acre site. 🐕 Cars can be parked by caravans and tents. Awnings permitted. No noise after 22.30. Campers' lounge.

Glamping available: Wooden pod. **Changeover days:** Any day

Additional glamping information: No smoking in pod. Cars can be parked by pod.

WADEBRIDGE

Map 2 SW97

Places to visit

Prideaux Place, PADSTOW, PL28 8RP, 01841 532411
www.prideauxplace.co.uk

Cornwall's Regimental Museum, BODMIN, PL31 1EG, 01208 72810
www.cornwalls-regimentalmuseum.org

Great for kids: Pencarrow, BODMIN, PL30 3AG, 01208 841369
www.pencarrow.co.uk

Crealy Adventure Park & Resort, CLYST ST MARY, EX5 1DR, 01395 233200
www.crealy.co.uk

The Laurels Holiday Park

▶▶▶▶ 92%

tel: 01208 813341 & 07957 154578 **Padstow Road, Whitecross PL27 7JQ**
email: info@thelaurelsholidaypark.co.uk **web:** www.thelaurelsholidaypark.co.uk
dir: A39 onto A389 signed Padstow, follow signs. Site entrance 1st right.

A very smart and well-equipped park with individual pitches screened by hedges
and young shrubs. The enclosed dog walk is of great benefit to pet owners, and the
Camel (cycle) Trail and Padstow are not far away. An excellent base if visiting the
Royal Cornwall Showground. Four holiday cottages are also available.

Open: Easter or April to 31 October **Last arrival:** 20.00 (or by dark if earlier)
Last departure: 11.00

Pitches: * 🚐 from £21; 🚌 from £21; ▲ from £17; 15 hardstanding pitches;
10 seasonal pitches

Leisure: 🅰

Facilities: 🏠 ⊙ 🏳 ✳ 🚻 WiFi

Services: 🔌 🔲 🧺 🛢 🛇

Within 3 miles: 🎣 🏌 🎳 ⛷ 🚲 🗓 🏪

Additional site information: 2.2 acre site. 🐕 Cars can be parked by caravans and tents.
Awnings permitted. Family park, no group bookings, no commercial vehicles. Wet suit
dunking bath and drying area. Bakery delivery daily in peak season only.

Lowarth Glamping

▶▶▶▶ 85% GLAMPING ONLY

tel: 01208 812011 & 07733 272148 **Chapel Farm, Edmonton PL27 7JA**
email: avrilrea@gmail.com **web:** www.lowarthglamping.co.uk
dir: A39 from Wadebridge towards Truro. After roundabout take 1st right signed
Edmonton, pass Quarryman pub on right and cottages, 1st right, 300 yards, 1st right at
Lowarth sign.

This site is in a secluded paddock in a peaceful location just outside Wadebridge
and enjoys stunning panoramic views across rolling countryside towards Bodmin
Moor. Avril Rea is the very proud owner and she does everything to ensure that a
stay here will be a glamping holiday with a difference; high levels of customer care
are assured. The six comfortable Lotus Belle tents, set in their own little garden
('lowarth' means garden in Cornish), are beautifully furnished in an understated,
contemporary style, with comfortable double beds with duvets, soft rugs, a wood-
burning stove plus a fully-equipped kitchen annexe. There is a separate wooden
cabin housing spotless unisex toilets and showers, a dish-washing room and
laundry, and a Shiatsu treatment cabin (with views across the Camel Estuary).
A fire pit with seating proves popular for evening get togethers.

Open: April to September **Last arrival:** 22.00 **Last departure:** 11.00

Leisure: 🖵

Facilities: 🏠 ⊙ 🏳 ✕ 🍳 🚻 WiFi

Within 3 miles: 🏌 🗓 🏪 🚲

Accommodation available: Lotus Belle tents from £40.

Changeover days: Mondays to Fridays, Saturdays

Additional site information: 0.5 acre site. 🚫 No pets. Social tent furnished with TV/DVD.
Cars can be parked by tents.

Little Bodievc Holiday Park

▶▶▶ 84%

tel: 01208 812323 **Bodieve Road PL27 6EG**
email: info@littlebodieve.co.uk **web:** www.littlebodieve.co.uk
dir: From A39 roundabout on Wadebridge by-pass take B3314 signed Rock and Port
Isaac, site 0.25 mile on right.

Rurally located with pitches in three large grassy paddocks, this family park is
close to the Camel Estuary. The licensed clubhouse provides bar meals, with an
entertainment programme in high season, and there is a swimming pool with sun
terrace plus a separate waterslide and splash pool. This makes a good base from
which to visit the Royal Cornwall Showground.

Open: mid March to October (restricted service: early and late season — shop, pool and
clubhouse closed) **Last arrival:** 21.00 **Last departure:** 11.00

Pitches: 🚐 🚌 ▲

Leisure: 🏊 🎣 🎵

Facilities: ⊙ 🏳 ✳ ♿ 🗓 🚻 🚻 WiFi

Services: 🔌 🔲 🍴 🍽 🍺 🧺 🛢 🛇 T

Within 3 miles: 🎣 🏌 🎳 ⊚ ⛷ 🗓

Additional site information: 22 acre site. 🐕 Cars can be parked by caravans and tents.
Awnings permitted. Families and couples only. Crazy golf.

WATERGATE BAY
Map 2 SW86

Places to visit
Carnewas at Bedruthan (NT), TRENANCE, PL27 7UW, 01637 860563
www.nationaltrust.org.uk/carnewas-at-bedruthan/

Premier Park

Watergate Bay Touring Park
▶▶▶▶▶ 91% HOLIDAY CENTRE

tel: 01637 860387 **TR8 4AD**
email: email@watergatebaytouringpark.co.uk
web: www.watergatebaytouringpark.co.uk
dir: *From Bodmin on A30 follow Newquay airport signs. Continue past airport, left at T-junction, site 0.5 mile on right. (Note: for sat nav use TR8 4AE).*

A well-established park above Watergate Bay, where acres of golden sand, rock pools and surf are all contribute to making this a holidaymakers' paradise. The toilet facilities are appointed to a high standard and include top quality family/disabled rooms; there is a well-stocked shop and café, an inviting swimming pool, and a wide range of activities including tennis. There is regular entertainment in the clubhouse and outdoor facilities are tailored for all ages.

Watergate Bay Touring Park

Open: March to November (restricted service: March to Spring bank holiday and September to October – restricted bar, café, shop and pool) **Last arrival:** 22.00 **Last departure:** noon

Pitches: 🚐 🚐 ▲; 14 hardstanding pitches
Leisure: 🏊 🏊 💦 🎣 🎱 ⬛ 🎵 ⚽ ⛳
Facilities: ⊙ 🅿 ✳ ♿ 🖺 🍴 WiFi
Services: 🔌 🔋 🔧 🍽 ⚙ 🛒 ♨ 🛢 🗑 Ⓣ
Within 3 miles: 🎣 ⛳ 🎱 ≈

Additional site information: 30 acre site. 🚌 Free mini bus to beach during main school holidays.

See advert below

LEISURE: 🏊 Indoor swimming pool 🏊 Outdoor swimming pool 🛝 Children's playground 🖐 Kids' club 🎾 Tennis court 🎱 Games room ⬜ Separate TV room 🏌 golf course 🚩 Pitch n putt 🚣 Boats for hire 🚲 Bikes for hire 🎬 Cinema 🎵 Entertainment 🎣 Fishing ◎ Mini golf 🏄 Watersports 🏋 Gym 🏟 Sports field ⛳ Stables
FACILITIES: 🛁 Baths/Shower ⊙ Electric shaver sockets 🅿 Hairdryer ✳ Ice Pack Facility 🍼 Baby facilities ♿ Disabled facilities 🆂 Shop on site or within 200yds 🍴 BBQ area 🪑 Picnic area WiFi WiFi

WHITE CROSS
Map 2 SW96

Places to visit

Trerice, TRERICE, TR8 4PG, 01637 875404
www.nationaltrust.org.uk/trerice

Great for kids: Dairy Land Farm World, NEWQUAY, TR8 5AA, 01872 510246
www.dairylandfarmworld.com

Platinum Park

Piran Meadows Resort and Spa
▶▶▶▶▶ HOLIDAY HOME PARK

tel: 01726 860415 **TR8 4LW**
email: enquiries@piranmeadows.co.uk **web:** www.piranmeadows.co.uk
dir: *From A30 take A392 toward Newquay. At crossroads in White Cross left, under rail bridge, site on right.*

A stunning development that provides excellent standards and facilities for couples and families. Generously spaced, superbly equipped lodges and static holiday homes are equipped with both practical and thoughtful extras and have unrivalled countryside views. The stylish main building, with a welcoming reception, is decorated and furnished with quality and comfort, and the many facilities include a modern swimming pool, special areas and attractions for children, and the excellent Serenity Spa offering a wide range of treatments. The 'Go Active' sports programme has its own instructors and the restaurant, with bar, has a spacious outdoor area for alfresco dining.

Open: All year

Holiday Homes: Sleep 8 Bedrooms 4 Bathrooms 3 Toilets 3 Two-ring burner Dishwasher Washing Machine Microwave Freezer TV Sky/Freeview DVD player WiFi Linen included Towels included Electricity included Gas included

Leisure: 🏊 🎡 👐 🎶 🏸 🎯 Spa
Facilities: 👩‍🦽 🚿 WiFi
Within 3 miles: 🎣 ↺
Additional site information: 🐕

WIDEMOUTH BAY

Places to visit

Penhallam Manor, WEEK ST MARY, EX22 6XW
www.english-heritage.org.uk/daysout/properties/penhallam-manor

WIDEMOUTH BAY
Map 2 SS20

Cornish Coasts Caravan & Camping Park
▶▶▶ 86%

tel: 01288 361380 **Middle Penlean, Poundstock EX23 0EE**
email: admin@cornishcoasts.co.uk **web:** www.cornishcoasts.co.uk
dir: *From Bude take A39 towards Wadebridge. Approximately 5 miles to site on right (0.5 mile south of Rebel Cinema on left).*

Situated on the A39 midway between Padstow and the beautiful surfing beaches of Bude and Widemouth Bay, this is a quiet park with lovely terraced pitches that make the most of the stunning views over the countryside to the sea. The reception is in a 13th-century cottage, and the park is well equipped and tidy, with the well maintained and quirky toilet facilities (note the mosaic vanity units) housed in a freshly painted older-style building.

Open: April to October **Last arrival:** 22.00 **Last departure:** 10.30

Pitches: 🚐 🚙 ▲; 8 hardstanding pitches **Facilities:** ☺ 🚿 ⚒ 👩‍🦽 💲 🚽 🐕 WiFi
Services: 🔌 🗑 🧺 🛢 🗑 🚽 **Within 3 miles:** 🎣 🌳 ↺ ◎ 🚣 🎣 🎯

Additional site information: 3.5 acre site. 🐕 Cars can be parked by caravans and tents. Awnings permitted. Quiet after 22.00. Post office.

Penhalt Farm Holiday Park
▶▶▶ 78%

tel: 01288 361210 **EX23 0DG**
email: info@penhaltfarm.co.uk **web:** www.penhaltfarm.co.uk
dir: *From Bude on A39 take 2nd right to Widemouth Bay road, left at end by Widemouth Manor signed Millook onto coastal road. Site 0.75 mile on left.*

Splendid views of the sea and coast can be enjoyed from all pitches on this sloping but partly level site, set in a lovely rural area on a working farm. About one mile away is one of Cornwall's finest beaches which proves popular with all the family as well as surfers.

Open: Easter to October

Pitches: 🚐 from £16; 🚙 from £16; ▲ from £16; 12 hardstanding pitches
Leisure: 🎣 **Facilities:** 🏪 ☺ 🚿 ⚒ 👩‍🦽 💲 🚽
Services: 🔌 🗑 🧺 🛢 🗑 **Within 3 miles:** 🎣 🌳 ↺ 🚣 🎣 🎯

Additional site information: 8 acre site. 🐕 Cars can be parked by caravans and tents. Awnings permitted. No rollerblades, no noise after midnight. Pool table, netball, air hockey and table tennis.

Cumbria

Cumbria means the Lake District really – a rumpled, rugged landscape that is hard to beat for sheer natural beauty and grandeur. It is almost certainly England's best known and most scenic national park, famous for Lake Windermere, the country's largest lake, and Derwentwater, described as the 'Queen of the English Lakes.'

The Lake District is a region of Britain that leaves some visitors relaxed, others completely exhausted. The list of activities and places to visit is endless. The old adage 'always leave something to come back for' is certainly apt in this remote corner of the country.

This region has long been inextricably associated with poets, artists and writers. Not surprisingly, it was this beautiful countryside that inspired William Wordsworth, Samuel Taylor Coleridge, Arthur Ransome and Robert Southey. Born in the Cumbrian town of Cockermouth, Wordsworth and his sister Dorothy moved to Dove Cottage in Grasmere in 1799. Their annual rent was £5. The poet later moved to Rydal Mount in Ambleside, a family home with a 4-acre garden and a charming setting on the banks of Rydal Water. Today, both Dove Cottage and Rydal Mount are among the most visited of all the Lake District attractions. Another house with strong literary links is Hill Top, the 17th-century farmhouse home of Beatrix Potter who moved here in 1905. Located near Windermere, Hill Top and its surroundings sparked Potter's imagination and she painstakingly reproduced much of what she saw and cherished in her charming book illustrations. Tom Kitten, Samuel Whiskers and Jemima Puddleduck were all created here and the success of the 2006 film about Potter's life has introduced her extraordinary work to new audiences.

Walkers are spoilt for choice in Cumbria and the Lake District. The 70-mile Cumbria Way follows the valley floors rather than the mountain summits, while the 190-mile Coast to Coast has just about every kind of landscape and terrain imaginable. The route, pioneered by the well-known fell walker and writer Alfred Wainwright, cuts across the Lake District, the Yorkshire Dales and the North York Moors, spanning the width of England between St Bees on the Cumbrian west coast, and Robin Hood's Bay on the North Yorkshire and Cleveland Heritage Coast. The region is also popular with cyclists and there are a great many cycle hire outlets and plenty of routes available.

As with any popular scenic region of the country, the Lake District has an abundance of attractions but there are plenty of places within its boundaries and outside them where you can experience peace, tranquillity and a true sense of solitude. The southern half of Cumbria is often overlooked in favour of the more obvious attractions of the region. The Lune Valley, for example, remains as lovely as it was when Turner came here to paint. In the 19th century, writer John Ruskin described the view from 'The Brow', a walk running behind Kirkby Lonsdale's parish church, as 'one of the loveliest scenes in England.'

The Cumbrian coast is also one of the county's secret gems. Overlooking the Solway Firth and noted in the area for its wide cobbled streets and spacious green, the town of Silloth is one of the finest examples of a Victorian seaside resort in the north of England and yet outside Cumbria few people know its name. There are other historic towns along this coastline, including Whitehaven, Workington and Maryport. The Roman defences at Ravenglass are a reminder of the occupation, as is the Cumbrian section of Hadrian's Wall where it follows the county's northern coast. Well worth a visit is the ancient and historic city of Carlisle. Once a Roman camp – its wall still runs north of the city – it was captured during the Jacobean rising of 1745. The cathedral dates back to the early 12th century.

◁ Lake Windermere

CUMBRIA

AMBLESIDE
Map 18 NY30

Places to visit

The Armitt Museum & Library, AMBLESIDE, LA22 9BL, 015394 31212
www.armitt.com

Beatrix Potter Gallery, HAWKSHEAD, LA22 0NS, 015394 36355
www.nationaltrust.org.uk/beatrix-potter-gallery-and-hawkshead

Platinum Park

Skelwith Fold Caravan Park
▶▶▶▶▶

tel: 015394 32277 **LA22 0HX**
email: info@skelwith.com **web:** www.skelwith.com
dir: *From Ambleside on A593 towards Coniston, left at Clappersgate onto B5286 (Hawkshead road). Site 1 mile on right.*

In the grounds of a former mansion, this park is in a beautiful setting close to Lake Windermere. Touring areas are dotted in paddocks around the extensively wooded grounds, and the all-weather pitches are set close to the many facility buildings; the premium pitches are quite superb. There is a five-acre family recreation area, which has spectacular views of Loughrigg Fell. Two excellent safari tents and four S-pods are for hire.

Open: March to 15 November **Last arrival:** dusk **Last departure:** noon
Pitches: 🚐 🚍 🏠; 130 hardstanding pitches; 30 seasonal pitches
Leisure: 🎠 ⛳ 🎯 ⚽ **Facilities:** 🛁 ☉ 🚿 ☀ ⚕ 🛍 🍴 🏕 🧺 WiFi
Services: 🔌 🗑 🚮 ⛽ 🔥 🛒 🗑 Ⓣ
Within 3 miles: ♨ 🏌 ♻ ◎ 🚣 ⛸ 📅

Additional site information: 130 acre site. 🐾 Cars can be parked by caravans. Awnings permitted.

Glamping available: Safari tents, S-pods

The Croft Caravan & Campsite
▶▶▶▶ 81%

tel: 015394 36374 **North Lonsdale Road, Hawkshead LA22 0NX**
email: enquiries@hawkshead-croft.com
dir: *From B5285 in Hawkshead turn into site opposite main public car and coach park.*

In the historic village of Hawkshead, which is a popular destination for Beatrix Potter fans, this former working farm has a large tent and touring field, bordering a beck and the sound of running water and birdsong are welcome distractions. Most pitches are fully serviced with water, electricity, TV hook-up and waste water disposal. The smart amenity block provides family bathrooms. In an adjoining field there are stylish wood-clad lodges.

Open: March to January **Last arrival:** 20.30 **Last departure:** noon
Pitches: 🚐 🚍 🏕; 26 hardstanding pitches
Leisure: 🎣 **Facilities:** 🛁 ☉ 🚿 ☀ ♿ 🧺 WiFi
Services: 🔌 🗑 🚮
Within 3 miles: ♻ 🛍

Additional site information: 5 acre site. 🐾 Dogs must be kept on a lead at all times. Cars can be parked by caravans and tents. Awnings permitted. No noise 23.00–07.00.

Hawkshead Hall Farm
▶▶▶ 82%

tel: 015394 36221 **Hawkshead LA22 0NN**
email: enquiries@hawksheadhall-campsite.co.uk
web: www.hawksheadhall-campsite.co.uk
dir: *From Ambleside take A593 signed Coniston, then B5286 signed Hawkshead. Site signed on left just before Hawkshead. Or from Coniston take B5285 to T-junction. Left, then 1st right into site.*

A lovely site that is situated on a working Lakeland farm in a perfect location for those looking for an active holiday in the heart of one of the most beautiful parts of the Lake District National Park. The campsite lies just 10 minutes away, by foot, from the small attractive village of Hawkshead; a path has been created to enable guests to walk safely off-road into the village to shop or explore. There are pitches for tourers and for tents, and this busy site has very good amenities, with spotlessly clean, well-appointed toilets and a spacious, comfortable TV room, with free WiFi.

Open: March to January **Last arrival:** 21.00 **Last departure:** noon
Pitches: * 🚐 from £25; 🚍 from £25; 🏕 from £20
Leisure: 🖵
Facilities: 🛁 ☉ 🚿 ☀ WiFi
Services: 🔌 🗑
Within 3 miles: ♻ ♨ 🚣 ⛸ 🛍

Additional site information: 3 acre site. 🐾 Dogs must be kept on a lead at all times. Cars can be parked by caravans and tents. Awnings permitted. No noise 23.00–07.00.

Low Wray National Trust Campsite
▶▶▶ 80%

tel: 015394 32733 & 32039 **Low Wray LA22 0JA**
email: campsite.bookings@nationaltrust.org.uk **web:** www.ntlakescampsites.org.uk
dir: *3 miles southwest of Ambleside on A593 to Clappersgate, then B5286. Approximately 1 mile left at Wray sign. Site approximately 1 mile on left.*

Set picturesquely on the wooded shores of Lake Windermere, this site is a favourite with tenters and watersport enthusiasts. The toilet facilities are housed in wooden cabins, and tents can be pitched in wooded glades with lake views or on open grassland; here there are wooden camping pods and a mini-reservation of tipis and solar-heated bell tents, in conjunction with third-party companies. In partnership with Quest 4 Adventure, the site provides many outdoor activities that are available for families (bookable during school holidays). Fresh bread is baked daily on site, and opposite the reception there is a rustic, covered area with a pizza oven. The site is accessible to campervan and small motorhomes only; caravans are not accommodated.

Open: week before Easter to October **Last arrival:** variable **Last departure:** 11.00
Pitches: 🚍 🏕 🏠
Leisure: 🎯
Facilities: 🛁 ☉ 🚿 ☀ ♿ 🛍 🏕
Services: 🗑 🛒 ♻
Within 3 miles: ♻ ◎ 🚣 ⛸ 📅

Additional site information: 10 acre site. 🐾 Awnings permitted. No groups larger than 4 unless a family group with children. No noise between 23.00–07.00. Launching area for sailing craft, canoes, paddle boards for hire, orienteering course. Freshly baked pastries, bacon butties, tea and coffee available.

Glamping available: 2 safari tents. **Changeover days:** Friday and Monday
Additional glamping information: Safari tents: minimum stay 3 nights.

LEISURE: 🏊 Indoor swimming pool 🏊 Outdoor swimming pool 🎠 Children's playground 🧒 Kids' club 🎾 Tennis court 🎱 Games room 🖵 Separate TV room
⛳ golf course 🏌 Pitch n putt 🚣 Boats for hire 🚲 Bikes for hire 🎬 Cinema 🎭 Entertainment 🎣 Fishing ◎ Mini golf 🏄 Watersports 🏋 Gym 🏅 Sports field ♻ Stables
FACILITIES: 🛁 Baths/Shower ☉ Electric shaver sockets 🚿 Hairdryer ☀ Ice Pack Facility 🍼 Baby facilities ♿ Disabled facilities 🛍 Shop on site or within 200yds
🔥 BBQ area 🍴 Picnic area WiFi WiFi

APPLEBY-IN-WESTMORLAND
Map 18 NY62

Places to visit

Acorn Bank Garden and Watermill, TEMPLE SOWERBY, CA10 1SP, 017683 61893
www.nationaltrust.org.uk/acorn-bank

Great for kids: Wetheriggs Animal Rescue, BARNARD CASTLE, DL12 9TY,
01833 627444, www.wetheriggsanimalrescue.co.uk

Premier Park

Wild Rose Park

▶▶▶▶▶ 82%

tel: 017683 51077 **Ormside CA16 6EJ**
email: reception@wildrose.co.uk **web:** www.harrisonholidayhomes.co.uk
dir: *In Burrells on B6260 (between Appleby and Hoff) follow site signs.
Left, site signed.*

Situated in the Eden Valley, this large leisure group-run park has been carefully
landscaped and offers superb facilities maintained to an extremely high
standard, including four wooden wigwams for hire. There are several individual
pitches, and extensive views from most areas of the park. Traditional stone walls
and the planting of lots of indigenous trees help the site to blend into the
environment; wildlife is actively encouraged. There is a stylish reception with
adjacent internet café, the Pennine View bar with slate floor and pub games
(and where dogs are welcome) and a choice of adults-only and family
entertainment rooms have all been added. Please note, tents are not accepted.

Open: All year (restricted service: November to March – shop closed, restaurant
has reduced hours. Pool closed 6 September to 27 May) **Last arrival:** 22.00
Last departure: 11.00

Pitches: 🚐 🚍 🏠; 140 hardstanding pitches

Leisure: 🏊 🎣 🏓 🎵 🎯

Facilities: 🏪 ☺ 🅿 ✳ ⚲ 🛉 WiFi

Services: 🔌 🗄 🍴 🍽 🏪 🎫 ⚓ 🔒 🐾 🚾

Within 3 miles: 🎣 🏌

Additional site information: 85 acre site. 🐾 No dangerous dogs. Cars can be parked
by caravans. Awnings permitted. No unaccompanied teenagers, no group bookings, no
noise after 22.30.

Glamping available: Wooden wigwams. **Changeover days:** Friday

BARROW-IN-FURNESS

Places to visit

The Dock Museum, BARROW-IN-FURNESS, LA14 2PW, 01229 876400
www.dockmuseum.org.uk

Furness Abbey, BARROW-IN-FURNESS, LA13 0PJ, 01229 823420
www.english-heritage.org.uk/daysout/properties/furness-abbey

Great for kids: South Lakes Safari Zoo, DALTON-IN-FURNESS, LA15 8JR,
01229 466086, www.safarizoo.co.uk

BARROW-IN-FURNESS
Map 18 SD26

South End Caravan Park

▶▶▶▶ 84%

tel: 01229 472823 **Walney Island LA14 3YQ**
email: enquiries@secp.co.uk **web:** www.walneyislandcaravanpark.co.uk
dir: *M6 junction 36, A590 to Barrow, follow signs for Walney Island. Cross bridge, turn
left. Site 6 miles south.*

A friendly family-owned and run park next to the sea and close to a nature reserve,
on the southern end of Walney Island. It offers an extensive range of quality
amenities including an adult lounge, and high standards of cleanliness and
maintenance.

Open: March to October (restricted service: March to Easter and October – pool closed)
Last arrival: 22.00 **Last departure:** noon

Pitches: 🚐 🚍; 15 hardstanding pitches; 34 seasonal pitches

Leisure: 🏊 🎱 🎣 ⚲

Facilities: 🏪 ☺ ✳ ⚲ WiFi

Services: 🔌 🗄 🍴 🏪 🎫 🔒 🐾 🚾

Within 3 miles: 🎣 🏌 ♻ ⛳

Additional site information: 7 acre site. 🐾 Cars can be parked by caravans. Awnings
permitted. Bowling green, snooker table.

PITCHES: 🚐 Caravans 🚍 Motorhomes 🏕 Tents 🏠 Glamping accommodation **SERVICES:** 🔌 Electric hook-up 🗄 Launderette 🍴 Licensed bar
🔒 Calor Gas 🐾 Campingaz 🚾 Toilet fluid 🍽 Café/Restaurant 🏪 Fast Food/Takeaway 🎫 Battery charging ⚓ Motorhome service point
* 2019 prices 💳 No credit or debit cards 🐕 Dogs permitted 🚫 No dogs

BEWALDETH — Map 18 NY23

Places to visit

Mirehouse, KESWICK, CA12 4QE, 017687 72287
www.mirehouse.com

Wordsworth House and Garden, COCKERMOUTH, CA13 9RX, 01900 824805
www.nationaltrust.org.uk/wordsworthhouse

Great for kids: Lake District Wildlife Park, BASSENTHWAITE, CA12 4RD,
017687 76239, www.lakedistrictwildlifepark.com

Premier Park

Keswick Reach Lodge Retreat
▶▶▶▶▶ 93% HOLIDAY HOME PARK

tel: 01768 766510 **Bewaldeth CA13 9SY**
email: reception@keswickreach.co.uk **web:** www.keswickreach.co.uk
dir: Signed from A591, south of Bothel.

This retreat was opened in 2016, and the creative architecture and landscaping transformed a former caravan and camping site into a must-visit destination for lovers of wildlife and outdoor activities. The stylish one to four-bedroom lodges are very well spaced and angled to create optimum privacy and have stunning views; some are designated as pet friendly. An ornamental lake and areas that attract wildlife have been created, and the only distractions are running water and birdsong. The unique slate- and local stone-built activities centre houses a smart reception, shop, a stylish bar and brasserie and a well-equipped spa with treatments, sauna, gym and hot tub.

Open: All year

Holiday Homes: Two-ring burner Dishwasher Washing Machine Tumble dryer Microwave Freezer TV Sky/Freeview DVD player WiFi Linen included Towels included Electricity included Gas included Woodburner

Leisure: Spa

Additional site information:

BOWNESS-ON-WINDERMERE

See Windermere

CARLISLE

Places to visit

Lanercost Priory, BRAMPTON, CA8 2HQ, 01697 73030
www.english-heritage.org.uk/daysout/properties/lanercost-priory

Tullie House Museum & Art Gallery Trust, CARLISLE, CA3 8TP, 01228 618718
www.tulliehouse.co.uk

CARLISLE — Map 18 NY35

Green Acres Caravan Park
▶▶▶▶ 89%

tel: 01228 675418 & 07720 343820 **High Knells, Houghton CA6 4JW**
email: info@caravanpark-cumbria.com **web:** www.caravanpark-cumbria.com
dir: M6 junction 44, A689 east towards Brampton for 1 mile. Left at Scaleby sign. Site 1 mile on left.

A small, adults-only touring park in rural surroundings close to the M6 with distant views of the fells. A convenient stopover, this pretty park is run by keen, friendly owners who maintain high standards throughout. The site has a caravan and motorhome pressure-washer area, a field and woodland dog walk and two superb unisex shower rooms which include a toilet and wash basin.

Open: April to October **Last arrival:** 20.00 **Last departure:** noon

Pitches: from £19; from £19; from £14; 35 hardstanding pitches; 17 seasonal pitches

Leisure: **Facilities:** **Services:** **Within 3 miles:**

Additional site information: 3 acre site. Adults only. Cars can be parked by caravans and tents. Awnings permitted. No group bookings. Woodland walk (joins public footpath).

CARTMEL — Map 18 SD37

Places to visit

Holker Hall & Gardens, HOLKER, LA11 7PL, 015395 58328
www.holker.co.uk

Hill Top, NEAR SAWREY, LA22 0LF, 015394 36269
www.nationaltrust.org.uk/hilltop

Great for kids: Lakes Aquarium, LAKESIDE, LA12 8AS, 015395 30153
www.lakesaquarium.co.uk

Greaves Farm Caravan Park
▶▶▶ 83%

tel: 015395 36587 **Field Broughton LA11 6HR**
email: info@greavesfarmcaravanpark.co.uk **web:** www.greavesfarmcaravanpark.co.uk
dir: M6 junction 36, A590 signed Barrow. Approximately 1 mile before Newby Bridge, turn left at end of dual carriageway signed Cartmel and Holker. Site 2 miles on left just before church.

A small family-owned park close to a working farm in a peaceful rural area. Motorhomes are parked in a paddock which has spacious hardstandings, and there is a large field for tents and caravans. This basic park is carefully maintained, offers electric pitches (6amp), and there is always a sparkle to the toilet facilities. Static holiday caravans are available for hire. (Please note, sat nav (including Garmin Camper) directions should not be used for accessing this site; follow directions given here).

Open: March to October **Last arrival:** 21.00 **Last departure:** noon

Pitches: from £19; from £19; from £19; 9 hardstanding pitches

Facilities: **Services:** **Within 3 miles:**

Additional site information: 3 acre site. Cars can be parked by caravans and tents. Awnings permitted. Couples and families only. No open fires, no noise after 22.30. Separate chalet for dishwashing, small freezer and fridge available.

CROOKLANDS
Map 18 SD58

Places to visit

Levens Hall, LEVENS, LA8 0PD, 015395 60321
www.levenshall.co.uk

RSPB Leighton Moss & Morecambe Bay Nature Reserve, SILVERDALE, LA5 0SW, 01524 701601, www.rspb.org.uk/leightonmoss

Waters Edge Caravan Park
▶▶▶▶ 84%

tel: 015395 67708 **LA7 7NN**
email: stay@watersedgecaravanpark.co.uk **web:** www.watersedgecaravanpark.co.uk
dir: M6 junction 36, A65 towards Kirkby Lonsdale, at 2nd roundabout follow signs for Crooklands and Endmoor. Site 1 mile on right at Crooklands garage, just after 40mph limit.

A truly lovely site bordered by streams and woodland. Despite being an oasis of calm, the site is just a short distance from the M6 and is ideal either as a stopover or for longer stays. There is a wonderful reception that shares space with a small shop, behind which is a comfortable bar. The pitches are excellent and very well maintained, as are the spotlessly clean toilets.

Open: March to 14 November (restricted service: low season – bar may be closed on weekdays) **Last arrival:** 22.00 **Last departure:** noon

Pitches: 🚐 🚙 ▲; 26 hardstanding pitches, 10 seasonal pitches

Leisure: ♦ ⬜ **Facilities:** 🏚 ☺ ⸮ ✳ ♿ 🛒 🚻 🏛 WiFi

Services: 🔌 🗑 🍴 🛢 🚰 ⊤

Within 3 miles: ⚡ ∪

Additional site information: 3 acre site. 🐕 Cars can be parked by caravans. Awnings permitted. No noise after midnight.

CUMWHITTON
Map 18 NY55

Places to visit

Lanercost Priory, BRAMPTON, CA8 2HQ, 01697 73030
www.english-heritage.org.uk/daysout/properties/lanercost-priory

Cairndale Caravan Park
▶▶▶ 72%

tel: 01768 896280 **CA8 9BZ**
dir: Exit A69 at Warwick Bridge on unclassified road through Great Corby to Cumwhitton, left at village sign, site 1 mile.

Lovely grass site set in the tranquil Eden Valley with good views to distant hills. The all-weather touring pitches have electricity, and are located close to the immaculately maintained toilet facilities. Static holiday caravans for hire.

Open: March to October **Last arrival:** 22.00

Pitches: * 🚐 from £18; 🚙 from £18; 5 hardstanding pitches

Facilities: 🏚 ☺ ✳ **Services:** 🔌 🛢

Within 3 miles: ↓ ⚡ ≋ ⋝

Additional site information: 2 acre site. 🐕 🚫 Cars can be parked by caravans. Awnings permitted.

FLOOKBURGH
Map 18 SD37

Places to visit

Holker Hall & Gardens, HOLKER, LA11 7PL, 015395 58328
www.holker.co.uk

Premier Park

Lakeland Leisure Park
▶▶▶▶▶ 88% HOLIDAY CENTRE

tel: 01539 558556 **Moor Lane LA11 7LT**
email: lakeland@haven.com **web:** www.haven.com/lakeland
dir: On B5277 through Grange-over-Sands to Flookburgh. Left at village square, site in 1 mile.

A leisure park with full range of activities and entertainment, making this flat, grassy site ideal for families. The touring area, which includes 24 fully-serviced pitches, is quietly situated away from the main amenities, but the swimming pools and evening entertainment are just a short stroll away. In addition to a choice of takeaway food options, the stylish Lakeside Bay bar/bistro serves a wide range of hot and cold dishes and also features a section dedicated to the memory of Arthur Wainwright. There is an adventure trail, aerial adventure activities and a lake offering non-motorised watersports.

Open: mid March to end October (restricted service: mid March to May and September to October – reduced activities, outdoor pool closed) **Last arrival:** anytime **Last departure:** 10.00

Pitches: 🚐 🚙 ▲; 24 hardstanding pitches

Leisure: ≋ ≈ 🎡 ✋ 🏊 ↓ 🎵 ☺

Facilities: 🏚 ☺ ⸮ ✳ ♿ 🛒 🚻 🏛 🐾 WiFi

Services: 🔌 🗑 🍴 🍽 🚰 🛢 ⊤

Within 3 miles: ⚡ ∪ ◎ ≋

Additional site information: 105 acre site. 🐕 Maximum 2 dogs per booking, certain dog breeds banned. No commercial vehicles, no bookings by persons under 21 years unless a family booking.

GREAT LANGDALE — Map 18 NY20

Places to visit

Hardknott Roman Fort, BOOT
www.english-heritage.org.uk/daysout/properties/hardknott-roman-fort

The Armitt Museum & Library, AMBLESIDE, LA22 9BL, 015394 31212
www.armitt.com

Great Langdale National Trust Campsite

►►► 80%

tel: 015394 32733 & 37668 **LA22 9JU**
email: campsite.bookings@nationaltrust.org.uk
web: www.nationaltrust.org.uk/features/great-langdale-campsite
dir: *From Ambleside, A593 to Skelwith Bridge, right onto B5343, approximately 5 miles to New Dungeon Ghyll Hotel. Site on left 500 metres after hotel.*

Situated in arguably the Lake District's loveliest dale, sheltered by mature trees and surrounded by stunning fell views, this site is an ideal base for campers, climbers and fell walkers. The large grass tent area includes hardstandings for campervans and small motorhomes. There is a separate area for groups, and one for families that has a children's play area. Attractive wooden cabins house the toilets, the reception and shop (selling fresh baked bread and pastries) and drying rooms. There are wooden camping pods, and in conjunction with third-party companies, there are also yurts and tipis for hire. It is a gentle 10-minute walk to The Sticklebarn Tavern, the only National Trust run pub.

Open: All year **Last departure:** 11.00

Pitches: 🚌 ⛺ 🛖

Leisure: 🛝 🚲

Facilities: 🛁 ⊙ ✱ ♿ 🛍

Services: 🔌 🧺 🔒 🍃

Within 3 miles: 🎣

Additional site information: 9 acre site. 🐕 Awnings permitted. No noise between 23.00–07.00, no groups of 4 or more unless a family with children. Freshly baked pastries, bacon butties, tea and coffee available daily.

Additional glamping information: Wooden pods, yurts and tipis.

HOLMROOK

Places to visit

Great for kids: Ravenglass & Eskdale Railway, RAVENGLASS, CA18 1SW, 01229 717171, www.ravenglass-railway.co.uk

HOLMROOK — Map 18 SD09

Seven Acres Caravan Park

►►► 78%

tel: 01946 822777 **CA19 1YD**
email: reception@seacote.com **web:** www.sevenacrespark.co.uk
dir: *Site signed on A595 between Holmrook and Gosforth.*

This sheltered park is close to quiet west Cumbrian coastal villages and beaches, and also handy for Eskdale and Wasdale. There is a good choice of pitches, some with hedged bays for privacy and some with coastal views. The park has a heated toilet block.

Open: All year **Last arrival:** 21.00 **Last departure:** 10.00

Pitches: 🚐 from £21; 🚌 from £21; ⛺ from £10; 20 hardstanding pitches

Facilities: 🛁 ⊙ ⛱ **Services:** 🔌 🧺

Within 3 miles: ⛳ 🎣 🐴 ◎ 🛍

Additional site information: 7 acre site. 🐕 Cars can be parked by caravans and tents. Awnings permitted.

KESWICK — Map 18 NY22

Places to visit

The Derwent Pencil Museum, KESWICK, CA12 5NG, 017687 73626
www.pencilmuseum.co.uk

Honister Slate Mine, BORROWDALE, CA12 5XN, 017687 77230
www.honister.com

Great for kids: Mirehouse, KESWICK, CA12 4QE, 017687 72287
www.mirehouse.com

Premier Park

Castlerigg Hall Caravan & Camping Park

►►►►► 91%

tel: 017687 74499 **Castlerigg Hall CA12 4TE**
email: info@castlerigg.co.uk **web:** www.castlerigg.co.uk
dir: *1.5 miles southeast of Keswick on A591, turn right at sign. Site 200 metres on right after Heights Hotel.*

Situated in the heart of the Lake District with truly breathtaking views across Derwentwater to Catbells and other well-known Lakeland fells, this really is a superb location for anyone interested in exploring the area on foot, bike or by vehicle. As well as superb toilet blocks and pitches there is a well-stocked shop and an excellent indoor campers' kitchen. In addition there are pods and caravans for hire. There is outstanding quality across all aspects of the operation.

Castlerigg Hall Caravan & Camping Park

Open: mid March to 7 November **Last arrival:** 21.00 **Last departure:** 11.30

Pitches: 🚐 🚑 🛖 🏕; 68 hardstanding pitches

Leisure: 🏓 ⛳ **Facilities:** 📷 😊 🚱 ✳ ♿ 🅂 WiFi

Services: 🔌 🛢 🔋 ⛽ 💧 🚿 🅃

Within 3 miles: 🎣 ⚓ ⤳ ◎ 🛥 🚣 🗓

Additional site information: 8 acre site. 🐕 Dogs must not be left unattended. Cars can be parked by caravans and tents. Awnings permitted. No noise after 22.30. Campers' kitchen, sitting room, gallery. Car hire can be arranged.

Glamping available: Wooden pods.

Additional glamping information: Standard pods sleep 2 adults and 1 child; Family pods sleep 2 adults and 2 children; Castle pods sleep 2 adults and 2 children (no pets permitted). Maximum of 2 dogs permitted in standard and family pods. Cars can be parked by pods.

See advert below

Burns Farm Caravan Park
►►► 77%

tel: 017687 79225 & 79112 **St Johns in the Vale CA12 4RR**
email: linda@burns-farm.co.uk **web:** www.burns-farm.co.uk
dir: *Exit A66 signed Castlerigg Stone Circle, Youth Centre and Burns Farm. Site on right in 0.5 mile.*

Just a short distance from the A66, Burns Farm is in an excellent location for those wishing to explore the northern area of the beautiful Lake District National Park. Some of England's most iconic mountains, Blencathra and Skiddaw, are a short distance from the site as is the 4000-year-old Castlerigg Stone Circle with its spectacular views. The amenity block is of a very high standard, with modern spotlessly clean toilets, a laundry and covered pot-wash area. The pitches are all on level grass with good drainage; touring pitches have electric hook-up as do eight of the pitches in the tent field.

Open: March to 4 November **Last departure:** noon (peak season)

Pitches: 🚐 🚑 🛖

Facilities: 📷 😊 ✳ ♿ 🪑 WiFi

Services: 🔌 🛢 🔋 🔋

Within 3 miles: 🎣 ⚓ ⤳ ◎ 🛥 🚣 🗓 🅂

Additional site information: 2.5 acre site. 🐕 🐕 Cars can be parked by caravans and tents. Awnings permitted. No noise after midnight.

KIRKBY LONSDALE	Map 18 SD67

Places to visit

Sizergh, SIZERGH, LA8 8AE, 015395 60951
www.nationaltrust.org.uk/sizergh

Premier Park

Woodclose Caravan Park
▶▶▶▶▶ 89%

tel: 015242 71597 **High Casterton LA6 2SE**
email: info@woodclosepark.com **web:** www.woodclosepark.com
dir: *On A65, 0.25 mile after Kirkby Lonsdale towards Skipton, park on left.*

A peaceful, well-managed park set in idyllic countryside within the beautiful Lune Valley, and centrally located for exploring the Lakes and Dales. Ideal for that 'back to nature' experience, with riverside walks, on-site woodland walks for both families and dogs, and top notch amenity blocks with fully serviced cubicles with one allocated for the Glamping Pod village and camping field. The generous pitches are surrounded by mature trees and seasonal planting. Parts of the site are havens for wildlife.

Open: March to early November **Last arrival:** 21.00 (no arrivals before 13.00) **Last departure:** noon

Pitches: 🚐 from £18.50; 🚙 from £18.50 🏠; 20 hardstanding pitches; 22 seasonal pitches

Leisure: ⚙ ⚽

Facilities: 🛁 ☉ 🦱 ✳ ♿ 🆂 🛎 🌳 🐾 WiFi

Services: 🔌 🗑 ⬇ 🛢 🧴

Within 3 miles: 🎣 ⚲ ∪

Additional site information: 9 acre site. 🐾 Cars can be parked by caravans. Awnings permitted. Crock boxes for hire. Car hire can be arranged.

Glamping available: 10 wooden pods.

Additional glamping information: 2 night minimum stay. Selection of pods, some dog friendly, some fully en suite.

New House Caravan Park
▶▶▶▶ 82%

tel: 015242 71590 **LA6 2HR**
email: colinpreece9@aol.com
dir: *1 mile southeast of Kirkby Lonsdale on A65, turn right into site entrance 300 yards after Whoop Hall Inn.*

Colourful floral displays greet new arrivals, creating an excellent first impression at this former farm, which has been carefully changed to provide well-spaced pitches, with hardstandings sheltered by surrounding mature trees and shrubs. An ideal base for exploring the Yorkshire Dales and the Lake District.

Open: All year **Last arrival:** 21.00 **Last departure:** noon

Pitches: * 🚐 from £18; 🚙 from £18; 50 hardstanding pitches

Facilities: 🛁 ☉ 🦱 ✳ ♿ WiFi

Services: 🔌 🗑 🛎 ⬇ 🛢 🧴 ⊤

Within 3 miles: 🎣 ⚲ 🆂

Additional site information: 3 acre site. 🐾 🐕 Cars can be parked by caravans. Awnings permitted. No cycling.

MEALSGATE	Map 18 NY24

Places to visit

Jennings Brewery Tour and Shop, COCKERMOUTH, CA13 9NE, 01900 820362
www.jenningsbrewery.co.uk

Wordsworth House and Garden, COCKERMOUTH, CA13 9RX, 01900 824805
www.nationaltrust.org.uk/wordsworthhouse

Larches Caravan Park
▶▶▶▶ 84%

tel: 016973 71379 **CA7 1LQ**
dir: *On A595 (Carlisle to Cockermouth road).*

This over 18s-only park is set in wooded rural surroundings on the fringe of the Lake District National Park. Touring units are spread out over two sections. The friendly family-run park offers constantly improving facilities, including a well-stocked shop that also provides a very good range of camping and caravanning spares.

Open: March to October (restricted service: in early and late season) **Last arrival:** 21.30 **Last departure:** noon

Pitches: 🚐 from £21.90; 🚙 from £21.90; ⛺ from £17.50; 30 hardstanding pitches

Facilities: 🛁 ☉ 🦱 ✳ ♿ 🆂

Services: 🔌 🗑 🛎 🛢 🧴 ⊤

Within 3 miles: 🎣 ⚲ ∪

Additional site information: 20 acre site. Adults only. 🐾 🐕 Cars can be parked by caravans and tents. Awnings permitted.

MILNTHORPE	Map 18 SD48

Places to visit

RSPB Leighton Moss & Morecambe Bay Nature Reserve, SILVERDALE, LA5 0SW, 01524 701601, www.rspb.org.uk/leightonmoss

Levens Hall, LEVENS, LA8 0PD, 015395 60321
www.levenshall.co.uk

Hall More Caravan Park
▶▶▶▶ 81%

tel: 01524 781453 & 784221 **Hale LA7 7BP**
email: enquiries@pureleisure-holidays.co.uk **web:** www.pureleisure-holidays.co.uk
dir: *M6 junction 35, A6 towards Milnthorpe for 4 miles. Left at Lakeland Wildlife Oasis, follow brown signs.*

Major investment in the last couple of years has enhanced the facilities and improved standards on this long-established holiday destination, which is set on former meadowland and surrounded by mature trees. This rural park provides neat, well-spaced pitches with colourful hedged areas and pretty seasonal flowers. The site is adjacent to a fishery where fly-fishing for trout is possible, and a farm with stables that offers pony trekking is nearby. There are seven wooden camping pods for hire.

Open: March to January **Last arrival:** 22.00 **Last departure:** 10.00

Pitches: 🚐 🚙 🏠; 7 hardstanding pitches

Leisure: 🎣 🐎

LEISURE: 🏊 Indoor swimming pool 🏊 Outdoor swimming pool ⚙ Children's playground 👦 Kids' club ⚲ Tennis court 🎱 Games room ▭ Separate TV room 🎣 golf course 🏌 Pitch n putt ⛵ Boats for hire 🚲 Bikes for hire ⊟ Cinema 🎵 Entertainment 🎣 Fishing ⊙ Mini golf 🏄 Watersports 🏋 Gym 🏵 Sports field ∪ Stables
FACILITIES: 🛁 Baths/Shower ☉ Electric shaver sockets 🦱 Hairdryer ✳ Ice Pack Facility 🍼 Baby facilities ♿ Disabled facilities 🆂 Shop on site or within 200yds 🛎 BBQ area 🌳 Picnic area WiFi WiFi

Facilities: ☺ ⚑ ☀

Services: ⊞ 🗑 🍽 ⚒ 🛢 🧴

Within 3 miles: ⚓ 🎣 ∪ ⑊

Additional site information: 4 acre site. 🐕 Cars can be parked by caravans. Awnings permitted.

Glamping available: Wooden pods.

NETHER WASDALE   Map 18 NY10

Places to visit

Ravenglass & Eskdale Railway, RAVENGLASS, CA18 1SW, 01229 717171
www.ravenglass-railway.co.uk

Hardknott Roman Fort, BOOT,
www.english-heritage.org.uk/daysout/properties/hardknott-roman-fort

---

Church Stile Farm & Holiday Park
►►►►   82%

tel: 01946 726252 **Church Stile CA20 1ET**
email: info@churchstile.com **web:** www.churchstile.com
dir: *M6 junction 36, (follow signs for Western Lakes) A590, A5092, A595 (towards Whitehaven). In Gosforth follow Nether Wasdale signs. Pass 2 pubs. Site immediately after church.*

A superb secluded park surrounded by mature trees, hedging and Lakeland-stone walls in a peaceful valley setting. The combination of indigenous trees and plants creates stunning displays to complement the beauty of the surrounding hills. A renowned farm shop with a wide range of local produce is situated within the stylish reception and café. The site offers two shepherd's huts, a bell tent and pods for hire.

Open: March to 15 October **Last arrival:** 21.00 **Last departure:** 11.00

Pitches: 🚌 from £15; ▲ from £9; 🏠 see prices below; 16 hardstanding pitches

Leisure: ⚑ ☉   **Facilities:** 🏢 ☺ ⚑ ☀ ⅋ 🗑 🚻 ⛱ 🚐 WiFi

Services: ⊞ 🗑 🍽 ⚒ 🧴   **Within 3 miles:** 🎣 🚣

Additional site information: 10 acre site. 🐕 Cars can be parked by tents. Awnings permitted. No noise after 23.00. Picnic tables, table tennis, woodland walk.

Glamping available: Shepherd's hut from £160; bell tent from £35; pods from £45.
Changeover days: Friday, Saturday, Monday

Additional glamping information: Shepherd's huts: price for 3 nights at weekend or 4 nights midweek. Bell tent: minimum stay 2 nights (3 nights on bank holiday weekends). Pods: minimum stay 2 nights. Cars can be parked by glamping units.

PATTERDALE   Map 18 NY31

Places to visit

Aira Force and Ullswater (NT), PENRITH, 017684 82067
www.nationaltrust.org.uk/aira-force-and-ullswater

Sykeside Camping & Caravan Park
►►►   81%

tel: 017684 82239 **Brotherswater CA11 0NZ**
email: info@sykeside.co.uk **web:** www.sykeside.co.uk
dir: *Direct access from A592 (Windermere to Ullswater road) at foot of Kirkstone Pass.*

A campers' delight, this family-run park is sited at the foot of Kirkstone Pass, under the 2,000ft Hartsop Dodd in a spectacular area with breathtaking views. The park has mainly grass pitches with a few hardstandings, and for those campers without a tent there is bunkhouse accommodation, yurts and tipis for hire. There's a small campers' kitchen and the bar serves breakfast and bar meals. There is abundant wildlife.

Open: All year **Last arrival:** 22.30 **Last departure:** 12.00

Pitches: 🚐 from £20; 🚌 from £20; ▲ from £15.75 🏠; 25 hardstanding pitches

Facilities: 🏢 ☺ ⚑ ☀ 🗑 🚻 ⛱ WiFi   **Services:** ⊞ 🗑 🍽 🍴 🛢 🔋 🧴 🍺

Within 3 miles: 🎣 🚣 🚶

Additional site information: 10 acre site. 🐕 Cars can be parked by caravans and tents. Awnings permitted. No noise after 23.00. Laundry and drying room.

Glamping available: 2 yurts; tipis. **Changeover days:** Monday and Friday

Additional glamping information: Yurts: available from March to November, sleep 6, minimum stay 3 nights. Cars can be parked by glamping units.

PITCHES: 🚐 Caravans   🚌 Motorhomes   ▲ Tents   🏠 Glamping accommodation   **SERVICES:** ⊞ Electric hook-up   🗑 Launderette   🍽 Licensed bar
🛢 Calor Gas   🧴 Campingaz   ⊤ Toilet fluid   🍴 Café/Restaurant   🍺 Fast Food/Takeaway   🔋 Battery charging   ⚒ Motorhome service point
* 2019 prices   🚫 No credit or debit cards   🐕 Dogs permitted   ⊗ No dogs

PENRITH
Map 18 NY53

Places to visit

Dalemain House & Gardens, DALEMAIN, CA11 0HB, 017684 86450
www.dalemain.com

Shap Abbey, SHAP, CA10 3NB, 0370 333 1181
www.english-heritage.org.uk/daysout/properties/shap-abbey

Great for kids: The Rheged Centre, PENRITH, CA11 0DQ, 01768 868000
www.rheged.com

Premier Park

Lowther Holiday Park
►►►►► 87%

tel: 01768 863631 **Eamont Bridge CA10 2JB**
email: alan@lowther-holidaypark.co.uk **web:** www.lowther-holidaypark.co.uk
dir: *3 miles south of Penrith on A6.*

A secluded natural woodland site with lovely riverside walks and glorious countryside all around. The park is home to a rare colony of red squirrels, and trout fishing is available on the two-mile stretch of the River Lowther which runs through it. A birdwatch scheme, with a coloured brochure, has been introduced, that invites guests to spot some of the 30 different species that can be seen on the park. Fully-serviced pitches are available.

Open: early March to mid November **Last arrival:** 22.00 **Last departure:** 22.00

Pitches: 🚐 🚃 ▲; 🏠 see prices below; 50 hardstanding pitches; 80 seasonal pitches

Leisure: 🎱 🎣 🎵 🎿 ⚽ **Facilities:** 🛁 ⊙ 🚿 ✳ ⟍ 🏪 🎪 🚙 WiFi

Services: 🚗 🔌 🍽 🍴 ⚙ 🧺 ⬇ 💧 ⟋ T **Within 3 miles:** 🎣 U ◎ ⛵ 🎠

Additional site information: 50 acre site. 🐾 Cars can be parked by caravans and tents. Awnings permitted. Families only. No commercial vehicles, rollerblades or skateboards, no cats.

Glamping available: Wooden pods from £38.

Additional glamping information: Cars can be parked by pods.

Flusco Wood
►►►► 87%

tel: 017684 80020 & 07818 552931 **Flusco CA11 0JB**
email: info@fluscowood.co.uk **web:** www.fluscowood.co.uk
dir: *From Penrith to Keswick on A66 turn right signed Flusco. Approximately 800 metres, up short incline to right. Site on left.*

Flusco Wood is set in mixed woodland with outstanding views towards Blencathra and the fells around Keswick. It combines two distinct areas, one of which has been designed specifically for touring caravans in neat glades with hardstandings, all within close proximity of the excellent log cabin-style toilet facilities. The abundant wildlife includes breeding red squirrels. 15 superb lodges are also for hire.

Open: 22 March to October **Last arrival:** 20.00 **Last departure:** noon

Pitches: 🚐 🚃; 36 hardstanding pitches; 20 seasonal pitches

Facilities: ⊙ 🚿 ✳ ⟍ 🏪 🎪 **Services:** 🚗 🔌 💧 T **Within 3 miles:** 🎠

Additional site information: 24 acre site. 🐾 Cars can be parked by caravans. Awnings permitted. Quiet site, not suitable for large groups. Internet access available.

PENTON
Map 21 NY47

Places to visit

Lanercost Priory, BRAMPTON, CA8 2HQ, 01697 73030
www.english-heritage.org.uk/daysout/properties/lanercost-priory

Twin Willows
►►► 80%

tel: 01228 577313 & 07850 713958 **The Beeches CA6 5QD**
email: davidson_b@btconnect.com
dir: *M6 junction 44, A7 signed Longtown, right into Netherby Street, 6 miles to Bridge Inn pub. Right then 1st left, site 300 yards on right.*

Located close to Longtown, Twin Willows is a spacious park in a rural location on a ridge overlooking the Scottish border. All facilities, including all-weather pitches, are of a high quality. The park is suited to those who enjoy being away-from-it-all yet at the same time like to explore the area's rich history. A seasonal marquee is erected to hold regular barbecue and hog roast parties.

Open: All year **Last arrival:** 22.00 **Last departure:** 10.00

Pitches: 🚐 🚃 ▲ 🏠; 16 hardstanding pitches; 10 seasonal pitches

Leisure: 🎿 ⚽ **Facilities:** 🛁 ⊙ 🚿 ✳ ⟍ 🏪 🎪 WiFi

Services: 🚗 🔌 🍴 🧺 ⬇ 💧 ⟋ T **Within 3 miles:** 🎣 U 🏪

Additional site information: 3 acre site. 🐾 Cars can be parked by caravans and tents. Awnings permitted.

Glamping available: Wooden pods. **Changeover days:** Saturday

Additional glamping information: Cars can be parked by wooden pods.

LEISURE: 🏊 Indoor swimming pool 🏊 Outdoor swimming pool 🎠 Children's playground 👋 Kids' club 🎾 Tennis court 🎱 Games room ⬜ Separate TV room
🎣 golf course ⛳ Pitch n putt ⛵ Boats for hire 🚲 Bikes for hire 🎬 Cinema 🎵 Entertainment 🎣 Fishing ◎ Mini golf 🏄 Watersports 🏋 Gym 🏟 Sports field ♨ Stables
FACILITIES: 🛁 Baths/Shower ⊙ Electric shaver sockets 🚿 Hairdryer ✳ Ice Pack Facility 🍼 Baby facilities ⟍ Disabled facilities 🏪 Shop on site or within 200yds
🎪 BBQ area 🍴 Picnic area WiFi WiFi

POOLEY BRIDGE

Map 18 NY42

Places to visit

Dalemain House & Gardens, DALEMAIN, CA11 0HB, 017684 86450
www.dalemain.com

Great for kids: The Rheged Centre, PENRITH, CA11 0DQ, 01768 868000
www.rheged.com

Premier Park

Park Foot Caravan & Camping Park

▶▶▶▶▶ 89% HOLIDAY CENTRE

tel: 017684 86309 **Howtown Road CA10 2NA**
email: holidays@parkfoottullswater.co.uk **web:** www.parkfoottullswater.co.uk
dir: *M6 junction 40, A66 towards Keswick, then A592 to Ullswater. Turn left for Pooley Bridge, right at church, right at crossroads signed Howtown. Alternatively from Penrith take A6 to Shap, then B5320 to Pooley Bridge, turn left towards Howton site 1 mile on left.*

A gorgeous location right beside Ullswater and the wonderful fells, this site is perfect for those that wish to explore the many paths in the area; there is a lovely walk from the park's shorefront to picturesque Pooley Bridge from where the Ullswater steamer departs. There is a range of excellent touring pitches for caravans, motorhomes and tents, with high quality amenities in each of the touring areas. Pony-trekking is possible from the site and electric bicycles are available for those who think the hills are just a bit too steep. With a well-stocked shop, a very good restaurant and bar, as well as entertainment for all the family, this site certainly is a high quality, family-owned holiday centre.

Open: March to October (restricted service: March to April and mid September to October – clubhouse open weekends only) **Last arrival:** 22.00 **Last departure:** noon

Pitches: 🚐 from £22; 🚌 from £22; ▲ from £15; 50 hardstanding pitches

Leisure: ⚒ ✋ 🏊 🎣 ▢ 🎱 ♫ ⌕ ⚽

Facilities: 🛁 ⊙ ⌁ ✳ ⚅ ⑤ 🗚 WiFi

Services: ⚡ ⑤ 🍽 †◉¹ 🏠 ⚞ ⚒ 🔋 ⌀ T

Within 3 miles: ∪ ⚞ ⚘

Additional site information: 40 acre site. 🐕 Families and couples only. Boat launch, pony-trekking, pool table, table tennis, kids' club in summer holidays.

Waterfoot Caravan Park

▶▶▶▶ 84%

tel: 017684 86302 **CA11 0JF**
email: bookings@waterfootpark.co.uk **web:** www.waterfootpark.co.uk
dir: *M6 junction 40, A66 for 1 mile, A592 for 4 miles, site on right before lake. (Note: do not leave A592 until site entrance; sat nav is not compatible).*

A quality touring park with neat, hardstanding pitches (most are fully serviced) in a grassy glade within the wooded grounds of an elegant Georgian mansion. The toilet facilities are clean and well maintained, and the lounge bar, with a separate family room, enjoys lake views. A path leads to Ullswater, and Dalemain House and Gardens, Pooley Bridge and Aira Force waterfall are all close by. Wooden wigwam pods and Hive Cabins (for two adults and two children) are available for hire. Please note that there is no access via Dacre.

Open: March to 14 November **Last arrival:** 21.30 **Last departure:** noon

Pitches: 🚐 from £17.30; 🚌 from £17.30; 🏠 see prices below; 32 hardstanding pitches

Leisure: ⚒ 🎣 ♫ ⊙ **Facilities:** 🛁 ⊙ ⌁ ✳ ⚅ ⑤ 🗚 ⚡ WiFi

Services: ⚡ ⑤ 🍽 🏠 ⚞ ⚒ 🔋 ⌀ T **Within 3 miles:** ⚓ ⌕ ∪ ◎ ⚞ ⚘ 目

Additional site information: 22 acre site. 🐕 Cars can be parked by caravans. Awnings permitted. No tents. Coffee lounge, fish and chips mobile unit (peak season only), table tennis, badminton nets, pool table. Car hire can be arranged.

Glamping available: Wooden wigwams from £58 **Changeover days:** Any day
Additional glamping information. Minimum stay 2 nights at weekends. Cars can be parked by wigwams.

PITCHES: 🚐 Caravans 🚌 Motorhomes ▲ Tents 🏠 Glamping accommodation **SERVICES:** ⚡ Electric hook-up ⑤ Launderette 🍽 Licensed bar
🔥 Calor Gas ⌀ Campingaz T Toilet fluid †◉¹ Café/Restaurant ⚞ Fast Food/Takeaway 🔋 Battery charging ⚒ Motorhome service point
* 2019 prices ⊗ No credit or debit cards 🐕 Dogs permitted ⊗ No dogs

SILLOTH

Map 18 NY15

Places to visit

RSPB Campfield Marsh, BOWNESS-ON-SOLWAY, CA7 5AG, 01697 351330
www.rspb.org.uk/reserves-and-events/reserves-a-z/campfield-marsh

Premier Park

Stanwix Park Holiday Centre

▶▶▶▶▶ 92% HOLIDAY CENTRE

tel: 016973 32666 **Greenrow CA7 4HH**
email: enquiries@stanwix.com **web:** www.stanwix.com
dir: *1 mile southwest on B5300. From A596 (Wigton bypass), follow signs to Silloth on B5302. In Silloth follow signs to site, approximately 1 mile on B5300.*

A large well-run family park within easy reach of the Lake District. Attractively laid out, with lots of amenities to ensure a lively holiday, including a 4-lane automatic, 10-pin bowling alley, and a choice of indoor and outdoor swimming pools. There are excellent touring areas with hardstandings, one in a peaceful glade well away from the main leisure complex, a campers' kitchen and clean,

well-maintained toilet facilities. Four camping pods are available to hire in Skiddaw touring field.

Stanwix Park Holiday Centre

Open: All year (restricted service: closed 25-26 December for tourers; November to February (except New Year) – no entertainment, shop closed) **Last arrival:** 21.00
Last departure: 11.00

Pitches: ⊞ from £22.10; ⊞ from £22.10; ▲ from £22.10; ⌂ see prices below; 95 hardstanding pitches; 28 seasonal pitches

Leisure: ⌂ ⛱ ⩜ ✋ ⬡ ⬟ ⬜ ⬢ ⬟ ♫ ⬡ Spa

Facilities: ⬛ ⊙ ✳ ⬠ ⑤ ⬜ ⬟ WiFi

Services: ⬢ ⬜ ⬟ ⬛ ⑩ ⬜ ⬟ ⬜ T

Within 3 miles: ⬟ ⬡ ◎

Additional site information: 26 acre site. ⬟ Families only. Amusement arcade, bowling alley, leisure centre.

Glamping available: Wooden pods from £30. **Changeover days:** Any day

Additional glamping information: Wooden pods sleep 4. Pet friendly pods available. No charge for pets. Own camping equipment required. Cars can be parked by pods.

See advert below

LEISURE: ⬡ Indoor swimming pool ⛱ Outdoor swimming pool ⩜ Children's playground ⬟ Kids' club ⬟ Tennis court ⬢ Games room ⬜ Separate TV room ⬟ golf course ⬟ Pitch n putt ⬟ Boats for hire ⬟ Bikes for hire ⬟ Cinema ♫ Entertainment ⬟ Fishing ◎ Mini golf ⬟ Watersports ⬟ Gym ⬟ Sports field ⬟ Stables
FACILITIES: ⬛ Baths/Shower ⊙ Electric shaver sockets ⬟ Hairdryer ✳ Ice Pack Facility ⬟ Baby facilities ⬠ Disabled facilities ⑤ Shop on site or within 200yds ⬟ BBQ area ⬟ Picnic area WiFi WiFi

Hylton Caravan Park

►►►► 88%

tel: 016973 32666 **Eden Street CA7 4AY**
email: enquiries@stanwix.com **web:** www.stanwix.com
dir: *On entering Silloth on B5302 follow signs for site, approximately 0.5 mile on left, at end of Eden Street.*

A smart, modern touring park with excellent toilet facilities including several bathrooms. This high quality park is a sister site to Stanwix Park, which is just a mile away and offers all the amenities of a holiday centre, which are available to Hylton tourers.

Open: March to November **Last arrival:** 21.00 **Last departure:** 11.00

Pitches: 🚐 from £21.40; 🚌 from £21.40; ⛺ from £21.40; 23 hardstanding pitches; 20 seasonal pitches

Leisure: 🛝

Facilities: 🛁 ☺ ♿ WiFi

Services: 🔌 🧺 🚰

Within 3 miles: ⛳ 🎣 ◎ [$]

Additional site information: 18 acre site. 🐕 Cars can be parked by caravans and tents. Awnings permitted. Families only. Use of facilities at Stanwix Park Holiday Centre.

ULVERSTON

Places to visit

The Dock Museum, BARROW-IN-FURNESS, LA14 2PW, 01229 876400
www.dockmuseum.org.uk

Furness Abbey, BARROW-IN-FURNESS, LA13 0PJ, 01229 823420
www.english-heritage.org.uk/daysout/properties/furness-abbey

Great for kids: South Lakes Safari Zoo, DALTON-IN-FURNESS, LA15 8JR, 01229 466086, www.safarizoo.co.uk

ULVERSTON — Map 18 SD27

Premier Park

Bardsea Leisure Park

►►►►► 89%

tel: 01229 584712 & 484363 **Priory Road LA12 9QE**
email: reception@bardsealeisure.co.uk **web:** www.bardsealeisure.co.uk
dir: *M6 junction 36, A590 towards Barrow. At Ulverston take A5087, site 1 mile on right.*

This attractively landscaped former quarry creates a quiet and very sheltered site; set on the southern edge of the town, it is convenient for both the coast and the Lake District. Many of the generously-sized pitches offer all-weather, full facilities. The superb amenity blocks provide excellent privacy. The site has a well-stocked caravan accessories shop. Please note, this site does not accept tents.

Open: All year **Last arrival:** 22.00 **Last departure:** noon

Pitches: 🚐 🚌; 83 hardstanding pitches; 50 seasonal pitches

Leisure: ⚽ **Facilities:** 🛁 ☺ 💨 ✱ ♿ [$] 🪑 WiFi

Services: 🔌 🧺 🍔 🔋 🚰 🛢 ⊘ [T]

Within 3 miles: ⛳ 🎣 U ⊟

Additional site information: 5 acre site. 🐕 Cars can be parked by caravans. Awnings permitted. No noise after 22.30.

WASDALE HEAD — Map 18 NY10

Places to visit

Muncaster Castle, RAVENGLASS, CA18 1RQ, 01229 717614
www.muncaster.co.uk

Wasdale Head National Trust Campsite

🛖

►►► 80%

tel: 015394 32733 & 01946 726220 **CA20 1EX**
email: lakescampsites@nationaltrust.org.uk **web:** www.ntlakescampsites.org.uk
dir: *From A595 north towards Whitehaven turn left at Gosforth; from Whitehaven south on A595 right at Holmrook for Santon Bridge, follow signs to Wasdale Head.*

This site is set in a remote and beautiful spot at Wasdale Head, under the stunning Scafell peaks at the head of the deepest lake in England. The clean, well-kept facilities are set centrally amongst open grass pitches and trees, where seven camping pods (including four family pods) and two Nordic-style tipis are also located. There are hardstandings for motorhomes and eight electric hook-ups for tents. A hot food van operates at weekends during the summer months. The renowned Wasdale Head Inn is close by.

Open: All year (restricted service: November to February – shop open reduced hours at weekends) **Last arrival:** 21.00 **Last departure:** 11.00

Pitches: 🚌 ⛺ 🛖; 10 hardstanding pitches

Facilities: 🛁 ☺ 💨 ✱ ♿ [$]

Services: 🔌 🧺 🍔 🔋 🛢 ⊘

Additional site information: 5 acre site. 🐕 No groups of more than 4 unless a family with children. Pop-up café at weekends. 3rd party outdoor activities by West Lake Adventure Ltd.

Glamping available: Wooden pods, tipis.

WATERMILLOCK Map 18 NY42

Places to visit

Aira Force and Ullswater (NT), PENRITH, 017684 82067
www.nationaltrust.org.uk/aira-force-and-ullswater

Dalemain House & Gardens, DALEMAIN, CA11 0HB, 017684 86450
www.dalemain.com

Premier Park

The Quiet Site 🛖

▶▶▶▶▶ 87%

tel: 07768 727016 **Ullswater CA11 0LS**
email: info@thequietsite.co.uk **web:** www.thequietsite.co.uk
dir: *M6 junction 40, A66 signed Workington. At next roundabout left onto A592 signed Ullswater. 5 miles (Ullswater on left), turn right at Brackenrigg Inn signed Bennethead. Approximately 1.5 miles to site on right.*

A lovely site with breathtaking views across Ullswater, and less than 20 minutes away by car there are access points to some of the best fell walking in the Lake District; maps of walks closer by are provided by the site including the 20-mile circular Ullswater Way that passes the impressive 20-metre high Aira Force. Caravans, motorhomes and tents enjoy very good level terraced pitches, and at the top of the site there are camping pods and comfortable 'Hobbit Holes' for hire. This is a site justifiably proud of its green credentials; they have a biomass boiler that heats all the water for their well-appointed toilet block. Free WiFi is available across the whole site, and there is also a popular bar.

Open: All year (restricted service: low season – bar may close on weekdays)
Last arrival: 21.00 **Last departure:** noon (or 11.00 for pods)

Pitches: * 🚐 from £20; 🚌 from £20; ⛺ from £20; 🛖 see prices below; 60 hardstanding pitches; 15 seasonal pitches

Leisure: 🎱 📺 🚲 ⚽

Facilities: 🔌 💨 ❄ ♿ [$] ⛱ [WiFi]

Services: ⚡ 🌀 🍷 🛒 🍳 ⬇ 🛢 🍃 [T]

Within 3 miles: 🎣 🌊 ⛵

Additional site information: 10 acre site. 🐕 Cars can be parked by caravans and tents. Awnings permitted. Quiet from 22.00. Pool table, soft play area for toddlers, caravan storage. Car hire can be arranged.

Glamping available: Bell tents from £40; wooden pods from £40; hobbit houses from £70. **Changeover days:** Any day

Additional glamping information: Minimum stay – 2 nights at weekends. Cars can be parked by glamping units.

Ullswater Holiday Park 🛖

▶▶▶▶ 84%

tel: 017684 86666 **High Longthwaite CA11 0LR**
email: info@ullswaterholidaypark.co.uk **web:** www.ullswaterholidaypark.co.uk
dir: *M6 junction 40, A66 signed Workington. At next roundabout left onto A592 signed Ullswater. 5 miles. (Ullswater on left for 2 miles), turn right at phone box signed Longthwaite. Site 0.5 mile on right.*

A pleasant rural site with its own nearby boat launching and marine storage facility, making it ideal for sailors. The family-owned and run park enjoys fell and lake views, and there is a bar, a stylish café, a splendid undercover area for campers, and a shop on site. Many of the pitches are fully serviced and there are wooden cabins with barbecues. Please note that the Marine Park is one mile from the camping area.

Open: March to 14 November (restricted service: low season – bar open at weekends only)
Last arrival: 21.00 **Last departure:** noon

Pitches: 🚐 from £17; 🚌 from £17; ⛺ from £17; 🛖 see prices below; 58 hardstanding pitches

Leisure: 🛝 🎱

Facilities: 🛁 🔌 💨 ❄ ♿ [$] ⛱ [WiFi]

Services: ⚡ 🌀 🍷 🛒 🍳 🛢 🍃 [T]

Within 3 miles: 🎣 🐴 🌊 ⛵

Additional site information: 12 acre site. 🐕 Cars can be parked by caravans and tents. Awnings permitted. No open fires, no noise after 23.30. Boat launching and moorings in 1 mile.

Glamping available: Cabins from £37. **Changeover days:** Any day

Additional glamping information: Some cabins are dog friendly. Cars can be parked by cabins.

Cove Caravan & Camping Park

▶▶▶▶ 83%

tel: 017684 86549 **Ullswater CA11 0LS**
email: info@cove-park.co.uk **web:** www.cove-park.co.uk
dir: *M6 junction 40, A66 signed Workington. At next roundabout left onto A592 signed Ullswater. 5 miles (Ullswater on left), turn right at Brackenrigg Inn signed Bennethead. Approximately 1.5 miles to site on left.*

A peaceful family site in an attractive and elevated position with extensive fell views and glimpses of Ullswater Lake. Extensive ground works have been carried out in order to provide spacious, mostly level pitches. Pretty, seasonal flowers are planted amid the wide variety of mature trees and shrubs.

Open: March to October **Last arrival:** 21.00 **Last departure:** noon

Pitches: 🚐 from £20; 🚌 from £20; ⛺ from £15; 27 hardstanding pitches; 10 seasonal pitches

Leisure: 🛝

Facilities: 🛁 🔌 💨 ❄ ♿ 🍖 ⛱

Services: ⚡ 🌀 🛢 🍃

Within 3 miles: 🎣 🐴 🌊 ⛵ [$]

Additional site information: 3 acre site. 🐕 Cars can be parked by caravans and tents. Awnings permitted. No groups, no open fires, no noise after 22.30.

WINDERMERE

Map 18 SD49

Places to visit

Holehird Gardens, WINDERMERE, LA23 1NP, 015394 46008
www.holehirdgardens.org.uk

Blackwell The Arts & Crafts House, BOWNESS-ON-WINDERMERE, LA23 3JT,
015394 46139, www.blackwell.org.uk

Great for kids: Brockhole on Windermere, WINDERMERE, LA23 1LJ,
015394 46601, www.brockhole.co.uk

Premier Park

Park Cliffe Camping & Caravan Estate

▶▶▶▶▶ 91%

tel: 015395 31344 **Birks Road, Tower Wood LA23 3PG**
email: info@parkcliffe.co.uk **web:** www.parkcliffe.co.uk
dir: *M6 junction 36, A590. Right at Newby Bridge onto A592. 3.6 miles right into site.
(Note: due to difficult access from main road this is the only advised direction for
approaching the site).*

A lovely hillside park set in 25 secluded acres of fell land. The camping area is
sloping and uneven in places, but well drained and sheltered; some pitches
have spectacular views of Lake Windermere and the Langdales. The park offers
a high level of customer care and is very well equipped for families (family
bathrooms), and there is an attractive bar and brasserie restaurant serving
quality food; 10 wooden pods and three static holiday caravans are for hire.

Open: March to mid November (weekends and school holidays – facilities fully open)
Last arrival: 22.00 **Last departure:** noon

Pitches: 🚐 from £27; 🚍 from £27; ▲ from £21; 🏠 see prices below;
60 hardstanding pitches; 25 seasonal pitches

Leisure: 🎦 🔍 **Facilities:** 🛁 ☉ 🌁 ❋ ᴴ 🖇 🚻 🛒 WiFi
Services: 🔌 🗑 🍴 🍽 🛒 ⬆️ 🔋 🧴 Ⓣ **Within 3 miles:** ᴸ 🐾 ◎ ⛳ ♨ 🎏

Additional site information: 25 acre site. 🐕 Cars can be parked by caravans and
tents. Awnings permitted. No noise 23.00–07.30. Off licence, bathrooms for hire.

Glamping available: Wooden pods from £44. **Changeover days:** Any day

Additional glamping information: Different size pods available – standard (no beds,
sleeps 2); family (no beds, sleeps 2 adults and 3 children); premier (double bed, bunk
beds, trundle bed, sleeps 2 adults and 3 children). Cars can be parked by pods.

Premier Park

Hill of Oaks & Blakeholme

▶▶▶▶▶ 85%

tel: 015395 31578 **LA12 8NR**
email: enquiries@hillofoaks.co.uk **web:** www.hillofoaks.co.uk
dir: *M6 junction 36, A590 towards Barrow. At roundabout signed Bowness turn right
onto A592. Site approximately 3 miles on left.*

A secluded, heavily wooded park on the shores of Lake Windermere. Pretty
lakeside picnic areas, woodland walks and a play area make this a delightful
park that's perfect for families; there are excellent serviced pitches, a licensed
shop and a heated toilet block; both the ladies' and gents' amenities have
quality fittings and very good privacy options. There are very high spec pods
available for hire and WiFi is available throughout all areas of park. Watersport
activities include sailing and canoeing, with private jetties for boat launching.
The private pier provides a regular ferry service to Bowness.

Open: March to 14 November (restricted service: Christmas and New Year – self
catering only) **Last departure:** noon

Pitches: 🚐 from £19.50; 🚍 from £19.50; 🏠 see prices below;
46 hardstanding pitches

Leisure: 🎦 🐾 ◎
Facilities: 🛁 ☉ 🌁 ❋ ᴴ 🖇 🚻 WiFi
Services: 🔌 🗑 ⬆️ 🔋 Ⓣ
Within 3 miles: ᴸ ∪ ◎ ⛳ ♨ 🎏

Additional site information: 31 acre site. 🐕 Cars can be parked by caravans.
Awnings permitted. No tents (except trailer tents), no groups. Daily lake cruise in peak
season – Lakeside Pier connections to Ambleside and Bowness on Windermere. Car
hire can be arranged.

Glamping available: 5 lakeside glamping pods from £295.

Changeover days: Monday, Friday

Additional glamping information: Wooden pods sleep 4. Minimum stay 3 nights. Each
pod has underfloor heating, TV, shower, toilet, sofa bed, table, chairs, patio furniture
and a kitchen with two-ring cooker, microwave and fridge. Towels and linen are
included. Cars can be parked by pods.

PITCHES: 🚐 Caravans 🚍 Motorhomes ▲ Tents 🏠 Glamping accommodation **SERVICES:** 🔌 Electric hook-up 🗑 Launderette 🍴 Licensed bar
🛒 Calor Gas ⊘ Campingaz Ⓣ Toilet fluid 🍽 Café/Restaurant 🛒 Fast Food/Takeaway 🔋 Battery charging ⬆️ Motorhome service point
* 2019 prices 🚫 No credit or debit cards 🐕 Dogs permitted ⊗ No dogs

DERBYSHIRE

BAKEWELL
Map 16 SK26

Places to visit

Chatsworth, CHATSWORTH, DE45 1PP, 01246 565300
www.chatsworth.org

Greenhills Holiday Park
▶▶▶▶ 84%

tel: 01629 813052 & 813467 **Crowhill Lane DE45 1PX**
email: info@greenhillsholidaypark.co.uk **web:** www.greenhillsholidaypark.co.uk
dir: *1 mile northwest of Bakewell on A6. Signed before Ashford-in-the-Water, onto unclassified road on right.*

A well-established park set in lovely countryside within the Peak District National Park. Many pitches enjoy uninterrupted views, and there is easy access to all facilities, including the spotlessly clean amenity blocks. This site includes an excellent area with 52 hardstanding pitches, that has great views. The clubhouse, shop and children's playground are popular features.

Open: February to November (restricted service: February to April and October to November – bar and shop closed) **Last arrival:** 22.00 **Last departure:** noon
Pitches: 🚐 🚗 ▲; 85 hardstanding pitches; 50 seasonal pitches **Leisure:** 🎠 ⚽
Facilities: 🛁 ⊙ 🌣 ❄ ⅙ 🔥 🍴 WiFi **Services:** 🔌 🗑 🗑 🍴 ⬆ ⬇ 🔒 🌿 T
Within 3 miles: ⅃ ✎ ↻ ◎

Additional site information: 8 acre site. 🐾 Cars can be parked by caravans and tents. Awnings permitted.

BIRCHOVER
Map 16 SK26

Places to visit

Haddon Hall, HADDON HALL, DE45 1LA, 01629 812855
www.haddonhall.co.uk

The Heights of Abraham, MATLOCK BATH, DE4 3PD, 01629 582365
www.heightsofabraham.com

Barn Farm Campsite
▶▶▶▶▶ 84%

tel: 01629 650245 **Barn Farm DE4 2BL**
email: gilberthh@msn.com **web:** www.barnfarmcamping.com
dir: *From A6 take B5056 towards Ashbourne. Follow brown signs to site.*

An interesting park on a former dairy farm with the many and varied facilities housed in high quality conversions of old farm buildings. The three large and well-maintained touring fields offer sweeping views across the Peak District National Park. There is an excellent choice of privacy cubicles, including shower and washbasin cubicles, a fully serviced family room, and even a shower and sauna. There are five stylish, self-catering camping barns for hire.

Open: April to October **Last arrival:** 21.00 **Last departure:** 11.00
Pitches: 🚐 🚗 ▲; 13 hardstanding pitches
Leisure: 🎠 🔍 ⬜ ⚽
Facilities: 🛁 ⊙ 🌣 ❄ ⅙ 🔥 🍴
Services: 🔌 🗑 🍴 🔒 🌿 T
Within 3 miles: ⅃ ✎ ↻ ◎ ⅃ ⅃

Additional site information: 15 acre site. 🐾 Cars can be parked by caravans and tents. Awnings permitted. No music after 22.30, minimum noise 22.30–07.00. Vending machines, sauna, sunbed. Internet access available.

BUXTON
Map 16 SK07

Places to visit

Poole's Cavern (Buxton Country Park), BUXTON, SK17 9DH, 01298 26978
www.poolescavern.co.uk

Great for kids: Go Ape Buxton, BUXTON, SK17 9DH, 01603 895500
www.goape.co.uk/buxton

Lime Tree Park
▶▶▶▶ 91%

tel: 01298 22988 **Dukes Drive SK17 9RP**
email: info@limetreeparkbuxton.com **web:** www.limetreeparkbuxton.com
dir: *1 mile south of Buxton, between A515 and A6.*

A very attractive and well-designed site, set on the side of a narrow valley in an elevated location, with separate, neatly landscaped areas for statics, tents, touring caravans and motorhomes. There's good attention to detail throughout including the clean toilets and showers, an excellent motorhome service point, and WiFi is free of charge. Its backdrop of a magnificent old railway viaduct and views over Buxton and the surrounding hills, make this a sought-after destination. There are eight static caravans, a pine lodge and two apartments available for holiday lets.

LEISURE: 🏊 Indoor swimming pool 🏊 Outdoor swimming pool 🎠 Children's playground 🎣 Kids' club 🎾 Tennis court 🎱 Games room 📺 Separate TV room ⅃ golf course 🏌 Pitch n putt ⛵ Boats for hire 🚲 Bikes for hire 🎬 Cinema 🎵 Entertainment 🎣 Fishing ◎ Mini golf 🚤 Watersports 🏋 Gym ♻ Sports field ↻ Stables
FACILITIES: 🛁 Baths/Shower ⊙ Electric shaver sockets 🌣 Hairdryer ❄ Ice Pack Facility 👶 Baby facilities ⅙ Disabled facilities 🏪 Shop on site or within 200yds 🍴 BBQ area 🍴 Picnic area WiFi WiFi

Open: March to October **Last arrival:** 18.00 **Last departure:** noon

Pitches: 🚐 from £25; 🚍 from £25; ⛺ from £18; 22 hardstanding pitches

Leisure: 🎱 🎣 🎪

Facilities: 📷 ⊙ 🚿 ☀ ♿ 🏧 WiFi

Services: 🔌 🗄 🧺 🔋 🛒 ⊘ 🅣

Within 3 miles: 🎿 ∪ ⊚ 🚴

Additional site information: 10.5 acre site. 🐕 Cars can be parked by caravans and tents. Awnings permitted. No noise after 22.00, no fires.

Beech Croft Farm
▶▶▶▶ 90%

tel: 01298 85330 **Beech Croft, Blackwell in the Peak SK17 9TQ**
email: mail@beechcroftfarm.co.uk **web:** www.beechcroftfarm.co.uk
dir: Exit A6 midway between Buxton and Bakewell. Site signed.

A small terraced farm site with lovely Peak District views. There's a fine stone-built toilet block with ultra-modern fittings, underfloor heating and additional unisex facilities, hardstanding pitches, gravel roads, a campers' shelter, and a super tarmac pathway leading from the camping field to the toilet block. All the tent pitches have hook-up via a pre-payment card system. There's a boot, dog and bike wash, a campers' cabin with microwave and hot drinks machine, and the old phone box now houses a defibrillator. This makes an ideal site for those touring or walking in the Peak District.

Open: All year (restricted service: November to February – tents not accepted)
Last arrival: 20.00 **Last departure:** noon

Pitches: * 🚐 from £23; 🚍 from £23; ⛺ from £16; 30 hardstanding pitches

Leisure: 🎱 ⚽

Facilities: 📷 ⊙ ☀ ♿ 🏧 🍴 WiFi

Services: 🔌 🗄 ⚓ 🔋 ⊘ 🅣

Additional site information: 3 acre site. 🐕 Cars can be parked by caravans and tents. Awnings permitted. No noise after 22.00.

HOPE
Map 16 SK18

Pindale Farm Outdoor Centre
▶▶▶ 79%

tel: 01433 620111 **Pindale Road S33 6RN**
email: info@pindalefarm.co.uk **web:** www.pindalefarm.co.uk
dir: From A6187 in Hope follow Pindale sign between church and Woodroffe Arms. Site 1 mile on left.

Set around a 13th-century farmhouse and a former lead mine pump house (now converted to a self-contained bunkhouse for up to 60 people), this simple, off-the-beaten-track site is an ideal base for walking, climbing, caving and various outdoor pursuits. Around the farm are several deeply wooded areas available for tents, and old stone buildings that have been converted to house modern toilet facilities.

Open: March to October **Pitches:** ⛺ from £8

Facilities: 📷 ⊙ ☀ WiFi **Services:** 🔌 🗄

Within 3 miles: ∪ 🏧

Additional site information: 4 acre site. 🐕 Cars can be parked by tents. Awnings permitted. No anti-social behaviour, noise must be kept to minimum after 21.00, no fires. Charge for WiFi.

Lickpenny Caravan Site
▶▶▶▶ 92%

tel: 01629 583040 **Lickpenny Lane, Tansley DE4 5GF**
email: enquiries@lickpennycaravanpark.co.uk **web:** www.lickpennycaravanpark.co.uk
dir: From Matlock take A615 towards Alfreton for 3 miles. Site signed to left, into Lickpenny Lane, right into site near end of road.

A picturesque site in the grounds of an old plant nursery with areas broken up and screened by a variety of shrubs; there are spectacular views which are best enjoyed from the upper terraced areas. The pitches, several fully serviced, are spacious, well screened and well marked, and facilities are kept to a very good standard. The bistro/coffee shop is popular with visitors.

Open: All year **Last arrival:** 20.00 **Last departure:** noon (later departures until 17.00 – charges apply)

Pitches: 🚐 from £20; 🚍 from £20; 80 hardstanding pitches; 20 seasonal pitches

Leisure: 🎱

Facilities: 📷 ⊙ 🚿 ♿ 🏧 🍴 WiFi

Services: 🔌 🗄 🧺 ⚓ 🛒 🅣

Within 3 miles: 🎿 🎣 ∪ ⊚ 🚴

Additional site information: 16 acre site. 🐕 Cars can be parked by caravans. Awnings permitted. No noise after 23.00, 1 car per pitch. Child's bath available, woodland walk. Car hire can be arranged.

NEWHAVEN
Map 16 SK16

Places to visit

Haddon Hall, HADDON HALL, DE45 1LA, 01629 812855
www.haddonhall.co.uk

Newhaven Holiday Park
▶▶▶▶ 84%

tel: 01298 84300 **SK17 ODT**
email: hello@newhavenholidaypark.co.uk **web:** www.newhavenholidaypark.co.uk
dir: *Between Ashbourne and Buxton at junction of A515 and A5012.*

Pleasantly situated within the Peak District National Park, this park has mature trees screening the three touring areas. Very good toilet facilities cater for touring vans and a large tent field, and there's a restaurant adjacent to the site. The static caravans on the site are privately owned.

Open: March to October **Last arrival:** Sunday to Thursday 19.30, Friday 20.00
Last departure: noon

Pitches: 🚐 from £19; 🚎 from £19; ▲ from £15; 95 hardstanding pitches; 40 seasonal pitches

Leisure: 𝐀 🔍

Facilities: 🛁 ⊙ 🛖 ✶ 🗐 🍴 🏕

Services: 🚫 🔄 ⛽ 🔒 🧺 🚰 Ⓣ

Within 3 miles: 🛖 ∪ 🏊

Additional site information: 30 acre site. 🐕 Cars can be parked by caravans and tents. Awnings permitted. No noise after 23.00.

RIDDINGS
Map 16 SK45

Places to visit

Denby Pottery Village, DENBY, DE5 8NX, 01773 740799
www.denbypottery.com

Midland Railway Butterley, RIPLEY, DE5 3QZ, 01773 747674
www.midlandrailway-butterley.co.uk

Riddings Wood Caravan and Camping Park
▶▶▶▶ 85%

tel: 01773 605160 **Bullock Lane DE55 4BP**
email: info@riddingswoodcaravanandcampingpark.co.uk
web: www.riddingswoodcaravanandcampingpark.co.uk
dir: *M1 junction 27, A608 signed Heanor. Right onto B600 signed Alfreton and Selston. Left onto B6016 signed Jacksdale. Through Jacksdale towards Ridding. Site on right.*

Located close to both Derby and Nottingham, this site's layout can be described as a sloping amphitheatre. It is surrounded by the mature trees of Riddings Wood on all sides and has a fabulous panoramic view looking down towards Jacksdale. Beyond the sweeping driveway and security barrier, you'll find a smart chalet-style reception, neat gravel hardstandings, manicured grass tent pitches, and a modern and stylish amenity block with quality shower and toilet facilities. Picnic benches are scattered around the park for campers to use, and fully serviced pitches are available. Lodges, sleeping up to four people, are available for hire; exclusive use of a hot tub is included in the price. A local bus service runs every nine minutes from the site entrance to both Derby and Nottingham.

Open: March to December (for tourers) **Last arrival:** 22.00 **Last departure:** 11.30

Pitches: 🚐 from £23; 🚎 from £23; ▲ from £19; 26 hardstanding pitches; 4 seasonal pitches

Leisure: 𝐀 🎡

Facilities: 🛁 ⊙ 🛖 ✶ 🗐 🏕 🍴 WiFi

Services: 🚫 🔄 ⛽ 🚰 🔒

Within 3 miles: 🛖 ∪ 🏊

Additional site information: 11.5 acre site. 🐕 Dogs must be on a lead. Cars can be parked by caravans and tents. Awnings permitted. Children must be accompanied by an adult at all times. Rubbish must be placed in designated areas. No noise after 23.00.

RIPLEY
Map 16 SK35

Places to visit

Midland Railway Butterley, RIPLEY, DE5 3QZ, 01773 747674
www.midlandrailway-butterley.co.uk

Denby Pottery Village, DENBY, DE5 8NX, 01773 740799
www.denbypottery.com

Golden Valley Caravan & Camping Park

▶▶▶▶ 86%

tel: 01773 513881 & 746786 **Coach Road DE55 4ES**
email: enquiries@goldenvalleycaravanpark.co.uk
web: www.goldenvalleycaravanpark.co.uk
dir: *M1 junction 26, A610 to Codnor. Right at lights. Right into Alfreton Road. In 1 mile left into Coach Road, park on left. (Note: it is advisable to ignore sat nav for last few miles and follow these directions).*

This superbly landscaped park is set within 30 acres of woodland in the Amber Valley. The fully serviced pitches are set out in informal groups in clearings amongst the trees. The park has a cosy bar and bistro with outside patio, a fully-stocked fishing lake, an innovative and well-equipped play area, an on-site jacuzzi and fully-equipped fitness suite. There is also a wildlife pond and a nature trail; nine new camping pods are available for hire.

Open: All year (restricted service: low season – bar and café open, children's activities at weekends only) **Last arrival:** 20.00 (call site if later) **Last departure:** noon

Pitches: 🚐 from £22; 🚎 from £22; ▲ from £15; 🏠 see prices below; 45 hardstanding pitches; 12 seasonal pitches

Leisure: 𝐀 🔍 ▯ 🎣 🏌

Facilities: 🏪 ⊙ 🪃 ✳ ♿ 🖸 🎏 🏕 WiFi

Services: 🔌 🖸 🍺 🍽 🛒 🔋 ⚡ 🛢 🧴 Ⓣ

Within 3 miles: ⚓ ∪ ◎ ≒ 🎎

Additional site information: 30 acre site. 🐕 Cars can be parked by caravans and tents. Awnings permitted. No vehicles on grass, no open fires or disposable BBQs, no noise after 22.30. Zip slide, tractor train, log flume ride, bouncy castle, paddle boats, crazy golf, segways (high season only).

Glamping available: Wooden pod from £35; Wooden barrel pod from £70.

Additional glamping information: Wooden pod sleeps 2, wooden barrel pod sleeps 4. No dogs, no smoking, no fires. Own sleeping equipment and camping accessories required.

ROSLISTON   Map 10 SK21

Places to visit

Ashby-de-la-Zouch Castle, ASHBY-DE-LA-ZOUCH, LE65 1BR, 01530 413343
www.english-heritage.org.uk/daysout/properties/ashby-de-la-zouch-castle

Great for kids: Conkers, MOIRA, DE12 6GA, 01283 216633
www.visitconkers.com

Beehive Woodland Lakes
▶▶▶▶ 86%

tel: 01283 763981 **DE12 8HZ**
email: info@beehivefarm-woodlandlakes.co.uk
web: www.beehivefarm-woodlandlakes.co.uk
dir: *From A444 in Castle Gresley into Mount Pleasant Road. Follow Rosliston signs for 3.5 miles through Linton. Left at T-junction signed Beehive Farms.*

A small, informal and continually developing caravan area secluded from an extensive woodland park in the heart of the National Forest National Park. The toilet facilities include four family rooms. Young children will enjoy the playground, whilst anglers can pass many a happy hour fishing at the park's three lakes. There are also five camping pods available to hire.

Open: All year **Last arrival:** 20.00 (18.00 in low season) **Last departure:** noon

Pitches: 🔌 from £21; 🚐 from £21; 🏕 from £21; 🛖 see prices below; 46 hardstanding pitches; 18 seasonal pitches

Leisure: 🎱 ✎

Facilities: 🏪 ⊙ 🪃 ✳ ♿ 🖸 🏕 WiFi

Services: 🔌 🖸 🍽 🔋 🛢 🧴 Ⓣ

Within 3 miles: ⚓ ◎ 🎎

Additional site information: 2.5 acre site. 🐕 Cars can be parked by caravans and tents. Awnings permitted. Takeaway food delivered to site.

Glamping available: Wooden pods from £40.

Additional glamping information: Wooden pods sleep 4 (suitable for families). No pets. Cars can be parked by pods.

SHARDLOW   Map 11 SK43

Places to visit

Melbourne Hall & Gardens, MELBOURNE, DE73 8EN, 01332 862502
www.melbournehall.com

Shardlow Marina Caravan Park
▶▶▶ 75%

tel: 01332 792832 **London Road DE72 2GL**
email: admin@shardlowmarina.co.uk
dir: *M1 junction 24a, A50 signed Derby. Exit from A50 junction 1 at roundabout signed Shardlow. Site 1 mile on right.*

A large marina site with restaurant facilities, situated on the Trent and Merseyside Canal. Pitches are on grass surrounded by mature trees, and for the keen angler, the site offers fishing within the marina. The attractive grass touring area overlooks the marina.

Open: March to January **Last arrival:** 17.00 **Last departure:** noon

Pitches: 🔌 from £18; 🚐 from £18; 🏕 from £18; 26 hardstanding pitches; 10 seasonal pitches

Leisure: ✎

Facilities: 🏪 ⊙ ✳ 🖸 WiFi

Services: 🔌 🖸 🍺 🍽 🔋 🛢 🧴 Ⓣ

Within 3 miles: ⚓ ∪ ◎ ≒

Additional site information: 25 acre site. 🐕 Maximum of 2 dogs per unit, dogs must not be left unattended or tied up outside. Cars can be parked by caravans and tents. Awnings permitted. Office closed between 13.00–14.00.

PITCHES: 🔌 Caravans 🚐 Motorhomes 🏕 Tents 🛖 Glamping accommodation **SERVICES:** 🔌 Electric hook-up 🖸 Launderette 🍺 Licensed bar
🛢 Calor Gas 🧴 Campingaz Ⓣ Toilet fluid 🍽 Café/Restaurant 🛒 Fast Food/Takeaway 🔋 Battery charging ⚡ Motorhome service point
* 2019 prices 🚫 No credit or debit cards 🐕 Dogs permitted ⊗ No dogs

Devon

With magnificent coastlines, two historic cities and the world-famous Dartmoor National Park, Devon sums up all that is best about the British landscape. For centuries it has been a fashionable and much loved holiday destination – especially south Devon's glorious English Riviera.

When the crime writer Agatha Christie was born in Torquay on Devon's glorious south coast, the town was a popular seaside resort. It was 1890, the start of Queen Victoria's last decade as monarch, and Torquay was a fashionable destination for all sorts of people, those looking for a permanent home by the sea as well as holidaymakers in search of long hours of sunshine and a mild climate. In many ways, Torquay remains much the same today and its impressive setting still evokes a sense of its Victorian heyday. A local steam train attraction adds to the atmosphere; you can travel from Paignton to Dartmouth, alighting on the way at the small station at Churston, just as Hercule Poirot does in Christie's 1930s detective novel *The ABC Murders*. The Queen of Crime herself used this station when she had a summer home nearby. The house, Greenway, overlooks a glorious sweep of the River Dart and is now managed as a popular visitor attraction by the National Trust.

Close to the English Riviera lies Dartmoor, one of the south-west's most spectacular landscapes. The contrast between the traditional attractions of the coast and this expanse of bleak, brooding moorland could not be greater. The National Park, which contains Dartmoor, covers 365 square miles and includes many fascinating geological features – isolated granite tors and two summits exceeding 2,000 feet among them. Dartmoor's waterfalls, including the tumbling Whitelady Waterfall at Lydford Gorge, can be seen in full spate even in the depths of winter. Everywhere you venture on Dartmoor, there are stone circles, burial chambers and mysterious clues to the distant past. The place oozes antiquity. Sir Arthur Conan Doyle set his classic Sherlock Holmes story *The Hound of the Baskervilles* on Dartmoor, and Agatha Christie stayed at a local hotel for two weeks at the height of the First World War in order to finish

writing her first detective novel *The Mysterious Affair at Styles*, first published in 1920.

Not surprisingly, Dartmoor equates with walking and the opportunities are enormous. For something really adventurous, try the Two Moors Way. This long-distance route begins at Ivybridge and crosses the National Park to enter neighbouring Exmoor, which straddles the Devon/Somerset border. At Lynton and Lynmouth the trail connects with the South West Coast Path, which takes walkers on a breathtaking journey to explore north Devon's gloriously rugged coastline, renowned for its extraordinary collection of peaks and outcrops. Cycling in the two National Parks is also extremely popular and there is a good choice of off-road routes taking you to the heart of Dartmoor and Exmoor.

Devon's towns and cities offer a pleasing but stimulating alternative to the rigours of the countryside. There are scores of small market towns in the region – for example there is Tavistock with its popular farmers' market, one of many in the county. Plymouth lies in Devon's south-west corner and is a striking city and naval port. Much of its transformation over the years is a reminder of the devastation it suffered, together with Exeter, during the Second World War. The city places particular emphasis, of course, on the Spanish Armada and the voyage of the Pilgrim Fathers to America.

On the theme of sailing, Devon is synonymous with this most invigorating of boating activities. Salcombe, on the county's south coast, is a sailing playground. Situated on a tree-fringed estuary beneath lush rolling hills, the town thrives on boats – it hosts the week-long Salcombe Regatta in August. It's even suitable for swimming, with several sandy beaches and sheltered bays.

◁ Combe Martin Beach, Exmoor National Park

DEVON

ASHBURTON
Map 3 SX77

Places to visit

Compton Castle, COMPTON, TQ3 1TA, 01803 661906
www.nationaltrust.org.uk/comptoncastle

Great for kids: Prickly Ball Farm, NEWTON ABBOT, TQ12 6BZ, 01626 362319
www.pricklyballfarm.com

Parkers Farm Holiday Park
►►►► 88%

tel: 01364 654869 **Higher Mead Farm TQ13 7LJ**
email: parkersfarm@btconnect.com **web:** www.parkersfarmholidays.co.uk
dir: *From Exeter on A38, 2nd left after Plymouth sign (29 miles), signed Woodland and Denbury. From Plymouth on A38 take A383 Newton Abbot exit, turn right, across bridge, rejoin A38, then as above.*

A well-developed site terraced into rising ground with stunning views across rolling countryside to the Dartmoor tors. Part of a working farm, this park offers excellent fully serviced hardstanding pitches, which make the most of the fine views; it is beautifully maintained and has good quality toilet facilities, a popular games room and a bar/restaurant that serves excellent meals. Large family rooms with two shower cubicles, a large sink and a toilet are especially appreciated by families with small children. There are regular farm walks when all the family can meet and feed the various animals.

Open: Easter to end October (restricted service: low season – bar and restaurant open at weekends only) **Last arrival:** 22.00 **Last departure:** 10.00

Pitches: 🚐 from £15; 🚌 from £15; ▲ from £13; 20 hardstanding pitches

Leisure: 🅰 🖐 🔍 ▭ 🎵 ⊛

Facilities: 🛁 ⊙ 🗲 ✳ ⅋ 🖾 🍖 🎪 ⚡ WiFi

Services: 🗨 🔋 🍴 🍽 ⬆ 🎪 ⬇ 🔒 🅰 T

Within 3 miles: 🎣

Additional site information: 25 acre site. 🐾 Cars can be parked by caravans and tents. Awnings permitted. Large field available for dog walking.

River Dart Country Park
►►►► 88%

tel: 01364 652511 **Holne Park TQ13 7NP**
email: info@riverdart.co.uk **web:** www.riverdart.co.uk
dir: *M5 junction 31, A38 towards Plymouth. In Ashburton at Peartree junction follow brown site signs. Site 1 mile on left. (Note: Peartree junction is 2nd exit at Ashburton; do not exit at Linhay junction as narrow roads are unsuitable for caravans).*

Set in 90 acres of magnificent parkland that was once part of a Victorian estate, with many specimen and exotic trees, this peaceful, hidden-away touring park occupies several camping areas, all served with good quality toilet facilities. In spring, the park is a blaze of colour from the many azaleas and rhododendrons. There are numerous outdoor activities for all ages including abseiling, caving and canoeing, plus high quality, well-maintained facilities. The open moorland of Dartmoor is only a few minutes away.

Open: April to September (restricted service: low and mid season – reduced opening hours at shop and café bar) **Last arrival:** 21.00 **Last departure:** 11.00

Pitches: 🚐 from £16.50; 🚌 from £16.50; ▲ from £16.50; 34 hardstanding pitches

---

Leisure: 🅰 🖐 🔍 ⚽ 🎣

Facilities: 🛁 ⊙ 🗲 ✳ ⅋ 🖾 🍖 WiFi

Services: 🗨 🔋 🍴 🍽 ⬆ 🎪 ⬇ 🔒 🅰 T

Within 3 miles: ⅃ ∪

Additional site information: 90 acre site. 🐾 Dogs must be kept on leads at all times. Cars can be parked by caravans and tents. Awnings permitted. Adventure playground, dare devil activities, cycle track.

ASHILL
Map 3 ST01

Places to visit

Coldharbour Mill Working Wool Museum, UFFCULME, EX15 3EE, 01884 840960
www.coldharbourmill.org.uk

Leafy Fields Glamping
►►►► 80% GLAMPING ONLY

tel: 07842 320981 **Ingleton Farm, Ashill Moor EX15 3NP**
email: leafyfieldsglamping@yahoo.com **web:** www.leafyfieldsglamping.com
dir: *Phone for directions.*

Located in the small hamlet of Ashill in the Blackdown Hills, Leafy Fields is a very tranquil, well laid out and rural glamping site with a relaxing back-to-nature atmosphere and a good choice of accommodation. Two safari lodges, six bell tents and a shepherd's hut (new for 2018) are neatly arranged in a pleasant meadow with toilet and shower facilities close at hand in a converted stable block. The bell tents are fully equipped and have a small kitchen unit outside, and there are six toilets/showers allocated to each bell tent. The larger safari lodges sleep six, have a kitchen area and are very well equipped, plus they have en suite toilets and showers and an alfresco decking area. The interiors are well presented and there is an electric radiator in all units. The site maintenance is excellent and there is a small children's play area and a family room with a sensory playroom. Fire pits and logs are also available.

Open: All year (booking advisable: July to September) **Last arrival:** 18.00 **Last departure:** 11.00

Leisure: 🅰

Facilities: 🛁 ⊙ ⅋

Within 3 miles: ⑤

Accommodation available: Safari tents x 2; bell tents; shepherd's hut.

Additional site information: ⊗ Sensory play room, rainy day room. Cars can be parked by units.

AXMINSTER

Places to visit

Branscombe - The Old Bakery, Manor Mill and Forge, BRANSCOMBE, EX12 3DB, 01752 346585, www.nationaltrust.org.uk/branscombe

Allhallows Museum, HONITON, EX14 1PG, 01404 44966
www.honitonmuseum.co.uk

LEISURE: 🏊 Indoor swimming pool 🏊 Outdoor swimming pool 🅰 Children's playground 🖐 Kids' club ⅃ Tennis court 🔍 Games room ▭ Separate TV room
⅃ golf course ⅊ Pitch n putt ⛵ Boats for hire 🚲 Bikes for hire 🎬 Cinema 🎵 Entertainment 🎣 Fishing ◎ Mini golf 🏄 Watersports 🏋 Gym ⊛ Sports field ∪ Stables
FACILITIES: 🛁 Baths/Shower ⊙ Electric shaver sockets 🗲 Hairdryer ✳ Ice Pack Facility 🍼 Baby facilities ⅋ Disabled facilities ⑤ Shop on site or within 200yds
🍖 BBQ area 🧺 Picnic area WiFi WiFi

AXMINSTER
Map 4 SY29

Platinum Park

Hawkchurch Resort & Spa
▶▶▶▶ HOLIDAY HOME PARK

tel: 01297 678402 **Hawkchurch EX13 5UL**
email: reception@hawkchurchresort.co.uk **web:** www.hawkchurchresort.co.uk
dir: *From A35 between Axminster and Charmouth take B3165 signed Crewkerne. Left signed Hawkchurch.*

This superb park is located in lovely countryside near Axminster and the Jurassic Coast and enjoys views over the Axe Valley. The luxury lodges are fully equipped and have en suite facilities. There are excellent leisure facilities – the Ezina Spa offering a wide range of luxury treatments, plus a spa pool and gym. In addition, there is a good restaurant, The Beeches, as well as an alfresco eating and drinking area.

Open: All year

Holiday Homes: Sleep 8 Two-ring burner Dishwasher Washing Machine Tumble dryer Microwave Freezer TV Sky/Freeview DVD player WiFi Linen included Towels included Electricity included Gas included

Leisure: 🏊 🏌 Spa

Additional site information: 🐕

Andrewshayes Holiday Park
▶▶▶▶ 89%

tel: 01404 831225 **Dalwood EX13 7DY**
email: info@andrewshayes.co.uk **web:** www.andrewshayes.co.uk
dir: *3 miles from Axminster towards Honiton on A35, right at Taunton Cross signed Dalwood and Stockland. Site 150 metres on right.*

An attractive family park within easy reach of Lyme Regis, Seaton, Branscombe and Sidmouth in an ideal touring location. This popular park offers modern toilet facilities, a quiet, cosy bar and takeaway service, and an excellent play area for children that's set beside the swimming pool, bar and restaurant area. There are two camping pods for hire.

Open: 24 March to 3 November (restricted service: off-peak season – shop and bar reduced hours and takeaway availability limited) **Last arrival:** 22.00
Last departure: 10.30

Pitches: * 🚐 from £21.50; 🚍 from £21.50; ⛺ from £21.50; 🏠 see prices below; 105 hardstanding pitches; 100 seasonal pitches

Leisure: 🏊 🏌 🎣 ⚽
Facilities: 🏪 ⊙ 🍴 ✳ ♿ 🛁 🎍 🛒 WiFi
Services: 🔌 🗄 🍺 🍽 🍔 🧺 🔒 🚰
Within 3 miles: 🐾

Additional site information: 12 acre site. 🐕 Cars can be parked by caravans and tents. Awnings permitted. Children under 12 must be supervised by an adult in the pool. Table tennis, woodland walk.

Glamping available: Wooden pods from £50.

Additional glamping information: Wooden pods: minimum stay 2 nights, offer lighting, heater, kettle, electric sockets, BBQ, picnic table and private decking area. No dogs allowed. Cars can be parked by pods.

BERRYNARBOR
Map 3 SS54

Places to visit

Great for kids: Watermouth Castle & Family Theme Park, ILFRACOMBE, EX34 9SL, 01271 867474, www.watermouthcastle.com

Combe Martin Wildlife Park & Dinosaur Park, COMBE MARTIN, EX34 0NG, 01271 882486, https://cmwdp.co.uk

Mill Park Touring Caravan & Camping Park

▶▶▶ 87%

tel: 01271 882647 **Mill Lane EX34 9SH**
email: cnquiries@millpark.com **web:** www.millpark.com
dir: *M5 junction 27, A361 towards Barnstaple. Right onto A399 towards Combe Martin. At Sawmills Inn take turn opposite Berrynarbor sign.*

Under enthusiastic ownership, this well managed park is set in an attractive wooded valley with a stream that runs into a lake where coarse fishing is available. There is a quiet bar and restaurant with a family room, a very pleasant camping meadow, an excellent children's play area, and clean and tidy toilet facilities. The park has lakeside wooden pods (cocoons), wooden pods (glampods) and Lotus Belle tents for hire. The site is located two miles from Combe Martin and Ilfracombe and just a stroll across the road from the small harbour at Watermouth.

Open: March to October **Last arrival:** 21.00 **Last departure:** 10.00

Pitches: * 🚐 from £20; 🚍 from £20; ⛺ from £20; 🏠 see prices below; 20 hardstanding pitches; 40 seasonal pitches

Leisure: 🏌 🎣 🎮
Facilities: 🏪 ⊙ 🍴 ✳ ♿ 🛁 🎍 WiFi
Services: 🔌 🗄 🍺 🧺 🔋 🔒 🚰 🚰
Within 3 miles: ⛳ 🏌 🐎 🏊 🎣 🚶

Additional site information: 30 acre site. 🐕 Cars can be parked by caravans and tents. Awnings permitted. No open fires, no groundsheets/footprints under tents. Fresh coffee and croissants everyday, family bathroom, accessible wetroom.

Glamping available: Lotus Belle tents from £50; wooden cocoons from £40, wooden pods from £45.

Additional glamping information: Lotus Belle tents: no dogs allowed. Lotus Belle tents, wooden cocoons and wooden pods offer fridge, heater, kettle, light, electricity, BBQ and picnic table. Cars can be parked by glamping units.

PITCHES: 🚐 Caravans 🚍 Motorhomes ⛺ Tents 🏠 Glamping accommodation **SERVICES:** 🔌 Electric hook-up 🗄 Launderette 🍺 Licensed bar 🔋 Calor Gas 🚰 Campingaz 🚽 Toilet fluid 🍽 Café/Restaurant 🍔 Fast Food/Takeaway 🔋 Battery charging 🚐 Motorhome service point * 2019 prices 🚫 No credit or debit cards 🐕 Dogs permitted 🚫 No dogs

BRAUNTON
Map 3 SS43

Places to visit

Marwood Hill Gardens, BARNSTAPLE, EX31 4EA, 01271 342528
www.marwoodhillgarden.co.uk

Great for kids: Combe Martin Wildlife Park & Dinosaur Park, COMBE MARTIN,
EX34 0NG, 01271 882486
https://cmwdp.co.uk

Premier Park

Hidden Valley Park
▶▶▶▶▶ 91%

Best of British

tel: 01271 813837 **West Down EX34 8NU**
email: info@hiddenvalleypark.com **web:** www.hiddenvalleypark.com
dir: *Direct access from A361, 8 miles from Barnstaple and 2 miles from Mullacott Cross.*

A delightful, well-appointed family site set in a wooded valley, with superb toilet facilities and a café. The park is set in a very rural, natural location not far from the beautiful coast around Ilfracombe. The woodland is home to nesting buzzards and woodpeckers, and otters have taken up residence by the lake. WiFi is available. There are three fully equipped timber cabins for hire, and the Lakeside Restaurant and Bar serves good home-cooked meals.

Open: All year **Last arrival:** 21.00 **Last departure:** 10.30

Pitches: 🚐 🚍 ▲; 50 hardstanding pitches; 15 seasonal pitches

Leisure: 🎠

Facilities: 🛁 ⊙ 🅿 ✳ ⅋ 🛒 🍴 🅆🄸🄵🄸

Services: 🔌 🔲 🔌 🍴 ♨ ♒ 🛒 ⊘ 🅃

Within 3 miles: ↥ 🏌 ∪ ◎ 🤽 🄷

Additional site information: 32 acre site. 🐕 Cars can be parked by caravans and tents. Awnings permitted.

Lobb Fields Caravan & Camping Park
▶▶▶ 83%

tel: 01271 812090 **Saunton Road EX33 1HG**
email: info@lobbfields.com **web:** www.lobbfields.com
dir: *At crossroads in Braunton take B3231 towards Croyde. Site signed on right.*

Located between Braunton and the miles of golden sands at Saunton, this bright, tree-lined park with gently-sloping grass pitches is a dog-friendly site and offers 180 pitches in two areas. There are a number of seasonal pitches and caravan storage available. Apart from relaxing and enjoying the views in this UNESCO World Biosphere area, there's plenty of surfing and cycling to be had with the 30-mile Tarka Trail cycle route nearby.

Open: March to October **Last arrival:** 22.00 **Last departure:** 10.30

Pitches: * 🚐 from £16; 🚍 from £16; ▲ from £12; 12 hardstanding pitches; 18 seasonal pitches

Leisure: 🎠

Facilities: 🛁 ⊙ 🅿 ✳ ⅋ 🅆🄸🄵🄸

Services: 🔌 🔲 ♨ 🛒 ⊘ 🛒 ♒

Within 3 miles: ↥ 🏌 ∪ 🤽 🕼

Additional site information: 14 acre site. 🐕 Cars can be parked by caravans and tents. Awnings permitted. No under 18s unless accompanied by an adult, no fires, no noise after 23.00. Surfing boards and wet suits for hire, wet suit washing areas.

BRIDESTOWE
Map 3 SX58

Places to visit

Lydford Castle and Saxon Town, LYDFORD, EX20 4BH, 0370 333 1181
www.english-heritage.org.uk/daysout/properties/lydford-castle-and-saxon-town

Museum of Dartmoor Life, OKEHAMPTON, EX20 1HQ, 01837 52295
www.museumofdartmoorlife.org.uk

Bridestowe Caravan Park
▶▶▶ 77%

tel: 01837 861261 **EX20 4ER**
email: ali.young53@btinternet.com **web:** www.glebe-park.co.uk
dir: *Exit A30 at A386 and Sourton Cross junction, follow B3278 signed Bridestowe, left in 3 miles. In village centre, left onto unclassified road for 0.5 mile.*

A small, well-established park in a rural setting close to Dartmoor National Park. This mainly static park has a small, peaceful touring space, and there are many

LEISURE: 🏊 Indoor swimming pool 🏊 Outdoor swimming pool 🎠 Children's playground 👐 Kids' club 🎾 Tennis court 🎱 Games room 📺 Separate TV room
↥ golf course 🏌 Pitch n putt 🚣 Boats for hire 🚲 Bikes for hire 🎬 Cinema 🎵 Entertainment 🎣 Fishing ◎ Mini golf 🤽 Watersports 🏋 Gym 🏐 Sports field ∪ Stables
FACILITIES: 🛁 Baths/Shower ⊙ Electric shaver sockets 🅿 Hairdryer ✳ Ice Pack Facility 🍼 Baby facilities ⅋ Disabled facilities 🛒 Shop on site or within 200yds
🍴 BBQ area 🅿 Picnic area 🅆🄸🄵🄸 WiFi

activities to enjoy in the area including fishing and riding. Part of the National Cycle Route 27 (the Devon Coast to Coast) passes close to this park.

Open: March to December **Last arrival:** 22.30 **Last departure:** noon

Pitches: 🚐 🚌 ⛺; 3 hardstanding pitches

Leisure: 🎱

Facilities: 🛁 🪒 ❄ 🛒

Services: 🔌 🧺 🔋 🛢 🔥

Additional site information: 1 acre site. 🐕 ⊘💳 Cars can be parked by caravans and tents. Awnings permitted.

BRIDGERULE — Map 2 SS20

Places to visit

Penhallam Manor, WEEK ST MARY, EX22 6XW
www.english-heritage.org.uk/daysout/properties/penhallam-manor

Hedley Wood Caravan & Camping Park

►►► 87%

tel: 01288 381404 **EX22 7ED**
email: maria.damsell@hedleywood.co.uk **web:** www.hedleywood.co.uk
dir: *From Exeter take A30 to Launceston, B3254 towards Bude. Left into Tackbear Road signed Marhamchurch and Widemouth (at Devon, Cornwall border). Site on right.*

Set in a very rural location about four miles from Bude, this relaxed site has a peaceful, easy-going atmosphere. Pitches are in separate paddocks, some with extensive views, and this wooded park is quite sheltered in the lower areas. The restaurant/club house is a popular place to relax.

Open: All year (restricted service: except in main holidays – shop, bar and restaurant may be closed) **Last arrival:** anytime **Last departure:** anytime

Pitches: 🚐 🚌 ⛺; 30 hardstanding pitches; 29 seasonal pitches

Leisure: 🛝 🎱 📺

Facilities: 🛁 🪒 🚿 ❄ ♿ 🛒 ♨ 🪑 WiFi

Services: 🔌 🧺 🍷 🍴 🍔 🔋 ⛽ 🛢 🔥 [T]

Within 3 miles: ⛳ 🎣 🐎

Additional site information: 16.5 acre site. 🐕 Dog kennels, dog walk. Cars can be parked by caravans and tents. Awnings permitted. Nature trail and caravan storage.

BROADWOODWIDGER

Places to visit

Lydford Gorge, LYDFORD, EX20 4BH, 01822 820320
www.nationaltrust.org.uk/lydford-gorge

Launceston Steam Railway, LAUNCESTON, PL15 8DA, 01566 775665
www.launcestonsr.co.uk

Great for kids: Tamar Otter & Wildlife Centre, LAUNCESTON, PL15 8GW, 01566 785646, www.tamarotters.co.uk

BROADWOODWIDGER — Map 3 SX48

Roadford Lake

►►► 81%

tel: 01409 211507 **Lower Goodacre PL16 0JL**
email: info@swlakestrust.org.uk **web:** www.southwestlakes.co.uk
dir: *Exit A30 between Okehampton and Launceston at Roadford Lake signs, cross dam wall, site 0.25 mile on right.*

Located right at the edge of Devon's largest inland water, this popular rural park is well screened by mature trees and shrubs. There is an excellent watersports school for sailing, windsurfing, rowing and kayaking, with hire and day launch facilities. This is an ideal location for brown trout fly fishing.

Open: March to October **Last arrival:** late arrivals by prior arrangement
Last departure: 11.00

Pitches: 🚐 🚌 ⛺; 13 hardstanding pitches **Leisure:** 🎣

Facilities: 🛁 🪒 🚿 ❄ ♿ ♨ 🪑 WiFi **Services:** 🔌 🧺 🍴

Within 3 miles: 🌊 ⛵ 🛒

Additional site information: 3 acre site. 🐕 Cars can be parked by caravans and tents. Awnings permitted. Off-ground BBQs only, no open fires. Climbing wall, archery, high ropes, watersports.

BUCKFASTLEIGH — Map 3 SX76

Places to visit

Buckfast Abbey, BUCKFASTLEIGH, TQ11 0EE, 01364 645500
www.buckfast.org.uk

Great for kids: Buckfast Butterflies & Dartmoor Otter Sanctuary, BUCKFASTLEIGH, TQ11 0DZ, 01364 642916
www.ottersandbutterflies.co.uk

Churchill Farm Campsite

►► 90%

tel: 01364 642844 & 07977 113175 **TQ11 0EZ**
email: apedrick@btinternet.com **web:** www.churchillfarmcampsite.com
dir: *From A38 follow Buckfast Abbey signs. Pass Abbey entrance on right, at top of hill left into no-through road. Pass Abbey entrance, up hill, left at crossroads to site entrance opposite Holy Trinity Church.*

A working family farm in a relaxed and peaceful setting, with keen, friendly owners. Set on the hills above Buckfast Abbey, this attractive park is maintained to a good standard. The spacious pitches in the neatly trimmed paddock enjoy extensive country views towards Dartmoor, and the clean, simple toilet facilities include smart showers and a family room. This is a hidden gem for those who love traditional camping. Close to a local bus service and within walking distance of Buckfastleigh, the Abbey and the South Devon Steam Railway. This site is within a Site of Special Scientific Interest (SSSI).

Open: Easter to September **Last arrival:** 20.00 **Last departure:** noon

Pitches: * 🚐 from £14; 🚌 from £14; ⛺ from £14

Facilities: 🛁 🪒 ❄ ♿

Services: 🔌 🔋

Within 3 miles: 🛒

Additional site information: 3 acre site. 🐕 ⊘💳 Cars can be parked by caravans and tents. Awnings permitted. No ball games. BACS transfer possible. Internet access available.

BUCKFASTLEIGH *continued*

Beara Farm Caravan & Camping Site
► 85%

tel: 01364 642234 **Colston Road TQ11 0LW**
dir: *From Exeter take Buckfastleigh exit at Dart Bridge, follow South Devon Steam Railway and Butterfly Farm signs. 200 metres after South Devon Steam Railway entrance take 1st left into Old Totnes Road, 0.5 mile, right at red brick cottages signed Beara Farm. Approximately 1 mile to site.*

A very good farm park, with clean unisex facilities, run by very keen and friendly owners. A well-trimmed camping field offers peace and quiet. Close to the River Dart and the Dart Valley Steam Railway line, within easy reach of the sea and moors. Please note that the approach to the site is narrow, with passing places, and care needs to be taken.

Open: All year **Last arrival:** 21.00 **Last departure:** anytime

Pitches: 🚐 🚌 ▲; 1 hardstanding pitch

Facilities: 🚿 ☺ ☼ 🎍 🏕

Services: 🚽

Within 3 miles: ✐ ⑤

Additional site information: 3.63 acre site. 🐕 🐾 Cars can be parked by caravans and tents. Awnings permitted. No noise after 22.30. Access to River Dart.

CLAYHIDON
Map 4 ST11

Places to visit
Coldharbour Mill Working Wool Museum, UFFCULME, EX15 3EE, 01884 840960
www.coldharbourmill.org.uk

Kingsmead Centre Camping
►►►► 75%

tel: 01823 421630 **EX15 3TR**
email: contact@kingsmeadcentre.com **web:** www.kingsmeadcentre.com
dir: *M5 junction 26, follow Blackmoor signs at roundabout. At T-junction left signed Blackmoor. Left at Blackmoor sign. Right at T-junction. Left at next T-junction. Right at Kingsmead Centre sign.*

Located in the middle of a forest, this well-maintained site offers two good, clean toilet blocks and caters for everyone, with a good mix of pitches for tents, caravans and motorhomes, plus the added attraction of a yurt and two Lotus Belle tents for hire. There are two fishing lakes on the site.

Open: All year **Last arrival:** 21.00 **Last departure:** 11.00

Pitches: 🚐 🚌 ▲ 🏠; 7 hardstanding pitches

Leisure: ✐

Facilities: 🚿 ☺ ☼ ⚕ ⑤ 🎍 WiFi

Services: 🚽 ⑤ ⚓ 🔒 T

Within 3 miles: ↧ ↺

Additional site information: 7 acre site. 🐕 Cars can be parked by caravans and tents. Awnings permitted. No amplified music; no noise after 21.00 (Monday to Friday) or after 22.00 (Saturday to Sunday). Fire pits available for hire.

Glamping available: 2 Lotus Belle tents; 1 yurt.

Additional glamping information: Cars can be parked by glamping units.

CLYST ST MARY
Map 3 SX99

Places to visit
Exeter Cathedral, EXETER, EX1 1HS, 01392 285983
www.exeter-cathedral.org.uk

Exeter's Underground Passages, EXETER, EX1 1GA, 01392 665887
www.exeter.gov.uk/passages

Great for kids: The World of Country Life, EXMOUTH, EX8 5BY, 01395 274533
www.worldofcountrylife.co.uk

Premier Park

Crealy Adventure Park and Resort
►►►►► 90%

tel: 01395 234888 **Sidmouth Road EX5 1DR**
email: fun@crealy.co.uk **web:** www.crealy.co.uk
dir: *M5 junction 30, A3052 signed Exmouth. At roundabout take A3052 signed Seaton. Follow brown Crealy Great Adventure Park signs. Turn right.*

A quality park with excellent toilet facilities, spacious, fully serviced pitches and good security, situated adjacent to the popular Crealy Adventure Park; free or discounted entry is available for all campers. Pre-erected luxury safari cabins are for hire, and also in the Camelot Village there are medieval-style pavillion tents for a real glamping holiday. In addition there are 17 spacious lodges with hot tubs for all the family to enjoy. For children, there is a unique 'own pony' and 'character breakfast' experience, plus there's a new multi-use games area and adventure golf. There is a clubhouse, located next to reception, and a new bar and restaurant opened in 2018. Free WiFi is available and free kennel accommodation is offered on request. The park is within a short drive of Exeter and the seaside attractions at Sidmouth.

Open: All year **Last arrival:** 20.00 **Last departure:** 10.00

Pitches: 🚐 🚌 ▲ 🏠; 21 hardstanding pitches

Leisure: 🎵 ⚙

Facilities: ☞ ☼ ⚕ ⑤ 🏕 WiFi

Services: 🚽 ⑤ 🍴 🍽 🍺 🔒 ⌀ T

Within 3 miles: ↧ ✐

Additional site information: 14.65 acre site. 🐕 Cars can be parked by caravans and tents. Awnings permitted. Underfloor heating in bathrooms. Crealy Adventure Park within walking distance.

Glamping available: Safari cabins, medieval pavillions.

COMBE MARTIN

Places to visit
Arlington Court, ARLINGTON, EX31 4LP, 01271 850296
www.nationaltrust.org.uk/arlington-court

Great for kids: Combe Martin Wildlife Park & Dinosaur Park, COMBE MARTIN, EX34 0NG, 01271 882486
https://cmwdp.co.uk

LEISURE: 🏊 Indoor swimming pool 🏊 Outdoor swimming pool 🛝 Children's playground ✋ Kids' club 🎾 Tennis court 🎱 Games room 📺 Separate TV room ↧ golf course 🎯 Pitch n putt 🚣 Boats for hire 🚲 Bikes for hire 🎬 Cinema 🎵 Entertainment ✐ Fishing ◉ Mini golf 🏄 Watersports 💪 Gym ⚽ Sports field ↺ Stables
FACILITIES: 🚿 Baths/Shower ☺ Electric shaver sockets ✄ Hairdryer ☼ Ice Pack Facility 🚼 Baby facilities ⚕ Disabled facilities ⑤ Shop on site or within 200yds 🎍 BBQ area 🏕 Picnic area WiFi WiFi

COMBE MARTIN

Map 3 SS54

Premier Park

Stowford Farm Meadows
▶▶▶▶▶ 91%

Best of British

tel: 01271 882476 **Berry Down EX34 0PW**
email: enquiries@stowford.co.uk **web:** www.stowford.co.uk
dir: M5 junction 27, A361 to Barnstaple. Take A39 from town centre towards Lynton, in 1 mile left onto B3230. Right at garage at Lynton Cross onto A3123, site 1.5 miles on right.

A very gently sloping, grassy, sheltered and south-facing site approached down a wide, well-kept driveway. This family-friendly site is set in 500 acres of rolling countryside and offers many quality amenities including a large swimming pool and horse riding. A woodland walk is an added attraction, as is the Petorama, an undercover mini zoo, with its variety of friendly animals. There's also a "new and used" caravan sales centre, a comprehensive caravan accessory shop, and VW campervan conversion centre.

Open: All year (restricted service: in winter at certain times – bars closed and catering not available) **Last arrival:** 20.00 **Last departure:** 11.00
Pitches: 🚐 from £16; 🚙 from £18; 🏕 from £16; 130 hardstanding pitches; 330 seasonal pitches

Leisure: 🏊 🎣 ⚓ ♪ ⚽
Facilities: 🛁 ☉ 🅿 ❄ ♿ 🖨 🛒 WiFi
Services: 🔌 🔄 🍺 🍽 🍔 🚗 ⚡ ⚓ 🔋 🚰 🅃
Within 3 miles: ⚓ ∪ ◎

Additional site information: 100 acre site. 🐕 Maximum of 3 dogs permitted. Cars can be parked by caravans and tents. Awnings permitted. No noise after 23.00, 10mph speed limit on site. Caravan accessory shop, storage, workshop and sales.

Premier Park

Newberry Valley Park
▶▶▶▶▶ 89%

tel: 01271 882334 **Woodlands EX34 0AT**
email: relax@newberryvalleypark.co.uk **web:** www.newberryvalleypark.co.uk
dir: M5 junction 27, A361 towards Barnstaple. Right at North Aller roundabout onto A399, through Combe Martin to sea. Left into site.

A family owned and run touring park on the edge of Combe Martin, with all its amenities just a five-minute walk away. The park is set in a wooded valley with its own coarse fishing lake and has a stunning toilet block with underfloor heating and excellent unisex privacy cubicles. There is a wooden hut, named Lily, and a shepherd's hut, named Rose, located in a quiet spot and available to hire. The safe beaches of Newberry and Combe Martin are reached by a short footpath opposite the park entrance, where the South West Coastal Path passes.

Open: 15 March to October (restricted service: low season – office hours limited)
Last arrival: variable (last arrival time is dusk in winter) **Last departure:** 11.00
Pitches: * 🚐 from £18; 🚙 from £18; 🏕 from £8; 🏠 see prices below; 40 hardstanding pitches; 18 seasonal pitches
Leisure: 🎱 🎣
Facilities: 🛁 ☉ 🅿 ❄ ♿ 🖨 🚗 🛒 WiFi
Services: 🔌 🔄 ⚓ 🚰 🅃
Within 3 miles: ⚓ ∪ 🚣 🚵

Additional site information: 20 acre site. 🐕 Cars can be parked by caravans and tents. Awnings permitted. No camp fires. Kitchen preparation area, fridge and microwave available; fresh bread and butchery delivery. Car hire can be arranged.

Glamping available: Wooden hut from £39; shepherd's hut from £49.
Changeover days: Any day

Additional glamping information: Minimum stay 3 nights. Cars can be parked by huts.

PITCHES: 🚐 Caravans 🚙 Motorhomes 🏕 Tents 🏠 Glamping accommodation **SERVICES:** 🔌 Electric hook-up 🔄 Launderette 🍺 Licensed bar 🔥 Calor Gas 🔥 Campingaz 🅃 Toilet fluid 🍽 Café/Restaurant 🍔 Fast Food/Takeaway 🔋 Battery charging ⚡ Motorhome service point * 2019 prices 🚫 No credit or debit cards 🐕 Dogs permitted 🚫 No dogs

CROYDE
Map 3 SS43

Places to visit
Marwood Hill Gardens, BARNSTAPLE, EX31 4EA, 01271 342528
www.marwoodhillgarden.co.uk

Great for kids: Watermouth Castle & Family Theme Park, ILFRACOMBE, EX34 9SL, 01271 867474
www.watermouthcastle.com

Bay View Farm Caravan & Camping Park

▶▶▶▶ 84%

tel: 01271 890501 **EX33 1PN**

email: info@bayviewfarm.co.uk **web:** www.bayviewfarm.co.uk
dir: M5 junction 27, A361, through Barnstaple to Braunton, left onto B3231. Site at entrance to Croyde.

A very busy and popular park close to surfing beaches and rock pools, with a public footpath leading directly to the sea. Set in a stunning location with views out over the Atlantic to Lundy Island, it is just a short stroll from Croyde. The facilities are clean and well maintained; a family bathroom is available. There is a fish and chip shop on site. Please note that dogs are not permitted.

Open: March to October **Last arrival:** 21.30 **Last departure:** 11.00

Pitches: 🚐 🚑 ▲ 🏠; 40 hardstanding pitches; 15 seasonal pitches

Leisure: ⚊

Facilities: 🛁 ☉ 🇵 ✳ ☕ 🛍 WiFi

Services: 🚽 🗄 🕸 🎀 🔒 🐾 Ⓣ

Within 3 miles: 🛳 🚣 ⛳ ∪ ◎ 🎣 🎪

Additional site information: 10 acre site. ⊗ Cars can be parked by caravans and tents. Awnings permitted. No noise after midnight. Fresh produce available in high season.

Glamping available: Wooden pods.

Additional glamping information: Cars can be parked by pods.

CULLOMPTON

See Kentisbeare

DARTMOUTH

Places to visit
Dartmouth Castle, DARTMOUTH, TQ6 0JN, 01803 833588
www.english-heritage.org.uk/daysout/properties/dartmouth-castle

DARTMOUTH
Map 3 SX85

Premier Park

Woodlands Grove Caravan & Camping Park

▶▶▶▶▶ 92%

tel: 01803 712598 **Blackawton TQ9 7DQ**
email: holiday@woodlandsgrove.com **web:** www.woodlandsgrove.co.uk
dir: From Dartmouth take A3122, 4 miles. Or from A38 take A385 to Totnes. Then A381 towards Salcombe, after Halwell take A3122 towards Dartmouth, site signed (brown tourist signs).

A quality caravan and tent park with smart toilet facilities (including excellent family rooms), spacious pitches, including decent hardstandings and good attention to detail throughout, all set in an extensive woodland environment with a terraced grass camping area. Free entry to the adjoining Woodlands Theme Park makes an excellent package holiday for families, but also good for adults travelling without children who are perhaps seeking a low season break. Please check with the site with reference to their minimum stay policy. There is a bus stop at the entrance.

Open: 23 March to 28 October **Last arrival:** 21.30 **Last departure:** 11.00

Pitches: 🚐 from £18; 🚑 from £18; ▲ from £18; 129 hardstanding pitches

Leisure: ⚊ ♜ ▭ 🎵 **Facilities:** 🛁 ☉ 🇵 ✳ ☕ 🛍 WiFi

Services: 🚽 🗄 🍽 🕸 🎀 ⚗ 🔒 🐾 Ⓣ **Within 3 miles:** 🛳 ◎

Additional site information: 16 acre site. ⌁ Cars can be parked by caravans and tents. Awnings permitted. No open fires, fire pits or chimeneas, quiet 22.30 to 08.00. Falconry centre, woodland walk, zoo-farm, dog kennels, theme park.

DAWLISH

Map 3 SX97

Places to visit

Powderham Castle, POWDERHAM, EX6 8JQ, 01626 890243
www.powderham.co.uk

Cofton Holidays

▶▶▶▶▶ 92%

tel: 01626 890111 & 0800 085 8649 **Starcross EX6 8RP**
email: info@coftonholidays.co.uk **web:** www.coftonholidays.co.uk
dir: *On A379 (Exeter to Dawlish road), 3 miles from Dawlish.*

This park is set in a rural location surrounded by spacious open grassland, with plenty of well-kept flowerbeds throughout. Most pitches overlook either the swimming pool complex or the coarse fishing lakes and woodlands. All the purpose-built toilet blocks offer smart modern facilities and the on-site pub serves drinks, meals and snacks for all the family, and a mini-market caters for most shopping needs.

Open: All year **Last arrival:** 20.00 **Last departure:** 11.00
Pitches: 🚐 🚍 ⛺; 60 hardstanding pitches; 110 seasonal pitches
Leisure: 🏊 ⛵ 🎣 ♘ 🎶 🎱 🎯 ⚽
Facilities: 🏪 ☉ ☂ ✳ ♿ 🚿 🚻 🛒 WiFi
Services: 🔌 🔋 🍴 🍽 🛒 🛒 ⚓ 🏍 🅃 **Within 3 miles:** 🚣 ◎ 🛶 🎿 🎯

Additional site information: 45 acre site. ⊀ Cars can be parked by caravans and tents. Awnings permitted. Soft play area, sauna and steam room, bowlingo.

Lady's Mile Holiday Park

▶▶▶▶▶ 88%

tel: 01626 863411 **EX7 0LX**
email: info@ladysmile.co.uk **web:** www.ladysmile.co.uk
dir: *1 mile north of Dawlish on A379.*

A family owned and run touring park with a wide variety of pitches, including some that are fully serviced. There are plenty of activities for everyone, including two swimming pools with waterslides, a children's splash pool, a well-equipped gym, a sauna in the main season, a large adventure playground, extensive restaurant facilities, and a bar with entertainment in high season. Facilities are kept very clean, and the surrounding beaches are easily accessed. Holiday homes, high quality wooden pods and safari tents are also available.

Open: All year (restricted service: November to 22 March – facilities reduced)
Last arrival: 20.00 **Last departure:** 11.00
Pitches: 🚐 🚍 ⛺ 🏠; 100 hardstanding pitches; 200 seasonal pitches
Leisure: 🏊 ⛵ 🎣 ♘ 🎣 🎶 🎯 ⚽ Spa
Facilities: 🏪 ☉ ☂ ♿ 🚿 🚻 🛒 WiFi
Services: 🔌 🔋 🍴 🍽 🛒 🛒 ⚓ 🏍 🅃
Within 3 miles: 🚣 ◎ ∪ ◎ 🛶 🎿 🎯

Additional site information: 60 acre site. ⊀ Cars can be parked by caravans and tents. Awnings permitted. No noise after 23.00. Bowling alley.

Glamping available: Safari tents, wooden pods.

Changeover days: Friday, Saturday, Monday

Additional glamping information: Safari tents: king-size four-poster bed and hot tub. Cars can be parked by glamping units.

PITCHES: 🚐 Caravans 🚍 Motorhomes ⛺ Tents 🏠 Glamping accommodation **SERVICES:** 🔌 Electric hook-up 🔋 Launderette 🍸 Licensed bar
🛢 Calor Gas 🔥 Campingaz 🅃 Toilet fluid 🍽 Café/Restaurant 🍟 Fast Food/Takeaway 🔋 Battery charging ⚡ Motorhome service point
* 2019 prices 🚫 No credit or debit cards ⊀ Dogs permitted 🚫 No dogs

DAWLISH *continued*

Leadstone Camping
▶▶▶▶ 85%

tel: 01626 864411 **Warren Road EX7 0NG**
email: leadstonecampng@gmail.com **web:** www.leadstonecamping.co.uk
dir: *M5 junction 30, A379 to Dawlish. Before village turn left on brow of hill, signed Dawlish Warren. Site 0.5 mile on right.*

A traditional, mainly level, grassy camping park approximately a half-mile walk from the sands and dunes at Dawlish Warren – a nature reserve and Blue Flag beach. This mainly tented park has been run by the same friendly family for many years, and is an ideal base for touring south Devon. A regular bus service from outside the gate takes in a wide area. The smart, well-equipped timber cabin toilet facility includes some privacy cubicles. There is a pub a short walk away.

Open: 24 May to 2 September **Last arrival:** 22.00 **Last departure:** noon
Pitches: * 🚐 from £29; 🚐 from £24; ▲ from £20; 14 seasonal pitches
Leisure: ⚲
Facilities: 🛁 ⊙ 🏴 ⚹ ♿ WiFi
Services: 🔌 🛢 🧺 ♒ 🔒 🗑 ⊤
Within 3 miles: 🎣 ⚲ ◎ ⑤

Additional site information: 8 acre site. 🐾 Cars can be parked by caravans and tents. Awnings permitted. No noise after 23.00. Only portable and disposable BBQs permitted.

DREWSTEIGNTON Map 3 SX79

Places to visit

Castle Drogo, DREWSTEIGNTON, EX6 6PB, 01647 433306
www.nationaltrust.org.uk/castle-drogo

Finch Foundry, STICKLEPATH, EX20 2NW, 01837 840046
www.nationaltrust.org.uk/finch-foundry

Premier Park

Woodland Springs Adult Touring Park
▶▶▶▶▶ 92%

tel: 01647 231695 **Venton EX6 6PG**
email: enquiries@woodlandsprings.co.uk **web:** woodlandsprings.co.uk
dir: *Exit A30 at Whiddon Down junction onto A382 towards Moretonhampstead. Site 1.5 miles on left.*

An attractive and very well managed park in a rural area within Dartmoor National Park. This site is surrounded by woodland and farmland, and is very peaceful. The toilet block offers superb facilities, including four fully serviced cubicles, some suitable for disabled visitors. Guests can expect high levels of customer care. Two glamping pods and additional toilet and shower facilities are also available. Please note, children are not accepted here.

Open: All year **Last arrival:** 20.00 **Last departure:** 11.00
Pitches: * 🚐 from £21; 🚐 from £24; ▲ from £17.50; 🏠 see prices below; 50 hardstanding pitches; 20 seasonal pitches
Facilities: 🛁 ⊙ 🏴 ⚹ ♿ 🗑 🧺 🚽 WiFi
Services: 🔌 🛢 🧺 ♒ 🗑 🔒 ⊘ ⊤
Within 3 miles: ⚲

Additional site information: 6 acre site. Adults only. 🐾 Cars can be parked by caravans and tents. Awnings permitted. No fires, no noise 23.00–08.00. Day kennels, freezer, coffee vending machine.

Glamping available: Wooden pods from £40.

Additional glamping information: Cars can be parked by pods.

EAST ALLINGTON

Places to visit

Kingsbridge Cookworthy Museum, KINGSBRIDGE, TQ7 1AW, 01548 853235
www.kingsbridgemuseum.org.uk

Great for kids: Woodlands Family Theme Park, DARTMOUTH, TQ9 7DQ, 01803 712598, www.woodlandspark.com

---

LEISURE: 🏊 Indoor swimming pool 🏊 Outdoor swimming pool ⚲ Children's playground 🧒 Kids' club 🎾 Tennis court 🎱 Games room 📺 Separate TV room ⛳ golf course 🏌 Pitch n putt 🚣 Boats for hire 🚲 Bikes for hire 🎬 Cinema 🎵 Entertainment 🎣 Fishing ◎ Mini golf 🏄 Watersports 💪 Gym ⚽ Sports field ♘ Stables
FACILITIES: 🛁 Baths/Shower ⊙ Electric shaver sockets 🏴 Hairdryer ⚹ Ice Pack Facility 🍼 Baby facilities ♿ Disabled facilities ⑤ Shop on site or within 200yds 🍖 BBQ area 🎍 Picnic area WiFi WiFi

EAST ALLINGTON | Map 3 SX74

Mounts Farm Touring Park
▶▶▶ 80%

tel: 01548 521591 **The Mounts TQ9 7QJ**
email: mounts.farm@lineone.net **web:** www.mountsfarm.co.uk
dir: A381 from Totnes towards Kingsbridge (Note: ignore signs for East Allington). At 'Mounts', site 0.5 mile on left.

A neat, grassy park divided into four paddocks by mature natural hedges. Three of the paddocks are for the tourers and campers, and the fourth is a children's play area. The laundry, toilets and well-stocked little shop are in converted farm buildings. There's an on-site snack bar and Calor Gas retailer.

Open: mid March to end October **Last arrival:** 22.00 **Last departure:** 16.00
Pitches: ⊞ ⇔ ▲; 10 seasonal pitches
Leisure: ⊕
Facilities: ⊙ ℙ ✳ 🛍
Services: ⊕ 🗐 🛒 🔒 ⌀ Ⓣ
Within 3 miles: ℐ ∪ ≋ ✦ 🎋

Additional site information: 7 acre site. ㅋ Cars can be parked by caravans and tents. Awnings permitted. Camping accessories shop on site.

EAST WORLINGTON | Map 3 SS71

Places to visit
Knightshayes, KNIGHTSHAYES, EX16 7RQ, 01884 254665
www.nationaltrust.org.uk/knightshayes

Yeatheridge Farm Caravan Park
▶▶▶▶ 87%

tel: 01884 860330 **EX17 4TN**
email: info@yeatheridge.co.uk **web:** www.yeatheridge.co.uk
dir: M5 junction 27, A361, at 1st roundabout at Tiverton take B3137 for 9 miles towards Witheridge. Fork left 1 mile after Nomansland onto B3042. Site on left in 3.5 miles. (Note: do not enter East Worlington)

A well-kept park in a remote woodland setting on the edge of the Tamar Valley. It is peacefully located at the end of a private, half mile, tree-lined drive; it offers superb on-site facilities, including an excellent restaurant and bar area with outside seating, a large children's play area, and high levels of customer care from the hands-on owners. The toilets are immaculate and well maintained, plus there is an indoor swimming pool, sauna and a good information and games room — all have a friendly atmosphere. Two fishing lakes are also available.

Open: 15 March to end September **Last arrival:** 22.00 **Last departure:** 10.00
Pitches: ⊞ ⇔ ▲; 8 hardstanding pitches
Leisure: ≋ ● ℐ ⊕
Facilities: ⊞ ⊙ ℙ ✳ ♿ 🛍 🍴 🚼 WiFi
Services: ⊕ 🗐 🍺 🍽 🛒 🛒 ⌄ 🔒 ⌀ Ⓣ
Within 3 miles: ∪

Additional site information: 12 acre site. ㅋ Cars can be parked by caravans and tents. Awnings permitted.

EXETER
See Kennford

HOLSWORTHY | Map 3 SS30

Places to visit
Dartington Crystal, GREAT TORRINGTON, EX38 7AN, 01805 626242 www.dartington.co.uk

RHS Garden Rosemoor, GREAT TORRINGTON, EX38 8PH, 01805 624067 www.rhs.org.uk/rosemoor

Great for kids: The Milky Way Adventure Park, CLOVELLY, EX39 5RY, 01237 431255, www.themilkyway.co.uk

Headon Farm Caravan Site
▶▶▶ 87%

tel: 01409 254477 **Headon Farm, Hollacombe EX22 6NN**
email: reader@headonfarm.co.uk **web:** www.headonfarm.co.uk
dir: From Holsworthy A388 signed Launceston. 0.5 mile, at hill brow left into Staddon Road. 1 mile (follow site signs) turn right signed Ashwater. 0.5 mile, left at hill brow. Site in 25 yards.

Set on a working farm in a quiet rural location. All pitches have extensive views of the Devon countryside, yet the park is only two and a half miles from the market town of Holsworthy, and within easy reach of roads to the coast and beaches of north Cornwall.

Open: All year **Last arrival:** 19.00 **Last departure:** noon
Pitches: ⊞ from £18.50; ⇔ from £18.50; ▲; 11 hardstanding pitches
Leisure: ⊕
Facilities: ⊞ ⊙ ✳ 🎋 WiFi
Services: ⊕ 🛒
Within 3 miles: ⌄ ℐ ∪ 🛍 🗐

Additional site information: 2 acre site. ㅋ Cars can be parked by caravans and tents. Awnings permitted. Breathable groundsheets only. Caravan and motorhome storage (outside or undercover). Car hire can be arranged.

Noteworthy Farm Caravan and Campsite
▶▶ 80%

tel: 01409 253731 & 07811 000071 **Noteworthy, Bude Road EX22 7JB**
email: enquiries@noteworthy-devon.co.uk **web:** www.noteworthy-devon.co.uk
dir: On A3072 between Holsworthy and Bude. 3 miles from Holsworthy on right.

This campsite is owned by a friendly young couple with their own children. There are good views from the quiet rural location, and simple toilet facilities. The local bus stops outside the gate on request.

Open: All year **Last departure:** 11.00
Pitches: * ⊞ from £16; ⇔ from £16; ▲ from £16; 3 hardstanding pitches
Leisure: ℐ **Facilities:** ⊞ ⊙ ✳ **Services:** ⊕ 🗐 **Within 3 miles:** ⌄ ∪ ≋ 🛍

Additional site information: 5 acre site. ㅋ ⊘ Cars can be parked by caravans and tents. Awnings permitted. No open fires, no noise after 22.30. Dog grooming available.

PITCHES: ⊞ Caravans ⇔ Motorhomes ▲ Tents ⋔ Glamping accommodation **SERVICES:** ⊕ Electric hook-up 🗐 Launderette 🍺 Licensed bar
🔒 Calor Gas ⌀ Campingaz Ⓣ Toilet fluid 🍽 Café/Restaurant 🍔 Fast Food/Takeaway 🛒 Battery charging ⌄ Motorhome service point
* 2019 prices ⊘ No credit or debit cards ㅋ Dogs permitted ⊗ No dogs

ILFRACOMBE
Map 3 SS54

Places to visit

Arlington Court, ARLINGTON, EX31 4LP, 01271 850296
www.nationaltrust.org.uk/arlington-court

Exmoor Zoological Park, BLACKMOOR GATE, EX31 4SG, 01598 763352
www.exmoorzoo.co.uk

Great for kids: Watermouth Castle & Family Theme Park, ILFRACOMBE,
EX34 9SL, 01271 867474
www.watermouthcastle.com

Premier Park

Hele Valley Holiday Park
▶▶▶▶▶ 86%

tel: 01271 862460 **Hele Bay EX34 9RD**
email: holidays@helevalley.co.uk **web:** www.helevalley.co.uk
dir: M5 junction 27, A361, through Barnstaple and Braunton to Ilfracombe. Take A399
towards Combe Martin. Follow brown Hele Valley signs. In 400 metres sharp right to
T-junction. Park on left.

A deceptively spacious park set in a picturesque valley with glorious tree-lined
hilly views from most pitches. High quality toilet facilities are provided, and the
park is within walking distance of a lovely beach and on a regular bus route.
Camping pods are available to hire. The harbour and other attractions of
Ilfracombe are just a mile away.

Open: Easter to end October **Last arrival:** 18.00 **Last departure:** 11.00
Pitches: 🚐 from £24; 🚙 from £19; ▲ from £19; 🏠 see prices below;
18 hardstanding pitches
Leisure: /Λ **Facilities:** 🚿 ⊙ 🗲 ✻ ⎕ 🛋 ㅠ 🅆🄸🄵🄸
Services: 🔌 🗑 🎣 ⚓ 🌀
Within 3 miles: ⌊ 🏌 ∪ ◎ ⚓ ⛵ 🎂 目 🅂

Additional site information: 17 acre site. 🚗 Cars can be parked by caravans and
tents. Awnings permitted. Groups, motorhomes and tourers by arrangement only.
Nature trail, postal collection. Car hire can be arranged.
Glamping available: Wooden pods from £34. **Changeover days:** Any day
Additional glamping information: Wooden pods are double glazed, heated (electricity
included in price) and have a small decking area with table, chairs and brazier. Cars
can be parked by pods.

Sunnymead Farm Camping & Touring Site
▶▶▶▶ 79%

tel: 01271 879845 & 07826 184874 **Morthoe Road EX34 8NZ**
email: info@sunnymead-farm.co.uk **web:** www.sunnymead-farm.co.uk
dir: From A361 between Ilfracombe and Braunton, at Mullacott Cross roundabout, take
B3343 signed Woolacombe. Site approximately 1 mile on right, just after Veterinary
Hospital; opposite Highways Guest House.

Peace and tranquillity abound at this small farm site that's set in the beautiful
north Devon countryside with easy reach to Ilfracombe and Woolacombe. 30 grass
pitches are set around a well mown and tended paddock, most have electric
hook-up and some enjoy superb sea views. Expect spotlessly clean toilet facilities
and a traditional camping atmosphere.

Open: Easter to October (restricted service: low season – reduced hours at
reception/shop) **Last arrival:** 19.00 (arrival until 21.00 by prior arrangement only)
Last departure: 10.30
Pitches: * 🚐 from £14; 🚙 from £14; ▲ from £14; 12 hardstanding pitches;
9 seasonal pitches
Leisure: /Λ **Facilities:** 🚿 ⊙ ✻ 🛋 🅂
Services: 🔌 🎣 **Within 3 miles:** ⌊ 🏌 ∪ ◎ ⚓ 目 🅂

Additional site information: 3 acre site. 🚗 Cars can be parked by caravans and tents.
Awnings permitted. Booking advisable during school holidays. Storage facilities, 2 static
caravans.

KENNFORD
Map 3 SX98

Places to visit

Canonteign Falls, CHUDLEIGH, EX6 7RH, 01647 252434
www.canonteignfalls.co.uk

Custom House Visitor Centre, EXETER, EX2 4AN, 01392 271611
www.exeter.gov.uk/customhouse

Great for kids: Crealy Adventure Park & Resort, CLYST ST MARY, EX5 1DR,
01395 233200, www.crealy.co.uk

Premier Park

Kennford International Holiday Park
▶▶▶▶▶ 84%

tel: 01392 833046 **EX6 7YN**
email: ian@kennfordinternational.com **web:** www.kennfordinternational.co.uk
dir: At end of M5 take A38, site signed at Kennford slip road.

Screened from the A38 by trees and shrubs, this park offers pitches divided by
hedging for privacy. A high quality toilet block complements the park's facilities.
A good, centrally located base for exploring the coast and touring the
countryside of Devon, and Exeter is easily accessible via buses that stop nearby.

Open: All year **Last arrival:** 21.00 (winter – check with site for arrival times)
Last departure: 11.00
Pitches: 🚐 from £16; 🚙 from £16; ▲ from £16; 9 hardstanding pitches
Leisure: /Λ **Facilities:** 🚿 ⊙ 🛋 🅆🄸🄵🄸
Services: 🔌 🗑 🎣 ⚓ ⊤ **Within 3 miles:** ⌊ 🏌 ∪ 🎂 目 🅂

Additional site information: 15 acre site. 🚗 Cars can be parked by caravans and
tents. Awnings permitted.

KENTISBEARE
Map 3 ST00

Places to visit

Killerton House & Garden, KILLERTON, EX5 3LE, 01392 881345
www.nationaltrust.org.uk/killerton

Custom House Visitor Centre, EXETER, EX2 4AN, 01392 271611
www.exeter.gov.uk/customhouse

Great for kids: Diggerland, CULLOMPTON, EX15 2PE, 0871 227 7007 (*calls cost 10p per minute plus your phone company's access charge*)
www.diggerland.com

Forest Glade Holiday Park
►►►► 83%

tel: 01404 841381 **EX15 2DT**
email: enquiries@forest-glade.co.uk **web:** www.forest-glade.co.uk
dir: *Tent traffic: from A373 turn left past Keepers Cottage Inn (2.5 miles east of M5 junction 28). (Note: due to narrow roads, touring caravans and larger motorhomes must approach from Honiton direction. Phone site for access details).*

A quiet, attractive park in a forest clearing with well-kept gardens and beech hedge screening. One of the main attractions is the site's immediate proximity to the forest which offers magnificent hillside walks with surprising views over the valleys. There's an undercover heated swimming pool, a good children's play area and large games room; camping pods are available for hire. Please note, that because the roads are narrow around the site, it is best to phone the site for suitable route details.

Open: mid March to end October (restricted service: low season – limited shop hours)
Last arrival: 21.00 **Last departure:** noon

Pitches: 🚐 🚍 ▲ 🏠; 40 hardstanding pitches; 28 seasonal pitches

Leisure: 🏖 🎢 ♨ ♣ ⊕

Facilities: 🏠 ⊙ ⊙ 🖙 ❄ ♿ 🛉 🚻 ➡ WiFi

Services: 🔌 🗊 🚽 🧺 ⚡ 🔋 🌿 Ⓣ

Within 3 miles: ✐ 🌙

Additional site information: 26 acre site. 🐕 Cars can be parked by caravans and tents. Awnings permitted. Families and couples only. Adventure and soft play areas, wildlife information room, paddling pool.

Glamping available: Wooden pods. **Changeover days:** Any day

Additional glamping information: Wooden pods: no dogs permitted. Cars can be parked by pods.

KINGSBRIDGE
Map 3 SX74

Places to visit

Kingsbridge Cookworthy Museum, KINGSBRIDGE, TQ7 1AW, 01548 853235
www.kingsbridgemuseum.org.uk

Overbeck's, SALCOMBE, TQ8 8LW, 01548 842893
www.nationaltrust.org.uk/overbecks

Premier Park

Parkland Caravan and Camping Site
►►►►► 85%

tel: 01548 852723 & 07968 222008 **Sorley Green Cross TQ7 4AF**
email: enquiries@parklandsite.co.uk **web:** www.parklandsite.co.uk
dir: *A384 to Totnes, A381 towards Kingsbridge. 12 miles, at Stumpy Post Cross roundabout turn right, 1 mile. Site 200 yards on left after Sorley Green Cross.*

Expect a high level of customer care at this family-run park set in the glorious South Hams countryside; it has panoramic views over Salcombe and the rolling countryside towards Dartmoor. The immaculately maintained grounds offer generous grass pitches, hardstandings and super pitches (RVs can be accommodated), and a dedicated touring field has 10 fully-serviced pitches. The on-site shop sells seasonal produce, everyday provisions, pre-ordered hampers and camping supplies. There is an excellent café; the toilet facilities feature quality cubicles, family washrooms, a bathroom and a fully-fitted disabled suite. Babysitting is available by arrangement. A bus stops close to the site entrance, which is handy for exploring the local towns and villages.

Open: All year **Last arrival:** 20.00 **Last departure:** 11.30

Pitches: * 🚐 from £25; 🚍 from £25; ▲ from £25; 30 hardstanding pitches; 25 seasonal pitches

Leisure: 🎢 ♣ ▭

Facilities: 🏠 ⊙ 🖙 ❄ ♿ 🛉 🚻 ➡ WiFi

Services: 🔌 🗊 🍴 🧺 ⚡ 🔋 🌿 Ⓣ

Within 3 miles: 🎣 ✐ 🌙 ◎ ⛳ 🎿 🎯

Additional site information: 3 acre site. 🚫 Cars can be parked by caravans and tents. Awnings permitted. No camp fires, no noise after 23.00, children must be accompanied by an adult when using facilities, site gates closed 23.00–07.00. Use of fridge freezers, campers' kitchen, coffee shop, freshly baked croissants, short term caravan storage facility, electric car-charging point. Car hire can be arranged.

KINGSBRIDGE *continued*

Premier Park

Island Lodge Caravan & Camping Site
►►►►► 82%

tel: 01548 852956 & 07968 222007 **Stumpy Post Cross TQ7 4BL**
email: islandlodgesite@gmail.com **web:** www.islandlodgesite.co.uk
dir: *Take A381 from Totnes towards Kingsbridge. In 12 miles, at roundabout (Stumpy Post Cross) right, 300 metres left into lane, site signed. 200 metres on left.*

A small, peaceful and well-established park, with extensive views over the South Hams, which has been run by the same family for many years. The site has a security barrier, low-level lighting around the park, good hardstanding pitches, and a motorhome service point. The immaculate toilet facilities are of good quality. A scenic 35-minute walk will take you to Kingsbridge, or the Kingsbridge bus stops close to the site. There are several dog-friendly beaches nearby.

Open: All year (restricted service: November to March – shop has basic supplies only)
Last arrival: 20.00 **Last departure:** 11.30

Pitches: 🚐 from £27; 🚏 from £27; ⛺ from £27; 4 hardstanding pitches; 24 seasonal pitches

Leisure: 🅰

Facilities: 🛁 ☺ 🚿 ✳ ⚒ ⑤ 🎪 WiFi

Services: 🚰 🗒 🛒 ⚐ 🛢 🦯 🔳

Within 3 miles: 🛶 🎣 ⛳ ◎ 🚵 ⛷ 🎡

Additional site information: 2 acre site. 🐕 Restrictions on certain dog breeds. 🐾 Cars can be parked by caravans and tents. Awnings permitted. No generators. Play area open 09.00–21.00. Electronic security barrier closed overnight. 24-hour CCTV, secure caravan storage yard, boat park, local brewery with off license 200 yards from site. Car hire can be arranged.

LYNTON

Places to visit

Arlington Court, ARLINGTON, EX31 4LP, 01271 850296
www.nationaltrust.org.uk/arlington-court

Great for kids: Exmoor Zoological Park, BLACKMOOR GATE, EX31 4SG, 01598 763352, www.exmoorzoo.co.uk

LYNTON — Map 3 SS74

Channel View Caravan and Camping Park
►►►► 72%

tel: 01598 753349 **Manor Farm EX35 6LD**
email: relax@channel-view.co.uk **web:** www.channel-view.co.uk
dir: *On A39 from Barbrook towards Hillsford Bridge. Approximately 0.5 mile to site on left.*

On the top of the cliffs overlooking the Bristol Channel, this is a well-maintained park on the edge of Exmoor, and close to both Lynton and Lynmouth. Pitches can be selected from either those in a hidden hedged area or those with panoramic views over the coast.

Open: 15 March to 15 November **Last arrival:** 22.00 **Last departure:** noon

Pitches: 🚐 🚏 ⛺; 15 hardstanding pitches

Facilities: 🛁 ☺ 🚿 ✳ ⚒ ⑤ WiFi

Services: 🚰 🗒 🛒 ⚐ 🛢 🦯 🔳

Within 3 miles: 🎣 ∪ ◎ ⛷ 🎡

Additional site information: 6 acre site. 🐕 Cars can be parked by caravans and tents. Awnings permitted. Groups by prior arrangement only. Parent and baby room.

MODBURY — Map 3 SX65

Places to visit

Kingsbridge Cookworthy Museum, KINGSBRIDGE, TQ7 1AW, 01548 853235
www.kingsbridgemuseum.org.uk

Overbeck's, SALCOMBE, TQ8 8LW, 01548 842893
www.nationaltrust.org.uk/overbecks

Pennymoor Camping & Caravan Park
►►► 87%

tel: 01548 830542 **PL21 0SB**
email: enquiries@pennymoor-camping.co.uk **web:** www.pennymoor-camping.co.uk
dir: *Exit A38 at Wrangaton Cross. Left, then right at crossroads. After by-passing Ermington, turn left onto A379, through Modbury, left at Harraton Cross. Site on left.*

Owned and run by the same family since 1935, this well-established, rural and lovingly tended park is tucked away in the South Hams; it is close to glorious beaches and has good views over rolling countryside to Dartmoor in the distance. On part level, part gently sloping grass, Pennymoor is an ideal base for exploring south Devon and offers everything for a relaxing and peaceful family stay, with spotless, well-maintained toilets, a fully-equipped children's play area, a well-stocked shop, site-wide WiFi and a relaxing atmosphere. Prices quoted include four people.

Open: 15 March to 15 November (restricted service: 15 March to mid May – only one toilet and shower block open) **Last arrival:** 20.00 (later arrival times by prior arrangement)
Last departure: 11.00

Pitches: 🚐 from £14; 🚏 from £14; ⛺ from £14; 3 hardstanding pitches

Leisure: 🅰

Facilities: 🛁 ☺ 🚿 ✳ ⚒ ⑤ WiFi

Services: 🚰 🗒 🍴 🛒 ⚐ 🦯 🔳

Within 3 miles: 🛶

Additional site information: 12.5 acre site. 🐕 Cars can be parked by caravans and tents. Awnings permitted. No skateboards or scooters, no noise after 22.00. Emergency phone, table tennis. Flogas. Caravans for hire and sale.

LEISURE: 🏊 Indoor swimming pool 🏊 Outdoor swimming pool 🅰 Children's playground 🧒 Kids' club 🎾 Tennis court 🎱 Games room 📺 Separate TV room
🏌 golf course 🏌 Pitch n putt ⛵ Boats for hire 🚲 Bikes for hire 🎬 Cinema 🎶 Entertainment 🎣 Fishing ◎ Mini golf ⛷ Watersports 🏋 Gym 🏟 Sports field ∪ Stables
FACILITIES: 🛁 Baths/Shower ☺ Electric shaver sockets 🚿 Hairdryer ✳ Ice Pack Facility 🍼 Baby facilities ⚒ Disabled facilities ⑤ Shop on site or within 200yds
🍖 BBQ area 🧺 Picnic area WiFi WiFi

MORTEHOE
Map 3 SS44

See also Woolacombe

Places to visit

Marwood Hill Gardens, BARNSTAPLE, EX31 4EA, 01271 342528
www.marwoodhillgarden.co.uk

Great for kids: Watermouth Castle & Family Theme Park, ILFRACOMBE,
EX34 9SL, 01271 867474, www.watermouthcastle.com

North Morte Farm Caravan & Camping Park
►►►► 90%

tel: 01271 870381 **North Morte Road EX34 7EG**
email: info@northmortefarm.co.uk **web:** www.northmortefarm.co.uk
dir: From B3343 into Mortehoe, right at post office. Site 500 yards on left.

Set in spectacular coastal countryside close to National Trust land and 500 yards
from Rockham Beach. This attractive park is very well run and maintained by
friendly family owners, and the quaint village of Mortehoe with its cafés, shops and
pubs, is just a five-minute walk away.

Open: April to October **Last arrival:** 22.00 **Last departure:** noon

Pitches: 🚐 from £15.50; 🚍 from £13; ▲ from £13; 25 hardstanding pitches;
13 seasonal pitches

Leisure: ⚠

Facilities: 🏠 ⊙ 🏳 ✳ ♿ 🗊 🐕 WiFi

Services: 🔌 🗊 🔋 🛒 ⬆ 🔒 🍃 Ⓣ

Within 3 miles: ↓ 🎣 ∪ ◎ 🖽

Additional site information: 22 acre site. 🐕 Cars can be parked by caravans and tents.
Awnings permitted. No large groups.

NEWTON ABBOT

Places to visit

Bradley Manor, NEWTON ABBOT, TQ12 1LX, 01803 661907
www.nationaltrust.org.uk/bradley

Great for kids: Prickly Ball Farm, NEWTON ABBOT, TQ12 6BZ, 01626 362319
www.pricklyballfarm.com

NEWTON ABBOT
Map 3 SX87

Platinum Park

Dornafield
►►►►►

Best of British

tel: 01803 812732 **Dornafield Farm, Two Mile Oak TQ12 6DD**
email: enquiries@dornafield.com **web:** www.dornafield.com
dir: From Newton Abbot take A381 signed Totnes for 2 miles. At Two Mile Oak Inn right,
left at crossroads in 0.5 mile. Site on right.

An immaculately kept park in a tranquil wooded valley between Dartmoor and
Torbay, divided into three areas. At the heart of the 30-acre site is Dornafield, a
14th-century farmhouse, adapted for campers' to use but still retaining much
charm. The friendly family owners are always available for help or to give advice.
The site has superb facilities in two ultra-modern toilet blocks. On site there is
the Quarry Café which provides takeaway food two nights a week. This is a quiet
and peaceful location convenient for Torbay, Dartmoor and the charming coastal
villages of the South Hams. A bus service to Totnes or Newton Abbot runs nearby.

Open: 14 March to 8 November **Last arrival:** 22.00 **Last departure:** 11.00

Pitches: 🚐 from £22; 🚍 from £22; ▲ from £20; 119 hardstanding pitches;
26 seasonal pitches

Leisure: ⚠ 🎱 🎾 **Facilities:** 🏠 ⊙ 🏳 ✳ ♿ 🗊 🍴 WiFi

Services: 🔌 🗊 🔋 🛒 ⬆ 🔒 🍃 Ⓣ **Within 3 miles:** ↓ 🎣

Additional site information: 30 acre site. 🐕 Cars can be parked by caravans and
tents. Awnings permitted. No commercial vehicles; no sign-written vehicles. Table
tennis, secure caravan storage (all year), freshly baked bread.

NEWTON ABBOT *continued*

Platinum Park

Ross Park
▶▶▶▶▶

tel: 01803 812983 **Park Hill Farm, Ipplepen TQ12 5TT**
email: enquiries@rossparkcaravanpark.co.uk **web:** www.rossparkcaravanpark.co.uk
dir: *North of Ipplepen on A381 follow brown site signs and sign for Woodland opposite Essar garage.*

A top-class park in every way, with large secluded pitches, high quality toilet facilities (which include excellent family rooms) and colourful flower displays throughout — note the wonderful floral walk to the toilets. The beautiful tropical conservatory also offers a breathtaking show of colour. There's a conservation walk through glorious wild flower meadows, replete with nature trail, a dog shower/grooming area, and six fully serviced pitches. This very rural park enjoys superb views of Dartmoor, and good quality meals to suit all tastes and pockets are served in the restaurant. Expect high levels of customer care — this park gets better each year. Home-grown produce and honey are sold in the shop. A bus, which stops close to the entrance, runs to Totnes and Newton Abbot.

Open: March to 2 January (restricted service: 1st 3 weeks in March, November and December (except Christmas and New Year) — restaurant and bar closed)
Last arrival: 21.00 **Last departure:** 11.00

Pitches: 🚐 from £19; 🚌 from £19; ▲ from £19; 110 hardstanding pitches

Leisure: ⚲ 🔍 ▭ ⚙

Facilities: 🏠 ☉ 🌡 ✳ ⚕ ⑤ ♨ 🗵 WiFi

Services: ⚡ 🔋 📶 🍴 ⚓ 🛒 ♿ ⬛ ⬥ 🅣

Within 3 miles: ⛳ 🏌 ⛵ ☕

Additional site information: 32 acre site. 🐎 Cars can be parked by caravans and tents. Awnings permitted. Bikes, skateboards and scooters only permitted on leisure field. Snooker, table tennis, badminton.

Twelve Oaks Farm Caravan Park
▶▶▶▶ 83%

tel: 01626 335015 & 07976 440456 **Teigngrace TQ12 6QT**
email: info@twelveoaksfarm.co.uk **web:** www.twelveoaksfarm.co.uk
dir: *A38 from Exeter left signed Teigngrace (only), 0.25 mile before Drumbridges roundabout. 1.5 miles, through village, site on left. Or from Plymouth pass Drumbridges roundabout, take slip road for Chudleigh Knighton. Right over bridge, rejoin A38 towards Plymouth. Left for Teigngrace (only), then as above.*

An attractive small park on a working farm close to Dartmoor National Park, and bordered by the River Teign. The tidy pitches are located amongst trees and shrubs, and the modern facilities are very well maintained. There are two well-stocked fishing lakes and children will enjoy visiting all the farm animals. Close by is Stover Country Park and also the popular Templar Way walking route.

Open: All year **Last arrival:** 21.00 **Last departure:** 10.30

Pitches: 🚐 from £17; 🚌 from £17; ▲ from £17; 25 hardstanding pitches

Leisure: 🎣 ⚲ ✒

Facilities: 🏠 ☉ 🌡 ✳ ⚕ ⑤ ♨ WiFi

Services: ⚡ 🔋 ⬥ ⬛ 🅣

Within 3 miles: ⛳ ☕ ◎ 🎣 ☕

Additional site information: 2 acre site. 🐎 Cars can be parked by caravans and tents. Awnings permitted. No noise after 23.00, no fire pits.

LEISURE: 🏊 Indoor swimming pool 🏊 Outdoor swimming pool ⚲ Children's playground 🧒 Kids' club 🎾 Tennis court 🎱 Games room ▭ Separate TV room
⛳ golf course ⛳ Pitch n putt ⛵ Boats for hire 🚲 Bikes for hire 🎬 Cinema 🎵 Entertainment ✒ Fishing ◎ Mini golf 🏄 Watersports 🏋 Gym 🏟 Sports field ☕ Stables
FACILITIES: 🏠 Baths/Shower ☉ Electric shaver sockets 🌡 Hairdryer ✳ Ice Pack Facility 👶 Baby facilities ⚕ Disabled facilities ⑤ Shop on site or within 200yds
♨ BBQ area 🗵 Picnic area WiFi WiFi

OTTERY ST MARY

Map 3 SY19

Places to visit

Cadhay, OTTERY ST MARY, EX11 1QT, 01404 813511
www.cadhay.org.uk

Cuckoo Down Farm Glamping 🏕

►►►► 81% GLAMPING ONLY

tel: 01271 27743 **Lower Broad Oak Road, West Hill EX11 1UE**
email: enquiries@cuckoodownfarm.co.uk **web:** www.cuckoodownfarm.co.uk
dir: *M5, A30 signed Honiton, after airport on left, left signed Daisymount and Ottery St Mary. At mini roundabout, last exit (under bridge). At next mini roundabout follow West Hill sign. 0.5 mile, left into Bendarroch Road. 3rd right into School Lane, right at end, immediately left into Elsdon Lane. At end, straight over onto track. 0.5 mile, fork right to site (bumpy road).*

On arrival at Cuckoo Down Farm the first thing that strikes you is the peace and tranquillity and the far-reaching views from the very spacious, 6-acre glamping meadow. There are four safari tents sleeping six and two yurts sleeping four; all units are kitted out with style. Each has a wood-burning stove, rugs and scatter cushions to make them cosy and comfortable, and down duvets and quilts on the beds. Each unit has a decked outside area, a fully-equipped kitchen cabin and a compost toilet, showers, fridges, freezers, washing machine and tumble drier are located in a nearby barn, which also has a small 'honesty' shop of essentials.

Open: 30 March to 30 October **Last arrival:** 18.00 (later arrivals by prior arrangement) **Last departure:** 10.00

Facilities: 🚿 ✱ ♿ 🪑

Within 3 miles: ⛳ 🎣 🐎 🌊 ⛵ 🛍

Accommodation available: 4 safari tents from £95; 2 yurts from £75.

Changeover days: Monday, Friday

Additional site information: 27 acre site. 🐕 No noise after midnight. Holistic therapies, yoga, on-site catering, woodland walk, forest school. Some safari tents have wood-fired hot tubs. All glamping units have own toilets, yurts share a shower block but safari tents have own hot shower. Wood-burning stoves in all units and camp fires are allowed.

PAIGNTON

Map 3 SX86

Places to visit

Dartmouth Steam Railway & River Boat Company, PAIGNTON, TQ4 6AF, 01803 555872, www.dartmouthrailriver.co.uk

Kents Cavern, TORQUAY, TQ1 2JF, 01803 215136
www.kents-cavern.co.uk

Great for kids: Paignton Zoo Environmental Park, PAIGNTON, TQ4 7EU, 01803 697500, www.paigntonzoo.org.uk

Premier Park

Beverley Park Caravan & Camping Park

Best of British

►►►►► 88%

tel: 01803 843887 **Goodrington Road TQ4 7JE**
email: info@beverley-holidays.co.uk **web:** www.beverley-holidays.co.uk
dir: *On A380, A3022, 2 miles south of Paignton left into Goodrington Road. Beverley Park on right.*

A high quality family-run park with extensive views of the bay and plenty of on-site amenities. The park boasts indoor and outdoor heated swimming pools, plus good bars and restaurants. The toilet facilities are modern and very clean and include excellent fully serviced family rooms. The park complex is attractively laid out with the touring areas divided into nicely screened areas.

Open: All year **Last arrival:** 21.00 **Last departure:** 10.00

Pitches: 🚐 from £20; 🚌 from £20; ⛺ from £14; 49 hardstanding pitches

Leisure: 🏊 🏊 🛝 ✋ 🎾 📺 🎵 🏓 🍸 ⚽ Spa

Facilities: 🚿 ☺ 📞 ✱ ♿ 🛍 🪑 🐕 [Wi-fi]

Services: 🔌 🧺 🍷 🍴 🍔 🚰 🛢 🍃 [T]

Within 3 miles: ⛳ 🎣 🐎 🎯 🌊 ⛵ 🛍

Additional site information: 12 acre site. 🐕 Cars can be parked by caravans and tents. Awnings permitted. Hot tub, sauna, steam room, gym, soft play, crazy golf.

PAIGNTON *continued*

Whitehill Country Park
▶▶▶▶ 85%

tel: 01803 782338 **Stoke Road TQ4 7PF**
email: info@whitehill-park.co.uk web: www.whitehill-park.co.uk
dir: *A385 through Totnes towards Paignton. Turn right by Parkers Arms into Stoke Road towards Stoke Gabriel. Site on left in approximately 1.5 miles.*

A family-owned and run park set in rolling countryside, with many scenic beaches just a short drive away. This extensive country park covers 40 acres with woodland walks and nature trails, an excellent outdoor swimming pool with splash pad and poolside spa, a café, a bar and restaurant plus summer entertainment. It offers ideal facilities, including luxury caravans, lodges and camping pods (dog-friendly accommodation is available) for an excellent holiday.

Open: Easter to October **Last arrival:** 21.00 **Last departure:** 10.00

Pitches: 🚐 from £18.45; 🚌 from £18.45; ⛺ from £15.50; 🏠 see prices below; 30 hardstanding pitches; 40 seasonal pitches

Leisure: 🏊 🅰 🔍 🖵 🎵 **Facilities:** 🛁 🌡 ✳ ♿ 🔼 🎡 🛒 WiFi

Services: 🔌 🔄 🍴 🍽 🔥 ♨ 🚽 🛢 🧴 🗓

Within 3 miles: ↓ 🚲 🐎 ⛳ 🎣 🏖 🎿 🏕

Additional site information: 40 acre site. 🐕 Cars can be parked by caravans and tents. Awnings permitted. Letter box trail, craft room, table tennis, soft play area, woodland walking trails, poolside spa and splash pad. Picnic area. Freshly baked bread available.

Glamping available: 6 wooden pods from £37. **Changeover days:** Any day

Additional glamping information: Wooden pods offer fold-out beds, heating, lighting, plug socket and outdoor furniture.

Places to visit
Saltram, PLYMPTON, PL7 1UH, 01752 333500
www.nationaltrust.org.uk/saltram

Riverside Caravan Park
▶▶▶▶ 85%

tel: 01752 344122 **Leigham Manor Drive PL6 8LL**
email: office@riversidecaravanpark.com web: www.riversidecaravanpark.com
dir: *From A38 at Marsh Mills roundabout, follow signs for Plympton (B3416) and brown 'Riverside' signs. At lights left into Riverside Road signed 'Riverside'. 400 metres, right into Leighham Manor Drive (River Plym on right) to site on right.*

A well-groomed site on the outskirts of Plymouth on the banks of the River Plym, in a surprisingly peaceful location surrounded by woodland. The toilet facilities are appointed to a very good standard, and include private cubicles, plus there's a good games room and bar/restaurant serving food. This park is an ideal stopover for the ferries to France and Spain, and makes an excellent base for touring Dartmoor and the coast. The local bus stop is just a 10-minute walk from the site.

Open: All year (restricted service: October to Easter – bar, restaurant, takeaway and pool closed) **Last arrival:** 22.00 **Last departure:** 11.00

Pitches: 🚐 🚌 ⛺; 63 hardstanding pitches **Leisure:** 🏊 🔍 🖵

Facilities: ⊙ 🌡 ✳ ♿ 🔼 WiFi **Services:** 🔌 🔄 🍴 🍽 🔥 ♨ 🚽 🛢 🧴 🗓

Within 3 miles: ↓ 🚲 🐎 ⛳ 🎣 🏖 🎿 🏕

Additional site information: 11 acre site. 🐕 Cars can be parked by caravans and tents. Awnings permitted.

PRINCETOWN
Map 3 SX57

Places to visit

The Garden House, YELVERTON, PL20 7LQ, 01822 854769
www.thegardenhouse.org.uk

Merrivale Prehistoric Settlement, MERRIVALE, PL20 6ST,
www.english-heritage.org.uk/daysout/properties/
merrivale-prehistoric-settlement

The Plume of Feathers Inn
▶▶ 78%

tel: 01822 890240 **Plymouth Hill PL20 6QQ**
email: contact@theplumeoffeathersdartmoor.co.uk
web: www.theplumeoffeathersdartmoor.co.uk
dir: Site accessed from B3212 roundabout (by Plume of Feathers Inn) in centre of Princetown.

Set amidst the rugged beauty of Dartmoor, and behind the village pub, this campsite boasts good toilet facilities and all the amenities of the inn. The Plume of Feathers is Princetown's oldest building, and serves food all day in an atmospheric setting – try the 'camp and breakfast' deal that's on offer. This campsite is mainly for tents.

Open: All year **Last arrival:** 23.00 **Last departure:** noon

Pitches: ⇔ Å

Services: ⊕ ⊖

Additional site information: 5 acre site. ☛

SALCOMBE
Map 3 SX73

Places to visit

Overbeck's, SALCOMBE, TQ8 8LW, 01548 842893
www.nationaltrust.org.uk/overbecks

Kingsbridge Cookworthy Museum, KINGSBRIDGE, TQ7 1AW, 01548 853235
www.kingsbridgemuseum.org.uk

Karrageen Caravan & Camping Park
▶▶▶▶ 84%

tel: 01548 561230 **Bolberry, Malborough TQ7 3EN**
email: phil@karrageen.co.uk **web:** www.karrageen.co.uk
dir: At Malborough on A381, sharp right through village, in 0.6 mile right again, 0.9 mile, site on right.

A small friendly, family-run park with secluded hidden dells for tents and terraced grass pitches giving extensive sea and country views. This park is a well-stocked shop and an excellent toilet block that has two cubicled units – one suitable for families and for less able visitors. This park is just one mile from the beach and pretty hamlet of Hope Cove and is a really peaceful park from which to explore the South Hams coast.

Open: Easter to September **Last arrival:** 21.00 **Last departure:** 11.30

Pitches: ⇔ ⇔ Å

Facilities: ⊕ ⊖ ⌽ ⋇ ⅋ ⓢ ☶ WiFi

Services: ⊕ ⊖ ⊟ ▣ ⊘ ⊺

Within 3 miles: ↕ ⌁ ⇶ ⇸

Additional site information: 7.5 acre site. ☛ ⊛ Cars can be parked by caravans and tents. Awnings permitted. Noise to be kept to a minimum after 22.00. Freshly baked bread and croissants available. BACS payments accepted.

Bolberry House Farm Caravan & Camping Park
▶▶▶ 83%

tel: 01548 561251 **Bolberry TQ7 3DY**
email: enquiries@bolberryparks.co.uk **web:** www.bolberryparks.co.uk
dir: At Malborough on A381 turn right signed Hope Cove and Bolberry. Take left fork after village signed Soar and Bolberry. Right in 0.6 mile. Site signed in 0.5 mile.

A very popular park in a peaceful setting on a coastal farm with sea views, fine cliff walks and nearby beaches. Customers are assured of a warm welcome and the nicely tucked-away portaloo facilities are smart and beautifully maintained. Hardstandings are available. A mobile fish and chip van calls weekly in high season. There's a super dog-walking area.

Open: Easter to October **Last arrival:** 20.00 **Last departure:** 11.30

Pitches: ⇔ ⇔ Å; 7 hardstanding pitches

Facilities: ⊕ ⌽ ⋇ ⓢ WiFi

Services: ⊕ ⊟ ⊺

Within 3 miles: ↕ ⌁ ⊚ ⇶ ⇸ Ħ

Additional site information: 6 acre site. ☛ Dogs must not be left unattended. ⊛ Cars can be parked by caravans and tents. Awnings permitted. Minimum noise 22.00–08.30. Shop on site (high season only).

Higher Rew Caravan & Camping Park
▶▶▶ 83%

tel: 01548 842681 **Higher Rew, Malborough TQ7 3BW**
email: enquiries@higherrew.co.uk **web:** www.higherrew.co.uk
dir: A381 to Malborough. Right at Townsend Cross, follow signs to Soar. 1 mile, left at Rew Cross, 0.5 mile, site on right.

A long-established park in a remote location within sight of the sea. The spacious, open touring field has some tiered pitches in the sloping grass, and there are lovely countryside or sea views from every pitch. The friendly family owners are continually improving the facilities.

Open: Easter to October **Last arrival:** 22.00 **Last departure:** noon

Pitches: ⇔ from £17; ⇔ from £17; Å from £16

Leisure: ⚑ ⊛ ⊛

Facilities: ⊕ ⌽ ⋇ ⓢ WiFi

Services: ⊕ ⊟ ⊞ ⊺ ⊘ ⊺

Within 3 miles: ⌁ ⇶ ⇸

Additional site information: 5 acre site. ☛ ⊛ Cars can be parked by caravans and tents. Awnings permitted. Minimum noise after 23.00. Play barn with table tennis. Freshly baked bread and croissants available in high season. Internet access available.

SAMPFORD PEVERELL Map 3 ST01

Places to visit

Tiverton Castle, TIVERTON, EX16 6RP, 01884 253200
www.tivertoncastle.com

Tiverton Museum of Mid Devon Life, TIVERTON, EX16 6PJ, 01884 256295
www.tivertonmuseum.org.uk

Great for kids: Diggerland, CULLOMPTON, EX15 2PE, 0871 227 7007 (*calls cost 10p per minute plus your phone company's access charge*)
www.diggerland.com

Premier Park

Minnows Touring Park
►►►►► 88%

tel: 01884 821770 **Holbrook Lane EX16 7EN**
email: admin@minnowstouringpark.co.uk **web:** www.minnowstouringpark.co.uk
dir: *M5 junction 27, A361 signed Tiverton and Barnstaple. In 600 yards take 1st slip road, right over bridge, site ahead.*

A small, well-sheltered park, peacefully located amidst fields and mature trees. The toilet facilities are of a high quality in keeping with the rest of the park, and there is a good laundry. The park has direct gated access to the canal towpath; a brisk 20-minute walk leads to a choice of pubs and a farm shop, and the bus stop is 15 minutes away. All pitches are hardstanding with some large enough for American RVs; fully serviced pitches are also available. The park has WiFi.

Open: 6 March to 6 November **Last arrival:** 20.00 (earliest arrival 13.00) **Last departure:** noon

Pitches: * 🚐 from £18; 🚙 from £18; ▲ from £14; 59 hardstanding pitches

Leisure: ⚠

Facilities: 🛁 ☉ 🗠 ❄ ♿ Ⓢ 🎐 WiFi

Services: 🔌 🗑 🛒 ⬆ 🔒 Ⓣ

Within 3 miles: ⌁ ✐ 🚤

Additional site information: 5.5 acre site. 🐕 Cars can be parked by caravans and tents. Awnings permitted. No cycling, no groundsheets on grass. Caravan storage, fishing and boating permits available. Car hire can be arranged.

SHALDON Map 3 SX97

Places to visit

'Bygones', TORQUAY, TQ1 4PR, 01803 326108
www.bygones.co.uk

Babbacombe Model Village, TORQUAY, TQ1 3LA, 01803 315315
www.model-village.co.uk

Coast View Holiday Park
►►►► 82% HOLIDAY HOME PARK

tel: 01626 818350 **Torquay Road TQ14 0BG**
email: holidays@coastview.co.uk **web:** www.southwestholidayparks.co.uk
dir: *M5 junction 31, A38 then A380 towards Torquay. A381 towards Teignmouth. Right in 4 miles at lights, over Shaldon Bridge. In 0.75 mile, up hill, site on right.*

Set high on the cliffs above Shaldon and with spectacular views across Teignmouth Bay and the Jurassic Coast, this popular holiday home park makes the most of the stunning location, with quality park homes spaciously laid out on neat terraces, each with a glass sheltered decked area from which to soak up the glorious sea views. Serious investment across the park has seen significant improvements in recent years including fully equipped statics and luxury lodges and the opening of an impressive and very smart complex featuring a restaurant and bar and indoor swimming pool.

Open: March to November **Last arrival:** 20.00 **Last departure:** 10.00

Holiday Homes: Sleep 4 Bedrooms 2 Bathrooms 2 Microwave TV WiFi Linen included Towels included Electricity included Gas included

Changeover days: Friday, Saturday, Monday

Leisure: 🌊 Spa

Facilities: WiFi

Within 3 miles: ⌁ ✐ Ⓢ 🎐

Additional site information: 33 acre site. 🐕

SIDMOUTH

Places to visit

Branscombe - The Old Bakery, Manor Mill and Forge, BRANSCOMBE, EX12 3DB, 01752 346585, www.nationaltrust.org.uk/branscombe

Otterton Mill, OTTERTON, EX9 7HG, 01395 568521
www.ottertonmill.com

Great for kids: Pecorama Pleasure Gardens, BEER, EX12 3NA, 01297 21542
www.pecorama.co.uk

SIDMOUTH
Map 3 SY18

Platinum Park

Oakdown Country Holiday Park

▶ ▶ ▶ ▶ ▶

tel: 01297 680387 **Gatedown Lane, Weston EX10 0PT**
email: enquiries@oakdown.co.uk **web:** www.oakdown.co.uk
dir: *Exit A3052, 2.5 miles east of junction with A375.*

A quality, friendly, well-maintained park with good landscaping and plenty of maturing trees that make it well screened from the A3052. Pitches are grouped in groves surrounded by shrubs, with a 50-pitch development replete with an upmarket toilet block. The park has excellent facilities including a spacious reception building, a 9-hole par 3 golf course and a good shop and café. There are four-berth wooden pods and a toilet cabin for the pods, and two shepherd's huts for hire. The park's conservation areas, with their natural flora and fauna, offer attractive walks, and there is a hide by the Victorian reed bed for both casual and dedicated birdwatchers.

Oakdown Country Holiday Park

Open: April to October **Last arrival:** 22.00 **Last departure:** 10.30

Pitches: 🚐 from £13.90; 🚍 from £13.90; ▲ from £13.90; 🏠 see prices below; 90 hardstanding pitches; 35 seasonal pitches

Leisure: 🅰 🔍 ⛱ ♨

Facilities: 🏪 ⊙ ⊙ 🅿 ⚒ ♿ 🚿 🛒 📶 WiFi

Services: 🚐 🔋 📶 🍴 🎮 ⬆ 🛢 🔄 T

Within 3 miles: 🦮 🕐 🎯 🅿 ⛳ 🎣 🏇

Additional site information: 16 acre site. 🐕 Cars can be parked by caravans and tents. Awnings permitted. No bikes, skateboards, drones or kite flying. Microwave available, field trail to donkey sanctuary

Glamping available: Wooden pods from £40; shepherd's huts from £90.

Changeover days: Any day

Additional glamping information. Shepherd's huts: Linen supplied, TV and microwave. Patio area with table and chairs. Cars can be parked by pods and huts.

See advert below

PITCHES: 🚐 Caravans 🚍 Motorhomes ▲ Tents 🏠 Glamping accommodation **SERVICES:** 🔌 Electric hook-up 🅻 Launderette 🍺 Licensed bar
🔥 Calor Gas 🔥 Campingaz T Toilet fluid 🍴 Café/Restaurant 🍟 Fast Food/Takeaway 🔋 Battery charging ⬆ Motorhome service point
* 2019 prices 🚫 No credit or debit cards 🐕 Dogs permitted 🚫 No dogs

SIDMOUTH *continued*

Premier Park

Salcombe Regis Caravan & Camping Park
►►►►► 85%

tel: 01395 514303 **Salcombe Regis EX10 0JH**
email: contact@salcombe-regis.co.uk **web:** www.salcombe-regis.co.uk
dir: *A375 to Sidford onto A3052 towards Lyme Regis, 1 mile, turn right at brown Salcombe Regis/campsite sign. From Lyme Regis towards Sidford on A3052 turn left after Donkey Sanctuary (Note: it is advisable to follow brown tourist signs not sat nav).*

Set in quiet countryside with glorious views, this spacious park has well-maintained facilities and a good mix of grass and hardstanding pitches. A footpath runs from the park to the coastal path and the beach. There is a self-catering holiday cottage and static caravans for hire. This is a perfect location for visiting Sidmouth, Lyme Regis and the coastal area of southeast Devon.

Open: Easter to end October **Last arrival:** 20.15 **Last departure:** noon

Pitches: * 🚐 from £16.50; 🚐 from £16.50; ▲ from £16.50;
40 hardstanding pitches; 30 seasonal pitches

Leisure: ⚠

Facilities: 🏠 ☉ 🇫 ✳ ﹠ ⑤ 🍴 ﹏ WiFi

Services: 🔌 🗓 🛒 ᛩ 🔋 🖉 🅃

Within 3 miles: ↓ ✐ ∪ ◎ 🎿 🛶 🎏

Additional site information: 16 acre site. 🐾 Cars can be parked by caravans and tents. Awnings permitted. Quiet at 22.00, no noise from 23.00. No open fires, no drones or remote controlled planes or helicopters. Putting green, table tennis, goal posts, badminton. Croissants baked to order. Car hire can be arranged.

SOURTON CROSS	Map 3 SX59

Places to visit

Lydford Gorge, LYDFORD, EX20 4BH, 01822 820320
www.nationaltrust.org.uk/lydford-gorge

Okehampton Castle, OKEHAMPTON, EX20 1JA, 01837 52844
www.english-heritage.org.uk/daysout/properties/okehampton-castle

---

Bundu Camping & Caravan Park
►►► 84%

tel: 01837 861747 **EX20 4HT**
email: bundu@btconnect.com **web:** www.bundu.co.uk
dir: *From A30, west of Okehampton towards Launceston, left onto A386 signed Tavistock. 1st left and left again.*

The welcoming, friendly owners set the tone for this well-maintained site, ideally positioned on the border of the Dartmoor National Park. Along with fine views, there's well-maintained toilet facilities, level grassy pitches and two bell tents for hire; the Granite Way cycle track (from Lydford to Okehampton) that runs along the old railway line passes the edge of the park. There is a bus stop and cycle hire a few minutes' walk away. Dogs are accepted.

Open: All year **Last arrival:** 21.00 **Last departure:** noon

---

Pitches: 🚐 from £16; 🚐 from £16; ▲ from £10; 🏠 see prices below;
16 hardstanding pitches

Facilities: 🏠 ☉ 🇫 ✳ ﹠ ⑤ 🍴 ﹏ WiFi

Services: 🔌 🗓 🛒 🔋 🖉 🅃

Within 3 miles: ↓ ✐ 🎏

Additional site information: 4.5 acre site. 🐾 Cars can be parked by caravans and tents. Awnings permitted.

Glamping available: Bell tents from £40. **Changeover days:** Any day

Additional glamping information: No dogs in bell tents. Cars can be parked by tents.

SOUTH MOLTON	Map 3 SS72

Places to visit

Quince Honey Farm, SOUTH MOLTON, EX36 3AZ, 01769 572401
www.quincehoneyfarm.co.uk

Cobbaton Combat Collection, CHITTLEHAMPTON, EX37 9RZ, 01769 540740
www.cobbatoncombat.co.uk

Great for kids: Exmoor Zoological Park, BLACKMOOR GATE, EX31 4SG,
01598 763352, www.exmoorzoo.co.uk

Premier Park

Riverside Caravan & Camping Park
►►►►► 92%

tel: 01769 579269 **Marsh Lane, North Molton Road EX36 3HQ**
email: relax@exmoorriverside.co.uk **web:** www.exmoorriverside.co.uk
dir: *M5 junction 27, A361 towards Barnstaple. Site signed 1 mile before South Molton on right.*

A family-run park set alongside the River Mole and in 70 acres of landscaped parkland with 10 acres of woodland trails. This is an ideal base for exploring Exmoor, as well as north Devon's golden beaches. It offers 58 premium, fully serviced pitches for RVs, motorhomes, caravans and campervans, 40 jumbo grass pitches with electricity for tents, a large camping field and rally field, an award-winning shower block, the Country Club restaurant and bar, family entertainment, caravan storage and a collection service. There is a public

---

footpath linking the park to South Molton and the local bus stops at the park entrance.

Riverside Caravan & Camping Park

Open: All year **Last arrival:** 22.00 **Last departure:** 11.00

Pitches: from £18; from £18; from £10; 54 hardstanding pitches

Leisure: ⚒ 🎵 ✐ ⚽

Facilities: 🛁 ⊙ 🛇 ✗ 👤 🛗 🛒 🖨 WiFi

Services: 🔌 🔲 🍺 🍴 🍟 🛒 ⚡ 🔋 🚰 ⓣ

Within 3 miles: 🔱 ♻ 🏌 🗓

Additional site information: 70 acre site. Cars can be parked by caravans and tents. Awnings permitted. Quiet after 23.00. Woodland and valley walks.

See advert below

STARCROSS

See Dawlish

STOKE GABRIEL   Map 3 SX85

Places to visit

Berry Pomeroy Castle, TOTNES, TQ9 6NJ, 01803 866618
www.english-heritage.org.uk/daysout/properties/berry-pomeroy-castle

Totnes Elizabethan House Museum, TOTNES, TQ9 5RU, 01803 863821
www.devonmuseums.net/totnes

Great for kids: Paignton Zoo Environmental Park, PAIGNTON, TQ4 7EU, 01803 697500, www.paigntonzoo.org.uk

Higher Well Farm Holiday Park
▶▶▶ 86%

tel: 01803 782289 **Waddeton Road TQ9 6RN**
email: higherwell@talk21.com **web:** www.higherwellfarmholidaypark.co.uk
dir: *From Exeter A380 to Paignton, turn right onto A385 for Totnes, in 0.5 mile left for Stoke Gabriel, follow signs.*

Set on a quiet farm yet only four miles from Paignton, this rural holiday park is on the outskirts of the picturesque village of Stoke Gabriel. A toilet block, with some en suite facilities, is an excellent amenity, and tourers are sited in an open field with very good views.

Open: 13 April to 2 November **Last arrival:** 22.00 **Last departure:** 10.00

Pitches: from £14; from £14; from £14; 3 hardstanding pitches

Facilities: 🛁 ⊙ 🛇 ✗ 👤 🔲

Services: 🔌 🔲 🛒 ⚡ 🔋 ⓣ

Within 3 miles: 🔱 ✐

Additional site information: 10 acre site. Cars can be parked by caravans and tents. Awnings permitted. No commercial vehicles. Pets must not be left unattended in caravans, motorhomes or tents.

PITCHES: 🚐 Caravans 🚐 Motorhomes ⛺ Tents ⛺ Glamping accommodation **SERVICES:** 🔌 Electric hook-up 🔲 Launderette 🍺 Licensed bar
🛢 Calor Gas ⚡ Campingaz ⓣ Toilet fluid 🍴 Café/Restaurant 🍟 Fast Food/Takeaway 🔋 Battery charging ⚡ Motorhome service point
* 2019 prices 🚫 No credit or debit cards 🐕 Dogs permitted 🚫 No dogs

STOKE GABRIEL *continued*

Broadleigh Farm Park
▶▶▶ 84%

tel: 01803 782110 **Coombe House Lane, Aish TQ9 6PU**
email: enquiries@broadleighfarm.co.uk web: www.broadleighfarm.co.uk
dir: *From Exeter on A38 then A380 towards Torbay. Right onto A385 for Totnes. In 0.5 mile right at Whitehill Country Park. Site approximately 0.75 mile on left.*

Set in a very rural location on a working farm bordering Paignton and Stoke Gabriel. The large sloping field with a timber-clad toilet block in the centre is sheltered and peaceful, surrounded by rolling countryside but handy for the beaches. There is also an excellent rally field with good toilets and showers.

Open: March to October **Last arrival:** 21.00 **Last departure:** 11.00

Pitches: 🚐 🚏 ▲ **Facilities:** 🛁 ☉ 🖉 ✳ 🌄 💲 🚽 🎍 🛜 WiFi

Services: 🔌 🗑 🧺

Within 3 miles: 🏌 🗡 ◎ 🏊 🚣 🎣

Additional site information: 7 acre site. 🚗 Cars can be parked by caravans and tents. Awnings permitted. Fish and chip van Saturdays in high season, basic essentials shop.

TAVISTOCK	Map 3 SX47

Places to visit

Morwellham Quay, MORWELLHAM, PL19 8JL, 01822 832766
www.morwellham-quay.co.uk

Premier Park

Woodovis Park
▶▶▶▶▶ 91%   Best of British

tel: 01822 832968 **Gulworthy PL19 8NY**
email: info@woodovis.com web: www.woodovis.com
dir: *A390 from Tavistock signed Callington and Gunnislake. At hill top right at roundabout signed Lamerton and Chipshop. Site 1 mile on left.*

A well-kept park in a remote woodland setting on the edge of the Tamar Valley. Peacefully located at the end of a private, half-mile, tree-lined drive, it offers superb on-site facilities and high levels of customer care from the owners. The toilets are immaculate and well maintained, plus there is an indoor swimming pool, sauna and a good information and games room, all creating a friendly atmosphere. Facilities include electric bike hire and a charging point for electric cars. 2-berth and 4-berth wooden pods are available for hire.

Open: 16 March to 3 November **Last arrival:** 20.00 **Last departure:** 11.00

Pitches: * 🚐 from £21; 🚏 from £21; ▲ from £21; 🏠 see prices below; 28 hardstanding pitches; 8 seasonal pitches

Leisure: 🏊 🎪 🎾 🎯 🎮 **Facilities:** 🛁 ☉ 🖉 ✳ 🌄 💲 🎍 WiFi

Services: 🔌 🗑 🧺 🧺 🚽 🔥 🚿 T **Within 3 miles:** 🏌 🗡 🏊 🚣 🎣

Additional site information: 14.5 acre site. 🚗 Cars can be parked by caravans and tents. Awnings permitted. No open fires. Pétanque court, outdoor table tennis, archery, water-walking, infrared therapy cabin, hot tub, circus skills workshops and story telling (in school holidays).

Glamping available: Wooden pods from £59. **Changeover days:** Any day

Additional glamping information: Wooden pods: 1 night stay not possible for Fridays or Saturdays. Cars can be parked by pods.

Premier Park

Harford Bridge Holiday Park
▶▶▶▶▶ 85%

tel: 01822 810349 & 07773 251457 **Peter Tavy PL19 9LS**
email: stay@harfordbridge.co.uk web: www.harfordbridge.co.uk
dir: *A386 from Tavistock towards Okehampton, 2 miles, right signed Peter Tavy, site 200 yards on right.*

This beautiful, spacious park is set beside the River Tavy in the Dartmoor National Park. Pitches are located beside the river and around the copses, and the park is very well equipped for holidaymakers. An adventure playground and games room keep children entertained, and there is fly-fishing and a free tennis court. Studio lodges (S-pods) and a lovely, authentic shepherd's hut complete with fridge and woodburner are available to let.

Open: All year (restricted service: 14 November to 15 March — no camping or touring pitches available (holiday caravans, lodges and studio lodges only)) **Last arrival:** 18.00 **Last departure:** noon

Pitches: 🚐 🚏 ▲ 🏠; 20 hardstanding pitches; 5 seasonal pitches

Leisure: 🎪 🎾 🎮 🖵 🎣 🎯

Facilities: 🛁 ☉ 🖉 ✳ 🌄 💲 🎍 🛜 WiFi

Services: 🔌 🗑 🧺 🚽 🔥 🚿 T

Within 3 miles: 🏌 🚶 🚣 🎣

Additional site information: 16 acre site. 🚗 Cars can be parked by caravans and tents. Awnings permitted. Baguettes, croissants, snacks, sweets, cold drinks, ices and grocery basics available. Expedition groups and rallies welcome by prior arrangement.

Glamping available: Shepherd's hut; studio lodges (S-pods).

Changeover days: Saturday

Additional glamping information: No smoking or vaping in shepherd's hut or studio lodges. Adults only. Cars can be parked by glamping units.

LEISURE: 🏊 Indoor swimming pool 🏊 Outdoor swimming pool 🎪 Children's playground 🧒 Kids' club 🎾 Tennis court 🎮 Games room 🖵 Separate TV room 🏌 golf course 🏌 Pitch n putt 🚣 Boats for hire 🚲 Bikes for hire 🎬 Cinema 🎵 Entertainment 🎣 Fishing ◎ Mini golf 🏊 Watersports 🏋 Gym 🏟 Sports field ⛺ Stables
FACILITIES: 🛁 Baths/Shower ☉ Electric shaver sockets 🖉 Hairdryer ✳ Ice Pack Facility 🍼 Baby facilities 🌄 Disabled facilities 💲 Shop on site or within 200yds 🍖 BBQ area 🎍 Picnic area 🛜 WiFi

Premier Park

Langstone Manor Camping & Caravan Park
▶▶▶▶▶ 83%

tel: 01822 613371 **Moortown PL19 9JZ**
email: jane@langstonemanor.co.uk **web:** www.langstonemanor.co.uk
dir: Take B3357 from Tavistock to Princetown. Approximately 1.5 miles turn right at crossroads, follow signs. Over bridge, cattle grid, up hill, left at sign, left again to park (Note: it is advisable not to follow sat nav).

A secluded and very peaceful site set in the well-maintained grounds of a manor house in Dartmoor National Park. Many attractive mature trees provide screening within the park, yet the west-facing terraced pitches on the main park enjoy the superb summer sunsets. There are excellent toilet facilities plus a popular lounge bar offering a very good menu of reasonably priced evening meals. Plenty of activities and places of interest can be found within the surrounding moorland. Dogs are accepted. Twelve wooden pods in a wooded setting are available for hire; three mega-pods have en suite facilities.

Open: 15 March to 15 November (restricted service: bar and restaurant open daily 16.00 to 21.00) **Last arrival:** 21.00 **Last departure:** 11.00

Pitches: 🚐 from £18; 🚐 from £18; ▲ from £18; 🏠 see prices below; 18 hardstanding pitches

Leisure: 🎡 🎯 🎣 **Facilities:** 🏠 ☺ 🍴 ※ ♿ 🚿 🚻 🛒 WiFi

Services: 🔌 🔋 🍴 🍽 🍟 🛒 ⛟ 🚰 T

Within 3 miles: ⅃ 🎣 U ◎ 🚴 🎢 £

Additional site information: 6.5 acre site. 🐕 Cars can be parked by caravans and tents. Awnings permitted. Cycle shed. Baguettes, croissants etc available. Car hire can be arranged.

Glamping available: Wooden pods from £45; mega pods from £90.

Changeover days: Any day

Additional glamping information: Cars can be parked by pods.

TEDBURN ST MARY Map 3 SX89

Places to visit

Finch Foundry, STICKLEPATH, EX20 2NW, 01837 840046
www.nationaltrust.org.uk/finch-foundry

Castle Drogo, DREWSTEIGNTON, EX6 6PB, 01647 433306
www.nationaltrust.org.uk/castle-drogo

Springfield Holiday Park
▶▶▶▶ 86%

tel: 01647 24242 **EX6 6EW**
email: info@springfieldcaravanpark.co.uk **web:** www.springfield-park.co.uk
dir: M5 junction 31, A30 towards Okehampton. Exit A30 at Cheriton Bishop sign. Follow brown tourist signs to site. (Note: for sat nav use EX6 6JN).

Set in a quiet rural location with countryside views, this park continues to be upgraded to a smart standard. It has the advantage of being close to Dartmoor National Park, with village pubs and stores less than a mile away. There is a very inviting heated outdoor swimming pool.

Open: 15 March to 30 October **Last arrival:** 21.00 **Last departure:** noon
Pitches: 🚐 🚐 ▲; 38 hardstanding pitches; 25 seasonal pitches

Leisure: 🏊 🎡 🎣 **Facilities:** 🏠 ※ 🚿 🚻 🛒 WiFi
Services: 🔌 🔋 🍴 🍽 🚰 ⛟ 🚰 ◎
Within 3 miles: ⅃ 🎣 U 🛒

Additional site information: 9 acre site. 🐕 Cars can be parked by caravans and tents. Awnings permitted.

TIVERTON

See East Worlington

TORQUAY Map 3 SX96

See also Newton Abbot

Places to visit

Torre Abbey Historic House & Gallery, TORQUAY, TQ2 5JE, 01803 293593
www.torre-abbey.org.uk

'Bygones', TORQUAY, TQ1 4PR, 01803 326108
www.bygones.co.uk

Widdicombe Farm Touring Park
▶▶▶▶ 90%

tel: 01803 558325 **Marldon TQ3 1ST**
email: info@widdicombefarm.co.uk **web:** www.widdicombefarm.co.uk
dir: On A380, midway between Torquay and Paignton.

A friendly family-run park on a working farm with good quality facilities, extensive views and easy access as there are no narrow roads. The level pitches are terraced to take advantage of the views towards the coast and Dartmoor. This is the only adult touring park within Torquay, and is also handy for Paignton and Brixham. There's a bus service from the park to the local shopping centre and Torquay's harbour. It has a small shop, a restaurant and a bar with entertainment from Easter to the end of September. Club WiFi is available throughout the park and The Nippy Chippy van calls regularly.

Open: mid March to end October **Last arrival:** 20.00 **Last departure:** 11.00

Pitches: 🚐 from £15.50; 🚐 from £15.50; ▲ from £13; 180 hardstanding pitches; 20 seasonal pitches

Leisure: 🎵 **Facilities:** ☺ 🍴 ※ ♿ £ 🚻 WiFi
Services: 🔌 🔋 🍴 🍽 🍟 🚰 ⛟ 🔋 ⊘ T **Within 3 miles:** ⅃ 🎣 ◎ 🚴 🎢 🎢

Additional site information: 8 acre site. Adults only. 🐕 Most dog breeds accepted (contact site for details). Cars can be parked by caravans and tents. Awnings permitted. No groups.

WHIDDON DOWN

Map 3 SX69

Places to visit

Castle Drogo, DREWSTEIGNTON, EX6 6PB, 01647 433306
www.nationaltrust.org.uk/castle-drogo

Finch Foundry, STICKLEPATH, EX20 2NW, 01837 840046
www.nationaltrust.org.uk/finch-foundry

Dartmoor View Holiday Park

►►► 84%

tel: 01647 588026 **EX20 2QL**
email: dartmoorviewtouring@haulfryn.co.uk **web:** www.dartmoorviewtouring.co.uk
dir: *From M5 junction 31, take A30 to Okehampton. At Whiddon Down take left junction through village. Turn right at small roundabout. Park is 400 metres on right.*

Located just off the A30 near Okehampton, on the northern edge of Dartmoor, this immaculate 20-acre park certainly lives up to its name, and more. Although predominantly a static park, the 26 designated pitches (hardstandings with electric, and some with water and waste drainage) for touring caravans and motorhomes are secluded in a separate, well-landscaped field, replete with a spotlessly clean and well-equipped amenity block. Dogs and children are very welcome and there's a children's play area and a heated outdoor swimming pool which has a sun-deck area. Dartmoor View is the ideal base for those keen to explore Dartmoor on foot or by bike.

Open: March to October **Last arrival:** 18.00 **Last departure:** 11.00

Pitches: 🚐 🚌; 26 hardstanding pitches; 26 seasonal pitches

Leisure: 🏊 🛝 🎱 📺 🎣 ⚽ **Facilities:** 🛁 💨 ♿ 🧺 [WiFi]

Services: 🚿 🗑 **Within 3 miles:** [S]

Additional site information: 20 acre site. 🐕 Cars can be parked by caravans. Awnings permitted. 10mph speed limit.

See advert opposite

WOOLACOMBE

Map 3 SS44

See also Mortehoe

Places to visit

Great for kids: Combe Martin Wildlife Park & Dinosaur Park, COMBE MARTIN, EX34 0NG, 01271 882486
https://cmwdp.co.uk

Premier Park

Warcombe Farm Caravan & Camping Park

►►►►► 90%

tel: 01271 870690 **Station Road, Mortehoe EX34 7EJ**
email: info@warcombefarm.co.uk **web:** www.warcombefarm.co.uk
dir: *On B3343 towards Woolacombe turn right towards Mortehoe. Site less than 1 mile on right.*

Extensive views over the Bristol Channel can be enjoyed from the open areas of this attractive park, while other pitches are sheltered in paddocks with maturing trees. The site has 14 excellent super pitches with hardstandings. The superb sandy, Blue Flag beach at Woolacombe Bay is only a mile and a half away, and there is a fishing lake with direct access from some pitches. The local bus stops outside the park entrance.

Open: 15 March to October **Last arrival:** 21.00 **Last departure:** 11.00

Pitches: 🚐 from £16; 🚌 from £16; ⛺ from £16; 82 hardstanding pitches
12 seasonal pitches

Leisure: 🛝 🎣 ⚽

Facilities: 🛁 🔌 💨 ❄ ♿ [S] 🍖 🧺 [WiFi]

Services: 🚿 🗑 🍴 🧺 🛒 ⚓ 🔒 🌿 [T]

Within 3 miles: 🏌 🐴 ◎ 🌊 ⛵ 🎬

Additional site information: 35 acre site. 🐕 Cars can be parked by caravans and tents. Awnings permitted. No noise after 22.30. Car hire can be arranged.

LEISURE: 🏊 Indoor swimming pool 🏊 Outdoor swimming pool 🛝 Children's playground 👋 Kids' club 🎾 Tennis court 🎱 Games room 📺 Separate TV room 🏌 golf course ⛳ Pitch n putt ⛵ Boats for hire 🚲 Bikes for hire 🎬 Cinema 🎭 Entertainment 🎣 Fishing ◎ Mini golf 🌊 Watersports 🏋 Gym ⚽ Sports field 🐴 Stables
FACILITIES: 🛁 Baths/Shower 🔌 Electric shaver sockets 💨 Hairdryer ❄ Ice Pack Facility 👶 Baby facilities ♿ Disabled facilities [S] Shop on site or within 200yds 🍖 BBQ area 🧺 Picnic area [WiFi] WiFi

IT'S ALL ABOUT THE VIEW...
Dartmoor Touring Pitches

NO HIDDEN EXTRAS

CALL THE SALES TEAM FOR EXCLUSIVE OFFERS THROUGHOUT THE YEAR

Terms & conditions apply.

- ✓ 26 superb touring pitches
- ✓ 20 acres of landscaped grounds
- ✓ **FREE** outdoor swimming pool
- ✓ **FREE** hot water, showers & electric
- ✓ Minutes from Dartmoor National Park
- ✓ Okehampton 15 mins, Exeter 25 mins

Call **01647 588026** or book online
at **dartmoorviewtouring.co.uk**

DARTMOOR VIEW
Whiddon Down, Okehampton, Devon EX20 2QL

PITCHES: 🚐 Caravans 🚍 Motorhomes 🅰 Tents ⛺ Glamping accommodation   SERVICES: 🔌 Electric hook-up 🧺 Launderette 🍺 Licensed bar
🔥 Calor Gas 🔥 Campingaz 🅃 Toilet fluid 🍽 Café/Restaurant 🍟 Fast Food/Takeaway 🔋 Battery charging ⚙ Motorhome service point
* 2019 prices 🚫 No credit or debit cards 🐕 Dogs permitted 🚫 No dogs

WOOLACOMBE *continued*

Premier Park

Twitchen House Holiday Village
▶▶▶▶▶ 90% HOLIDAY CENTRE

tel: 01271 872302 **Mortehoe Station Road, Mortehoe EX34 7ES**
email: goodtimes@woolacombe.com **web:** www.woolacombe.com
dir: *M5 junction 27, A361 to Ilfracombe. From Mullacott Cross roundabout take B3343 (Woolacombe road) to Turnpike Cross junction. Take right fork, site 1.5 miles on left.*

A very attractive, seaside park with excellent leisure facilities, all-weather activities and entertainment. The touring area features many fully serviced pitches and 80 that are available for tents; they have either sea views or a woodland countryside outlook. There are super pitches with TV aerial, water, drainage, electricity and a night light. The shower rooms have underfloor heating and individual cubicles, plus there's a sauna, steam room, launderette, washing up area and chemical disposal facilities. There's an entertainment lounge, indoor soft play area, a cinema, pottery painting studio and many all-weather activities. Visitors can also use the amenities at the other three villages owned by Woolacombe Bay Holiday Parks and a bus service connects them all with the beach.

Open: mid March to October (restricted service: mid March to mid May and September to October — outdoor pool closed) **Last arrival:** midnight **Last departure:** 10.00
Pitches: * 🚐 from £10; 🚎 from £10; ▲ from £10; 110 hardstanding pitches
Leisure: 🏊 ⛱ 🎢 ✋ 🎯 ▢ 🎵 🎣 🏏 ⚽ 🎾 🎱
Facilities: 🛁 ☺ ☔ ✳ ⛐ ⓢ 🍴 🚜 ➡ 📶
Services: 🔌 🗑 🍽 🍴 🛒 🎪 ⚓ 🌀 🆃
Within 3 miles: ⬇ ∪ ◎ ⛸ ⚓ 🎱

Additional site information: 45 acre site. ⛩ Table tennis, sauna, swimming and surfing lessons, climbing wall, bungee trampoline, kiddy karts, cinema, flumes, splash pads, outdoor gym, wildlife and bushcraft activities. Internet access available.

See adverts on page 163 and the inside front cover

Premier Park

Woolacombe Bay Holiday Village & Spa
▶▶▶▶▶ 88% HOLIDAY HOME PARK 🏰

tel: 01271 872302 **Sandy Lane EX34 7AH**
email: goodtimes@woolacombe.com **web:** www.woolacombe.com
dir: *M5 junction 27, A361 to Ilfracombe. At Mullacott roundabout take 1st exit to Woolacombe. Follow Mortehoe signs.*

This park has spectacular sea views and a superb selection of activities and facilities. A new Surf Village was developed for the 2018 and 2019 season offering a premium selection of caravan holiday homes plus new surf lodges with private hot tubs, and a unique surf pod in a coastal-theme setting. The park has invested in an entertainment complex with a panoramic terrace, ocean bar, a 2D and 3D cinema, fitness gym, craft centre, soft play area and indoor pirate ship fun pool. Guests here can use all the facilities offered by the other three villages (just minutes away) owned by Woolacombe Bay Holiday Parks plus there is a bus service connecting them all with the beach. There's all-weather activities (many are free) and sports facilities for all ages. Please note, Woolacombe Bay Holiday Village & Spa no longer accepts tourers — pitches are available at Twitchen House Holiday Village, Golden Coast Holiday Village, and Easewell Farm Holiday Village.

Open: mid March to October (restricted service: mid March to mid May and September to October — outdoor pool closed) **Last arrival:** midnight **Last departure:** 10.00

Accommodation available: Caravans, apartments and surf lodges (sleep 8, depending on model). Cars can be parked by apartments, surf lodges and surf pod. From £169 (short breaks); from £339 (7 nights).

Leisure: 🏊 ⛱ 🎢 ✋ 🎲 🎣 🎵 🏏 ⚽ 🎾 ☺ 🎱 ⛸ Spa
Facilities: 🛁 ☺ ☔ ✳ ⛐ ⓢ 🍴 🚜 ➡ 📶
Services: 🗑 🍽 🍴 🛒
Within 3 miles: ⬇ ∪ ◎ ⛸ ⚓ 🎱

Additional site information: 8.5 acre site. Pet friendly accommodation available. Site not ideal for guests with mobility problems due to hills and stairs. Bungee trampoline, climbing wall, 2D and 3D cinema, gym, spa, heated pools, toddler fun pool, Water Walkerz, sun terrace, pottery painting, kiddy karts, pirate ship, Segways and zorbing. Internet access available.

Glamping available: Surf pod located in surf village.

Additional glamping information: Surf pod: sleeps 4 and are fully equipped. Cars can be parked by pod.

See adverts on page 163 and the inside front cover

LEISURE: 🏊 Indoor swimming pool ⛱ Outdoor swimming pool 🎢 Children's playground ✋ Kids' club 🎾 Tennis court 🎱 Games room ▢ Separate TV room ⬇ golf course 🏏 Pitch n putt ⚓ Boats for hire 🚲 Bikes for hire 🎬 Cinema 🎵 Entertainment 🎣 Fishing ◎ Mini golf ⛸ Watersports 🏋 Gym ⚽ Sports field ∪ Stables
FACILITIES: 🛁 Baths/Shower ☺ Electric shaver sockets ☔ Hairdryer ✳ Ice Pack Facility 🚜 Baby facilities ⛐ Disabled facilities ⓢ Shop on site or within 200yds 🍴 BBQ area 🪑 Picnic area 📶 WiFi

Premier Park

Golden Coast Holiday Village

►►►►► 87% HOLIDAY CENTRE

tel: 01271 872302 **Station Road EX34 7HW**
email: goodtimes@woolacombe.com **web:** www.woolacombe.com
dir: M5 junction 27, A361 to Ilfracombe. At Mullacott roundabout 1st exit to Woolacombe.

A seaside holiday village, set beside a three-mile sandy beach, that offers excellent leisure facilities together with the amenities available at the other three villages owned by Woolacombe Bay Holiday Parks. There is a neat touring area with a unisex toilet block that has underfloor heating and individual cubicles – all maintained to a high standard; the super pitches have water, drainage, electricity, TV aerial and night light. The sports complex features ten-pin bowling, high ropes course, climbing wall, surfing simulator and adventure golf and much more, there are over 40 free activities available to try. Please note, pets are only allowed in the pet-friendly accommodation, not on the touring pitches.

Open: February to November (restricted service: February to May and mid September to November – outdoor pool closed) **Last arrival:** midnight **Last departure:** 10.00

Pitches: * 🚐 from £21; 🚙 from £21; ⛺ from £21; 89 hardstanding pitches

Leisure: 🏊 🏖 ⛰ ✋ 🎣 🎱 🏓 🎹 🎨 🎯 ⚽

Facilities: 🏠 ⊙ 🚿 ✳ ♿ 🛒 🍴 🔌 WiFi

Services: 🔌 🗑 🍴 🍽 🍺 🛒 ♻ T

Within 3 miles: ♨ ∪ ◎ 🚴 🎣 日

Additional site information: 10 acre site. 🐕 Dogs only in pet-friendly accommodation. No pets allowed on caravan, motorhome or tent pitches. Sauna, fishing, snooker, cinema, bungee trampoline, 3 level soft play area, sports complex, outdoor gym, swimming and surfing lessons, surf simulator, pottery, painting, ten-pin bowling. Internet access available.

See adverts on page 163 and the inside front cover

Easewell Farm Holiday Village

►►► 85%

tel: 01271 872302 **Mortehoe Station Road, Mortehoe EX34 7EH**
email: goodtimes@woolacombe.com **web:** www.woolacombe.com
dir: M5 junction 27, A361 to Ilfracombe. At Mullacott roundabout 1st exit to Woolacombe. Follow Mortehoe signs.

A peaceful cliff-top park with superb views that offers full facility pitches for caravans and motorhomes – there are super pitches with TV aerial, water, drainage, electricity and a night light. The shower rooms have individual cubicles plus there's a washing up area, launderette and chemical disposal facilities. The park offers a traditional campsite experience in a rural setting and also has a professional sea view 9-hole (18 tee) par 33 golf course and direct access to the South West Coast Path which runs through the grounds. There is an indoor heated pool with a toddler pool, outdoor adventure play area, convenience store and a sports bar plus you can use the facilities and activities at the other nearby three villages owned by Woolacombe Bay Holiday Parks. There is also a bus that connects them all and the beach.

Open: March to end October (restricted service: at Easter) **Last arrival:** 22.00 **Last departure:** 10.00

Pitches: * 🚐 from £6; 🚙 from £6; ⛺ from £6; 186 hardstanding pitches

Leisure: 🏊 ⛰ ✋ 🎹 🎯

Facilities: 🏠 ⊙ 🚿 ✳ ♿ 🛒 🍴 🔌 WiFi

Services: 🔌 🗑 🍴 🍽 🍺 🛒 ♻ T

Within 3 miles: 🎣 ∪ ◎ 🚴 🎣 日

Additional site information: 17 acre site. 🐕 Cars can be parked by caravans and tents. Awnings permitted. Toddlers' pool, amusement arcade, pool table and surf lessons. Professional golf course, indoor bowls, darts and outdoor adventure play area. Internet access available.

See adverts on page 163 and the inside front cover

WOOLACOMBE *continued*

Europa Park
► ► ► 80%

tel: 01271 871425 **Beach Rd EX34 7AN**
email: holidays@europapark.co.uk **web:** www.europapark.co.uk
dir: *M5 junction 27, A361 through Barnstaple to Mullacott Cross. Left onto B3343 signed Woolacombe. Site on right at Spa shop/garage.*

A very lively family-run site that's handy for the beach at Woolacombe, and that caters well for surfers; it may not be suitable for a quieter type of stay, so please make sure the site meets your holiday requirements before making your booking. Set in a stunning location high above the bay, it provides a wide range of accommodation including surf cabins (sleep 2–6), surf pods (sleep 1–2), surf lodges (sleep up to 12) and generous touring pitches. Visitors can enjoy the indoor pool and sauna, games room, restaurant/café/bar and clubhouse.

Open: All year **Last arrival:** 23.00 **Last departure:** 10.00

Pitches: 🚐 🚙 ⛺ 🏠; 10 hardstanding pitches; 20 seasonal pitches

Leisure: 🏊 🎱 🎵

Facilities: 🛁 ☺ ♿ ⑤ 🚿 🍴 **WiFi**

Services: 🔌 🗑 🚽 🍽 ⚙ 🛒 ⛽ 🔒 🧺 T

Within 3 miles: ⛳ 🎣 ⛵ ◎ 🚣 ✈ 🎪

Additional site information: 16 acre site. 🐕 Cars can be parked by caravans and tents. Awnings permitted. No noise after midnight, no campfires. Beer deck, off licence, pub, big-screen TV, hot tub. Car hire can be arranged.

Glamping available: Surf pods.

Additional glamping information: Cars can be parked by pods.

Escape to North Devon

Right next to Woolacombe's three miles of golden sandy beach

What we've got to offer...

- Sea view touring & super pitches
- Level pitches with easy access
- 400 all weather pitches
- 16 amp electric hookups
- Modern amenity blocks
- Over 40 **FREE** activities

 Stay at one Park and you get to use the facilities on all four of our award winning Holiday Parks...

Golden Coast | Woolacombe Bay | Twitchen House | Easewell Farm

Pitches from just

£6

per night

Call **01271 872 302**
or visit **woolacombe.com**

 *We're here*

WOOLACOMBE BAY
HOLIDAY PARKS

For more information please see our listings on p160 & 161.

PITCHES: 🚐 Caravans 🚐 Motorhomes ⛺ Tents ⛺ Glamping accommodation **SERVICES:** 🔌 Electric hook-up 🧺 Launderette 🍺 Licensed bar
🔋 Calor Gas ⛽ Campingaz 🚽 Toilet fluid 🍽️ Café/Restaurant 🍔 Fast Food/Takeaway 🔋 Battery charging 🚐 Motorhome service point
* 2019 prices 💳 No credit or debit cards 🐕 Dogs permitted 🚫 No dogs

Dorset

Dorset means rugged varied coastlines and high chalk downlands with more than a hint of Thomas Hardy, its most famous son. Squeezed in among the cliffs and set amid some of Britain's most beautiful scenery is a chain of picturesque villages and seaside towns.

Along the coast you'll find the Lulworth Ranges, which run from Kimmeridge Bay in the east to Lulworth Cove in the west. Walking is the most obvious and rewarding recreational activity here, but the British Army firing ranges mean that access to this glorious landscape is restricted. This is Britain's Jurassic Coast, a UNESCO World Heritage Site and Area of Outstanding Natural Beauty, noted for its layers of shale and numerous fossils embedded in the rock. Among the best-known natural landmarks on this stretch of the Dorset coast is Durdle Door, a rocky arch that has been shaped and sculpted to perfection by the elements. The whole area has the unmistakable stamp of prehistory. The landscape and coastal views may be spectacular but the up-and-down nature of the walking here is often physically demanding.

This designated coastline stretches from Swanage and the Isle of Purbeck to east Devon, offering miles of breathtaking scenery. Beyond the seaside town of Weymouth is Chesil Beach, a long shingle reef running for 10 miles between Portland and Abbotsbury. The beach is covered by a vast wall of shingle left by centuries of dramatic weather-induced activity along the Devon and Dorset coast. Beyond Bridport and West Bay, where the hugely successful TV series *Broadchurch* is filmed, lies quaint Lyme Regis, with its sturdy breakwater, known as The Cobb. It's the sort of place where Georgian houses and pretty cottages jostle with historic pubs and independently run shops. With its blend of architectural styles and old world charm, Lyme Regis looks very much like a film set. Perhaps that is why film producers chose this setting as a location for the making of *The French Lieutenant's Woman* in 1981. Jeremy Irons and Meryl Streep starred in the film, based on the novel by John Fowles.

Away from Dorset's magical coastline lies a landscape with a very different character and atmosphere, but one that is no less appealing. Here, winding, hedge-lined country lanes lead beneath lush, green hilltops to snug, sleepy villages hidden from view and the wider world. The main roads lead to the country towns of Sherborne, Blandford Forum, Wareham and Shaftesbury and in September these routes fill with even more traffic as the county prepares to host the annual Dorset Steam Fair. This famous event draws many visitors who come to admire the various vintage and classic vehicles on display. The same month is also set aside for the two-day County Show, an eagerly anticipated annual fixture.

Inland there are further links with literature. Dorset is justifiably proud of the achievements of Thomas Hardy, and much of the county is immortalised in his writing. He was born at Higher Bockhampton, near Dorchester, and this quaint old cob-and-thatch cottage was where the writer lived until he was 34. As a child, Hardy spent much of his time here reading and writing poems about the countryside. The cottage contains the desk where he wrote *Far from the Madding Crowd*. In later years Hardy lived at Max Gate on the edge of Dorchester and here he was visited by many distinguished writers of the day, including Rudyard Kipling and Virginia Woolf. Even the Prince of Wales called on him one day in 1923. Both homes are now in the care of the National Trust.

One of Thomas Hardy's great friends was T. E. (Thomas Edward) Lawrence, better known as Lawrence of Arabia, who lived nearby in a modest cottage known as Clouds Hill. The cottage, also managed by the National Trust, was Lawrence's secluded retreat from the world, where he could read and play music.

◁ Lyme Regis

DORSET

ALDERHOLT
Map 5 SU11

Places to visit

Breamore House & Countryside Museum, BREAMORE, SP6 2DF, 01725 512858
www.breamorehouse.com

Great for kids: Rockbourne Roman Villa, ROCKBOURNE, SP6 3PG, 01725 518541
www.hampshireculturaltrust.org.uk/rockbourne-roman-villa

Premier Park

Hill Cottage Farm Camping and Caravan Park
►►►►► 85%

tel: 01425 650513 & 07714 648690 **Sandleheath Road SP6 3EG**
email: hillcottagefarmcaravansite@supanet.com
web: www.hillcottagefarmcampingandcaravanpark.co.uk
dir: Take B3078 west of Fordingbridge. Exit at Alderholt, site in 0.25 mile on left after railway bridge.

Set within extensive grounds, this rural and beautifully landscaped park offers fully serviced pitches set in individual hardstanding bays with mature dividing hedges to give adequate pitch privacy. The upgraded modern toilet block is kept immaculately clean, and there's a good range of leisure facilities. In high season there is an area available for tents; rallies are very welcome. A function room with a skittle alley is available, and there is a fully-equipped shepherd's hut for hire. The park is well situated for exploring the New Forest.

Open: March to November **Last arrival:** 20.00 **Last departure:** 11.00

Pitches: 🚐 🚏 ▲ 🏠; 35 hardstanding pitches

Leisure: 🛝 🎱 🎣

Facilities: 🛁 ☺ 📡 ✳ ♿ 🏧 🚿 🎪 WiFi

Services: 🔌 🔲 ⬆ 🛒 🗑 🇹

Within 3 miles: ⛳ ↻ 🏊

Additional site information: 40 acre site. 🐾 Cars can be parked by caravans and tents. Awnings permitted. No noise after 22.30. Freshly baked baguettes and croissants available. Car hire can be arranged.

Glamping available: Shepherd's hut.

Additional glamping information: Cars can be parked by hut.

BERE REGIS

Places to visit

Kingston Lacy, WIMBORNE, BH21 4EA, 01202 883402
www.nationaltrust.org.uk/kingston-lacy

Priest's House Museum and Garden, WIMBORNE, BH21 1HR, 01202 882533
www.priest-house.co.uk

Great for kids: Monkey World-Ape Rescue Centre, WOOL, BH20 6HH,
01929 462537, www.monkeyworld.org

BERE REGIS
Map 4 SY89

Rowlands Wait Touring Park
►►► 88%

tel: 01929 472727 **Rye Hill BH20 7LP**
email: enquiries@rowlandswait.co.uk **web:** www.rowlandswait.co.uk
dir: From A35 or A31 to Bere Regis, follow Bovington Tank Museum signs. 0.75 mile, at top of Rye Hill turn right. 200 yards to site.

This park lies in a really attractive setting overlooking Bere Regis and the Dorset countryside, and is set amongst undulating areas of trees and shrubs. It is located within a few miles of The Tank Museum (Bovingdon Camp) with its mock battles, and is also very convenient for visiting the Dorchester, Poole and Swanage areas. The toilet facilities include two family rooms. The park has fully-equipped tents (a pop-up Glampotel as they call them) each with a shower, toilet and wash basin, as well as a wood-burning stove.

Open: mid March to October (winter by prior arrangement) (restricted service: November to February – own facilities required) **Last arrival:** 21.00 **Last departure:** noon

Pitches: 🚐 🚏 ▲; 🏠 see prices below; 3 hardstanding pitches; 23 seasonal pitches

Leisure: 🛝 🎱

Facilities: 🛁 ☺ 📡 ✳ ♿ 🏧 WiFi

Services: 🔌 🔲 ⬆ 🛒 🗑 🇹

Within 3 miles: ⛳

Additional site information: 8 acre site. 🐾 Cars can be parked by caravans and tents. Awnings permitted. No open fires. Pool table, table tennis, hot drinks, fresh bread to order, woodland walks, cycling trails from site.

Glamping available: 4 bell tents from £169; 2 safari tents.

Additional glamping information: Bell tents and safari tents are en suite, fully equipped and have log-burners. Cars can be parked by tents.

BLANDFORD FORUM

Map 4 ST80

Places to visit

Kingston Lacy, WIMBORNE, BH21 4EA, 01202 883402
www.nationaltrust.org.uk/kingston-lacy

Old Wardour Castle, TISBURY, SP3 6RR, 01747 870487
www.english-heritage.org.uk/daysout/properties/old-wardour-castle

Great for kids: Monkey World-Ape Rescue Centre, WOOL, BH20 6HH,
01929 462537, www.monkeyworld.org

The Inside Park

▶▶▶▶ 86%

tel: 01258 453719 **Down House Estate DT11 9AD**
email: mail@theinsidepark.co.uk **web:** www.theinsidepark.co.uk
dir: *From Blandford Forum follow Winterborne Stickland signs. Site in 1.5 miles.*

An attractive, well-sheltered and quiet park, half a mile along a country lane in a
wooded valley, yet close to Blandford Forum. The spacious pitches are divided by
mature trees and shrubs, and the amenities are housed in an 18th-century coach
house and stables. There are some lovely woodland walks within the park, an
excellent fenced play area for children and a dog-free area; four dog kennels are
available for daily hire. This site makes the perfect base for anyone visiting the
Blandford Steam Fair in August, and there are over six miles of private waymarked
farm walks for guests to enjoy.

Open: Easter to October **Last arrival:** 22.00 **Last departure:** noon

Pitches: ⇔ from £20; ⇔ from £20; ▲ from £20

Leisure: ⚠ 🔍 **Facilities:** 🛁 ☉ 🖉 ✳ ♿ ⑤ 📶

Services: 🔌 ⑤ 🛒 ♨ 🔒 ⊘ Ⓣ **Within 3 miles:** ↓ 🖉 ∪

Additional site information: 12 acre site. 🐾 Cars can be parked by caravans and tents.
Awnings permitted. Kennels (charges apply).

BRIDPORT

Places to visit

Dorset County Museum, DORCHESTER, DT1 1XA, 01305 756827
www.dorsetcountymuseum.org

Abbotsbury Subtropical Gardens, ABBOTSBURY, DT3 4LA, 01305 871387
http://abbotsbury-tourism.co.uk/gardens/

Great for kids: Abbotsbury Swannery, ABBOTSBURY, DT3 4JG, 01305 871858
www.abbotsbury-tourism.co.uk/swannery

BRIDPORT

Map 4 SY49

Platinum Park

Highlands End Holiday Park

▶▶▶▶▶

tel: 01308 422139 & 426947 **Eype DT6 6AR**
email: holidays@wdlh.co.uk **web:** www.wdlh.co.uk
dir: *1 mile west of Bridport on A35, follow signs for Eype. Site signed.*

A well-screened site with magnificent cliff-top views over the Channel and the
Dorset coast, adjacent to National Trust land and overlooking Lyme Bay. The
pitches are mostly sheltered by hedging and are well spaced on hardstandings.
The excellent facilities include a stylish bar and restaurant, indoor pool, leisure
centre and The Cowshed Café, a very good coffee shop. A new addition is a soft-
play area for children. There is a mixture of statics and tourers, but the tourers
enjoy the best cliff-top positions, including gravel hardstanding pitches
overlooking Lyme Bay. Ten luxury lodges, and wooden pods that sleep four, are
available for hire.

Open: March to November **Last arrival:** 22.00 **Last departure:** 11.00

Pitches: ⇔ ⇔ ▲ 🏠; 45 hardstanding pitches **Leisure:** 🏊 ⚠ ⚉ 🔍 ♫ ⚽ ⚽

Facilities: 🛁 ☉ 🖉 ✳ ♿ ⑤ 📶

Services: 🔌 ⑤ 🍴 🍽 🛒 ♨ 🔒 ⊘ Ⓣ **Within 3 miles:** ↓ 🖉 ⚓ 🖽

Additional site information: 9 acre site. 🐾 Cars can be parked by caravans and
tents. Awnings permitted. Steam room, sauna, pitch and putt.

Glamping available: Wooden pods.

Changeover days: Monday, Friday, Saturday (Saturday only in peak season)

Additional glamping information: Cars can be parked by pods.

Premier Park

Freshwater Beach Holiday Park

▶▶▶▶▶ 92% HOLIDAY CENTRE

tel: 01308 897317 **Burton Bradstock DT6 4PT**
email: office@freshwaterbeach.co.uk **web:** www.freshwaterbeach.co.uk
dir: *Take B3157 from Bridport towards Burton Bradstock. Site 1.5 miles from Crown
roundabout on right.*

A family holiday centre sheltered by a sand bank and enjoying its own private
beach. The park offers a wide variety of leisure and entertainment programmes
for all the family, plus the Jurassic Fun Centre with indoor pool, gym, 6-lane

LEISURE: 🏊 Indoor swimming pool 🏊 Outdoor swimming pool ⚠ Children's playground 👶 Kids' club ⚉ Tennis court 🔍 Games room ⬜ Separate TV room
↓ golf course ⛳ Pitch n putt ⚓ Boats for hire 🚲 Bikes for hire 🎦 Cinema ♫ Entertainment 🎣 Fishing ◎ Mini golf ⚑ Watersports 🏋 Gym ⚽ Sports field ∪ Stables
FACILITIES: 🛁 Baths/Shower ☉ Electric shaver sockets 🖉 Hairdryer ✳ Ice Pack Facility 👶 Baby facilities ♿ Disabled facilities ⑤ Shop on site or within 200yds
🍴 BBQ area 🖽 Picnic area 📶 WiFi

bowling alley, restaurant and bar is excellent. There is an adults-only Sunset Lounge Bar and Cellar function room. The park is well placed at one end of the Weymouth to Bridport coastal area with spectacular views of Chesil Beach. There are three immaculate toilet blocks with excellent private rooms.

Freshwater Beach Holiday Park

Open: mid March to mid November **Last arrival:** 22.00 **Last departure:** 10.00

Pitches: from £25; from £25; from £25, 25 hardstanding pitches

Leisure: Spa

Facilities: WiFi

Services: **Within 3 miles:**

Additional site information: 40 acre site. Families and couples only. Large TV, kids' club in high season and bank holidays.

See advert on page 167

Graston Copse Holiday Park

▶ ▶ ▶ 90%

tel: 01308 426912 & 422139 **Annings Lane, Burton Bradstock DT6 4QP**
email: holidays@wdlh.co.uk **web:** www.wdlh.co.uk
dir: *From Dorchester take A35 to Bridport. In Bridport follow 'Westbound through traffic' sign at mini roundabout. At next roundabout left onto B3157 to Burton Bradstock. In village, left at Anchor Inn, 2nd right into Annings Lane. 1 mile to site.*

This small, peaceful site offering good facilities for families, is located near the village of Burton Bradstock making it a perfect base for visiting the stunning cliffs and beaches along the Jurassic coastline. The facilities are modern and spotlessly clean. Wooden pods that sleep four, a well-equipped safari tent and a Lotus Belle tent are available for hire. Please note, extra care is needed if driving through Burton Bradstock to the site.

Open: 28 April to 5 September **Last arrival:** 22.00 **Last departure:** 11.00

Pitches:

Facilities: WiFi

Services:

Within 3 miles:

Additional site information: 9 acre site. Cars can be parked by caravans and tents. Awnings permitted.

Glamping available: Wooden pods, safari tent, Lotus Belle tent.

Changeover days: Monday, Friday, Saturday (Saturday only in peak season)

Additional glamping information: No dogs permitted in glamping units. Cars can be parked by glamping units.

CERNE ABBAS   Map 4 ST60

Places to visit

Athelhampton House & Gardens, ATHELHAMPTON, DT2 7LG, 01305 848363
www.athelhampton.co.uk

Hardy's Cottage, DORCHESTER, DT2 8QJ, 01305 262366
www.nationaltrust.org.uk/hardys-cottage

Great for kids: Maiden Castle, DORCHESTER, DT2 9PP, 0370 333 1181
www.english-heritage.org.uk/daysout/properties/maiden-castle

Lyons Gate Caravan and Camping Park

▶ ▶ ▶ ▶ 81%

tel: 01300 345260 **DT2 7AZ**
email: info@lyons-gate.co.uk **web:** www.lyons-gate.co.uk
dir: *Direct access from A352, 3 miles north of Cerne Abbas, site signed.*

A peaceful park with pitches set out around the four attractive coarse fishing lakes. It is surrounded by mature woodland, with many footpaths and bridleways. A smart new café and shop are proving a very popular additional facility. Other easily accessible attractions include the Cerne Giant carved into the hills, the old market town of Dorchester and the superb sandy beach at Weymouth.

Open: All year **Last arrival:** 20.00 **Last departure:** 11.30

Pitches: ; 24 hardstanding pitches

Leisure:

Facilities: WiFi

Services:

Within 3 miles:

Additional site information: 10 acre site. Cars can be parked by caravans and tents. Awnings permitted.

Giants Head Caravan & Camping Park

▶ ▶ ▶ 80%

tel: 01300 341242 & 07970 277730
Giants Head Farm, Old Sherborne Road DT2 7TR
email: holidays@giantshead.co.uk **web:** www.giantshead.co.uk
dir: *From Dorchester to Cerne Abbas avoiding bypass, at Top O'Town roundabout take A352 (Sherborne road), in 500 yards right fork at BP (Loder's) garage and Lidl store.*

A pleasant, though rather basic, park set in Dorset downlands near the Cerne Giant (the famous landmark figure cut into the chalk) and with stunning views. There is a smart toilet block which is kept very clean and a new shower block opened for the 2018 season. This is a good stopover site especially for tenters and backpackers on The Ridgeway National Trail. The site also offers 'Treasure Trail' routes for Dorset. Holiday chalets are available to let.

Open: Easter to October **Last arrival:** 21.00 unless by prior arrangement
Last departure: noon

Pitches: from £14; from £14; from £14

Facilities: **Services:**

Within 3 miles:

Additional site information: 4 acre site. Dogs must be on leads at all times. Owners must clean up after their pets – bin provided. Cars can be parked by caravans and tents. Awnings permitted. Ice cream and catering vans on site at busy times.

PITCHES: Caravans Motorhomes Tents Glamping accommodation **SERVICES:** Electric hook-up Launderette Licensed bar
Calor Gas Campingaz Toilet fluid Café/Restaurant Fast Food/Takeaway Battery charging Motorhome service point
* 2019 prices No credit or debit cards Dogs permitted No dogs

CHARMOUTH

Map 4 SY39

Places to visit

Forde Abbey, THORNCOMBE, TA20 4LU, 01460 221290
www.fordeabbey.co.uk

Great for kids: Abbotsbury Swannery, ABBOTSBURY, DT3 4JG, 01305 871858
www.abbotsbury-tourism.co.uk/swannery

Premier Park

Wood Farm Caravan & Camping Park

▶▶▶▶▶ 94%

Best of British

tel: 01297 560697 **Axminster Road DT6 6BT**
email: reception@woodfarm.co.uk **web:** www.woodfarm.co.uk
dir: *Accessed directly from A35 roundabout, on Axminster side of Charmouth.*

This top quality park, the perfect place to relax, is set amongst mature native trees with the various levels of the ground falling away into a beautiful valley below. The park offers excellent facilities including family rooms and fully serviced pitches. Everything throughout the park is spotless. At the bottom end of the park there is an indoor swimming pool and leisure complex, plus the licensed, conservatory-style Offshore Café. There's a very good children's play room and excellent play area, in addition to tennis courts and a well-stocked, coarse-fishing lake. The park is well positioned on the Heritage Coast near Lyme Regis. Static holiday homes are also available for hire.

Open: Easter to October **Last arrival:** 19.00 **Last departure:** noon
Pitches: * from £17.50; from £17.50; from £16; 175 hardstanding pitches;

20 seasonal pitches

Leisure:
Facilities: WiFi
Services: T
Within 3 miles:

Additional site information: 13 acre site. Cars can be parked by caravans and tents. Awnings permitted. No bikes, skateboards, scooters or roller skates. Dog bowls provided on café terrace, dog shower, dog walks with waste bags provided.

See advert opposite

Premier Park

Newlands Holidays

▶▶▶▶▶ 86%

tel: 01297 560259 **DT6 6RB**
email: enq@newlandsholidays.co.uk **web:** www.newlandsholidays.co.uk
dir: *6.4 miles west of Bridport on A35.*

A very smart site with excellent touring facilities, set on gently sloping ground in hilly countryside near the sea. Level and very spacious pitches are available. During the high season, the park offers a full entertainment programme, and boasts a clubhouse, an indoor swimming pool and an outdoor pool with water slide. Lodges, apartments and motel rooms are available, plus there are four camping pods for hire.

Open: mid March to October **Last arrival:** 21.00 **Last departure:** 10.00
Pitches: from £16; from £16; from £16; see prices below; 72 hardstanding pitches; 40 seasonal pitches

---

LEISURE: Indoor swimming pool Outdoor swimming pool Children's playground Kids' club Tennis court Games room Separate TV room golf course Pitch n putt Boats for hire Cinema Entertainment Fishing Mini golf Watersports Gym Sports field Stables
FACILITIES: Baths/Shower Electric shaver sockets Hairdryer Ice Pack Facility Baby facilities Disabled facilities Shop on site or within 200yds BBQ area Picnic area Wi-fi Internet access

Leisure: 🏊 ⛱ 🎿 ✋ 🔍 🖥 🎵 ⚽

Facilities: 🏪 ☺ 🅿 ❄ ♿ 🛒 🚻 🛗 WiFi

Services: 🔌 🗄 🍺 🍴 🏬 🧳 🔋 🗑 T

Within 3 miles: 🚶 🎣 ∪ ◎ ⛳ ✈ 日

Additional site information: 23 acre site. 🐕 Cars can be parked by caravans and tents. Awnings permitted. Kids' club during school holidays, freshly baked bread available. On-site nature trail. Car hire can be arranged.

Glamping available: Wooden pods from £56. **Changeover days:** Any day

Additional glamping information: Cars can be parked by pods.

See advert on page 172

Manor Farm Holiday Centre
▶▶▶▶ 85%

tel: 01297 560226 **DT6 6QL**
email: enquiries@manorfarmholidaycentre.co.uk
web: www.manorfarmholidaycentre.co.uk
dir: *From east: A35 into Charmouth, site 0.75 mile on right.*

Set just a short walk from the safe sand and shingle beach at Charmouth, this popular family park offers a good range of facilities. There is an indoor-outdoor swimming pool plus café, a fully-equipped gym and sauna. Children certainly enjoy the activity area and the park also offers a lively programme in the extensive bar and entertainment complex. In addition there are 16 luxury cottages available for hire and smart lodges for sale.

Open: All year (restricted service: mid March to end October – statics only)
Last arrival: 20.00 **Last departure:** 10.00

Pitches: 🚐 from £16; 🚍 from £16; 🏕 from £16; 80 hardstanding pitches; 100 seasonal pitches

Leisure: 🏊 ⛱ 🎿 🔍 🎵 🏇 Spa

Facilities: 🏪 ☺ 🅿 ❄ ♿ 🚻 WiFi

Services: 🔌 🗄 🍺 🍴 🏬 🔋 🗑 T

Within 3 miles: 🚶 🎣 ∪ ◎ ⛳ ✈ 日 🛒

Additional site information: 30 acre site. 🐕 Cars can be parked by caravans and tents. Awnings permitted. No skateboards.

STAY A WHILE IN DELIGHTFUL DORSET

CHIDEOCK   Map 4 SY49

Places to visit

Mapperton, BEAMINSTER, DT8 3NR, 01308 862645
www.mapperton.com

Premier Park

Golden Cap Holiday Park
▶▶▶▶▶   86%

tel: 01308 422139 & 426947 **Seatown DT6 6JX**
email: holidays@wdlh.co.uk **web:** www.wdlh.co.uk
dir: On A35, in Chideock follow Seatown signs, site signed.

A grassy site, overlooking the sea and beach and surrounded by National Trust parkland. This uniquely placed park slopes down to the sea, although pitches are generally level. A slight dip hides the view of the beach from the back of the park, but this area benefits from having trees, scrub and meadows, unlike the barer areas closer to the sea which do have a spectacular outlook. There is a smart toilet and shower block, plus there's a shop and café and takeaway. Three luxury lodges, with outstanding views, and different types of glamping accommodation are available, including two impressive Premier Pods. This makes an ideal base for touring Dorset and Devon. Lake fishing is possible (a licence can be obtained locally).

Open: March to November **Last arrival:** 22.00 **Last departure:** 11.00
Pitches: 🚐 🚚 ▲ ♨; 24 hardstanding pitches
Leisure: ⚑ ✎
Facilities: 🛁 ☉ ⌒ ⚘ ♿ 🛍 ⊞ WiFi
Services: 🔌 🗑 ⚒ 🧺 🔒 ⬚ ⊤
Within 3 miles: ⚓

Additional site information: 11 acre site. ⚡ Cars can be parked by caravans and tents. Awnings permitted.
Glamping available: Wooden pods; safari tents; Lotus Belle tents.
Changeover days: Monday, Friday, Saturday (Saturday only in peak season)
Additional glamping information: Cars can be parked by glamping units.

CHRISTCHURCH

Places to visit

Red House Museum & Gardens, CHRISTCHURCH, BH23 1BU, 01202 482860
www.hampshireculturaltrust.org.uk

Great for kids: Oceanarium, BOURNEMOUTH, BH2 5AA, 01202 311993
www.oceanarium.co.uk

LEISURE: 🏊 Indoor swimming pool   🏊 Outdoor swimming pool   🎠 Children's playground   👦 Kids' club   🎾 Tennis court   🎱 Games room   📺 Separate TV room   ⛳ golf course   🏑 Pitch n putt   🚣 Boats for hire   🚲 Bikes for hire   🎬 Cinema   🎵 Entertainment   🎣 Fishing   ⛳ Mini golf   🏄 Watersports   💪 Gym   ⚽ Sports field   ⛺ Stables
FACILITIES: 🛁 Baths/Shower   ☉ Electric shaver sockets   ⌒ Hairdryer   ❄ Ice Pack Facility   🍼 Baby facilities   ♿ Disabled facilities   🛍 Shop on site or within 200yds   🍖 BBQ area   ⊞ Picnic area   WiFi WiFi

Premier Park

Meadowbank Holidays
▶▶▶▶▶   87%

tel: 01202 483597 **Stour Way BH23 2PQ**
email: enquiries@meadowbankholidays.co.uk **web:** www.meadowbank-holidays.co.uk
dir: *A31 onto A338 towards Bournemouth. 5 miles, left towards Christchurch on B3073. Right at 1st roundabout into St Catherine's Way, becomes River Way. 3rd right into Stour Way to site.*

A very smart park on the banks of the River Stour, with a colourful display of hanging baskets and flower-filled tubs placed around the superb reception area. The toilet block is excellent, with modern, stylish facilities. There's a choice of pitch sizes including luxury, fully serviced ones. There is also an excellent play area, a cycle storage facility, a good shop on site and coarse fishing. Statics are available for hire. The park is well located in a peaceful area and very convenient for visiting nearby Christchurch, the south coast and the New Forest.

Open: March to October **Last arrival:** 21.00 **Last departure:** noon

Pitches: 🚐 🚐; 22 hardstanding pitches

Leisure: ⚑ 🔍 ✐

Facilities: 🖰 ☉ ℉ ♿ ⑤ 🗪 ⛟ WiFi

Services: ⚡ ⑤ 🎪 ⛟ 🛢 ⌀ T

Within 3 miles: ⚓ ∪ ◎ ⛷ ✠ ⊟

Additional site information: 2 acre site. Cars can be parked by caravans. Awnings permitted. No pets. Table tennis, riverside walk. Car hire can be arranged.

Places to visit
Brownsea Island, BROWNSEA ISLAND, BH13 7EE, 01202 707744
www.nationaltrust.org.uk/brownsea-island

Corfe Castle, CORFE CASTLE, BH20 5EZ, 01929 481294
www.nationaltrust.org.uk/corfecastle

Great for kids: Swanage Railway, SWANAGE, BH19 1HB, 01929 425800
www.swanagerailway.co.uk

Corfe Castle Camping & Caravanning Club Site
▶▶▶▶   93%

tel: 01929 480280 & 024 7647 5426 **Bucknowle BH20 5PQ**
email: corfecastle.site@campingandcaravanningclub.co.uk
web: www.campingandcaravanningclub.co.uk/corfecastle
dir: *A351 from Wareham towards Swanage for 4 miles. Right at foot of Corfe Castle signed Church Knowle. 0.75 mile, right at Corfe Castle C&CC Site sign.*

This lovely campsite, where non-members are also very welcome, is set in woodland near the famous Corfe Castle at the foot of the Purbeck Hills. It has a stone reception building, which has a really comfortable information lounge, on-site shop and modern toilet and shower facilities, which are spotless. Although the site is sloping, pitches are level and include spacious hardstandings. The site is perfect for anyone visiting the many attractions of the Purbeck area, including the award-winning beaches at Studland and Swanage, and the seaside towns of Poole, Bournemouth and Weymouth. There is also a station at Corfe for the Swanage Steam Railway. The site is pet friendly.

Open: March to October **Last arrival:** 20.00 (later arrivals by prior arrangement only) **Last departure:** noon

Pitches: 🚐 from £8.65; 🚐 from £8.65; ⚊ from £8.65; 43 hardstanding pitches

Leisure: ⚑

Facilities: 🖰 ☉ ℉ ✳ ♿ ⑤

Services: ⚡ ⑤ 🎪 ⛟ 🛢 ⌀ T

Within 3 miles: ⚓ ∪ ◎ ⛷ ✠ ⊟

Additional site information: 6 acre site. 🐕 Cars can be parked by caravans and tents. Awnings permitted. Site gates closed 23.00–07.00. Bread and newspapers can be ordered. Local sausages, bacon, ice cream and free-range eggs available.

PITCHES: 🚐 Caravans   🚐 Motorhomes   ⚊ Tents   ⛺ Glamping accommodation   **SERVICES:** ⚡ Electric hook-up   ⑤ Launderette   🍷 Licensed bar
🛢 Calor Gas   ⌀ Campingaz   T Toilet fluid   🍽 Café/Restaurant   🎪 Fast Food/Takeaway   ⛟ Battery charging   ⛟ Motorhome service point
* 2019 prices   ⊘ No credit or debit cards   🐕 Dogs permitted   ⊗ No dogs

CORFE CASTLE *continued*

Woodyhyde Camp Site
▶▶▶ 81%

tel: 01929 480274 **Valley Road BH20 5HT**
email: camp@woodyhyde.co.uk web: www.woodyhyde.co.uk
dir: *From Corfe Castle towards Swanage on A351, site approximately 1 mile on right.*

A large grassy campsite in a sheltered location for tents and motorhomes only, divided into three paddocks – one is dog free. This site offers traditional camping in a great location between Corfe Castle and Swanage, and the Swanage steam railway that runs past the site adds interest for campers. There is a well-stocked shop on site, a modern toilet and shower block, and there's a regular bus service that stops near the site entrance. Electric hook-ups and some hardstandings are available and glamping accommodation is also offered, consisting of yurts and a shepherd's hut.

Open: March to October **Last departure:** noon

Pitches: 🚐 from £20; ▲ from £20; 🏠; 25 hardstanding pitches

Facilities: 🛁 ☉ 🏳 ✳ ♿ $ WiFi

Services: 🚰 🚿 🧺 ⛽ 🔒 🗑 T

Within 3 miles: ⚓ ✏ ∪ ◎ 🚣 🎣 🎯 🗐

Additional site information: 13 acre site. 🐕 Cars can be parked by tents. Awnings permitted. No noise after 23.00, no open fires.

Glamping available: 1 shepherd's hut; 5 yurts.

See advert opposite

DORCHESTER

See Cerne Abbas

DRIMPTON Map 4 ST40

Places to visit

Forde Abbey, THORNCOMBE, TA20 4LU, 01460 221290
www.fordeabbey.co.uk

Mapperton, BEAMINSTER, DT8 3NR, 01308 862645
www.mapperton.com

Oathill Farm Touring and Camping Site
▶▶▶▶ 84%

tel: 01460 30234 & 07403 415986 **Oathill TA18 8PZ**
email: oathillfarm@btconnect.com web: www.oathillfarmleisure.co.uk
dir: *From Crewkerne take B3165. Site on left just after Clapton.*

This small peaceful park borders Somerset and Devon, with the Jurassic Coast at Lyme Regis, Charmouth and Bridport only a short drive away. The modern facilities are spotless and there are hardstandings and fully serviced pitches available. There is also a very pleasant camping area which has two additional hardstandings. Lucy's Tea Room serves breakfast and meals. The well-stocked, landscaped fishing ponds prove a hit with anglers. Three luxury lodges are available.

Open: All year (restricted service: winter – shop not fully stocked) **Last arrival:** 20.00 **Last departure:** noon

Pitches: 🚐 🚐 ▲; 18 hardstanding pitches; 8 seasonal pitches

Leisure: ✏ ⚽ ◎

Facilities: 🛁 ☉ 🏳 ✳ $ 🍖 🏓 WiFi

Services: 🚰 🚿 🍽 🧺 ⛽ 🔒 🗑 T

Within 3 miles: ⚓ ∪

Additional site information: 10 acre site. 🐕 Cars can be parked by caravans and tents. Awnings permitted. No washing lines, no quad bikes, no noise after 23.00. Separate recreational areas, dog walking area.

St Leonards Farm Caravan & Camping Park

►►►► 84%

tel: 01202 872637 **Ringwood Road, West Moors BH22 0AQ**
email: enquiries_stleonards@yahoo.co.uk **web:** www.stleonardsfarmpark.com
dir: *From Ringwood on A31 (dual carriageway) towards Ferndown, exit left into slip road at site sign. From Wimborne Minster on A31 at roundabout (junction of A31 & A347) follow signs for Ringwood (A31) (pass Texaco garage on left) to next roundabout. 3rd exit (ie double back towards Ferndown) exit at slip road for site.*

A private road accessed from the A31 leads to this well-screened park divided into paddocks that have spacious pitches. The site has an excellent, secure children's soft-play area and a new indoor play barn. There is a toilet and shower block with excellent family/disabled rooms, and a late arrival point with electricity and water. A shepherd's hut, complete with a fully-equipped utility cabin, is available for hire. The park is well located for visiting nearby Bournemouth and the New Forest National Park.

St Leonards Farm Caravan & Camping Park

Open: 7 February to 6 January (restricted service: 31 October to 6 January, 7 February to 31 March — site open only from Friday to Sunday) **Last arrival:** late arrivals by prior arrangement **Last departure:** noon

Pitches: 🚐 🚐 🏕 🛖; 15 hardstanding pitches; 30 seasonal pitches

Leisure: 🎿 ⚽ **Facilities:** 🖳 ☺ 🍴 ☀ ♿ 🚻

Services: 🔌 🔲 🚿 🛢 🗑 **Within 3 miles:** ⚓ 🏌 ∪ 🏪

Additional site information: 12 acre site. 🐾 No dogs in July and August. Cars can be parked by caravans and tents. Awnings permitted. No large groups, no noise after 23.00, no disposable BBQs, no gazebos.

Glamping available: Shepherd's hut. **Changeover days:** Monday

Additional glamping information: Cars can be parked by shepherd's hut.

PITCHES: 🚐 Caravans 🚐 Motorhomes 🏕 Tents 🛖 Glamping accommodation **SERVICES:** 🔌 Electric hook-up 🔲 Launderette 🍺 Licensed bar
🛢 Calor Gas 🗑 Campingaz 🇹 Toilet fluid 🍴 Café/Restaurant 🍔 Fast Food/Takeaway 🔋 Battery charging ⛟ Motorhome service point
* 2019 prices 🚫 No credit or debit cards 🐾 Dogs permitted 🚫 No dogs

HOLDITCH
Map 4 ST30

Places to visit
Forde Abbey, THORNCOMBE, TA20 4LU, 01460 221290
www.fordeabbey.co.uk

Premier Park

Crafty Camping
►►►►► 85% GLAMPING ONLY

tel: 01460 221102 **Woodland Workshop, Yonder Hill TA20 4NL**
email: enquiries@mallinson.co.uk **web:** www.mallinson.co.uk
dir: *From A358 between Axminster and Chard, in Tytherleigh into Broom Lane signed Holditch (becomes Holditch Lane). Through Holditch, after Manor Farm, after sharp left bend, car park on left in 200 yards. (Note: it is advisable not to use sat nav).*

Crafty Camping offers a unique holiday adventure in peaceful and beautiful surroundings. If you have a desire to experience a different type of holiday, then this adults-only site could fit the bill. Choose from fully-equipped yurts, each with their own toilet and shower facilities, or bell tents and a tipi, which share excellent communal facilities, or book 'the jewel in the crown', a spectacular tree house. Here there's a double bed, toilet and shower facilities, including a copper bath, a wood-burning stove, and a decked area with table and chairs, hammock, pizza oven and even an open-air shower. There is a spiral staircase to an upper level, which has a sauna and a hot tub – you can even get to the forest floor via a slide! There is also a communal kitchen and eating area, and woodland craft courses are also available. Although hidden away in the hamlet of Holditch, it is close to Axminster, Lyme Regis and the Jurassic Coast. The Woodman's Treehouse was filmed for *George Clarke's Amazing Spaces* for Channel 4 and has been shortlisted for various design awards.

Open: All year **Earliest arrival:** After 15.00 **Last departure:** 11.00

Leisure: 🔍 ⌐

Facilities: 🛁 ✳ ☷ 🎋 WiFi

Within 3 miles: ⌕ Ⓢ 🔲

Accommodation available: Bell tents from £97; tipis from £139; yurts from £139; treehouse from £495.

Changeover days: Monday, Wednesday, Friday

Additional site information: 14 acre site. Adults only. No pets, no children, no noise. Green woodcraft courses, wood-fired pizza oven, sauna yurt.

HURN
Map 5 SZ19

Places to visit
Red House Museum & Gardens, CHRISTCHURCH, BH23 1BU, 01202 482860
www.hampshireculturaltrust.org.uk

Oceanarium, BOURNEMOUTH, BH2 5AA, 01202 311993
www.oceanarium.co.uk

Fillybrook Farm Touring Park
►► 85%

tel: 01202 478266 **Matchams Lane BH23 6AW**
email: enquiries@fillybrookfarm.co.uk **web:** www.fillybrookfarm.co.uk
dir: *M27 junction 1, A31 to Ringwood, then Poole, left immediately after Texaco Garage signed Verwood and B3081, left into Hurn Lane signed Matchams. Site on right in 4 miles.*

A small adults-only and very dog-friendly park that's well located on the edge of Hurn Forest, with Bournemouth, Christchurch, Poole and the New Forest within easy reach. Fillybrook provides a pleasant, peaceful camping environment, and the facilities are both modern and very clean. A dry-ski slope, with an adjoining restaurant and small bar, is a short walk from the site. There is also a separate rally field.

Open: Easter to October **Last arrival:** 20.00 **Last departure:** 11.00

Pitches: 🚐 from £20; 🚌 from £20; ▲ from £20

Facilities: 🛁 ⊙ ℉ ✳

Services: 🖳 🗓

Within 3 miles: ⌕ ℐ ↺ Ⓢ 🔲

Additional site information: 1 acre site. Adults only. 🐕 🚭 Cars can be parked by caravans and tents. Awnings permitted. No large groups, no commercial vehicles, no campfires.

LYME REGIS

See also Charmouth

Places to visit
Pecorama Pleasure Gardens, BEER, EX12 3NA, 01297 21542
www.pecorama.co.uk

Shute Barton (NT), SHUTE, EX13 7PT, 01752 346585
www.nationaltrust.org.uk/shute-barton

Great for kids: Pecorama Pleasure Gardens, BEER, EX12 3NA, 01297 21542
www.pecorama.co.uk

LEISURE: 🏊 Indoor swimming pool 🏊 Outdoor swimming pool ⅄ Children's playground 🏏 Kids' club 🎾 Tennis court 🎱 Games room 📺 Separate TV room
⌕ golf course ⛳ Pitch n putt 🚣 Boats for hire 🚲 Bikes for hire 🎬 Cinema 🎵 Entertainment ℐ Fishing ◉ Mini golf 🏄 Watersports 🏋 Gym 🏟 Sports field ↺ Stables
FACILITIES: 🛁 Baths/Shower ⊙ Electric shaver sockets ℉ Hairdryer ✳ Ice Pack Facility 🍼 Baby facilities 👤 Disabled facilities Ⓢ Shop on site or within 200yds
🍖 BBQ area 🎋 Picnic area WiFi WiFi

LYME REGIS Map 4 SY39

Shrubbery Touring Park 🛖

▶▶▶▶ 91%

tel: 01297 442227 **Rousdon DT7 3XW**
email: info4shrubberypark@yahoo.co.uk **web:** www.shrubberypark.co.uk
dir: *3 miles west of Lyme Regis on A3052 (coast road).*

Mature trees enclose this peaceful park, which has distant views of the lovely countryside. The modern facilities are well kept and include beautifully appointed family rooms, the hardstanding pitches are spacious, and there is plenty of space for children to play in the grounds. There is a small area set aside for adults only and there are two camping pods for hire. Well located for visiting Lyme Regis, Sidmouth and Seaton, the park is right on the Jurassic Coast bus route, which is popular with visitors to this area.

Open: April to October **Last arrival:** 21.00 **Last departure:** 11.00

Pitches: * 🚐 from £14.25; 🚌 from £14.25; ⛺ from £14.25; 🛖 see prices below; 40 hardstanding pitches; 12 seasonal pitches

Leisure: 🛝

Facilities: 🛁 ☺ 💨 ✲ ♿ [$] [WiFi]

Services: 🔌 🧺 🚰 🛢 🔥 [T]

Within 3 miles: ⛳ 🎣 🐎 ◎ 🌊 ⛵

Additional site information: 10 acre site. 🐕 Cars can be parked by caravans and tents. Awnings permitted. No groups (except rallies), no motor scooters, roller skates or skateboards. Crazy golf.

Glamping available: 2 wooden pods from £37.

Additional glamping information: Wooden pods – one with double bed and two singles. Both offer electric sockets, heating, lighting and picnic bench. No pets permitted. Cars can be parked by pods.

Hook Farm Caravan & Camping Park 🛖

▶▶▶ 86%

tel: 01297 442801 **Gore Lane, Uplyme DT7 3UU**
email: info@hookfarmcamping.com **web:** www.hookfarmcamping.com
dir: *A35 onto B3165 towards Lyme Regis and Uplyme at Hunters Lodge pub. In 2 miles right into Gore Lane, site 400 yards on right.*

Set in a peaceful and very rural location, this popular farm site enjoys lovely views of Lym Valley and is just a mile from the seaside at Lyme Regis. There are modern toilet facilities at the top and bottom of the site, and good on-site amenities. Most pitches are level due to excellent terracing – it is a great site for tents but also suited to motorhomes and caravans. A shepherd's hut is now available for hire. Please note, it is advised that if arriving in a motorhome or if towing a caravan that sat nav is not used; there are many narrow roads that only have a few passing places.

Open: March to October **Last arrival:** 20.00 **Last departure:** 10.30

Pitches: * 🚐 from £23.50; 🚌 from £23.50; ⛺ from £15; 🛖 see prices below; 4 hardstanding pitches

Leisure: 🛝

Facilities: 🛁 ☺ 💨 ✲ ♿ [$] [WiFi]

Services: 🔌 🧺 🚰 🛢 🔥 [T]

Within 3 miles: ⛳ 🎣 🐎 ◎ 🌊 ⛵ 🛍

Additional site information: 5.5 acre site. 🐕 No dangerous dog breeds. Cars can be parked by caravans and tents. Awnings permitted. No groups of 4 adults or more. Freshly baked bread and pastries, visiting takeaway food in peak season, river walk into Lyme Regis. Car hire can be arranged.

Glamping available: Shepherd's hut from £55.

Additional glamping information: Sleeps 2. No pets. 2 night minimum booking.

LYTCHETT MATRAVERS Map 4 SY99

Places to visit

Brownsea Island, BROWNSEA ISLAND, BH13 7EE, 01202 707744
www.nationaltrust.org.uk/brownsea-island

Poole Museum, POOLE, BH15 1BW, 01202 262600
www.boroughofpoole.com/museums

Great for kids: Swanage Railway, SWANAGE, BH19 1HB, 01929 425800
www.swanagerailway.co.uk

Huntick Farm Caravan Park

▶▶▶▶ 82%

tel: 01202 622222 **Huntick Road BH16 6BB**
email: huntickcaravans@btconnect.com **web:** www.huntick.co.uk
dir: *Site between Lytchett Minster & Lytchett Matravers. From A31 take A350 towards Poole. Follow Lytchett Minster signs, then Lytchett Matravers signs. Into Huntick Road by Rose & Crown pub.*

A really attractive, small park surrounded by woodland and located a mile from the village of Lytchett Matravers. The park offers excellent toilet and shower facilities as well as a smart reception. You can be sure of a warm welcome by the staff, and the park's delightful rural location makes it a peaceful base for touring in this lovely county.

Open: April to October **Last arrival:** 21.00 **Last departure:** noon

Pitches: 🚐 🚌 ⛺; 13 seasonal pitches

Leisure: ⚽

Facilities: 🛁 ☺ ✲ [WiFi]

Services: 🔌 🛢

Within 3 miles: ⛳ 🐎 [$] 🧺

Additional site information: 4 acre site. 🐕 Cars can be parked by caravans and tents. Awnings permitted. No gazebos. Ball games permitted only on games field, no noise 22.00–08.00.

OWERMOIGNE

Map 4 SY78

Places to visit

RSPB Nature Reserve Radipole Lake and Wild Weymouth Discovery Centre, WEYMOUTH, DT4 7TZ, 01305 778313
www.rspb.org.uk

Clouds Hill, BOVINGTON CAMP, BH20 7NQ, 01929 405616
www.nationaltrust.org.uk/clouds-hill

Great for kids: Weymouth Sea Life Adventure Park & Marine Sanctuary, WEYMOUTH, DT4 7SX
www2.visitsealife.com/weymouth

Sandyholme Holiday Park

▶▶▶ 87%

tel: 01308 422139 & 426947 **Moreton Road DT2 8HZ**
email: holidays@wdlh.co.uk **web:** www.wdlh.co.uk
dir: From A352 (Wareham to Dorchester road) turn towards Owermoigne. Site on left in 1 mile.

A pleasant quiet site surrounded by trees and within easy reach of the coast at Lulworth Cove, and handy for several seaside resorts, including Weymouth, Portland, Purbeck and Swanage. The facilities are good, including a children's play area, small football pitch, shop and tourist information. A well-appointed safari tent and a Lotus Belle tent are available for hire.

Open: 18 March to 6 November (restricted service: at Easter) **Last arrival:** 22.00
Last departure: 11.00

Pitches: ⛺ ⛟ ⛺ ⛺; 20 seasonal pitches

Leisure: 🎱 ⚽

Facilities: 🛁 ☉ 🎣 ✳ ♿ 🖫 🍴 📶

Services: 🚽 🗑 🛒 🖕 🛢 🌿 📺

Within 3 miles: ⛳

Additional site information: 6 acre site. 🚗 Cars can be parked by caravans and tents. Awnings permitted. Table tennis, wildlife lake, football pitch.

Glamping available: Safari tent; Lotus Belle tent.

POOLE

See also Wimborne Minster

Places to visit

Brownsea Island, BROWNSEA ISLAND, BH13 7EE, 01202 707744
www.nationaltrust.org.uk/brownsea-island

Poole Museum, POOLE, BH15 1BW, 01202 262600
www.boroughofpoole.com/museums

Great for kids: Oceanarium, BOURNEMOUTH, BH2 5AA, 01202 311993
www.oceanarium.co.uk

POOLE

Map 4 SZ09

Platinum Park

South Lytchett Manor Caravan & Camping Park

▶▶▶▶▶

tel: 01202 622577 **Dorchester Road, Lytchett Minster BH16 6JB**
email: info@southlytchettmanor.co.uk **web:** www.southlytchettmanor.co.uk
dir: Exit A35 onto B3067, 1 mile east of Lytchett Minster, 600 yards on right after village.

Year-on year improvements are made here to exceed guest expectations and new investment includes the upgrading of the interiors of the amenity blocks with stylish fittings and the introduction of an on-site bakery to provide fresh croissants and pastries daily. Situated in the grounds of a historic manor house, the site has modern facilities that are spotless and well maintained. There's a TV hook-up on every pitch and free WiFi across the park. A warm and friendly welcome awaits at this lovely park which is well located for visiting Poole and Bournemouth; the Jurassic X53 bus route (Exeter to Poole) has a stop just outside the park. Four stylishly furnished and well-equipped Romany caravans, replete with double bed and two singles plus kitchen and fridge, are available for hire.

Open: March to 2 January **Last arrival:** 21.00 **Last departure:** 11.00
Pitches: ⛺ ⛟ ⛺ ⛺; 90 hardstanding pitches; 4 seasonal pitches

---

LEISURE: 🏊 Indoor swimming pool 🏊 Outdoor swimming pool 🛝 Children's playground 🧒 Kids' club 🎾 Tennis court 🎱 Games room 📺 Separate TV room 🏌 golf course 🏌 Pitch n putt 🚤 Boats for hire 🚲 Bikes for hire 🎬 Cinema 🎵 Entertainment 🎣 Fishing ◎ Mini golf 🏄 Watersports 🏋 Gym 🏟 Sports field ♘ Stables
FACILITIES: 🛁 Baths/Shower ☉ Electric shaver sockets 🎣 Hairdryer ✳ Ice Pack Facility 🍼 Baby facilities ♿ Disabled facilities 🛒 Shop on site or within 200yds 🍴 BBQ area 🍴 Picnic area 📶 WiFi

Leisure: ⚑ 🎣 🖵 ⚽ ☉
Facilities: ☉ 🚿 ✳ ♿ $ 🚻 WiFi
Services: 🔌 🔲 🧺 ⚓ 🔋 ✦ T
Within 3 miles: ⚓ ✎ ∪ 🏌 目

Additional site information: 22 acre site. 🐕 Cars can be parked by caravans and tents. Awnings permitted. No camp fires or Chinese lanterns, no noise after 22.30. Table tennis, football nets. Car hire can be arranged.

Glamping available: Romany caravans.

Additional glamping information: One unit is dog friendly. Please advise site in advance of any allergies. Cars can be parked by caravans.

See advert below

Rockley Park
▶▶▶▶▶ 94% HOLIDAY HOME PARK

tel: 0800 197 2075 **Hamworthy BH15 4LZ**
email: rockleypark@haven.com **web:** www.haven.com/rockleypark
dir: *M27 junction 1, A31 to Poole centre, then follow signs to site.*

A complete holiday experience, including a wide range of day and night entertainment, and plenty of sports and leisure activities, notably watersports. There is also mooring and launching from the park. A great base for all the family, set in a good location for exploring Poole and Bournemouth, offering something for all ages, and there are a wide choice of quality eating outlets.

Open: March to 2 January

Holiday Homes: Two-ring burner Microwave Freezer TV Sky/Freeview WiFi

Changeover days: Fridays, Saturdays, Mondays

Leisure: ≋ ≋ Spa

Facilities: $ 🚻 ♨ WiFi

Within 3 miles: 🔲

Additional site information: 🐕 Most dog breeds accepted (please check when booking). Dogs must be kept on leads at all times. The facilities provided in the holiday homes may differ depending on the grade.

PITCHES: 🚐 Caravans 🚙 Motorhomes ⛺ Tents ⛺ Glamping accommodation **SERVICES:** 🔌 Electric hook-up 🔲 Launderette 🍺 Licensed bar
🔥 Calor Gas ✿ Campingaz T Toilet fluid 🍽 Café/Restaurant 🍟 Fast Food/Takeaway 🔋 Battery charging ⚡ Motorhome service point
* 2019 prices ⊘ No credit or debit cards 🐕 Dogs permitted ⊗ No dogs

PORTESHAM
Map 4 SY68

Places to visit

Tutankhamun Exhibition, DORCHESTER, DT1 1UW, 01305 269571
www.tutankhamun-exhibition.co.uk

Maiden Castle, DORCHESTER, DT2 9PP, 0370 333 1181
www.english-heritage.org.uk/daysout/properties/maiden-castle

Great for kids: Teddy Bear Museum, DORCHESTER, DT1 1JU, 01305 266040
www.teddybearmuseum.co.uk

Portesham Dairy Farm Campsite
►►►► 83%

tel: 01305 871297 **DT3 4HG**
email: info@porteshamdairyfarm.co.uk **web:** www.porteshamdairyfarm.co.uk
dir: *From Dorchester take A35 towards Bridport. In 5 miles left at Winterbourne Abbas,
follow Portesham signs. Through village, left at Kings Arms pub, site 350 yards on right.*

Located at the edge of the picturesque village of Portesham close to the Dorset
coast, this family-run, level park is part of a small working farm in a quiet rural
location. Fully serviced and seasonal pitches are available. There is an excellent
pub and a country store just a short walk from the site, and a bus stop outside of
the park. This quiet park is close to Abbotsbury Swannery and well situated for
visiting many areas of the west Dorset coast.

Open: All year **Last arrival:** 21.00 **Last departure:** 11.00
Pitches: * 🚐 from £17; 🚏 from £17; ▲ from £15; 61 hardstanding pitches;
70 seasonal pitches
Leisure: 𝄞
Facilities: 🖻 ⊙ ℱ ☀ ⑤ WiFi
Services: 🔌 🔲 🔒
Within 3 miles: 𝒫

Additional site information: 8 acre site. 🐾 Cars can be parked by caravans and tents.
Awnings permitted. No commercial vehicles, groups accepted by prior arrangement only,
no camp fires, minimum noise after 22.00. Caravan storage.

PUNCKNOWLE

Places to visit

Hardy's Cottage, DORCHESTER, DT2 8QJ, 01305 262366
www.nationaltrust.org.uk/hardys-cottage

Abbotsbury Swannery, ABBOTSBURY, DT3 4JG, 01305 871858
www.abbotsbury-tourism.co.uk/swannery

Great for kids: Dinosaur Museum, DORCHESTER, DT1 1EW, 01305 269880
www.thedinosaurmuseum.com

PUNCKNOWLE
Map 4 SY58

Home Farm Caravan and Campsite
►►► 81%

tel: 01308 897258 **Home Farm, Rectory Lane DT2 9BW**
web: www.caravanandcampingwestdorset.co.uk
dir: *From Dorchester towards Bridport on A35, left at start of dual carriageway, at hill
bottom right to Litton Cheney. Through village, 2nd left to Puncknowle (Hazel Lane).
Left at T-junction, left at phone box. Site 150 metres on right. Caravan route: approach
via A35 Bridport, then Swyre on B3157, continue to Swyre Lane and Rectory Lane.*

This quiet site, hidden away on the edge of a little hamlet, has good facilities and
is an excellent place to camp; hardstanding pitches are available. It offers
sweeping views of the Dorset countryside from most pitches, and is just five miles
from Abbotsbury, and one and a half miles from the South West Coast Path. This is
a really good base from which to tour this attractive area. There is an excellent pub
in the village, just a short walk from the campsite.

Open: April to 6 October **Last arrival:** 20.00 (arrivals until 21.00 by prior arrangement
only) **Last departure:** noon
Pitches: 🚐 from £18; 🚏 from £18; ▲ from £14; 2 hardstanding pitches;
14 seasonal pitches
Facilities: 🖻 ⊙ ℱ ☀ 🛏
Services: 🔌 🔒 🖉
Within 3 miles: 𝒫 ⑤

Additional site information: 6.5 acre site. 🐾 Dogs must be kept on leads at all times.
🚗 Cars can be parked by caravans and tents. Awnings permitted. No cats, no wood-
burning fires, skateboards, rollerblades, motorised toys, drones or loud music. Calor Gas
exchange.

ST LEONARDS
Map 5 SU10

Places to visit

Rockbourne Roman Villa, ROCKBOURNE, SP6 3PG, 01725 518541
www.hampshireculturaltrust.org.uk/rockbourne-roman-villa

Red House Museum & Gardens, CHRISTCHURCH, BH23 1BU, 01202 482860
www.hampshireculturaltrust.org.uk

Great for kids: Moors Valley Country Park and Forest, RINGWOOD, BH24 2ET,
01425 470721, www.moors-valley.co.uk

Premier Park

Shamba Holidays
►►►►► 88%

tel: 01202 873302 **230 Ringwood Road BH24 2SB**
email: enquiries@shambaholidays.co.uk **web:** www.shambaholidays.co.uk
dir: *From Poole on A31, pass Woodman Pub on left, straight on at roundabout (keep in
left lane), immediately left into East Moors Lane. Site 1 mile on right.*

This top quality park is situated in a popular location near the south coast and
is handy for visiting Bournemouth, Poole or Christchurch, as well as the New
Forest. The toilet and shower block is excellent and offers some of the best
facilities you will find in the country. There is a lovely indoor-outdoor swimming

LEISURE: 🏊 Indoor swimming pool 🏊 Outdoor swimming pool 𝄞 Children's playground ✋ Kids' club 🎾 Tennis court 🎱 Games room ▭ Separate TV room
⛳ golf course ⛳ Pitch n putt 🚣 Boats for hire 🚲 Bikes for hire 🎬 Cinema 🎵 Entertainment 🎣 Fishing ⛳ Mini golf 🏄 Watersports 🏋 Gym ⚽ Sports field ♨ Stables
FACILITIES: 🖻 Baths/Shower ⊙ Electric shaver sockets ℱ Hairdryer ☀ Ice Pack Facility 🛏 Baby facilities ♿ Disabled facilities ⑤ Shop on site or within 200yds
🍖 BBQ area 🛏 Picnic area WiFi WiFi

pool as well as a very tasteful clubhouse which serves food, and has entertainment in the main season. You can always be assured of a warm welcome.

Open: All year (restricted service: low and mid season – some facilities only open at weekends) **Last arrival:** 20.00 (later arrivals by prior arrangement only) **Last departure:** 11.00

Pitches: * 🚐 from £25; 🚌 from £25; ⛺ from £25; 10 hardstanding pitches; 40 seasonal pitches

Leisure: 🏊 🏊 🛝 🎱 ♫ ⚽

Facilities: 🚿 ☺ 💇 ❄ ♿ 🛒 🍼 WiFi

Services: 🔌 🧺 🍷 🍴 🍔 🔋 ⛽ 🛢 🔥 [T]

Within 3 miles: 🎣 ⛳ 🐎

Additional site information: 7 acre site. 🐕 Cars can be parked by caravans and tents. Awnings permitted. No large groups or commercial vehicles, no noise after 23.00. Fresh bread delivered daily. Entertainment 4 nights in low season, 5 nights in high season.

Back of Beyond Touring Park

►►►► 93% 🛖

tel: 01202 876968 **234 Ringwood Rd BH24 2SB**
email: info@backofbeyondtouringpark.co.uk **web:** www.backofbeyondtouringpark.co.uk
dir: *From east: on A31 over Little Chef roundabout, pass St Leonard's Hotel, at next roundabout U-turn into lane immediately left. Site at end of lane. From west: on A31 pass Texaco garage and Woodman Inn, immediately left to site.*

This lovely adults-only park, a member of the Tranquil Parks group, is set in 30 acres of woodland and offers plenty of pleasant walks. Visitors are sure to receive a warm welcome from the owners and their team. In addition to good caravan and motorhome pitches, there are some excellent areas for tents. The site has a fishing lake and a picnic area, and the whole area is a haven for wildlife. The facilities are well appointed and very clean. There are fish and chip and pizza nights as well as BBQ evenings. A secluded and separate glamping area offers camping pods, a yurt, bell tents and lodges for hire – all have their own spacious decking areas.

Open: March to October **Last arrival:** 19.00 **Last departure:** 11.00

Pitches: 🚐 from £20; 🚌 from £20; ⛺ from £15; 🛖 see prices below; 34 seasonal pitches

Leisure: 🎣 🌴 ⛳

Facilities: 🚿 ☺ 💇 ❄ ♿ 🛒 🧺 WiFi

Services: 🔌 🧺 🍔 🔋 ⛽ 🛢 🔥 [T]

Within 3 miles: 🐎 ◎ 🏄 🚴

Additional site information: 30 acre site. Adults only. 🐕 Cars can be parked by caravans and tents. Awnings permitted. No commercial vehicles, no groups, no noise after 22.30. Visiting food vans, coffee and tea available, morning bakery. Licensed to sell alcohol. Car hire can be arranged.

Glamping available: Bell tents (unfurnished) from £22; pod (furnished) from £37; lodges from £42; yurt from £37. **Changeover days:** Any day

Additional glamping information: For further information on dog-friendly accommodation, please phone for details. Wood burner in yurt. Cars can be parked by glamping units.

SHAFTESBURY — Map 4 ST82

Places to visit

Shaftesbury Abbey Museum & Garden, SHAFTESBURY, SP7 8JR, 01747 852910 www.shaftesburyabbey.org.uk

Premier Park

Dorset Country Holidays

►►►►► 88% GLAMPING ONLY 🛖

tel: 01747 851523 & 01225 290924 **Sherborne Causeway SP7 9PX**
email: info@dche.co.uk **web:** www.blackmorevalecaravanandcampingpark.co.uk
dir: *From Shaftesbury's Ivy Cross roundabout take A30 signed Sherborne. Site 2 miles on right.*

Blackmore Vale Caravan & Camping Park (see next entry) has a separate glamping area (Dorset Country Holidays) which is well screened from the main park and is run by its own 24/7, dedicated team. The accommodation varies, two luxury yurts, of British design and manufacture offer excellent insulation, heating and lighting; they have double beds, two single futons, some have fridges and TV and are carpeted. Set on wooden decking, each comes with picnic benches and a BBQ and guests receive a welcome breakfast pack and towelling gowns. In addition, there are three bell tents, including one large family bell tent, a geo dome plus a 'country kabin' – all are fully equipped to a high standard. There's a modern and well-appointed toilet and shower room block. Customer service here is excellent and guests are welcomed with refreshments and can be collected from the local railway station. Deluxe glamping packages and massage breaks are now also available.

Open: All year **Last arrival:** 21.00 **Last departure:** noon

Accommodation available: Bell tents, yurts, cabin, geo dome.

Additional site information: 1 acre site. 🐕

Blackmore Vale Caravan & Camping Park

►►►► 86%

tel: 01747 851523 & 01225 290924 **Sherborne Causeway SP7 9PX**
email: info@dche.co.uk **web:** www.blackmorevalecaravanpark.co.uk
dir: *From Shaftesbury's Ivy Cross roundabout take A30 signed Sherborne. Site 2 miles on right.*

This small park set in open countryside just outside Shaftesbury (famous for the steep, cobbled street known as Gold Hill) offers a wide range of camping opportunities, including touring pitches (some with large hardstandings), and an area where there are six luxury lodges. The facilities are modern and very clean, and a fully-equipped gym is available to all customers. There is a separate glamping area (see previous entry) with a dedicated team to look after guests.

Open: All year **Last arrival:** 21.00

Pitches: 🚐 🚌 ⛺; 7 hardstanding pitches

Leisure: ⛳ 🏋

Facilities: 🚿 ☺ 💇 ❄ ♿ 🛒 🍽 🧺

Services: 🔌 🧺 🔋 🛢 🔥 [T]

Additional site information: 3 acre site. 🐕 Cars can be parked by caravans and tents. Awnings permitted. No noise after 23.00. Caravan sales and accessories.

SHAFTESBURY *continued*

Lower Liston Farm Touring Park
▶▶▶ 78%

tel: 01747 851865 & 07725 500963 **Lower Liston Farm, Semley Hollow SP7 9AG**
email: lowerlistoncamping@outlook.com **web:** www.lowerlistonfarm.co.uk
dir: *From Shaftesbury towards Warminster A350, 2 miles from Shaftesbury. Gate on the left before Rail Bridge.*

A small, well managed, family run, adults-only site located on a working sheep farm and equestrian centre just off the A350, north of Shaftesbury. With just 12 pitches (6 grass; 6 hardstandings), the site has basic but clean toilet and shower facilities and provides a peaceful rural base for exploring the north Dorset and Wiltshire countryside. Natural, organic meadows with an abundance of wildlife surround this farm site and a network of footpaths radiate from the farm. Dogs are very welcome.

Open: March to November **Last arrival:** 19.00 (later arrivals by prior arrangement)
Last departure: noon

Pitches: * 🚐 from £20; 🚚 from £20; 6 hardstanding pitches

Facilities: 🚿 🧖 🍴 🪑 WiFi

Services: 🔌 🛒 🚽 🔒 T

Within 3 miles: 🎣 ⛳ 🎯 🛒 🛍

Additional site information: 2 acre site. Adults only. 🐕 Cars can be parked by caravans. Awnings permitted. Woodland walks, free-range eggs.

SIXPENNY HANDLEY

Places to visit

Larmer Tree Gardens, TOLLARD ROYAL, SP5 5PT, 01725 516971
www.larmertree.co.uk

Shaftesbury Abbey Museum & Garden, SHAFTESBURY, SP7 8JR, 01747 852910
www.shaftesburyabbey.org.uk

Great for kids: Moors Valley Country Park and Forest, RINGWOOD, BH24 2ET, 01425 470721, www.moors-valley.co.uk

---

SIXPENNY HANDLEY   Map 4 ST91

Church Farm Caravan & Camping Park
▶▶▶▶ 85%

tel: 01725 552563 & 07766 677525 **The Bungalow, Church Farm SP5 5ND**
email: churchfarmcandcpark@hotmail.co.uk **web:** www.churchfarmcandcpark.co.uk
dir: *1 mile south of Handley Hill roundabout. Exit for Sixpenny Handley, right by school, site 300 yards by church.*

A spacious park located within the Cranborne Chase Area of Outstanding Natural Beauty; the site is split into several camping areas including one for adults only. There is a first-class facility block with good private facilities, an excellent café and restaurant, and a function room, Hanlega's. The pretty village of Sixpenny Handley, with all its amenities, is just 200 yards away, and the site is well positioned for visiting the Great Dorset Steam Fair, the New Forest National Park, Bournemouth, Poole and Stonehenge.

Open: All year (restricted service: November to March – 10 vans maximum)
Last arrival: 21.00 **Last departure:** 11.00

Pitches: 🚐 🚚 ⛺; 4 hardstanding pitches; 5 seasonal pitches

Facilities: 🚿 ☉ ❄ ♿ 🍴 WiFi

Services: 🔌 🛢 🚽 🍴 🍽 🛒 🚽 🔒 🌱 T

Within 3 miles: ♿ 🛍

Additional site information: 10 acre site. 🐕 Cars can be parked by caravans and tents. Awnings permitted. Quiet after 23.00. Use of fridge freezer and microwave.

SWANAGE

Places to visit

Corfe Castle, CORFE CASTLE, BH20 5EZ, 01929 481294
www.nationaltrust.org.uk/corfecastle

Brownsea Island, BROWNSEA ISLAND, BH13 7EE, 01202 707744
www.nationaltrust.org.uk/brownsea-island

Great for kids: Swanage Railway, SWANAGE, BH19 1HB, 01929 425800
www.swanagerailway.co.uk

LEISURE: 🏊 Indoor swimming pool   🏊 Outdoor swimming pool   /⋀ Children's playground   🖐 Kids' club   🎾 Tennis court   🎱 Games room   📺 Separate TV room
🏌 golf course   ⛳ Pitch n putt   🚣 Boats for hire   🚲 Bikes for hire   🎬 Cinema   🎵 Entertainment   🎣 Fishing   ◎ Mini golf   🏄 Watersports   🏋 Gym   🏟 Sports field   ⛹ Stables
FACILITIES: 🚿 Baths/Shower   ☉ Electric shaver sockets   🗲 Hairdryer   ❄ Ice Pack Facility   🛒 Baby facilities   ♿ Disabled facilities   🛍 Shop on site or within 200yds
🍴 BBQ area   🍴 Picnic area   WiFi WiFi

SWANAGE

Map 5 SZ07

Premier Park

Ulwell Cottage Caravan Park

▶▶▶▶▶ 88%

tel: 01929 422823 **Ulwell Cottage, Ulwell BH19 3DG**
email: enq@ulwellcottagepark.co.uk **web:** www.ulwellcottagepark.co.uk
dir: *From Bournemouth via Sandbanks chain ferry onto B3351 towards Swanage. Through Studland, fork left follow Swanage signs. Site on right. Or from Wareham on A351 to Swanage, left at seafront towards Studland (Shore Road becomes Ulwell Road). Approximately 2 miles, left at campsite sign.*

Sitting under the Purbeck Hills and surrounded by scenic walks, this park is only two miles from the beach. It is a family-run and caters well for families and couples, and offers a toilet and shower block complete with good family rooms (heated in winter), all appointed to a high standard. There are fully serviced pitches and a good indoor swimming pool; the village inn offers a good range of meals. There is a camping pod for hire and, suitable for a couple, a stylish self-contained S-pod with a decking area.

Open: March to 7 January (Easter to 31 October – shop has variable opening times)
Last arrival: 22.00 **Last departure:** 11.00

Pitches: 🚐 from £18; 🚌 from £18; ⛺ from £15; 🏠 see prices below; 23 hardstanding pitches

Leisure: 🏊 ⛰ ✈ **Facilities:** 🏠 ☉ 🌡 ✳ ♿ 🛡 🚿 🐶 WiFi

Services: 🔌 🖨 🗐 🍴 🧺 🛢 🌀

Within 3 miles: ↓ 🎣 ∪ ◎ 🥐 🛶 🐎 🎌

Additional site information: 13 acre site. 🐕 Cars can be parked by caravans and tents. Awnings permitted. No bonfires or fireworks.

Glamping available: Wooden pods from £45; cabin (S-pod).

Changeover days: Variable

Additional glamping information: Linen only supplied if requested. Cars can be parked by pods.

Herston Caravan & Camping Park

▶▶▶ 85%

tel: 01929 422932 **Washpond Lane BH19 3DJ**
email: office@herstonleisure.co.uk **web:** www.herstonleisure.co.uk
dir: *From Wareham on A351 towards Swanage. Washpond Lane on left just after 'Welcome to Swanage' sign.*

Set in a rural area, with extensive views of the Purbecks, this tree-lined park has fully serviced pitches plus large camping areas. There is a toilet and shower block with excellent family rooms, a bar and restaurant, takeaway and barbecue food, and entertainment in the high season. Herston Halt, a stop for the famous Swanage Steam Railway between the town centre and Corfe Castle, is within walking distance.

Open: All year

Pitches: 🚐 from £18; 🚌 from £18; ⛺ from £10; 17 hardstanding pitches

Facilities: 🏠 ☉ 🌡 ✳ ♿ 🛡 🚿 🐶 WiFi

Services: 🔌 🖨 🗐 🍴 🚚 🧺 🔋 🛠 T

Within 3 miles: ↓ 🎣 ∪ ◎ 🥐 🛶 🎌

Additional site information: 10 acre site. 🐕 Cars can be parked by caravans and tents. Awnings permitted. No noise after 23.00.

Acton Field Camping Site

▶▶ 80%

tel: 01929 424184 **Acton Field, Langton Matravers BH19 3HS**
email: enquiries@actonfieldcampsite.co.uk **web:** www.actonfieldcampsite.co.uk
dir: *From A351 right after Corfe Castle onto B3069 to Langton Matravers, 2nd right after village (bridleway sign).*

This informal campsite, bordered by farmland on the outskirts of Langton Matravers, offers good toilet facilities. There are superb views of the Purbeck Hills and towards the Isle of Wight, and a footpath leads to the coastal path. The site occupies what was once a stone quarry so rock pegs may be required. Its location and views make it a wonderful place to camp.

Open: Early May bank holiday weekend, Spring bank holiday weekend, early July to end August (organised groups from Easter to end October) **Last arrival:** 22.00
Last departure: noon

Pitches: 🚐 from £18; 🚌 from £16; ⛺ from £8

Facilities: ☉ ✳

Services: 🔌 🔋

Within 3 miles: ↓ 🎣 ∪ ◎ 🥐 🛶 🎌 🛢 🗐

Additional site information: 7 acre site. 🐕 🚫 Cars can be parked by caravans and tents. Awnings permitted. No open fires, no noise after 23.00. Mobile grocer calls during school summer holidays. Phone charger on site.

THREE LEGGED CROSS
Map 5 SU00

Places to visit
Moors Valley Country Park and Forest, RINGWOOD, BH24 2ET, 01425 470721
www.moors-valley.co.uk

Woolsbridge Manor Farm Caravan Park
►►►► 84%

tel: 01202 826369 **BH21 6RA**
email: woolsbridge@btconnect.com **web:** www.woolsbridgemanorcaravanpark.co.uk
dir: *From Ringwood take A31 towards Ferndown. Approximately 1 mile, follow signs for Three Legged Cross and Horton. Site 2 miles on right.*

A small farm site with spacious pitches on a level field. This quiet site is an excellent central base for touring the New Forest National Park, Salisbury and the south coast, and is close to Moors Valley Country Park for outdoor family activities. The facilities are good and very clean and there are excellent family rooms available.

Open: March to October **Last arrival:** 20.00 **Last departure:** 10.30
Pitches: 🚐 🚙 ⛺ **Leisure:** ⚖ ✐
Facilities: 🛁 ⊙ ☂ ✳ ⚓ 🖵 WiFi
Services: 🔌 🔲 🧺 🛢 ⌀ T
Within 3 miles: ⚓ ∪

Additional site information: 6.75 acre site. Cars can be parked by caravans and tents. Awnings permitted. Car hire can be arranged.

See advert opposite

WAREHAM
Map 4 SY98

Places to visit
Brownsea Island, BROWNSEA ISLAND, BH13 7EE, 01202 707744
www.nationaltrust.org.uk/brownsea-island

Platinum Park

Wareham Forest Tourist Park
►►►►►

tel: 01929 551393 **North Trigon BH20 7NZ**
email: holiday@warehamforest.co.uk **web:** www.warehamforest.co.uk
dir: *From A35 between Bere Regis and Lytchett Minster follow Wareham sign into Sugar Hill. Site on left.*

A woodland park within the tranquil Wareham Forest, with its many walks and proximity to Poole, Dorchester and the Purbeck coast. Two luxury blocks, with combined washbasin and toilets for total privacy, are maintained to a high standard of cleanliness. A heated outdoor swimming pool, off licence, shop and games room add to the enjoyment of a stay on this top quality park. There is a bike wash and a separate dog wash with hot water. Its location and high standards make this one of the leading parks in the country.

Open: All year (restricted service: limited services available in off-peak season)
Last arrival: 21.00 **Last departure:** 11.00
Pitches: 🚐 🚙 ⛺; 70 hardstanding pitches; 70 seasonal pitches
Leisure: ⚖ 🎡 🔍
Facilities: 🛁 ⊙ ☂ ✳ ⚓ 🖵 WiFi
Services: 🔌 🔲 🧺 ⌀ 🛢 T
Within 3 miles: ⚓ ✐ ∪ ✈ 🎬

Additional site information: 55 acre site. Cars can be parked by caravans and tents. Awnings permitted. Families and couples only, no group bookings. Table tennis. Fresh bread and croissants available in high season.

Birchwood Tourist Park

▶▶▶▶ 85%

tel: 01929 554763 **Bere Road, Coldharbour BH20 7PA**
email: birchwoodtouristpark@hotmail.com **web:** www.birchwoodtouristpark.co.uk
dir: *From Poole (A351) or Dorchester (A352) on north side of railway line at Wareham, follow Bere Regis signs. 2nd park after 2.25 miles.*

Birchwood Tourist Park

Open: All year **Last arrival:** 21.00 **Last departure:** 11.00 (until 16.00 – fee applies)

Pitches: 🚐 from £19.50; 🚐; ▲ from £15.50; 25 hardstanding pitches; 50 seasonal pitches

Leisure: 🛝 🎣 ⚽

Facilities: 🏪 ☉ ✳ ⑤ 🎡 WiFi

Services: 🔌 🗑 🏧 🚿 ⚡ 🔋 ⛽ 🚐 T

Within 3 miles: ⚓ 🏌 ⛸ 🎯

Set in 50 acres of parkland located within Wareham Forest, this site offers direct access to areas that are ideal for walking, mountain biking and horse and pony riding. This is a spacious open park, ideal for families, with plenty of room for young people to play games, including football, and there is a small pool for children and a games room. The modern facilities are in two central locations and are very clean. The site has a good security barrier system. The park is only a short drive from Bournemouth and Swanage.

Additional site information: 25 acre site. 🐕 Cars can be parked by caravans and tents. Awnings permitted. No groups on bank holidays, no generators or camp fires. Dogs on leads, no noise after 22.00, barrier entry system. Paddling pool, table tennis. Shop/reception open for 2-3 hours daily.

See advert on page 186

PITCHES: 🚐 Caravans 🚐 Motorhomes ▲ Tents 🏕 Glamping accommodation **SERVICES:** 🔌 Electric hook-up ⑤ Launderette 🍺 Licensed bar 🔋 Calor Gas ⊘ Campingaz T Toilet fluid 🍽 Café/Restaurant 🏧 Fast Food/Takeaway 🔋 Battery charging ⚡ Motorhome service point * 2019 prices ⊘ No credit or debit cards 🐕 Dogs permitted ⊗ No dogs

WAREHAM *continued*

Norden Farm Touring Caravan and Camping Site

►►►► 82%

tel: 01929 480098 **Norden Farm, Corfe Castle BH20 5DS**
email: campsite@nordenfarm.com **web:** www.nordenfarm.com
dir: *On A351 from Wareham towards Swanage, 3.5 miles to site on right.*

This delightful farm site offers traditional camping but with excellent toilet and shower facilities. It is a very dog-friendly site and is ideally suited for those who enjoy country pursuits. Its location is very close to Corfe Castle so it's very convenient for visiting the Isle of Purbeck and Swanage (the Swanage Railway runs seasonal trains from Swanage through to Wareham). There is a holiday cottage for hire.

Open: March to October (weather depending) (restricted service: early March to late October – 1 shower block may be closed) **Last arrival:** 22.00 **Last departure:** 11.00 (flexible departure times available in low season)

Pitches: * 🚃 from £17; 🚌 from £17; ⛺ from £10

Leisure: 🛝 🎣 ⚽ **Facilities:** 🛁 🔌 💨 ❄ ♿ 🛒 🍖 [WiFi]

Services: 🚐 🧼 🧺 🚽 🔋 🛢 🍃 [T] **Within 3 miles:** ⛳ 🚣 🎬

Additional site information: 10 acre site. 🐕 Cars can be parked by caravans and tents. Awnings permitted. Strict 5mph speed limit on site, no noise after 23.00. Fresh bakery deliveries daily, hot shower washroom for dogs, footpaths to local attractions.

East Creech Farm Campsite

►►► 85%

tel: 01929 480519 **East Creech Farm, East Creech BH20 5AP**
email: farmhouse@eastcreechfarm.co.uk **web:** www.eastcreechfarm.co.uk
dir: *From Wareham on A351 south towards Swanage. On bypass at 3rd roundabout take Furzebrook/Blue Pool Road exit, site approximately 2 miles on right.*

This grassy park set in a peaceful location beneath the Purbeck Hills, with extensive views towards Poole and Brownsea Island. The park boasts bright, clean toilet facilities, a woodland play area, a farm shop selling milk, eggs and bread, and a children's play area. There are also four coarse fishing lakes teeming with fish. A good tearoom, The Cake Room, adjacent to the site, is open in the main season. The park is close to Norden Station on the Swanage to Norden steam railway line, and is well located for visiting Corfe Castle, Swanage and the Purbeck coast.

Open: April to October **Last arrival:** 20.00 **Last departure:** noon

Pitches: * 🚃 from £16; 🚌 from £16; ⛺ from £16

Leisure: 🛝 🎣 **Facilities:** 🛁 🔌 💨 ❄

Services: 🚐 🧼 🍴 **Within 3 miles:** ⛳ 🏄 🚣 🎬 🛒

Additional site information: 4 acre site. 🐕 Cars can be parked by caravans and tents. Awnings permitted. No camp fires, no loud noise.

Ridge Farm Camping & Caravan Park

►►► 81%

tel: 01929 556444 **Barnhill Road, Ridge BH20 5BG**
email: enquiries@ridgefarm.co.uk **web:** www.ridgefarm.co.uk
dir: *From Wareham take B3075 towards Corfe Castle, cross river, into Stoborough, left to Ridge. Follow site signs for 1.5 miles.*

A quiet rural park, adjacent to a working farm and surrounded by trees and bushes. This away-from-it-all park is ideally located for touring this part of Dorset, and especially for birdwatchers, or those who enjoy walking and cycling. This site is perfect for visiting the Arne Nature Reserve, the Blue Pool and Corfe Castle. There are good supermarkets and shops in nearby Wareham.

Open: Easter to September **Last arrival:** 21.00 **Last departure:** noon

Pitches: 🚃 from £17; 🚌 from £17; ⛺ from £17; 2 hardstanding pitches; 20 seasonal pitches

Facilities: 🛁 🔌 💨 ❄ 🛒 **Services:** 🚐 🧼 🚽 [T]

Within 3 miles: ⛳ 🎣 🐴 🚣 🎬

Additional site information: 3.47 acre site. 🐕 Dogs by prior arrangement only. 💳 Cars can be parked by caravans and tents. Awnings permitted.

LEISURE: 🏊 Indoor swimming pool ⛱ Outdoor swimming pool 🛝 Children's playground ✋ Kids' club 🎾 Tennis court ♠ Games room 📺 Separate TV room ⛳ golf course 🏌 Pitch n putt 🚣 Boats for hire 🚲 Bikes for hire 🎬 Cinema 🎵 Entertainment 🎣 Fishing ◎ Mini golf 🏄 Watersports 🏋 Gym ⚽ Sports field 🐴 Stables
FACILITIES: 🛁 Baths/Shower 🔌 Electric shaver sockets 💨 Hairdryer ❄ Ice Pack Facility 🍼 Baby facilities ♿ Disabled facilities 🛒 Shop on site or within 200yds 🍖 BBQ area 🪑 Picnic area [WiFi] WiFi

WEYMOUTH

Map 4 SY67

Places to visit

RSPB Nature Reserve Radipole Lake and Wild Weymouth Discovery Centre, WEYMOUTH, DT4 7TZ, 01305 778313
www.rspb.org.uk

Portland Castle, PORTLAND, DT5 1AZ, 01305 820539
www.english-heritage.org.uk/daysout/properties/portland-castle

Great for kids: Weymouth Sea Life Adventure Park & Marine Sanctuary, WEYMOUTH, DT4 7SX
www2.visitsealife.com/weymouth

Premier Park

Weymouth Bay Holiday Park

▶ ▶ ▶ ▶ ▶   93% HOLIDAY HOME PARK

tel: 01305 832271 **Preston DT3 6BQ**
email: weymouthbay@haven.com web: www.haven.com/weymouthbay
dir: *From A35 towards Dorchester take A354 signed Weymouth. Follow Preston signs onto A353. At Chalbury roundabout 1st left into Preston Road. Park on right.*

This well-located holiday park, just a short drive away from Weymouth beach, offers the complete holiday experience for the whole family. It has excellent indoor and outdoor pools complete with a Lazy River attraction. There is a good choice of eating outlets as well as a full entertainment programme, and an excellent range of sporting activities for all ages. Although a large holiday park, it is of exceptional quality and very well cared for, and guests can expect top customer service throughout their stay. The holiday homes are well appointed throughout. The park is conveniently placed for visiting Portland Bill, Lulworth Cove and Chesil Beach.

Open: mid March to October

Holiday Homes: Sleep 8 Bedrooms 2 Bathrooms 1 Toilets 1 Microwave Freezer TV Sky/Freeview DVD player WiFi Linen included Towels included Electricity included

Leisure: ▨ ☀ ▩ 🖐

Additional site information: 🐕 Most dog breeds accepted (please check when booking). Dogs must be kept on leads at all times. The facilities provided in the holiday homes may differ depending on the grade.

Premier Park

East Fleet Farm Touring Park

▶ ▶ ▶ ▶ ▶   92%

Best of British

tel: 01305 785768 **Chickerell DT3 4DW**
email: enquiries@eastfleet.co.uk web: www.eastfleet.co.uk
dir: *On B3157 (Weymouth to Bridport road), 3 miles from Weymouth.*

Set on a working organic farm and in a unique location on the shores of the Fleet Lagoon, overlooking Chesil Beach and the sea, with direct access to the South West Coast Path. There is a wide variety of pitches, including hardstandings and fully serviced pitches, and the largest family tents can be accommodated. This park offers excellent toilet and shower facilities with family rooms. There are

good play facilities for children, including a fenced play area for younger ones and a separate play barn with table tennis and other activities. The Old Barn has a tasteful bar and lovely patio area, where customers are welcome to take their own food, or order locally and have the food delivered to the bar. In addition, there is 'Festival Food', an area for pizzas and fish and chips, which is very popular with guests. The park is well positioned for visiting Weymouth and Portland, as well as other local attractions, such as the Abbotsbury Swannery and the Abbotsbury Subtropical Gardens. There is a fine drive along the coast road from East Fleet to Bridport with spectacular views of Chesil Beach.

Open: 16 March to October **Last arrival:** 22.00 **Last departure:** 10.30

Pitches: * 🚐 from £18.30; 🚐 from £18.30; ▲ from £18.30; 90 hardstanding pitches; 30 seasonal pitches

Leisure: ⅄ ⚊ ⚽

Facilities: 🏪 ⊙ 𝒫 ☼ 🔥 🚿 ▤ 🚻 WiFi

Services: 🔌 🅂 🍺 ♨ ▦ ⚡ 🛠 ⊘ 🅣

Within 3 miles: ↧ 🏇 U ◉ 🚤 ⅜ 🎣 🎡

Additional site information: 21 acre site. 🐕 Cars can be parked by caravans and tents. Awnings permitted. Camping and caravan accessories shop. Car hire can be arranged.

Premier Park

Littlesea Holiday Park

▶ ▶ ▶ ▶ ▶   88% HOLIDAY CENTRE

tel: 01305 774414 **Lynch Lane DT4 9DT**
email: littlesea@haven.com web: www.haven.com/littlesea
dir: *A35 onto A354 signed Weymouth. Right at 1st roundabout, 3rd exit at 2nd roundabout towards Chickerell. Left into Lynch Lane after lights. Site at far end of road.*

Just three miles from Weymouth with its lovely beaches and many attractions, Littlesea has a cheerful family atmosphere and fantastic facilities. Indoor and outdoor entertainment and activities are on offer for all the family, and the toilet facilities on the touring park are modern and spotlessly clean as well as being nice and warm. The touring section of this holiday complex is at the far end of the site adjacent to the South West Coast Path in a perfect location. An excellent base for visiting the many attractions close to Weymouth and Portland.

Open: end March to end October (restricted service: end March to May and September to end October – facilities may be reduced) **Last arrival:** 20.30 **Last departure:** 10.00

Pitches: 🚐 🚐 ▲; 🏕 see prices below

Leisure: ▨ ☀ ⅄ 🖐 🎱 🏐 🎵 ⚽

Facilities: 🏪 ⊙ 𝒫 ☼ 🔥 🚻 ▤ 🚻 WiFi

Services: 🔌 🅂 🍺 🍽 ▦ 🔋 ⊘ 🅣

Within 3 miles: ↧ 🏇 U ◉ 🚤 ⅜ 🎣 🎡

Additional site information: 100 acre site. 🐕 Maximum 2 dogs per booking, certain dog breeds banned. No commercial vehicles, no bookings by persons under 21 years unless a family booking, no boats.

Glamping available: Safari tents from £125.

Additional glamping information: Safari tents: minimum stay 3 nights.

WEYMOUTH *continued*

Premier Park

Seaview Holiday Park

►►►►► 87% HOLIDAY CENTRE

tel: 01305 832271 **Preston DT3 6DZ**
email: seaview@haven.com **web:** www.haven.com/seaview
dir: *A354 to Weymouth, follow signs for Preston and Wareham onto A353. Site 3 miles on right just after Weymouth Bay Holiday Park.*

A fun-packed holiday centre especially suited to families and for all ages, with plenty of activities and entertainment during the day or evening. Guests can use the facilities offered at the sister park, Weymouth Bay Holiday Park, which can be reached via a walkway from Seaview Holiday Park. There is a touring section for caravans, motorhomes and tents, the upper area having all fully serviced pitches, whilst the lower section is mainly for tents. There are also six fully-equipped safari tents in this area for anyone wishing to try a glamping experience.

Open: mid March to end October (restricted service: mid March to May and September to end October – some facilities may be reduced) **Last arrival:** midnight **Last departure:** 10.00

Pitches: ; see prices below; 35 hardstanding pitches

Leisure:

Facilities: WiFi

Services:

Within 3 miles:

Additional site information: 20 acre site. Maximum 2 dogs per booking, certain dog breeds banned. No commercial vehicles, no bookings by persons under 21 years unless a family booking.

Glamping available: Safari tents from £125. **Changeover days:** Fridays and Mondays

Additional glamping information: Safari tents: minimum stay 3 nights. Price shown is for 3 nights. Kitchen equipment included.

Bagwell Farm Touring Park

►►►► 89%

tel: 01305 782575 **Knights in the Bottom, Chickerell DT3 4EA**
email: aa@bagwellfarm.co.uk **web:** www.bagwellfarm.co.uk
dir: *From A354 follow signs for Weymouth town centre, then B3157 to Chickerell and Abbotsbury, 1 mile after Chickerell turn left into site 500 yards after Victoria Inn.*

This well located park is set in a small valley with access to the South West Coast Path and is very convenient for visiting Weymouth and Portland. It has excellent facilities including a good shop, pets' corner, children's play area plus the Red Barn bar and restaurant. A good range of hardstandings is available, including 25 super pitches, which are very spacious and can take the longest units. This is an excellent place to stay at any time of the year.

Open: All year (restricted service: winter – bar closed) **Last arrival:** 21.00 **Last departure:** 11.00

Pitches: ; 35 hardstanding pitches; 70 seasonal pitches

Leisure:

Facilities: WiFi

Services:

Within 3 miles:

Additional site information: 14 acre site. Cars can be parked by caravans and tents. Awnings permitted. Families and couples only, no noise after 23.00. Wet suit shower, campers' shelter, dog wash. Car hire can be arranged.

Pebble Bank Caravan Park

►►►► 88%

tel: 01305 774844 **Camp Road, Wyke Regis DT4 9HF**
email: info@pebblebank.co.uk **web:** www.pebblebank.co.uk
dir: *A354 to Weymouth, B3155 signed Portland. At lights into Wyke Road signed Wyke Regis. Straight on at roundabout, 1st left into Camp Road. Site on left. Or from Portesham take B3157 signed Weymouth. Right onto B3156 (Lanehouse Rocks Road). Right into Camp Road.*

This site, although only one and a half miles from Weymouth, is in a peaceful location overlooking Chesil Beach and The Fleet, and is an excellent place to stay. The site has a bar and restaurant with an alfresco decking area and fabulous views. The toilet and shower block is very modern and spotlessly clean and 12 hardstandings are available. The park is adjacent to the South West Coast Path, making it a good base for walkers.

Open: Easter to mid October (restricted service: bar open in high season and at weekends only in low season) **Last arrival:** 18.00 **Last departure:** 11.00

Pitches:

Leisure:

Facilities: WiFi

Services:

Within 3 miles:

Additional site information: 4 acre site. Cars can be parked by caravans and tents. Awnings permitted.

West Fleet Holiday Farm

►►► 92%

tel: 01305 782218 **Fleet DT3 4EF**
email: aa@westfleetholidays.co.uk **web:** www.westfleetholidays.co.uk
dir: *From Weymouth take B3157 towards Abbotsbury for 3 miles. Past Chickerell turn left at mini roundabout to Fleet, site 1 mile on right.*

A spacious farm site with both level and sloping pitches divided into paddocks and screened by hedges. This site has good views of the Dorset countryside, and is a relaxing place for a family holiday, particularly suited to tents, especially family-sized tents, and small motorhomes or campervans. The Barn Clubhouse has a bar, restaurant and entertainment area. There is an excellent and very popular outdoor swimming pool, which is great for families, and modern, toilet facilities. WiFi is also available.

Open: Easter to September (restricted service: mid and low season – clubhouse closed; low season – pool closed) **Last arrival:** 21.00 **Last departure:** 11.00 (Later departures only out of high season)

Pitches: 🚐 from £14; 🚍 from £14; ▲ from £14

Leisure: 🏊 🎱 🎵 ⚽

Facilities: 📷 ⊙ 🖲 ✳ ♿ 🛉 **WiFi**

Services: 🔌 🔲 🍽 🍴 🎫 ⬆ 🔒 🧹 🇹

Within 3 miles: 🛶

Additional site information: 12 acre site. 🐕 Dogs restricted to certain areas. Cars can be parked by caravans and tents. Awnings permitted. Non-family groups by arrangement only.

Rosewall Camping
▶▶▶ 90%

tel: 01305 832248 **East Farm Dairy, Osmington Mills DT3 6HA**
email: holidays@weymouthcamping.com **web:** www.weymouthcamping.com
dir: *Take A353 towards Weymouth. At Osmington Mills sign (opposite garage) turn left, 0.25 mile, site on 1st right.*

This well-positioned sloping tent site, just a few miles to the east of Weymouth, is adjacent to the South West Coast Path and affords great sea views from virtually every pitch. There are excellent toilet and shower facilities including a block at the bottom of the campsite. There is a well-stocked shop and for those that like horse riding or are thinking of learning how to ride, there is Rosewall Equestrian near the site entrance. This is a great place to bring a tent and makes a good base for exploring this area.

Open: Easter to October (restricted service: April to May and September to October – shop opening times vary) **Last arrival:** 22.00 **Last departure:** 10.00

Pitches: 🚍 from £18; ▲ from £18

Leisure: 🎱 ✏

Facilities: 📷 ⊙ ✳ ♿ 🛉

Services: 🔲 📥 🔒 🧹

Within 3 miles: 🛶 🚣 ⚓ 🎣

Additional site information: 13 acre site. 🐕 Cars can be parked by tents. Awnings permitted. Families and couples only, no noise after 23.00. Riding stables and coarse fishing.

Sea Barn Farm
▶▶▶ 83%

tel: 01305 782218 **Fleet Road, Fleet DT3 4ED**
email: aa@seabarnfarm.co.uk **web:** www.seabarnfarm.co.uk
dir: *From Weymouth take B3157 towards Abbotsbury for 3 miles. Past Chickerell turn left at mini roundabout into Fleet Road, site 1 mile on left.*

This site is set high on the Dorset coast and has spectacular views over Chesil Beach, The Fleet and Lyme Bay, and it is also on the South West Coast Path. Optional use of the clubhouse and swimming pool (in high seaon) at West Fleet Holiday Farm is available. The pitches are sheltered by hedging, and there is an excellent toilet facility block, and plenty of space for outdoor games. This site is suitable mainly for tents, especially large family tents, and small motorhomes or campervans.

Open: 15 March to October **Last arrival:** 21.00 **Last departure:** 11.00

Pitches: 🚐 from £14; 🚍 from £14; ▲ from £14

Facilities: 📷 ⊙ 🖲 ✳ ♿ 🛉 🏧 **WiFi**

Services: 🔌 🔲 🔒 🧹 🇹

Within 3 miles: 🛶

Additional site information: 12 acre site. 🐕 Dogs must be kept on leads at all times. Cars can be parked by caravans and tents. Awnings permitted. Non-family groups by prior arrangement only. Use of West Fleet facilities including outdoor pool, motorhome service point, bar and restaurant (open in high season – contact site for details).

WIMBORNE MINSTER — Map 5 SZ09

Places to visit

Kingston Lacy, WIMBORNE, BH21 4EA, 01202 883402
www.nationaltrust.org.uk/kingston-lacy

Priest's House Museum and Garden, WIMBORNE, BH21 1HR, 01202 882533
www.priest-house.co.uk

Premier Park

Wilksworth Caravan Park

▶▶▶▶▶ 90%

Best of British

tel: 01202 885467 **Cranborne Road BH21 4HW**
email: ww.reception@shorefield.co.uk
web: www.shorefield.co.uk/camping-touring-holidays/our-parks/wilksworth-caravan-park
dir: *1 mile north of Wimborne on B3078.*

A popular and attractive park peacefully set in the grounds of a listed house in the heart of rural Dorset. This spacious site has much to offer visitors, including an excellent heated swimming pool, tennis courts, takeaway and café, a bar and restaurant plus an excellent Tiny Town play area for young children. The modern toilet facilities contain en suite rooms and good family rooms.

Open: April to October (restricted service: October – shop closed) **Last arrival:** 20.00 **Last departure:** 11.00

Pitches: 🚐 🚎 ▲; 20 hardstanding pitches

Leisure: ⌔ ⽊ 🏊 ⚽

Facilities: 🛁 ⊙ ☞ ☀ ☦ ⑤ 🎪 📶

Services: 🔌 🗑 🍽 🛒 🛠 🚽 🛢 🗑 🅣

Within 3 miles: ⌔ ✎ ⊥ 🎣

Additional site information: 11 acre site. 🐕 Maximum of 2 dogs per pitch. Cars can be parked by caravans. Awnings permitted. No noise 23.00–07.00. Paddling pool, volley ball, mini-football pitch.

Charris Camping & Caravan Park

▶▶▶▶ 91%

tel: 01202 885970 **Candys Lane, Corfe Mullen BH21 3EF**
email: bookings@charris.co.uk **web:** www.charris.co.uk
dir: *From A31 (Wimborne bypass) at roundabout (junction with B3078, south of Wimborne Minster) into Wimborne Road signed Corfe Mullen. Right at crossroads into Candys Lane. Site on right.*

A sheltered park of grassland lined with trees on the edge of the Stour Valley, with Poole and the south coast resorts only a short drive away. Customers can be assured of a warm welcome at this well located park. The facilities are very clean, some hardstandings are available, and social get-togethers are held for customers including barbecues which prove very popular. In addition to the top quality toilet and shower block, the park continues to make improvements, proving it to be a top place to stay.

Open: All year **Last arrival:** 21.00 **Last departure:** 11.00

Pitches: 🚐 🚎 ▲; 🏠 see prices below; 12 hardstanding pitches; 10 seasonal pitches

Facilities: 🛁 ⊙ ☞ ☀ ☦ ⑤ 🎪 📶

Services: 🔌 🗑 🛒 🛢 🗑 🅣

Within 3 miles: ⌔ ✎ ⌣

Additional site information: 3.5 acre site. 🐕 Cars can be parked by caravans and tents. Awnings permitted. No noise after 23:00. Earliest arrival 11.00.

Glamping available: Shepherd's hut from £46.

Additional glamping information: Cars can be parked by shepherd's hut.

Springfield Touring Park

▶▶▶ 86%

tel: 01202 881719 **Candys Lane, Corfe Mullen BH21 3EF**
email: john.clark18@btconnect.com **web:** www.springfieldtouringpark.co.uk
dir: *From Wimborne Minster towards Dorchester on A31 (Wimborne bypass) after Caravan Sales and Accessories shop, then garage, take 1st left in Candys Lane. Follow brown campsite signs.*

A small touring park with extensive views over the Stour Valley and a quiet and friendly atmosphere. It is well positioned for visiting Poole, Bournemouth or the really lovely town of Wimborne. The park is maintained immaculately, has a well-stocked shop, and is a great place to stay.

Open: April to 14 October **Last arrival:** 21.00 **Last departure:** 11.00

Pitches: 🚐 from £23; 🚎 from £23; ▲ from £23; 38 hardstanding pitches

Leisure: ⽊

Facilities: 🛁 ⊙ ☞ ☀ ☦ ⑤

Services: 🔌 🗑 🛒

Within 3 miles: ⌔ ✎ ⌣ ⊥ 🎣

Additional site information: 3.5 acre site. 🐕 🚫 Cars can be parked by caravans and tents. Awnings permitted. No skateboards.

WOOL · Map 4 SY88

Places to visit

Lulworth Castle & Park , LULWORTH, BH20 5QS, 01929 400352
www.lulworth.com/visit/places-to-visit/castle-and-park

Great for kids: Monkey World-Ape Rescue Centre, WOOL, BH20 6HH,
01929 462537, www.monkeyworld.org

Whitemead Caravan Park
►►►► 88%

tel: 01929 462241 **East Burton Road BH20 6HG**
email: book@whitemeadcaravanpark.co.uk
dir: From A352 (opposite petrol station) in Wool into East Burton Road signed East
Burton. Site on right.

This quality park situated in the village of Wool is well placed for visiting the many
attractions of the area and also has the advantage of a train station within walking
distance – a great alternative to driving and easy for visiting Poole or Weymouth.
The facilities are excellent and spotlessly clean. There is a good shop selling basic
provisions, wine and camping accessories. The site is also close to Bovington Tank
Museum.

Open: 14 March to October **Last arrival:** 19.00 **Last departure:** 11.00

Pitches: * 🚐 from £21; 🚐 from £21; ⛺ from £16.50; 10 hardstanding pitches;
24 seasonal pitches

Leisure: ⚲ ⚲

Facilities: 🏠 ☺ ℱ ☀ ♿ 🛁 🎋 WiFi

Services: 🔌 🗑 ⚡ 🛢 🍃 T

Within 3 miles: ⚓ ∪

Additional site information: 🐕 Cars can be parked by caravans and tents. Awnings
permitted. No pit fires, no ball games. River walks, bridle path. Debit cards accepted (no
credit cards).

COUNTY DURHAM

BARNARD CASTLE · Map 19 NZ01

Places to visit

Barnard Castle, BARNARD CASTLE, DL12 8PR, 01833 638212
www.english-heritage.org.uk/daysout/properties/barnard-castle

The Bowes Museum, BARNARD CASTLE, DL12 8NP, 01833 690606
www.thebowesmuseum.org.uk

Pecknell Farm Caravan Park
►►► 82%

tel: 01833 638357 **Lartington DL12 9DF**
dir: 1.5 miles from Barnard Castle. From A66 take B6277. Site on right 1.5 miles from
junction with A67.

A small, well laid out site on a working farm in beautiful rural meadowland, with
spacious marked pitches on level ground. There are many walking opportunities
that start directly from this friendly site.

Open: April to October **Last arrival:** 20.00 **Last departure:** noon

Pitches: 🚐 from £15; 🚐 from £15; 5 hardstanding pitches

Facilities: 🏠 ☺ ℱ **Services:** 🔌 🛢

Within 3 miles: ⚓ ℱ ∪ ◎ 🎋 ⛳ 🗑

Additional site information: 1.5 acre site. 🐕 Maximum of 2 dogs. 🚗 Cars can be
parked by caravans. Awnings permitted. No noise after 22.30.

ESSEX

BRADFIELD · Map 13 TM13

Places to visit

RSPB Stour Estuary, RAMSEY, CO12 5ND, 01206 391153
www.rspb.org.uk/reserves-and-events/reserves-a-z/stour-estuary

Strangers Home
►►► 82%

tel: 01255 870304 & 07762 956134 **The Street CO11 2US**
email: joannmeri@aol.com **web:** www.strangershome.co.uk
dir: From Manningtree take B1352 towards Harwich. Strangers Home pub and campsite
on right in village centre.

A level, well maintained and improving small campsite located behind the
Strangers Home pub on the edge of pretty Bradfield, close to the Stour Estuary,
Flatford Mill and historic Harwich. There are spacious hardstandings, electricity to
all pitches, upgraded toilets in rustic outbuildings, and summer bike storage is
available. Children can use the excellent village play area, 100 yards along
the road.

Open: March to 14 January **Last arrival:** flexible **Last departure:** flexible

Pitches: 🚐 🚐 ⛺; 22 seasonal pitches

Leisure: ⚲ 🎵 **Facilities:** 🏠 🎋 🎋

Services: 🔌 🗑 🍴 ⚡ **Within 3 miles:** ℱ ∪ 🗑

Additional site information: 4 acre site. 🐕 Cars can be parked by caravans and tents.
Awnings permitted. No noise after 23.00. Seasonal live entertainment in pub.

MERSEA ISLAND

Map 7 TM01

Places to visit

Layer Marney Tower, LAYER MARNEY, CO5 9US, 01206 330784
www.layermarneytower.co.uk

Premier Park

Waldegraves Holiday Park

►►►►► 82% HOLIDAY CENTRE

tel: 01206 382898 & 381195 **CO5 8SE**

email: holidays@waldegraves.co.uk **web:** www.waldegraves.co.uk
dir: A12 junction 26, B1025 to Mersea Island across The Strood. Left to East Mersea, 2nd right, follow tourist signs to site.

A spacious and pleasant site located between farmland and its own private beach on the Blackwater Estuary. There are well-maintained standard grass pitches and a limited selection of hardstanding and serviced pitches – some have hedges to offer a greater level of privacy; the pitches are flat and spacious. There are excellent facilities including the restaurant, bar, shop, coarse fishing lakes, entertainment, a boat slipway, a heated outdoor swimming pool and fibre optic WiFi.

Open: March to November (restricted service: March to June and September to November (except bank holidays and school half terms) — pool, shop and clubhouse reduced opening hours; pool open May to September weather permitting)
Last arrival: 22.00 **Last departure:** 13.00

Pitches: * 🚐 from £20; 🚐 from £20; ▲ from £20; 25 hardstanding pitches; 100 seasonal pitches

Leisure: 🏊 🛝 👋 🔍 ⚲ 🏓 🎵 🎣 ⚽

Facilities: 🛁 ☉ 🪒 ✳ ♿ 🛒 🍽 🛏 ♨ WiFi

Services: 🔌 🗄 🏴 🍴 🍺 🛒 🚾 ♨ 🗑 T

Within 3 miles: ↻ ◎ ⛷ 🎿

Additional site information: 25 acre site. 🐕 No groups of under 21s. Boating lake, slipway, driving range, crazy golf, foot golf, family games room, family entertainment. Car hire can be arranged.

Fen Farm Caravan Site

►►►► 86%

tel: 01206 383275 **Moore Lane, East Mersea CO5 8FE**
email: havefun@fenfarm.co.uk **web:** www.fenfarm.co.uk
dir: B1025 from Colchester to Mersea Island, left signed East Mersea. 1st right after Dog and Pheasant pub into Moore Lane. (Note: road is tidal, please check tide times).

The first tents were pitched at Fen Farm in 1923 and over the years the farm has entirely become a caravan park. Enjoying an enviable location beside the Blackwater Estuary, it has a unique atmosphere with a mixture of meadow, woodland and marine shore, and varied wildlife to match each environment. There are two excellent solar-heated toilet blocks which include three family rooms and privacy cubicles; the newest block is constructed in the local style of black clapboard and a red tile roof. There is a woodland dog walk and two well-equipped play areas, while crabbing in the beach pools is a popular pastime. The site also includes an electric car charger.

Open: mid March to October **Last arrival:** dusk

Pitches: * 🚐 from £19; 🚐 from £19; ▲ from £19; 3 hardstanding pitches; 65 seasonal pitches

Leisure: 🛝 ⚽

Facilities: 🛁 ☉ 🪒 ✳ ♿ 🛒 WiFi

Services: 🔌 🗄 🚾 🛒 ♨ 🗑 T

Within 3 miles: 🎣 ◎

Additional site information: 25 acre site. 🐕 Cars can be parked by caravans and tents. Awnings permitted. No open fires, no noise after 23.00.

Seaview Holiday Park

►►► 80%

tel: 01206 382534 & 07733 333940 **Seaview Avenue, West Mersea CO5 8DA**
web: www.seaviewholiday.co.uk
dir: From A12 (Colchester) onto B1025 (Mersea Island), cross causeway, left towards East Mersea, 1st right, follow signs.

With sweeping views across the Blackwater Estuary, this interesting, well-established park has its own private beach, complete with boat slipway and attractive beach cabins, a shop, café and a stylish clubhouse that offers evening meals and drinks in a quiet, family atmosphere. The touring area is well maintained and has 40 fully serviced pitches.

Open: April to October **Last arrival:** 18.00 (phone site if later arrival is expected) **Last departure:** noon

Pitches: ⌂ ⛟; 40 hardstanding pitches

Facilities: 🏠 ♿ 💲 WiFi

Services: 🔌 🎫 🍽 🕪 🍴 🚮 ⚒

Within 3 miles: ↕ 🎣 ⟳ 🎿

Additional site information: 30 acre site. 🐕 Cars can be parked by caravans. Awnings permitted. No noise after midnight, no boats or jet skis. Private beach.

ST OSYTH
Map 7 TM11

Places to visit

The Beth Chatto Gardens, COLCHESTER, CO7 7DB, 01206 822007 www.bethchatto.co.uk

Colne Estuary National Nature Reserve, BRIGHTLINGSEA, 0300 060 3900 www.essexwt.org.uk/reserves/colne-point

Great for kids: Colchester Zoo, COLCHESTER, CO3 0SL, 01206 331292 www.colchesterzoo.org

The Orchards Holiday Park
▶▶▶▶ 83% HOLIDAY CENTRE

tel: 01255 820651 **CO16 8LJ**
email: theorchards@haven.com **web:** www.haven.com/theorchards
dir: From Clacton-on-Sea take B1027 towards Colchester. Left after petrol station, straight on at crossroads in St Osyth. Follow signs to Point Clear. Park in 3 miles.

The Orchards offers good touring facilities with a centrally heated toilet block which includes a laundry, play area and two very spacious family rooms. The touring pitches are generously sized. There's also direct access to all the leisure, entertainment and dining outlets available on this large popular holiday park on the Essex coast.

Open: end March to end October (restricted service: end March to May and September to October – some facilities may be reduced) **Last arrival:** anytime **Last departure:** 10.00

Pitches: ⌂ ⛟ ⛺

Leisure: ≋ ≋ ⌂ ↕ ♪ 🎣 ⚽

Facilities: 🏠 ☉ 🎣 ♿ 💲 🍴 🚻 WiFi

Services: 🔌 🎫 🍽 🍴 🚮 🔒

Within 3 miles: ⟳ ◎ 🎿

Additional site information: 140 acre site. 🐕 Maximum of 2 dogs per booking, certain dog breeds banned. No commercial vehicles, no bookings by persons under 21 years unless a family booking.

GLOUCESTERSHIRE

BERKELEY
Map 4 ST69

Places to visit

WWT Slimbridge Wetland Centre, SLIMBRIDGE, GL2 7BT, 01453 891900 www.wwt.org.uk/slimbridge

Dr Jenner's House, Museum and Garden, BERKELEY, GL13 9BN, 01453 810631 www.jennermuseum.com

Great for kids: Berkeley Castle & Butterfly House, BERKELEY, GL13 9BQ, 01453 810303, www.berkeley-castle.com

Hogsdown Farm Caravan & Camping Park
▶▶▶ 81%

tel: 01453 810224 **Hogsdown Farm, Lower Wick GL11 6DD**
web: www.hogsdownfarm.co.uk
dir: M5 junction 14 (Falfield), A38 towards Gloucester. Through Stone and Woodford. After Newport turn right signed Lower Wick.

A pleasant site, with good toilet facilities, located between Bristol and Gloucester. It is well positioned for visiting Berkeley Castle and the Cotswolds, and makes an excellent overnight stop when travelling to or from the West Country.

Open: All year **Last arrival:** 21.00 **Last departure:** 16.00

Pitches: ⌂ from £14; ⛟ from £14; ⛺ from £11.50; 12 hardstanding pitches

Leisure: ⌂

Facilities: 🏠 ☉ ❄

Services: 🔌 🎫 🛄 🔒

Within 3 miles: ↕ 🎣 ⟳ 💲

Additional site information: 5 acre site. 🐕 Cars can be parked by caravans and tents. Awnings permitted. No skateboards or bikes.

CHELTENHAM — Map 10 SO92

Places to visit

Holst Birthplace Museum, CHELTENHAM, GL52 2AY, 01242 524846
www.holstmuseum.org.uk

Sudeley Castle, Gardens & Exhibitions, WINCHCOMBE, GL54 5JD, 01242 604244
www.sudeleycastle.co.uk

Briarfields Motel & Touring Park
►►►► 90%

tel: 01242 235324 **Gloucester Road GL51 0SX**
email: reception@briarfields.net **web:** www.briarfields.net
dir: *M5 junction 11, A40 towards Cheltenham. At roundabout left onto B4063, site 200 metres on left.*

This is a well-designed, level, adults-only park, with a motel, where the facilities are modern and very clean. It is well-positioned between Cheltenham and Gloucester, with easy access to the Cotswolds. And, being close to the M5, it makes a perfect overnight stopping point.

Open: All year **Last arrival:** 22.00 **Last departure:** 11.00
Pitches: 🚐 from £18; 🚍 from £18; ▲ from £16; 72 hardstanding pitches
Facilities: 🛁 ⊙ 🄵 ✳ ঙ 🖺 🍴 WiFi
Services: 🔌 🖸 ↓
Within 3 miles: 🛴 🖉 ∪ 🎣 🗓

Additional site information: 5 acre site. Adults only. Cars can be parked by caravans and tents. Awnings permitted. No noise 22.00–08.00. Car hire can be arranged.

CIRENCESTER — Map 5 SP00

Places to visit

New Brewery Arts, CIRENCESTER, GL7 1JH, 01285 657181
www.newbreweryarts.org.uk

Corinium Museum, CIRENCESTER, GL7 2BX, 01285 655611
www.coriniummuseum.org

Mayfield Park
►►►► 90%

tel: 01285 831301 & 07483 327535 **Cheltenham Road GL7 7BH**
email: enquiries@mayfieldpark.co.uk **web:** www.mayfieldpark.co.uk
dir: *In Cirencester at roundabout junction of A429 and A417, take A417 signed Cheltenham and A435. Right onto A435 signed Cheltenham, follow brown camping signs, pass golf course, site on left.*

A much improved and gently sloping park on the edge of the Cotswolds that offers level pitches and a warm welcome. Popular with couples and families, it has a reception area, a small shop selling essentials and offers well-appointed fully serviced hardstanding pitches and caravans for hire. This lovely park makes an ideal base for exploring the Cotswolds and its many attractions, and for walking the nearby Monarch's Way and the Cotswold Way long-distance paths.

Open: All year

Pitches: 🚐 from £12; 🚍 from £12; ▲ from £12; 22 hardstanding pitches; 21 seasonal pitches
Leisure: Ⓐ
Facilities: 🛁 ⊙ 🄵 ✳ ঙ 🖺 🍴 WiFi
Services: 🔌 🖸 🛒 ↓ 🔒 ⌀ Ⓣ
Within 3 miles: 🛴

Additional site information: 13 acre site. Cars can be parked by caravans and tents. Awnings permitted. No bikes, scooters or skateboards, no noise after 23.00, minimum 3 nights stay for bank holidays.

GLOUCESTER — Map 10 SO81

Places to visit

Museum of Gloucester, GLOUCESTER, GL1 1HP, 01452 396131
www.thecityofgloucester.co.uk/things-to-do/museum-of-gloucester-p137013

RSPB Highnam Woods, GLOUCESTER, GL2 8AA, 01594 562852
www.rspb.org.uk/reserves-and-events/reserves-a-z/highnam-woods

Great for kids: National Waterways Museum Gloucester, GLOUCESTER, GL1 2EH, 01452 318200
www.canalrivertrust.org.uk/gloucester-waterways-museum

Red Lion Caravan & Camping Park
►►► 69%

tel: 01452 731810 & 01299 400787 **Wainlode Hill, Norton GL2 9LW**
email: redlion.loveri@btconnect.com **web:** www.redlioncaravancampingpark.co.uk
dir: *Exit A38 at Norton, follow road to river.*

An attractive meadowland park, adjacent to a traditional pub, with the River Severn just across a country lane. There is a private lake for freshwater fishing. This makes an ideal touring base.

Open: All year **Last arrival:** 21.30 **Last departure:** 11.00
Pitches: 🚐 🚍 ▲; 10 hardstanding pitches; 60 seasonal pitches
Leisure: Ⓐ
Facilities: 🛁 ⊙ 🄵 ✳ 🖺 🍴
Services: 🔌 🖸 🍴 🍽 ⚙ ⌀ Ⓣ
Within 3 miles: 🛴 🖉

Additional site information: 24 acre site. Cars can be parked by caravans and tents. Awnings permitted. No noise after 22.00, no open fires.

NEWENT

Places to visit

Odda's Chapel, DEERHURST, 0370 333 1181
www.english-heritage.org.uk/daysout/properties/oddas-chapel

Westbury Court Garden, WESTBURY-ON-SEVERN, GL14 1PD, 01452 760461
www.nationaltrust.org.uk/westbury-court-garden

Great for kids: International Centre for Birds of Prey, NEWENT, GL18 1JJ, 01531 820286, www.icbp.org

NEWENT — Map 10 SO72

Pelerine Caravan and Camping
▶▶▶ 86%

tel: 01531 822761 & 07909 914262 **Ford House Road GL18 1LQ**
email: pelerine@hotmail.com **web:** www.newent.biz
dir: *1 mile from Newent.*

A pleasant, French-themed site divided into separate areas (Rue de Pelerine and Avenue des Families), plus one for adults only; there are some hardstandings and electric hook-ups in each area. Facilities are very good, especially for families. It is close to several vineyards, and well positioned in the north of the Forest of Dean with Tewkesbury, Cheltenham and Ross-on-Wye within easy reach.

Open: March to November **Last arrival:** 22.00 **Last departure:** 16.00

Pitches: 🚐 from £22; 🚎 from £22; ⛺ from £15; 2 hardstanding pitches; 20 seasonal pitches

Facilities: 🏪 ⊙ 📡 ⚒ ☀ ⚿ ♨ WiFi

Services: 🔌 🔲 🔋 Within 3 miles: ⚓ 🏊 ∪ 🍴 💲

Additional site information: 5 acre site. 🐕 Dogs must be on leads at all times. Cars can be parked by caravans and tents. Awnings permitted. Woodburners, chimneas, burning pits available.

SLIMBRIDGE — Map 4 SO70

Places to visit

WWT Slimbridge Wetland Centre, SLIMBRIDGE, GL2 7BT, 01453 891900 www.wwt.org.uk/slimbridge

Great for kids: Berkeley Castle & Butterfly House, BERKELEY, GL13 9BQ, 01453 810303, www.berkeley-castle.com

Tudor Caravan & Camping
▶▶▶▶ 88%

tel: 01453 890483 **Shepherds Patch GL2 7BP**
email: aa@tudorcaravanpark.co.uk **web:** www.tudorcaravanpark.com
dir: *M5 junctions 13 and 14, follow WWT Slimbridge Wetland Centre signs. Site at rear of Tudor Arms pub.*

This park benefits from one of the best locations in the county, situated right alongside the Sharpness to Gloucester canal and just a short walk from the famous Wildfowl & Wetlands Trust at Slimbridge. The site has two areas, one for adults only, and a more open area with a facility block. There are both grass and gravel pitches complete with electric hook-ups. Being beside the canal, there are excellent walks plus the National Cycle Network route 41 can be accessed from the site. There is a pub and restaurant adjacent to the site.

Open: All year **Last arrival:** 20.00 **Last departure:** 11.00

Pitches: 🚐 from £15; 🚎 from £15; ⛺ from £8; 48 hardstanding pitches; 4 seasonal pitches

Leisure: ✏

Facilities: 🏪 ⊙ 📡 ⚒ ☀ ⚿ ♨ 🛒 🎋 WiFi

Services: 🔌 🔲 🔋 🍴 🛒 🔋 ⚒ 🛢 🚿 T

Within 3 miles: ∪ 🏊

Additional site information: 8 acre site. 🐕 Cars can be parked by caravans and tents. Awnings permitted. Debit cards accepted (no credit cards).

STONEHOUSE — Map 4 SO80

Places to visit

Painswick Rococo Garden, PAINSWICK, GL6 6TH, 01452 813204 www.rococogarden.org.uk

WWT Slimbridge Wetland Centre, SLIMBRIDGE, GL2 7BT, 01453 891900 www.wwt.org.uk/slimbridge

Apple Tree Park Caravan and Camping Site
▶▶▶▶ 89%

tel: 01452 742362 & 07708 221457 **A38, Claypits GL10 3AL**
email: appletreepark@hotmail.co.uk **web:** www.appletreepark.co.uk
dir: *M5 junction 13, A38. Take 1st exit at roundabout. Site in 0.7 mile on left (400 metres beyond filling station).*

This is a family-owned park conveniently located on the A38, not far from the M5. A peaceful site with glorious views of the Cotswolds, it offers modern and spotlessly clean toilet facilities with underfloor heating. The park is well located for visiting Wildfowl & Wetlands Trust at Slimbridge and makes an excellent stopover for M5 travellers. There is a bus stop directly outside the park which is handy for those with motorhomes who wish to visit nearby Gloucester and Cheltenham.

Open: All year **Last arrival:** 21.00 **Last departure:** noon

Pitches: 🚐 🚎 ⛺; 14 hardstanding pitches; 10 seasonal pitches

Leisure: ⚽

Facilities: 🏪 ⊙ 📡 ⚒ ☀ ⚿ 💲 WiFi

Services: 🔌 🚿 🛢 🚿 T

Within 3 miles: ✏ 🏊 🏊

Additional site information: 6.5 acre site. 🐕 Cars can be parked by caravans and tents. Awnings permitted. Minimum noise after 22.30.

GREATER MANCHESTER

LITTLEBOROUGH
Map 16 SD91

Places to visit
Standedge Tunnel and Visitor Centre, MARSDEN, HD7 6NQ, 01484 844298
http://canalrivertrust.org.uk/enjoy-the-waterways/museums-and-attractions/
standedge-tunnel-and-visitor-centre-west-yorkshire

Hollingworth Lake Caravan Park
▶▶▶ 76%

tel: 01706 378661 **Round House Farm, Rakewood Road OL15 0AT**
email: info@hollingworthlakecaravanpark.com
dir: *From Littleborough or Milnrow (M62 junction 21), follow Hollingworth Lake Country Park signs to Fishermans Inn and The Wine Press. Take 'No Through Road' to Rakewood, then 2nd right.*

A popular park adjacent to Hollingworth Lake, at the foot of the Pennines, within easy reach of many local attractions. Backpackers walking the Pennine Way are welcome at this family-run park, and there are also large rally fields.

Open: All year **Last arrival:** 20.00 **Last departure:** noon

Pitches: 🚐 from £15; 🚚 from £15; ▲ from £10; 25 hardstanding pitches

Leisure: ✪

Facilities: 🛁 ☉ ✳ ♿ 🏧 🛒

Services: 🔌 🗑 🛒 ⬇ 🔒 🧺 ⊺

Within 3 miles: 🎣 ✎ ♻ ⛵ ≋

Additional site information: 5 acre site. 🐾 Maximum of 1 dog per pitch. 🚗 Cars can be parked by caravans and tents. Awnings permitted. Family groups only. Pony trekking.

HAMPSHIRE

BRANSGORE

Places to visit
Sammy Miller Museum, NEW MILTON, BH25 5SZ, 01425 620777
www.sammymiller.co.uk

Red House Museum & Gardens, CHRISTCHURCH, BH23 1BU, 01202 482860
www.hampshireculturaltrust.org.uk

Great for kids: Moors Valley Country Park and Forest, RINGWOOD, BH24 2ET, 01425 470721, www.moors-valley.co.uk

BRANSGORE
Map 5 SZ19

Harrow Wood Farm Caravan Park
▶▶▶ 86%

tel: 01425 672487 **Harrow Wood Farm, Poplar Lane BH23 8JE**
email: harrowwood@caravan-sites.co.uk **web:** www.caravan-sites.co.uk
dir: *From Ringwood take B3347 towards Christchurch. At Sopley, left for Bransgore, to T-junction. Turn right. Straight on at crossroads. Left in 400 yards (just after garage) into Poplar Lane.*

A well laid-out, well-drained and spacious site in a pleasant rural position adjoining woodland and fields. Facilities are well appointed and very clean. Free on-site coarse fishing is available at this peaceful park. Well located for visiting Christchurch, the New Forest National Park and the south coast.

Open: March to 6 January **Last arrival:** 22.00 **Last departure:** noon

Pitches: 🚐 from £19; 🚚 from £19; ▲ from £19; 60 hardstanding pitches

Leisure: ✎

Facilities: 🛁 ☉ ☂ ✳ ♿ WiFi

Services: 🔌 🗑 🛒 ⬇ 🔒

Within 3 miles: 🅂

Additional site information: 6 acre site. 🚫 Cars can be parked by caravans and tents. Awnings permitted. No open fires.

FORDINGBRIDGE

Places to visit
Rockbourne Roman Villa, ROCKBOURNE, SP6 3PG, 01725 518541
www.hampshireculturaltrust.org.uk/rockbourne-roman-villa

Breamore House & Countryside Museum, BREAMORE, SP6 2DF, 01725 512858
www.breamorehouse.com

Great for kids: Moors Valley Country Park and Forest, RINGWOOD, BH24 2ET, 01425 470721, www.moors-valley.co.uk

FORDINGBRIDGE
Map 5 SU11

Premier Park

Sandy Balls Holiday Village

▶▶▶▶▶ 90%

tel: 01442 508850 **Sandy Balls Estate Ltd, Godshill SP6 2JZ**
email: post@sandyballs.co.uk **web:** www.awayresorts.co.uk
dir: *M27 junction 1, B3078, B3079, 8 miles to Godshill. Site 0.25 mile after cattle grid.*

A large, mostly wooded New Forest holiday complex with good provision of touring facilities on terraced, well laid-out fields. Pitches are fully serviced with shingle bases, and groups can be sited beside the river and away from the main site. There are excellent sporting, leisure and entertainment facilities for the whole family including a jacuzzi, sauna, beauty therapy, horse riding and children's activities. There's also a bistro, information centre and ready-erected tents, lodges and camping pods for hire. This a large holiday village with something for all ages – children and teenagers love it here as there is so much to keep them occupied.

Open: All year (restricted service: November to February – number of pitches reduced, activities limited but swimming pool and leisure centre open) **Last arrival:** 22.30 **Last departure:** 11.00

Pitches: 🚐 🚍 ▲ 🏠; 225 hardstanding pitches

Leisure: 🌊 ⚖ 🎣 🎱 🎾 🎵 ♪ 🏇 ⚽ Spa

Facilities: 🏪 ☺ 🚰 ⚒ 🛁 🛒 🚻 WiFi

Services: 🔌 🗑 🍴 🍽 🍺 🔋 🔧 🛒 🌿 T Within 3 miles: ♻ 🏊

Additional site information: 120 acre site. 🐕 Cars can be parked by caravans and tents. Awnings permitted. Groups by prior arrangement only, no gazebos, no noise after 23.00. Freshly baked bread available.

Glamping available: Safari tent; wooden pods. **Changeover days:** Friday (3, 7 and 14 night stays); Monday (4 night stays)

Additional glamping information: Cars can be parked by pods and tent.

HAMBLE-LE-RICE
Map 5 SU40

Riverside Holidays
▶▶▶▶ 83%

tel: 023 8045 3220 **Satchell Lane SO31 4HR**
email: enquiries@riversideholidays.co.uk **web:** www.riversideholidays.co.uk
dir: *M27 junction 8, follow signs to Hamble on B3397. Left into Satchell Lane, site in 1 mile.*

A small peaceful park set alongside the River Hamble and next to a marina that offers a unique place to stay in this attractive area. There is a well-appointed central facility block with separate and spacious fully serviced rooms for ladies and gents. There is a convenient pub and restaurant right beside the site plus good walks along the river.

Open: March to October **Last arrival:** 22.00 **Last departure:** 11.00

Pitches: 🚐 🚍 ▲ **Facilities:** 🏪 ☺ 🚰 ⚒ 🛁 WiFi

Services: 🔌 🗑 🔋 🛒 T Within 3 miles: 🏇 ♻ 🏊 📶 🅿

Additional site information: 3 acre site. 🐕 Cars can be parked by caravans and tents. Awnings permitted. Chargeable WiFi.

LINWOOD
Map 5 SU10

Places to visit
The New Forest Centre, LYNDHURST, SO43 7NY, 023 8028 3444
www.newforestcentre.org.uk

Furzey Gardens, MINSTEAD, SO43 7GL, 023 8081 2464
www.furzey-gardens.org

Great for kids: Paultons Park, OWER, SO51 6AL, 023 8081 4442
www.paultonspark.co.uk

Red Shoot Camping Park
▶▶▶ 89%

tel: 01425 473789 **BH24 3QT**
email: enquiries@redshoot-campingpark.com **web:** www.redshoot-campingpark.com
dir: *A31 onto A338 towards Fordingbridge and Salisbury. Right at brown signs for caravan park towards Linwood on unclassified roads, site signed.*

Located behind the Red Shoot Inn in one of the most attractive parts of the New Forest, this park is in an ideal spot for nature lovers and walkers. It is personally supervised by friendly owners, and offers many amenities including a children's play area. There are modern and spotless facilities plus a smart reception and shop selling fresh bread, croissants and local farm produce.

Open: March to October **Last arrival:** 19.00 **Last departure:** 13.00

Pitches: 🚐 🚍 ▲

Leisure: 🛝

Facilities: 🏪 ☺ 🚰 ⚒ 🛁 🛒

Services: 🔌 🗑 🍴 🍽 🔋 🔧 🛒 🌿 T

Within 3 miles: 🏇 ♻ 🏊

Additional site information: 3.5 acre site. 🐕 Cars can be parked by caravans and tents. Awnings permitted. Quiet after 22.30. Freshly baked bread and croissants. Car hire can be arranged.

PITCHES: 🚐 Caravans 🚍 Motorhomes ▲ Tents 🏠 Glamping accommodation **SERVICES:** 🔌 Electric hook-up 🗑 Launderette 🍺 Licensed bar
🛒 Calor Gas 🌿 Campingaz T Toilet fluid 🍽 Café/Restaurant 🍴 Fast Food/Takeaway 🔋 Battery charging 🔧 Motorhome service point
* 2019 prices 🚫 No credit or debit cards 🐕 Dogs permitted ⊗ No dogs

RINGWOOD

See St Leonards (Dorset)

ROMSEY Map 5 SU32

Places to visit

Sir Harold Hillier Gardens, AMPFIELD, SO51 0QA, 01794 369318
www.hilliergardens.org.uk

Mottisfont, MOTTISFONT, SO51 0LP, 01794 340757
www.nationaltrust.org.uk/mottisfont

Great for kids: Longdown Activity Farm, ASHURST, SO40 7EH, 023 8029 2837
www.longdownfarm.co.uk

Green Pastures Farm Camping & Touring Park

►►► 85%

tel: 023 8081 4444 **Ower SO51 6AJ**
email: enquiries@greenpasturesfarm.com **web:** www.greenpasturesfarm.com
dir: *M27 junction 2. Follow Salisbury signs, 0.5 mile, follow brown tourist signs for Green Pastures. Also signed from A36 and A3090 at Ower.*

This pleasant site offers a variety of easily accessed pitches, including those with electric hook-up. There is a code access security barrier to the site. Green Pastures is well located for visiting Paultons Park, Southampton and the New Forest National Park, and being close to the M27 it is convenient for overnight stops. There are kennels where dogs can be left while you visit the theme park or go shopping.

Open: 13 March to October **Last arrival:** 20.00 **Last departure:** 11.00

Pitches: 🚙 from £21; 🚐 from £21; ⛺ from £14; 6 hardstanding pitches

Facilities: 🛁 ✱ ♿ [$] [WiFi]

Services: 🔌 🧺 🍽 🚰 🔒 🍃 [T]

Within 3 miles: ⛳ 🎣

Additional site information: 6 acre site. 🐕 Cars can be parked by caravans and tents. Awnings permitted. No water games, no fire pits, only off-ground BBQs permitted. Coffee van Saturday mornings.

WARSASH Map 5 SU40

Places to visit

Explosion Museum of Naval Firepower, GOSPORT, PO12 4LE, 023 9283 9766
www.historicdockyard.co.uk/site-attractions/off-site-attractions/explosion-museum-of-naval-firepower

Portchester Castle, PORTCHESTER, PO16 9QW
www.english-heritage.org.uk/daysout/properties/portchester-castle

Great for kids: Blue Reef Aquarium, PORTSMOUTH, PO5 3PB, 023 9287 5222
www.bluereefaquarium.co.uk

Dibles Park

►►►► 86%

tel: 01489 575232 **Dibles Rd SO31 9SA**
email: dibles.park@btconnect.com **web:** www.diblespark.co.uk
dir: *M27 junction 9, at roundabout 5th exit (Parkgate A27), 3rd roundabout 1st exit, 4th roundabout 2nd exit. Site 500 yards on left. Or M27 junction 8, at roundabout 1st exit (Parkgate), next roundabout 3rd exit (Brook Lane), 4th roundabout 2nd exit. Site 500 yards on left.*

A small peaceful touring park adjacent to a private residential park. The facilities are excellent and spotlessly clean, and the spacious pitches are hardstanding with electric and can take the largest RVs. A warm welcome awaits visitors to this well-managed park, which is very convenient for the Hamble, the Solent and very well positioned for an overnight stay if heading for the cross-channel ferry port at Portsmouth, which is about 14 miles away. WiFi is available. The park also offers free leaflets of the many excellent walks around the area.

Open: All year **Last arrival:** Anytime **Last departure:** 11.00

Pitches: * 🚙 from £22; 🚐 from £22; ⛺ from £18; 11 hardstanding pitches

Facilities: 🛁 ⊙ 💨 ✱ [WiFi]

Services: 🔌 🧺 🚰 🔒 🍃

Within 3 miles: 🎣 ∪ 🏄 ⛵ 🎬 [$]

Additional site information: 0.75 acre site. 🐕 No dog walking on site. Cars can be parked by caravans and tents. Awnings permitted. No noise after 23.00, no children's ball games, no cycling, no scooters.

LEISURE: 🏊 Indoor swimming pool 🏊 Outdoor swimming pool 🛝 Children's playground 👋 Kids' club 🎾 Tennis court 🎱 Games room 📺 Separate TV room ⛳ golf course ⛳ Pitch n putt ⛵ Boats for hire 🚲 Bikes for hire 🎬 Cinema 🎵 Entertainment 🎣 Fishing ◎ Mini golf 🏄 Watersports 🏋 Gym ⚽ Sports field ∪ Stables
FACILITIES: 🛁 Baths/Shower ⊙ Electric shaver sockets 💨 Hairdryer ✱ Ice Pack Facility 🚼 Baby facilities ♿ Disabled facilities [$] Shop on site or within 200yds 🍖 BBQ area ⛩ Picnic area [WiFi] WiFi

HERTFORDSHIRE

HODDESDON
Map 6 TL30

Places to visit

RSPB Rye Meads, STANSTEAD ABBOTTS, SG12 8JS, 01992 708383
www.rspb.org.uk/reserves-and-events/reserves-a-z/rye-meads

Lee Valley Caravan Park Dobbs Weir

►►►► 83%

tel: 03000 030 619 **Charlton Meadows, Essex Road EN11 0AS**
email: dobbsweircampsite@vibrantpartnerships.co.uk
web: www.visitleevalley.org.uk/en/content/cms/where-to-stay-and-short-breaks
dir: *From A10 follow Hoddesdon signs, at 2nd roundabout left signed Dobbs Weir. At next roundabout take 3rd exit. 1 mile to site on right.*

This site provides much needed camping facilities close to London. Situated on level ground beside the River Lee, the park has a modernised toilet block with good facilities (and additional toilets were added in 2018), a large timber chalet housing the reception and shop, an extremely innovative motorhome service point. 12 wooden wigwams, three family safari tents and two luxury lodges are available for hire. On-site fishing is available and there's free WiFi.

Open: March to January **Last arrival:** 20.00 **Last departure:** 11.00 (later departures by prior arrangement)

Pitches: 🚐 from £15; 🚍 from £15; ▲ from £15; 🛖 see prices below; 21 hardstanding pitches

Leisure: ⌂ 🎣 🎾

Facilities: 🖥 ⊙ ✳ ♿ 🛒 🏛 🪑 WiFi

Services: 🔌 🔲 ↻ 🔋 🪛 ℹ

Within 3 miles: ⛵ 🎿

Additional site information: 11 acre site. 🐕 Cars can be parked by caravans and tents. Awnings permitted. No commercial vehicles. Under 18s must be accompanied by an adult. Fire pit hire. Fresh produce in shop.

Glamping available: Wooden wigwams from £75; safari tents from £105.

Additional glamping information: Safari tents have cooking galleys. Cars can be parked by tents and wigwams.

PITCHES: 🚐 Caravans 🚍 Motorhomes ▲ Tents 🛖 Glamping accommodation **SERVICES:** 🔌 Electric hook-up 🔲 Launderette 🍺 Licensed bar
🔥 Calor Gas ⊘ Campingaz 🔲 Toilet fluid 🍽 Café/Restaurant 🍟 Fast Food/Takeaway 🔋 Battery charging ↻ Motorhome service point
* 2019 prices 🚫 No credit or debit cards 🐕 Dogs permitted 🚫 No dogs

Isle of Wight

There is a timeless quality to the Isle of Wight. For many it embodies the spirit and atmosphere of English seaside holidays over the years, and being an island, it has a unique and highly distinctive identity. Small and intimate – it's just 23 miles by 13 miles – it's a great place to get away-from-it-all, and with its mild climate, long hours of sunshine and colourful architecture, it has something of a continental flavour.

The Isle of Wight is probably most famous for the world's premier sailing regatta. Cowes Week, which takes place at the height of summer, is a key annual fixture in the country's sporting calendar, with the regatta drawing more than 1,000 boats and around 100,000 spectators. It is a hugely colourful event attracting Olympic veterans, weekend sailors and top names from the worlds of sport and the media. Various spectator boats offer good views of the action, but for something less hectic and more sedate, take to the island's 65-mile Coast Path, which offers a continual, unfolding backdrop of magnificent coastal scenery and natural beauty. The sea is seen at numerous points along the route and during Cowes Week, you get constant views of the energetic sailing activity. The regatta is held in the first week of August.

The Isle of Wight Coast Path is a good way to explore the island's varied coastline at any time of the year. Even in the depths of winter, the weather conditions are often favourable for walking. Much of the trail in the southern half of the island represents a relatively undemanding walk over majestic chalk downs. Beyond Freshwater Bay the coast is largely uninhabited with a palpable air of isolation. It is on this stretch that walkers can appreciate how the elements have shaped and weathered the island over many centuries. Away from the coast an intricate network of paths offers the chance to discover a rich assortment of charming villages, hidden valleys and country houses. In all, the Isle of Wight has more than 500 miles of public rights of way and over half the island is acknowledged as an Area of Outstanding Natural Beauty. There is an annual walking festival in May and a weekend walking festival in October. Cycling is also extremely popular here, with the Round the Island Cycle Route attracting many enthusiasts. The route runs for 49 miles and there are starting points at Yarmouth, Cowes and Ryde.

Away from walking and cycling, the Isle of Wight offers numerous attractions and activities. You could plan a week's itinerary on the island and not set foot on the beach. The island's history is a fascinating and crucial aspect of its story. It was long considered as a convenient stepping stone for the French in their plan to invade the mainland, and various fortifications – including Fort Victoria and Yarmouth Castle – reflect its key strategic role in the defence of our coastline. Carisbrooke Castle at Newport – the island's capital – is where Charles I was held before his execution in 1649.

The Isle of Wight has been a fashionable destination for the rich and famous over the years, and members of royalty made their home here. Queen Victoria and Prince Albert boosted tourism hugely when they chose the island as the setting for their summer home, Osborne House, which is now open to the public. Elsewhere, there are echoes of the Isle of Wight's fascinating literary links. Charles Dickens is said to have written six chapters of *David Copperfield* in the village of Bonchurch, near Ventnor, and the Victorian Poet Laureate Alfred Lord Tennyson lived at Faringford House, near Freshwater Bay. He claimed that the air on the coast here was worth 'sixpence a pint.'

◁ Bembridge

ISLE OF WIGHT

BRIGHSTONE
Map 5 SZ48

Places to visit

Mottistone Gardens, MOTTISTONE, PO30 4ED, 01983 741302
www.nationaltrust.org.uk/mottistone-gardens-and-estate

Grange Farm
▶▶▶▶ 81%

tel: 01983 740296 **Grange Chine PO30 4DA**
email: grangefarmholidays@gmail.com **web:** www.grangefarmholidays.com
dir: *From Freshwater Bay take A3055 towards Ventnor, 5 miles (pass Isle of Wight Pearl). Site in approximately 0.5 mile on right.*

This family-run site is set in a stunning location on the southwest coast of the island in Brighstone Bay. The facilities are very good. For children there is an imaginative play area and a wide range of animals to see including llamas and water buffalo. This site is right on the coastal path and ideally located for those who like walking and cycling. There are camping pods for hire plus static homes on a lower level by the beach.

Open: March to October **Last arrival:** noon **Last departure:** noon

Pitches: 🚐 🚌 ⛺ 🏠; 8 hardstanding pitches

Facilities: ☺ ⚲ ✳ Ⓢ 🍽 🛋 WiFi

Services: 🔌 🔘 🛒 🛁 🔒 🧼 Ⓣ

Within 3 miles: 🚵 🛶

Additional site information: 8 acre site. 🐾 Cars can be parked by caravans and tents. Awnings permitted. No fires. Bakery.

Glamping available: Wooden pods.

FRESHWATER
Map 5 SZ38

Places to visit

Yarmouth Castle, YARMOUTH, PO41 0PB, 01983 760678
www.english-heritage.org.uk/daysout/properties/yarmouth-castle

Dimbola Museum & Galleries, FRESHWATER, PO40 9QE, 01983 756814
www.dimbola.co.uk

Great for kids: The Needles Park, ALUM BAY, PO39 0JD, 01983 752401
www.theneedles.co.uk

Heathfield Farm Camping
▶▶▶▶ 88%

tel: 01983 407822 **Heathfield Road PO40 9SH**
email: web@heathfieldcamping.co.uk **web:** www.heathfieldcamping.co.uk
dir: *2 miles west from Yarmouth ferry port on A3054, left to Heathfield Road, entrance 200 yards on right.*

A well located park in the far west of the island, perfect for visiting the Needles, Freshwater, Totland and Tennyson Down. There are large grass pitches (many over 200 square metres) giving plenty of space, and the facilities are modern, well appointed and very clean. There is also a good backpackers' area for camping with picnic tables, and a children's play area. The local town of Freshwater has an excellent supermarket and good range of shops. The closest ferry point is at Yarmouth but the site is easily reached from all ferry ports.

Open: May to September **Last arrival:** 20.00 **Last departure:** 11.00

Pitches: 🚐 from £16; 🚌 from £16; ⛺ from £14

Leisure: 🎠 ⚽

Facilities: 🛁 ☺ ⚲ ✳ ♿ 🍽 🛋 WiFi

Services: 🔌 🔘 🛁 🧼

Within 3 miles: 🎣 🚵 U ◎ 🛶 🎣 Ⓢ

Additional site information: 10 acre site. 🐾 Cars can be parked by caravans and tents. Awnings permitted. Car hire can be arranged.

NEWBRIDGE
Map 5 SZ48

Places to visit

Newtown Old Town Hall, NEWTOWN, PO30 4PA, 01983 531785
www.nationaltrust.org.uk/newtown-national-nature-reserve-and-old-town-hall

Great for kids: Yarmouth Castle, YARMOUTH, PO41 0PB, 01983 760678
www.english-heritage.org.uk/daysout/properties/yarmouth-castle

Platinum Park

The Orchards Holiday Caravan Park
▶▶▶▶▶

tel: 01983 531331 & 531350 **Main Road PO41 0TS**
email: info@orchards-holiday-park.co.uk **web:** www.orchards-holiday-park.co.uk
dir: A3054 from Yarmouth, right in 3 miles at Horse & Groom Inn. Follow signs to
Newbridge. Entrance opposite post office. Or from Newport, 6 miles, via B3401.

A really excellent, well-managed park set in a peaceful village location amid
downs and meadowland, with glorious downland views. The pitches are terraced
and offer a good provision of hardstandings, including those that are water
serviced. There is a high quality facility centre offering excellent, spacious
showers and family rooms, plus there is access for less able visitors to all site
facilities and disabled toilets. The park has indoor and outdoor swimming pools,
a takeaway and licensed shop. Static homes are available for hire and 'ferry
plus stay' packages are on offer. The site is just 10 minutes from the Wightlink
ferry terminal in Yarmouth and there are buses that stop at the entrance
every hour.

Open: 31 March to 30 October (restricted service: March to late May and mid/late
September to October — outdoor pool closed) **Last arrival:** 23.00 **Last departure:** 11.00
Pitches: 🚐 from £18; 🚍 from £18; ▲ from £18; 52 hardstanding pitches
Leisure: 🏊 🏊 ⋔ 🎣 ⚽
Facilities: 🛁 ⊙ 🎣 ✳ ♿ 🏪 🚻 ♨ WiFi
Services: 🔌 🔄 🍽 🚮 🏧 ⚓ 🛒 🅃
Within 3 miles: ♿

Additional site information: 15 acre site. ⌇ Cars can be parked by caravans and
tents. Awnings permitted. No cycling, no noise after midnight. Table tennis room,
Fin2Fit mermaid experience, poolside coffee shop, pool room, arcade, play areas.
Car hire can be arranged.

NEWPORT
Map 5 SZ48

Places to visit

Carisbrooke Castle, CARISBROOKE, PO30 1XY, 01983 522107
www.english-heritage.org.uk/daysout/properties/carisbrooke-castle

Premier Park

Wight Glamping Holidays
▶▶▶▶▶ 85% GLAMPING ONLY

tel: 01983 532507 **Everland, Long Lane PO30 2NW**
email: info@wightglampingholidays.co.uk **web:** www.wightglampingholidays.co.uk
dir: From Cowes to Newport on A3020. In Newport follow Sandown A3054 signs. Take
middle lane at lights (signed Sandown and A3054). At roundabout 1st exit into
Fairlee Road (A3054) signed Ryde. Right into Staples Road. Left into Long Lane
signed Sandown and Brading.

Situated in the heart of the island with open countryside views over a valley, this
site (Everlands Camping) comprises four Lotus Belle tents. Standing on their
individual decking areas, each of the carpeted tents is very well equipped with a
king-size bed, plus a sofa which can be converted to either another king-size
bed or two singles. The bed linen and covers are of the highest quality and each
tent is also equipped with a table and four chairs, plus good storage space for
clothes. The heating and lighting is electric. Adjoining at the rear is a separate
utility tent with a fridge and cooking unit. Externally, each tent has a picnic
table and easy chairs as well as the use of a BBQ. There is a separate high
quality toilet and shower block with two shower rooms plus two toilet and wash
basin rooms — a dishwashing area is behind this small block. Cars are parked
adjacent to the glamping area but do not spoil the views or the setting.

Open: May to September **Last arrival:** 22.00 **Last departure:** 11.00
Facilities: 🛁 ⊙ 🚻 🏧
Within 3 miles: ♿ 🎣 ∪ ⛵ 🅷 🏧 🛒
Accommodation available: Lotus Belle tents.
Additional site information: 1 acre site. ⊗ 🚫 Minimum stay 3 nights.

PITCHES: 🚐 Caravans 🚍 Motorhomes ▲ Tents ⋔ Glamping accommodation **SERVICES:** 🔌 Electric hook-up 🅾 Launderette 🍸 Licensed bar
🔥 Calor Gas 🌿 Campingaz 🅃 Toilet fluid 🍽 Café/Restaurant 🍔 Fast Food/Takeaway 🔋 Battery charging ⚓ Motorhome service point
* 2019 prices 🚫 No credit or debit cards ⌇ Dogs permitted ⊗ No dogs

RYDE
Map 5 SZ59

Places to visit
Nunwell House & Gardens, BRADING, PO36 0JQ, 01983 407240
www.nunwellhouse.co.uk

Bembridge Windmill, BEMBRIDGE, PO35 5SQ, 01983 873945
www.nationaltrust.org.uk/bembridge-windmill

Great for kids: Robin Hill Country Park, ARRETON, PO30 2NU, 01983 527352
www.robin-hill.com

Platinum Park

Whitefield Forest Touring Park
▶▶▶▶▶

tel: 01983 617069 **Brading Road PO33 1QL**
email: pat&louise@whitefieldforest.co.uk **web:** www.whitefieldforest.co.uk
dir: *From Ryde follow A3055 towards Brading, after Tesco roundabout site in 0.5 mile on left.*

This park is beautifully laid out in the Whitefield Forest, and offers a wide variety of pitches, including 26 fully serviced pitches, as well as family rooms; it is conveniently located on a bus route. It offers excellent modern facilities which are kept spotlessly clean. The park takes great care to retain the natural beauty of the forest, and is a haven for wildlife; red squirrels can be spotted throughout the park, including along the nature walk. Activities such as foraging, bushcraft and cycle rides for children and adults are available at certain times of the year.

Open: 5 April to 7 October **Last arrival:** 21.00 **Last departure:** 11.00
Pitches: 🚐 from £18.50; 🚙 from £18.50; ▲ from £18.50; 40 hardstanding pitches
Leisure: /⚠\
Facilities: 🛁 ⊙ 🪒 ✳ ઠ 🅂 WiFi
Services: 🔌 🗑 🧺 ⬆ ■ ⌀ T
Within 3 miles: ⅃ 🏌 ∪ ≋ ≑ 🎌

Additional site information: 23 acre site. 🚗 Cars can be parked by caravans and tents. Awnings permitted.

Roebeck Country Park
▶▶▶ 83%

tel: 01983 562505 & 07768 491187 **Gatehouse Road, Upton PO33 4BP**
email: info@roebeckcountrypark.co.uk **web:** www.roebeckcountrypark.co.uk
dir: *From Fishbourne ferry turn right, at T-junction left at lights onto A3054 towards Ryde. At lights into right lane, straight on into Pellhurst Road (follow Sandown (A3055) signs). At T-junction right into Upton Road. At mini roundabout straight on into Gatehouse Road (site signed).*

Roebeck Country Park is located approximately two miles south of Ryde on the northeast side of the island and just five minutes from the beach. It offers a peaceful camping environment for families and couples and the facilities are very clean. Pitches with hook-ups are available and there is a small kitchen with fridge, kettle and microwave. There is another road that large units can use by prior arrangement with the warden. There's a well-stocked fishing lake and luxury lodges.

Open: All year **Last arrival:** by prior arrangement **Last departure:** by prior arrangement
Pitches: 🚐 🚙 ▲; 4 hardstanding pitches; 22 seasonal pitches
Leisure: ⚽
Facilities: 🪒 ✳ ઠ 🍴 🎌 WiFi
Services: 🔌 🗑 🧺 ■ ⌀ T
Within 3 miles: ⅃ 🏌 ∪ ◎ ≋ ≑ 🎌 🅂

Additional site information: 13.8 acre site. 🚗 Cars can be parked by caravans and tents. Awnings permitted.

SANDOWN

Places to visit
Nunwell House & Gardens, BRADING, PO36 0JQ, 01983 407240
www.nunwellhouse.co.uk

Bembridge Windmill, BEMBRIDGE, PO35 5SQ, 01983 873945
www.nationaltrust.org.uk/bembridge-windmill

Great for kids: Dinosaur Isle, SANDOWN, PO36 8QA, 01983 404344
www.dinosaurisle.com

LEISURE: 🏊 Indoor swimming pool 🏊 Outdoor swimming pool /⚠\ Children's playground 👋 Kids' club 🎾 Tennis court 🎱 Games room 📺 Separate TV room
⅃ golf course 🏌 Pitch n putt 🚣 Boats for hire 🚲 Bikes for hire 🎬 Cinema 🎵 Entertainment 🎣 Fishing ◎ Mini golf 🏄 Watersports 💪 Gym ✪ Sports field ∪ Stables
FACILITIES: 🛁 Baths/Shower ⊙ Electric shaver sockets 🪒 Hairdryer ✳ Ice Pack Facility 🛒 Baby facilities ઠ Disabled facilities 🅂 Shop on site or within 200yds
🍴 BBQ area 🎌 Picnic area WiFi WiFi

SANDOWN
Map 5 SZ58

Old Barn Touring Park
▶▶▶▶ 79%

tel: 01983 866414 **Cheverton Farm, Newport Road PO36 9PJ**
email: mail@oldbarntouring.co.uk **web:** www.oldbarntouring.co.uk
dir: *On A3056 from Newport, site on left after Apse Heath roundabout.*

A terraced site with several secluded camping areas that are divided by hedges. This site is well positioned for visiting the eastern side of the island, and customers can be sure of a warm welcome from the friendly staff. Rallies are very welcome.

Open: Easter to September **Last arrival:** 21.00 **Last departure:** noon

Pitches: 🚐 from £19; 🚍 from £19; ▲ from £19; 9 hardstanding pitches; 6 seasonal pitches

Leisure: 🎣 ▢ **Facilities:** 🏪 ⊙ 🅟 ☀ ♿ WiFi

Services: 🔌 🗑 ⚏ ⚒ 🔋 ⚗ **Within 3 miles:** ⚓ 🏌 ∪ ◎ ⚑ ⚓ 💲

Additional site information: 5 acre site. 🐕 Cars can be parked by caravans and tents. Awnings permitted. Car hire can be arranged.

SHANKLIN
Map 5 SZ58

Places to visit

Shanklin Chine, SHANKLIN, PO37 0PF, 01983 866432
www.shanklinchine.co.uk

Ventnor Botanic Garden, VENTNOR, PO38 1UL, 01983 855397
www.botanic.co.uk

Great for kids: Dinosaur Isle, SANDOWN, PO36 8QA, 01983 404344
www.dinosaurisle.com

Ninham Country Holidays
▶▶▶▶ 88%

tel: 01983 864243 **Ninham PO37 7PL**
email: office@ninham-holidays.co.uk **web:** www.ninham-holidays.co.uk
dir: *Signed from A3056 (Newport to Sandown road). Note: for sat nav use PO36 9PJ.*

Enjoying a lofty rural location with fine country views, this delightful, spacious park occupies two separate, well-maintained areas in a country park setting near the sea and beach. It has an excellent toilet and shower block in The Orchards that has a good layout of pitches; there is also a good outdoor pool, a games room and an excellent children's play area. Willow Brook is a separate camping area with a toilet and well appointed shower block. This is a great place for families and close to Shanklin and Sandown.

Ninham Country Holidays

Open: May to September **Last arrival:** 20.00 **Last departure:** 10.00

Pitches: * 🚐 from £19.50; 🚍 from £19.50; ▲ from £12 **Leisure:** 🏊 🎮 🎣 ▢ ⚽

Facilities: 🏪 ⊙ 🅟 ☀ ♿ WiFi **Services:** 🔌 🗑 ⚏ ⚒ 🔋 ⚗

Within 3 miles: ⚓ ∪ ◎ ⚑ ⚓ 💲

Additional site information: 12 acre site. 🐕 Cars can be parked by caravans and tents. Awnings permitted. Recycling obligatory.

See advert on page 206

TOTLAND BAY
Map 5 SZ38

Places to visit

Dimbola Museum & Galleries, FRESHWATER, PO40 9QE, 01983 756814
www.dimbola.co.uk

Mottistone Gardens, MOTTISTONE, PO30 4ED, 01983 741302
www.nationaltrust.org.uk/mottistone-gardens-and-estate

Great for kids: Yarmouth Castle, YARMOUTH, PO41 0PB, 01983 760678
www.english-heritage.org.uk/daysout/properties/yarmouth-castle

Stoats Farm Caravan & Camping
▶▶▶ 78%

tel: 01983 755258 **PO39 OHE**
email: bookings@stoats-farm.co.uk **web:** www.stoats-farm.co.uk
dir: *0.75 mile south of Totland. (Note: it is advisable for caravans and motorhomes to approach via Moons Hill; do not approach via Weston Lane which is narrow).*

A friendly, personally run site in a quiet country setting close to Alum Bay, Tennyson Down and The Needles. It has good laundry and shower facilities, and the shop, although small, is well stocked. Popular with families, walkers and cyclists, it makes the perfect base for campers wishing to explore this part of the island.

Open: April to October **Pitches:** 🚐 🚍 ▲ **Facilities:** 🏪 ⊙ 🅟 ☀ ♿ 💲 🍴

Services: 🔌 🗑 ⚏ ⚒ ⚗ **Within 3 miles:** ⚓ 🏌 ∪ ◎ ⚑ ⚓

Additional site information: 10 acre site. 🐕 Cars can be parked by caravans and tents. Awnings permitted. No loud noise after 23.00. No camp fires unless appropriate equipment used (check with site manager). Campers' fridge available, service wash laundry.

WOOTTON BRIDGE

Map 5 SZ59

Places to visit

Osborne House, OSBORNE HOUSE, PO32 6JX, 01983 200022
www.english-heritage.org.uk/daysout/properties/osborne

Carisbrooke Castle, CARISBROOKE, PO30 1XY, 01983 522107
www.english-heritage.org.uk/daysout/properties/carisbrooke-castle

Great for kids: Robin Hill Country Park, ARRETON, PO30 2NU, 01983 527352
www.robin-hill.com

Platinum Park

Woodside Bay Lodge Retreat

►►►►► HOLIDAY HOME PARK

tel: 01983 885220 **Lower Woodside Road PO33 4JT**
email: reception@woodside-bay.co.uk **web:** www.woodside-bay.co.uk
dir: *From A3054 between Ryde and Newport, turn right into New Road, becomes Lower Woodside Road.*

This luxury park is located on the northeast shore of the Isle of Wight near Wootton Bridge – the setting is absolutely fabulous and the sloping terrain offers lovely views over the Solent. The restaurant and its position on the park is ideal and if the weather's good you can enjoy your meal or drinks on a covered veranda along with the views. There is a quality spa and gym plus an alfresco eating area, The Braai. Accommodation offered is a variety of luxury fully-equipped lodges sleeping 4, 6 or 8 plus and two spectacular tree houses that sleep two.

Open: All year

Holiday Homes: Two-ring burner Dishwasher Washing Machine Tumble dryer Microwave Freezer TV Sky/Freeview DVD player WiFi Linen included Towels included Electricity included Gas included Woodburner

Leisure: 🏋 **Spa**

Additional site information: 🐕

Kite Hill Farm Caravan & Camping Park

►►► 87%

tel: 01983 883261 **Firestone Copse Road PO33 4LE**
email: welcome@kitehillfarm.co.uk **web:** www.kitehillfarm.co.uk
dir: *Signed from A3054 at Wootton Bridge, between Ryde and Newport.*

The park, on a gently sloping field, is tucked away behind the owners' farm, just a short walk from the village and attractive river estuary. The facilities are excellent and very clean, and even include a defibrillator at reception. This park provides a pleasant relaxing atmosphere for a stay on the island and is well located for visiting Cowes and the many attractions on this part of the island. Rallies are welcome here.

Open: All year **Last arrival:** anytime **Last departure:** noon

Pitches: * 🚐 from £18.50; 🚌 from £18.50; ⛺ from £15

Leisure: 🛝 **Facilities:** 🛁 ⊙ ❄ ♿ **Services:** 🧺 🗑 🔌 🔒 🍃

Within 3 miles: ⛳ 🎣 ∪ ◎ 🌊 ⛵ 🎬 [S]

Additional site information: 12.5 acre site. 🐕 Cars can be parked by caravans and tents. Awnings permitted. Owners must clean up after their pets.

YARMOUTH

See Newbridge

KENT

ASHFORD
Map 7 TR04

Places to visit

Kent & East Sussex Railway, TENTERDEN, TN30 6HE, 01580 765155
www.kesr.org.uk

Great for kids: Port Lympne Wild Animal Park, LYMPNE, CT21 4LR,
0844 842 4647 (*calls cost 7p per minute plus your phone company's
access charge*)
www.aspinallfoundation.org/portlympne

REGIONAL WINNER – SOUTH EAST ENGLAND
AA CAMPSITE OF THE YEAR 2019

Premier Park

Broadhembury Caravan & Camping Park

▶▶▶▶▶ 90%

tel: 01233 620859 **Steeds Lane, Kingsnorth TN26 1NQ**
email: holidaypark@broadhembury.co.uk **web:** www.broadhembury.co.uk
dir. *M20 junction 10, A2070 towards Brenzett. Straight on at 1st roundabout. Left at
2nd roundabout (ignore fork left). Straight on at next roundabout. Left at 2nd
crossroads in village*

A well-run and well-maintained small family park surrounded by open pasture;
it is neatly landscaped with pitches sheltered by mature hedges. There is a
well-equipped campers' kitchen adjacent to the spotless toilet facilities, which
were upgraded for 2018, and children will love the play areas, games room and
football pitch. The adults-only area, close to the excellent reception building,
includes popular fully serviced hardstanding pitches; this area has its own
first-class, solar heated toilet block.

Broadhembury Caravan & Camping Park

Open: All year **Last arrival:** 21.00 (late arrivals to use designated area)
Last departure: noon

Pitches: * 🚐 from £20.80; 🚐 from £20.80; ▲ from £20.00; 🏠 see prices below;
20 hardstanding pitches

Leisure: 🎱 🎣 ⬜ ⚽

Facilities: 🏠 ⊙ ℙ ❄ ♿ ⑤ WiFi

Services: 🔌 🔲 🍺 📠 ⬆ 🧺 🧪 T

Within 3 miles: 🚶 ℙ ∪ ◎ 🎿 🎣 📅

Additional site information. 10 acre site. 🚗 Cars can be parked by caravans and
tents. Awnings permitted. No noise after 22.00. Bakery, table tennis, pool, skittle alley
and air hockey. Car hire can be arranged.

Glamping available: Lotus Belle tents from £40. **Changeover days:** Sunday to Friday

Additional glamping information: Lotus Belle tents: minimum stay 2 nights. Double
bed, 2 single beds or 1 double bed. Fully equipped. Bed linen can be hired. BBQ and
picnic table. Cars can be parked by tents.

PITCHES: 🚐 Caravans 🚐 Motorhomes ▲ Tents 🏠 Glamping accommodation **SERVICES:** 🔌 Electric hook-up 🔲 Launderette 🍺 Licensed bar
🔥 Calor Gas 🌀 Campingaz T Toilet fluid 🍽 Café/Restaurant 🍟 Fast Food/Takeaway 🔋 Battery charging 🔧 Motorhome service point
* 2019 prices ⊘ No credit or debit cards 🐕 Dogs permitted ⊗ No dogs

AYLESFORD
Map 6 TQ75

Places to visit

Aylesford Priory, AYLESFORD, ME20 7BX, 01622 717272
www.thefriars.org.uk

Premier Park

Kits Coty Glamping

►►►►► 88% GLAMPING ONLY

tel: 01634 685862 **84 Collingwood Road, Kits Coty Estate ME20 7ER**
email: info@kitscotyglamping.co.uk **web:** www.kitscotyglamping.co.uk
dir: *M2 junction 3, A229 towards Maidstone, follow Eccles and Burham signs. Under motorway bridge, 1st right signed Kits Coty Estate. 1st left into Salisbury Road (before joining M2). 2nd left into Beresford Road. Right at T-junction to site at end.*

Established in a lush paddock opposite the owners' house, Kits Coty Glamping is located in glorious North Downs countryside between Maidstone and Chatham, with far-reaching views across the Medway Valley. The well landscaped paddock is home to a shepherd's hut (traditionally decorated and with a double bed and log-burning stove), three spacious bell tents and 'Gretel', a woodland-themed cabin. Careful thought has been given to the space between the units and the attention to detail is excellent, as is the customer care from hands-on owners Ami and Mark, who are passionate about their unique glamping patch. The bell tents have quality mattresses, chest of drawers, electric lighting and stove, Egyptian cotton sheets, cosy duvets, throws and blankets – these are very colourful in the spacious and fun Festival and Marrakesh tents; the Mamadou tent just sleeps two. Each unit has a decked area outside, with chairs, a picnic bench and rustic log seats around a brazier. The facility cabin houses a well-equipped washing-up area that also contains every conceivable cooking utensil plus a fridge and freezer, kettle, microwave and toaster. There are also two spacious fully serviced wet rooms and two extra toilet and washbasin cubicles. There's a great outdoor space for ball games in a separate paddock, which also contains the communal eating area, chill-out room and a large fire pit.

Open: April to September **Last arrival:** 22.00 **Last departure:** 10.30

Accommodation available: Bell tents, shepherd's hut, camping cabin.

Additional site information: 1 acre site. ☼ Some glamping units are dog friendly – please contact site for details.

DETLING
Map 7 TQ75

Places to visit

Leeds Castle, MAIDSTONE, ME17 1PL, 01622 765400
www.leeds-castle.com

Maidstone Museum, MAIDSTONE, ME14 1LH, 01622 602838
www.museum.maidstone.gov.uk

Great for kids: Kent Life, MAIDSTONE, ME14 3AU, 01622 763936
www.kentlife.org.uk

Oak View Caravan Park

►►► 87%

tel: 01622 631298 **Scragged Oak Road ME14 3HB**
email: bookings@scraggedoak.co.uk
dir: *From M20 junction 7, A429 towards Ramsgate. After Detling left signed Bredhurst into Scragged Oak Road.*

Situated on top of the North Downs, adjacent to the Kent Showground, this peaceful park has a smart toilet block and provides a handy overnight stop for the ferries and Channel Tunnel. The experienced and enthusiastic wardens are gradually improving the park, adding hardstanding pitches and refurbishing the water/waste stations.

Open: March to October **Last arrival:** 22.00 **Last departure:** noon

Pitches: * 🚐 from £18; 🚌 from £18; ▲ from £18; 22 hardstanding pitches

Facilities: 🛆 ☉ 🍽 ⚒ & 🖺 🛒 WiFi

Services: 🖳 🗓 🛒 🛠 🛡 🌣 T

Within 3 miles: 🖉

Additional site information: 6 acre site. ☼ Cars can be parked by caravans and tents. Awnings permitted. No unaccompanied children in toilet block, no noise after 22.30, no gazebos, no wood burning. Freshly baked bread, croissants and sausage rolls available; dog shower.

FOLKESTONE

Places to visit

Dover Castle & Secret Wartime Tunnels, DOVER, CT16 1HU, 01304 211067
www.english-heritage.org.uk/daysout/properties/dover-castle

Dymchurch Martello Tower, DYMCHURCH, TN29 0NU,
www.english-heritage.org.uk/daysout/properties/dymchurch-martello-tower

Great for kids: Port Lympne Wild Animal Park, LYMPNE, CT21 4LR,
0844 842 4647 (*calls cost 7p per minute plus your phone company's access charge*)
www.aspinallfoundation.org/portlympne

LEISURE: 🏊 Indoor swimming pool 🏊 Outdoor swimming pool 🎢 Children's playground 👶 Kids' club 🎾 Tennis court 🎱 Games room 📺 Separate TV room
⛳ golf course 🏌 Pitch n putt 🚣 Boats for hire 🚴 Bikes for hire 🎬 Cinema 🎵 Entertainment 🎣 Fishing ⛳ Mini golf 🏄 Watersports 🏋 Gym 🏟 Sports field 🎠 Stables
FACILITIES: 🛆 Baths/Shower ☉ Electric shaver sockets 🍽 Hairdryer ✳ Ice Pack Facility 👶 Baby facilities & Disabled facilities 🖺 Shop on site or within 200yds
🛒 BBQ area 🛖 Picnic area WiFi WiFi

FOLKESTONE
Map 7 TR23

Little Switzerland Camping & Caravan Site
▶▶ 80%

tel: 01303 252168 **Wear Bay Road CT19 6PS**
email: btony328@aol.com
web: www.caravancampingsites.co.uk/kent/littleswitzerland.htm
dir: M20 junction 13, A259 (Folkestone Harbour). At 2nd roundabout follow brown Country Park sign (A260). Right at next roundabout (Country Park). 8th left into Swiss Way, site signed.

Set on a narrow plateau below the White Cliffs and above The Warren, this unique site offers sheltered, traditional camping in secluded dells and enjoys fine views across the English Channel to the French coast — probably best enjoyed from the grassy alfresco area at the popular café. The toilet facilities are basic and unsuitable for less able visitors.

Open: March to October **Last arrival:** midnight **Last departure:** noon

Pitches: 🚐 🚌 ⛺

Facilities: ⊙ ⚒ 🍴 WiFi

Services: 🔌 🗑 🍽 🍴 🛒 🧺 ⚱ 🔋 ⊘ T

Within 3 miles: 🛶 ✒ ∪ ◎ ⛷ ⛳ 🎣 💰

Additional site information: 3 acre site. 🐕 ⊗ Cars can be parked by caravans and tents. Awnings permitted. No open fires, no noise after 22.30.

LEYSDOWN-ON-SEA
Map 7 TR07

Priory Hill
▶▶▶ 74%

tel: 01795 510267 **Wing Road ME12 4QT**
email: info@prioryhill.co.uk **web:** www.prioryhill.co.uk
dir: M2 junction 5, A249 signed Sheerness, then A2500 to Eastchurch, then B2231 to Leysdown, follow brown tourist signs.

A small well-maintained touring area on an established family-run holiday park close to the sea, with views of the north Kent coast. Amenities include a clubhouse and a swimming pool. The pitch price includes membership of the clubhouse with live entertainment, and use of the indoor swimming pool.

Open: March to October **Last arrival:** 18.00 **Last departure:** noon

Pitches: 🚐 🚌 ⛺

Leisure: 🏊 🎣 ▭ ♪ ⚽

Facilities: 📷 ⊙ ⚱ 💰 🛒 WiFi

Services: 🔌 🗑 🍽 🍴 🛒 🔋 ⊘

Within 3 miles: ✒ ◎

Additional site information: 1.5 acre site. 🐕 Cars can be parked by caravans and tents. Awnings permitted. Cakes and fresh coffee available.

MARDEN

Places to visit
Scotney Castle, LAMBERHURST, TN3 8JN, 01892 893820
www.nationaltrust.org.uk/scotneycastle

MARDEN
Map 6 TQ74

Premier Park

Tanner Farm Touring Caravan & Camping Park
▶▶▶▶▶ 90%

tel: 01622 832399 **Tanner Farm, Goudhurst Road TN12 9ND**
email: enquiries@tannerfarmpark.co.uk **web:** www.tannerfarmpark.co.uk
dir: From A21 or A229 onto B2079. Midway between Marden and Goudhurst.

At the heart of a 150-acre Wealden farm, this extensive, long-established touring park is peacefully tucked away down a quiet farm drive deep in unspoilt Kent countryside, yet close to Sissinghurst Castle and within easy reach of London (Marden station is three miles away). Perfect for families, as it has farm animals, two excellent play areas and a recreation/wet weather room (with TV); it offers quality toilet blocks with privacy cubicles, a good shop, spacious hardstandings (12 fully serviced), and high levels of security and customer care. Two camping pods are available.

Open: All year (restricted service: winter months — no tents accepted) **Last arrival:** 20.00 **Last departure:** noon

Pitches: 🚐 🚌 ⛺ 🏠; 34 hardstanding pitches; 13 seasonal pitches

Leisure: 🎱 🎣 ▭ ⚽

Facilities: 📷 ⊙ ⚱ ⚒ ⚱ 💰 WiFi

Services: 🔌 🗑 🔋 ⊘ T

Within 3 miles: ✒

Additional site information: 15 acre site. 🐕 Cars can be parked by caravans and tents. Awnings permitted. No groups, 1 car per pitch, no commercial vehicles. Recreation room with table football and TV. Woodland walks.

Glamping available: Wooden pods.

Additional glamping information: Wooden pods sleep 2. Minimum stay 2 nights Friday to Sunday. Cars can be parked by pods.

MINSTER ON SEA
Map 7 TQ97

Plough Leisure Caravan Park
▶▶ 74%

tel: 01795 872895 & 07788 986547 **Plough Road ME12 4JF**
email: andyjames@live.co.uk **web:** www.ploughleisurecaravanpark.com
dir: M2 junction 5, A429 signed Sheerness. Right at roundabout signed Leysdown onto A2500. Left signed Minster onto B2008. At roundabout take 1st exit. Right at phone box and brown camping sign into Plough Road. Site on left.

Tucked away on the edge of Minster and well placed to visit the island's marshes and coastline, this small touring site is part of a neatly maintained static park and offers well-spaced pitches, a good play area and a games field for children, and portacabin toilet and shower facilities.

Open: March to 1 October **Last arrival:** anytime **Last departure:** anytime

Pitches: 🚐 🚌 ⛺ **Leisure:** 🎱 ⚽ **Facilities:** 📷 ⊙ ⚒ ⚱ 🍴 🍽

Services: 🔌 🗑 🧺 ⚱ 🔋 ⊘ **Within 3 miles:** 🛶 ✒ 💰

Additional site information: 4 acre site. ⊗ Cars can be parked by caravans and tents. Awnings permitted. Noise to a minimum after 22.00. No fires on grass.

PITCHES: 🚐 Caravans 🚌 Motorhomes ⛺ Tents 🏠 Glamping accommodation **SERVICES:** 🔌 Electric hook-up 🗑 Launderette 🍽 Licensed bar
🔋 Calor Gas ⊘ Campingaz T Toilet fluid 🍴 Café/Restaurant 🛒 Fast Food/Takeaway 🔋 Battery charging ⚱ Motorhome service point
* 2019 prices ◎ No credit or debit cards 🐕 Dogs permitted ⊗ No dogs

ROCHESTER
Map 6 TQ76

Places to visit

Guildhall Museum, ROCHESTER, ME1 1PY, 01634 332900
www.guildhallmuseumrochester.co.uk

Upnor Castle, UPNOR, ME2 4XG, 01634 718742
www.english-heritage.org.uk/daysout/properties/upnor-castle

Great for kids: Diggerland, STROOD, ME2 2NU, 0871 227 7007 (*calls cost 10p per minute plus your phone company's access charge*)
www.diggerland.com

Allhallows Leisure Park
▶▶▶▶ 82% HOLIDAY HOME PARK

tel: 01634 270385 **Allhallows-on-Sea ME3 9QD**
email: allhallows@haven.com **web:** www.haven.com/allhallows
dir: *M25 junction 2, A2 signed Rochester, A289 signed Gillingham. A228 signed Grain. Follow site signs.*

Located in a peaceful country park setting close to Rochester, Allhallows is a static-only holiday park offering a wide range of sporting and leisure activities for all the family, including swimming pools, tennis courts, a 9-hole golf course and fencing. Children will love the kids' club and play area, while there is a restaurant and bar with evening entertainment for adults.

Open: March to October

Holiday Homes: Sleep 8 Bedrooms 2 Bathrooms 1 Toilets 1 Dishwasher Microwave Freezer TV Sky/Freeview DVD player Linen included Electricity included Gas included

Leisure: 🏊 🏖 🎠 👋 🎾 🎱 🎵

Facilities: ♿ 🏪 🚼 WiFi

Within 3 miles: ⛹ ◎ 🖥

Additional site information: 188 acre site. 🐕 Most dog breeds accepted (please check when booking). Dogs must be kept on leads at all times. The facilities provided in the holiday homes may differ depending on the grade.

ST NICHOLAS AT WADE

Places to visit

Reculver Towers & Roman Fort, RECULVER, CT6 6SU, 01227 740676
www.english-heritage.org.uk/daysout/properties/reculver-towers-and-roman-fort

Upnor Castle, UPNOR, ME2 4XG, 01634 718742
www.english-heritage.org.uk/daysout/properties/upnor-castle

Great for kids: Diggerland, STROOD, ME2 2NU, 0871 227 7007 (*calls cost 10p per minute plus your phone company's access charge*)
www.diggerland.com

ST NICHOLAS AT WADE
Map 7 TR26

St Nicholas Camping Site
▶▶ 78%

tel: 01843 847245 **Court Road CT7 0NH**
web: www.stnicholascampingsite.co.uk
dir: *Signed from A299 and A28, site at west end of village near church.*

A gently-sloping field with mature hedging, on the edge of the village close to the shop. This pretty site offers good facilities, including a family/disabled room, and is conveniently located close to primary routes and the north Kent coast.

Open: Easter to October **Last arrival:** 22.00 **Last departure:** 14.00

Pitches: 🚐 from £22; 🚃 from £21; ⛺ from £18; 6 seasonal pitches

Leisure: 🎠

Facilities: 🏪 ☺ 🅿 ☀ ♿

Services: 🔧 🔒 🧺 T

Within 3 miles: 🎣 ⛹ 🖥

Additional site information: 3 acre site. 🐕 🚗 Cars can be parked by caravans and tents. Awnings permitted. No music after 22.30. Baby changing area.

WHITSTABLE
Map 7 TR16

Places to visit

Westgate Towers Museum & Viewpoint, CANTERBURY, CT1 2BZ, 01227 458629
www.onepoundlane.co.uk

The Canterbury Tales, CANTERBURY, CT1 2TG, 01227 696002
www.canterburytales.org.uk

Great for kids: Druidstone Park, CANTERBURY, CT2 9JR, 01227 765168
www.druidstone.net

Homing Park
▶▶▶▶ 84%

tel: 01227 771777 **Church Lane, Seasalter CT5 4BU**
email: info@homingpark.co.uk **web:** www.homingpark.co.uk
dir: *Exit A299 for Whitstable and Canterbury, left at brown camping-caravan sign into Church Lane. Site entrance has 2 large flag poles.*

A small touring park close to Seasalter Beach and Whitstable, which is famous for its oysters. All pitches are generously sized and fully serviced, and most are

---

LEISURE: 🏊 Indoor swimming pool 🏖 Outdoor swimming pool 🎠 Children's playground 👋 Kids' club 🎾 Tennis court 🎱 Games room 📺 Separate TV room
🏌 golf course 🏌 Pitch n putt ⛵ Boats for hire 🚲 Bikes for hire 🎬 Cinema 🎵 Entertainment 🎣 Fishing ◎ Mini golf 🏄 Watersports 🏋 Gym 🏟 Sports field ⛹ Stables
FACILITIES: 🏪 Baths/Shower ☺ Electric shaver sockets 🖐 Hairdryer ☀ Ice Pack Facility 🚼 Baby facilities ♿ Disabled facilities 🖥 Shop on site or within 200yds
🍖 BBQ area 🧺 Picnic area WiFi WiFi

separated by hedging and shrubs. A clubhouse and swimming pool are available on site with a small cost for the use of the swimming pool. Wooden camping pods, for four or six people, are available for hire; their outwardly sloping walls adds to the internal space.

Open: Easter to October **Last arrival:** 20.00 **Last departure:** 11.00

Pitches: 🚐 from £23; 🚌 from £23; ⚊ from £23; 🏠 see prices below

Leisure: 🏊 🎱 ♨ **Facilities:** 🏠 ⊙ 🕐 ✳ ♿ WiFi

Services: 🔌 🗑 🍴 🍽 🔒 **Within 3 miles:** ⚓ 🎣 ∪ 🏇 🎢 🎯 💲

Additional site information: 12.6 acre site. 🐕 Cars can be parked by caravans and tents. Awnings permitted. No commercial vehicles, no tents larger than 8 berths or 5 metres wide, no unaccompanied minors, no cycles or scooters.

Glamping available: Wooden pods from £35. **Changeover days:** Any day

Additional glamping information: Minimum stay 2 nights (3 nights at bank holiday weekends). Cars can be parked by pods.

WROTHAM HEATH — Map 6 TQ65

Places to visit

Ightham Mote, IGHTHAM, TN15 0NT, 01732 810378
www.nationaltrust.org.uk/ightham-mote

St Leonard's Tower, WEST MALLING, ME19 6PE,
www.english-heritage.org.uk/daysout/properties/st-leonards-tower

Great for kids: Kent Life, MAIDSTONE, ME14 3AU, 01622 763936
www.kentlife.org.uk

Gate House Wood Touring Park
▶▶▶ 81%

tel: 01732 843062 **Ford Lane TN15 7SD**
email: contact@gatehousewoodtouringpark.com
web: www.gatehousewoodtouringpark.com
dir: M26 junction 2a, A20 south towards Maidstone, through lights at Wrotham Heath. 1st left signed Trottiscliffe, left at next junction into Ford Lane. Site 100 yards on left.

A well-sheltered and mature site in a former quarry surrounded by tall deciduous trees and gorse banks. The well-designed facilities include a reception, shop and smart toilets, 11 hardstandings, and there is good entrance security and high levels of customer care. The colourful flower beds and hanging baskets are impressive and give a positive first impression. Conveniently placed for the M20 and M25 and a fast rail link to central London.

Open: March to October **Last arrival:** 21.00 **Last departure:** noon

Pitches: 🚐 🚌 ⚊

Leisure: 🎱

Facilities: 🏠 ⊙ 🕐 ✳ ♿ 💲 🚿 WiFi

Services: 🔌 🗑 ↻ 🔒 🧴 🅃

Within 3 miles: ⚓ 🎣 ∪ 🏇 🎢

Additional site information: 3.5 acre site. 🐕 Cars can be parked by caravans and tents. Awnings permitted. No commercial vehicles, no noise after 23.00, no camp fires, soft balls only. Fresh bread and newspapers to order at peak times only. Car hire can be arranged.

LANCASHIRE

See also sites under Greater Manchester and Merseyside

BLACKPOOL — Map 18 SD33

See also Lytham St Annes and Thornton

Places to visit

Madame Tussauds Blackpool, BLACKPOOL, FY1 5AA,
www.madametussauds.com/Blackpool

Great for kids: Blackpool Zoo, BLACKPOOL, FY3 8PP, 01253 830830
www.blackpoolzoo.org.uk

Premier Park

Marton Mere Holiday Village
▶▶▶▶ 88% HOLIDAY CENTRE

tel: 01253 767544 **Mythop Road FY4 4XN**
email: martonmere@haven.com **web:** www.haven.com/martonmere
dir: M55 junction 4, A583 towards Blackpool. Right at Clifton Arms lights into Mythop Road. Site 150 yards on left.

A very attractive holiday centre in an unusual setting on the edge of the mere, with plenty of birdlife to be spotted. The site has a stylish Mediterranean seaside-themed Boathouse Restaurant and the on-site entertainment is tailored for all ages, and includes a superb show bar. There's a regular bus service into Blackpool for those who want to explore further afield. The separate touring area is well equipped with hardstandings and electric pitches, and there are good quality facilities, including a superb amenity block.

Open: mid March to end October (restricted service: March to end May and September to October – reduced facilities, splash zone closed) **Last arrival:** 22.00 **Last departure:** 10.00

Pitches: 🚐 🚌; 82 hardstanding pitches

Leisure: 🏊 🎱 🎿 🎵

Facilities: 🏠 ⊙ 🕐 ✳ ♿ 💲 🚿 WiFi

Services: 🔌 🗑 🍴 🍽 🍔 🔒 🧴

Within 3 miles: ⚓ 🎣 ∪ ◎ 🏇 🎢 🎯

Additional site information: 30 acre site. 🐕 Maximum of 2 dogs per booking, certain dog breeds banned. No commercial vehicles, no bookings by persons under 21 years unless a family booking.

BLACKPOOL *continued*

Manor House Caravan Park
►►►► 82%

tel: 01253 764723 **Kitty Lane, Marton Moss FY4 5EG**
email: manorhousecaravanpark@outlook.com **web:** www.manorhousecaravanpark.co.uk
dir: *At roundabout at end of M55 junction 4, take A5230 signed Squires Gate. At next roundabout take 3rd exit (Blackpool/Squires Gate/A5230). In 0.5 mile left at lights into Midgeland Road. 500 yards, straight on at crossroads. 250 yards, right into Kitty Lane. In 250 yards, site on right. (Note: it is advisable not to follow sat nav).*

A sympathetically converted former small holding close to both Lytham St Annes and Blackpool, this peacefully located adults-only park is surrounded by high neat hedges and generous sized hardstanding pitches ensure optimum privacy. A warm welcome is assured by the resident owners and although there is no shop or launderette, both services are within a 10-minute drive. There are caravan pitches and motorhome pitches. Please note that tents are not accepted.

Open: February to November **Last arrival:** 20.00 **Last departure:** 11.30

Pitches: 🚐 from £22; 🚙 from £22; 10 hardstanding pitches

Facilities: 🛁 🍴

Services: 📷 ⛏

Within 3 miles: ⚓ 🎣 ⟳ ◉ 🛥 🎮 💷 🛍

Additional site information: 1 acre site. Adults only. 🐾 Pets accepted by prior arrangement only. Cars can be parked by caravans. Awnings permitted. No ball games or loud music.

BOLTON LE SANDS

Places to visit

Lancaster Maritime Museum, LANCASTER, LA1 1RB, 01524 382264
www.lancashire.gov.uk/museums

Lancaster City Museum, LANCASTER, LA1 1HT, 01524 64637
www.lancashire.gov.uk/museums

Great for kids: Lancaster Castle, LANCASTER, LA1 1YJ, 01524 64998
www.lancastercastle.com

BOLTON LE SANDS   Map 18 SD46

Bay View Holiday Park
►►►► 87%

tel: 01524 732854 & 701508 **LA5 9TN**
email: info@holgates.co.uk **web:** www.holgates.co.uk
dir: *M6 junction 25, A6 through Carnforth to Bolton-le-Sands. Site on right.*

A high quality, family-oriented seaside destination with fully serviced all-weather pitches, many of which have views of Morecambe Bay and the Cumbrian hills. A stylish bar/restaurant is just one of the park's amenities, and there is a wide range of activities and attractions on offer within a few miles. This makes a good choice for a family holiday by the sea; two family pods are available to hire.

Open: All year (restricted service: at quieter times – restaurant and bar reduced hours)
Last arrival: 20.00 **Last departure:** noon

Pitches: 🚐 from £23.50; 🚙 from £23.50; ⛺ from £19; 🏠 see prices below; 50 hardstanding pitches; 127 seasonal pitches

Leisure: 🎪 🎱 🖵 ⚽ 🎣

Facilities: 🛁 ⊙ ✳ ♿ 💷 🍴 🚼 WiFi

Services: 📷 🔲 ⛏ 🍴 ⬆ 🚲 ⛏ 🔒 🌿 🔳

Within 3 miles: ⚓ 🎣 ⟳ 🛥 🎮 💷

Additional site information: 10 acre site. 🐾 Cars can be parked by caravans and tents. Awnings permitted. No noise after 23.00. Car hire can be arranged.

Glamping available: 2 wooden pods from £35. **Changeover days:** Saturday

Additional glamping information: Wooden pods (sleep 2 adults and 3 children) offer light, heater, electrical sockets and pull-out bed/sofa. No dogs in pods. Cars can be parked by pods.

Red Bank Farm
►►► 81%

tel: 01524 823196 **LA5 8JR**
email: mark.archer@hotmail.co.uk **web:** www.redbankfarm.co.uk
dir: *From Morecambe take A5015 towards Carnforth. After Hest Bank left into Pastures Lane (follow brown site sign). Over rail bridge, right (follow site sign). At T-junction left into The Shore to site at end.*

A gently sloping grassy field with mature hedges, close to the sea shore and a RSPB reserve. This farm site has smart toilet facilities, a superb view across Morecambe Bay to the distant Lake District hills, and is popular with tenters. Archers Café serves a good range of cooked food, including home-reared marsh lamb dishes.

LEISURE: 🏊 Indoor swimming pool   🏊 Outdoor swimming pool   🎪 Children's playground   👦 Kids' club   ☺ Tennis court   🎱 Games room   🖵 Separate TV room
⚓ golf course   ⛳ Pitch n putt   🚤 Boats for hire   🚲 Bikes for hire   🎬 Cinema   🎵 Entertainment   🎣 Fishing   ◉ Mini golf   🛥 Watersports   🏋 Gym   ⚽ Sports field   ⟳ Stables
FACILITIES: 🛁 Baths/Shower   ⊙ Electric shaver sockets   ✳ Hairdryer   ✳ Ice Pack Facility   🚼 Baby facilities   ♿ Disabled facilities   💷 Shop on site or within 200yds
🍴 BBQ area   ⚘ Picnic area   WiFi WiFi

Open: March to October **Last arrival:** 22.00

Pitches: 🚐 from £14; 🏕 from £14

Facilities: 🛁 ⊙ 🏳 ❄ WiFi

Services: 🔌 🗑 🍽 🏭

Within 3 miles: ⚓ 🎣 🚣 ⚑ 🛒

Additional site information: 3 acre site. 🐕 Cars can be parked by tents. Awnings permitted. No noise after 22.30. Pets' corner.

CAPERNWRAY
Map 18 SD57

Places to visit

Leighton Hall, CARNFORTH, LA5 9ST, 01524 734474
www.leightonhall.co.uk

RSPB Leighton Moss & Morecambe Bay Nature Reserve, SILVERDALE, LA5 0SW, 01524 701601, www.rspb.org.uk/leightonmoss

---

REGIONAL WINNER – NORTH WEST ENGLAND AA CAMPSITE OF THE YEAR 2019

Premier Park

Old Hall Caravan Park
▶▶▶▶▶ 91%

tel: 01524 733276 **LA6 1AD**

email: hello@oldhallcaravanpark.co.uk **web:** www.oldhallcaravanpark.co.uk

dir: M6 junction 35, A601(M) follow signs for Over Kellet, at T-junction left onto B6254. In Over Kellet left at village green signed Capernwray. Site 1.5 miles on right.

A lovely secluded park set in a clearing amongst trees at the end of a half-mile long drive. This peaceful park is home to a wide variety of wildlife, and there are marked walks in the woods. A pathway over a meandering brook through woodland separates the reception from the touring area. All pitches are fully serviced and the stylish amenity block contains superb combined shower, toilet and washbasin rooms with excellent fixtures and fittings. The facilities are well maintained by the friendly owners, and booking is advisable. Please note, on bank holidays a minimum stay of three nights is required.

Open: March to October (restricted service: November to January – seasonal tourers can stay longer by prior arrangement) **Last arrival:** 9.30 **Last departure:** noon

Pitches: * 🚐 from £22; 🚐 from £22; 38 hardstanding pitches; 30 seasonal pitches

Leisure: 🎠

Facilities: 🛁 ⊙ 🏳 ⚐ WiFi

Services: 🔌 🗑 🔋 ⚒ 🔒

Within 3 miles: 🎣 🚣 🚣 ⚑ 🛒

Additional site information: 3 acre site. 🐕 Cars can be parked by caravans. Awnings permitted. No skateboards, rollerblades or roller boots. Woodland walk, information room.

COCKERHAM

Places to visit

Lancaster Cathedral, LANCASTER, LA1 3BT, 01524 384820
www.lancastercathedral.org.uk

COCKERHAM
Map 18 SD45

Moss Wood Caravan Park
▶▶▶▶ 88%

tel: 01524 791041 **Crimbles Lane LA2 0ES**

email: info@mosswood.co.uk **web:** www.mosswood.co.uk

dir: M6 junction 33, A6, approximately 4 miles to site. From Cockerham take A588 west. Left into Crimbles Lane to site.

A tree-lined grassy park with sheltered, level pitches, located on peaceful Cockerham Moss. A spacious air-conditioned licensed shop at the entrance stocks a variety of local produce including cheeses, smoked bacon and ales. The modern toilet block is attractively clad in stained wood, and the facilities include cubicle washing units and a launderette. A private lake is also available for coarse fishing enthusiasts.

Open: March to October **Last arrival:** 20.00 **Last departure:** 16.00

Pitches: 🚐 from £23.30; 🚐 from £23.30; 31 hardstanding pitches; 12 seasonal pitches

Leisure: 🏳 ⚽ **Facilities:** 🛁 ⊙ 🏳 ♿ 🗑 🍴 WiFi

Services: 🔌 🗑 🔋 ⚒ Ⓣ

Within 3 miles: ⚓ ♻

Additional site information: 25 acre site. 🐕 Cars can be parked by caravans. Awnings permitted. Woodland walks, fishing lake, nature trail.

CROSTON
Map 15 SD41

Places to visit

Harris Museum & Art Gallery, PRESTON, PR1 2PP, 01772 258248
www.harrismuseum.org.uk

Rufford Old Hall, RUFFORD, L40 1SG, 01704 821254
www.nationaltrust.org.uk/ruffordoldhall

Royal Umpire Caravan Park
▶▶▶▶ 82%

tel: 01772 600257 **Southport Road PR26 9JB**

email: info@royalumpire.co.uk **web:** www.harrisonholidays.com

dir: From north: M6 junction 28 (from south: M6 junction 27), onto B5209, right onto B5250.

A large park with tree- or hedge-lined bays for touring caravans and motorhomes, plus a large camping field in open countryside. There are many areas for children's activities and several pubs and restaurants are within walking distance. Four camping pods are available for hire.

Open: All year **Last arrival:** 20.00 **Last departure:** 16.00

Pitches: 🚐 🚐 🏕 🏠; 180 hardstanding pitches

Leisure: 🎠 ⚽ **Facilities:** 🛁 ⊙ 🏳 ❄ ♿ 🗑

Services: 🔌 🗑 ⚒ 🔒 ⚐

Within 3 miles: ⚓ 🎣 ♻ 🚣 ⚑ 🛒

Additional site information: 60 acre site. 🐕 Cars can be parked by caravans and tents. Awnings permitted.

Glamping available: Wooden pods.

Additional glamping information: Wooden pods offer fridge, microwave, toaster, kettle, crockery, electric heater, TV. Own bedding and towels required. Pets accepted in 1 pod only. Cars can be parked by pods.

ESPRICK
Map 18 SD43

Places to visit
Blackpool Zoo, BLACKPOOL, FY3 8PP, 01253 830830
www.blackpoolzoo.org.uk

Charoland Farm
►►►► 81%

tel: 07876 196434 & 01253 836595 **Greenhalgh Lane, Greenhalgh PR4 3HL**
email: enquiries@charolandfarm.co.uk **web:** www.charolandfarm.co.uk
dir: *Exit M55 junction 3 onto A585 signed Fleetwood. Left into Greenhalgh Lane.*

A hedge-screened, adults-only touring park based on an award-winning beef cattle and sheep farm, ideally located for touring the many Fylde Coast attractions. All pitches are firm and surrounded by attractive seasonal shrubs and flowers, and level approaches to facilities benefit less mobile visitors. Please note that there is no laundry facility at this park.

Open: March to October **Last arrival:** 20.00 **Last departure:** 17.00
Pitches: 🚐 from £18; 🚍 from £18; ⛺ from £18; 10 hardstanding pitches
Facilities: 🛁 ⊙ ✳ ♿ 🍴 ⊞
Services: 🚽
Within 3 miles: ✐ ⑤

Additional site information: 0.5 acre site. Adults only. 🐾 Pets by prior arrangement. ⊛ Cars can be parked by caravans and tents. Awnings permitted. No commercial vehicles. No ball games.

FAR ARNSIDE

Places to visit
Rufford Old Hall, RUFFORD, L40 1SG, 01704 821254
www.nationaltrust.org.uk/ruffordoldhall

RSPB Leighton Moss & Morecambe Bay Nature Reserve, SILVERDALE, LA5 0SW, 01524 701601, www.rspb.org.uk/leightonmoss

---

FAR ARNSIDE
Map 18 SD47

Hollins Farm Camping & Caravanning
►►►►► 88%
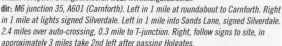

tel: 01524 701767 & 701508 **LA5 0SL**
email: reception@holgates.co.uk **web:** www.holgates.co.uk
dir: *M6 junction 35, A601 (Carnforth). Left in 1 mile at roundabout to Carnforth. Right in 1 mile at lights signed Silverdale. Left in 1 mile into Sands Lane, signed Silverdale. 2.4 miles over auto-crossing, 0.3 mile to T-junction. Right, follow signs to site, in approximately 3 miles take 2nd left after passing Holgates.*

Hollins Farm is a long established park that continues to be upgraded by the owners. There are 50 fully serviced hardstanding pitches for tourers and 25 fully serviced tent pitches; the excellent amenity block provides very good facilities and privacy options. It has a traditional family camping feel and offers high standard facilities; most pitches have views towards Morecambe Bay, and WiFi is available throughout the park. Two family pods (Daisy and Buttercup) are available for hire. The leisure and recreation facilities of the nearby, much larger, sister park (Silverdale Caravan Park at Silverdale) can be accessed by guests here.

Open: 14 March to 7 November **Last arrival:** 20.00 **Last departure:** noon
Pitches: 🚐 from £35; 🚍 from £35; ⛺ from £35; 🏠 see prices below; 5 hardstanding pitches; 38 seasonal pitches
Leisure: 🎿 🔍 ▭
Facilities: 🛁 ⊙ ✳ ♿ 🍴 WiFi
Services: 🚽 🔋 ⬆ 🛢 ⊘ Ⓣ
Within 3 miles: ↓ ✐ ∪ ◎ ⚓ ⑤

Additional site information: 30 acre site. 🐾 Cars can be parked by caravans and tents. Awnings permitted. No unaccompanied children, no fire pits or chimeneas, no gazebos, no commercial vehicles at reception after unloading, no noise after 22.30.

Glamping available: Wooden pods from £40.

Additional glamping information: Wooden pods offer sofa bed and heater.

FLEETWOOD

Places to visit
Blackpool Zoo, BLACKPOOL, FY3 8PP, 01253 830830
www.blackpoolzoo.org.uk

FLEETWOOD
Map 18 SD34

Premier Park

Cala Gran Holiday Park
►►►► 86% HOLIDAY HOME PARK

tel: 01253 872555 **Fleetwood Road FY7 8JY**
email: calagran@haven.com **web:** www.haven.com/calagran
dir: *M55 junction 3, A585 signed Fleetwood. At 4th roundabout (Nautical College on left) take 3rd exit. Park 250 yards on left.*

Cala Gran is a lively holiday park close to Blackpool with a range of quality holiday caravans and apartments. The park is all about fun, and the entertainment includes live music, comedy shows and resident DJs, while for children there are swimming pools and a SplashZone, a pick and paint room, climbing wall, and also a sports range for supervised archery and fencing.

Open: mid March to 30 October

Holiday Homes: Sleep 8 Bedrooms 2 Bathrooms 1 Toilets 1 Microwave Freezer TV Sky/Freeview

Leisure: 🏊 🎢 🎯 🎣 🎵 **Facilities:** 🄂 🌂 **WiFi** **Within 3 miles:** 🚲 ◎ 🗒

Additional site information: 🐕 Most dog breeds accepted (please check when booking). Dogs must be kept on leads at all times. The facilities provided in the holiday homes may differ depending on the grade.

GARSTANG
Map 18 SD44

Places to visit

Lancaster Maritime Museum, LANCASTER, LA1 1RB, 01524 382264
www.lancashire.gov.uk/museums

Lancaster City Museum, LANCASTER, LA1 1HT, 01524 64637
www.lancashire.gov.uk/museums

Great for kids: Lancaster Castle, LANCASTER, LA1 1YJ, 01524 64998
www.lancastercastle.com

Bridge House Marina & Caravan Park
►►►► 83%

tel: 01995 603207 **Nateby Crossing Lane, Nateby PR3 0JJ**
email: info@bridgehousemarina.co.uk **web:** www.bridgehousemarina.co.uk
dir: *Exit A6 at pub and Knott End sign, immediately right into Nateby Crossing Lane, over canal bridge to site on left.*

Set in attractive countryside by the Lancaster Canal, you drive through an extensive boatyard with lots of historical interest, to arrive at this carefully landscaped park. It has excellent pitches, including some that are fully serviced. The park also has a good on-site café and children's play area.

Open: March to 4 January **Last arrival:** 22.00 **Last departure:** 13.00

Pitches: 🚐 from £23; 🚐 from £23; 42 hardstanding pitches; 20 seasonal pitches

Leisure: 🎢 ⊙ **Facilities:** 🚿 ⊙ 🄿 ❄ ⅄ 🄂 **WiFi**

Services: 🔌 🄂 🍺 🍽 ♨ ⚓ 🌀 ⊺ **Within 3 miles:** 🚲 🗒 ⚓

Additional site information: 4 acre site. 🐕 Cars can be parked by caravans. Awnings permitted.

LANCASTER
Map 18 SD46

Places to visit

Lancaster Maritime Museum, LANCASTER, LA1 1RB, 01524 382264
www.lancashire.gov.uk/museums

Lancaster City Museum, LANCASTER, LA1 1HT, 01524 64637
www.lancashire.gov.uk/museums

Great for kids: Lancaster Castle, LANCASTER, LA1 1YJ, 01524 64998
www.lancastercastle.com

New Parkside Farm Caravan Park
►►► 83%

tel: 015247 70723 **Denny Beck, Caton Road LA2 9HH**
email: enquiries@newparksidefarm.co.uk **web:** www.newparksidefarm.co.uk
dir: *M6 junction 34, A683 towards Caton and Kirkby Lonsdale. Site 1 mile on right.*

A few minutes from M6 and an ideal stopover en route to or from Scotland, this rural and peaceful park is set in the Lune Valley and is near the historic city of Lancaster and the Forest of Bowland. This friendly, family-run park is part of a working farm and has generously sized pitches (both grass and hardstanding) and a smart amenity block.

Open: March to October **Last arrival:** 20.00 **Last departure:** 16.00

Pitches: 🚐 🚐 🏕; 40 hardstanding pitches

Facilities: 🚿 ⊙ 🄿

Services: 🔌 🄂

Within 3 miles: 🚲 🗒 🗒 🄂 🄂

Additional site information: 4 acre site. 🐕 🚗 Cars can be parked by caravans and tents. Awnings permitted. No football.

LONGRIDGE
Map 18 SD63

Places to visit
Brockholes Nature Reserve, SAMLESBURY, PR5 0AG, 01772 872000
www.brockholes.org

Beacon Fell View Holiday Park
►►►► 81% HOLIDAY CENTRE

tel: 01772 783233 **110 Higher Road PR3 2TF**
email: beacon@hagansleisure.co.uk web: www.hagansleisure.co.uk
dir: *At junction of Dilworth Road (B6243) and King Street in Longridge into Higher Road. Site on right.*

Located on the outskirts of Longridge with fine views of the surrounding fells, this long-established family holiday destination has a good range of all-weather attractions for both adults and children. In addition to holiday homes, the touring areas have good hardstanding pitches for caravans or motorhomes with electric hook-ups to all.

Open: March to 11 November **Last arrival:** 22.00 **Last departure:** 11.00

Pitches: 🚐 from £18; 🚙 from £18; ⛺ from £18; 56 hardstanding pitches; 12 seasonal pitches

Leisure: 🏊 🎢 👋 🎯 🎵 🏌

Facilities: 🚿 ☉ ⚲ ⓢ 🚾 🍴 WiFi

Services: 🔌 🗑 🍴 🛒 🛅

Within 3 miles: 🎣 ◎ 🎱

Additional site information: 32 acre site. 🐕 Dogs must be kept on leads at all times. Quiet between 22.00–07.00.

LYTHAM ST ANNES
Map 18 SD32

Places to visit
Blackpool Zoo, BLACKPOOL, FY3 8PP, 01253 830830
www.blackpoolzoo.org.uk

Eastham Hall Holiday Park
►►►► 86%

tel: 01253 737907 **Saltcotes Road FY8 4LS**
email: info@easthamhall.co.uk web: www.easthamhall.co.uk
dir: *M55 junction 3. Straight over 3 roundabouts onto B5259. Through Wrea Green and Moss Side, site 1 mile after level crossing.*

A large family-run park in a tranquil rural setting, surrounded by trees and mature shrubs. The pitch density is very good and most are fully serviced, plus the amenity

---

LEISURE: 🏊 Indoor swimming pool 🏊 Outdoor swimming pool 🎢 Children's playground 👋 Kids' club 🎾 Tennis court 🎱 Games room ▭ Separate TV room 🏌 golf course 🏌 Pitch n putt 🚣 Boats for hire 🚲 Bikes for hire 🎬 Cinema 🎵 Entertainment 🎣 Fishing ◎ Mini golf 🏄 Watersports 🏋 Gym ⚽ Sports field ♘ Stables
FACILITIES: 🚿 Baths/Shower ☉ Electric shaver sockets 💈 Hairdryer ❄ Ice Pack Facility 🍼 Baby facilities ♿ Disabled facilities ⓢ Shop on site or within 200yds 🍴 BBQ area 🍴 Picnic area WiFi WiFi

blocks have been appointed to a high standard. Please note, this site does not accept tents.

Eastham Hall Holiday Park

Open: March to 1 December (restricted service: 20 February to 1 March and 2 December to 3 January holiday homes only) **Last arrival:** 20.00 **Last departure:** noon

Pitches: 🚐 🚉; 101 hardstanding pitches; 77 seasonal pitches

Leisure: 🅰 ✪ **Facilities:** 🛁 ☉ ☂ ✳ ♿ ⓢ 🚮 WiFi

Services: 🔌 🗄 🛢 🌱 Ⓣ **Within 3 miles:** ↓ ⌇ ∪ ◎ ⚲ ✈

Additional site information: 30 acre site. 🐾 Dogs must be kept on leads at all times. Cars can be parked by caravans. Awnings permitted. No tents, no noise after 23.00, 10mph speed limit. Football field, dog exercise area. Local produce, newspapers available.

See advert opposite

MORECAMBE   Map 18 SD46

Places to visit

Leighton Hall, CARNFORTH, LA5 9ST, 01524 734474
www.leightonhall.co.uk

Lancaster City Museum, LANCASTER, LA1 1HT, 01524 64637
www.lancashire.gov.uk/museums

Venture Caravan Park

▶▶▶▶ 79%

tel: 01524 412986 **Langridge Way, Westgate LA4 4TQ**

email: mark@venturecaravanpark.co.uk **web:** www.venturecaravanpark.co.uk

dir: *M6 junction 34, A683, follow Morecambe signs. At 1st roundabout 1st exit, at 2nd roundabout 1st exit. At major crossroads (at lights) turn right into Morecambe Road. At next roundabout 1st left into Westgate. After fire station (on right) turn right into Langridge Way.*

A large family park close to the town centre, with good modern facilities, including a small indoor heated pool, a licensed clubhouse and a family room with children's entertainment. The site has many statics, some of which are for holiday hire. Please note, tents are not accepted.

Open: All year (restricted service: in winter – only one toilet block open) **Last arrival:** 22.00 **Last departure:** noon

Pitches: 🚐 from £22; 🚉 from £22; 40 hardstanding pitches; 25 seasonal pitches

Leisure: 🏊 🅰 🔍 ⚲ **Facilities:** 🛁 ☉ ☂ ✳ ♿ ⓢ 🚮 WiFi

Services: 🔌 🗄 🍽 🍺 🚮 ⚡ 🔋 Ⓣ **Within 3 miles:** ↓ ⌇ 🎌

Additional site information: 17.5 acre site. 🐾 Cars can be parked by caravans. Awnings permitted. Amusement arcade, off licence, seasonal entertainment.

SILVERDALE

Map 18 SD47

Places to visit

Leighton Hall, CARNFORTH, LA5 9ST, 01524 734474
www.leightonhall.co.uk

Great for kids: RSPB Leighton Moss & Morecambe Bay Nature Reserve,
SILVERDALE, LA5 0SW, 01524 701601
www.rspb.org.uk/leightonmoss

Platinum Park

Silverdale Caravan Park

▶▶▶▶▶

tel: 01524 701508 **Middlebarrow Plain, Cove Road LA5 0SH**
email: caravan@holgates.co.uk **web:** www.holgates.co.uk
dir: *M6 junction 35, A601(M) follow Kirkby Lonsdale (B6254) signs. At T-junction right
to Carnforth. In Carnforth centre at crossroads, straight on (Silverdale). 1 mile, left
into Sands Lane (Silverdale). 2.4 miles, over automatic level crossing. Right at
T-junction, follow Holgates sign. 1 mile left, 0.5 mile right into Cove Road,
0.7 mile to site.*

A superb family holiday destination set in extensive wooded countryside
overlooking the sea. All areas of the park are maintained in excellent condition
with mature trees, shrubs and pretty, seasonal flowers creating a peaceful and
relaxing atmosphere. The pitch density is generous and the spotlessly clean
amenity blocks, which were completely refurbished for the 2018 season, are
conveniently located. There's an indoor swimming pool, well-stocked licensed
mini-market, smart bar and bistro, an internet room, bowling alley with
amusements and a toddlers' soft ball area. Family camping pods are available
for hire.

Silverdale Caravan Park

Open: All year **Last arrival:** 20.00 **Last departure:** noon

Pitches: 🚐 from £37.50; 🚌 from £37.50; ▲ from £37.50; 🏠 see prices below;
80 hardstanding pitches; 2 seasonal pitches

Leisure: 🏊 🎢 🎱 🎵 ⛳ ⚽

Facilities: 🛁 ☉ 🪒 ✳ ♿ 🛢 🍴 🛒 WiFi

Services: 🔌 🗑 🍽 🍴 🛒 ⬆ 🔒 🧺 T

Within 3 miles: 🚲 🏌 ∪ ◎ 🏄

Additional site information: 100 acre site. 🐕 Cars can be parked by caravans and
tents. Awnings permitted. No unaccompanied children, no gazebos, no fire pits or
chimeneas, no noise after 22.30. Sauna, spa pool, steam room, bowling alley,
ice cream parlour, indoor play area.

Glamping available: Wooden pods from £45.

Additional glamping information: Wooden pods offer a sofa bed, heater and lighting.

See advert on page 217

THORNTON
Map 18 SD34

Places to visit
Blackpool Zoo, BLACKPOOL, FY3 8PP, 01253 830830
www.blackpoolzoo.org.uk

Premier Park

Kneps Farm Holiday Caravan Park
▶▶▶▶▶ 84%

tel: 01253 823632 **River Road, Stanah FY5 5LR**
email: enquiries@knepsfarm.co.uk web: www.knepsfarm.co.uk
dir: *Exit A585 at roundabout onto B5412 to Little Thornton. Right at mini roundabout after school into Stanah Road, over 2nd mini roundabout, leading to River Road.*

In the same family ownership for over 50 years, this is a quality park quietly located adjacent to the River Wyre and the Wyre Estuary Country Park, and handily placed for the attractions of Blackpool and the Fylde coast. It offers a well-stocked shop, an excellent toilet block with immaculate facilities, and a mixture of hard and grass pitches (no tents are accepted), plus there are 4-berth and 6-berth wooden pods for hire.

Open: March to mid November (restricted service: March and early November – shop closed) **Last arrival:** 20.00 **Last departure:** noon
Pitches: ⊞ from £22; ⊞ from £22; ⋔ see prices below; 40 hardstanding pitches; 5 seasonal pitches
Leisure: ⋔
Facilities: 🏪 ☉ ⵗ ✱ ⅋ 🖳 🚿 WiFi
Services: 🔌 🔄 🛒 ⅄ ⬤ ⌀ T
Within 3 miles: ⅄ ⌀ ≋ 🎏

Additional site information: 10 acre site. 🐕 Maximum of 3 dogs (chargeable) per unit. Cars can be parked by caravans. Awnings permitted. No commercial vehicles. No gazebos or shade sails, complete quiet after midnight.

Glamping available: Wooden pods from £35. **Changeover days:** Any day

Additional glamping information: Wooden pods: minimum advanced booking 2 nights (3 for bank holidays). Arrival 15:00, depart noon. Standard pods sleep 3; family pods sleep 4. Own beds, bedding and other equipment required. No smoking/vaping, no pets, no unaccompanied teenagers. Cars can be parked by pods.

LEICESTERSHIRE
See also Wolvey (Warwickshire)

CASTLE DONINGTON

Places to visit
Calke Abbey, CALKE, DE73 7LE, 01332 863822
www.nationaltrust.org.uk/calke-abbey

Ashby-de-la Zouch Castle, ASHBY-DE-LA-ZOUCH, LE65 1BR, 01530 413343
www.english-heritage.org.uk/daysout/properties/ashby-de-la-zouch-castle

CASTLE DONINGTON
Map 11 SK42

Donington Park Farmhouse
▶▶▶ 75%

tel: 01332 862409 **Melbourne Road, Isley Walton DE74 2RN**
email: info@parkfarmhouse.co.uk web: www.parkfarmhouse.co.uk
dir: *M1 junction 24, pass airport to Isley Walton, right towards Melbourne. Site 0.5 mile on right.*

A secluded touring site, at the rear of a hotel beside Donington Park Racing Circuit, which is very popular on race days so booking is essential. Reception for the campsite is at the hotel. Please note that there are no laundry facilities and both day and night flights from nearby East Midlands Airport may cause disturbance.

Open: 27 December to 23 December (restricted service: closed for 7 days in early June; winter – hardstanding only) **Last arrival:** 21.00 **Last departure:** noon
Pitches: ⊞ from £20; ⊞ from £20; ⋏ from £16; 50 hardstanding pitches
Facilities: 🏪 ☉ ✱ ⅋ **Services:** 🔌 🛒 🍽 ⅄ ⬤ T
Within 3 miles: ⅄ ⌀ 🛒

Additional site information: 10 acre site. 🐕 Dogs must be on leads at all times. Cars can be parked by caravans and tents. Awnings permitted. No noise between 23.00 and 08.00. Bread and milk available, on-site hotel with bar and WiFi. Internet access available.

MELTON MOWBRAY
Map 11 SK71

Premier Park

Eye Kettleby Lakes
▶▶▶▶▶ 93%

tel: 01664 565900 **Eye Kettleby LE14 2TN**
email: info@eyekettlebylakes.com web: www.eyekettlebylakes.com
dir: *From Melton Mowbray take A607 towards Leicester. In approximately 2 miles left signed Great Dalby and Eye Kettleby Lakes. Site 1 mile on left.*

A haven for lovers of coarse fishing and walking, this long-established leisure destination, located in the hamlet of Eye Kettleby, provides very high standards. There are eight fishing lakes as well as designated walking areas and accommodation located in lodges, a glamping forest and touring fields. Touring pitches are fully serviced and divided by mature hedges to provide optimum privacy. The top-notch amenity blocks provide excellent standards in respect of fittings and privacy. A large Scandinavian log building houses a reception, shop, café and clubhouse where regular entertainment is provided.

Open: All year **Last arrival:** 22.00 **Last departure:** noon
Pitches: ⊞ from £25.50; ⊞ from £25.50; ⋏ from £22; ⋔ see prices below; 130 hardstanding pitches
Leisure: ⌖ ▱ 🎣 ♫ ⌀
Facilities: 🏪 ☉ ⵗ ✱ ⅋ 🖳 🎏 WiFi
Services: 🔌 🔄 🍽 🍽 ⬤ T **Within 3 miles:** ⅄ ↻ 🎏

Additional site information: 150 acre site. Adults only. 🐕 Cars can be parked by caravans and tents. Awnings permitted. Cycle routes, coarse/specimen fishing.

Glamping available: Wooden pods from £62.50. **Changeover days:** Any day (weekends in July and August – minimum 3-day stay)

Additional glamping information: Wooden pods have fitted bathroom.

LINCOLNSHIRE

ANCASTER
Map 11 SK94

Places to visit

Belton House Park & Gardens, BELTON, NG32 2LS, 01476 566116
www.nationaltrust.org.uk/belton-house

Woodland Waters
►►►► 83%

tel: 01400 230888 **Willoughby Road NG32 3RT**
email: info@woodlandwaters.co.uk **web:** www.woodlandwaters.co.uk
dir: On A153, west of junction with B6403.

On an impressive estate, with a wide variety of mature trees and five beautifully landscaped fishing lakes, this popular holiday destination provides lodges (the six new Wood View lodges were introduced for the 2018 season), lodge rooms and level touring areas with smart modern amenity blocks. A pub and clubhouse, with restaurant, are additional benefits.

Open: All year **Last arrival:** 20.00 **Last departure:** noon

Pitches: 🚐 🚙 ⛺; 5 hardstanding pitches

Leisure: 🎱 🎣 ✎

Facilities: ⊙ ☂ ⌂ ♿ 🛁 ▦ ⛱ WiFi

Services: 🔌 🗑 🚽 🍴 🛒 🎀 🔒 🌱

Within 3 miles: ♪ ∪

Additional site information: 72 acre site. 🐕 Cars can be parked by caravans and tents. Awnings permitted. No noise after 23.00.

BOSTON
Map 12 TF34

Places to visit

Battle of Britain Memorial Flight Visitor Centre, CONINGSBY, LN4 4SY, 01522 782040, www.lincolnshire.gov.uk/bbmf

Tattershall Castle, TATTERSHALL, LN4 4LR, 01526 342543
www.nationaltrust.org.uk/tattershall-castle

Long Acres Touring Park
►►►► 92%

Best of British

tel: 01205 871555 **Station Road, Old Leake PE22 9RF**
email: info@long-acres.co.uk **web:** www.long-acres.co.uk
dir: From A16 take B1184 at Sibsey (by church); approximately 1 mile at T-junction turn left. 1.5 miles, after level crossing take next right into Station Road. Park entrance approximately 0.5 mile on left.

A small, rural, adults-only park in an attractive setting within easy reach of Boston, Spalding and Skegness. Excellent shelter is provided by the high, mature boundary hedging. The park has a smart toilet block which is very clean and has an appealing interior with modern, upmarket fittings and a new laundry room. A holiday cottage is available to let. Long Acres is a member of the Tranquil Parks group.

Open: March to 8 January **Last arrival:** 20.00 **Last departure:** 11.00

Pitches: * 🚐 from £20; 🚙 from £20; ⛺ from £20; 40 hardstanding pitches

Facilities: 🛁 ⊙ ☂ ⌂ ♿ WiFi

Services: 🔌 🗑 🚽 🔒

Within 3 miles: ✎ 🏪

Additional site information: 3 acre site. Adults only. 🐕 Cars can be parked by caravans and tents. Awnings permitted.

Orchard Park
►►►► 85%

tel: 01205 290328 **Frampton Lane, Hubbert's Bridge PE20 3QU**
email: info@orchardpark.co.uk **web:** www.orchardpark.co.uk
dir: On B1192 between A52 (Boston to Grantham road) and A1121 (Boston to Sleaford road).

Ideally located for exploring the unique Fenlands, this continually improving park has two lakes — one for fishing and the other set aside for conservation. The attractive restaurant and bar are popular with visitors and Jan's Café is open for snacks during the day.

Open: All year (restricted service: December to February — bar, shop and café closed)
Last arrival: 20.00 **Last departure:** 16.00

Pitches: * 🚐 from £20; 🚙 from £20; ⛺ from £10; 15 hardstanding pitches

Leisure: 🎣 ♫ ✎ ⚽

Facilities: 🛁 ⊙ ☂ ⌂ ♿ 🛒 ▦ ⛱ WiFi

Services: 🔌 🗑 🚽 🍴 🛒 🎀 🚽 🔒 🌱 T

Within 3 miles: ♪ ∪ ◉

Additional site information: 51 acre site. Adults only. 🐕 Cars can be parked by caravans and tents. Awnings permitted. No washing lines.

LEISURE: 🏊 Indoor swimming pool 🏊 Outdoor swimming pool 🎠 Children's playground 🙌 Kids' club 🎾 Tennis court 🎱 Games room 📺 Separate TV room ⛳ golf course ⛳ Pitch n putt 🚣 Boats for hire 🚲 Bikes for hire 🎬 Cinema ♫ Entertainment ✎ Fishing ◉ Mini golf 🏄 Watersports 🏋 Gym ⚽ Sports field ∪ Stables
FACILITIES: 🛁 Baths/Shower ⊙ Electric shaver sockets ☂ Hairdryer ❄ Ice Pack Facility 🎀 Baby facilities ♿ Disabled facilities 🏪 Shop on site or within 200yds ▦ BBQ area ⛱ Picnic area WiFi WiFi

CAISTOR
Map 17 TA10

Platinum Park

Caistor Lakes Leisure Park
►►►►►

tel: 01472 859626 **99a Brigg Road LN7 6RX**
email: info@caistorlakes.co.uk web: www.caistorlakes.co.uk
dir: *From Caistor bypass follow Immingham and Humber Bridge signs onto A1173. 1st left signed Brigg (A1084) into Grimsby Road (becomes High Street, then Brigg Road). Site on left.*

This is a stunning seven-acre park that was developed beside established fishing lakes. The passionate owners have created a very impressive park – there's excellent landscaping and first-class facilities that include smart hardstanding pitches and modern, low-level buildings housing the professionally-run reception, the top-notch toilets and showers, a shop selling essentials and fishing supplies, and a smart 100-seat restaurant with views across the lakes and Lincolnshire Wolds. There are five luxury lodges with hot tubs available for hire.

Open: All year **Last arrival:** 17.00 **Last departure:** 15.00

Pitches: ♘ from £22; ♙ from £22, 28 hardstanding pitches

Leisure: ♙ **Facilities:** 🏠 🅿 ♿ **WiFi**

Services: ♘ ☎ 🍴 ♨

Within 3 miles: ♘ 🖈

Additional site information: 7 acre site. Adults only. 🐕 Cars can be parked by caravans. Awnings permitted. No swimming in lakes, no bikes.

Wolds View Touring Park
►►►► 88%

tel: 01472 851099 **115 Brigg Road LN7 6RX**
email: phil@wvtp.co.uk web: www.woldsviewtouringpark.co.uk
dir: *From A46, at Caistor, follow Brigg and A1084 signs. 1st left signed Brigg and Caistor. Through Caistor, continue on A1084. Approximately 1 mile, site on left.*

Set in the Lincolnshire Wolds with spectacular views, Wolds View is extremely welcoming, really modern and tidy, with good wide access, stoned roads, and good shrubbery and hedging throughout. The facilities block is a beautiful, purpose-designed wooden building, painted cornflower blue – at one end is a fabulous café and coffee shop serving a variety of drinks, breakfasts and home-made cakes, and at the other end are light, modern and spotless toilet and shower facilities, and a professionally managed reception.

Open: All year **Last arrival:** 20.00 (18.00 weekdays) **Last departure:** 13.00

Pitches: ♘ from £20; ♙ from £20; ♙ from £20; ♙ see prices below; 20 hardstanding pitches

Facilities: 🏠 ☺ 🅿 ❄ ♿ 🅂 🍴 🛎 **WiFi**

Services: ♘ ☎ 🍴 ♨ ⚓ 🔋 🔒 🅃 **Within 3 miles:** ♙ ♘

Additional site information: 4.5 acre site. Adults only. 🐕 Cars can be parked by caravans and tents. Awnings permitted. No groups. No noise after 23.00.

Glamping available: 1 wooden pod from £65. **Changeover days:** Any day

Additional glamping information: Wooden pod: minimum stay 2 nights. King-size bed, TV, toaster, microwave, tea and coffee making facilities, oil radiator, 2 chairs, outdoor patio set. Own bedding required. Cars can be parked by pod.

CLEETHORPES
Map 17 TA30

Places to visit
Fishing Heritage Centre, GRIMSBY, DN31 1UZ, 01472 323345
www.thefishingheritagecentre.com

Premier Park

Thorpe Park Holiday Centre
►►►►► 85% HOLIDAY CENTRE

tel: 01472 813395 **DN35 0PW**
email: thorpepark@haven.com web: www.haven.com/thorpepark
dir: *From A180 at Cleethorpes take unclassified road signed 'Humberstone and Holiday Park'.*

A large static site, adjacent to the beach, with touring facilities, including fully serviced pitches and pitches with hardstandings. This holiday centre offers excellent recreational and leisure activities including an indoor pool, archery range, climbing wall, lake coarse fishing and a 9-hole golf course. The Carousel bar and restaurant with its unique fairground theme is popular, along with several very good takeaway food options.

Open: mid March to end October (restricted service: mid March to May and September to end October – some facilities may be reduced) **Last arrival:** anytime **Last departure:** 10.00

Pitches: ♘ ♙ ♙; 81 hardstanding pitches

Leisure: 🏊 🎣 🏹 🖐 ♙ 🎵 ♙ ⛳

Facilities: 🏠 ☺ 🅿 ♿ 🅂 🍴

Services: ♘ ☎ 🍴 ♨ 🛎 🔒 ✏

Within 3 miles: ♘ ♙ ♙ 🍴

Additional site information: 300 acre site. 🐕 Maximum 2 dogs per booking, certain dog breeds banned. No commercial vehicles, no bookings by persons under 21 years unless a family booking. Internet access available.

GREAT CARLTON · Map 17 TF48

Places to visit

Cadwell Park Circuit, LOUTH, LN11 9SE, 01507 343248
www.cadwellpark.co.uk

West End Farm

▶▶▶ 87%

tel: 01507 450949 & 07766 278740 **Salters Way LN11 8BF**
email: info@westendfarm.co.uk web: www.skegnessmablethorpecaravancamping.com
dir: *From Gayton Top on A157 follow Great Carlton signs. Follow brown sign for West End Farm. Site on right in 0.5 mile.*

A neat and well-maintained four-acre touring park situated on the edge of the Lincolnshire Wolds. Surrounded by mature trees and bushes and well away from the busy main roads, yet connected by walking and cycling paths, it offers enjoyable peace and quiet close to the popular holiday resort of Mablethorpe. The site has good, clean facilities throughout and there's a passionate approach to everything 'green', with a reed bed sewage system, wild areas, bird and bat boxes and wildlife identification charts.

Open: 28 March to 2 October **Last arrival:** 20.30 **Last departure:** 14.00
Pitches: * 🚐 from £16; 🚏 from £16; ▲ from £16; 4 seasonal pitches
Facilities: 🛁 📠 ✳ 🍴 🛆
Services: 🔌 🗑 🚽 ⬇ 🅣
Within 3 miles: ⅃ 🎣 ∪ ◎ 🛒

Additional site information: 4 acre site. 🐕 Cars can be parked by caravans and tents. Awnings permitted. No fires, quiet after 22.30. Fridge available. Internet access available.

LANGWORTH · Map 17 TF07

Places to visit

The Collection: Art & Archaeology in Lincolnshire, LINCOLN, LN2 1LP, 01522 782040, www.thecollectionmuseum.com

Lincoln Cathedral, LINCOLN, LN2 1PX, 01522 561600
http://lincolncathedral.com

Barlings Country Holiday Park

▶▶▶▶ 86%

tel: 01522 753200 & 07931 227673 **Barlings Lane LN3 5DF**
email: info@barlingscountrypark.co.uk web: www.barlingscountrypark.co.uk
dir: *From Lincoln take A158 towards Horncastle. In Langworth right into Barlings Lane signed Barlings and Reepham.*

Set in rural Lincolnshire and only a short car journey from Lincoln, this idyllic 26-acre site offers both seasonal and touring pitches positioned around four lakes. With wildlife in abundance, the park is well landscaped, with beautifully mown grass and trimmed shrubs, a wooden reception chalet, spotlessly clean, older-style

toilet facilities, including family rooms, and fishing from purpose-built jetties on two of the lakes. Lodges, static caravans and glamping cabins, with hot tubs, are available to hire.

Open: All year **Last arrival:** 18.00 (late arrivals can be arranged) **Last departure:** noon
Pitches: 🚐 🚏 ▲; 🏠 see prices below; 43 hardstanding pitches; 40 seasonal pitches
Leisure: 🎣 ⚽ ✪ **Facilities:** 🛁 ⊙ 🛆 🍴 WiFi
Services: 🔌 🗑 🚽 ⬇ 🛒 🅣
Within 3 miles: 🛒

Additional site information: 26 acre site. 🐕 Cars can be parked by caravans and tents. Awnings permitted. No music after 22.00, quiet 23.00–08.00. Mobile shop Friday 11–11.30 only, ice cream van (summer).

Glamping available: 2 small cabins from £75. **Changeover days:** Any day
Additional glamping information: Small cabins offer hot tubs. Cars can be parked by cabins.

MABLETHORPE · Map 17 TF58

Places to visit

Great for kids: Skegness Natureland Seal Sanctuary, SKEGNESS, PE25 1DB, 01754 764345, www.skegnessnatureland.co.uk

Premier Park

Golden Sands Holiday Park

▶▶▶▶▶ 88% HOLIDAY CENTRE

tel: 01507 477871 **Quebec Road LN12 1QJ**
email: goldensands@haven.com web: www.haven.com/goldensands
dir: *From centre of Mablethorpe turn left into Quebec Road (seafront road). Site on left.*

A large, well-equipped seaside holiday park with many all-weather attractions and a good choice of entertainment and eating options, including the stylish Quayside Bar and Restaurant. The large touring area is serviced by two amenity blocks and is close to the mini market and laundry. Just across the road is The Marblethorpe Seal Sanctuary and Wildlife Centre.

Open: mid March to end October **Last arrival:** anytime **Last departure:** 10.00
Pitches: 🚐 🚏 ▲; 20 hardstanding pitches
Leisure: 🏊 🏊 🎢 👶 🎱 🎵 🎣
Facilities: 🛁 ⊙ 📠 ✳ 🛆 🛒 WiFi
Services: 🔌 🗑 🍴 🍽 🎰 🚽 ⬇ 🅣
Within 3 miles: ⅃ ◎ 🎳

Additional site information: 23 acre site. 🐕 Maximum 2 dogs per booking, certain dog breeds banned. No commercial vehicles, no bookings by persons under 21 years unless a family booking. Mini bowling alley, snooker and pool, amusement arcade.

LEISURE: 🏊 Indoor swimming pool 🏊 Outdoor swimming pool 🎢 Children's playground 👶 Kids' club 🎾 Tennis court 🎱 Games room 🖵 Separate TV room ⅃ golf course 🏌 Pitch n putt 🚣 Boats for hire 🚲 Bikes for hire 🎬 Cinema 🎵 Entertainment 🎣 Fishing ◎ Mini golf 🏄 Watersports 🏌 Gym ✪ Sports field ∪ Stables
FACILITIES: 🛁 Baths/Shower ⊙ Electric shaver sockets 📠 Hairdryer ✳ Ice Pack Facility 🛒 Baby facilities 🛆 Disabled facilities 🛒 Shop on site or within 200yds 🍴 BBQ area 🍴 Picnic area WiFi WiFi

Kirkstead Holiday Park

▶▶▶ 85%

tel: 01507 441483 **North Road, Trusthorpe LN12 2QD**
email: mark@kirkstead.co.uk **web:** www.kirkstead.co.uk
dir: *From Mablethorpe town centre take A52 south towards Sutton-on-Sea. 1 mile, sharp right by phone box into North Road. Site signed in 300 yards.*

A well-established family-run park catering for all age groups, just a few minutes' walk from Trusthorpe and the sandy beaches of Mablethorpe. The main touring area, which is serviced by good quality toilet facilities, has 37 fully serviced pitches on what was once the football pitch, and here toilets have been installed. The site is particularly well maintained.

Open: March to November **Last arrival:** 21.00 **Last departure:** 11.00

Pitches: 🚐 from £12; 🚍 from £12; ▲ from £10; 3 hardstanding pitches; 30 seasonal pitches

Leisure: 🛝 🎣 🎵 ⚽

Facilities: 🚿 ☺ 🐾 ✳ ♿ 🛁 🛒 �️ WiFi

Services: 🔌 🔲 🗑️ 🍴 🍽️ 🏭 🔋 🛠️

Within 3 miles: 🎣 🏌️ 🎯 ⦿ ☕ 🗓️

Additional site information: 12 acre site. 🐕 No dogs in tents. Cars can be parked by caravans and tents. Awnings permitted.

MARSTON Map 11 SK84

Places to visit

Belton House Park & Gardens, BELTON, NG32 2LS, 01476 566116
www.nationaltrust.org.uk/belton-house

Newark Air Museum, NEWARK-ON-TRENT, NG24 2NY, 01636 707170
www.newarkairmuseum.org

Wagtail Country Park

▶▶▶▶ 93%

tel: 01400 251123 & 07814 481088 **Cliff Lane NG32 2HU**
email: info@wagtailcountrypark.co.uk **web:** www.wagtailcountrypark.co.uk
dir: *From A1 exit at petrol station signed Barkston and Marston, right signed Barkston into Green Lane, right into Cliff Lane.*

A peaceful site near the village of Marston, surrounded by trees and where birdsong is the only welcome distraction. The touring areas are neatly laid out and enhanced by mature shrubs and pretty, seasonal flowers. There is a stunning facilities block that includes four family rooms, and five smart, new lodges were added in 2018. There is a separate adults-only area, and coarse fishing is also available.

Open: All year **Last arrival:** anytime (earliest arrival noon) **Last departure:** 11.00

Pitches: 🚐 🚍; 76 hardstanding pitches; 6 seasonal pitches

Leisure: 🎣

Facilities: 🚿 ☺ 🐾 ♿ 🛁 🍴 🌭 �️ WiFi

Services: 🔌 🔲 🛠️ 🛒 T

Within 3 miles: 🎣

Additional site information: 30 acre site. 🐕 Cars can be parked by caravans. Awnings permitted. No noise after 23.00. Fishing bait, basic essentials, milk and ice creams available.

SKEGNESS Map 17 TF56

Places to visit

Skegness Natureland Seal Sanctuary, SKEGNESS, PE25 1DB, 01754 764345
www.skegnessnatureland.co.uk

The Village-Church Farm Museum, SKEGNESS, PE25 2HF, 01754 766658
www.churchfarmvillage.org.uk

Eastview Caravan Park

▶▶▶▶ 81%

tel: 01754 875324 & 07710 336145 **Trunch Lane, Chapel St Leonards PE24 5UA**
email: enquiries@eastviewcaravans.co.uk **web:** www.eastviewcaravans.co.uk
dir: *A52 from Skegness to Chapel St Leonards. Turn left into Trunch Lane. 2nd caravan park on left.*

Set in 15 acres and only a short walk from one of Lincolnshire's finest beaches, Eastview Caravan Park is neat and tidy and a good all-round campsite. It has beautifully mown grass, well-trimmed shrubbery and spotlessly clean and modern toilet facilities. There is a children's playground and a shop. It is well placed for exploring both the coast and the countryside, especially the beautiful Lincolnshire Wolds.

Open: March to October **Last arrival:** 17.00 (Friday 20.00) **Last departure:** 10.30 (later departures until 17.00 – fee applies).

Pitches: * 🚐 from £20; 🚍 from £20; ▲ from £18.50; 56 hardstanding pitches; 116 seasonal pitches

Facilities: ☺ ✳ ♿ 🌭 WiFi **Services:** 🔌 🔲 🛠️ 🛒 T

Within 3 miles: 🎣 🏌️ 🎯 ⦿ ☕ 🗓️

Additional site information: 15 acre site. 🐕 Maximum 2 dogs per pitch. Cars can be parked by caravans and tents. Awnings permitted. No motorised scooters, BB guns or kites. BBQs to be at least 1 foot off ground, quiet after 22.30.

TATTERSHALL
Map 17 TF25

Places to visit

Tattershall Castle, TATTERSHALL, LN4 4LR, 01526 342543
www.nationaltrust.org.uk/tattershall-castle

Tattershall Lakes Country Park
▶▶▶▶ 90%

tel: 01526 348800 **Sleaford Road LN4 4LR**
email: tattershall.holidays@awayresorts.co.uk **web:** www.tattershall-lakes.com
dir: *Access from A153 in Tattershall.*

Set amongst woodlands, lakes and parkland on the edge of Tattershall in the heart of the Lincolnshire Fens, this mature country park has been created from old gravel pits and the flat, well-drained and maintained touring area offers plenty of space

for campers. There's a lot to entertain the youngsters as well as the grown-ups, with good fishing on excellent lakes, a 9-hole golf course, water-skiing and jet-skiing lakes and an indoor heated pool with spa facilities. Three fully-equipped bell tents (sleeping 2-4) and two canvas cottages (sleeping 2-8) are available for hire.

Open: end March to end October (restricted service: off-peak season – reduced services)
Last arrival: 19.00 **Last departure:** 10.00

Pitches: ⬛ ⬛ ⬛ ⬛; 2 hardstanding pitches

Leisure: 🏊 🚣 🎣 🖥 🎵 🏹 ⚽ Spa   **Facilities:** ☺ 🚿 ♿ 🖥 🚻 🪑 🛒 WiFi

Services: 🔌 🚽 🍴 🍽 🛒 🔒   **Within 3 miles:** ↨ 🎣 🛶 🐟 🎯

Additional site information: 365 acre site. 🐾 Cars can be parked by caravans and tents. Awnings permitted. No excessive noise after midnight.

Glamping available: Bell tents; safari tents (canvas cottage).

Additional glamping information: Safari tents: includes hot tub.

THORPE ST PETER — Map 17 TF46

Places to visit

Gunby Hall and Gardens, SPILSBY, PE23 5SS, 01754 890102
www.nationaltrust.org.uk/gunby-estate-hall-and-gardens

Grooby's Pit

▶▶▶▶ 90%

tel: 07427 137463 & 07449 488234 **Bridgefoot Farm, Steeping Road PE24 4QT**
web: www.fishskegness.co.uk
dir: *Use the A52 to Wainfleet St Mary, turning left onto the B1195. Follow the road through Wainfleet and continue to Thorpe St Peter passing the church on your right. Turn left at the crossroads signposted for Thorpe Culvert railway station (Station Road). Go over the railway crossing, then turn right into Steeping Road. Grooby's Pit is on the left hand side.*

A small adults-only park developed from scratch around two fishing lakes by Neil and Tracy Murton. A peaceful haven in the heart of rural Lincolnshire, the park comprises spacious handstanding pitches (five are seasonal) and bespoke glamping pods set beside the lakes, that have good security, smartly appointed toilet and shower blocks, good laundry facilities, high levels of customer care, and an exclusive feel. Dogs are welcome on the park and the site now features an enclosed dog exercise area for use by one customer at a time.

Open: 15 March to 31 October (restricted service: bank holidays. 3 night minimum stay Friday to Monday) **Last arrival:** 20.00 **Last departure:** 11.30

Pitches: * 🚐 from £19; 🚐 from £19; 🏠 see prices below; 12 hardstanding pitches; 5 seasonal pitches

Leisure: 🎣

Facilities: 🏚 ☺ ⚑ ⚒ ⌐

Services: 🔌 🅾

Within 3 miles: ⛳ 🏬

Additional site information: 7 acre site. Adults only. 🦮 Dogs must be on a 2-metre maximum lead. Cars can be parked by caravans. Awnings permitted. No noise after 22.00. Barrier doesn't operate between 22.00–07.00. 2 fishing lakes, BBQs for purchase, fresh eggs.

Glamping available: Pods from £60; Deluxe pods from £85 (2 night minimum stay).

Changeover days: Any day

Additional glamping information: Pods: furnished, bespoke settee/bed, heater, fridge, microwave, kettle, outside patio, firepit, 2 private fishing pegs. Deluxe pods: In addition – toilet and washbasin, kitchen with sink, fridge/freezer, toaster, 2 ring ceramic hob and extractor, TV/DVD player, private decked fishing platform. Maximum 2 people in each pod, no smoking, no dogs allowed.

WADDINGHAM — Map 17 SK99

Places to visit

Gainsborough Old Hall, GAINSBOROUGH, DN21 2NB, 01522 782040
www.english-heritage.org.uk/daysout/properties/gainsborough-old-hall

Brandy Wharf Leisure Park

▶▶▶ 72%

tel: 01673 818010 **Brandy Wharf DN21 4RT**
email: brandywharflp@freenetname.co.uk **web:** www.brandywharfleisurepark.co.uk
dir: *From A15 onto B1205 through Waddingham. Site in 3 miles.*

A delightful site in a very rural area on the banks of the River Ancholme, where fishing is available. The toilet block has unisex rooms with combined facilities as well as a more conventional ladies and gents with washbasins and toilets. All the grassy pitches have electricity, and there's a play and picnic area. This site will appeal to bikers, groups, music lovers, and families – children's natural play is encouraged. Advance booking is necessary for weekend pitches.

Open: All year (restricted service: November to Easter – no tents) **Last arrival:** dusk **Last departure:** 17.00

Pitches: * 🚐 from £18; 🚐 from £18; 🛖 from £15

Leisure: 🎠 ⚽ 🎣

Facilities: 🏚 ☺ ⚒ ♿ 🚿 ⌐ **WiFi**

Services: 🔌 🅾 🚮 🛢 ⊘

Within 3 miles: ⚓ ⛳ ⚓ 🏬

Additional site information: 5 acre site. 🦮 Cars can be parked by caravans and tents. Awnings permitted. No disposable BBQs on grass, no music after 23.00. Boat mooring and slipway, canoe hire, pedalos, pets' corner. Camping – children under 10 are free of charge.

PITCHES: 🚐 Caravans 🚐 Motorhomes 🛖 Tents 🏠 Glamping accommodation **SERVICES:** 🔌 Electric hook-up 🅾 Launderette 🍺 Licensed bar
🛢 Calor Gas ⊘ Campingaz 🅃 Toilet fluid 🍽 Café/Restaurant 🍟 Fast Food/Takeaway 🔋 Battery charging ⚡ Motorhome service point
* 2019 prices 🚫 No credit or debit cards 🦮 Dogs permitted 🚫 No dogs

WOODHALL SPA
Map 17 TF16

Places to visit

Tattershall Castle, TATTERSHALL, LN4 4LR, 01526 342543
www.nationaltrust.org.uk/tattershall-castle

Battle of Britain Memorial Flight Visitor Centre, CONINGSBY, LN4 4SY, 01522 782040, www.lincolnshire.gov.uk/bbmf

Premier Park

Woodhall Country Park

▶ ▶ ▶ ▶ ▶ 93%

tel: 01526 353710 **Stixwould Road LN10 6UJ**
email: info@woodhallcountrypark.co.uk **web:** www. woodhallcountrypark.co.uk
dir: *In Woodhall Spa at roundabout in High Street take Stixwould Road. 1 mile, site on right, just before Village Limits pub.*

A peaceful and attractive touring park situated just a short walk from Woodhall Spa. The owners transformed part of the woodland area into a countryside retreat for campers who wish to get away from a hectic lifestyle. Well organised and well laid out, the park offers fishing lakes, three superb log cabin amenity blocks, fully serviced pitches and high levels of customer care. There's a strong ethos towards sustainability and a bio-mass boiler provides all the heating and hot water to the amenity blocks, plus there are bird hides around the park. There are camping pods, superb bespoke quality lodges and four new, fully-equipped 'Hideaways' available for hire. A mobile van, offering wood-fired pizzas, is a feature on Friday nights.

Open: March to November **Last arrival:** 20.00 **Last departure:** noon

Pitches: 🚗 from £22; 🚐 from £22; ▲ from £18; 🏠 see prices below; 88 hardstanding pitches

Leisure: 𝄃 🎨 🎣 ⚽ 🌐

Facilities: 🛁 ⊙ 🪒 ✳ ⚸ 𝖲 🧺 ⊓ WiFi

Services: 🚐 🔄 🛒 🚿 T

Within 3 miles: 🏌 ∪ ◎ 🎏

Additional site information: 80 acre site. 🐾 Cars can be parked by caravans. Awnings permitted. No fires, Chinese lanterns or fireworks, no noise between 23.00–07.00. BBQs must be off ground. Walking and cycling trail, food preparation room including worktops, freezer, kettle, grill and microwave.

Glamping available: Wooden pods from £25; cabins from £59.

Additional glamping information: Minimum stay 2 nights; check in from 15.00, check out by 11.00. Cabins have their own kitchen. Cars can be parked by pods and cabins.

See advert on page 224

Petwood Caravan Park

▶ ▶ ▶ ▶ 90%

tel: 01526 354799 **Off Stixwould Road LN10 6QH**
email: info@petwoodcaravanpark.co.uk **web:** www. petwoodcaravanpark.com
dir: *From Lincoln take A15 towards Sleaford. Left onto B1188 signed Woodhall Spa. In approximately 7.5 miles at Metheringham left onto B1189 (signed Billinghay). 3.7 miles, left onto B1191 (Woodhall Spa). In approximately 6 miles at roundabout in Woodhall Spa, 1st exit into Stixwould Road. In 0.3 mile left into Jubilee Park, follow site signs.*

Covering seven immaculate acres of beautifully manicured grounds, Petwood Caravan Park is a hidden gem located behind a much larger touring park in the heart of Woodhall Spa. There are 98 pitches, each with electric hook-ups and fresh water taps; 16 have spacious hardstandings suitable for caravans and motorhomes. There is a modern reception and shop, and two excellent heated toilet blocks, each containing a spotlessly maintained disabled/family room. Dogs are welcome at no extra charge.

Open: 5 April to 20 October **Last arrival:** 20.00 **Last departure:** noon

Pitches: * 🚗 from £19; 🚐 from £19; ▲ from £19; 16 hardstanding pitches; 20 seasonal pitches

Facilities: 🛁 ⊙ 🪒 ✳ ⚸ 𝖲 WiFi

Services: 🚐 🔄 🛁

Within 3 miles: 🏌 🎣 ◎ 🎏

Additional site information: 7 acre site. 🐾 Cars can be parked by caravans and tents. Awnings permitted. No rollerblades, skateboards, hoverboards or segways. No noise after 22.00.

LONDON

E4 CHINGFORD — Map 6 TQ39

Places to visit

Waltham Abbey Gatehouse, Bridge & Entrance to Cloisters, WALTHAM ABBEY, EN9 1XQ
www.english-heritage.org.uk/daysout/properties/waltham-abbey-gatehouse-and-bridge

Lee Valley Campsite

🏕

►►►► 81%

tel: 020 8529 5689 **Sewardstone Road, Chingford E4 7RA**
email: sewardstonecampsite@vibrantpartnerships.co.uk
web: www.visitleevalley.org.uk/wheretostay
dir: *M25 junction 26, A112. Site signed.*

Overlooking King George's Reservoir and close to Epping Forest, this popular and very peaceful park features very good modern facilities and excellent hardstanding pitches including nine that are able to accommodate larger motorhomes. This impressive park is maintained to a high standard and there is glamping accommodation in a separate shady glade. A bus calls at the site hourly to take passengers to the nearest tube station, and Enfield is easily accessible.

Open: March to January **Last arrival:** 20.00 **Last departure:** 11.00 (late departures by prior arrangement)

Pitches: 🚐 from £15; 🚌 from £15; ⛺ from £15; 🏕; 65 hardstanding pitches

Leisure: 🛝 🚲 **Facilities:** 🚻 ⊙ 💨 ✲ ♿ [$] WiFi

Services: 🔌 🧺 🔋 ⬇ 🛢 🔥 [T] **Within 3 miles:** ⛳ 🎣 U ≋ H

Additional site information: 12 acre site. 🐕 Cars can be parked by caravans and tents. Awnings permitted. Under 18s must be accompanied by an adult, no commercial vehicles. Fresh produce available, bike hire, fire pit.

Glamping available: 2 and 4 berth wooden pods.

Additional glamping information: Cars can be parked by pods.

N9 EDMONTON — Map 6 TQ39

Places to visit

Queen Elizabeth's Hunting Lodge, LONDON, E4 7QH, 020 7332 1911
www.cityoflondon.gov.uk/eppingforest

Lee Valley Camping & Caravan Park

🏕

►►►► 81%

tel: 020 8803 6900 **Meridian Way N9 0AR**
email: edmontoncampsite@vibrantpartnerships.co.uk
web: www.visitleevalley.org.uk/wheretostay
dir: *M25 junction 25, A10 south, 1st left onto A1055, approximately 5 miles to Leisure Complex. From A406 (North Circular), north on A1010, left after 0.25 mile, right into Pickets Lock Lane.*

A pleasant, open site within easy reach of London yet peacefully located close to two large reservoirs. There are excellent gravel access roads to the camping field, good signage and lighting and smart toilets. The site has the advantage of being next to an 18-hole golf course and a multi-screen cinema. There are also camping pods (cocoons), ready-erected tents and small timber cabins for hire. A convenient bus stop provides a direct service to central London.

Open: All year **Last arrival:** 20.00 **Last departure:** 11.00 (late departures by prior arrangement)

Pitches: 🚐 from £15; 🚌 from £15; ⛺ from £15; 🏕; 54 hardstanding pitches

Leisure: 🛝 ⛳

Facilities: 🚻 ⊙ 💨 ✲ ♿ [$] ⛩ WiFi

Services: 🔌 🧺 🍴 🔋 ⬇ 🛢 [T] **Within 3 miles:** H

Additional site information: 7 acre site. 🐕 Cars can be parked by caravans and tents. Awnings permitted. Under 18s must be accompanied by an adult. Foot golf, fresh produce available.

Glamping available: Wooden pods (cocoons and cabins).

Additional glamping information: Cars can be parked by pods.

MERSEYSIDE

SOUTHPORT — Map 15 SD31

Places to visit

RSPB Marshside, SOUTHPORT, PR9 9PJ, 01704 211690
www.rspb.org.uk/reserves-and-events/reserves-a-z/marshside

British Lawnmower Museum, SOUTHPORT, PR8 5AJ, 01704 501336
www.lawnmowerworld.com

Great for kids: Dunes Splash World, SOUTHPORT, PR8 1RX, 01704 537160
www.splashworldsouthport.com

Premier Park

Riverside Holiday Park

►►►►► 86% HOLIDAY CENTRE

tel: 01704 228886 **Southport New Road PR9 8DF**
email: reception@harrisonleisureuk.com **web:** www.riversideleisurecentre.co.uk
dir: *M6 junction 27, A5209 towards Parbold and Burscough, right onto A59. Left onto A565 at lights in Tarleton. Continue to dual carriageway. At roundabout straight across, site 1 mile on left.*

A family-friendly park north of Southport, with many indoor attractions, including a swimming pool, sauna, steam room and jacuzzi, plus a clubhouse. The generously sized pitches are located on neat landscaped grounds and served by a conveniently located modern amenity block. Free WiFi is provided in an attractive café.

Open: 14 February to January **Last arrival:** 17.00 **Last departure:** 11.00

Pitches: 🚐 🚌; 130 hardstanding pitches

Leisure: 🏊 🛝 ✋ 🎱 🎵 🎣

Facilities: 🚻 💨 ♿ [$] 🍖 WiFi

Services: 🔌 🧺 🍷 🍴 🍔

Within 3 miles: ⛳ U ≋

Additional site information: 80 acre site. 🐕 One car per pitch. Cash payments not accepted.

SOUTHPORT *continued*

Willowbank Holiday Home & Touring Park

►►►► 87%

tel: 01704 571566 **Coastal Road, Ainsdale PR8 3ST**
email: info@willowbankcp.co.uk **web:** www.willowbankcp.co.uk
dir: *From A565 between Formby and Ainsdale exit at Woodvale lights onto coast road, site 150 metres on left. From north: M6 junction 31, A59 towards Preston, A565, through Southport and Ainsdale, right at Woodvale lights.*

Set in woodland on a nature reserve next to sand dunes, this constantly improving park is a peaceful and relaxing holiday destination with mature trees, shrubs and colourful seasonal flowers surrounding neat pitches and modern amenity blocks.

Open: 14 February to 31 January **Last arrival:** 20.30 **Last departure:** noon

Pitches: 🚐 from £17.30; 🚌 from £17.30; 61 hardstanding pitches

Leisure: 🛝 ⚽

Facilities: 🛁 🪒 💨 ❄ ♿ 🧺 [WiFi]

Services: 🛠 🧺 🚰 🛍 🌿

Within 3 miles: ⛳ 🎣 🐴 ◎ 🌊 ⛵ 🎬 🛒

Additional site information: 8 acre site. 🐕 No dangerous dog breeds, maximum of 2 dogs, no cats. Cars can be parked by caravans. Awnings permitted. Cannot accommodate continental door entry units, no commercial vehicles, only one car parked by caravan. Cycling trail.

LEISURE: 🏊 Indoor swimming pool 🏊 Outdoor swimming pool 🛝 Children's playground ✋ Kids' club 🎾 Tennis court 🎱 Games room 📺 Separate TV room ⛳ golf course ⛳ Pitch n putt ⛵ Boats for hire 🚲 Bikes for hire 🎬 Cinema 🎵 Entertainment 🎣 Fishing ◎ Mini golf 🌊 Watersports 🏋 Gym ⚽ Sports field 🐴 Stables
FACILITIES: 🛁 Baths/Shower 🪒 Electric shaver sockets 💨 Hairdryer ❄ Ice Pack Facility 👶 Baby facilities ♿ Disabled facilities 🛒 Shop on site or within 200yds 🍖 BBQ area 🧺 Picnic area [WiFi] WiFi

Hurlston Hall Country Caravan Park
▶▶▶▶ 80%

tel: 01704 840400 & 842829 **Southport Road L40 8HB**
email: info@hurlstonhall.co.uk **web:** www.hurlstonhallcaravanpark.co.uk
dir: *On A570, 3 miles from Ormskirk towards Southport.*

A peaceful tree-lined touring park next to a static site in attractive countryside about 10 minutes' drive from Southport. The park is maturing well, with fairly large trees and a coarse fishing lake, and the excellent on-site facilities include golf, a bistro, a well-equipped health centre, a bowling green and model boat lake. Please note, neither tents nor dogs are accepted at this site.

Open: 1 March to 31 October **Last arrival:** 20.30 (last arrival 18.30 at weekends and bank holidays) **Last departure:** 17.00

Pitches: 🚐 🚐

Leisure: ≋ ⚓ ⚲ 🏌 Spa

Facilities: 🖾 ☺ ♿

Services: ⚡ 🔲 🍴 🍽 🔒

Within 3 miles: 💲

Additional site information: 5 acre site. ⊗ Cars can be parked by caravans. Awnings permitted. Internet access available.

PITCHES: 🚐 Caravans 🚐 Motorhomes 🛆 Tents 🏠 Glamping accommodation **SERVICES:** ⚡ Electric hook-up 🔲 Launderette 🍴 Licensed bar
🔒 Calor Gas ⊘ Campingaz 🛙 Toilet fluid 🍽 Café/Restaurant 🍟 Fast Food/Takeaway 🔋 Battery charging ⚡ Motorhome service point
* 2019 prices ⊗ No credit or debit cards 🐕 Dogs permitted ⊗ No dogs

Norfolk

Think of Norfolk, and the theme of water – in particular the Norfolk Broads, a complex network of mostly navigable rivers and man-made waterways – usually springs to mind. This delightfully unspoiled region attracts thousands of visitors every year, as does the North Norfolk Coast, designated an Area of Outstanding Natural Beauty and probably the finest of its kind in Europe.

'A long way from anywhere' and 'a remote corner of England that has been able to hold on to its traditions and ancient secrets,' are two of the apt descriptions that apply to this spacious corner of the country that still seems a separate entity, as if it is strangely detached from the rest of the country.

The coastline here represents a world of lonely beaches, vast salt marshes and extensive sand dunes stretching to the far horizon. It remains essentially unchanged, a stark reminder of how this area has long been vulnerable to attack and enemy invasion.

The highly successful thriller writer Jack Higgins chose this theme as the subject of his hugely popular adventure yarn *The Eagle has Landed*, published in 1975. The book, about a wartime Nazi plot to kidnap and assassinate Winston Churchill while he is spending the weekend at a country house near the sea in this part of East Anglia, vividly conveys the strange, unsettling atmosphere of the North Norfolk Coast.

Walking is the best way to gain a flavour of that atmosphere and visit the story's memorable setting. The 93-mile Peddars Way and North Norfolk Coast Path is one of Britain's most popular national trails. Made up of two paths strung together to form one continuous route, the trail begins near Thetford on the Suffolk/Norfolk border and follows ancient tracks and sections of Roman road before reaching the coast near Hunstanton. Cycling is another popular pastime in this region and in places you can combine it with a local train ride. One option, for example, is to cycle beside the Bure Valley Railway on a 9-mile trail running from Aylsham to Wroxham, returning to the start by train. There is also the North Norfolk Coast Cycleway between King's Lynn and Cromer, among other routes.

Norfolk prides itself on its wealth of historic houses, the most famous being Sandringham, where Her Majesty the Queen and her family spend Christmas. The Grade II listed house, which is surrounded by 20,000 acres, has been the private home of four generations of monarchs since 1862. 'Dear old Sandringham, the place I love better than anywhere in the world,' wrote King George V. The house and gardens are open to visitors. Among the other great houses in the region are Holkham Hall – the magnificent Palladian home of the Earls of Leicester – and the National Trust properties of Blickling Hall and Felbrigg Hall.

Many of Norfolk's towns have a particular charm and a strong sense of community. The quiet market towns of Fakenham and Swaffham are prime examples, and there is also Thetford, with its popular museum focusing on the iconic TV comedy series *Dad's Army*. Much of the filming for this cherished BBC production took place in the town and in nearby Thetford Forest. On the coast, you'll find a string of quaint villages and small towns. Wells-next-the-Sea is a popular destination for many visitors to Norfolk, as is Blakeney, renowned for its mudflats and medieval parish church, dedicated to the patron saint of seafarers, standing guard over the village and the estuary of the River Glaven. With its iconic pier, a key feature of coastal towns, Cromer is a classic example of a good old fashioned seaside resort where rather grand Victorian hotels look out to sea. Together with Sheringham, Cromer hosts a Crab and Lobster Festival in May.

NORFOLK

BARNEY | Map 13 TF93

Places to visit

Baconsthorpe Castle, BACONSTHORPE, NR25 9LN,
www.english-heritage.org.uk/daysout/properties/baconsthorpe-castle

Holkham Hall, HOLKHAM, NR23 1AB, 01328 710227
www.holkham.co.uk

Great for kids: Roarr! Dinosaur Adventure, LENWADE, NR9 5JW, 01603 876310
www.roarrdinosauradventure.co.uk

Premier Park

The Old Brick Kilns
►►►►► 93%

tel: 01328 878305 **Little Barney Lane NR21 0NL**
email: enquiries@old-brick-kilns.co.uk **web:** www.old-brick-kilns.co.uk
dir: From A148 (Fakenham to Cromer road) follow brown tourist signs to Barney, left into Little Barney Lane. Site at end of lane.

This award-winning, secluded and peaceful park is approached via a quiet, leafy country lane. The park is on two levels with its own boating and fishing pool and many mature trees. Excellent, well-planned toilet facilities can be found in three beautifully appointed blocks and there is a short dog walk around the site. In Barney's Restaurant & Bar, food and drink (including takeaways) are available on selected nights of the week (ask on check-in). The shop sells basic essentials including freshly baked bread and newspapers. Please note, due to a narrow access road, no arrivals are accepted until after 1.30pm. There are also four self-catering holiday cottages and B&B available.

Open: 15 March to 2 January (restricted service: Easter to September — bar food and takeaway available on selected nights only) **Last arrival:** 21.00 **Last departure:** 11.00
Pitches: ⊞ from £18; ⊠ from £18; ▲ from £16; 65 hardstanding pitches; 7 seasonal pitches
Leisure: ⚞ ⚲ ⚮ ✎ ⚲
Facilities: ⚞ ⊙ ⚲ ✳ ⚲ ⚲ ⚰ ⚲ ⚲ ⚲ **WiFi**
Services: ⚲ ⚲ ⚲ ⚲ ⚲ ⚲ ⚲ ⚲ ⚲ ⚲ ⚲ **T**

Additional site information: 12.73 acre site. ⚲ Cars can be parked by caravans and tents. Awnings permitted. No gazebos. Outdoor draughts, chess and family games. Freshly baked bread available.

BELTON | Map 13 TG40

Places to visit

Burgh Castle, BURGH CASTLE, NR31 9PZ, 0370 333 1181
www.english-heritage.org.uk/daysout/properties/burgh-castle

Premier Park

Rose Farm Touring & Camping Park
►►►►► 86%

tel: 01493 738292 **Stepshort NR31 9JS**
email: office@rosefarmtouringpark.com **web:** www.rosefarmtouringpark.com
dir: From A143 follow signs to Belton. In Belton, from mini roundabout on New Road into Stepshort, site on right.

A former railway line is the setting for this very peaceful, beautifully presented site which enjoys rural views. It is brightened with many flower and herb beds. The toilet facilities are smart, spotlessly clean, inviting to use and include family rooms. The customer care here is exceptional and wooden cabins are available for hire.

Open: All year **Last arrival:** 21.00 **Last departure:** 14.00
Pitches: ⊞ from £12; ⊠ from £12; ▲ from £12; ⚲ 26 hardstanding pitches; 60 seasonal pitches
Leisure: ⚲ ⚮
Facilities: ⚞ ⊙ ⚲ ✳ ⚲ **WiFi**
Services: ⚲ ⚲ ⚲ ⚲
Within 3 miles: ⚲ ⚲ ⚲ ⚲ ⚲ ⚲

Additional site information: 10 acre site. ⚲ No dog fouling, dogs must be on leads at all times. Cars can be parked by caravans and tents. Awnings permitted.

Glamping available: Cabins (summerhouses).

Additional glamping information: Summerhouses: cabin for daily, weekly, or seasonal hire (includes fridge, TV, microwave, wardrobe, bunk beds, sofa bed, toaster, kettle). Cars can be parked by cabins.

Wild Duck Holiday Park
►►►► 81% HOLIDAY CENTRE

tel: 01493 780268 **Howards Common NR31 9NE**
email: wildduck@haven.com **web:** www.haven.com/wildduck
dir: A47 to Great Yarmouth, 3rd exit at Asda roundabout, straight on at next 2 roundabouts. Left onto A143 signed Beccles. Right at lights, 2 miles to dual carriageway, right at roundabout signed Belton. Straight on at mini roundabout. Right at T-junction, left at next T-junction. Park 200 yards on right.

This a large holiday complex with plenty to do for all ages both indoors and out. It's a level grassy site with well laid-out facilities and set in a forest with small, cleared areas for tourers. Clubs for children and teenagers, sporting activities and evening shows all add to the fun of a stay here. There are 10 fully-equipped safari tents for hire, each with its own stone-built barbecue and facility block.

Open: 16 March to 5 November (restricted service: mid March to May and September to early November — some facilities may be reduced) **Last arrival:** 21.00
Last departure: 10.00
Pitches: ⊞ ⊠ ▲; ⚲ see prices below
Leisure: ⚲ ⚲ ⚲ ⚲ ⚲ ⚲

LEISURE: ⚲ Indoor swimming pool ⚲ Outdoor swimming pool ⚲ Children's playground ⚲ Kids' club ⚲ Tennis court ⚲ Games room ⚲ Separate TV room
⚲ golf course ⚲ Pitch n putt ⚲ Boats for hire ⚲ Bikes for hire ⚲ Cinema ⚲ Entertainment ⚲ Fishing ⚲ Mini golf ⚲ Watersports ⚲ Gym ⚲ Sports field ⚲ Stables
FACILITIES: ⚲ Baths/Shower ⊙ Electric shaver sockets ⚲ Hairdryer ✳ Ice Pack Facility ⚲ Baby facilities ⚲ Disabled facilities ⚲ Shop on site or within 200yds
⚲ BBQ area ⚲ Picnic area **WiFi** WiFi

Facilities: 🚿 ⊙ 💨 ❄ ♿ [$] 🪑 [WiFi]

Services: 🔌 🧺 🍷 🍴 🍔 🛢

Within 3 miles: ⛳ 🎣 U ◎ ⛵

Additional site information: 97 acre site. 🐕 Maximum 2 dogs per booking, certain dog breeds banned. No commercial vehicles, no bookings by persons under 21 years unless a family booking.

Glamping available: Safari tents from £119. **Changeover days:** Mondays, Fridays

Additional glamping information: Safari tents: minimum stay 3 nights.

BURNHAM DEEPDALE — Map 13 TF84

Places to visit

Brancaster Estate (NT), BRANCASTER STAITHE, PE31 8BW, 01263 740241 www.nationaltrust.org.uk/brancaster-estate

RSPB Nature Reserve Titchwell Marsh, TITCHWELL, PE31 8BB, 01485 210779 www.rspb.org.uk/reserves-and-events/reserves-a-z/titchwell-marsh

Great for kids: Wells & Walsingham Light Railway, WELLS-NEXT-THE-SEA, NR23 1QB, 01328 711630, www.wellswalsinghamrailway.co.uk

Deepdale Backpackers & Camping

►►►► 88%

tel: 01485 210256 **Deepdale Farm PE31 8DD**
email: stay@deepdalebackpackers.co.uk **web:** www.deepdalebackpackers.co.uk
dir: *On south side of A149 (coast road), opposite church, between Hunstanton and Wells-next-the-Sea.*

Within the heart of this notable tourist destination, near craft and food shops, a petrol station and visitor centre, which are all part of the Deepdale Estate, this park is a must for lovers of peace and tranquillity. The touring areas, spread over four distinctive fields, all offer generous pitch sizes, and most are equipped with electric hook-ups. There are also five fully serviced pitches capable of accommodating RVs. Three separate amenity blocks provide superb decor, fixtures and fittings and have excellent privacy options. The site is located a short stroll from the coastal path.

Open: All year **Last arrival:** 21.00 **Last departure:** 11.00

Pitches: 🚐 from £8; ⛺ from £8; 7 hardstanding pitches

Leisure: 🎰 ♫

Facilities: 🚿 ⊙ 💨 ❄ ♿ [$] [WiFi]

Services: 🔌 🧺 🍴 🍔 🔋 ⤓ 🛢 🍃 [T]

Within 3 miles: ⛳ 🎣 🏄 ⛵

Additional site information: 8 acre site. 🐕 Cars can be parked by tents. Awnings permitted. Quiet policy after 22.00. Visitor information centre.

CAISTER-ON-SEA — Map 13 TG51

Places to visit

Caister Roman Fort, CAISTER-ON-SEA, NR30 5RN, 0370 333 1181 www.english-heritage.org.uk/daysout/properties/caister-roman-fort

Thrigby Hall Wildlife Gardens, FILBY, NR29 3DR, 01493 369477 www.thrigbyhall.co.uk

Premier Park

Caister-on-Sea Holiday Park

►►►►► 88% HOLIDAY CENTRE

tel: 01493 728931 **Ormesby Road NR30 5NH**
email: caister@haven.com **web:** www.haven.com/caister
dir: *A1064 signed Caister-on-Sea. At roundabout 2nd exit onto A149, at next roundabout 1st exit onto Caister bypass, at 3rd roundabout 3rd exit to Caister-on-Sea. Park on left.*

An all-action holiday park located beside the beach north of the resort of Great Yarmouth, yet close to the attractions of the Norfolk Broads. The touring area offers 46 fully serviced pitches and a modern, well-appointed, purpose-built toilet block. Customer care is of an extremely high standard with a full time, experienced and caring warden. Please note, this park does not accept tents.

Open: mid March to end October **Last arrival:** anytime **Last departure:** 10.00

Pitches: 🚐 🚌; 49 seasonal pitches

Leisure: 🌊 ✋ 🎰 ♫

Facilities: 🚿 ⊙ 💨 ♿ [$] 🪑 👶 [WiFi]

Services: 🔌 🧺 🍷 🍴 🍔 ⤓ 🛢

Within 3 miles: ⛳ 🎣 Ⓜ ⛵ ☰

Additional site information: 138 acre site. 🐕 Maximum 2 dogs per booking, certain dog breeds not accepted. No tents, no commercial vehicles, no bookings by persons under 21 years unless a family booking.

CLIPPESBY
Map 13 TG41

Places to visit

Fairhaven Woodland & Water Garden, SOUTH WALSHAM, NR13 6DZ, 01603 270449, www.fairhavengarden.co.uk

Caister Roman Fort, CAISTER-ON-SEA, NR30 5RN, 0370 333 1181 www.english-heritage.org.uk/daysout/properties/caister-roman-fort

Premier Park

Clippesby Hall
▶▶▶▶▶ 93%

tel: 01493 367800 **Hall Lane NR29 3BL**
email: holidays@clippesby.com **web:** www.clippesbyhall.com
dir: *From A47 follow tourist signs for The Broads. At Acle roundabout take A1064, in 2 miles left onto B1152, 0.5 mile left opposite village sign, site 400 yards on right.*

A lovely country house estate with secluded pitches hidden among the trees or in sheltered sunny glades. The toilet facilities, appointed to a very good standard, provide a wide choice of cubicles. Amenities include a coffee shop with both WiFi and wired internet access, a family bar and restaurant and family golf. Excellent hardstanding pitches are available as the park is open all year. There are pine lodges and cottages for holiday lets.

Open: All year (restricted service: November to March – coffee shop, bar and restaurant closed) **Last arrival:** 17.30 **Last departure:** 11.00

Pitches: 🚐 🚍 🛆; 41 hardstanding pitches

Leisure: 🏊 🅰 🎠 🔎 🏏 🎵 🎡 ⚽

Facilities: 🛁 ⊙ 🗜 ✳ ⚿ ⑤ 🎴 🚙 WiFi

Services: 🔌 🗑 🍴 🍲 🛒 🧺 ⏏ 🔒 🌿 🆃

Within 3 miles: 🎣 🏌 U ◎ 🚤 ✈

Additional site information: 30 acre site. 🐕 Cars can be parked by caravans and tents. Awnings permitted. No groups, no noise after 23.00, no camp fires. Table tennis, cycle trail.

CROMER
Map 13 TG24

Places to visit

RNLI Henry Blogg Museum, CROMER, NR27 9ET, 01263 511294 www.rnli.org/henryblogg

Felbrigg Hall, FELBRIGG, NR11 8PR, 01263 837444 www.nationaltrust.org.uk/felbrigg-hall

Forest Park
▶▶▶▶ 83%

tel: 01263 513290 **Northrepps Road NR27 0JR**
email: info@forest-park.co.uk **web:** www.forest-park.co.uk
dir: *A140 from Norwich, left at T-junction signed Cromer, right signed Northrepps, right then immediately left, left at T-junction, site on right.*

Surrounded by forest, this gently sloping park offers a wide choice of pitches. Visitors have the use of a heated indoor swimming pool, a stylish café and a large clubhouse which provides entertainment.

Open: 15 March to 15 January **Last arrival:** 21.00 **Last departure:** 11.00

Pitches: 🚐 from £17.50; 🚍 from £17.50; 🛆 from £17.50; 🏠 see prices below; 5 hardstanding pitches

Leisure: 🏊 🅰 🎵

Facilities: 🛁 ⊙ 🗜 ✳ ⚿ ⑤ 🎴 WiFi

Services: 🔌 🗑 🍴 🍲 🛒 🧺 ⏏ 🔒 🌿 🆃

Within 3 miles: 🎣 🏌 ◎ 🚤 ✈ 🎿

Additional site information: 100 acre site. 🐕 Cars can be parked by caravans and tents. Awnings permitted. Freshly baked bread and croissants available. Woodland walk.

Glamping available: Wooden wigwams from £85. **Changeover days:** Any day

Additional glamping information: Wooden wigwams: very short walk to dedicated car park.

Manor Farm Caravan & Camping Site
▶▶▶▶ 83%

tel: 01263 512858 **East Runton NR27 9PR**
email: stay@manorfarmcampsite.co.uk **web:** www.manorfarmcaravansite.co.uk
dir: *1 mile west of Cromer, exit A148 or A149 (recommended towing route) at Manor Farm sign.*

A well-established, family-run site on a working farm enjoying panoramic sea views. There are good modern facilities across the site, including three smart toilet blocks with two quality family rooms and privacy cubicles, two good play areas and a large expanse of grass for games – the park is very popular with families. Care must be taken on approaching the site, which is along a 0.5 mile long farm track; if required, please ask for directions from reception.

Open: Easter to September **Last arrival:** 20.30 **Last departure:** noon

Pitches: 🚐 from £15.50; 🚍 from £15.50; 🛆 from £15.50

LEISURE: 🏊 Indoor swimming pool 🏊 Outdoor swimming pool 🅰 Children's playground 🙌 Kids' club 🎾 Tennis court 🎱 Games room ▭ Separate TV room 🏌 golf course 🛝 Pitch n putt ⛵ Boats for hire 🚲 Bikes for hire 🎬 Cinema 🎵 Entertainment 🎣 Fishing ◎ Mini golf 🚤 Watersports 🏋 Gym ⚽ Sports field U Stables
FACILITIES: 🛁 Baths/Shower ⊙ Electric shaver sockets 🗜 Hairdryer ✳ Ice Pack Facility 🚙 Baby facilities ⚿ Disabled facilities ⑤ Shop on site or within 200yds 🎴 BBQ area 🅿 Picnic area WiFi WiFi

Leisure: 🛝 🎰 ⚽

Facilities: 📺 ⊙ ❄ ♿

Services: 🔌 🧺 🔋 🔥 🍃

Within 3 miles: ⛳ 🎣 🎯 🏊 🏛 $

Additional site information: 17 acre site. 🐕 Cars can be parked by caravans and tents. Awnings permitted. No groups, no noise after 23.00. 1 dog-free field available.

DOWNHAM MARKET — Map 12 TF60

Places to visit

WWT Welney Wetland Centre, WELNEY, PE14 9TN, 01353 860711 www.wwt.org.uk/welney

Oxburgh Hall, OXBOROUGH, PE33 9PS, www.nationaltrust.org.uk/oxburgh-hall

Lakeside Caravan Park & Fisheries

►►►► 83%

tel: 01366 383491 & 387074 **Sluice Rd, Denver PE38 0DZ**
email: bookings@westhallfarmholidays.co.uk **web:** www.westhallfarmholidays.co.uk
dir: *Exit A10 towards Denver, follow signs to Denver Windmill, site on right.*

A peaceful, continually improving park set around five pretty fishing lakes. There are several grassy touring areas which are sheltered by mature hedging and trees, a function room for social get-togethers, a shop, laundry and children's play area. Electric hook-up pitches are available and rallies are welcome.

Open: All year (restricted service: October to March) **Last arrival:** 21.00 **Last departure:** 10.30

Pitches: 🚐 🚌 ⛺

Leisure: 🛝 🎣

Facilities: 📺 ⊙ 🚿 ❄ ♿ $ 🧺 [WiFi]

Services: 🔌 🧺 🔋 🔥 🍃 [T]

Within 3 miles: ⛳ 🏊 🚤

Additional site information: 30 acre site. 🐕 Cars can be parked by caravans and tents. Awnings permitted. No noise after 23.00. Fishing tackle and bait, caravan accessories, caravan storage. Newspapers, bread and milk available.

FAKENHAM — Map 13 TF92

Places to visit

Houghton Hall & Gardens, HOUGHTON, PE31 6UE, 01485 528569 www.houghtonhall.com

Great for kids: Pensthorpe Natural Park, FAKENHAM, NR21 0LN, 01328 851465 www.pensthorpe.co.uk

Caravan Club M.V.C. Site

►►► 83%

tel: 01328 862388 **Fakenham Racecourse NR21 7NY**
email: caravan@fakenhamracecourse.co.uk **web:** www.fakenhamracecourse.co.uk
dir: *From B1146, south of Fakenham follow brown Racecourse signs (with tent and caravan symbols), leads to site entrance.*

A very well laid-out site set around the racecourse, with a grandstand offering smart, modern toilet facilities. Tourers move to the centre of the course on race days, and enjoy free racing, and there's a wide range of sporting activities in the club house.

Open: All year **Last arrival:** 21.00 **Last departure:** noon

Pitches: 🚐 🚌 ⛺; 25 hardstanding pitches; 22 seasonal pitches

Leisure: 🎾 ⛳

Facilities: 📺 ⊙ 🚿 ❄ ♿ $ 🍖 [WiFi]

Services: 🔌 🧺 🍷 🍽 ⛽ 🔥 🍃 [T]

Within 3 miles: 🎣 🏛

Additional site information: 11.4 acre site. 🐕 Maximum 2 dogs per pitch. Cars can be parked by caravans and tents. Awnings permitted. TV aerial hook-ups.

GREAT YARMOUTH

Map 13 TG50

Places to visit

Time and Tide Museum of Great Yarmouth Life, GREAT YARMOUTH, NR30 3BX, 01493 743930, www.museums.norfolk.gov.uk

Great for kids: Sea Life Great Yarmouth, GREAT YARMOUTH, NR30 3AH, 01493 330631, www.pensthorpe.co.uk

Premier Park

Seashore Holiday Park
►►►►► 87% HOLIDAY HOME PARK

tel: 01493 851131 **North Denes NR30 4HG**
email: seashore@haven.com **web:** www.haven.com/seashore
dir: *A149 from Great Yarmouth to Caister. Right at 2nd lights signed seafront and racecourse. Continue to sea, turn left. Park on left.*

Bordered by sand dunes and with direct access to a sandy beach, Seashore Holiday Park is located in Great Yarmouth, yet it is easy to take day trips to the peaceful Norfolk Broads. Facilities include excellent water activities and bike hire for children and lively evening entertainment for adults. There is a good range of holiday homes for hire to suit both couples and families.

Open: mid March to October

Holiday Homes: Sleep 8 Bedrooms 3 Bathrooms 1 Toilets 1 Two-ring burner Microwave Freezer TV Sky/Freeview WiFi

Leisure: 🏊 🅰 👋 🎾 🎵 ⚽

Within 3 miles: ◎ 🎱

Additional site information: 🐕 Most dog breeds accepted (please check when booking). Dogs must be kept on leads at all times. The facilities provided in the holiday homes may differ depending on the grade.

The Grange Touring Park
►►►► 82%

tel: 01493 730306 & 730023 **Yarmouth Road, Ormesby St Margaret NR29 3QG**
email: info@grangetouring.co.uk **web:** www.grangetouring.co.uk
dir: *From A149, 3 miles north of Great Yarmouth. Site at junction of A149 and B1159, signed.*

A mature, ever improving park with a stunning display of shrubs and trees, located just one mile from the sea and within easy reach of both coastal attractions and the Norfolk Broads. The level pitches have WiFi and electric hook-ups and include hardstanding pitches. There are clean, modern toilets including three spacious family rooms, and an electric car charging point.

Open: Easter to October **Last arrival:** 21.00 **Last departure:** 14.00

Pitches: 🚐 from £10; 🚏 from £10; ⛺ from £7; 7 hardstanding pitches; 2 seasonal pitches

Leisure: 🅰 **Facilities:** 🛁 ☺ 🚿 ✳ ♿ WiFi

Services: 🔌 🗑 🍽 ⚌ 🛒 🛍 ⊘

Within 3 miles: 🎣 🏌 ∪ ◎ 🛍

Additional site information: 3.5 acre site. 🐕 Cars can be parked by caravans and tents. Awnings permitted. No football, no open fires. Table tennis, bar/restaurant adjoining.

HOPTON ON SEA

Map 13 TM59

Places to visit

St Olave's Priory, ST OLAVES, NR31 9HE, 0370 333 1181
www.english-heritage.org.uk/daysout/properties/st-olaves-priory

Premier Park

Hopton Holiday Village
►►►►► 94% HOLIDAY HOME PARK

tel: 01502 730214 **NR31 9BW**
email: hopton@haven.com **web:** www.haven.com/hopton
dir: *Site signed from A47 between Great Yarmouth and Lowestoft.*

Located between Lowestoft and Great Yarmouth, close to beaches and the town attractions, this lively holiday park offers excellent sport activities, including a 9-hole golf course and tennis coaching, plus popular evening entertainment in the form of shows, music and dancing. There is a nature walk and a wide range of quality holiday homes is available for rental.

Open: mid March to 30 October

Holiday Homes: Sleep 8 Bedrooms 2 Bathrooms 1 Toilets 1 Microwave Freezer TV Sky/Freeview

Prices: Low season from £79

Changeover days: Monday, Friday, Saturday

Leisure: 🏊 🏊 🅰 👋 🎾 🎵

Facilities: 🛍 📺 WiFi

Within 3 miles: 🛍

Additional site information: 🐕 Most dog breeds accepted (please check when booking). Dogs must be kept on leads at all times. The facilities provided in the holiday homes may differ depending on the grade.

HUNSTANTON

Places to visit

Lynn Museum, KING'S LYNN, PE30 1NL, 01553 775001
www.museums.norfolk.gov.uk

Norfolk Lavender, HEACHAM, PE31 7JE, 01485 570384
www.norfolk-lavender.co.uk

Great for kids: Hunstanton Sea Life Sanctuary, HUNSTANTON, PE36 5BH, 01485 533576, www.visitsealife.com/hunstanton

---

LEISURE: 🏊 Indoor swimming pool 🏊 Outdoor swimming pool 🅰 Children's playground 👋 Kids' club 🎾 Tennis court 🎱 Games room ▭ Separate TV room 🏌 golf course 🚩 Pitch n putt ⛵ Boats for hire 🚲 Bikes for hire ▤ Cinema 🎵 Entertainment 🎣 Fishing ◎ Mini golf 🏄 Watersports ⛳ Gym 🏉 Sports field ∪ Stables
FACILITIES: 🛁 Baths/Shower ☺ Electric shaver sockets 🚿 Hairdryer ✳ Ice Pack Facility 🍼 Baby facilities ♿ Disabled facilities 🛍 Shop on site or within 200yds 🍖 BBQ area 🌲 Picnic area WiFi WiFi

HUNSTANTON
Map 12 TF64

AA HOLIDAY CENTRE OF THE YEAR 2019

Premier Park

Searles Leisure Resort

▶▶▶▶▶ 92% HOLIDAY CENTRE

tel: 01485 534211 **South Beach Road PE36 5BB**
email: bookings@searles.co.uk **web:** www.searles.co.uk
dir: *A149 from King's Lynn to Hunstanton. At roundabout follow signs for South Beach. Straight on at 2nd roundabout. Site on left.*

A large seaside holiday complex with well managed facilities, adjacent to sea and beach. The tourers have their own areas, including two excellent toilet blocks, and pitches are individually marked by small maturing shrubs for privacy. A wide range of food options is available from takeaway choices to more formal dining and wide ranging indoor and outdoor activities include a full entertainment programme for all ages.

Open: All year (restricted service: December to March (except February half term) – limited facilities. Outdoor pool open May to September only)
Pitches: ⛟ from £14; ⛺ from £14; ▲ from £17; ⋒ see prices below; 91 hardstanding pitches
Leisure: 🎱 ⛵ ⌂ ⬆ ⬇ 🎯 ⚐ ♨ 🎵 ✎ 🎾 ✪
Facilities: 🖥 ✳ ⛐ ⑤ 🍴 ⋒ **WiFi**
Services: 🔌 🔄 🍺 🍽 🍔 🔋 ⬆ 🛢 ⌀ ⊤
Within 3 miles: ∪ ◎ ⬆

Additional site information: 50 acre site. 🐕 Restrictions on certain dog breeds (contact site for details).
Glamping available: Wooden pods from £24.

KING'S LYNN
Map 12 TF62

See also Stanhoe

Places to visit
Bircham Windmill, GREAT BIRCHAM, PE31 6SJ, 01485 578393
www.birchamwindmill.co.uk

Castle Rising Castle, CASTLE RISING, PE31 6AH, 01553 631330
www.english-heritage.org.uk/daysout/properties/castle-rising-castle

Premier Park

King's Lynn Caravan and Camping Park

▶▶▶▶▶ 85%

tel: 01553 840004 **New Road, North Runcton PE33 0RA**
email: klcc@btconnect.com **web:** www.kl-cc.co.uk
dir: *From King's Lynn take A47 signed Swaffham and Norwich, in 1.5 miles turn right signed North Runcton. Site 100 yards on left.*

Set in approximately 10 acres of parkland, this developing camping park is situated on the edge of North Runcton, just a few miles south of the historic town of King's Lynn. The three very extensive touring fields are equipped with

150 electric hook-ups and one field is reserved for rallies. There is an eco-friendly toilet block which is powered by solar panels and an air-sourced heat pump which also recycles rainwater – this in itself proves a source of great interest to visitors. There are eight high quality camping pods and 14 superb pine lodges for hire.

Open: All year **Last arrival:** flexible **Last departure:** flexible
Pitches: ⛟ ⛺ ▲ ⋒; 2 hardstanding pitches; 54 seasonal pitches
Leisure: ⌂ ▢
Facilities: 🖥 ☺ ⛐ ✳ ⅙ ⑤ **WiFi**
Services: 🔌 🔄 🍺 ⬆ 🛢 ⌀ ⊤
Within 3 miles: ⬇ ✐ ∪ ⬆

Additional site information: 9 acre site. 🐕 Cars can be parked by caravans and tents. Awnings permitted. No skateboards or fires.
Glamping available: Wooden pods.
Additional glamping information: No smoking in wooden pods; no dogs in wooden pods.

NORTH WALSHAM
Map 13 TG23

Places to visit
Blickling Estate, BLICKLING, NR11 6NF, 01263 738030
www.nationaltrust.org.uk/blickling

Mannington Gardens, SAXTHORPE, NR11 7BB, 01263 584175
www.manningtongardens.co.uk

Premier Park

Two Mills Touring Park
▶▶▶▶▶ 88%

tel: 01692 405829 **Yarmouth Road NR28 9NA**
email: enquiries@twomills.co.uk **web:** www.twomills.co.uk
dir: *In North Walsham at lights on A149 follow Norwich sign into Norwich Road. At mini roundabout, right into Grammar School Road. At mini roundabout (Lidl supermarket opposite) right into Yarmouth Road. Site on left in approximately 1 mile (after police station and hospital).*

An intimate, beautifully presented park set in superb countryside in a peaceful, rural spot, which is also convenient for touring. The 'Top Acre' section is maturing and features fully serviced pitches with panoramic views over the site, an immaculate toilet block and good planting, plus the layout of pitches and facilities is excellent. A cabin-style building houses a fully-equipped disabled room. The very friendly owners keep the park in immaculate condition. Please note, this park is for adults only.

Open: March to 3 January **Last arrival:** 18.00 **Last departure:** noon
Pitches: ⛟ from £21; ⛺ from £21; ▲ from £21; 81 hardstanding pitches; 30 seasonal pitches
Facilities: 🖥 ☺ ⛐ ✳ ⅙ ⑤ ⨆ **WiFi**
Services: 🔌 🔄 🍺 ⬆ 🛢 ⌀ ⊤
Within 3 miles: ✐

Additional site information: 7 acre site. Adults only. 🐕 Maximum 2 dogs per pitch. Cars can be parked by caravans and tents. Awnings permitted. Library, DVDs, tea and coffee facilities.

PITCHES: ⛟ Caravans ⛺ Motorhomes ▲ Tents ⋒ Glamping accommodation **SERVICES:** 🔌 Electric hook-up 🔄 Launderette 🍺 Licensed bar 🔋 Calor Gas ⌀ Campingaz ⊤ Toilet fluid 🍴 Café/Restaurant 🍔 Fast Food/Takeaway 🔋 Battery charging ⬆ Motorhome service point
* 2019 prices ⊘ No credit or debit cards 🐕 Dogs permitted ⊗ No dogs

SCRATBY Map 13 TG51

Places to visit

Time and Tide Museum of Great Yarmouth Life, GREAT YARMOUTH, NR30 3BX, 01493 743930, www.museums.norfolk.gov.uk

Great for kids: Caister Roman Fort, CAISTER-ON-SEA, NR30 5RN, 0370 333 1181
www.english-heritage.org.uk/daysout/properties/caister-roman-fort

Scratby Hall Caravan Park

►►►► 84%

tel: 01493 730283 **NR29 3SR**
email: scratbyhall@aol.com **web:** www.scratbyhall.co.uk
dir: *5 miles north of Great Yarmouth. Exit A149 onto B1159, site signed.*

A beautifully maintained park situated on former gardens and farmland with high wall or hedge surroundings to improve privacy and wind resistance. The well-spaced lush grass pitches include many with full services, and the amenity block includes unisex shower toilet and washbasin rooms. The park also benefits from a well-stocked shop, popular children's play area and outdoor swimming pool.

Open: Easter to end September (restricted service: Easter to 3rd week July and September – pool closed; shop hours reduced outside peak season) **Last arrival:** 21.00 **Last departure:** noon

Pitches: 🚐 from £11; 🚌 from £11; ⛺ from £11

Leisure: 🏊 🛝

Facilities: 🛁 🔌 💨 ❄ ♿ [$] [WiFi]

Services: ⚡ 🫧 🛏 🔒 ♻ [T]

Within 3 miles: ⛳ 🎣 🐴 ⛵

Additional site information: 5 acre site. 🐕 Cars can be parked by caravans and tents. Awnings permitted. No commercial vehicles, no noise after 23.00. Food preparation room, family/privacy bathroom.

STANHOE Map 13 TF83

Places to visit

Norfolk Lavender, HEACHAM, PE31 7JE, 01485 570384
www.norfolk-lavender.co.uk

Walsingham Abbey Grounds & Shirehall Museum, LITTLE WALSINGHAM, NR22 6BP, 01328 820510
www.walsinghamabbey.com

The Rickels Caravan & Camping Park

►►► 85%

tel: 01485 518671 **Bircham Road PE31 8PU**
email: therickelscaravanandcampingpark@hotmail.co.uk
dir: *Take A149 (south of King's Lynn) signed Cromer (and A148). Right at roundabout onto A148 signed Fakenham and Cromer. Left on B1153 signed Flitcham and Great Bircham. In Great Bircham right onto B115 signed Stanhoe. At crossroads (junction with B1454) straight across (Stanhoe). Site on left.*

Set in three acres of grassland, with sweeping country views and a pleasant, relaxing atmosphere fostered by being a site for adults only. The meticulously maintained grounds and facilities are part of the attraction, and the slightly sloping land has some level areas and sheltering for tents. A field is available to hire for rallies.

Open: All year **Last arrival:** 21.00 **Last departure:** 11.00

Pitches: 🚐 from £12; 🚌 from £12; ⛺ from £12

Leisure: 📺

Facilities: 🛁 🔌 ❄ [WiFi]

Services: ⚡ 🫧 🛏 🔒 ♻

Within 3 miles: 🎣 [$]

Additional site information: 3 acre site. Adults only. 🐕 ⊘ Cars can be parked by caravans and tents. Awnings permitted. No groundsheets.

SWAFFHAM
Map 13 TF80

Places to visit

Gressenhall Farm and Workhouse, GRESSENHALL, NR20 4DR, 01362 869263
www.museums.norfolk.gov.uk/Gressenhall

Castle Acre Priory, CASTLE ACRE, PE32 2XD, 01760 755394
www.english-heritage.org.uk/daysout/properties/castle-acre-castle-acre-priory

---

Breckland Meadows Touring Park
►►►► 82%

tel: 01760 721246 **Lynn Road PE37 7PT**
email: info@brecklandmeadows.co.uk **web:** www.brecklandmeadows.co.uk
dir: *In Swaffham from A1065 northbound at lights turn into Lynn Street (pass Asda on left, petrol station on right). Site on right in approximately 1 mile. Or from A47 eastbound: follow Swaffham sign. Site on left in 0.75 mile after Swaffham village sign. Or from A47 westbound: at roundabout (east of Swaffham) left signed Norwich Road. Straight on at lights in Swaffham centre into Lynn Street (pass Asda on left, petrol station on right). Site on right in approximately 1 mile.*

An immaculate, well-landscaped little park on the edge of Swaffham. The toilet block is a very impressive facility, replete with quality fixtures and fittings, spacious cubicles, including a family and disabled room, a large, well-equipped laundry, and a high tech, and very efficient, hot water system. Planned planting creates optimum privacy and the hardstandings are particularly spacious. Leading directly from the site is Swaefas Way, a pleasant walk with, or without, a dog.

Open: All year **Last arrival:** 19.00 **Last departure:** noon
Pitches: 🚐 from £15.50; 🚌 from £15.50; ▲ from £8; 35 hardstanding pitches; 5 seasonal pitches
Facilities: 🏠 ⊙ ✳ ⚐ 🖲 🚻 🎍 WiFi
Services: 🔌 🗄 🛒 🛢 🚿 🗑
Within 3 miles: ⚓ ⚲

Additional site information: 3 acre site. Adults only. 🐕 Dogs must be on leads at all times and exercised off site. Cars can be parked by caravans and tents. Awnings permitted. Newspaper deliveries.

SYDERSTONE
Map 13 TF83

Places to visit

Creake Abbey, NORTH CREAKE, NR21 9LF, 0370 333 1181
www.english-heritage.org.uk/daysout/properties/creake-abbey

The Garden Caravan Site
►►► 80%

tel: 07788 438968 **Barmer Hall Farm PE31 8SR**
email: nlmason@tiscali.co.uk **web:** www.gardencaravansite.co.uk
dir: *Signed from B1454 at Barmer between A148 and Docking, 1 mile north of Syderstone.*

In the tranquil setting of a former walled garden beside a large farmhouse, with mature trees and shrubs, this is a secluded site surrounded by woodland. The site is run mainly on trust, with a daily notice indicating which pitches are available, and an honesty box for basic foods. An ideal site for the discerning camper, and well placed for touring north Norfolk.

Open: March to November **Last arrival:** 21.00 **Last departure:** noon
Pitches: * 🚐 from £21; 🚌 from £21; ▲ from £21
Facilities: 🏠 ⊙ ⚐ ✳ ⚐ 🎍
Services: 🔌 🛒 🚿 🛢
Within 3 miles: ⚓ ⊙ 🗓 💲

Additional site information: 3.5 acre site. 🐕 Maximum 2 dogs per pitch. 🚫 Cars can be parked by caravans and tents. Awnings permitted. Maximum tent width 5 metres. Cold drinks, ice creams and eggs available.

WORTWELL
Map 13 TM28

Places to visit

Bressingham Steam & Gardens, BRESSINGHAM, IP22 2AA, 01379 686900
www.bressingham.co.uk

Little Lakeland Caravan Park
►►►► 88%

tel: 01986 788646 **IP20 0EL**
email: info@littlelakeland.co.uk **web:** www.littlelakelandcaravanparkandcamping.co.uk
dir: *From west: exit A143 at sign for Wortwell. In village turn right 300 yards after garage. From east: from A143 left onto B1062, then right. After 800 yards turn left.*

A well-kept and pretty site built round a fishing lake, and accessed by a lake-lined drive. The 25 individual pitches are sited in hedged enclosures for complete privacy, and the purpose-built toilet facilities are excellent.

Open: All year **Last arrival:** 20.00 **Last departure:** 11.30
Pitches: 🚐 🚌 ▲; 6 hardstanding pitches; 17 seasonal pitches
Leisure: 🎣 ⚲
Facilities: 🏠 ⊙ ⚐ ✳ ⚐ 🖲 WiFi
Services: 🔌 🗄 🛒 🛢 🚿 🗑
Within 3 miles: ⚓ 🚲

Additional site information: 4.5 acre site. 🐕 Cars can be parked by caravans and tents. Awnings permitted. No noise after 22.30. Library.

NORTHAMPTONSHIRE

BULWICK   Map 11 SP99

Places to visit

Kirby Hall, DEENE, NN17 3EN, 01536 203230
www.english-heritage.org.uk/daysout/properties/kirby-hall

Deene Park, DEENE, NN17 3EW, 01780 450361
www.deenepark.com

Premier Park

New Lodge Farm Caravan & Camping Site
▶▶▶▶▶ 86%

tel: 01780 450493 **New Lodge Farm NN17 3DU**
email: shop@newlodgefarm.com **web:** www.newlodgefarm.com
dir: *On A43 between Corby (5 miles) and Stamford (8 miles) turn right at Laxton and Harringworth junction. Site signed.*

Simon and Sarah Singlehurst have worked hard to create this beautiful adults-only site on their working farm in rural Northamptonshire. The result is impressive – large, fully serviced and level pitches (26 with hardstandings), all with views over the farm and rolling countryside. The heated toilet and amenity block is located in a beautifully restored stone barn, as is the site reception. There's an award-winning farm shop that sells home-reared meats, bread, cakes and locally grown fruit and vegetables. Attached to the shop is a cosy licensed café with a patio area overlooking the site – here breakfasts, lunches and afternoon teas are served. Nobbies Nook is a landscaped riverside chill-out area. The site is situated in the heart of Rockingham Forest, making this a good base for visiting Stamford, Oundle and Uppingham.

Open: 21 March to 27 October **Last arrival:** 20.00 **Last departure:** noon

Pitches: 🚐 🚍 ▲; 26 hardstanding pitches; 10 seasonal pitches

Facilities: 🏠 ⊙ 🌀 ✳ ⚐ Ⓢ 🎁 WiFi

Services: 🔌 🔄 🍴 🔣 🌐 🛒 🛁 💧 🔥 ⊘ Ⓣ

Within 3 miles: 🚶 🎣 ∪

Additional site information: 4 acre site. Adults only. 🐾 Cars can be parked by caravans and tents. Awnings permitted. No noise after 23.00. Farm shop and butchery. Car hire can be arranged.

NORTHUMBERLAND

BAMBURGH

Places to visit

Chillingham Wild Cattle Park, CHILLINGHAM, NE66 5NP, 01668 215250
www.chillinghamwildcattle.com

Bamburgh Castle, BAMBURGH, NE69 7DF, 01668 214515
www.bamburghcastle.com

Great for kids: Alnwick Castle, ALNWICK, NE66 1NG, 01665 511100
www.alnwickcastle.com

BAMBURGH   Map 21 NU13

Waren Caravan & Camping Park
▶▶▶▶ 90%

tel: 01668 214366 & 214224 **Waren Mill NE70 7EE**
email: waren@meadowhead.co.uk **web:** www.meadowhead.co.uk
dir: *2 miles east of town. From A1 onto B1342 signed Bamburgh. Take unclassified road past Waren Mill, signed Budle.*

An especially attractive, family- and dog-friendly park sheltered within the grassy embankments of a former quarry and with truly stunning sea views over the beautiful Burdle Bay. As well as a footpath leading to the sandy beach there are excellent walking and cycling opportunities in the surrounding area. The park offers excellent facilities – fully serviced pitches, an on-site restaurant serving a good breakfast and smart toilet and shower blocks, which include several family bathrooms. There are also wooden wigwams for hire.

Open: March to October (restricted service: March to Spring bank holiday and October – splash pool closed) **Last arrival:** 20.00 **Last departure:** noon

Pitches: 🚐 from £10; 🚍 from £10; ▲ from £10; 🏠 see prices below; 41 hardstanding pitches

Leisure: 🏊 🎠 🎧 ♣ ⚽

Facilities: 🏠 ⊙ 🌀 ✳ ⚐ Ⓢ 🎁 🍴 🛒 WiFi

Services: 🔌 🔄 🍴 🔣 🌐 🛒 🛁 💧 🔥 ⊘ Ⓣ

Within 3 miles: 🚶 🎣 ∪ ◎ 🏄

Additional site information: 4 acre site. 🐾 Cars can be parked by caravans and tents. Awnings permitted. No noise after 23.00. 100 acres of private heathland. Fire pits for hire, BBQ hut for hire, freshly baked bread available. Car hire can be arranged.

Glamping available: Wooden wigwams from £15.50. **Changeover days:** Any day

Additional glamping information: Wooden wigwams sleep 5. Cars can be parked by wigwams.

Glororum Caravan Park
▶▶▶▶ 88%

tel: 01670 860256 **Glororum Farm NE69 7AW**
email: enquiries@northumbrianleisure.co.uk **web:** www.northumbrianleisure.co.uk
dir: *Exit A1 at junction with B1341 (Purdy's Lodge). In 3.5 miles left onto unclassified road. Site 300 yards on left.*

A pleasantly situated site in an open countryside setting with good views of Bamburgh Castle. A popular holiday destination where tourers have their own separate area – 43 excellent, well-spaced, fully serviced pitches have a lush grass

LEISURE: 🏊 Indoor swimming pool 🏊 Outdoor swimming pool Ⓐ Children's playground ✋ Kids' club 🎾 Tennis court ♣ Games room ▭ Separate TV room
🚶 golf course ⛳ Pitch n putt 🚣 Boats for hire 🚲 Bikes for hire 🎬 Cinema 🎧 Entertainment 🎣 Fishing ◎ Mini golf 🏄 Watersports 💪 Gym 🏈 Sports field ∪ Stables
FACILITIES: 🏠 Baths/Shower ⊙ Electric shaver sockets 🌀 Hairdryer ✳ Ice Pack Facility 🛒 Baby facilities ⚐ Disabled facilities Ⓢ Shop on site or within 200yds
🍴 BBQ area 🎁 Picnic area WiFi WiFi

area in addition to the hardstanding. This field also has an excellent purpose-built amenity block with a smartly clad interior and modern, efficient fittings.

Open: March to end November **Last arrival:** 18.00 **Last departure:** noon

Pitches: 🚐 from £25; 🚍 from £25; 43 hardstanding pitches; 30 seasonal pitches

Leisure: 🎱

Facilities: ☉ ♿ ✻ ✗ ⓢ 🗃

Services: ⚡ 🔲 ∅ 🅣

Within 3 miles: ↨ 🎣 ↻ ⛷ ⥄

Additional site information: 6 acre site. 🐕 Cars can be parked by caravans. Awnings permitted. No commercial vehicles, no noise after 23.00.

BELFORD
Map 21 NU13

Places to visit

Bamburgh Castle, BAMBURGH, NE69 7DF, 01668 214515
www.bamburghcastle.com

Lindisfarne Castle, HOLY ISLAND [LINDISFARNE], TD15 2SH, 01289 389244
www.nationaltrust.org.uk/lindisfarne-castle

Great for kids: Alnwick Castle, ALNWICK, NE66 1NG, 01665 511100
www.alnwickcastle.com

Platinum Park

South Meadows Caravan Park

▶▶▶▶▶

tel: 01668 213326 **South Road NE70 7DP**
email: info@southmeadows.co.uk **web:** www.southmeadows.co.uk
dir: From A1 between Alnwick and Berwick-upon-Tweed take B6349 towards Belford, at right bend site signed, turn left, site on right.

An excellent, justifiably very popular site that is ideally situated to exploit the many beauties and attractions of the nearby Northumbrian coast. It is set in open countryside with generous, very well laid out pitches set amongst attractive beech hedging. There is a great adventure playground for children of all ages and even two very good dog walks on site, one through bluebell woodland. For the 2018 season a new toilet block was added.

Open: All year **Last departure:** 16.00

Pitches: 🚐 🚍 ⛺; 46 hardstanding pitches; 63 seasonal pitches

Leisure: ⚠ 🎱

Facilities: 🏠 ☉ ♿ ✻ ✗ ⓢ 🗃 **WiFi**

Services: ⚡ 🔲 ⭝ ⚓ ∅ 🅣

Within 3 miles: ↨ ↻

Additional site information: 50 acre site. 🐕 Cars can be parked by caravans and tents. Awnings permitted. Minimum noise after 23.00, under 12s must be supervised in toilet blocks. Woodland walk, football and recreation field, cycle route.

BELLINGHAM
Map 21 NY88

Places to visit

Wallington, CAMBO, NE61 4AR, 01670 773600
www.nationaltrust.org.uk/wallington

Premier Park

Bellingham Camping & Caravanning Club Site

▶▶▶▶▶ 90%

tel: 01434 220175 & 024 7647 5426 **Brown Rigg NE48 2JY**
email: bellingham.site@campingandcaravanningclub.co.uk
web: www.campingandcaravanningclub.co.uk/bellingham
dir: From A69 take A6079 north to Chollerford and B6320 to Bellingham. Pass Forestry Commission land, site 0.5 mile south of Bellingham.

A beautiful and peaceful campsite set in the glorious Northumberland National Park. It is exceptionally well managed by the enthusiastic owners who offer high levels of customer care, maintenance and cleanliness. The excellent toilet facilities are spotlessly clean, and there are family washrooms, a recreation room, a campers' kitchen, a drying room, and star-gazing equipment for customers to use. There are four camping pods for hire. This is a perfect base for exploring an undiscovered part of England, and it is handily placed for visiting the beautiful Northumberland coast.

Open: March to 4 January **Last arrival:** 20.00 **Last departure:** noon

Pitches: 🚐 from £7.85; 🚍 from £7.85; ⛺ from £7.85; 🏠 see prices below; 42 hardstanding pitches

Leisure: ⚠ 🎱 ▭

Facilities: 🏠 ☉ ♿ ✻ ✗ ⓢ **WiFi**

Services: ⚡ 🔲 ⭝ ⚓ ∅ 🅣

Within 3 miles: ↨ 🎣

Additional site information: 5 acre site. 🐕 Cars can be parked by caravans and tents. Awnings permitted. Site gates closed and quiet time from 23.00 to 07.00. BBQs permitted, no open fires. Only septic tank soft (green) toilet fluids to be used. Communal modern kitchen, centrally heated indoor social space, drying room.

Glamping available: Wooden pods from £45.

Additional glamping information: Wooden pods: minimum stay 2 nights, sleeps either 3 adults or 2 adults and 2 children. Pods are well insulated and carpeted with electric heating and lighting. No fixed beds provided. Deals available for selected stays.

PITCHES: 🚐 Caravans 🚍 Motorhomes ⛺ Tents 🏠 Glamping accommodation **SERVICES:** ⚡ Electric hook-up 🔲 Launderette 🍺 Licensed bar
🔋 Calor Gas ∅ Campingaz 🅣 Toilet fluid 🍽 Café/Restaurant 🍔 Fast Food/Takeaway ⚓ Battery charging ⭝ Motorhome service point
* 2019 prices 🚫 No credit or debit cards 🐕 Dogs permitted ⊗ No dogs

BERWICK-UPON-TWEED Map 21 NT95

Places to visit

Berwick-upon-Tweed Barracks, BERWICK-UPON-TWEED, TD15 1DF, 01289 304493
www.english-heritage.org.uk/daysout/properties/berwick-upon-tweed-barracks-and-main-guard

REGIONAL WINNER – NORTH EAST ENGLAND
AA CAMPSITE OF THE YEAR 2019

Premier Park

Ord House Country Park

►►►►► 92%

tel: 01289 305288 **East Ord TD15 2NS**
email: enquiries@ordhouse.co.uk **web:** www.ordhouse.co.uk
dir: *From A1 (Berwick bypass), or from A698, at roundabout (south of River Tweed) follow East Ord sign, then brown site signs.*

Set within the grounds of 18th-century Ord House, this very well-run park takes great pride in the quality of its landscaping and in the siting and spacing of touring pitches, some of which are fully serviced. The toilet blocks are truly superb. Youngsters are well catered for with a fantastic adventure playground, mini golf and a football field. A broad range of meals is available in Maguires Bar & Grill where there is also a soft toy play area for children. Wooden wigwams, each sleeping four, are available for hire.

Open: All year **Last arrival:** 23.00 **Last departure:** noon

Pitches: 🚐 🚌 ⛺ 🏕; 46 hardstanding pitches; 30 seasonal pitches

Leisure: ⚽

Facilities: 🛁 🔌 💨 ❄ ♿ 🛒 🧺 [WiFi]

Services: 🗨 🗄 🍷 🍽 🍔 ⬇ 🔒 ♻

Within 3 miles: ⛳ 🎣 ◎ 🚣 🎬

Additional site information: 42 acre site. 🐕 Cars can be parked by caravans and tents. Awnings permitted. No noise after midnight. Crazy golf, table tennis.

Glamping available: Wooden wigwams.

Additional glamping information: Cars can be parked by wigwams.

Premier Park

Berwick Holiday Park

►►►►► 89% HOLIDAY HOME PARK

tel: 01289 307113 **Magdalene Fields TD15 1NE**
email: berwick@haven.com **web:** www.haven.com/berwick
dir: *From A1 follow Berwick-upon-Tweed signs. At Morrisons/McDonalds roundabout take 2nd exit. At mini roundabout straight on, into North Road (pass Shell garage on left). At next mini roundabout 1st exit into Northumberland Avenue. Park at end.*

A very friendly, welcoming static-only holiday park with excellent entertainment and leisure facilities for all ages, and with direct access to the beach on the edge of Berwick. Exciting family activities and entertainment include the FunWorks Amusement Centre, Nature Rockz and a multisports court. Everything here is of a high standard – the holiday homes, the landscaping and the facilities – customer feedback on their holiday experience is very positive.

Open: mid March to 30 October

Holiday Homes: Sleep 8 Bedrooms 2 Bathrooms 1 Toilets 1 Microwave Freezer TV Sky/Freeview DVD player Linen included Electricity included Gas included

Leisure: 🏊 🌊 🛝 ✋ 🚲

Additional site information: 🐕 Most dog breeds accepted (please check when booking). Dogs must be kept on leads at all times. The facilities provided in the holiday homes may differ depending on the grade.

Premier Park

Haggerston Castle Holiday Park

►►►►► 84% HOLIDAY CENTRE

tel: 01289 381333 **Beal TD15 2PA**
email: haggerstoncastle@haven.com **web:** www.haven.com/haggerstoncastle
dir: *On A1, 7 miles south of Berwick-upon-Tweed, site signed.*

A large holiday centre with a very well equipped touring park, offering comprehensive holiday activities. The entertainment complex contains amusements for the whole family, and there are several bars, an adventure playground, boating on the lake, a children's club, a 9-hole golf course, tennis courts, and various eating outlets. Please note that this site does not accept tents.

Open: mid March to end October (restricted service: mid March to May and September to October – some facilities may be reduced) **Last arrival:** anytime **Last departure:** 10.00

Pitches: 🚐 🚌; 140 hardstanding pitches

Leisure: 🏊 🛝 ✋ 🎾 ⛳ 🎵 🎣 🏋 Spa

Facilities: 🛁 🔌 💨 ❄ ♿ 🛒 🧺 👶 [WiFi]

Services: 🗨 🗄 🍷 🍽 🍔 ⬇ 🔒 [T]

Within 3 miles: 🐎 ◎ 🚣

Additional site information: 100 acre site. 🐕 Max 2 dogs per booking, certain dog breeds banned. No commercial vehicles, no bookings by persons under 21 years unless a family booking.

Old Mill Caravan Site

►► 80%

tel: 01289 381295 & 07791 976535 **West Kyloe Farm, Fenwick TD15 2PF**
email: info@westkyloe.co.uk **web:** www.westkyloe.co.uk
dir: *A1 onto B6353 (9 miles south of Berwick-upon-Tweed) signed Lowick and Fenwick. Site 1.5 miles signed on left.*

Small, secluded site accessed through a farm complex, and overlooking a mill pond complete with resident ducks. Some pitches are in a walled garden, and the amenity block is basic but well kept. Delightful walks can be enjoyed on the 600-acre farm. A holiday cottage is also available.

Open: April to October **Last arrival:** 19.00 **Last departure:** 11.00

Pitches: * 🚐 from £20; 🚌 from £20; ⛺ from £15

Facilities: 🛁 🔌 ♿

Services: 🗨

Within 3 miles: 🛒

Additional site information: 2.5 acre site. 🐕 💳 Cars can be parked by caravans and tents. Awnings permitted. No gazebos or open fires. Wet room, farm walks (600 acres).

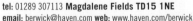

LEISURE: 🏊 Indoor swimming pool 🌊 Outdoor swimming pool 🛝 Children's playground ✋ Kids' club 🎾 Tennis court 🎱 Games room 📺 Separate TV room ⛳ golf course 🏌 Pitch n putt 🚣 Boats for hire 🚲 Bikes for hire 🎬 Cinema 🎵 Entertainment 🎣 Fishing ◎ Mini golf 🏄 Watersports 🏋 Gym ⚽ Sports field 🐎 Stables
FACILITIES: 🛁 Baths/Shower 🔌 Electric shaver sockets 💨 Hairdryer ❄ Ice Pack Facility 👶 Baby facilities ♿ Disabled facilities 🛒 Shop on site or within 200yds 🔥 BBQ area 🧺 Picnic area [WiFi] WiFi

HEXHAM — Map 21 NY96

Places to visit

Vindolanda (Chesterholm), BARDON MILL, NE47 7JN, 01434 344277
www.vindolanda.com

Temple of Mithras (Hadrian's Wall), CARRAWBROUGH, 0370 333 1181
www.english-heritage.org.uk/daysout/properties/temple-of-mithras-carraw-burgh-hadrians-wall

Great for kids: Housesteads Roman Fort, HOUSESTEADS, NE47 6NN,
01434 344363
www.english-heritage.org.uk/daysout/properties/housesteads-roman-fort-hadrians-wall

Hexham Racecourse Caravan Site

▶▶▶ 76%

tel: 01434 606847 & 606881 **Hexham Racecourse NE46 2JP**
email: hexrace.caravan@btconnect.com
dir: *From Hexham take B6305 signed Allendale and Alston. Left in 3 miles signed to racecourse. Site 1.5 miles on right.*

A part-level and part-sloping grassy site situated on a racecourse overlooking Hexhamshire Moors. The facilities, although clean, are of an older but functional type.

Open: May to September **Last arrival:** 20.00 **Last departure:** noon
Pitches: 🚐 from £15; 🚌 from £15; ▲ from £11; 20 seasonal pitches
Leisure: ⩘ 🔍
Facilities: 🏠 ☺ 🅿 ☼ 🗖 WiFi
Services: 🔌 🔄 🧺 🔋 🛢 ⌀
Within 3 miles: ↕ ✐ ◎ ⚓ 🖩 🅂

Additional site information: 4 acre site. 🐾 Cars can be parked by caravans and tents. Awnings permitted. No noise after 23.00.

WOOLER — Map 21 NT92

Places to visit

Chillingham Castle, CHILLINGHAM, NE66 5NJ, 01668 215359
www.chillingham-castle.com

Great for kids: Chillingham Wild Cattle Park, CHILLINGHAM, NE66 5NP,
01668 215250
www.chillinghamwildcattle.com

Riverside Leisure Park

▶▶▶ 83%

tel: 01668 281447 & 280000 **South Road NE71 6NJ**
email: reception@riverside-wooler.co.uk **web:** www.riverside-wooler.co.uk
dir: *From south: A1 to Morpeth, A697 signed Wooler and Coldstream. In Wooler, park on left. From north: Berwick-upon-Tweed on A1, 1st right signed Wooler (B6525). Through Wooler on A697. Park on right.*

This is the sister park to Thurston Manor Leisure Park at Dunbar in East Lothian. It is set in the heart of stunning Northumberland countryside on the edge of Wooler Water. Very much family orientated, the park offers excellent leisure facilities

including swimming pools, a bar and a restaurant, weekend entertainment and riverside and woodland walks. Fly fishing for rainbow trout is possible at the site's own lake. Please note, no tents are accepted. Wooden pods are available for hire.

Open: All year (restricted service: November to March — swimming pool closed)
Last departure: noon
Pitches: 🚐 from £38.50; 🚌 from £38.50; 🏕; 50 hardstanding pitches;
35 seasonal pitches
Leisure: 🏊 ⩘ 🤿 🔍 🗖 🎵 ✐ ⚽ Spa
Facilities: 🏠 ☺ 🅿 ☼ 👤 🛁 🔥 🗖 🚿 WiFi
Services: 🔌 🔄 🍺 🍴 🍔 🔋 🛢 ⌀ 🅃
Within 3 miles: ↕ ↻

Additional site information: 90 acre site. 🐾 Cars can be parked by caravans. Awnings permitted. No noise after 22.00.
Glamping available: Wooden pods.
Additional glamping information: Cars can be parked by pods.

NOTTINGHAMSHIRE

CHURCH LANEHAM — Map 17 SK07

Places to visit

Newark Air Museum, NEWARK-ON-TRENT, NG24 2NY, 01636 707170
www.newarkairmuseum.org

Doddington Hall, LINCOLN, LN6 4RU, 01522 694308
www.doddingtonhall.com

Trentfield Farm

▶▶▶ 84%

tel: 01777 228651 **DN22 0NJ**
email: post@trentfield.co.uk **web:** www.trentfield.co.uk
dir: *A1 onto A57 towards Lincoln for 6 miles. Left signed Laneham, 1.5 miles, through Laneham and Church Laneham (pass Ferryboat pub on left). Site 300 yards on right.*

A delightfully rural and level grass park tucked away on the banks of the River Trent. The park has its own river frontage with free coarse fishing available to park residents. The cosy local pub, which serves food, is under the same ownership.

Open: Easter to November **Last arrival:** 20.00 **Last departure:** noon
Pitches: * 🚐 from £24.50; 🚌 from £24.50; ▲ from £18; 20 seasonal pitches
Facilities: 🏠 ☺ 🅿 ☼ 👤 🅂 🗖 WiFi
Services: 🔌 🔄 🔋 ⚒
Within 3 miles: ↕ ✐ ↻

Additional site information: 34 acre site. 🐾 Cars can be parked by caravans and tents. Awnings permitted. No open fires or fire pits. 24-hour mini shop.

MANSFIELD Map 16 SK56

Places to visit

Sherwood Forest National Nature Reserve, EDWINSTOWE, NG21 9RN, 01623 824643, www.visitsherwood.co.uk

Tall Trees Touring Park

►►►► 77%

tel: 01623 626503 & 07770 661957 **Old Mill Lane, Forest Town NG19 0JP**
email: info@talltreestouringpark.co.uk **web:** www.talltreestouringpark.co.uk
dir: *A60 from Mansfield towards Worksop. In 1 mile turn right at lights into Old Mill Lane. Site in approximately 0.5 mile on left.*

A very pleasant park situated just on the outskirts of Mansfield and within easy walking distance of shops and restaurants. It is surrounded on three sides by trees and shrubs, and securely set at the back of the residential park. This site has a modern amenity block, a fishing lake to the rear of the site and an extra grassed area to give more space for caravans and tents.

Open: All year **Last arrival:** anytime **Last departure:** anytime

Pitches: 🚐 from £15; 🚌 from £15; ⛺ from £15; 10 hardstanding pitches; 5 seasonal pitches

Leisure: 🛝 ⛳ 🎣 ⚽

Facilities: 🛁 🔌 💨 ♿ 🧺 [WiFi]

Services: 🚙 🧼

Within 3 miles: 🐴 🎬 [S]

Additional site information: 10 acre site. 🐕 Cars can be parked by caravans and tents. Awnings permitted. No noise after midnight.

NEWARK

See Southwell

RADCLIFFE ON TRENT Map 11 SK63

Places to visit

Wollaton Hall, Gardens & Deer Park, NOTTINGHAM, NG8 2AE, 0115 876 3100 www.wollatonhall.org.uk

Great for kids: Green's Windmill, NOTTINGHAM, NG2 4QB, 0115 915 6878 www.nottinghamcity.gov.uk/greenswindmill

Thornton's Holt Camping Park

►►►► 83%

tel: 0115 933 2125 & 933 4204 **Stragglethorpe Road, Stragglethorpe NG12 2JZ**
email: camping@thorntons-holt.co.uk **web:** www.thorntons-holt.co.uk
dir: *At lights on A52 (3 miles east of Nottingham) follow Cropwell Bishop signs. Site 0.5 mile on left. Or from A46 (southeast of Nottingham) at Stragglethorpe junction follow Cropwell Bishop signs. Site 2.5 miles on right.*

A well-run family site in former meadowland, with pitches (hardstanding and also grass from April to October) located amid maturing trees and bushes that create a rural and peaceful setting. There is a children's play area, a laundry and a small shop. The smart toilet block is spacious and has plenty of hot water. The indoor swimming pool is a popular attraction.

Open: All year (restricted service: November to March – swimming pool and shop closed)
Last arrival: 20.00 **Last departure:** noon

Pitches: 🚐 from £21; 🚌 from £21; ⛺ from £17.50; 35 hardstanding pitches; 20 seasonal pitches

Leisure: 🏊 🛝

Facilities: 🛁 🔌 💨 ❄ ♿ [S] [WiFi]

Services: 🚙 🧼 🛏 ⬇ 🔒 🌿 [T]

Within 3 miles: ⛳ 🎣 🐴 🏄 🚣 🎬

Additional site information: 14 acre site. 🐕 Cars can be parked by caravans and tents. Awnings permitted. No noise after 22.00.

SOUTHWELL
Map 17 SK65

Places to visit

The Workhouse, SOUTHWELL, NG25 0PT, 01636 817260
www.nationaltrust.org.uk/theworkhouse

New Hall Farm Touring Park
▶▶▶ 84%

tel: 01623 883041 **New Hall Farm, New Hall Lane NG22 8BS**
email: enquiries@newhallfarm.co.uk **web:** www.newhallfarm.co.uk
dir: *From A614 at White Post Modern Farm Centre follow Southwell signs. Immediately after Edingley into New Hall Lane to site.*

A park on a working stock farm with the elevated pitching area enjoying outstanding panoramic views. It is within a short drive of medieval Newark and Sherwood Forest. A log cabin viewing gantry offers a place to relax and take in the spectacular scenery.

Open: March to October **Last arrival:** 21.00 **Last departure:** noon
Pitches: * 🚐 from £18; 🚍 from £18; ▲ from £15; 10 hardstanding pitches; 7 seasonal pitches
Facilities: ⊙ ✳ 🍴 🎋
Services: 🔌 🔲 📶
Within 3 miles: ⟟ 🚣 ∪ 🔳

Additional site information: 2.5 acre site. Adults only. 🐕 🚭 Cars can be parked by caravans and tents. Awnings permitted. Quiet after 22.00. Walking trail, cycling trail, viewing gantry, ice cream for sale on site.

TEVERSAL
Map 16 SK46

Places to visit

Hardwick Hall, HARDWICK HALL, S44 5QJ, 01246 850430
www.nationaltrust.org.uk/hardwick

Premier Park

Teversal Camping & Caravanning Club Site
▶▶▶▶▶ 93%

tel: 01623 551838 & 024 7647 5426 **Silverhill Lane NG17 3JJ**
email: teversal.site@campingandcaravanningclub.co.uk
web: www.campingandcaravanningclub.co.uk/teversal
dir: *M1 junction 28, A38 towards Mansfield. Left at lights onto B6027. At top of hill straight over at lights, left at Tesco Express. Right onto B6014, left at Carnarvon Arms, site on left.*

A top notch park with excellent purpose-built facilities and innovative, hands-on owners. Each pitch is spacious, the excellent toilet facilities are state-of-the-art, and there are views of, and access to, the countryside and nearby Silverhill Community Woods. Both the attention to detail and the all-round quality are truly exceptional – there is a special area for washing dogs and bikes. The site has a shop. Buses for Sutton Ashfield and Chesterfield stop just a five-minute walk from the site. A six-berth holiday caravan, luxury ready-erected safari tents and a log cabin are available for hire. Good pub food can be found only a few minutes' walk from the site.

Open: All year **Last arrival:** 20.00 **Last departure:** noon

---

Pitches: 🚐 from £8.65; 🚍 from £8.65; ▲ from £8.65; 🛖 see prices below; 92 hardstanding pitches
Leisure: ⚞ ⚽ ⊕
Facilities: 🏠 ⊙ 🍴 ✳ ⅙ 🔳 📶
Services: 🔌 🔲 ⅃ 🔋 ⊘ 🅃
Within 3 miles: ⟟ 🚣 ∪

Additional site information: 6 acre site. 🐕 Cars can be parked by caravans and tents. Awnings permitted. Site gates close from 23.00 to 07.00. Cycle trails nearby. Car hire can be arranged.

Glamping available: Safari tents from £44; Log cabin from £200 (for 3 nights).
Changeover days: Any day for safari tents; Monday and Friday for log cabin.

Additional glamping information: Safari tents: minimum stay 3 nights. Log cabin: minimum stay 3 nights (Friday to Monday), 4 nights (Monday to Friday). Cars can be parked by glamping units.

OXFORDSHIRE

BANBURY
Map 11 SP44

Places to visit

Banbury Museum, BANBURY, OX16 2PQ, 01295 753752
www.banburymuseum.org

Broughton Castle, BROUGHTON, OX15 5EB, 01295 276070
www.broughtoncastle.com

Great for kids: Deddington Castle, DEDDINGTON, 0370 333 1181
www.english-heritage.org.uk/daysout/properties/deddington-castle

Barnstones Caravan & Camping Site
▶▶▶▶ 84%

tel: 01295 750289 **Great Bourton OX17 1QU**
dir: *Take A423 from Banbury signed Southam. In 3 miles turn right signed Great Bourton and Cropredy, site 100 yards on right.*

A popular, neatly laid-out site with plenty of hardstandings, some fully serviced pitches, a smart up-to-date toilet block, and excellent rally facilities. Well run by a very personable owner, this is an excellent value park. The site is well positioned for stopovers or for visiting nearby Banbury.

Open: All year **Last arrival:** by arrangement **Last departure:** by arrangement
Pitches: * 🚐 from £14; 🚍 from £14; ▲ from £12; 44 hardstanding pitches
Leisure: ⚞ ⚽
Facilities: 🏠 ⊙ ✳ ⅙ 🍴 🎋 📶
Services: 🔌 🔲 ⅃ 🔋 ⅃ 🔋 ⊘
Within 3 miles: ⟟ 🚣 ∪ ◎ 🍴 ✲ 🎯 🔳

Additional site information: 3 acre site. 🐕 🚭 Cars can be parked by caravans and tents. Awnings permitted.

BLETCHINGDON | Map 11 SP51

Places to visit

Rousham House, ROUSHAM, OX25 4QX, 01869 347110
www.rousham.org

Museum of the History of Science, OXFORD, OX1 3AZ, 01865 277293
www.mhs.ox.ac.uk

Great for kids: Oxford University Museum of Natural History, OXFORD, OX1 3PW, 01865 272950, www.oum.ox.ac.uk

Greenhill Leisure Park
▶▶▶▶ 91%

tel: 01869 351600 **Greenhill Farm, Station Road OX5 3BQ**
email: info@greenhill-leisure-park.co.uk web: www.greenhill-leisure-park.co.uk
dir: *M40 junction 9, A34 south for 3 miles. Take B4027 to Bletchingdon. Site 0.5 mile after village on left.*

An all-year round park with spacious pitches, set in open countryside near the village of Bletchingdon and well placed for visiting Oxford and the Cotswolds. Fishing is available at the park's two well-stocked lakes and nearby river. This is a family-friendly park and certainly maintains the owner's 'where fun meets the countryside' philosophy. The facilities are very good and include an excellent reception, shop and café-bar, a beauty salon and photographic studio, and 12 fully serviced pitches.

Open: All year (restricted service: October to March – games room closed)
Last arrival: 21.00 (20.00 in winter) **Last departure:** noon

Pitches: 🚐 from £17; 🚌 from £17; ▲ from £17; 44 hardstanding pitches; 20 seasonal pitches

Leisure: /Ⅱ\ 🔍 ⌒

Facilities: 🛁 ⊙ ☇ ✳ ⅙ 🖻 ⏢ WiFi

Services: 🔌 🗑 🍴 ⁅◎⁆ ⚖ 🧺 ⚱ 🛢 ⌀ Ⓣ

Within 3 miles: ⅃

Additional site information: 7 acre site. 🐕 No dogs permitted from October to March. Cars can be parked by caravans and tents. Awnings permitted. No campfires or fire pits.

Diamond Caravan & Camping Park
▶▶▶▶ 86%

tel: 01869 350909 **Islip Road OX5 3DR**
email: warden@diamondpark.co.uk web: www.diamondpark.co.uk
dir: *M40 junction 9, A34 signed Oxford and Newbury. In 3 miles take B4027 to Bletchingdon. Site 1 mile on left.*

A well-run, quiet rural site in good level surroundings, and ideal for touring the Cotswolds, situated seven miles north of Oxford in the heart of the Thames Valley. This popular park is open all year, has excellent facilities, and offers a heated outdoor swimming pool, a games room for children and a small bar.

Open: All year (restricted service: September to May – bar and swimming pool closed)
Last arrival: dusk **Last departure:** 11.00

Pitches: 🚐 from £20; 🚌 from £20; ▲ from £20; 20 hardstanding pitches

Leisure: ⛱ /Ⅱ\ 🔍

Facilities: 🛁 ⊙ ☇ ✳ 🖻 ⏢ WiFi

Services: 🔌 🗑 🍴 ⚖ 🧺 ⚱ 🛢 ⌀ Ⓣ

Within 3 miles: ⅃ ⌒

Additional site information: 3 acre site. 🐕 ⊛ Cars can be parked by caravans and tents. Awnings permitted. No campfires, no groups occupying more than 3 pitches, no noise after 22.30.

BURFORD | Map 5 SP21

Places to visit

Minster Lovell Heritage Centre, MINSTER LOVELL, OX29 0RB, 01993 775262
http://minsterlovell.com

Cotswold Woollen Weavers, FILKINS, GL7 3JJ, 01367 860660
www.naturalbest.co.uk

Wysdom Touring Park
▶▶ 86%

tel: 01993 823207 **Cheltenham Road OX18 4JG**
web: www.wysdomtouringpark.co.uk
dir: *From roundabout on A40 in Burford take A361 towards Lechdale-on-Thames. Turn right signed Burford School. 100 yards to site.*

Owned by Burford School, this small adults-only park is very much a hidden gem being just a five-minute walk from Burford, one of prettiest towns in the Cotswolds. The pitches have good privacy; all have electricity and there are many hardstandings for caravans and motorhomes. The unisex toilet facilities are very clean. This makes a good base from which to explore the Cotswolds.

Open: All year **Last arrival:** 21.00 **Last departure:** noon

Pitches: 🚐 from £18; 🚌 from £18; 18 hardstanding pitches; 7 seasonal pitches

Facilities: 🛁 ⊙ WiFi

Services: 🔌

Within 3 miles: ⅃ 🖻 🗑

Additional site information: 2.5 acre site. Adults only. 🐕 Cars can be parked by caravans. Awnings permitted. Free book swap.

FRINGFORD
Map 11 SP62

Places to visit

Rousham House, ROUSHAM, OX25 4QX, 01869 347110
www.rousham.org

Stowe House, STOWE, MK18 5EH, 01280 818002
www.stowehouse.org

Great for kids: Buckinghamshire Railway Centre, QUAINTON, HP22 4BY, 01296 655720, www.bucksrailcentre.org

Glebe Leisure

►►► 80%

tel: 01869 277800 **Stratton Lane OX27 8RJ**
email: ann.herring@btinternet.com **web:** www.glebeleisure.co.uk
dir: *M40 junction 10, A43 (signed Northampton). At next roundabout take B4100 signed Bicester. 2nd right onto unclassified road signed Hethe and Stoke Lyne. Follow brown site signs.*

Glebe Leisure is a small, peaceful park in a good countryside location just a few miles from Bicester and the M40, making it an ideal overnight stopover site. It is also very popular with fishing enthusiasts due to the well-stocked lake, and with keen shoppers wishing to spend time at the Bicester Village shopping outlet, three miles away. The park comprises two well-tended fields – one with hardstandings and four camping pods, the other with neat, grassy pitches. The main toilet block offers clean, well-maintained facilities and there's a good motorhome service point.

Open: All year **Last arrival:** March to September 20.00; October to February 18.00
Last departure: anytime

Pitches: 🚐 from £23; 🚌 from £23; ⛺ from £20; 🛖 see prices below; 15 hardstanding pitches

Leisure: 🎣

Facilities: 🏪 ✲ ♿ ⛩ [WiFi]

Services: 🔌 [🧺] 🔋 ⤓

Within 3 miles: ⛳ U [H] [$]

Additional site information: 5 acre site. 🐕 Cars can be parked by caravans and tents. Awnings permitted. No noise or taxis after 23.00, no unaccompanied children in toilet block or around lakes. Dog walks.

Glamping available: Wooden pods from £35. **Changeover days:** Any day

Additional glamping information: Cars can be parked by pods.

HENLEY-ON-THAMES

Places to visit

Greys Court, HENLEY-ON-THAMES, RG9 4PG, 01491 628529
www.nationaltrust.org.uk/greys-court

Great for kids: River & Rowing Museum, HENLEY-ON-THAMES, RG9 1BF, 01491 415600, www.rrm.co.uk

HENLEY-ON-THAMES
Map 5 SU78

Premier Park

Swiss Farm Touring & Camping

►►►►► 94%

Best of British

tel: 01491 573419 **Marlow Road RG9 2HY**
email: info@swissfarmhenley.co.uk **web:** www.swissfarmhenley.co.uk
dir: *From Henley-on-Thames take A4155 towards Marlow. 1st left after rugby club.*

This park enjoys an excellent location within easy walking distance of the town and is perfect for those visiting the Henley Regatta (but booking is essential at that time). Pitches are spacious and well appointed, and include some that are fully serviced. There is a tasteful coffee shop and bar plus a nice outdoor swimming pool. There are wooden pods and a luxury lodge for hire.

Open: March to November (restricted service: March to May and October to November – pool closed) **Last arrival:** 21.00 **Last departure:** noon

Pitches: 🚐 🚌 ⛺ 🛖; 100 hardstanding pitches

Leisure: 🏊 Λ 🎣 **Facilities:** 🏪 ☺ 💨 ✲ ♿ [$] ⛩ [WiFi]

Services: 🔌 [🧺] 🍽 🍔 🔋 ⤓ 🔒 🔥 [T]

Within 3 miles: ⛳ ⛵ [H]

Additional site information: 6 acre site. 🐕 No dogs during spring half term and summer holidays. Cars can be parked by caravans and tents. Awnings permitted. No groups.

Glamping available: Wooden pods.

See advert on page 248

PITCHES: 🚐 Caravans 🚌 Motorhomes ⛺ Tents 🛖 Glamping accommodation **SERVICES:** 🔌 Electric hook-up [🧺] Launderette 🍷 Licensed bar 🔒 Calor Gas 🔥 Campingaz [T] Toilet fluid 🍽 Café/Restaurant 🍔 Fast Food/Takeaway 🔋 Battery charging ⤓ Motorhome service point
* 2019 prices 💳 No credit or debit cards 🐕 Dogs permitted 🚫 No dogs

STANDLAKE
Map 5 SP30

Places to visit

Buscot Park, BUSCOT, SN7 8BU, 01367 240786
www.buscotpark.com

Harcourt Arboretum, OXFORD, OX44 9PX, 01865 610305
www.harcourt-arboretum.ox.ac.uk

Great for kids: Cotswold Wildlife Park and Gardens, BURFORD, OX18 4JP, 01993 823006
www.cotswoldwildlifepark.co.uk

Platinum Park

Lincoln Farm Park Oxfordshire

▶▶▶▶▶

Best of British

tel: 01865 300239 **High Street OX29 7RH**
email: info@lincolnfarmpark.co.uk **web:** www.lincolnfarmpark.co.uk
dir: *Exit A415 between Abingdon and Witney (5 miles southeast of Witney). Follow brown campsite sign in Standlake.*

This attractively landscaped family-run park, located in a quiet village near the River Thames, offers a truly excellent camping or caravanning experience. There are top class facilities throughout the park. It has excellent leisure facilities in the Standlake Leisure Centre complete with two pools plus a gym and sauna, and there's a new spa/massage facility. This is the perfect base for visiting the many attractions in Oxfordshire and the Cotswolds. A warm welcome is assured from the friendly staff.

Open: February to November **Last arrival:** 20.00 **Last departure:** noon

Pitches: 🚐 from £22; 🚌 from £22; ⛺ from £22; 75 hardstanding pitches

Leisure: 🏊 🎢 🎣 🏌 Spa

Facilities: 🛁 ⊙ ☂ ✳ ♿ Ⓢ 🚏 WiFi

Services: 🔌 🗑 🛒 🔒 🧺 Ⓣ

Within 3 miles: 🎣 🚲 ⛳ 🏊 🎿

Additional site information: 9 acre site. 🐕 Cars can be parked by caravans and tents. Awnings permitted. No gazebos, no noise after 23.00. Information room.

LEISURE: 🏊 Indoor swimming pool ⛱ Outdoor swimming pool 🎢 Children's playground 👋 Kids' club 🎾 Tennis court 🎱 Games room 📺 Separate TV room 🏌 golf course 🏁 Pitch n putt 🚣 Boats for hire 🚲 Bikes for hire 🎬 Cinema 🎵 Entertainment 🎣 Fishing ◉ Mini golf 🏄 Watersports 🏋 Gym ✪ Sports field ⛓ Stables
FACILITIES: 🛁 Baths/Shower ⊙ Electric shaver sockets ☂ Hairdryer ✳ Ice Pack Facility 🍼 Baby facilities ♿ Disabled facilities Ⓢ Shop on site or within 200yds 🍖 BBQ area 🧺 Picnic area WiFi WiFi

RUTLAND

GREETHAM
Map 11 SK91

Places to visit
Rutland County Museum & Visitor Centre, OAKHAM, LE15 6HW, 01572 758440
www.rutland.gov.uk/museum

Oakham Castle, OAKHAM, LE15 6DR, 01572 757578
www.oakhamcastle.org

Premier Park

Rutland Caravan & Camping
▶▶▶▶▶ 88%

tel: 01572 813520 **Park Lane LE15 7FN**
email: info@rutlandcaravanandcamping.co.uk
web: www.rutlandcaravanandcamping.co.uk
dir: *From A1 onto B668 towards Greetham. Before Greetham turn right at crossroads, left to site.*

This pretty caravan park, built to a high specification and surrounded by well planted banks, continues to improve year after year due to the enthusiasm and vision of its owner. The site has a swimming pool, 40 fully serviced pitches and luxury lodges. From the spacious reception, café and the innovative play area to the high-spec toilet block, everything is of a very high standard. This spacious, grassy site is close to the Viking Way and other footpath networks, and is well situated for visiting Rutland Water and the many picturesque villages in the area.

Open: All year **Last arrival:** 20.00
Pitches: 🚐 🚙 ⛺; 65 hardstanding pitches, 20 seasonal pitches
Leisure: 🏊 🎡 🎣
Facilities: 🏠 ⊙ 🇵 ✳ ♿ ⓢ ⴲ WiFi
Services: 🔌 🔋 🍴 🚰 ⚓ 🪫 🚽 Ⓣ
Within 3 miles: ⅃ 🎣 ⥁ ◎ ⇟ ⥮

Additional site information: 5 acre site. 🐕 Cars can be parked by caravans and tents. Awnings permitted. No noise after 23.00. Dog shower. Car hire can be arranged.

WING
Map 11 SK80

Places to visit
Lyddington Bede House, LYDDINGTON, LE15 9LZ, 01572 822438
www.english-heritage.org.uk/daysout/properties/lyddington-bede-house

Great for kids: Oakham Castle, OAKHAM, LE15 6DR, 01572 757578
www.oakhamcastle.org

Wing Hall Caravan & Camping
▶▶▶ 74%

tel: 01572 737283 & 737090 **Wing Hall LE15 8RQ**
email: winghall1891@aol.com **web:** www.winghall.co.uk
dir: *From A1 take A47 towards Leicester, 14 miles, follow Morcott signs. In Morcott follow Wing signs. 2.5 miles, follow site signs.*

A deeply tranquil and rural park set in the grounds of an old manor house. The four grassy fields with attractive borders of mixed, mature deciduous trees have

exceptional views across the Rutland countryside and are within one mile of Rutland Water. There's a good farm shop which specialises in locally sourced produce, a licensed café, and there are high quality showers and a fully-equipped laundry. Children and tents are very welcome in what is a safe environment where there is space to roam.

Open: All year (restricted service: November to March – large motorhomes advised not to arrive if weather is very wet) **Last arrival:** 21.00 **Last departure:** noon
Pitches: 🚐 🚙 ⛺; 4 hardstanding pitches
Facilities: 🇵 ✳ ⓢ WiFi
Services: 🔌 🔋 🍴 🍽 ⚓ 🪫
Within 3 miles: ⅃ 🎣 ⥁ ⇟ ⥮

Additional site information: 11 acre site. 🐕 Cars can be parked by caravans and tents. Awnings permitted. Coarse fishing.

SHROPSHIRE

BRIDGNORTH
Map 10 SO79

Places to visit
Benthall Hall, BENTHALL, TF12 5RX, 01952 882159
www.nationaltrust.org.uk/benthall-hall

Great for kids: Dudmaston Estate, QUATT, WV15 6QN, 01746 780866
www.nationaltrust.org.uk/dudmaston-estate

Premier Park

Stanmore Hall Touring Park
▶▶▶▶▶ 88%

tel: 01746 761761 **Stourbridge Road WV15 6DT**
email: stanmore@morris-leisure.co.uk **web:** www.morris-leisure.co.uk
dir: *2 miles east of Bridgnorth on A458.*

An excellent park in peaceful surroundings offering outstanding facilities. The pitches, many fully serviced (with Freeview TV), are arranged around the lake close to Stanmore Hall. Arboretum standard trees include some magnificent Californian Redwoods and an oak tree that is nearly 700 years old. The site is handy for visiting Ironbridge, the Severn Valley Railway and the attractive market town of Bridgnorth.

Open: All year **Last arrival:** 20.00 (late arrival pitches available) **Last departure:** noon
Pitches: 🚐 🚙 ⛺; 68 hardstanding pitches; 12 seasonal pitches
Leisure: 🎡 ⚽
Facilities: 🏠 ⊙ 🇵 ✳ ♿ ⓢ 🚻 ⴲ WiFi
Services: 🔌 🔋 🚰 🪫 🚽 Ⓣ
Within 3 miles: ⅃ 🎣 ⥁ ⥮ 🎣

Additional site information: 12.5 acre site. 🐕 Maximum of 2 dogs per pitch. Cars can be parked by caravans and tents. Awnings permitted. Adult only section. Dog walk.

LYNEAL (NEAR ELLESMERE)　　　Map 15 SJ43

Places to visit

Old Oswestry Hill Fort, OSWESTRY, 0370 333 1181
www.english-heritage.org.uk/daysout/properties/old-oswestry-hill-fort

Great for kids: Hawkstone Historic Park & Follies, WESTON-UNDER-REDCASTLE, SY4 5JY, 01948 841700
www.hawkstoneparkfollies.co.uk

Fernwood Caravan Park
►►►►　86%

tel: 01948 710221 **SY12 0QF**
email: enquiries@fernwoodpark.co.uk **web:** www.fernwoodpark.co.uk
dir: *From A495 in Welshampton take B5063, over canal bridge, turn right, follow signs.*

A peaceful park set in wooded countryside, with a screened, tree-lined touring area and coarse fishing lake. The approach to the park passes colourful shrubs and flower beds, and part of the static area is tastefully arranged around a children's playing area. There is a small child-free touring area for those wanting complete relaxation, and the park has 40 acres of woodland where there are many walks to enjoy.

Open: March to November (restricted service: March and November – shop closed)
Last arrival: 21.00 **Last departure:** 17.00
Pitches: 🚐 from £26; 🚙 from £26; 8 hardstanding pitches; 30 seasonal pitches
Leisure: 🅰 🖊
Facilities: 🛁 ☉ 🖻 ✳ ♿ ⑤
Services: 🔌 ⑤ ⚓ 🔒 🔟
Within 3 miles: ⚡

Additional site information: 26 acre site. 🐴 Cars can be parked by caravans. Awnings permitted. No noise after 23.00. Guest WiFi available by site office.

MINSTERLEY　　　Map 15 SJ30

Places to visit

Powis Castle & Garden, WELSHPOOL, SY21 8RF, 01938 551944
www.nationaltrust.org.uk/powis-castle-and-garden

Great for kids: Stiperstones National Nature Reserve, SHREWSBURY, SY5 0NL, 01743 792294, www.naturalengland.org.uk

The Old School Caravan Park
►►►　86%

tel: 01588 650410 **Shelve SY5 0JQ**
web: www.theoldschoolcaravanpark.co.uk
dir: *6.5 miles southwest of Minsterley on A488. Site on left, 2 miles after village sign for Hope.*

Situated in the Shropshire Hills, an Area of Outstanding Natural Beauty, with many excellent walks starting directly from the site, and many cycle trails close by. Although a small site of just 1.5 acres, it is well equipped. It is a really beautiful park, often described as 'a gem', that has excellent facilities and offers all the requirements for a relaxing countryside holiday. The friendly owners, Terry and Jan, are always on hand to help out with anything. Nearby Snailbreach Mine offers guided tours on certain days. Please note that there is no laundry at this park.

Open: March to January **Last arrival:** 21.00 **Last departure:** 11.00
Pitches: 🚐 🚙 ⛺; 10 hardstanding pitches; 6 seasonal pitches
Facilities: 🛁 ☉ ✳ 🍴
Services: 🔌
Within 3 miles: 🖊 ♺ ⑤
Additional site information: 1.5 acre site. 🐴 ◉ Cars can be parked by caravans and tents. Awnings permitted. No ball games or cycle riding.

SHREWSBURY　　　Map 15 SJ41

Places to visit

Attingham Park Estate Town Walls (NT), SHREWSBURY, SY1 1TN, 01743 708162
www.nationaltrust.org.uk/attingham-park-estate-town-walls-tower

Great for kids: Wroxeter Roman City, WROXETER, SY5 6PH, 01743 761330
www.english-heritage.org.uk/daysout/properties/wroxeter-roman-city

Premier Park

Beaconsfield Farm Caravan Park
►►►►►　91%

tel: 01939 210370 & 210399 **Battlefield SY4 4AA**
email: mail@beaconsfieldholidaypark.co.uk **web:** www.beaconsfieldholidaypark.co.uk
dir: *At Hadnall, 1.5 miles northeast of Shrewsbury. Follow sign for Astley from A49.*

A purpose-built, adults-only (21 years and over) family-run park on farmland in open countryside. This pleasant park offers quality in every area, including superior toilets, heated indoor swimming pool, luxury lodges for hire and attractive landscaping. Fly and coarse fishing are available from the park's own lake. A large new restaurant is planned for 2019 to replace the popular Bothy Bistro, which enjoys an on-site and local following. Car hire is available directly

LEISURE: 🏊 Indoor swimming pool　🏊 Outdoor swimming pool　🅰 Children's playground　🧒 Kids' club　🎾 Tennis court　🎱 Games room　📺 Separate TV room
🏌 golf course　⛳ Pitch n putt　🚣 Boats for hire　🚲 Bikes for hire　🎬 Cinema　🎵 Entertainment　🎣 Fishing　⛳ Mini golf　🏄 Watersports　🏋 Gym　⚽ Sports field　🐴 Stables
FACILITIES: 🛁 Baths/Shower　☉ Electric shaver sockets　🖍 Hairdryer　✳ Ice Pack Facility　🍼 Baby facilities　♿ Disabled facilities　⑤ Shop on site or within 200yds
🍴 BBQ area　🧺 Picnic area　📶 WiFi

from the site, and there's a steam room, plus free WiFi. 12 luxury lodges are available for hire or sale.

Beaconsfield Farm Caravan Park

Open: All year **Last arrival:** 19.00 **Last departure:** 11.00

Pitches: 🚐 from £26; 🚍 from £26; 50 hardstanding pitches; 10 seasonal pitches

Leisure: 🏊 ⚽ ✏

Facilities: 🏠 🎣 ✳ ♿ 🧺 WiFi

Services: 🔌 🧺 🍴 🔧 🛢

Within 3 miles: 🎣 🎯 💲

Additional site information: 16 acre site. Adults only. 🐕 Cars can be parked by caravans. Awnings permitted.

REGIONAL WINNER – HEART OF ENGLAND AA CAMPSITE OF THE YEAR 2019

Premier Park

Oxon Hall Touring Park
▶▶▶▶▶ 90%

Best of British

tel: 01743 340868 **Welshpool Road SY3 5FB**
email: oxon@morris-leisure.co.uk **web:** www.morris-leisure.co.uk
dir: *Exit A5 (ring road) at junction with A458. Site shares entrance with Oxford Park and Ride.*

A delightful park with quality facilities, including a top-notch toilet block and a choice of grass and fully serviced pitches. The adults-only section proves very popular, and there is an inviting patio area next to reception and the shop, overlooking a small lake. This site is ideally located for a visit to Shrewsbury and the surrounding countryside, and the site also benefits from the Oxon Park & Ride being just a short walk away.

Open: All year **Last arrival:** 20.00 **Last departure:** noon

Pitches: 🚐 🚍 ▲; 72 hardstanding pitches

Facilities: 🏠 ☺ 🎣 ✳ ♿ 🧺 🛒 🍴 WiFi

Services: 🔌 🧺 🔧 🛢 ✿ T

Within 3 miles: 🎣 🎯 ∪ 🎯

Additional site information: 15 acre site. 🐕 Maximum of 2 dogs per pitch. Cars can be parked by caravans and tents. Awnings permitted.

Cartref Caravan & Camping
▶▶▶▶ 90%

tel: 01743 821688 & 07803 907061 **Cartref, Ford Heath SY5 9GD**
email: info@cartrefcaravansite.co.uk **web:** www.cartrefcaravansite.co.uk
dir: *From north: A5 from Oswestry towards Shrewsbury. At roundabout take A458 towards Welshpool. After petrol station turn left signed Shoothill and Ford Heath. Take 2nd right, site on left. From south: from A5 (west of Shrewsbury) take B4386 signed Montgomery. In 2 miles turn right signed Ford and Montford Bridge. Site on right in approximately 1 mile.*

Located in the peaceful hamlet of Ford Heath, less than five miles from Shrewsbury, this carefully designed, relaxing holiday destination provides separate adults-only and family areas suitable for caravans, motorhomes and tents. Pitches, most fully serviced, are enclosed by mature hedges and colourful shrubs to create optimum privacy. In addition to a well-equipped amenity block, a rustic-themed bar provides a wide range of wines, spirits and local ales, and the well-stocked shop offers the best local produce. Additional features include a safe meadow area for dog walking and a wildlife pond carefully planted to attract a variety of birds and animals including the Great Crested Newt.

Open: 2 March to 28 October **Last arrival:** 21.00 **Last departure:** 11.00 (later by prior arrangement)

Pitches: 🚐 from £21; 🚍 from £21; ▲ from £21; 38 hardstanding pitches; 15 seasonal pitches **Leisure:** ⛺

Facilities: 🏠 ☺ 🎣 ✳ ♿ 🧺 🛒 WiFi **Services:** 🔌 🧺 🔧 🍴 🔋 🛢 T

Additional site information: 7.7 acre site. 🐕 ⊛ Cars can be parked by caravans and tents. Awnings permitted. No ball games or cycling. Strict no noise policy between 23.00–8.00. Fresh baked bread to order. Local and walks information available.

TELFORD   Map 10 SJ60

Places to visit

Lilleshall Abbey, LILLESHALL, TF10 9HW,
www.english-heritage.org.uk/daysout/properties/lilleshall-abbey

---

Premier Park

Severn Gorge Park
▶▶▶▶▶ 81%

tel: 01952 684789 **Bridgnorth Road, Tweedale TF7 4JB**
email: info@severngorgepark.co.uk **web:** www.severngorgepark.co.uk
dir: *South of Telford take A442 towards Bridgnorth. Onto A4169 signed Telford Town Centre. Right at Cuckoo Oak roundabout into Bridgnorth Road (follow site signs). Site on right.*

A very pleasant wooded site in the heart of Telford, that is well screened and well maintained. The sanitary facilities are fresh and immaculate, and landscaping of the grounds is carefully managed. Although the touring section is small, this is a really delightful park to stay at, and it is also well positioned for visiting nearby Ironbridge and its museums. The Telford bus stops at the end of the drive.

Open: All year **Last arrival:** 20.00 by prior arrangement **Last departure:** noon

Pitches: 🚐 🚍; 12 hardstanding pitches **Facilities:** 🏠 ☺ 🎣 ✳ ♿

Services: 🔌 🧺 🔋 🔧 🛢 ✿ **Within 3 miles:** 🎣 🎯 ∪ ◎ ⛴ 🎯 💲

Additional site information: 6 acre site. Adults only. 🐕 Well behaved dogs only. Cars can be parked by caravans. Awnings permitted.

WEM
Map 15 SJ52

Places to visit

Hawkstone Historic Park & Follies, WESTON-UNDER-REDCASTLE, SY4 5JY, 01948 841700, www.hawkstoneparkfollies.co.uk

Attingham Park Estate Town Walls (NT), SHREWSBURY, SY1 1TN, 01743 708162 www.nationaltrust.org.uk/attingham-park-estate-town-walls-tower

Great for kids: Stiperstones National Nature Reserve, SHREWSBURY, SY5 0NL, 01743 792294 www.naturalengland.org.uk

Lower Lacon Caravan Park
►►► 81%

tel: 01939 232376 **SY4 5RP**
email: info@llcp.co.uk **web:** www.llcp.co.uk
dir: *A49 onto B5065. Site 3 miles on right.*

A large, spacious park with lively club facilities and an entertainments' barn, set safely away from the main road. The park is particularly suited to families, with an outdoor swimming pool and many farm animals including alpacas and kune kune pigs. Family-size wooden pods are available for hire.

Open: All year (restricted service: in winter – entertainment barn and café closed)
Last arrival: anytime **Last departure:** 17.00

Pitches: 🚐 from £25; 🚃 from £25; ▲ from £25; 🏠; 30 hardstanding pitches; 100 seasonal pitches

Leisure: ⬗ 🎠 ✋ 🔍 ⬛

Facilities: 🛁 ☉ 🚿 ✳ ⅋ Ⓢ WiFi

Services: 🔌 🗄 🚽 🍽 ⬛ 🛒 🛢 🌿 🔲

Within 3 miles: ⌁ 🖎 ◎

Additional site information: 57 acre site. 🐾 Cars can be parked by caravans and tents. Awnings permitted. No skateboards, no commercial vehicles, no sign-written vehicles. Crazy golf.

Glamping available: Wooden pods.

Additional glamping information: Cars can be parked by pods.

WENTNOR

Places to visit

Montgomery Castle, MONTGOMERY, 03000 256000 http://cadw.gov.wales/daysout/montgomerycastle/?lang=en

Great for kids: Shropshire Hills Discovery Centre, CRAVEN ARMS, SY7 9RS, 01588 676060 www.shropshirehillsdiscoverycentre.co.uk

WENTNOR
Map 15 SO39

The Green Caravan Park
►►► 81%

tel: 01588 650605 **SY9 5EF**
email: lin@greencaravanpark.co.uk **web:** www.greencaravanpark.co.uk
dir: *1 mile northeast of Bishop's Castle on A489. Right at brown tourist sign.*

A pleasant family-run site adjacent to a village pub, in a peaceful setting that's convenient for visiting Ludlow or Shrewsbury. The site is very family orientated, and has good facilities. The grassy pitches are mainly level – some hardstandings are available.

Open: Easter to October **Last arrival:** 21.00 **Last departure:** noon (fee charged for late departures)

Pitches: 🚐 from £17; 🚃 from £17; ▲ from £17; 6 hardstanding pitches; 42 seasonal pitches

Leisure: 🎠 ✎

Facilities: 🛁 ☉ 🚿 ✳ Ⓢ

Services: 🔌 🗄 🚽 🍽 ⬛ 🛒 🛢 🌿 🔲

Additional site information: 15 acre site. 🐾 Dogs must be kept on leads at all times except in exercise area. Cars can be parked by caravans and tents. Awnings permitted. No open fires, quiet from 22.00–08.00. Car hire can be arranged.

WHEATHILL
Map 10 SO68

Places to visit

Ludlow Castle, LUDLOW, SY8 1AY, 01584 873355 www.ludlowcastle.com

---

Premier Park

Wheathill Touring Park
►►►►► 90%

tel: 01584 823456 **WV16 6QT**
email: info@wheathillpark.co.uk **web:** www.wheathillpark.co.uk
dir: *On B4364 between Ludlow and Bridgnorth. (Note: sat nav may give directions to exit B4364, this should be ignored). Site entrance adjacent to Three Horseshoes Pub and well signed from B4364.*

Ideally located in open countryside between the historic towns of Bridgnorth and Ludlow, this development provides spacious, fully serviced pitches, most with stunning views. There is a top-notch amenity block in each field that have quality fittings and good privacy options. The park is situated adjacent to a pub serving a good range of ales and food. Please note, the on-site shop only sells caravan and camping spares but there's a licensed village shop within a 10-minute drive.

Open: 15 March to 15 December **Last arrival:** 19.00 **Last departure:** noon

Pitches: 🚐 🚃; 50 hardstanding pitches; 5 seasonal pitches

Facilities: 🛁 ☉ 🚿 ⅋ 🍴 🏮 WiFi

Services: 🔌 🗄 🛒 ⅄ 🛢 🌿 🔲

Within 3 miles: ✎ ♻ Ⓢ

Additional site information: 4 acre site. Adults only. 🐾 Cars can be parked by caravans. Awnings permitted.

Somerset

Somerset means 'summer pastures' — appropriate given that so much of this county remains rural and unspoiled. Ever popular areas to visit are the limestone and red sandstone Mendips Hills rising to over 1,000 feet, and by complete contrast, to the south and southwest, the flat landscape of the Somerset Levels.

At the heart of Somerset lies the city of Wells, one of the smallest in the country and surely one of the finest. The jewel in the city's crown is its splendid cathedral, with a magnificent Gothic interior; adorned with sculptures, the West Front is a masterpiece of medieval craftsmanship. Nearby are Vicar's Close, a delightful street of 14th-century houses, and the Bishop's Palace, which is 13th century and moated.

Radiating from Wells are numerous paths and tracks, offering walkers the chance to escape the noise and bustle of the city and discover Somerset's rural delights. Deep within the county are the Mendip Hills, 25 miles long by 5 miles wide, that have a distinctive character and identity.

One of Somerset's more adventurous routes, and a long-term favourite with walkers, is the West Mendip Way, running for 50 miles between the coast and the town of Frome. The starting point at Uphill is spectacular – a ruined hilltop church overlooking the coast near the classic seaside resort of Weston-Super-Mare. The town's famous pier replaces a previous structure destroyed by fire in 2008. Weston and Minehead, which lie on the edge of Exmoor National Park, are two traditional, much-loved holiday destinations on this stretch of coastline.

From Uphill, the West Mendip Way makes for Cheddar Caves and Gorge where stunning geological formations attract countless visitors who are left with a lasting impression of unique natural beauty. For almost a mile the gorge's limestone cliffs rise vertically above the road, in places giving Cheddar a somewhat sinister and oppressive air. Beyond Cheddar the trail heads for Wells. The choice of walks in Somerset is impressive, as is the range of cycle routes.

Descend to the Somerset Levels, an evocative lowland landscape that was the setting for the Battle of Sedgemoor in 1685. In the depths of winter this is a desolate place and famously prone to extensive flooding. There is also a palpable sense of the distant past among these fields and scattered communities. It is claimed that Alfred the Great retreated here after his defeat by the Danes.

One of Somerset's most famous features is the ancient, enigmatic Glastonbury Tor. Steeped in early Christian and Arthurian legend, the Isle of Avalon is one of a number of 'islands' rising above the Somerset Levels. This was once the site of the largest and richest monastery in medieval England and it is claimed that in this setting, Joseph of Arimathea founded the first Christian church in the country. Today, near this spot, modern-day pilgrims come for worship of a very different kind – every summer Glastonbury's legendary festival attracts big names from the world of music and large crowds who brave the elements to support them.

Away from the flat country are the Quantocks, once the haunt of poets. Samuel Taylor Coleridge wrote *The Ancient Mariner* while living in the area and William Wordsworth and his sister Dorothy visited on occasion and often accompanied their friend Coleridge on his country rambles among these hills. The Quantocks are noted for their gentle slopes, heather-covered moorland expanses and red deer. From the summit, the Bristol Channel is visible where it meets the Severn Estuary. So much of this hilly landscape has a timeless quality about it and large areas have hardly changed since Coleridge and William and Dorothy Wordsworth explored it on foot around the end of the 18th century.

◁ Selworthy Beacon, Exmoor National Park

SOMERSET

BATH
Map 4 ST76

See also Bishop Sutton

Places to visit

The Herschel Museum of Astronomy, BATH, BA1 2BL, 01225 446865
www.herschelmuseum.org.uk

Sally Lunn's Historic Eating House & Museum, BATH, BA1 1NX, 01225 461634
www.sallylunns.co.uk

Great for kids: Roman Baths & Pump Room, BATH, BA1 1LZ, 01225 477785
www.romanbaths.co.uk

Premier Park

Bath Mill Lodge Retreat
▶▶▶▶▶ 94% HOLIDAY HOME PARK

tel: 01225 333909 **Newton Road BA2 9JF**
email: reception@bathmill.co.uk **web:** www.bathmill.co.uk
dir: *From A36 from Bath towards Bristol at roundabout into Pennyquick Road signed Newton St Loe (Globe Inn on right). In 1 mile left into Newton Road. 1st left to park.*

Bath Mill offers very high quality lodge accommodation in a beautifully landscaped park close to Bath. The lodges are fully equipped to a very high standard and are available with two, three or four bedrooms, plus there are 'Studio Lodges', suitable for a couple, with king-size bed, sofa, a well-appointed bathroom and kitchen. There is an excellent bar and bistro and a well-equipped gym. It's a peaceful location that makes a perfect base for visiting Bath, Bristol and the Mendip Hills.

Open: All year

Holiday Homes: Sleep 8 Bedrooms 4 Two-ring burner Dishwasher Washing Machine Microwave Freezer TV Sky/Freeview WiFi Linen included Towels included Electricity included Gas included

Leisure: 🏋

Additional site information: 🐾

BISHOP SUTTON
Map 4 ST55

Places to visit

Wookey Hole Caves & Papermill, WOOKEY HOLE, BA5 1BB, 01749 672243
www.wookey.co.uk

Roman Baths & Pump Room, BATH, BA1 1LZ, 01225 477785
www.romanbaths.co.uk

Platinum Park

Bath Chew Valley Caravan Park
▶▶▶▶▶

tel: 01275 332127 **Ham Lane BS39 5TZ**
email: marc@bathchewvalley.co.uk **web:** www.bathchewvalley.co.uk
dir: *From A4 towards Bath take A39 towards Weston-Super-Mare. Right onto A368. 6 miles, right opposite The Red Lion into Ham Lane, site 250 metres on left.*

This peaceful adults-only park can be described as 'a park in a garden', with caravan pitches set amidst lawns, shrubs and trees. There are excellent private facilities – rooms with showers, wash basins and toilets – all are spotlessly clean and well maintained. There is a good woodland walk on the park, and a stylish fully-equipped lodge is available for hire. WiFi is available throughout the site and there is a free internet workstation. This site is well situated for visiting Bath, Bristol, Wells, Cheddar and Wookey Hole, and for walking in the Mendip Hills. Chew Valley Lake, noted for its top quality fishing, is close by.

Open: All year **Last arrival:** 19.00 **Last departure:** 11.00

Pitches: 🚐 from £24; 🚍 from £24; ▲ from £24; 4 seasonal pitches

Facilities: 🛁 ⊙ 🅿 ⚒ ♿ 🛒 🏧 🎍 WiFi

Services: 🔌 🛢 🍴 🛒 ⚱ 🛒 🔒 🧺 T

Within 3 miles: 🎣 🛶

Additional site information: 4.5 acre site. Adults only. 🐾 Awnings permitted. Lending library. Shop, pub and restaurant 200 metres from site. Car hire can be arranged.

BREAN

Places to visit

King John's Hunting Lodge, AXBRIDGE, BS26 2AP, 01934 732012
www.kingjohnshuntinglodge.co.uk

Weston Museum, WESTON-SUPER-MARE, BS23 1PR, 01934 621028
www.westonmuseum.org

Great for kids: The Helicopter Museum, WESTON-SUPER-MARE, BS24 8PP, 01934 635227
www.helicoptermuseum.co.uk

BREAN

Map 4 ST25

Platinum Park

Warren Farm Holiday Centre

▶▶▶▶▶ HOLIDAY CENTRE

tel: 01278 751227 **Brean Sands TA8 2RP**
emaš: info@warrenfarm.co.uk web: www.warrenfarm.co.uk
dir: *M5 junctÚn 22 , B3140 through Burnham-on-Sea to Berrow and Brean. Site 1.5 mŠes past Brean Leisure Park.*

A large famŠy-run holiday park just a short walk from the beach and divided up into several fields (pet-friendly and pet-free), each with its own designated tacŠities. The pitches are spacÚus and level and both grass pitches and hardstandings are avaŠable; there are good panoramic views of the Mendip HŠls and Brean Down. Luxury 'En suite Super Pitches' are also now avaŠable. The park has its own Beachcomber Inn with bar, restaurant and entertainment area. The site is perfect for famŠies and has an indoor play barn. Lake fishing is avaŠable on site and there is also a fishing tackle and bait shop.

Open: AprŠ to October **Last arrival:** 20.00 **Last departure:** 11.00
Pitches: 🚐 from £11; 🚐 from £11; ▲ from £11; 136 hardstanding pitches; 400 seasonal pitches

Leisure: 🎱 🎣 🎵 🎿 ⚽
FacŠities: 🛁 ☉ 🅿 ✳ 👶 💲 🎏 🛒 WiFi
Services: 🔌 🗑 🍺 🍽 🏪 🔋 🛗 🔒 🚿 T
Within 3 mŠes: 🏇 ∪ ≋

AdditÚnal site informatÚn: 100 acre site. 🐕 No commercial vehicles. Arcade, farm walk, clubhouse, entertainment. 'En suite Super Pitches' from £41.

See advert on page 258

Premier Park

Holiday Resort Unity

▶▶▶▶▶ 93% HOLIDAY CENTRE

tel: 01278 751235 **Coast Road, Brean Sands TA8 2RB**
emaš: admin@hru.co.uk web: www.hru.co.uk
dir: *M5 junctÚn 22, B3140 through Burnham-on-Sea, through Berrow to Brean. Site on left just before Brean Leisure Park.*

This is an excellent, famŠy-run holiday park offering very good touring facŠities plus a wide range of famŠy-oriented activities including bowling, RJ's entertainment club. There's plenty of eating outlets – The Tavern, RJ's, an American-themed diner, the beach-themed Bucket & Spade (especially suitable for smaller chŠdren), cafés and takeaway optÚns. Brean Splash Waterpark is situated directly opposite this touring park – a discounted entry price is avaŠable. Wooden camping pods, yurts, fully-equipped safari tents, and Euro tents are also avaŠable for hire. The park also holds 'themed' weekends and rallies are also welcome.

Open: February to November **Last arrival:** 21.00 **Last departure:** 10.00 (late departures – charges apply)
Pitches: 🚐 🚐 ▲ 🏕; 158 hardstanding pitches; 168 seasonal pitches
Leisure: 🏊 ≋ 🎱 🎿 🎣 ⚲ 🎵 🎿 ⚽
FacŠities: 🛁 ☉ 🅿 👶 💲 🛒 WiFi
Services: 🔌 🗑 🍺 🍽 🏪 🛗 🔒 🚿 T
Within 3 mŠes: ∪ ◎ 🎿

AdditÚnal site informatÚn: 200 acre site. 🐕 FamŠy parties of 3 or more must be over 21 years (young persons' policy applies). Arcade, soft play, dog walk.

Glamping avaŠable: Safari tents; Euro tents; wooden pods; yurts.

Changeover days: contact site for detaŠs

AdditÚnal glamping informatÚn: Safari tents: sleep 4. Wooden pods: sleep 2 adults and 2 chŠdren. Yurts: sleep 4 (2 single beds avaŠable on request). Euro tents: sleep 6 (some are pet-friendly). Cars can be parked by glamping units.

LEISURE: 🏊 Indoor swimming pool 🏊 Outdoor swimming pool 🛝 Children's playground 🙌 Kids' club 🎾 Tennis court 🎱 Games room 📺 Separate TV room
🏌 golf course ⛳ Pitch n putt ⚓ Boats for hire 🚲 Bikes for hire 🎬 Cinema 🎵 Entertainment 🎣 Fishing ◉ Mini golf 🏄 Watersports 🏋 Gym ⚽ Sports field ⛺ Stables
FACILITIES: 🛁 Baths/Shower ⊙ Electric shaver sockets 💈 Hairdryer ❄ Ice Pack Facility 🍼 Baby facilities ♿ Disabled facilities 🏪 Shop on site or within 200yds
🍖 BBQ area 🌲 Picnic area 📶 WiFi

BREAN *continued*

Northam Farm Caravan & Touring Park

►►►► 95%

tel: 01278 751244 **TA8 2SE**
email: stay@northamfarm.co.uk **web:** www.northamfarm.co.uk
dir: *M5 junction 22, B3140 to Burnham-on-Sea and Brean. Park on right 0.5 mile after Brean Leisure Park.*

An attractive site that's just a short walk from the sea and a long sandy beach. This quality park also has lots of children's play areas, and also owns the Seagull Inn about 600 yards away, which includes a restaurant and entertainment. There is a top quality fishing lake on site, which is very popular and has been featured on TV. The facilities on this park are excellent. A DVD of the site is available on request, free of charge. The park has a main caravan dealership plus full workshop and repair facility.

Open: March to October (restricted service: March and October – reduced hours for shop, café and takeaway) **Last arrival:** 20.00 **Last departure:** 10.30

Pitches: 🚐 from £14.50; 🚌 from £14.50; ⛺ from £12.50; 300 hardstanding pitches; 200 seasonal pitches

Leisure: 🛝 🎣 ⚽ **Facilities:** 🛁 ☺ 🚿 ✲ ♿ [$] 🪑 WiFi

Services: 🔌 🧺 🍷 🍴 🍟 🔋 🚰 🔥 ⛽ [T]

Within 3 miles: ⛳ 🐎 🎯 🎬

Additional site information: 30 acre site. 🐕 Cars can be parked by caravans and tents. Awnings permitted. Families and couples only, no commercial vehicles. Car hire can be arranged.

See advert opposite

BRIDGETOWN — Map 3 SS93

Places to visit

Dunster Castle, DUNSTER, TA24 6SL, 01643 821314
www.nationaltrust.org.uk/dunstercastle

Cleeve Abbey, WASHFORD, TA23 0PS, 01984 640377
www.english-heritage.org.uk/daysout/properties/cleeve-abbey

Premier Park

Exe Valley Caravan Site

►►►►► 87%

tel: 01643 851432 **Mill House TA22 9JR**
email: info@exevalleycamping.co.uk **web:** www.exevalleycamping.co.uk
dir: *From south: M5 junction 27, A361 signed Tiverton. 7 miles, right at roundabout signed Bampton. Left at Exeter Inn roundabout, 2 miles, take A396. Through Exebridge to Bridgetown, left after Badgers Holt Inn, site on right. (Note: for sat nav use TA22 9JN).*

Set in the Exmoor National Park, this adults-only park occupies an enchanting, peaceful spot in a wooded valley alongside the River Exe. There is free fly-fishing, an abundance of wildlife and excellent walks leading directly from the park. The site has good, spotlessly clean facilities. The inn opposite serves meals at lunchtime and in the evening.

Open: 15 March to 14 October **Last arrival:** 22.00 **Last departure:** 11.00

Pitches: 🚐 from £14.50; 🚌 from £14.50; ⛺ from £14.50; 13 hardstanding pitches; 1 seasonal pitch

Leisure: 🎣

Facilities: 🛁 ☺ 🚿 ✲ ♿ [$] 🍖 🪑 WiFi

Services: 🔌 🧺 🔋 🚰 🔥 ⛽ [T]

Within 3 miles: 🐎 ≋ ⚘

Additional site information: 4 acre site. Adults only. 🐕 💳 Cars can be parked by caravans and tents. Awnings permitted. 17th-century mill. TV sockets and cables.

BRIDGWATER
Map 4 ST23

Places to visit

Hestercombe Gardens, TAUNTON, TA2 8LG, 01823 413923
www.hestercombe.com

Coleridge Cottage, NETHER STOWEY, TA5 1NQ, 01278 732662
www.nationaltrust.org.uk/coleridgecottage

Great for kids: Tropiquaria Zoo, WASHFORD, TA23 0QB, 01984 640688
www.tropiquaria.co.uk

Mill Farm Caravan & Camping Park

►►►► 85%

tel: 01278 732286 **Fiddington TA5 1JQ**
web: www.millfarm.biz
dir: *From Bridgwater take A39 west, left at Cannington roundabout, 2 miles, right just beyond Apple Tree Inn towards Fiddington. Follow camping signs.*

A large holiday park with plenty to interest all the family, including indoor and outdoor pools, a boating lake, a gym, horse riding and a BMX track. There is also a clubhouse with bar, and a full entertainment programme in the main season. Although lively and busy in the high season, the park also offers a much quieter environment at other times; out of season, some activities and entertainment may not be available.

Open: mid March to 1 December **Last arrival:** 23.00 **Last departure:** 10.00

Pitches: from £14.50; from £14.50; from £14.50; 75 seasonal pitches

Leisure:

Facilities: WiFi

Services:

Within 3 miles:

Additional site information: 6 acre site. Cars can be parked by caravans and tents. Awnings permitted. No noise after 23.00. Canoeing, pool table, trampolines, fitness classes, saunas.

See advert opposite

BURNHAM-ON-SEA
Map 4 ST34

Places to visit

The Helicopter Museum, WESTON-SUPER-MARE, BS24 8PP, 01934 635227
www.helicoptermuseum.co.uk

King John's Hunting Lodge, AXBRIDGE, BS26 2AP, 01934 732012
www.kingjohnshuntinglodge.co.uk

Premier Park

Burnham-on-Sea Holiday Village

►►►►► 91% HOLIDAY CENTRE

tel: 01278 783391 **Marine Drive TA8 1LA**
email: burnhamonsea@haven.com **web:** www.haven.com/burnhamonsea
dir: *M5 junction 22, A38 towards Highbridge. Over mini roundabout, right onto B3139 to Burnham. After petrol station, left into Marine Drive. Park 400 yards on left.*

A large, family-orientated holiday village complex with a separate touring park containing 43 super pitches. There is a wide range of activities, including excellent indoor and outdoor pools, plus bars, restaurants and entertainment for all the family – there is plenty to do for all ages without even leaving the park. The coarse fishing lake is very popular, and the seafront at Burnham is only half a mile away. A wide range of well laid out holiday homes is available to rent and there's a Safari Village with fully-equipped safari tents for hire.

Open: mid March to end October (restricted service: mid March to May and September to end October – some facilities may be reduced) **Last arrival:** anytime **Last departure:** 10.00

Pitches: see prices below; 46 hardstanding pitches

Leisure:

Facilities: WiFi

Services:

Within 3 miles:

Additional site information: 94 acre site. No pets, no commercial vehicles, no bookings by persons under 21 years unless a family booking.

Glamping available: Safari tents from £125. **Changeover days:** Fridays and Mondays

Additional glamping information: Safari tents: minimum stay 3 nights. Price shown is for 3 nights. Includes 2 ring cooker, kettle, toaster, microwave and fridge.

CHEDDAR
Map 4 ST45

Places to visit

Cheddar Gorge (NT), CHEDDAR, 01934 744689
www.nationaltrust.org.uk/cheddar-gorge

Glastonbury Abbey, GLASTONBURY, BA6 9EL, 01458 832267
www.glastonburyabbey.com

Great for kids: Wookey Hole Caves & Papermill, WOOKEY HOLE, BA5 1BB,
01749 672243, www.wookey.co.uk

Platinum Park

Cheddar Woods Resort & Spa
▶▶▶▶▶ HOLIDAY HOME PARK

tel: 01934 742610 **Axbridge Road BS27 3DB**
email: enquiries@cheddarwoods.co.uk
web: www.darwinescapes.co.uk/parks/cheddar-woods-resort-spa/
dir: From M5 junction 22 follow signs for 'Cheddar Gorge & Caves' (8 miles). Site
midway between Cheddar and Axbridge on A371.

Situated in the beautiful Mendip Hills, Cheddar Woods is the perfect place to
relax and unwind, and this state-of-the-art park is an ideal location for family
holidays. Both large and smaller lodges are available for hire, all offering top
quality accommodation. There are excellent leisure facilities including a gym,
spa and swimming pool plus a 'Go Active' programme, and a pizza bar. In
addition, there is a very tasteful bar and good restaurant. The park is just
outside the village of Cheddar with its famous caves and is well positioned for
visiting Wells, Weston-Super-Mare and many other attractions in the area. It
should be noted this is a lodge-only park.

Open: All year
Holiday Homes: Sleep 8 Bedrooms 4 Bathrooms 2 Toilets 2 Two-ring burner
Dishwasher Washing Machine Tumble dryer Microwave Freezer TV Sky/Freeview DVD
player WiFi Linen included Towels included Electricity included Gas included
Woodburner
Prices: Low season from £355; High season from £909; Weekly from £600
Leisure: 🏊 ⛰ 🐟 ♨ 🎵 🏹 ⚽ Spa
Facilities: ♿ 💲
Within 3 miles: 🎣 ↻
Additional site information: 🐕

Mill Farm Caravan and Camping Park
Fiddington, Bridgwater, TA5 1JQ

Swimming * Riding * Boating

Friendly park with Lots
for children, making it
the ideal family park.

HIRE: Trampolines, Pony
rides, Canoes, Pool tables

FREE: Heated Swimming
Pool and Large water slide
Children's Boating Lake,
BMX track, Games room
and Hot showers

ALSO: Hot take-away and
shop during high season.

* Club with Entertainment
* Meadow for Rallies
* Holiday Cottages
* Caravan Storage
* Season Pitches

01278 732286   www.millfarm.biz

COWSLIP GREEN
Map 4 ST46

Places to visit

Clevedon Court, CLEVEDON, BS21 6QU, 01275 872257
www.nationaltrust.org.uk/clevedon-court

Bristol Museum & Art Gallery, BRISTOL, BS8 1RL, 0117 922 3571
www.bristolmuseums.org.uk

Brook Lodge Farm Camping & Caravan Park

►►► 92%

tel: 01934 862311 **BS40 5RB**
email: brooklodgefrm@gmail.com **web:** www.brooklodgefarm.com
dir: M5 junction 22, A38 to Churchill. Site 4 miles on right opposite Holiday Inn. Or M5 junction 18, follow Bristol Airport signs. From A38 towards Bridgwater (airport on right). Site 3 miles on left at bottom of hill.

A naturally sheltered country touring park sitting in a valley of the Mendip Hills, surrounded by trees and a historic walled garden. A friendly welcome is always assured by the family owners who are particularly keen on preserving the site's environment and have won a green tourism award. This park is particularly well placed for visiting the Bristol Balloon Festival, held in August, plus the many country walks in the area. There is also a separate glamping area, with bell tents, which has become very popular.

Open: March to October **Last arrival:** 21.00 **Last departure:** 11.45

Pitches: 🚐 🚾 ⛺ 🏠; 3 hardstanding pitches

Facilities: ⊙ 🅟 ✳ ⑤ 🛒 🎋 WiFi

Services: 🔌 ⑤ 🧺 🛒 🔒

Within 3 miles: ♨ 🎣 ∪

Additional site information: 4.5 acre site. 🐕 Dogs by prior arrangement only. Cars can be parked by caravans and tents. Awnings permitted. Cycle loan, walking maps available, fire pits.

Glamping available: Bell tents (contact site for more information)

CREWKERNE

See Drimpton (Dorset)

CROWCOMBE
Map 3 ST13

Places to visit

Cleeve Abbey, WASHFORD, TA23 0PS, 01984 640377
www.english-heritage.org.uk/daysout/properties/cleeve-abbey

Great for kids: Dunster Castle, DUNSTER, TA24 6SL, 01643 821314
www.nationaltrust.org.uk/dunstercastle

Premier Park

Quantock Orchard Caravan Park
►►►►► 78%

tel: 01984 618618 **Flaxpool TA4 4AW**
email: info@quantockorchard.co.uk **web:** www.quantock-orchard.co.uk
dir: Take A358 from Taunton, follow Minehead and Williton signs. In 8 miles left just past Flaxpool Garage. Site immediately on left.

This small family-run park is set at the foot of the beautiful Quantock Hills and makes an ideal base for touring Somerset, Exmoor and north Devon. It is also close to the West Somerset Railway. There is a lovely heated outdoor swimming pool, plus gym and fitness centre; bike hire is also available. There are static homes for hire.

Open: All year (restricted service: 10 September to 20 May – swimming pool closed) **Last arrival:** 22.00 **Last departure:** noon

Pitches: 🚐 🚾 ⛺; 30 hardstanding pitches

Leisure: 🏊 ⅊ 🎱 ⊡ 🏓 ⛳ Spa

Facilities: 🛁 ⊙ 🅟 ✳ ♿ ⑤ 🛒 🎋 WiFi

Services: 🔌 ⑤ 🧺 ⬆ 🔒 🖤 T

Within 3 miles: ♨ 🎣 ∪

Additional site information: 3.5 acre site. 🐕 Cars can be parked by caravans and tents. Awnings permitted. Off licence.

LEISURE: 🏊 Indoor swimming pool 🏊 Outdoor swimming pool ⅊ Children's playground 👶 Kids' club 🎾 Tennis court 🎱 Games room ⬚ Separate TV room ⛳ golf course 🏌 Pitch n putt 🚣 Boats for hire 🚲 Bikes for hire 🎬 Cinema 🎵 Entertainment 🎣 Fishing ◎ Mini golf 🏄 Watersports 💪 Gym 🏅 Sports field ∪ Stables
FACILITIES: 🛁 Baths/Shower ⊙ Electric shaver sockets 🅟 Hairdryer ✳ Ice Pack Facility 👶 Baby facilities ♿ Disabled facilities ⑤ Shop on site or within 200yds 🛒 BBQ area 🎋 Picnic area WiFi WiFi

DULVERTON

Map 3 SS92

Places to visit

Knightshayes, KNIGHTSHAYES, EX16 7RQ, 01884 254665
www.nationaltrust.org.uk/knightshayes

Great for kids: Tiverton Castle, TIVERTON, EX16 6RP, 01884 253200
www.tivertoncastle.com

Wimbleball Lake

►►► 84%

tel: 01398 371460 & 371116 **Brompton Regis TA22 9NU**
email: wimbleball@swlakestrust.org.uk **web:** www.swlakestrust.org.uk
dir: From A396 (Tiverton to Minehead road) take B3222 signed Dulverton Services, follow
signs to Wimbleball Lake. Ignore 1st entry (fishing), take 2nd entry signed tea room and
camping. (Note: care needed due to narrow roads).

A grassy site overlooking Wimbleball Lake, set high up on Exmoor National Park. The
camping area is adjacent to the visitor centre and café, which also includes the
camping toilets and showers. A new toilet block is due to open for 2019. The
camping field, with 14 electric hook-ups and two hardstandings, is in a quiet and
peaceful setting with good views of the lake, which is nationally renowned for its
trout fishing; boats can be hired with advance notice. There are two camping pods
and three Lotus Belle tents for hire.

Open: March to October **Last arrival:** 22.00 **Last departure:** 11.00

Pitches: 🚐 🚙 ⛺ 🏠; 2 hardstanding pitches

Leisure: ⚽

Facilities: 🚿 ☺ 🅿 ♿ 🔒 🛒 ♨

Services: 🔌 🗄 🍽 🛒

Within 3 miles: 🚲 () 👣 🎣

Additional site information: 1.25 acre site. 🐕 Dogs must be kept on leads at all times
and are not permitted in lake. Cars can be parked by caravans and tents. Awnings
permitted. No open fires, off-ground BBQs only, no swimming in lake. Watersports and
activity centre, birdwatching, cycling, lakeside walks and bushcraft. Internet access
available.

Glamping available: 2 wooden pods; 3 Lotus Belle tents.

Additional glamping information: Cars can be parked by pods and tents.

EXFORD

Places to visit

Dunster Castle, DUNSTER, TA24 6SL, 01643 821314
www.nationaltrust.org.uk/dunstercastle

West Somerset Railway, MINEHEAD, TA24 5BG, 01643 704996
www.west-somerset-railway.co.uk

Great for kids: Exmoor Zoological Park, BLACKMOOR GATE, EX31 4SG,
01598 763352, www.exmoorzoo.co.uk

EXFORD

Map 3 SS83

Westermill Farm

►►► 87%

tel: 01643 831238 & 07970 594808 **TA24 7NJ**
email: info@westermill.com **web:** www.westermill.com
dir: In Exford follow Porlock sign. Left in 0.25 mile, left to Westermill, sign on tree. Fork
left. (Note: this is the only recommended route).

An idyllic site for peace and quiet, in a sheltered valley in the heart of Exmoor,
which has won awards for conservation. Highly recommended for traditional
camping, although a few hardstandings and electric hook ups are available. There
are four waymarked walks over the 500-acre working farm and there's two miles of
shallow water of the River Exe to bathe or fish in (not coarse fishing). Self-catering
accommodation is also available. Please note, this site should only be approached
from Exford (other approaches are difficult).

Open: March to October (restricted service: November to May — smaller toilet block and
shop closed)

Pitches: 🚐 🚙 ⛺ from £18.50

Leisure: 🎣

Facilities: 🚿 ☺ 🅿 ☀ ♿ 🔒 🛒 📶

Services: 🔌 🗄 🛒 ♨

Additional site information: 12 acre site. 🐕 Well behaved dogs accepted. Cars can be
parked by caravans and tents. Awnings permitted. No noise after 23.00. 4 waymarked
walks, 500-acre farm.

FROME

Map 4 ST74

Places to visit

Stourhead, STOURHEAD, BA12 6QD, 01747 841152
www.nationaltrust.org.uk/stourhead

Nunney Castle, NUNNEY, 0370 333 1181
www.english-heritage.org.uk/dayout/properties/nunney-castle

Great for kids: Longleat, LONGLEAT, BA12 7NW, 01985 844400
www.longleat.co.uk

Seven Acres Caravan & Camping Site

►►► 85%

tel: 01373 464222 **Seven Acres, West Woodlands BA11 5EQ**
dir: From roundabout on A361 (Frome bypass) onto B3092 towards Maiden Bradley,
0.75 mile to site.

A level meadowland site beside the shallow River Frome, with a bridge across to an
adjacent field, and plenty of scope for families. The facilities are spotless. Set on
the edge of the Longleat Estate with its stately home, wildlife safari park and many
other attractions.

Open: March to October

Pitches: * 🚐 from £18; 🚙 from £18; ⛺ from £13; 16 hardstanding pitches

Facilities: 🚿 ☺ 🅿 ☀ ♨

Services: 🔌

Within 3 miles: 🎿 🚲 () 🎯 🛒 🗄

Additional site information: 3 acre site. 🐕 🚫 Cars can be parked by caravans and
tents. Awnings permitted.

PITCHES: 🚐 Caravans 🚙 Motorhomes ⛺ Tents 🏠 Glamping accommodation **SERVICES:** 🔌 Electric hook-up 🗄 Launderette 🍺 Licensed bar
🔥 Calor Gas 🧴 Campingaz Ⓣ Toilet fluid 🍽 Café/Restaurant 🍔 Fast Food/Takeaway 🔋 Battery charging 🔧 Motorhome service point
* 2019 prices 💳 No credit or debit cards 🐕 Dogs permitted 🚫 No dogs

GLASTONBURY
Map 4 ST53

Places to visit

Lytes Cary Manor, KINGSDON, TA11 7HU, 01458 224471
www.nationaltrust.org.uk/lytes-cary-manor

Fleet Air Arm Museum, YEOVILTON, BA22 8HT, 01935 840565
www.fleetairarm.com

Great for kids: Haynes International Motor Museum, SPARKFORD, BA22 7LH, 01963 440804, www.himm.co.uk

Platinum Park

The Old Oaks Touring Park
►►►►►

tel: 01458 831437 **Wick Farm, Wick BA6 8JS**
email: info@theoldoaks.co.uk **web:** www.theoldoaks.co.uk
dir: M5 junction 23, A39 to Glastonbury. After Street take A39 towards Wells. At 3rd roundabout follow Wick and Brindham signs. Site 1.5 miles on right. (Note: it is advisable not to use sat nav for last part of journey).

An exceptional adults-only park offering larger than average landscaped pitches (premier pitches have satellite HD TV), impeccably maintained grounds and wonderful views. The perfect 'get away from it all' spot where you can enjoy walking, cycling, fishing and touring or simply relaxing amid the abundant wildlife. The top class facilities include a well-stocked shop selling locally-sourced produce and home-baked cakes, a smart shower block with excellent wet rooms, WiFi, free walking and cycling maps, a half-acre fishing lake, a daily mini bus service to nearby towns and even a hot doggy shower! Glamping now comprises six 2-person, heated wooden 'camping cabins', two shepherd's huts and four new mini lodges, all beautifully equipped to a high standard.

Open: March to mid November (restricted service: March and October to November – reduced opening hours at shop and reception) **Last arrival:** 20.00 **Last departure:** noon

Pitches: 🚐 from £22; 🚌 from £22; ▲ from £22; 🏠 see prices below; 88 hardstanding pitches

Leisure: 🖵 🎣

Facilities: 🛁 ⊙ 🖤 ✳ 👶 ⑤ WiFi

Services: 🔌 🗑 🖬 🧺 ⚱ 🔒 🐾 Ⓣ

Additional site information: 15 acre site. Adults only. 🐕 Cars can be parked by caravans and tents. Awnings permitted. No groups, no noise after 22.30. Off licence, local produce boxes, caravan cleaning, dog owners' information pack, fish and chip nights, minibus. Car hire can be arranged.

Glamping available: Wooden pods from £59; shepherd's hut from £85; shepherd's hut with hot tub from £105; mini cedar lodges from £99; mini cedar lodges with hot tub from £119. **Changeover days:** any day

Additional glamping information: Each glamping unit has a fire pit and picnic bench and are dog friendly. Cars can be parked by glamping units.

Premier Park

Middlewick Farm
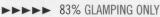
►►►►► 83% GLAMPING ONLY

tel: 01458 832351 **Wick Lane BA6 8JW**
email: hello@themiddlewick.co.uk **web:** www.themiddlewick.co.uk
dir: From Glastonbury take A361 towards Frome. After Millfield Prep School (on right) take next left signed Wick. Site on left in 1.5 miles.

A short walk past the cottages on this camping site brings you to the glamping area where there are three stylish E-den wooden camping cabins with good privacy and views of the Tor. Each has a double bed, small fridge, heater, cutlery and clothes storage, plus a porch and decking area with table, chairs and BBQ. In addition, each unit has a separate, spacious cabin with high spec toilet, washbasin and shower. There is also a shepherd's hut that accommodates additional guests. The site also has a function room, a very nice indoor swimming pool, and a pizza-oven for the popular pizza nights during the main season. The site offers a peaceful environment but is well located for visiting nearby Wells, Clarks Village or Weston-Super-Mare, all just a short drive away.

Open: All year **Last arrival:** 20.00 **Last departure:** 10.00

Leisure: 🏊

Facilities: 🛁 ⊙ 🖤 ✳ ⑤ 🛏 🏕 🛒 WiFi

Within 3 miles: ∪

Accommodation available: Wooden pods (E-den cabins); shepherd's hut.

Additional site information: 16 acre site. 🐕 Steam room.

Isle of Avalon Touring Caravan Park
►►►► 87%

tel: 01458 833618 **Godney Road BA6 9AF**
email: candicehatwell@hotmail.co.uk **web:** www.avaloncaravanpark.co.uk
dir: M5 junction 23, A39 to outskirts of Glastonbury, 2nd exit signed Wells at B&Q roundabout, straight on at next roundabout, 1st exit at next roundabout (B3151), site 200 yards on right.

A popular site, on the south side of this historic town, and within easy walking distance of the centre. It is a level park, with a separate tent field, that offers a quiet environment. It makes an ideal spot from which to explore the many local attractions that include Glastonbury Tor, Wells, Wookey Hole and Clarks Village. Approved caravan storage is available.

Open: All year **Last arrival:** 21.00 **Last departure:** 11.00

Pitches: 🚐 🚌 ▲; 70 hardstanding pitches

Facilities: ⊙ 🖤 ✳ 👶 ⑤ 🛏 🏕 WiFi

Services: 🔌 🗑 🖬 🧺 ⚱ 🐾 Ⓣ

Within 3 miles: 🎣 ∪ 🎾

Additional site information: 8 acre site. 🐕 Cars can be parked by caravans and tents. Awnings permitted. No ball games.

LEISURE: 🏊 Indoor swimming pool 🏊 Outdoor swimming pool ⚠ Children's playground 🧒 Kids' club 🎾 Tennis court 🎱 Games room 🖵 Separate TV room
🏌 golf course ⛳ Pitch n putt 🚣 Boats for hire 🚲 Bikes for hire 🎬 Cinema 🎵 Entertainment 🎣 Fishing ◎ Mini golf 🏄 Watersports 🏋 Gym 🏟 Sports field ∪ Stables
FACILITIES: 🛁 Baths/Shower ⊙ Electric shaver sockets 🖤 Hairdryer ✳ Ice Pack Facility 👶 Baby facilities 👶 Disabled facilities ⑤ Shop on site or within 200yds
🛒 BBQ area 🏕 Picnic area WiFi WiFi

HIGHBRIDGE Map 4 ST34

Places to visit

Huntspill River National Nature Reserve, WEST HUNTSPILL
www.gov.uk/government/publications/somersets-national-nature-reserves/somersets-national-nature-reserves#huntspill-river

Greenacre Place Touring Caravan Park

►►► 86%

tel: 01278 785227 & 07717 822852 **Bristol Road, Edithmead TA9 4HA**
email: info@greenacreplace.com **web:** www.greenacreplace.com
dir: *M5 junction 22, A38 signed Weston-Super-Mare and Burnham-on-Sea. At roundabout take A38 signed Highbridge and Bridgwater. Site on right.*

An excellent small adults-only park, very well located near to the M5 junction 22, making it great for visiting the Somerset Levels, Burnham-on-Sea, Brean, Cheddar or Clarks Village. It also makes an excellent stopover when travelling to and from the West Country. All 10 pitches have electric hook-ups and the small facility block is very well appointed and clean. There is free WiFi and also a two-bedroom cottage available for hire where children are accepted. The park is also well placed for anyone visiting the Somerset Carnivals held in November. Dogs are welcome.

Open: March to November **Last arrival:** 22.00 **Last departure:** 11.00

Pitches: 🚐 from £14; 🚌 from £14

Facilities: 🚿 ☺ ♿ [WiFi]

Services: 🔌

Within 3 miles: ⛳ 🎣 🐎 🎯 🏊 ⛵ ▤ 🛍 🧺

Additional site information: 0.5 acre site. Adults only. 🐕 Cars can be parked by caravans. Awnings permitted. Breathable groundsheets only, no ball games.

MARTOCK Map 4 ST41

Places to visit

Montacute House, MONTACUTE, TA15 6XP, 01935 823289
www.nationaltrust.org.uk/montacute-house

Great for kids: Fleet Air Arm Museum, YEOVILTON, BA22 8HT, 01935 840565
www.fleetairarm.com

Southfork Caravan Park

🛖

►►►► 86%

tel: 01935 825661 **Parrett Works TA12 6AE**
email: info@southforkcaravans.co.uk **web:** www.southforkcaravans.co.uk
dir: *From A303: approximately 2 miles after Cargate roundabout exit left A303, over fly-over, signed A356 Martock. At junction left, then after sharp bend, next right. Site approximately 1 mile on right. M25 junction 25: follow A358 signed Yeovil. At roundabout junction of A303/A358, 1st exit signed Andover/London. Follow A303, to junction then left to Martock.*

A neat, level mainly grass park in a quiet rural area, just outside the pretty village of Martock. Some excellent spacious hardstandings are available. The facilities are always spotless and the whole site is well cared for by the friendly owners, who will ensure your stay is a happy one, a fact borne out by the many repeat customers. The park is unique in that it also has a fully-approved caravan repair and servicing centre with accessory shop. There are also static caravans, a camping pod and a lodge available for hire. Caravan storage is also available.

Open: All year **Last arrival:** 22.30 **Last departure:** noon

Pitches: 🚐 from £16; 🚌 from £16; ⛺ from £16; 🛖 see prices below; 5 hardstanding pitches

Facilities: 🚿 ☺ 💨 ❄ 🛍 [WiFi]

Services: 🔌 🧺 🔋 🔥 🌿 [T]

Within 3 miles: ⛳ 🎣

Additional site information: 2 acre site. 🐕 Dogs must be kept on short leads at all times. Cars can be parked by caravans and tents. Awnings permitted. No loud noise after 22.30.

Glamping available: Wooden pod from £35.

Additional glamping information: 12 volt supply only, double beds. Cars can be parked by pod.

MINEHEAD Map 3 SS94

Places to visit

West Somerset Railway, MINEHEAD, TA24 5BG, 01643 704996
www.west-somerset-railway.co.uk

Dunster Castle, DUNSTER, TA24 6SL, 01643 821314
www.nationaltrust.org.uk/dunstercastle

Great for kids: Tropiquaria Zoo, WASHFORD, TA23 0QB, 01984 640688
www.tropiquaria.co.uk

Minehead & Exmoor Caravan & Camping Park

►►► 78%

tel: 01643 703074 **Porlock Road TA24 8SW**
email: enquiries@mineheadandexmoorcamping.co.uk
web: www.mineheadandexmoorcamping.co.uk
dir: *1 mile west of Minehead town centre take A39 towards Porlock. Site on right.*

A small terraced park, on the edge of Exmoor, spread over five small paddocks and screened by the mature trees that surround it. The level pitches provide a comfortable space for each unit on this family-run park. The site is very conveniently placed for visiting Minehead and the Exmoor National Park.

Open: March to October (restricted service: November to February – open certain weeks only (contact site for details)) **Last arrival:** 21.00 **Last departure:** 11.00

Pitches: 🚐 🚌 ⛺; 9 hardstanding pitches; 10 seasonal pitches

Leisure: 🛝

Facilities: 🚿 ☺ 💨 ❄ ♿

Services: 🔌 🔋 🔥 🌿

Within 3 miles: ⛳ 🎣 🎯 🏊 ▤ 🛍 🧺

Additional site information: 3 acre site. 🐕 💳 Cars can be parked by caravans and tents. Awnings permitted. No open fires or loud music. Tumble dryer available.

PORLOCK
Map 3 SS84

Places to visit

West Somerset Railway, MINEHEAD, TA24 5BG, 01643 704996
www.west-somerset-railway.co.uk

Dunster Castle, DUNSTER, TA24 6SL, 01643 821314
www.nationaltrust.org.uk/dunstercastle

Great for kids: Tropiquaria Zoo, WASHFORD, TA23 0QB, 01984 640688
www.tropiquaria.co.uk

Burrowhayes Farm Caravan & Camping Site & Riding Stables
▶▶▶▶ 94%

tel: 01643 862463 **West Luccombe TA24 8HT**
email: info@burrowhayes.co.uk **web:** www.burrowhayes.co.uk
dir: A39 from Minehead towards Porlock for 5 miles. Left at Red Post to Horner and West Luccombe, site 0.25 mile on right, immediately before humpback bridge.

A delightful site on the edge of Exmoor that slopes gently down to Horner Water. The farm buildings have been converted into riding stables from where escorted rides onto the moors can be taken; the excellent toilet facilities are housed in timber-clad buildings. Hardstandings are available – some are fully serviced and many of the hook-ups have TV points. There is a popular, well-stocked shop and many countryside walks can be accessed directly from the site.

Open: 15 March to October (restricted service: before Easter – caravan hire and riding not available) **Last arrival:** 22.00 **Last departure:** 11.00

Pitches: 🚐 from £20; 🚛 from £20; ▲ from £16; 16 hardstanding pitches
Facilities: 🚿 ⊙ 🗲 ✳ ♿ ⑤ 🍴 WiFi
Services: 🔌 🗑 🧺 ⚱ 🔒 🗑 Ⓣ
Within 3 miles: ⚓ 🎣 ∪ ◎

Additional site information: 8 acre site. 🐕 Cars can be parked by caravans and tents. Awnings permitted.

PRIDDY
Map 4 ST55

Places to visit

Glastonbury Abbey, GLASTONBURY, BA6 9EL, 01458 832267
www.glastonburyabbey.com

The Helicopter Museum, WESTON-SUPER-MARE, BS24 8PP, 01934 635227
www.helicoptermuseum.co.uk

Great for kids: Wookey Hole Caves & Papermill, WOOKEY HOLE, BA5 1BB,
01749 672243, www.wookey.co.uk

Cheddar Mendip Heights Camping & Caravanning Club Site
▶▶▶▶ 89%

tel: 01749 870241 & 024 7647 5426 **Townsend BA5 3BP**
email: cheddar.site@campingandcaravanningclub.co.uk
web: www.campingandcaravanningclub.co.uk/cheddar
dir: From A39 take B3135 to Cheddar. Left in 4.5 miles. Site 200 yards on right, signed.

A gently sloping site set high on the Mendip Hills and surrounded by trees. This excellent campsite offers really good facilities, including top notch family rooms and private cubicles which are spotlessly maintained. Fresh bread is baked daily and, along with pastries, can be ordered each morning from the well-stocked shop. The site is well positioned for visiting local attractions such as Cheddar, Wookey Hole, Wells and Glastonbury, and is popular with walkers. Self-catering caravans are available for hire.

Open: March to January **Last arrival:** 20.00 **Last departure:** noon

Pitches: 🚐 from £8.65; 🚛 from £8.65; ▲ from £8.65; 38 hardstanding pitches
Leisure: ⚠
Facilities: 🚿 ⊙ 🗲 ✳ ♿ ⑤ WiFi
Services: 🔌 🗑 🧺 🔒 🗑 Ⓣ
Within 3 miles: ⚓ ∪

Additional site information: 4.5 acre site. 🐕 Dogs must be on leads at all times. Cars can be parked by caravans and tents. Awnings permitted. Site gates closed 23.00–07.00. No fires, BBQs must be raised off the ground. Freshly baked bread and pastries, local preserves, bacon, sausages, lamb, beef, beer, cider and cheese available. Car hire can be arranged.

LEISURE: 🏊 Indoor swimming pool 🏊 Outdoor swimming pool 🎢 Children's playground 🧒 Kids' club 🎾 Tennis court 🎱 Games room 📺 Separate TV room
⛳ golf course 🏓 Pitch n putt 🚣 Boats for hire 🚲 Bikes for hire 🎬 Cinema 🎵 Entertainment 🎣 Fishing ⛳ Mini golf 🏄 Watersports 🏋 Gym ⚽ Sports field 🐎 Stables
FACILITIES: 🚿 Baths/Shower ⊙ Electric shaver sockets 🗲 Hairdryer ✳ Ice Pack Facility 👶 Baby facilities ♿ Disabled facilities ⑤ Shop on site or within 200yds
🍴 BBQ area 🪑 Picnic area WiFi WiFi

SHEPTON MALLET   Map 4 ST64

Places to visit

East Somerset Railway, CRANMORE, BA4 4QP, 01749 880417
www.eastsomersetrailway.com

The Bishop's Palace, WELLS, BA5 2PD, 01749 988111
www.bishopspalace.org.uk

Great for kids: Wookey Hole Caves & Papermill, WOOKEY HOLE, BA5 1BB, 01749 672243, www.wookey.co.uk

Greenacres Camping

▶▶   96%

tel: 01749 890497 **Barrow Lane, North Wootton BA4 4HL**
email: stay@greenacres-camping.co.uk **web:** www.greenacres-camping.co.uk
dir: *Approximately halfway between Glastonbury and Shepton Mallet on A361 turn at Steanbow Farm signed North Wootton. Or from A39 between Upper Coxley and Wells (at Brownes Garden Centre) into Woodford Lane. Follow North Wootton and site signs.*

An immaculately maintained site peacefully set within sight of Glastonbury Tor. It is mainly family orientated and there is plenty of space for children to play games in a very safe environment; many thoughtful extra facilities are provided such as play houses and a children's entertainment team in the high season. There is even a 'glow worm safari' at certain times of the year. Facilities are exceptionally clean and cycle hire is available. Please note, caravans and large motorhomes are not accepted.

Open: May to September **Last arrival:** 21.00 **Last departure:** 11.00
Pitches: 🚐 from £20; ⛺ from £20
Leisure: 🅰 🏊 ⊙
Facilities: 🛁 ⊙ ⌕ ☀ 🔥 🍴 🚪 WiFi
Services: 🔌 🛒 🔒 🍃
Within 3 miles: 🛶 🏌 ∪ 🎱 🛒

Additional site information: 4.5 acre site. ⊗ Cars can be parked by tents. Awnings permitted. No noise between 23.00–07.00. Fire pits, campfires, free use of fridges and freezers, book library. Car hire can be arranged.

SPARKFORD

Places to visit

Lytes Cary Manor, KINGSDON, TA11 7HU, 01458 224471
www.nationaltrust.org.uk/lytes-cary-manor

Haynes International Motor Museum, SPARKFORD, BA22 7LH, 01963 440804
www.himm.co.uk

SPARKFORD   Map 4 ST62

Long Hazel Park

▶▶▶▶   86%

tel: 01963 440002 **High Street BA22 7JH**
email: longhazelpark@hotmail.com **web:** www.longhazelpark.co.uk
dir: *Exit A303 at Hazlegrove roundabout, follow signs for Sparkford. Site 400 yards on left.*

A very neat, adults-only park next to the village inn in the high street. This attractive park is run by friendly owners to a very good standard. Many of the spacious pitches have hardstandings. There are also luxury lodges on site for hire or purchase. The site is close to the Haynes International Motor Museum and the Fleet Air Arm Museum.

Open: All year **Last arrival:** 21.00 **Last departure:** 11.00
Pitches: 🚐 🚍 ⛺; 30 hardstanding pitches; 21 seasonal pitches
Facilities: 🛁 ⊙ ⌕ ☀ 🔥 🍴 WiFi
Services: 🔌 🛒 🔒 🍃
Within 3 miles: 🛶 🏌 🛒

Additional site information: 3.5 acre site. Adults only. 🐕 Dogs must be kept on leads at all times and exercised outside the park. ⊗ Cars can be parked by caravans and tents. Awnings permitted. No open fires or fire pits, no noise after 22.00. Picnic tables available, camping spares.

Woodland Escape

▶▶▶▶   80% GLAMPING ONLY

tel: 01225 290924 **South Barrow BA22 7LR**
email: into@countryglampingholidays.co.uk **web:** www.woodlandescape.co.uk
dir: *Phone site (or see website) for detailed directions.*

Located just a mile from Sparkford, Woodland Escape is a back to basics 'off grid' glamping site tucked away in a wooded area, offering peace and tranquility for those wishing to get away from the hustle and bustle of everyday life. There are yurts, belle tents and a canvas lodge, well equipped on a 3-tier system of comfort (basic, classic and deluxe); all have cooking facilities, a barbecue, fire pit, picnic bench, plus a food hamper on arrival. The unisex toilets and showers are of a very good quality and there is hot tub hidden away in its own private glade. Dogs are very welcome.

Open: March to October **Last arrival:** 21.00 (by prior arrangement only)
Last departure: noon (by prior arrangement only)
Leisure: 🅰
Facilities: 🛁 ☀ 🍴
Within 3 miles: 🛒

Accommodation available: 7 bell tents from £53.50; 1 safari tent from £97.50; 2 yurts from £73.50.

Changeover days: Any day

Additional site information: 8.9 acre site. 🐕 Dogs must be kept on leads at all times. No noise after 23.00, respect for other guests. Hot tub, massage, board games, library, swingball, quoits, jenga, boules, giant xylophone, percussion pipes, giant connect 4, croquet, archery, welcome drinks, breakfast hampers, phone charging. Artisan food delivery to order. Cutlery and crockery, logs, kindling, charcoal, gas stoves available.

TAUNTON   Map 4 ST22

Places to visit

Hestercombe Gardens, TAUNTON, TA2 8LG, 01823 413923
www.hestercombe.com

Barrington Court, BARRINGTON, TA19 0NQ, 01460 241938
www.nationaltrust.org.uk/barrington-court

Cornish Farm Touring Park

▶▶▶▶ 87%

tel: 01823 327746 **Shoreditch TA3 7BS**
email: info@cornishfarm.com **web:** www.cornishfarm.com
dir: *M5 junction 25, A358 towards Taunton. Left at lights. 3rd left into Ilminster Road (follow Corfe signs). Right at roundabout, left at next roundabout. Right at T-junction, left into Killams Drive, 2nd left into Killams Avenue. Over motorway bridge. Site on left, access via 2nd entrance.*

This smart park provides really top quality facilities throughout. Although only two miles from Taunton, it is set in open countryside and is a very convenient base for visiting the many attractions of the area such as Clarks Village, Glastonbury and Cheddar Gorge. Also makes an excellent base for watching county cricket at the nearby Somerset County Ground.

Open: All year **Last arrival:** anytime **Last departure:** 11.30
Pitches: 🚐 from £18; 🚏 from £18; ▲ from £18; 25 hardstanding pitches
Facilities: 🏠 ☉ 🍽 ⅙ 🤝 WiFi
Services: 🔌 🗑 ⅃ 🔒 Ⓣ
Within 3 miles: ⅃ 🎣 ∪ ◎ 日 ⑤
Additional site information: 3.5 acre site. 🐕 Cars can be parked by caravans and tents. Awnings permitted.

Ashe Farm Camping & Caravan Site

▶▶▶ 82%

tel: 01823 443764 & 07891 989482 **Thornfalcon TA3 5NW**
email: info@ashefarm.co.uk **web:** www.ashefarm.co.uk
dir: *M5 junction 25, A358, east for 2.5 miles. Right at Nags Head pub. Site 0.25 mile on right.*

A well-screened site surrounded by mature trees and shrubs, with two large touring fields. The modern, upgraded facilities block includes toilets and showers plus a separate laundry room. This site is not far from the bustling market town of

Taunton, and handy for both south and north coasts. Also makes a good stopover for people travelling on the nearby M5.

Open: April to October **Last arrival:** 22.00 **Last departure:** noon
Pitches: 🚐 🚏 ▲; 11 hardstanding pitches
Leisure: ⚠ 🌡
Facilities: 🏠 ☉ 🍽 ✳ ⅙
Services: 🔌 🗑
Within 3 miles: ⅃ 🎣 ∪ ◎ 日 ⑤
Additional site information: 7 acre site. 🐕 🌳 Cars can be parked by caravans and tents. Awnings permitted. No camp fires, no noise after 22.00.

WATCHET   Map 3 ST04

Places to visit

West Somerset Railway, MINEHEAD, TA24 5BG, 01643 704996
www.west-somerset-railway.co.uk

Dunster Castle, DUNSTER, TA24 6SL, 01643 821314
www.nationaltrust.org.uk/dunstercastle

Great for kids: Tropiquaria Zoo, WASHFORD, TA23 0QB, 01984 640688
www.tropiquaria.co.uk

Premier Park

Doniford Bay Holiday Park

▶▶▶▶▶ 92% HOLIDAY HOME PARK

tel: 01984 632423 **TA23 0TJ**
email: donifordbay@haven.com **web:** www.haven.com/donifordbay
dir: *M5 junction 23, A38 towards Bridgwater, A39 towards Minehead. 15 miles, at West Quantoxhead, right after St Audries garage. Park 1 mile on right.*

This well-appointed holiday park, situated adjacent to a shingle and sand beach, offers a wide range of activities for the whole family. The holiday homes are spacious and well-appointed and there is plenty to keep children (of all ages) interested, including great indoor and outdoor pools, a multi-sports centre, slides and archery. The park has good eating outlets including a nice café/restaurant. Being close to the Exmoor National Park, it offers visitors the chance to seek out some of the best scenery in the county.

Open: mid March to end October

Holiday Homes: Sleep 8 Bedrooms 2 Bathrooms 1 Toilets 1 Microwave Freezer TV Sky/Freeview

Leisure: 🏊 🏊 ⚠ 🖐 🚴

Additional site information: 🐕 Most dog breeds accepted (please check when booking). Dogs must be kept on leads at all times.

Home Farm Holiday Centre

▶▶▶▶ 82%

tel: 01984 632487 **St Audries Bay TA4 4DP**
email: dib@homefarmholidaycentre.co.uk **web:** www.homefarmholidaycentre.co.uk
dir: *From Bridgwater take A39 to West Quantoxhead (approximately 15 miles), after garage, right onto B3191 signed Doniford. 0.25 mile, 1st right.*

In a hidden valley beneath the Quantock Hills, this park overlooks its own private beach. The atmosphere is friendly and quiet, and there are lovely sea views from

LEISURE: 🏊 Indoor swimming pool   🏊 Outdoor swimming pool   ⚠ Children's playground   🖐 Kids' club   🎾 Tennis court   🎱 Games room   📺 Separate TV room
⅃ golf course   ⛳ Pitch n putt   🚣 Boats for hire   🚲 Bikes for hire   🎬 Cinema   🎵 Entertainment   🎣 Fishing   ◎ Mini golf   🏄 Watersports   🏋 Gym   🏟 Sports field   ∪ Stables
FACILITIES: 🏠 Baths/Shower   ☉ Electric shaver sockets   🍽 Hairdryer   ✳ Ice Pack Facility   🍼 Baby facilities   ⅙ Disabled facilities   ⑤ Shop on site or within 200yds
🍖 BBQ area   🌳 Picnic area   WiFi WiFi

the level pitches. Flowerbeds, woodland walks and the Koi carp pond all enhance this very attractive site, along with a lovely indoor swimming pool, an excellent children's play area, and a beer garden.

Open: All year (restricted service: November to 1 March – no tents accepted; shop and bar closed) **Last arrival:** dusk **Last departure:** noon

Pitches: * 🚐 from £12; 🚍 from £12; 🏕 from £12; 35 hardstanding pitches

Leisure: 🏊 ⚔ 🎣

Facilities: 🚻 ⊙ 🕯 ✳ 🚿 🏧 WiFi

Services: 🔌 🗑 🍺 🔧 🛍 🧺 T

Additional site information: 45 acre site. 🐾 Cars can be parked by tents. Awnings permitted. No noise after 23.00. Table tennis, sea fishing, woodland walk, coastal path; baguettes, croissants and pain au chocolat available.

WELLS
Map 4 ST54

Places to visit
Glastonbury Abbey, GLASTONBURY, BA6 9EL, 01458 832267 www.glastonburyabbey.com

The Bishop's Palace, WELLS, BA5 2PD, 01749 988111 www.bishopspalace.org.uk

---

Premier Park

Wells Touring Park
▶▶▶▶▶ 92%

tel: 01749 676869 **Haybridge BA5 1AJ**
email: info@wellstouringpark.co.uk **web:** www.wellstouringpark.co.uk
dir: On A371 between Wells and Westbury-sub-Mendip.

This well established, adults-only holiday park has first-class toilet facilities and many hardstandings, some of which are fully serviced. It is a restful park set in countryside on the outskirts of Wells, and is within easy walking distance of the city centre, with its spectacular cathedral and Bishop's Palace. Cheddar Gorge, Bath, Bristol, Weston-Super-Mare, Wookey Hole and Glastonbury are all within easy driving distance. The site has a function room, The Lounge, which has free WiFi and a new coffee shop (opened in 2018), plus a hire car and an excellent doggy shower. Holiday cottages are available for hire and luxury lodges for sale.

Open: All year **Last arrival:** 20.00 **Last departure:** noon

Pitches: 🚐 🚍; 54 hardstanding pitches; 20 seasonal pitches

Leisure: 🖵

Facilities: 🚻 ⊙ 🕯 ✳ 🚿 🏧 🍴 🚏 WiFi

Services: 🔌 🗑 🚮 🛄 🛍 🧺 T

Within 3 miles: 🚶 🎣 🐾 ◎ 🎯

Additional site information: 7.5 acre site. Adults only. 🐾 Cars can be parked by caravans. Awnings permitted. No tents. Pétanque. Car hire can be arranged.

WESTON-SUPER-MARE
Map 4 ST36

Places to visit
Weston Museum, WESTON-SUPER-MARE, BS23 1PR, 01934 621028 www.westonmuseum.org

Great for kids: The Helicopter Museum, WESTON-SUPER-MARE, BS24 8PP, 01934 635227, www.helicoptermuseum.co.uk

---

Country View Holiday Park
▶▶▶▶ 88%

tel: 01934 627595 **Sand Road, Sand Bay BS22 9UJ**
email: info@cvhp.co.uk **web:** www.cvhp.co.uk
dir: M5 junction 21, A370 towards Weston-Super-Mare. Immediately into left lane, follow Kewstoke and Sand Bay signs. Straight over 3 roundabouts onto Lower Norton Lane. At Sand Bay right into Sand Road, site on right.

A pleasant open site in a rural area a few hundred yards from Sandy Bay and the beach. The park is also well placed for energetic walks along the coast at either end of the beach and is only a short drive away from Weston-Super-Mare. There is a touring section for tents, caravans and motorhomes with a toilet and shower block. There are hardstanding pitches plus grass pitches all with electricity. The facilities are excellent and well maintained, including a nice outdoor swimming pool and small tasteful bar. There is also a separate seasonal touring section with its own facility block.

Open: March to January **Last arrival:** 20.00 **Last departure:** noon

Pitches: 🚐 from £20; 🚍 from £20; 🏕 from £20; 150 hardstanding pitches; 90 seasonal pitches

Leisure: 🏊 🎣 🎵 ⚽ **Facilities:** 🚻 ⊙ 🕯 ✳ 🚿 🚏 WiFi

Services: 🔌 🗑 🚮 T **Within 3 miles:** 🚶 🎣 🐾 ◎ 🏌 🚴 🎯 🏧

Additional site information: 20 acre site. 🐾 Cars can be parked by caravans and tents. Awnings permitted.

WESTON-SUPER-MARE *continued*

West End Farm Caravan & Camping Park
►►► 84%

tel: 01934 822529 **Locking BS24 8RH**
email: robin@westendfarm.org **web:** www.westendcaravan.com
dir: *M5 junction 21 onto A370. Follow International Helicopter Museum signs. Right at roundabout, follow signs to site.*

A spacious and well laid out park bordered by hedges, with good landscaping, and well-kept facilities. Fully serviced pitches are available. There is a bus stop close to the site which is handily located next to a helicopter museum, and there's good access to Weston-Super-Mare and the Mendips.

Open: All year **Last arrival:** 21.00 (arrivals from noon) **Last departure:** noon

Pitches: 🚐 from £17; 🚐 from £17; ▲ from £17; 30 hardstanding pitches; 45 seasonal pitches

Leisure: 🏃

Facilities: 🚿 ☉ 🧑‍🦽 🛎️ WiFi

Services: 🚰 🗑️ ♨️ 🛒 ⊘

Within 3 miles: ⌄ ⌇ ∪ ◎ 🍴 🍴 📅 🛍️

Additional site information: 10 acre site. 🐕 Cars can be parked by caravans and tents. Awnings permitted. No noise after 22.00.

WINSFORD
Map 3 SS93

Places to visit
Dunster Castle, DUNSTER, TA24 6SL, 01643 821314
www.nationaltrust.org.uk/dunstercastle

Cleeve Abbey, WASHFORD, TA23 0PS, 01984 640377
www.english-heritage.org.uk/daysout/properties/cleeve-abbey

Great for kids: Tropiquaria Zoo, WASHFORD, TA23 0QB, 01984 640688
www.tropiquaria.co.uk

Halse Farm Caravan & Camping Park
►►►► 82%

tel: 01643 851259 **TA24 7JL**
email: info@halsefarm.co.uk **web:** www.halsefarm.co.uk
dir: *Signed from A396 at Bridgetown. In Winsford turn left, bear left past pub. 1 mile up hill, entrance on left immediately after cattle grid.*

A peaceful little site on Exmoor overlooking a wooded valley with glorious views. This moorland site is quite remote, but it provides good modern toilet facilities which are kept immaculately clean. This is a good base for exploring the Exmoor National Park, and Minehead, Porlock and Lynton are only a short drive away.

Open: 23 March to 31 October **Last arrival:** 22.00 **Last departure:** noon

Pitches: 🚐 from £16.50; 🚐 from £16.50; ▲ from £16.50

Leisure: 🛝

Facilities: 🚿 ☉ 📠 ❄️ 🧑‍🦽 WiFi

Services: 🚰 🗑️ 🛒 ⊘

Within 3 miles: ⌇ ∪ 🛍️

Additional site information: 3 acre site. 🐕 Cars can be parked by caravans and tents. Awnings permitted.

LEISURE: 🏊 Indoor swimming pool 🏊 Outdoor swimming pool 🛝 Children's playground 👦 Kids' club 🎾 Tennis court 🎱 Games room 📺 Separate TV room ⌄ golf course 🏌️ Pitch n putt ⛵ Boats for hire 🚲 Bikes for hire 🎬 Cinema 🎵 Entertainment 🎣 Fishing ◎ Mini golf 🏄 Watersports 🏋️ Gym 🏟️ Sports field ∪ Stables
FACILITIES: 🚿 Baths/Shower ☉ Electric shaver sockets 📠 Hairdryer ❄️ Ice Pack Facility 👶 Baby facilities 🧑‍🦽 Disabled facilities 🛍️ Shop on site or within 200yds 🍴 BBQ area 🍴 Picnic area WiFi WiFi

WIVELISCOMBE
Map 3 ST02

Places to visit

Cleeve Abbey, WASHFORD, TA23 0PS, 01984 640377
www.english-heritage.org.uk/daysout/properties/cleeve-abbey

Hestercombe Gardens, TAUNTON, TA2 8LG, 01823 413923
www.hestercombe.com

Premier Park

Waterrow Touring Park
▶▶▶▶▶ 92%

Best of British

tel: 01984 623464 **TA4 2AZ**
email: info@waterrowpark.co.uk **web:** www.waterrowpark.co.uk
dir: *M5 junction 25, A358 signed Minehead (bypassing Taunton), B3227 through Wiveliscombe. Site in 3 miles at Waterrow, 0.25 mile past Rock Inn.*

Under pro-active ownership, this really delightful park for adults has spotless facilities, plenty of spacious hardstandings, including fully serviced pitches and a motorhome service point. The River Tone runs along a valley beneath the park, accessed by steps to a nature area created by the owners, where fly-fishing is permitted. Watercolour painting workshops and other activities are available, and the local pub is a short walk away. There is also a bus stop just outside the site.

Open: All year **Last arrival:** 19.00 **Last departure:** 11.30
Pitches: 🚐 🚙 ▲; 40 hardstanding pitches
Facilities: ☺ 🏳 ⚒ ⚐ 🔥 [WiFi]
Services: 🔌 ⬚ ⚒ ⬆ 🔋 T
Within 3 miles: 🎣 💲

Additional site information: 8 acre site. Adults only. 🐕 Maximum 3 dogs per unit. Cars can be parked by caravans and tents. Awnings permitted. No gazebos. Caravan storage.

STAFFORDSHIRE

LONGNOR
Map 16 SK06

Places to visit

Poole's Cavern (Buxton Country Park), BUXTON, SK17 9DH, 01298 26978
www.poolescavern.co.uk

Haddon Hall, HADDON HALL, DE45 1LA, 01629 812855
www.haddonhall.co.uk

Premier Park

Longnor Wood Holiday Park
▶▶▶▶▶ 92%

tel: 01298 83648 & 07866 016567 **Newtown SK17 0NG**
email: info@longnorwood.co.uk **web:** www.longnorwood.co.uk
dir: *From A53 follow Longnor sign. Site signed from village, 1.25 miles.*

Enjoying a secluded and very peaceful setting in the heart of the Peak District National Park, this spacious adults-only park is a hidden gem. It is surrounded by beautiful rolling countryside and sheltered by woodland where there is a variety of wildlife to observe. Expect a warm welcome from the O'Neill family and excellent, well-maintained facilities, including spotlessly clean modern toilets, good hardstanding pitches, high levels of security, a putting green, badminton courts, a 4-acre dog walk (a dog wash is available too) and super walks from the park gate. The reception building includes a small shop. There are two fully-equipped log pods and six statics for hire.

Open: March to 10 January **Last arrival:** 19.00 **Last departure:** noon
Pitches: 🚐 from £26.50; 🚙 from £26.50; ▲ from £24.50; 🏠 see prices below; 47 hardstanding pitches; 13 seasonal pitches
Leisure: ⚽
Facilities: 📷 ☺ 🏳 ⚒ 💲 🔥 [WiFi]
Services: 🔌 ⬚ ⚒ ⬆ 🔋 ⊘ T
Within 3 miles: ⚡ 🎣 ⛳ ⛷ 🚴

Additional site information: 10.5 acre site. Adults only. 🐕 Cars can be parked by caravans and tents. Awnings permitted. No fires, no noise after 23.00. Car hire can be arranged.

Glamping available: 2 pods from £60. **Changeover days:** Any time
Additional glamping information: Pods: en suite bathroom, under-floor heating, double bed and linen, fully equipped kitchen unit, TV/DVD, large external deck, outside furniture. Cars can be parked by pods.

Suffolk

Suffolk is Constable country, where the county's crumbling, time-ravaged coastline spreads itself under wide skies to convey a wonderful sense of remoteness and solitude. Highly evocative and atmospheric, this is where rivers wind lazily to the sea and notorious 18th-century smugglers hid from the excise men.

It was the artist John Constable who was responsible for raising the region's profile in the 18th century. Constable immortalised these expansive flatlands in his paintings and today the marketing brochures and websites usually refer to the area as Constable Country. Situated on the River Stour at Flatford, Constable's mill is now a major tourist attraction in the area but a close look at the surroundings confirms rural Suffolk is little changed since the family lived here. Constable himself maintained that the Suffolk countryside 'made me a painter and I am grateful.'

Facing the European mainland and with easy access by the various rivers, the county's open, often bleak, landscape made Suffolk vulnerable in early times to attack from waves of invaders. In the Middle Ages, however, it prospered under the wool merchants: it was their wealth that built the great churches which dominate the countryside.

Walking is one of Suffolk's most popular recreational activities. It may be flat but the county has much to discover on foot – not least the isolated Heritage Coast, which can be accessed via the Suffolk Coast Path. Running along the edge of the shore, between Felixstowe and Lowestoft, the trail is a fascinating blend of ecology and military history. Near its southerly start, the path passes close to one of the National Trust's most unusual acquisitions – Orford Ness. Acquired by the Trust in 1993, and officially opened in 1995, this spectacular stretch of coastline had previously been closed to the public since 1915 when the Royal Flying Corps chose Orford Ness as the setting for military research. These days, it is a Site of Special Scientific Interest, recognised in particular for its rare shingle habitats. Visitors to Orford Ness cross the River Ore by National Trust ferry from Orford Quay.

Beyond Orford, the Suffolk Coast Path parts company with the North Sea, albeit briefly, to visit Aldeburgh. Nearby are Snape Maltings, renowned internationally as the home of the Aldeburgh Festival that takes place in June. Benjamin Britten lived at Snape and wrote *Peter Grimes* here. The Suffolk coast is where both the sea and the natural landscape have influenced generations of writers, artists and musicians. An annual literary festival is staged at Aldeburgh on the first weekend in March.

Back on the Suffolk coast, the trail makes for Southwold, with its distinctive, white-walled lighthouse standing sentinel above the town and its colourful beach huts and attractive pier that feature on many a promotional brochure. The final section of the walk is one of the most spectacular, with low, sandy cliffs, several shallow Suffolk broads and the occasional church tower peeping through the trees. Much of Suffolk's coastal heathland is protected as a designated Area of Outstanding Natural Beauty and shelters several rare creatures including the adder, the heath butterfly and the nightjar.

In addition to walking, there is a good choice of cycling routes. There is the Heart of Suffolk Cycle Route, which extends for 78 miles, while the National Byway, a 4,000-mile cycle route around Britain takes in part of Suffolk and is a very enjoyable way to explore the county.

For something less demanding, visit some of Suffolk's best-known towns. Bury St Edmunds, Sudbury and Ipswich feature prominently on the tourist trail, while Lavenham, Kersey and Debenham are a reminder of the county's important role in the wool industry and the vast wealth it yielded the wool merchants. In these charming old towns look out for streets of handsome, period buildings and picturesque, timber-framed houses.

◁ Dunwich coast

SUFFOLK

BUNGAY — Map 13 TM38

Places to visit

Norfolk & Suffolk Aviation Museum, FLIXTON, NR35 1NZ, 01986 896644
www.aviationmuseum.net

Outney Meadow Caravan Park

▶▶▶ 77%

tel: 01986 892338 **Outney Meadow NR35 1HG**
email: c.r.hancy@ukgateway.net **web:** www.outneymeadow.co.uk
dir: *In Bungay, site signed from roundabout junction of A143 and A144.*

Three pleasant grassy areas beside the River Waveney, with screened pitches. The central toilet block offers good modern facilities, especially in the ladies' section, and is open at all times. The views from the site across the wide flood plain could be straight out of a Constable painting. Canoeing and boating, coarse fishing and cycling are all available here.

Open: March to October **Last arrival:** 21.00 **Last departure:** 16.00

Pitches: 🚐 from £15; 🚐 from £15; ⛺ from £15; 7 hardstanding pitches; 15 seasonal pitches

Facilities: 🛁 ☺ 🚻 ❄ ♿ 🛍

Services: 🚾 🔌 🍴 🛒 🌿 T

Within 3 miles: 🎣 🚴 🚤 🎣

Additional site information: 6 acre site. 🐾 Cars can be parked by caravans and tents. Awnings permitted. Boat and canoe.

DUNWICH — Map 13 TM47

Places to visit

RSPB Nature Reserve Minsmere, WESTLETON, IP17 3BY, 01728 648281
www.rspb.org.uk/minsmere

Premier Park

Haw Wood Farm Caravan Park

▶▶▶▶▶ 92%

tel: 01502 359550 **Hinton IP17 3QT**
email: info@hawwoodfarm.co.uk **web:** www.hawwoodfarm.co.uk
dir: *Exit A12, 1.5 miles north of Darsham level crossing at Darsham shop and café. Site 0.5 mile on right.*

An unpretentious family-orientated park set in two large fields surrounded by low hedges. The amenity block is appointed to a very high standard – it includes an excellent reception with café, a good play area and top quality toilet and shower facilities. With year-on-year investment and high levels of customer care assured, the visitor's experience is constantly improving.

Open: March to 14 January **Last arrival:** 21.00 **Last departure:** 11.00

Pitches: 🚐 from £16; 🚐 from £16; ⛺ from £16; 14 hardstanding pitches; 30 seasonal pitches

Leisure: 🎢 ⛹

Facilities: 🛁 ☺ 🚻 ❄ ♿ 🛍 🍖 🪑 🐕 WiFi

Services: 🚾 🔌 🍴 🍽 🛒 ⛽ 🔒 🌿 T

Within 3 miles: 🎣 🚴 U

Additional site information: 15 acre site. 🐾 Cars can be parked by caravans and tents. Awnings permitted. No noise after 22.00. Fresh bread and pastries available. Rainy day craft tent, nature trail, books and board games, table tennis.

LEISURE: 🏊 Indoor swimming pool 🏊 Outdoor swimming pool 🎢 Children's playground 👋 Kids' club 🎾 Tennis court 🎱 Games room 📺 Separate TV room
🎣 golf course 🏌 Pitch n putt 🚤 Boats for hire 🚲 Bikes for hire 🎬 Cinema 🎭 Entertainment 🎣 Fishing 🎱 Mini golf 🏄 Watersports 🏋 Gym 🏟 Sports field U Stables
FACILITIES: 🛁 Baths/Shower ☺ Electric shaver sockets 🪒 Hairdryer ❄ Ice Pack Facility 🚼 Baby facilities ♿ Disabled facilities 🛍 Shop on site or within 200yds
🍖 BBQ area 🪑 Picnic area WiFi WiFi

FELIXSTOWE
Map 13 TM33

Places to visit

Ipswich Museum, IPSWICH, IP1 3QH, 01473 433551
www.cimuseums.org.uk/Ipswich-Museum

Christchurch Mansion, IPSWICH, IP4 2BE, 01473 433554
www.cimuseums.org.uk/Christchurch-Mansion

Peewit Caravan Park
▶▶▶ 86%

tel: 01394 284511 & 07793 967829 **Walton Avenue IP11 2HB**
email: peewitpark@gmail.com **web:** www.peewitcaravanpark.co.uk
dir: *A14 junction 62, follow sign for town centre. Site 100 metres on left.*

A grass touring area fringed by trees, with well-maintained grounds and a colourful floral display. This handy urban site is not overlooked by houses, and the toilet and shower facilities are clean and tidy. A function room contains a TV and library. The beach is a few minutes away by car.

Open: April (or Easter if earlier) to October **Last arrival:** 21.00 **Last departure:** 11.00 (later departures possible)

Pitches: * 🚐 from £17; 🚎 from £17; ▲ from £17, 4 hardstanding pitches

Leisure: ⚑

Facilities: 🛁 ☉ 🌡 ✳ ♿ WiFi

Services: 🔌 🔲 🔒

Within 3 miles: ↓ ♪ ◎ 🎣 🛒 🗓 £

Additional site information: 13 acre site. 🐾 Dogs must be kept on leads. Cars can be parked by caravans and tents. Awnings permitted. 5mph speed restriction on site, only foam footballs permitted. Boules area, bowling green, small play area. Car hire can be arranged

HOLLESLEY
Map 13 TM34

Places to visit

Woodbridge Tide Mill, WOODBRIDGE, IP12 1BY, 01394 388202
www.woodbridgetidemill.org.uk

Sutton Hoo, WOODBRIDGE, IP12 3DJ, 01394 389700
www.nationaltrust.org.uk/suttonhoo

Run Cottage Touring Park
▶▶▶▶ 88%

tel: 01394 411309 **Alderton Road IP12 3RQ**
email: info@runcottage.co.uk **web:** www.runcottage.co.uk
dir: *From A12 (Ipswich to Saxmundham road) onto A1152 at Melton. 1.5 miles, right at roundabout onto B1083. 0.75 mile, left to Hollesley. In Hollesley right into The Street, through village, down hill, over bridge, site 100 yards on left.*

Located in the peaceful village of Hollesley on the Suffolk coast, this landscaped adults-only park is set behind the owners' house. The generously-sized pitches, which include six new super pitches, are serviced by a well-appointed and immaculately maintained toilet block which includes two fully serviced cubicles. Another landscaped field offers 22 extra pitches, each with an electric hook-up and TV point, and seven hardstanding pitches. Two camping pods are available for hire. This site is handy for the National Trust's Sutton Hoo, and also by travelling a little further north, the coastal centre and beach at Dunwich Heath, and the RSPB bird reserve at Minsmere.

Open: All year **Last arrival:** 20.00 **Last departure:** 11.00

Pitches: 🚐 from £22; 🚎 from £22; ▲ from £20; 🏠 see prices below; 20 hardstanding pitches; 6 seasonal pitches

Facilities: 🛁 ☉ 🌡 ✳ ♿ WiFi

Services: 🔌 🔲 🔋 T

Within 3 miles: ↓ ♪ ∪ 🛒 £

Additional site information: 4.25 acre site. Adults only. 🐾 Cars can be parked by caravans and tents. Awnings permitted. No groundsheets. Satellite TV point on some pitches.

Glamping available: Wooden pods from £50.

Additional glamping information: Wooden pods: minimum stay 2 nights in summer. Microwave, toaster, tea and coffee, BBQ stand, bedding included. Cars can be parked by pods.

PITCHES: 🚐 Caravans 🚎 Motorhomes ▲ Tents 🏠 Glamping accommodation SERVICES: 🔌 Electric hook-up 🔲 Launderette 🍺 Licensed bar
🔥 Calor Gas ⊘ Campingaz T Toilet fluid 🍽 Café/Restaurant 🍔 Fast Food/Takeaway 🔋 Battery charging ⇅ Motorhome service point
* 2019 prices ⊘ No credit or debit cards 🐾 Dogs permitted ⊗ No dogs

KESSINGLAND Map 13 TM58

Places to visit

East Anglia Transport Museum, LOWESTOFT, NR33 8BL, 01502 518459
www.eatransportmuseum.co.uk

Maritime Museum, LOWESTOFT, NR32 1XG, 01502 569165
www.lowestoftmaritimemuseum.co.uk

Great for kids: Africa Alive!, LOWESTOFT, NR33 7TF, 01502 740291
www.africa-alive.co.uk

Heathland Beach Holiday Park

91%

tel: 01502 740337 **London Road NR33 7PJ**
email: reception@heathlandbeach.co.uk **web:** www.heathlandbeach.co.uk
dir: *From roundabout on A12 (1 mile north of Kessingland) take B1437 signed Kessingland (and brown camping signs). Site 1st left.*

A well-run and maintained park offering superb toilet facilities. The park is set in meadowland, with level grass pitches, and mature trees and bushes. There is direct access to the sea and beach, and good provisions for families on site with a heated swimming pool and three play areas. There is a well-stocked fishing lake, and sea fishing is also possible.

Open: April to October **Last arrival:** 21.00 **Last departure:** 11.00

Pitches: ; 7 hardstanding pitches

Leisure:

Facilities:

Services:

Within 3 miles:

Additional site information: 5 acre site. Only 1 dog per unit during peak times. Cars can be parked by caravans and tents. Awnings permitted. Table tennis. Fresh bread available.

LEISTON

Places to visit

Long Shop Museum, LEISTON, IP16 4ES, 01728 832189
www.longshopmuseum.co.uk

Leiston Abbey, LEISTON, IP16 4TD
www.english-heritage.org.uk/daysout/properties/leiston-abbey

Great for kids: Easton Farm Park, EASTON, IP13 0EQ, 01728 746475
www.eastonfarmpark.co.uk

LEISTON Map 13 TM46

Premier Park

Cakes & Ale

90%

tel: 01728 831655 **Abbey Lane, Theberton IP16 4TE**
email: reception@cakesandale.co.uk **web:** www.cakesandale.co.uk
dir: *From Saxmundham east on B1119. 3 miles, follow minor road over level crossing, turn right, in 0.5 mile straight on at crossroads, entrance 0.5 mile on left.*

A large, well spread out and beautifully maintained site on a former World War II airfield that has many trees and bushes. The spacious touring area includes plenty of hardstandings and 55 super pitches, and there is a good bar. There is a high-quality, solar-powered toilet block containing four fully serviced family rooms, seven cubicled toilet and washbasin rooms, dishwashing facilities, laundry and underfloor heating.

Open: April to end October (restricted service: low season – club, shop and reception reduced opening hours) **Last arrival:** 19.00 **Last departure:** 13.00

Pitches: from £30; ; 55 hardstanding pitches

Leisure: **Facilities:**

Services:

Within 3 miles: **Additional site information:** 45 acre site. Cars can be parked by caravans and tents. Awnings permitted. No group bookings, no noise between 21.00–08.00. Golf practice range, football pitch, boules, table tennis.

See advert opposite

LEISURE: Indoor swimming pool Outdoor swimming pool Children's playground Kids' club Tennis court Games room Separate TV room golf course Pitch n putt Boats for hire Bikes for hire Cinema Entertainment Fishing Mini golf Watersports Gym Sports field Stables
FACILITIES: Baths/Shower Electric shaver sockets Hairdryer Ice Pack Facility Baby facilities Disabled facilities Shop on site or within 200yds BBQ area Picnic area WiFi

PITCHES: 🚐 Caravans 🚍 Motorhomes 🔺 Tents 🏠 Glamping accommodation **SERVICES:** ⚡ Electric hook-up 🧺 Launderette 🍷 Licensed bar 🔥 Calor Gas 🔥 Campingaz 🚽 Toilet fluid 🍴 Café/Restaurant 🍔 Fast Food/Takeaway 🔋 Battery charging 🚐 Motorhome service point
* 2019 prices 🚫 No credit or debit cards 🐕 Dogs permitted 🚫 No dogs

LOWESTOFT

See Kessingland

SAXMUNDHAM
Map 13 TM36

Places to visit

Long Shop Museum, LEISTON, IP16 4ES, 01728 832189
www.longshopmuseum.co.uk

Leiston Abbey, LEISTON, IP16 4TD
www.english-heritage.org.uk/daysout/properties/leiston-abbey

Great for kids: RSPB Nature Reserve Minsmere, WESTLETON, IP17 3BY, 01728 648281, www.rspb.org.uk/minsmere

Marsh Farm Caravan Site
▶▶ 91%

tel: 01728 602168 **Sternfield IP17 1HW**
web: www.marshfarm-caravansite.co.uk
dir: A12 onto A1094 (Aldeburgh road), at Snape crossroads left signed Sternfield, follow signs to site.

A very pretty site overlooking reed-fringed lakes which offer excellent coarse fishing. The facilities are very well maintained and includes a basic but fully-equipped facility block; five new toilets were added in 2018. The park truly is a peaceful haven but no tents are allowed.

Open: February to November (weather dependent) **Last arrival:** 21.00
Last departure: 15.00

Pitches: 🚐 🚙

Leisure: 🎣

Facilities: 🚿 ⚡ ⑤ 🍖 🪑

Services: ⊙ 🛒

Within 3 miles: 🎣 ♨ 📅

Additional site information: 30 acre site. 🐕 🚭 Cars can be parked by caravans. Awnings permitted. Campers must report to reception on arrival. Site closed when freezing temperatures are forecast. Only 1 car per caravan on site. No tents accepted.

THEBERTON
Map 13 TM46

Places to visit

Leiston Abbey, LEISTON, IP16 4TD,
www.english-heritage.org.uk/daysout/properties/leiston-abbey

RSPB Nature Reserve Minsmere, WESTLETON, IP17 3BY, 01728 648281
www.rspb.org.uk/minsmere

Sycamore Park
▶▶▶ 80%

tel: 01728 635830 & 01502 380129 **Rearoff Pump Cottages, Main Road IP16 4RA**
email: enquiries@sycamorepark.co.uk **web:** www.sycamorepark.co.uk
dir: From A12 at Yoxford take B1122 towards Theberton.

Sycamore Park is a very peaceful site in the village of Theberton, within easy reach of Southwold and Aldeburgh, and only three miles from RSPB Minsmere. There are 20 electric hook-ups on grass pitches set out in a compact field surrounded by mature trees. The small, but high quality and very stylish, toilet block contains combined cubicled facilities and has underfloor heating.

Open: 3 March to 28 January **Last departure:** noon

Pitches: * 🚐 from £20; 🚙 from £20; ▲ from £20; 5 hardstanding pitches

Facilities: 🚿 🪑 WiFi

Services: ⊙

Within 3 miles: 🎣 ♨ ⚓ 📅 ⑤ 🏌

Additional site information: 2 acre site. Adults only. 🐕 🚭 Cars can be parked by caravans and tents. Awnings permitted.

WOODBRIDGE

Places to visit

Sutton Hoo, WOODBRIDGE, IP12 3DJ, 01394 389700
www.nationaltrust.org.uk/suttonhoo

Orford Castle, ORFORD, IP12 2ND, 01394 450472
www.english-heritage.org.uk/daysout/properties/orford-castle

Great for kids: Easton Farm Park, EASTON, IP13 0EQ, 01728 746475
www.eastonfarmpark.co.uk

WOODBRIDGE

Map 13 TM24

Premier Park

Moon & Sixpence

▶▶▶▶▶ 92%

tel: 01473 736650 **Newbourn Road, Waldringfield IP12 4PP**
email: info@moonandsixpence.eu **web:** www.moonandsixpence.co.uk
dir: *From roundabout on A12 (east of Ipswich) follow brown Moon & Sixpence signs (Waldringfield). In 1.5 miles left at crossroads, follow signs.*

A well-planned site, with tourers occupying a sheltered valley position around an attractive boating lake with a sandy beach. Toilet facilities are housed in a smart Norwegian-style cabin, and there is a laundry and dish-washing area. Leisure facilities include tennis courts, a bowling green, fishing, boating and a games room; there's also a lake, woodland trails, a cycle trail and 9-hole golf. The park has an adult only area, and a strict 'no groups and no noise after 9pm' policy. Please note, tents are not accepted.

Open: April to October (restricted service: low season – reduced opening hours at club, shop and reception) **Last arrival:** 20.00 **Last departure:** noon

Pitches: 🚐 from £24; 🚍 from £24; 6 hardstanding pitches

Leisure: ⚲ 🏊 🎣 ⚿ ⚽ **Facilities:** 🏪 ⊙ ⌁ ✳ 🛁 🍳 WiFi

Services: 🔌 🛢 🍺 🍽 🛒 🔋 ⛽ 🐕 ∅ **Within 3 miles:** ⌁ 🎣 ⚕ 🍴

Additional site information: 5 acre site. 🐕 Cars can be parked by caravans. Awnings permitted. No tents. No group bookings or commercial vehicles, quiet from 21.00–08.00. 10-acre sports area, 110-acre woods.

See advert on page 277

Moat Barn Touring Caravan Park

▶▶▶ 85%

tel: 01473 737520 **Dallinghoo Road, Bredfield IP13 6BD**
web: www.moatbarn.co.uk
dir: *Exit A12 at Bredfield, 1st right at village pump. Through village, 1 mile site on left.*

An attractive small park for adults only, set in idyllic Suffolk countryside, perfectly located for touring the heritage coastline and for visiting the National Trust's Sutton Hoo. The modern toilet block is well equipped and maintained. There are 10 tent pitches and the park is located on the popular Hull to Harwich cycle route; cycle hire is available.

Open: March to 15 January **Last arrival:** 22.00 **Last departure:** noon

Pitches: 🚐 🚍 ⛺; 10 seasonal pitches

Leisure: 🚴

Facilities: 🏪 ⊙ ⌁ ✳ WiFi

Services: 🔌 🔋 🐕

Within 3 miles: ⚓ ⌁ ⚕ ◎ 🏇 🍴 🛒 🎣

Additional site information: 2 acre site. Adults only. 🐕 ∅ Cars can be parked by caravans and tents. Awnings permitted. No ball games, only breathable groundsheets permitted.

Sussex

East and West Sussex are adjoining counties packed with interest. This is a land of stately homes and castles, miles of breezy chalk cliffs overlooking the English Channel, pretty rivers, picturesque villages and links to our glorious past. Since 2011 it has been the home of Britain's newest national park – the South Downs

Mention Sussex to many people and images of the South Downs immediately spring to mind – 'vast, smooth, shaven, serene,' as the writer Virginia Woolf described them. She and her husband lived at Monk's House in the village of Rodmell, near Lewes, and today, her modest home is managed by the National Trust and open to the public.

Close by, on the downs, is Charleston Farmhouse where Woolf's sister, the artist Vanessa Bell, lived a bohemian life as part of the renowned Bloomsbury group, whose members were mainly notable writers, artists and thinkers. Rudyard Kipling resided at Bateman's, near Burwash, and described the house as 'a good and peaceable place,' after moving there in 1902. 'We have loved it ever since our first sight of it,' he wrote later. Bateman's is also in the care of the National Trust, as is Uppark House at South Harting, near Petersfield. The writer H. G. Wells stayed at Uppark as a boy while his mother was employed there as housekeeper. Away to the east, inland from Hastings, lies Great Dixter, an ancient house in a magical garden. This was the home of the pioneering gardening writer Christopher Lloyd and today both Great Dixter and its garden are open to visitors.

There are a great many historic landmarks within Sussex, but probably the most famous is the battlefield where William, Duke of Normandy defeated Harold and his Saxon army to become William the Conqueror of England. By visiting Battle, near Hastings, you can, with a little imagination, picture the bloody events that led to his defeat. Before the Battle of Hastings, William vowed that if God gave him victory that day, he would build an abbey on the site of the battle at Senlac Field. This he did, with the high altar set up on the spot where Harold died. The abbey was enlarged and improved over the years and today is maintained by English Heritage.

In terms of walking in Sussex, this county is spoilt for choice. Studying the map reveals a multitude of routes – many of them to be found within the boundaries of the South Downs National Park – and an assortment of scenic long-distance trails leading towards distant horizons; all of them offer a perfect way to get to the heart of 'Sussex by the sea,' as it has long been known. The Monarch's Way, one of the region's most popular trails, broadly follows Charles II's escape route in 1651, while the most famous of them, the South Downs Way, follows hill paths and cliff-top tracks all the way from Winchester to Eastbourne. As well as a good range of walks, Sussex offers exhilarating cycle rides through the High Weald, along the South Downs Way and via coastal routes between Worthing and Rye. There is also the Forest Way through East Grinstead to Groombridge. If you enjoy cycling with the salty tang of the sea for company, try the ride between Chichester and West Wittering. You can vary the return journey by taking the Itchenor ferry to Bosham.

Sussex is renowned for its many pretty towns, of course. There is Arundel, littered with period buildings and dominated by the castle, the family home of the Duke of Norfolk, that dates back nearly 1,000 years. Midhurst, Lewes, Rye and Uckfield also have their charms, while the cities of Chichester and Brighton offer countless museums and fascinating landmarks. Brighton's best-known and grandest feature is surely the Royal Pavilion, created as the seaside palace of the Prince Regent (later George IV). The town's genteel Regency terraces and graceful crescents reflect his influence on Brighton. Often referred to as 'London by the sea,' the city has long enjoyed a colourful reputation and has been used as a location in many high profile and highly successful films, including *Brighton Rock* and *Quadrophenia*.

◁ Beachy Head

EAST SUSSEX

BATTLE
Map 7 TQ71

Places to visit

1066 Battle of Hastings Abbey & Battlefield, BATTLE, TN33 0AD, 01424 775705 www.english-heritage.org.uk/daysout/properties/1066-battle-of-hastings-abbey-and-battlefield

Great for kids: The Observatory Science Centre, HERSTMONCEUX, BN27 1RN, 01323 832731, www.the-observatory.org

Senlac Wood
▶▶▶ 81%

tel: 01424 773969 **Catsfield Road, Catsfield TN33 9LN**
email: senlacwood@xlninternet.co.uk **web:** www.senlacwood.co.uk
dir: A271 from Battle onto B2204 signed Bexhill. Site on left.

A woodland site with many secluded hardstanding bays and two peaceful grassy glades for tents. The toilet facilities have been upgraded and are clean and tidy. The site is ideal for anyone looking for seclusion and shade and it is well placed for visiting nearby Battle and the south coast beaches.

Open: March to October **Last arrival:** 22.00 **Last departure:** noon

Pitches: 🚐 from £15; 🚙 from £15; 🛖 from £15; 16 hardstanding pitches

Leisure: 🔍

Facilities: 🏠 ⊙ 🏳 ☀ 🪑 WiFi

Services: 🖲 🔌 🍽 🛒 🛎

Within 3 miles: ⌕ 🎣 ↻ 🛒

Additional site information: 20 acre site. 🐾 Cars can be parked by caravans and tents. Awnings permitted. No camp fires, no noise after 23.00. Caravan storage.

BEXHILL
Map 6 TQ70

Places to visit

RSPB Fore Wood, CROWHURST, TN33 9AG, 01892 752430 www.rspb.org.uk/reserves-and-events/reserves-a-z/fore-wood

Great for kids: The Observatory Science Centre, HERSTMONCEUX, BN27 1RN, 01323 832731, www.the-observatory.org

Premier Park

Kloofs Caravan Park
▶▶▶▶▶ 85%

tel: 01424 842839 **Sandhurst Lane TN39 4RG**
email: camping@kloofs.com **web:** www.kloofs.com
dir: From Bexhill take A259 towards Pevensey. At Little Common roundabout right into Peartree Lane. At crossroads left into Whydown Road. 300 yards left into Sandhurst Lane, site on right. (Note: Use postcode for sat nav).

Hidden away down a quiet lane, just inland from Bexhill and the coast, Kloofs is a friendly, family-run park surrounded by farmland and oak woodlands, with views extending to the South Downs from hilltop pitches. Developed by the Griggs family over the past 20 years, the site is well landscaped and thoughtfully laid out, with excellent hardstandings (some large enough for RVs and fully serviced) and spacious pitches, each with mini patio, bench and brick barbecue. Toilet facilities include a family shower room and a unisex block with privacy cubicles, a dog shower and drying room.

Open: All year (restricted service: some facilities not available in winter)
Last arrival: noon (later arrivals possible) **Last departure:** 11.00

Pitches: 🚐 🚙 🛖

Leisure: 🅰

Facilities: ⑤ WiFi

Additional site information: 22 acre site. 🐾 Dogs must be kept on leads at all times. Quiet from 22.00–07.00. No open fires, only off-ground BBQs permitted.

FURNER'S GREEN

Places to visit

Sheffield Park and Garden, SHEFFIELD PARK, TN22 3QX, 01825 790231 www.nationaltrust.org.uk/sheffieldpark

Nymans, HANDCROSS, RH17 6EB, 01444 405250 www.nationaltrust.org.uk/nymans

Great for kids: Bluebell Railway, SHEFFIELD PARK, TN22 3QL, 01825 720800 www.bluebell-railway.co.uk

FURNER'S GREEN
Map 6 TQ42

Heaven Farm
►► 83%

tel: 01825 790226 **TN22 3RG**
email: heavenfarmleisure@btinternet.com **web:** www.heavenfarm.co.uk
dir: *On A275 between Lewes and East Grinstead, 1 mile north of Sheffield Park Garden and Bluebell Railway.*

A delightful, small, rural site on a popular farm complex incorporating a farm museum, craft shop, tea room and nature trail. The good, clean toilet facilities are housed in well-converted outbuildings and chickens and ducks roam freely around the site. Ashdown Forest, the Bluebell Railway and Sheffield Park Garden are nearby.

Open: All year (restricted service: November to March – site may close due to bad weather) **Last arrival:** 21.00 **Last departure:** noon
Pitches: 🚐 from £20; 🚐 from £20; ⛺ from £20; 2 hardstanding pitches
Leisure: 🎣
Facilities: 🛁 ⊙ ⚒ ☕ ❴ 🎯 🞄 📶 WiFi
Services: 🔌 🍴 🖶 🔋 ⛽ 🅣
Within 3 miles: 🔱 ∪ ✈

Additional site information: 1.5 acre site. 🐕 Cars can be parked by caravans and tents. Awnings permitted. Credit and debit cards accepted only in shop and café. Fresh food shop open all year. Nature trail, 1.5 mile walk.

HASTINGS & ST LEONARDS
Map 7 TQ80

Places to visit
Shipwreck Museum, HASTINGS & ST LEONARDS, TN34 3DW, 01424 437452
www.shipwreckmuseum.co.uk

Great for kids: Blue Reef Aquarium, HASTINGS, TN34 3DW, 01424 718776
www.bluereefaquarium.co.uk

Premier Park

Combe Haven Holiday Park
►►►►► 87% HOLIDAY HOME PARK

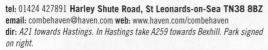

tel: 01424 427891 **Harley Shute Road, St Leonards-on-Sea TN38 8BZ**
email: combehaven@haven.com **web:** www.haven.com/combehaven
dir: *A21 towards Hastings. In Hastings take A259 towards Bexhill. Park signed on right.*

Close to a beach and the resort attractions of Hastings, this holiday park has been designed with families in mind. Activities include a pirates' adventure playground, heated swimming pools and a wealth of sports and outdoor activities.

Open: mid March to October
Holiday Homes: Sleep 8 Bedrooms 3 Bathrooms 1 Toilets 1 Microwave Freezer TV Sky/Freeview
Leisure: 🏊 🏊 ⚏ 👋 ⚽

Additional site information: 🐕 Most dog breeds accepted (please check when booking). Dogs must be kept on leads at all times. The facilities provided in the holiday homes may differ depending on the grade.

WEST SUSSEX

ARUNDEL
Map 6 TQ00

Places to visit
Arundel Castle, ARUNDEL, BN18 9AB, 01903 882173
www.arundelcastle.org

Harbour Park, LITTLEHAMPTON, BN17 5LL, 01903 721200
www.harbourpark.com

Great for kids: Look & Sea Visitor Centre, LITTLEHAMPTON, BN17 5AW, 01903 718984, www.lookandsea.co.uk

Ship & Anchor Marina
►► 79%

tel: 01243 551262 **Station Road, Ford BN18 0BJ**
email: enquiries@shipandanchormarina.co.uk
dir: *From A27 at Arundel take road south signed Ford. Site 2 miles on left after level crossing.*

Neatly maintained by the enthusiastic, hard working owner, this small, well located site has dated but spotlessly clean toilet facilities, a secluded tent area, and enjoys a pleasant position beside the Ship & Anchor pub and the tidal River Arun. There are good walks from the site to Arundel and the coast. River fishing is possible.

Open: March to October **Last arrival:** 21.00 **Last departure:** noon
Pitches: 🚐 from £22; 🚐 from £22; ⛺ from £22; 11 hardstanding pitches
Leisure: ⚏
Facilities: 🛁 ⊙ 🌐 ☕ ❴ 🎯
Services: 🔌 🍴 🖶 🔋 🛢 🐾 🅣
Within 3 miles: 🔱 🎣 ∪ ◎ 🍴 ✈ 🎱

Additional site information: 12 acre site. 🐕 🐾 Cars can be parked by caravans and tents. Awnings permitted. No music audible to others, no visitors. Pub on site.

BARNS GREEN
Map 6 TQ12

Places to visit

Parham House & Gardens, PULBOROUGH, RH20 4HS, 01903 742021
www.parhaminsussex.co.uk

Great for kids: Bignor Roman Villa, BIGNOR, RH20 1PH, 01798 869259
www.bignorromanvilla.co.uk

Sumners Ponds Fishery & Campsite
▶▶▶▶ 90%

tel: 01403 732539 **Chapel Road RH13 OPR**
email: bookings@sumnersponds.co.uk **web:** www.sumnersponds.co.uk
dir: From A272 at Coolham crossroads, north towards Barns Green. In 1.5 miles take 1st
left at small crossroads. 1 mile, over level crossing. Site on left just after right bend.

Dedication to provide high quality camping continues at this working farm set in
attractive surroundings on the edge of the quiet village of Barns Green. There are
three touring areas; one continues to develop and includes camping pods and extra
hardstandings, and another, which has a stunning modern toilet block, has
excellent pitches on the banks of one of the well-stocked fishing lakes. For a
glamping holiday there are wooden pods, a stunning fully-equipped safari tent,
lodges and shepherd's huts. There are many cycle paths on site and a woodland
walk has direct access to miles of footpaths. The Café by the Lake serves meals
from breakfast onwards. Horsham and Brighton are within easy reach.

Open: All year **Last arrival:** 20.00 **Last departure:** noon

Pitches: 🚐 from £23; 🚙 from £23; ▲ from £23; 🏕 see prices below;
45 hardstanding pitches

Leisure: 🎪 🖊

Facilities: 🚿 ⊙ 🗜 ✳ ♿ 🏪 🚽 WiFi

Services: 🔌 🗑 🛒 🍴 🛒 🛢 🚰 🌿 ⓣ

Within 3 miles: 🎣 ♻ ⛵

Additional site information: 100 acre site. 🐕 Well behaved dogs accepted. Cars can be
parked by caravans and tents. Awnings permitted. 1 car per pitch. No noise after 22.30.
Fishing lakes, footpaths.

Glamping available: 6 wooden pods from £35; 4 shepherd's huts from £120; 1 safari tent
from £210.

Additional glamping information: Wooden pods: minimum stay 1 night (2 nights at
weekends, school holidays), 3 nights at bank holiday weekends; Shepherd's huts:
minimum stay 2 nights (3 at weekends; 4 nights at Easter weekend); Safari tent
minimum stay 3 nights Friday to Monday (4 nights Monday to Friday; 7 nights Friday to
Friday or Monday to Monday); All units – electricity; no smoking. Shepherd's huts and
safari tent – log burners; no dogs. Wooden pods – electric heater. Cars can be parked by
glamping units.

CHICHESTER

Places to visit

Pallant House Gallery, CHICHESTER, PO19 1TJ, 01243 774557
www.pallant.org.uk

Chichester Cathedral, CHICHESTER, PO19 1PX, 01243 782595
www.chichestercathedral.org.uk

LEISURE: 🏊 Indoor swimming pool   🏊 Outdoor swimming pool   🎪 Children's playground   👐 Kids' club   🎾 Tennis court   🎱 Games room   📺 Separate TV room
🏌 golf course   ⛳ Pitch n putt   🚣 Boats for hire   🚲 Bikes for hire   🎬 Cinema   🎵 Entertainment   🎣 Fishing   ⊙ Mini golf   🏄 Watersports   💪 Gym   🏟 Sports field   ♻ Stables
FACILITIES: 🚿 Baths/Shower   ⊙ Electric shaver sockets   🗜 Hairdryer   ✳ Ice Pack Facility   🛒 Baby facilities   ♿ Disabled facilities   🏪 Shop on site or within 200yds
🛒 BBQ area   🍴 Picnic area   WiFi WiFi

CHICHESTER
Map 5 SU80

ENGLAND & OVERALL WINNER OF THE AA CAMPSITE OF THE YEAR 2019

Platinum Park

Concierge Camping
▶▶▶▶▶

Best of British

tel: 01243 573118 **Ratham Estate, Ratham Lane PO18 8DL**
email: service@conciergecamping.co.uk **web:** www.conciergecamping.co.uk
dir: *From A27 onto A259 to Bosham. In Bosham at roundabout into Station Road. Over railway line, over A27. At T-junction left onto B2146 signed West Ashling. 1st left into Ratham Lane.*

Developing this stunning park in a field adjoining their home has been a labour of love for owners, Tracey and Guy. It is a first-class, small park for 27 units offering large fully serviced pitches with some suitable for American RVs, and the attention to detail throughout is very impressive. Everything is high spec, from very spacious pitches and the reception, complete with a shop that sells daily-delivered local produce, coffee, drinks, late-arrival and breakfast hampers, and smart alfresco tables and chairs for all to use, to the state-of-the-art amenity block. Here you'll find full-length mirrors, ultra-efficient rain showers, an air-blade hand-drier, stylish washbasins and showers with temperature controls, piped radio and Ratham Estate toiletries plus an excellent family/disabled room.

Open: All year **Last arrival:** 18.00 (later arrival times by prior arrangement) (earliest arrival 13.00) **Last departure:** noon

---

Pitches: 🚐 from £32; 🚍 from £30; 27 hardstanding pitches
Facilities: 🏠 ⊙ 🅿 ♿ 🏧 🎐 📶 WiFi
Services: 🔌 🔋 🍽 🍴 🛒 T
Within 3 miles: ↓ ✎ ∪ 🎿 🎣 📅
Additional site information: 4 acre site. 🐕 Cars can be parked by caravans. Awnings permitted. No bookings accepted by under 18 years. No noise after 23.00. No awnings on the grass. Fresh pastries available each morning.

See advert opposite

Premier Park

Concierge Glamping
▶▶▶▶▶ 93% GLAMPING ONLY

tel: 01243 573118 **Ratham Estate, Ratham Lane PO18 8DL**
email: service@conciergecamping.co.uk **web:** www.conciergecamping.co.uk
dir: *From A27 onto A259 to Bosham. In Bosham at roundabout into Station Road. Over railway line, over A27. At T-junction left onto B2146 signed West Ashling. 1st left into Ratham Lane.*

Quality and attention to detail are very evident at Guy and Tracey Hodgkin's park near Chichester. They offer four stunning safari tents, idyllically situated in an adjoining meadow to the main site, beside a babbling chalk stream. These impressive 'lodges' are made from wood and top-quality canvas – they ooze style and comfort, with a range cooker, dishwasher, fridge-freezer, TV, underfloor heating and a Nespresso machine in the fully-fitted kitchen, a smart en suite shower room (with piped radio), and two good-size bedrooms; the twin-bedded room is situated at the top of a wooden staircase. Each tent has a large veranda, replete with stylish seating, picnic bench and barbecue, and overlook a stream.

Open: All year **Last arrival:** 18.00 **Last departure:** 10.00

Accommodation available: Safari Lodges from £435.

Changeover days: Monday and Friday

Additional site information: 4 acre site. 🐕 Booking advisable. Minimum stay 3 nights.

PITCHES: 🚐 Caravans 🚍 Motorhomes 🅰 Tents 🏠 Glamping accommodation **SERVICES:** 🔌 Electric hook-up 🔋 Launderette 🍺 Licensed bar
🔥 Calor Gas ⊘ Campingaz T Toilet fluid 🍴 Café/Restaurant 🍔 Fast Food/Takeaway 🔋 Battery charging 🔧 Motorhome service point
* 2019 prices 🚫 No credit or debit cards 🐕 Dogs permitted 🚫 No dogs

CHICHESTER *continued*

Ellscott Park

►►► 82%

tel: 01243 512003 **Sidlesham Lane, Birdham PO20 7QL**
email: camping@ellscottpark.co.uk **web:** www.ellscottpark.co.uk
dir: *From Chichester take A286 towards West Wittering. In approximately 4 miles left at Butterfly Farm sign, site 500 yards right.*

A well-kept park set in sheltered meadowland behind the owners' nursery and van storage area. The park, that attracts a peace-loving clientele, has spotless, well-maintained toilet facilities, and is handy for the beach, Chichester, Goodwood House, the racing at Goodwood and walking on the South Downs.

Open: April to 2nd week October **Last arrival:** in daylight **Last departure:** variable

Pitches: * 🚐 from £17; 🚌 from £17; ⛺ from £14; 26 seasonal pitches

Leisure: 🛝 ⚽

Facilities: 🛁 🔌 ❄ ♿ 🍖 🧺 [WiFi]

Services: 🚰 👕 🚮 🍃 [T]

Within 3 miles: ⛳ 🎣 🐎 ◎ 🌊 ⛵ [S]

Additional site information: 6 acre site. 🐕 🚗 Cars can be parked by caravans and tents. Awnings permitted. No commercial vehicles, site closed between 22.30–07.00. Car hire can be arranged.

HENFIELD

Places to visit

Bolney Wine Estate, BOLNEY, RH17 5NB, 01444 881575
www.bolneywineestate.com

HENFIELD

Map 6 TQ21

Blacklands Farm Caravan & Camping

►►► 74%

tel: 01273 493528 & 07773 792577 **Wheatsheaf Road BN5 9AT**
email: info@blacklandsfarm.co.uk **web:** www.blacklandsfarm.co.uk
dir: *A23, B2118, B2116 towards Henfield. Site approximately 4 miles on right.*

Tucked away, just off the B2116 east of Henfield, and well placed for visiting Brighton and exploring the South Downs National Park, this simple, grassy site has great potential and is gradually developing. There are spacious pitches down by the fishing lakes and the basic portaloos, smartly clad in wood, are clean and tidy – the owners are still planning to build a new toilet block.

Open: March to January **Last arrival:** 20.00 **Last departure:** anytime

Pitches: 🚐 🚌 ⛺; 10 hardstanding pitches

Leisure: 🛝 🚲 🎣 ⚽

Facilities: 🛁 💨 ❄ ♿ [S] 🍖 🧺 [WiFi]

Services: 🚰 🍃 [T]

Within 3 miles: ⛳ 🐎 👕

Additional site information: 5 acre site. 🐕 Cars can be parked by caravans and tents. Awnings permitted. No commercial vehicles, no noise after 23.00. Coffee machine.

HORSHAM

See Barns Green

PAGHAM

Places to visit

RSPB Pagham Harbour LNR, SIDLESHAM, PO20 7NE, 01243 641508
www.rspb.org.uk/reserves-and-events/reserves-a-z/pagham-harbour-local-nature-reserve

LEISURE: 🏊 Indoor swimming pool 🏖 Outdoor swimming pool 🛝 Children's playground 👶 Kids' club 🎾 Tennis court 🎱 Games room 📺 Separate TV room ⛳ golf course 🏌 Pitch n putt ⛵ Boats for hire 🚲 Bikes for hire 🎬 Cinema 🎭 Entertainment 🎣 Fishing ◎ Mini golf 🌊 Watersports 🏋 Gym ⚽ Sports field 🐎 Stables
FACILITIES: 🛁 Baths/Shower 🔌 Electric shaver sockets 💨 Hairdryer ❄ Ice Pack Facility 🍼 Baby facilities ♿ Disabled facilities [S] Shop on site or within 200yds 🍖 BBQ area 🧺 Picnic area [WiFi] WiFi

PAGHAM
Map 6 SZ89

Premier Park

Church Farm Holiday Park
▶▶▶▶▶ 90% HOLIDAY HOME PARK

tel: 01243 262635 **Church Lane PO21 4NR**
email: churchfarm@haven.com **web:** www.haven.com/churchfarm
dir: *At roundabout on A27 (south of Chichester) take B2145 signed Hunston and Selsey. At mini roundabout take 1st left signed North Mundham, Pagham and Bognor Regis. Site in approximately 3 miles.*

Close to Portsmouth, Chichester and south coast beaches, this relaxing and fun-packed holiday park is located close to Pagham Harbour Nature Reserve. On-site activities include golf on the 9-hole course, tennis coaching, shopping, kids' play areas and evening entertainment. There are a range of holiday caravans and apartments.

Open: 15 March to 31 October

Holiday Homes: Sleep 8 Bedrooms 2 Bathrooms 1 Toilets 1 Microwave Freezer TV Sky/Freeview

Leisure: 🐟 🥅 🎢 👋 🎯 **Additional site information:** 🐾

SELSEY
Map 0 3Z09

Places to visit
RSPB Pagham Harbour LNR, SIDLESHAM, PO20 7NE, 01243 641508
www.rspb.org.uk/reserves-and-events/reserves-a-z/pagham-harbour-local-nature-reserve

Fishbourne Roman Palace, FISHBOURNE, PO19 3QR, 01243 789829
www.sussexpast.co.uk

Warner Farm
▶▶▶▶ 82% HOLIDAY CENTRE

tel: 01243 604499 **Warner Lane PO20 9EL**
email: touring@bunnleisure.co.uk **web:** www.warnerfarm.co.uk
dir: *From B2145 in Selsey turn right into School Lane, follow signs.*

A well-screened touring site that adjoins the three static parks under the same ownership. A courtesy bus runs around the complex to entertainment areas and supermarkets. The park backs onto open grassland and offers modern toilet facilities and an excellent children's play area, and the leisure facilities with bar,

amusements and bowling alley, and swimming pool/sauna complex are also accessible to tourers.

Warner Farm

Open: March to January **Last arrival:** 17.30 **Last departure:** 10.00

Pitches: 🚐 from £32.50; 🚌 from £32.50; ⛺ from £20; 60 hardstanding pitches; 25 seasonal pitches

Leisure: 🐟 🥅 🎢 👋 🎯 🎱 🏹 🎯 🏊

Facilities: 🛁 ⊙ 🌡️ ✳️ ♿ 🍴 🚿 🏕️ 📶

Services: 🔌 🔲 🍴 🍽️ 🍔 🚰 🔋 🔄 🚽 **Within 3 miles:** 🏌️ 🚴 ⛳ ◎ 🏇 ⛵

Additional site information: 10 acre site. 🐾

See advert opposite

TYNE & WEAR

SOUTH SHIELDS
Map 21 NZ36

Places to visit
Arbeia Roman Fort & Museum, SOUTH SHIELDS, NE33 2BB, 0191 277 1410
https://arbeiaromanfort.org.uk

Souter Lighthouse & The Leas, WHITBURN, SR6 7NH, 0191 529 3161
www.nationaltrust.org.uk/souter-lighthouse-and-the-leas

Great for kids: Blue Reef Aquarium, TYNEMOUTH, NE30 4JF, 0191 258 1031
www.bluereefaquarium.co.uk

Lizard Lane Caravan & Camping Site
▶▶▶ 85%

tel: 0191 455 4455 & 455 1732 **Lizard Lane NE34 7AB**
email: lizardlanecaravanpark@gmail.com **web:** www.lizardlanecaravanpark.co.uk
dir: *2 miles south of town centre on A183 (Sunderland road).*

This improving site is located in an elevated position with good sea views. All touring pitches are fully serviced and the modern smart amenity block is equipped with superb fixtures and fittings. A shop is also provided.

Open: February to 28 January **Last arrival:** 18.00 **Last departure:** 11.00

Pitches: 🚐 from £22; 🚌 from £22; ⛺ from £22; 16 hardstanding pitches

Facilities: 🌡️ ✳️ ♿ 🍴 📶 **Services:** 🔌 🔲 🔋 🔒 🔄

Within 3 miles: 🏌️ 🚴 ⛳ ◎ 🏇 ⛵ 🎣

Additional site information: 2 acre site. 🐾 Cars can be parked by caravans and tents.

PITCHES: 🚐 Caravans 🚌 Motorhomes ⛺ Tents 🏕 Glamping accommodation **SERVICES:** 🔌 Electric hook-up 🔲 Launderette 🍷 Licensed bar 🔋 Calor Gas ⊘ Campingaz 🇹 Toilet fluid 🍽️ Café/Restaurant 🍔 Fast Food/Takeaway 🔋 Battery charging 🔄 Motorhome service point
* 2019 prices 🚫 No credit or debit cards 🐾 Dogs permitted 🚫 No dogs

WARWICKSHIRE

HARBURY
Map 11 SP35

Places to visit

Warwick Castle, WARWICK, CV34 4QU, 01926 495421
www.warwick-castle.com

Farnborough Hall, FARNBOROUGH, OX17 1DU, 01295 690002
www.nationaltrust.org.uk/farnborough-hall

Great for kids: British Motor Museum, GAYDON, CV35 0BJ, 01926 641188
www.britishmotormuseum.co.uk

Premier Park

Harbury Fields
▶▶▶▶▶ 85%

tel: 01926 612457 **Harbury Fields Farm CV33 9JN**
email: rdavis@harburyfields.co.uk web: www.harburyfields.co.uk
dir: *M40 junction 12, B4451 (signed Kineton and Gaydon). 0.75 mile, right signed Lightborne. 4 miles, right at roundabout onto B4455 (signed Harbury). 3rd right by petrol station, site in 700 yards by two cottages.*

This developing park is in a peaceful farm setting with lovely countryside views. All pitches are hardstanding and fully serviced, the reception is housed in an attractive wooden chalet, and the facility block has fully serviced cubicles. The park is well positioned for visiting Warwick and Royal Leamington Spa as well as NEC Birmingham and Stoneleigh Park. Stratford is just 10 miles away, and Upton House (NT) and Compton Valley Art Gallery are nearby.

Open: February to 1 December **Last arrival:** 20.00 **Last departure:** noon

Pitches: 🚐 🚏; 59 hardstanding pitches

Facilities: 🛁 ♿ WiFi

Services: 🔌 🗓 ⬇

Within 3 miles: ⬇ ✐ 🛒

Additional site information: 6 acre site. 🐾 Cars can be parked by caravans. Awnings permitted. No traffic noise midnight–07.30.

KINGSBURY

Places to visit

Drayton Manor Theme Park, TAMWORTH, B78 3TW, 01827 287979
www.draytonmanor.co.uk

Tamworth Castle, TAMWORTH, B79 7NA, 01827 709626
www.tamworthcastle.co.uk

Great for kids: Ash End House Children's Farm, MIDDLETON, B78 2BL, 0121 329 3240, www.childrensfarm.co.uk

KINGSBURY
Map 10 SP29

Tame View Caravan Site
▶ 69%

tel: 01827 873853 **Cliff B78 2DR**
dir: *From A51 (Tamworth to Kingsbury road). Approximately 1 mile north of Kingsbury into Cliff Hall Lane (opposite pub), 400 yards to site.*

A secluded spot overlooking the Tame Valley and river, sheltered by high hedges. Sanitary facilities are minimal but clean on this small park. The site is popular with many returning visitors who like a peaceful, basic site.

Open: All year **Last arrival:** 23.00 **Last departure:** 23.00

Pitches: 🚐 🚏 ⛺

Leisure: ✐

Facilities: 🛁 ✳ 🍴 🏓

Services: 🔌 🗑

Within 3 miles: ⬇ ⛳ ◎ ≋ ✈ 🗓 🛒 🎣

Additional site information: 3 acre site. 🐾 🐕 Cars can be parked by caravans and tents. Awnings permitted. No noise after midnight. Fishing, takeaway food can be ordered for delivery.

WOLVEY
Map 11 SP48

Places to visit

Arbury Hall, NUNEATON, CV10 7PT, 024 7638 2804
www.arburyestate.co.uk

Lunt Roman Fort, COVENTRY, CV8 3AJ, 024 7623 7548
www.luntromanfort.org

Great for kids: Coventry Transport Museum, COVENTRY, CV1 1JD, 024 7623 4270
www.transport-museum.com

Wolvey Villa Farm Caravan & Camping Park
▶▶▶ 80%

tel: 01455 220493 **LE10 3HF**
web: www.wolveycaravanpark.itgo.com
dir: *M6 junction 2, B4065 follow Wolvey signs. Or M69 junction 1 and follow Wolvey signs.*

A level grass site, surrounded by trees and shrubs, on the border of Warwickshire and Leicestershire. This quiet country site has its own popular fishing lake, and is convenient for visiting Coventry and Leicester.

Open: 1 March to 31 October **Last arrival:** 22.00 **Last departure:** noon

Pitches: 🚐 from £18; 🚏 from £18; ⛺ from £14; 24 hardstanding pitches

Leisure: 🎱 ✐ ⚽

Facilities: 🛁 ☉ 🖋 ✳ ♿ 🛒 🏓

Services: 🔌 🗓 🏷 ⬭ T

Within 3 miles: ⬇ ∪ ◎ 🏓

Additional site information: 7 acre site. 🐾 🐕 Cars can be parked by caravans and tents. Awnings permitted. No noise after 23.00. No fire pits, no twin axle vehicles. Putting green, off licence.

LEISURE: 🏊 Indoor swimming pool 🏊 Outdoor swimming pool 🎢 Children's playground 👪 Kids' club 🎾 Tennis court 🎱 Games room 📺 Separate TV room ⬇ golf course ⛳ Pitch n putt ⛵ Boats for hire 🚲 Bikes for hire 🎬 Cinema 🎵 Entertainment 🎣 Fishing ◎ Mini golf 🏄 Watersports 💪 Gym ⚽ Sports field ∪ Stables
FACILITIES: 🛁 Baths/Shower ☉ Electric shaver sockets 🖋 Hairdryer ✳ Ice Pack Facility 🍼 Baby facilities ♿ Disabled facilities 🛒 Shop on site or within 200yds 🍴 BBQ area 🏓 Picnic area WiFi WiFi

WEST MIDLANDS

MERIDEN
Map 10 SP28

Places to visit

Blakesley Hall, BIRMINGHAM, B25 8RN, 0121 348 8120
www.birminghammuseums.org.uk/blakesley

Packwood House, LAPWORTH, B94 6AT, 01564 782024
www.nationaltrust.org.uk/packwood-house

Somers Wood Caravan Park

▶▶▶▶ 92%

tel: 01676 522978 **Somers Road CV7 7PL**
email: enquiries@somerswood.co.uk **web:** www.somerswood.co.uk
dir: *M42 junction 6, A45 signed Coventry. Keep left, do not take flyover. Right onto A452 signed Meriden and Leamington. At next roundabout left onto B4102 (Hampton Lane). Site in 0.5 mile on left.*

A peaceful adults-only park set in the heart of England with spotless facilities. The park is well positioned for visiting the National Exhibition Centre (NEC), the NEC Arena and National Indoor Arena (NIA), and Birmingham is only 12 miles away. The park also makes an ideal touring base for Stratford-upon-Avon, Warwick and Coventry. Please note, tents are not accepted.

Open: All year **Last arrival:** variable **Last departure:** variable
Pitches: 🚐 from £21; 🚍 from £21; 48 hardstanding pitches
Facilities: 🏠 ⊙ 🅿 🕭 WiFi
Services: 🔌 🗑 🚰 ⚓ T
Within 3 miles: ↧ 🎣 ∪ 🎱 🛅

Additional site information: 4 acre site. Adults only. 🐕 Cars can be parked by caravans. Awnings permitted. No noise 22.30–08.00.

WILTSHIRE

AMESBURY

Places to visit

Stonehenge, STONEHENGE, SP4 7DE, 0370 333 1181
www.english-heritage.org.uk/daysout/properties/stonehenge

Heale Garden, MIDDLE WOODFORD, SP4 6NT, 01722 782504
www.healegarden.co.uk

Great for kids: Wilton House, WILTON [NEAR SALISBURY], SP2 0BJ, 01722 746728, www.wiltonhouse.com

AMESBURY
Map 5 SU14

Stonehenge Touring Park

▶▶▶ 90%

tel: 01980 620304 **Orcheston SP3 4SH**
email: stay@stonehengetouringpark.com **web:** www.stonehengetouringpark.com
dir: *From A360 towards Devizes turn right, follow lane, site at bottom of village on right.*

A quiet site adjacent to the small village of Orcheston near the centre of Salisbury Plain. There are modern and very clean facilities and an excellent on-site shop; some hardstandings are available. This is a well located site for visiting Stonehenge and nearby Salisbury plus it's less that an hour's drive from the heart of the New Forest National Park.

Open: All year **Last arrival:** 19.00 **Last departure:** 11.00
Pitches: 🚐 from £11.50; 🚍 from £11.50; ⛺ from £11.50; 13 hardstanding pitches
Leisure: 🅰
Facilities: 🏠 🗑 ⊙ 🅿 ⚡ ☀ ⛄ 🕭 S 🍴 WiFi
Services: 🔌 🗑 🚰 ⚓ 🛢 ⚓ 🐾 T
Within 3 miles: ∪

Additional site information: 2 acre site. 🐕 Cars can be parked by caravans and tents. Awnings permitted. No noise after 23.00.

BERWICK ST JAMES
Map 5 SU03

Places to visit

Stonehenge, STONEHENGE, SP4 7DE, 0370 333 1181
www.english-heritage.org.uk/daysout/properties/stonehenge

Stonehenge Campsite & Glamping Pods

▶▶▶▶ 81%

tel: 07786 734732 **SP3 4TQ**
email: stay@stonehengecampsite.co.uk **web:** www.stonehengecampsite.co.uk
dir: *From Stonehenge Visitor Centre take A303 west, 2 miles. Through Winterbourne Stoke. Left onto B3083 towards Berwick St James. Site on left in 0.5 mile.*

This small campsite is split into three areas and has good modern toilets and showers including a laundry facility. The lower end of the site has hardstandings for caravans and motorhomes plus five glamping pods, including the novel Festival Pod. The middle field is for tents, both for families and individuals, whilst the top area is for larger groups who can perhaps enjoy some of their holiday time sitting around open fires or fire pits. The site is close to Stonehenge and Longleat; there are plenty of excellent walks from the campsite and two good pubs nearby.

Open: Easter to end October **Last arrival:** 20.00 **Last departure:** 10.45
Pitches: 🚐 🚍 ⛺ 🏠; 12 hardstanding pitches
Facilities: 🏠 ⊙ 🅿 ☀ ⛄ 🍴 WiFi
Services: 🔌 🗑 🍔
Within 3 miles: 🎣 ∪ 🛅

Additional site information: 4 acre site. 🐕 Cars can be parked by caravans and tents. Awnings permitted. No noise 22.00 to 08.00, no music at any time. Fixed fire pits and mobile fire pits.

Glamping available: Wooden pods.

CALNE Map 4 ST97

Places to visit

Avebury Manor & Garden, AVEBURY, SN8 1RF, 01672 539250
www.nationaltrust.org.uk/avebury

Bowood House & Gardens, CALNE, SN11 0LZ, 01249 812102
www.bowood.org

Great for kids: Alexander Keiller Museum, AVEBURY, SN8 1RF, 01672 539250
www.nationaltrust.org.uk/avebury

Blackland Lakes Holiday & Leisure Centre

►►► 81%

tel: 01249 810943 **Stockley Lane SN11 0NQ**
email: enquiries@blacklandlakes.co.uk **web:** www.blacklandlakes.co.uk
dir: *From Calne take A4 towards Beckhampton and Avebury for 1.5 miles. In Quemerford right at brown camp sign and Stockley/Headington sign into Stockley Lane. Site 1 mile on left.*

A rural site surrounded by the North and West Downs. The park offers 15 fully serviced pitches and is divided into several paddocks separated by hedges, trees and fences, and there are two well-stocked carp fisheries for the angling enthusiast. There are some excellent walks close by, and the interesting market town of Devizes is just a few miles away.

Open: All year (restricted service: 30 October to 1 March – pre-paid bookings only)
Last arrival: 22.00 **Last departure:** noon

Pitches: 🚐 from £17.25; 🚌 from £18.25; ⛺ from £17.25; 16 hardstanding pitches; 25 seasonal pitches

Leisure: 🛝 🎣

Facilities: 🛁 🔌 💨 ❄ ♿ 🛒 🍖 🧺

Services: ⚡ 🫧 🍷 🔋 🚰 🔒 ♻ [T]

Within 3 miles: ⛳ 🐴

Additional site information: 15 acre site. 🐕 Cars can be parked by caravans and tents. Awnings permitted. No groups of under 25s. No noise after 22.30, no loud music. Wildfowl sanctuary, cycle trail, nature trail, pygmy goats. Licensed bar on bank holidays, Friday and Saturday in peak season.

COOMBE BISSETT Map 5 SU12

Places to visit

Breamore House & Countryside Museum, BREAMORE, SP6 2DF, 01725 512858
www.breamorehouse.com

Summerlands Caravan Park

►►► 78%

tel: 01722 718259 & 07718 014343 **College Farm, Rockbourne Road SP5 4LP**
email: enquiries@summerlandscaravanpark.co.uk
web: www.summerlandscaravanpark.co.uk
dir: *Signed from junction of A354 and Rockbourne Road. Approximately 6 miles south of Salisbury.*

Approached via a long private drive and situated well off the beaten track within the Cranborne Chase, yet close to Salisbury, this small, family-run park offers peace and quiet and superb views across rolling countryside. 26 level grass pitches are located in a neat meadow and the well-maintained toilet and shower facilities are kept spotlessly clean. There is also a well-equipped bell tent for hire. Dogs are welcome and there's plenty of space for children to play.

Open: April to October **Last arrival:** 21.00 **Last departure:** 11.00

Pitches: 🚐 from £14.85; 🚌 from £14.85; ⛺ from £14.85

Facilities: 🛁 🔌 💨 ❄ ♿

Services: ⚡ 🔋 🚰

Within 3 miles: 🛒

Additional site information: 3.3 acre site. 🐕 Cars can be parked by caravans and tents. Awnings permitted. No noise after 23.00. Vehicle access restrictions 23.00–07.00.

LACOCK Map 4 ST96

Places to visit

Lacock Abbey, Fox Talbot Museum & Village, LACOCK, SN15 2LG, 01249 730459
www.nationaltrust.org.uk/lacock

Corsham Court, CORSHAM, SN13 0BZ, 01249 701610
www.corsham-court.co.uk

Piccadilly Caravan Park

►►►► 85%

tel: 01249 730260 **Folly Lane West SN15 2LP**
email: info@piccadillylacock.co.uk **web:** www.piccadillylacock.co.uk
dir: *4 miles south of Chippenham just past Lacock. Exit A350 signed Gastard. Site 300 yards on left.*

A peaceful, pleasant site, well established and beautifully laid out, close to the village of Lacock and Lacock Abbey. Both the facilities and the grounds are immaculately maintained; there is very good screening. A section of the park has been developed to provide spacious pitches especially for tents, complete with its own toilet and shower block.

Open: Easter and April to October **Last arrival:** 20.00 **Last departure:** noon

Pitches: * 🚐 from £20; 🚌 from £20; ⛺ from £20; 12 hardstanding pitches

Leisure: 🛝 ⚽

Facilities: 🛁 🔌 💨 ❄ 📶

Services: ⚡ 🫧 🔋 🔒 ♻

Within 3 miles: ⛳ 🎣 🐴 🎬 🛒

Additional site information: 2.5 acre site. 🐕 🚷 Cars can be parked by caravans and tents. Awnings permitted. No excessive noise.

LANDFORD
Map 5 SU21

Places to visit

Furzey Gardens, MINSTEAD, SO43 7GL, 023 8081 2464
www.furzey-gardens.org

Mottisfont, MOTTISFONT, SO51 0LP, 01794 340757
www.nationaltrust.org.uk/mottisfont

Great for kids: Paultons Park, OWER, SO51 6AL, 023 8081 4442
www.paultonspark.co.uk

Premier Park

Greenhill Farm Caravan & Camping Park
►►►►► 87%

tel: 01794 324117 **Greenhill Farm, New Road SP5 2AZ**
email: info@greenhillfarm.co.uk **web:** www.greenhillfarm.co.uk
dir: *M27 junction 2, A36 towards Salisbury. Approximately 3 miles after Hampshire–Wiltshire border, pass Shoe Inn pub on right, BP garage on left, left into New Road, signed Nomansland, 0.75 mile on left.*

A tranquil, well-landscaped park hidden away in unspoilt countryside on the edge of the New Forest National Park. Pitches overlooking the fishing lake include hardstandings and are for adults only. The other section of the park is for families and includes a play area and games room. The site provides excellent toilet and shower blocks in both the family area and adults-only area. This site is also well placed for visiting Paultons Park at Ower.

Open: All year **Last arrival:** 21.30 **Last departure:** 11.00

Pitches: 🚐 from £21; 🚐 from £21; ▲ from £18; 🏠 see prices below;
50 hardstanding pitches

Leisure: 🎱 🎣 ⛱ 🎮 ⚽ ☺

Facilities: 🚿 ⊙ 📶 ✳ ♿ 🛒

Services: 🔌 �e 🍽 🍺 ⛽ ⬆ ⬇ 🚰 ⚡ 🔋 Ⓣ

Within 3 miles: ♨ ◎

Additional site information: 13 acre site. 🐕 Cars can be parked by caravans and tents. Awnings permitted. No noise after 23.00. Disposable BBQs, freshly baked bread available. Internet access available.

Glamping available: Wooden pods from £45.

Additional glamping information: Wooden pods accomodate up to 4 people, no dogs. Cars can be parked by pods.

SALISBURY
Map 5 SU12

See also Amesbury

Places to visit

The Salisbury Museum, SALISBURY, SP1 2EN, 01722 332151
www.salisburymuseum.org.com

Salisbury Cathedral, SALISBURY, SP1 2EJ, 01722 555120
www.salisburycathedral.org.uk

Coombe Touring Park
►►►► 91%

tel: 01722 328451 **Race Plain, Netherhampton SP2 8PN**
email: enquiries@coombecaravanpark.co.uk **web:** www.coombecaravanpark.co.uk
dir: *From Salisbury take A345 towards Blandford. Onto A3094 then follow Stratford Tony and site signs. After racecourse turn left. 700 yards to site on right. Or from A36 (west of Salisbury) onto A3094 (signed Bournemouth), at Netherhampton Corner follow Stratford Tony and racecourse signs. After racecourse turn left. 700 yards to site on right.*

A very neat and attractive site adjacent to the racecourse with views over the downs. The park is well landscaped with shrubs and maturing trees, and the very colourful beds are stocked from the owner's own greenhouse. This is a lovely quiet and peaceful park to stay on with an excellent toilet and shower block, plus a fully-equipped function room with a kitchen that makes for a welcome campers' retreat. There are four static homes available for hire.

Open: All year (restricted service: October to April – shop closed) **Last arrival:** 21.00
Last departure: noon

Pitches: * 🚐 from £20; 🚐 from £20; ▲ from £20; 6 hardstanding pitches

Leisure: 🎱

Facilities: 🚿 ⊙ 📶 ✳ ♿ 🛒 🍽 🏓

Services: 🔌 �e 🔋 ⚡

Within 3 miles: ♨ ∪

Additional site information: 8 acre site. 🐕 🚫 Cars can be parked by caravans and tents. Awnings permitted. No open fires, no mini motorbikes, no drones, no noise between 23.00–07.00. Table tennis, campers' kitchen, children's bathroom.

PITCHES: 🚐 Caravans 🚐 Motorhomes ▲ Tents 🏠 Glamping accommodation **SERVICES:** 🔌 Electric hook-up �e Launderette 🍺 Licensed bar
🔋 Calor Gas ⚡ Campingaz Ⓣ Toilet fluid 🍽 Café/Restaurant 🍔 Fast Food/Takeaway 🔋 Battery charging ⬇ Motorhome service point
* 2019 prices 🚫 No credit or debit cards 🐕 Dogs permitted 🚫 No dogs

SALISBURY *continued*

Alderbury Caravan & Camping Park

▶▶▶ 83%

tel: 01722 710125 **Southampton Road, Whaddon SP5 3HB**
email: alderbury@aol.com
dir: *Follow Whaddon signs from A36, 3 miles from Salisbury. Site opposite The Three Crowns pub.*

A pleasant, attractive park set in the village of Whaddon not far from Salisbury. The small site is well maintained and is ideally positioned near the A36 for overnight stops to and from the Southampton ferry terminals.

Open: All year **Last arrival:** 21.00 **Last departure:** 12.30

Pitches: 🚐 🚎 ▲; 12 hardstanding pitches **Facilities:** ⊙ ✳ ⅙ ☷ WiFi

Services: 🔌 🗑 ⬆ 🔒 🖉 **Within 3 miles:** ⅙ 🖉 ∪ ⅞ 🎄 🛍

Additional site information: 2 acre site. 🐾 Cars can be parked by caravans and tents. Awnings permitted. No open fires. Microwave and electric kettle available.

Stowford Manor Farm

▶▶ 76%

tel: 01225 752253 **Stowford, Wingfield BA14 9LH**
email: camping@stowfordmanorfarm.co.uk web: www.stowfordmanorfarm.co.uk
dir: *From Trowbridge take A366 west towards Radstock. Site on left in 3 miles.*

A very simple farm site set on the banks of the River Frome behind the farm courtyard. The owners are friendly and relaxed and the park enjoys a similarly comfortable ambience. Cream teas are available at the farmhouse. The unisex facilities are kept clean and tidy. Farleigh & District Swimming Club, one of the few remaining river swimming clubs, is just half a mile from the site.

Open: Easter to October **Last departure:** noon

Pitches: 🚐 🚎 ▲

Leisure: 🖉

Facilities: 🏠 ⊙ ✳ WiFi

Services: 🔌 🍴 ⬆

Within 3 miles: ⅙ ∪ ≋ ⅞ 🎄 🛍 ▣

Additional site information: 1.5 acre site. 🐾 Cars can be parked by caravans and tents. Awnings permitted. No open fires. Fishing, boating, river swimming. Fire bowl hire.

Brokerswood Country Park

▶▶▶▶ 85%

tel: 01373 822238 **Brokerswood BA13 4EH**
email: brokerswood.info@haulfryn.co.uk web: www.brokerswoodcountrypark.co.uk
dir: *M4 junction 17, south on A350. Right at Yarnbrook to Rising Sun pub at North Bradley, left at roundabout. Left on bend approaching Southwick, 2.5 miles, site on right.*

A popular site on the edge of an 80-acre woodland park with nature trails, fishing lakes and a good range of activities including archery, tree-top high rope course and kayaking. The adventure playground offers plenty of fun for all ages, and there is a miniature railway, an undercover play area and a breakfast bar. There are high quality toilet facilities.

Open: 7 April to 31 October **Last arrival:** 17.30 (later arrivals by prior arrangement only) **Last departure:** 11.00

Pitches: 🚐 🚎 ▲; 25 hardstanding pitches; 55 seasonal pitches

Leisure: ᴧ 🖉

Facilities: 🏠 🖉 ✳ ⅙ 🛁 ☷ 🎄 🚼 WiFi

Services: 🔌 🗑 🍴 ⬆ 🔒 ▣

Additional site information: 80 acre site. 🐾 Cars can be parked by caravans and tents. Awnings permitted. Maximum of 3 pitches per booking. Seasonal café/restaurant and takeaway food. Car hire can be arranged.

WORCESTERSHIRE

HONEYBOURNE — Map 10 SP14

Places to visit

Kiftsgate Court Garden, MICKLETON, GL55 6LN, 01386 438777
www.kiftsgate.co.uk

Hidcote Manor Garden, MICKLETON, GL55 6LR, 01386 438333
www.nationaltrust.org.uk/hidcote

Great for kids: Anne Hathaway's Cottage, SHOTTERY, CV37 9HH, 01789 338532
www.shakespeare.org.uk

Premier Park

Ranch Caravan Park

►►►►► 86%

tel: 01386 830744 **Station Road WR11 7PR**
email: enquiries@ranch.co.uk **web:** www.ranch.co.uk
dir: *From village crossroads towards Bidford, site 400 metres on left.*

An attractive and well-run park set amidst farmland in the Vale of Evesham and landscaped with trees and bushes. Tourers have their own excellent facilities in two locations, and the use of an outdoor heated swimming pool in peak season. There is also a licensed club serving meals. Please note that this site does not accept tents.

Open: March to November (restricted service: March to May and September to November – swimming pool closed, shorter club hours) **Last arrival:** 20.00 **Last departure:** noon

Pitches: 🚐 from £26.50; 🚌; 46 touring pitches; 23 seasonal pitches

Leisure: 🏊 🛝 🎱 📺 🎵 🎉 ⚽

Facilities: 🛁 ⊙ 🚿 ❄ ♿ [S]

Services: 🔌 🧺 🍷 🍴 🍔 🔋 ⬇ 🛢 🔥 [T]

Within 3 miles: ⛳ 🎣 🐎

Additional site information: 12 acre site. 🐕 Cars can be parked by caravans. Awnings permitted. No unaccompanied minors. Car hire can be arranged. Internet access available.

WORCESTER — Map 10 SO85

Places to visit

City Museum & Art Gallery, WORCESTER, WR1 1DT, 01905 25371
www.museumsworcestershire.org.uk

The Greyfriars' House and Garden, WORCESTER, WR1 2LZ, 01905 23571
www.nationaltrust.org.uk/greyfriars

Great for kids: West Midland Safari & Leisure Park, BEWDLEY, DY12 1LF, 01299 402114, www.wmsp.co.uk

Peachley Leisure Touring Park

►►► 87%

tel: 01905 641309 & 07764 540803 **Peachley Lane, Lower Broadheath WR2 6QX**
email: peachleyleisure@live.co.uk **web:** www.peachleyleisure.com
dir: *M5 junction 7, A44 (Worcester ring road) towards Leominster. Exit at sign for Elgar's Birthplace Museum. Pass museum, at crossroads turn right. In 0.75 mile at T-junction turn left. Park signed on right.*

The park is set in its own area in the grounds of Peachley Farm and has all hardstanding and fully serviced pitches. The 25 super pitches have 16 amp electricity, mains water and sewer. There are two fishing lakes, a really excellent quad bike course and outdoor giant draughts, chess and jenga. The park proves to be a peaceful haven, and is an excellent base from which to explore the area, which includes The Elgar Birthplace Museum, Worcester Racecourse and the Worcester Victorian Christmas Fayre (in late November); it is also convenient for Malvern's Three Counties Showground.

Open: All year **Last arrival:** 21.30 **Last departure:** 15.00

Pitches: 🚐 🚌 ⛺; 82 hardstanding pitches; 50 seasonal pitches

Leisure: 🎣 ⚽

Facilities: 🛁 ⊙ ❄ ♿ 🍖 🪑 [WiFi]

Services: 🔌 🧺 🍴 🛢

Within 3 miles: ⛳ 🐎 ◎ 🏄 🚤 目 [S]

Additional site information: 8 acre site. 🐕 Cars can be parked by caravans and tents. Awnings permitted. No skateboards, no riding on motorbikes or scooters. Table tennis.

Yorkshire

There is nowhere in the British Isles quite like Yorkshire. With such scenic and cultural diversity, it is almost a country within a country. For sheer scale, size and grandeur, there is nowhere to beat it. Much of it in the spectacular Pennines, Yorkshire is a land of glorious moors, gentle dales, ruined abbeys and picturesque market towns.

'My Yorkshire, a land of pure air, rocky streams and hidden waterfalls,' was how the celebrated vet Alf Wight described his adopted home. Wight was born in Sunderland but moved to the North Yorkshire market town of Thirsk soon after the outbreak of the Second World War. He fell in love with the place and in later years his affection for the beauty, spirit and character of this great county translated to the printed page when Wight, writing under the name of James Herriot, wrote eight best-selling volumes of memoirs about the life of a Yorkshire vet, which spawned two films and a long-running TV series. Today, thousands of visitors from near and far travel to the landscape he loved so dearly to see it all for themselves. His veterinary practice, and original home, in Thirsk is open to the public.

Not surprisingly, walking features prominently on the list of things to do in Yorkshire. There are countless footpaths and bridleways to explore and miles of long-distance trails across vast open moorland and through tranquil meandering valleys. The 81-mile Dales Way is a perfect way to discover the magnificent scenery of Wharfedale, Ribblesdale and Dentdale, while the Calderdale Way offers a fascinating insight into the Pennine heartland of industrial West Yorkshire. Most famous of all the region's longer routes is surely the Pennine Way, which opened 50 years ago in April 1965. Its inception was the most important achievement in the history of the Ramblers' Association, marking Britain's first national long-distance footpath.

The Pennine Way was the brainchild of Tom Stephenson, one-time secretary of the Association but his vision for a trail for everyone was a long time in the planning. Landowners regularly thwarted his attempts to make the landscape accessible to walkers and there were countless prosecutions for trespassing 'I could never understand how anyone could own a mountain,' Stephenson wrote. 'Surely it was there for everybody.'

One of the more surprising features to be found on the route of the Pennine Way is the ruined house known as Top Withins. This is thought to be the inspiration for *Wuthering Heights*, the Earnshaw home in Emily Brontë's stirring novel of the same name. The Brontë sisters knew the area well, and their home, now the Brontë Parsonage Museum, lies just a few miles from the ruins in the village of Haworth. The parsonage draws thousands of visitors every year; its atmospheric setting amid bleak moorland and gritstone houses vividly captures the spirit of this uniquely talented trio of writers.

An easier, more comfortable way of exploring much of Yorkshire's scenic landscape is by train. A ride on the famous Settle to Carlisle railway represents one of the region's most memorable train journeys. For a while during the late 1980s the future of this line was in serious doubt, when it seemed British Rail might close it because of soaring maintenance costs. Thanks to Michael Portillo, a noted railway enthusiast who was Secretary of State for Transport at the time, the line was saved. Essentially, the Settle to Carlisle railway is a lifeline for commuters and the people of the more remote communities of the western Dales, but it is also an extremely popular tourist attraction. Carriages are regularly filled with summer visitors in search of stunning scenery and they are not disappointed. Elsewhere in Yorkshire, a very different train recalls a very different age. In the National Railway Museum at York you'll find countless locomotives, including a replica of Stephenson's Rocket and the much-loved *Flying Scotsman*.

◁ Lower Wharfedale

EAST RIDING OF YORKSHIRE

BRANDESBURTON — Map 17 TA14

Places to visit

Beverley Guildhall, BEVERLEY, HU17 9XX, 01482 392783
www.eastriding.gov.uk/museums

Burton Constable Hall, SPROATLEY, HU11 4LN, 01964 562400
www.burtonconstable.com

Blue Rose Caravan Country Park

►►►► 91%

tel: 01964 543366 & 07504 026899 **Star Carr Lane YO25 8RU**
email: info@bluerosepark.com **web:** www.bluerosepark.com
dir: *From A165 at roundabout into New Road, signed Brandesburton, which becomes Star Carr Lane. In approximately 1 mile, site on left.*

High standards of customer care are assured at this neat and well-maintained adults-only site that is well placed for visiting Hornsea and the Yorkshire coastline. The park is within walking distance of Brandesburton and offers an idyllic stopover for caravanners wanting a peaceful break in the countryside.

Open: All year **Last arrival:** 20.00 **Last departure:** noon

Pitches: 🚐 🚌; 59 hardstanding pitches; 43 seasonal pitches

Facilities: 🛁 🔌 💨 ♿ 🍖 ⛱ [WiFi]

Services: 🔧 🧺 🍷 🛢 🍃 [T]

Within 3 miles: ⛳ 🎣 🐴 ◎ 🏄 ⛵ 🛒

Additional site information: 16 acre site. Adults only. 🐕 Cars can be parked by caravans. Awnings permitted.

Dacre Lakeside Park

►►► 88%

tel: 0800 180 4556 & 01964 543704 **YO25 8RT**
email: dacrepark@btconnect.com **web:** www.dacrepark.co.uk
dir: *From A165 (bypass) midway between Beverley and Hornsea, follow Brandesburton and brown site sign.*

A large lake popular with watersports enthusiasts is the focal point of this grassy site, which offers predominantly seasonal pitches – there are just three tent pitches and five caravan/motorhome pitches available. The clubhouse offers indoor activities; there's a fish and chip shop, a pub and a Chinese takeaway in the village, which is within walking distance. The six-acre lake is used for windsurfing, sailing, kayaking, canoeing and fishing. Camping pods are available for hire.

Open: March to October **Last arrival:** 21.00 **Last departure:** noon

Pitches: 🚐 🚌 ⛺ 🛖; 2 hardstanding pitches; 107 seasonal pitches

Leisure: 🛝 🎾 🎱 📺 🚲 🎵 🎣 ⚽

Facilities: 🛁 🔌 💨 ❄ ♿ [WiFi]

Services: 🔧 🧺 🍷 🍴 🛢

Within 3 miles: ⛳ 🐴 🏄 ⛵ 🛒

Additional site information: 8 acre site. 🐕 Cars can be parked by caravans and tents. Awnings permitted. No noise 23.00–08.00, no craft with engines permitted on lake.

Glamping available: Wooden pods.

BRIDLINGTON — Map 17 TA16

See also Rudston

Places to visit

Sewerby Hall & Gardens, BRIDLINGTON, YO15 1EA, 01262 673769
www.sewerbyhall.co.uk

RSPB Bempton Cliffs, BEMPTON, YO15 1JD, 01262 422212
www.rspb.org.uk/bemptoncliffs

Great for kids: Burton Agnes Hall, BURTON AGNES, YO25 4ND, 01262 490324
www.burtonagnes.com

Fir Tree Caravan Park

►►►► 81%

tel: 01262 676442 **Jewison Lane, Sewerby YO16 6YG**
email: info@flowerofmay.com **web:** www.flowerofmay.com
dir: *1.5 miles from centre of Bridlington. Left onto B1255 at Marton Corner. Site 600 yards on left.*

Fir Tree Caravan Park is a large, mainly static park that has a well laid out touring area with its own facilities. It has an excellent swimming pool complex and the adjacent bar-cum-conservatory serves meals. There is also a family bar, games room and outdoor children's play area. Please note, this park only offers seasonal touring pitches.

Open: March to October (restricted service: early and late season – bar and entertainment restrictions)

Pitches: 🚐; 45 hardstanding pitches; 45 seasonal pitches

Leisure: 🏊 🛝 🎱 📺 🎵 ⚽

Facilities: 🛁 🔌 ❄ ♿ 🛒 🍖 🍼 [WiFi]

Services: 🔧 🧺 🍷 🍴 🛍 🍟 🛢 🍃 [T]

Within 3 miles: ⛳ 🎣 🐴 ◎ 🏄 ⛵ 🎬

Additional site information: 22 acre site. 🐕 Dogs accepted by prior arrangement only. Cars can be parked by caravans. Awnings permitted. No noise after midnight.

FLAMBOROUGH
Map 17 TA27

Places to visit
RSPB Bempton Cliffs, BEMPTON, YO15 1JD, 01262 422212
www.rspb.org.uk/bemptoncliffs

Premier Park

Thornwick Bay Holiday Village
►►►►► 88% HOLIDAY CENTRE

tel: 01262 850569 **North Marine Road YO15 1AU**
email: thornwickbay@haven.com
dir: From Flamborough take B1255 (Tower Street) signed North landing. Site entrance on left in approximately 1 mile.

A large holiday village close to beach, with a superb range of attractions including indoor swimming pools, lake fishing and a sports zone. Eating options include the stylish Lighthouse Bar & Grill and The Yorkshire Café that serves espressos, lattes and muffins. The large cliff-top touring and camping areas are mainly level and grassed; there are a few hardstandings and fully services pitches plus two smart amenity blocks with family rooms.

Open: mid March to end October **Last arrival:** 22.00 **Last departure:** 10.00
Pitches: from £30; from £30; from £17; 57 hardstanding pitches
Leisure:
Facilities:
Services:
Within 3 miles:

Additional site information: 4 acre site. 2 dogs per booking, certain dog breeds banned. No commercial vehicles, no bookings by person under 21 years unless a family booking. Bakery, fishing lake, sports and nature activities, nature trails. Car hire can be arranged.

KINGSTON UPON HULL

See Sproatley

RUDSTON
Map 17 TA06

Places to visit
Sewerby Hall & Gardens, BRIDLINGTON, YO15 1EA, 01262 673769
www.sewerbyhall.co.uk

Thorpe Hall Caravan & Camping Site
►►►► 83%

tel: 01262 420393 & 420574 **Thorpe Hall YO25 4JE**
email: caravansite@thorpehall.co.uk **web:** www.thorpehall.co.uk
dir: From Bridlington take B1253 west for 5 miles.

A delightful, peaceful small park within the walled gardens of Thorpe Hall yet within a few miles of the bustling seaside resort of Bridlington. The site offers a games field, its own coarse fishery, and a games and TV lounge. There are numerous walks locally.

Open: March to October **Last arrival:** 22.00 **Last departure:** noon
Pitches:
Leisure:
Facilities:
Services:
Within 3 miles:

Additional site information: 4.5 acre site. Well behaved dogs only. Cars can be parked by caravans and tents. Awnings permitted. No ball games except on designated field, no noise 23.00–08.00, shop/reception open 09.00–11.30 and 16.30–20.30 (longer hours when busy). 4.5-acre golf practice area/games field. Car hire can be arranged.

SKIPSEA
Map 17 TA15

Places to visit
Hornsea Museum, HORNSEA, HU18 1AB, 01964 533443
www.hornseamuseum.com

Sewerby Hall & Gardens, BRIDLINGTON, YO15 1EA, 01262 673769
www.sewerbyhall.co.uk

Premier Park

Skirlington Leisure Park
►►►►► 89% HOLIDAY CENTRE

tel: 01262 468213 & 468466 **YO25 8SY**
email: info@skirlington.com **web:** www.skirlington.com
dir: From M62 towards Beverley then Hornsea. Between Skipsea and Hornsea on B1242.

A large, well-run seaside park set close to the beach in partly-sloping meadowland with young trees and shrubs. The site has five toilet blocks, a supermarket and an amusement arcade, plus entertainment occasionally in the clubhouse. The wide range of family amenities includes an indoor heated swimming pool complex with sauna, steam room and gym. A 10-pin bowling alley and indoor soft play area for children are added attractions.

Open: March to October (restricted service: diner and some facilities open from Friday to Sunday only (except school holidays and bank holidays)) **Last arrival:** 20.00 **Last departure:** 11.00
Pitches: ; 15 hardstanding pitches; 180 seasonal pitches
Leisure: Spa
Facilities:
Services:
Within 3 miles:

Additional site information: 140 acre site. No noise after 22.00. Putting green, fishing lake, arcade, mini bowling alley, Sunday market.

SPROATLEY
Map 17 TA13

Places to visit

Burton Constable Hall, SPROATLEY, HU11 4LN, 01964 562400
www.burtonconstable.com

Streetlife Museum Hull, KINGSTON UPON HULL, HU1 1PS, 01482 300300
www.hcandl.co.uk

Great for kids: The Deep, KINGSTON UPON HULL, HU1 4DP, 01482 381000
www.thedeep.co.uk

Burton Constable Holiday Park & Arboretum

►►►► 90%

tel: 01964 562508 **Old Lodges HU11 4LJ**
email: info@burtonconstable.co.uk **web:** www.burtonconstableholidaypark.co.uk
dir: A165 onto B1238 to Sproatley. For sat nav use HU11 4PG. Follow Park Road alongside
the Constable Arms for approximately 500 yards, follow signs to holiday park ahead.

Within the extensive estate of Constable Burton Hall, this large and secluded
holiday destination provides a wide range of attractions including fishing and
boating on the two 10-acre lakes, a snooker room, Mr Constable's Country Kitchen,
and a licensed bar with a designated family room. The grounds are immaculately
maintained and generous pitch density offers good privacy. Two luxury lodges and
nine pods (two with en suite facilities) are available for hire.

Open: March to mid February (restricted service: November to mid February – no tourers
or tents accepted) **Last arrival:** 18.00 (later by prior arrangement) **Last departure:** 11.00

Pitches: ⊞ from £22; ⊞ from £22; ▲ from £20; ⋒ see prices below;
26 hardstanding pitches; 14 seasonal pitches

Leisure: ⋒ ♫ ✐ ⚽

Facilities: ⌂ ☺ ⌿ ⅙ ⑤ ⨅ WiFi

Services: ⊡ ⑤ ⑩ ⑩ ⊞ ⛴ ⮥ ⧋ ⌀ Ⓣ

Within 3 miles: ♨ ∪

Additional site information: 90 acre site. ⌇ Cars can be parked by caravans and tents.
Awnings permitted. No fires, skateboards or rollerblades. Snooker, table tennis, woodland
walks, cycling, toddlers play area, night security warden. Beer garden and events at
Lakeside bar.

Glamping available: Wooden pods from £34. **Changeover days:** Any day

Additional glamping information: Deluxe pods with shower, toilet, washbasin and kitchen
are available, sleeps 5. Cars can be parked by pods.

TUNSTALL
Map 17 TA33

Places to visit

Burton Constable Hall, SPROATLEY, HU11 4LN, 01964 562400
www.burtonconstable.com

Premier Park

Sand le Mere Holiday Village
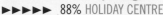

►►►►► 88% HOLIDAY CENTRE

tel: 01964 670403 **Southfield Lane HU12 0JF**
email: info@sand-le-mere.co.uk **web:** www.sand-le-mere.co.uk
dir: From Hull A1033 signed Withernsea, B1362 (Hull Road) signed Hedon. In Hedon
continue on B3162 towards Withernsea. Turn left signed Roos. In Roos take B1242.
Turn left at brown sign for site. In Tunstall right at T-junction, right into Seaside Lane
to site.

Ideally located between Withernsea and Bridlington, this impressive
development provides first-class indoor leisure facilities with swimming pool,
entertainment and a kiddies' soft ball area. Excellent level touring pitches,
including six that have their own private en suite wet room pods, are surrounded
by mature trees, and a lovely nature walk ensures that this rural destination can
be fully appreciated. Please note, this site does not accept tents.

Open: March to November **Last arrival:** 23.00 **Last departure:** 11.00

Pitches: ⊞ ⊞; 51 hardstanding pitches; 24 seasonal pitches

Leisure: ⌖ ⋒ ♨ ⚲ ⎁ ♫ ✐ ⚽ Spa

Facilities: ⌂ ⌿ ✳ ⅙ ⑤ ⨅ ⮝ WiFi

Services: ⊡ ⑤ ⑩ ⑩ ⊞ ⮥ ⌀

Within 3 miles: ♨ ◎

Additional site information: 135 acre site. ⌇ No noise after 23.00, speed limits
around site to be observed, no camp fires.

LEISURE: ⌖ Indoor swimming pool ⚲ Outdoor swimming pool ⋒ Children's playground ⚃ Kids' club ⚲ Tennis court ⚲ Games room ⎁ Separate TV room
♨ golf course ⛳ Pitch n putt ⛴ Boats for hire ⚲ Bikes for hire ⎁ Cinema ♫ Entertainment ✐ Fishing ◎ Mini golf ⚲ Watersports ⚲ Gym ⚽ Sports field ∪ Stables
FACILITIES: ⌂ Baths/Shower ☺ Electric shaver sockets ⌿ Hairdryer ✳ Ice Pack Facility ⮝ Baby facilities ⅙ Disabled facilities ⑤ Shop on site or within 200yds
⨅ BBQ area ⨅ Picnic area WiFi WiFi

NORTH YORKSHIRE

ACASTER MALBIS
Map 16 SE54

Places to visit

National Railway Museum, YORK, YO26 4XJ, 03330 161010
www.nrm.org.uk

York Minster, YORK, YO1 7HH, 01904 557200
www.yorkminster.org

Great for kids: Jorvik Viking Centre, YORK, YO1 9WT, 01904 615505
www.jorvik-viking-centre.com

Moor End Farm
▶▶ 76%

tel: 01904 706727 & 07860 405872 **YO23 2UQ**
email: dawnhhall@hotmail.co.uk **web:** www.moor-end-farm.co.uk
dir: At junction of A64 and A1237 at Copmanthorpe follow Acaster Malbis signs. In Copmanthorpe left into Station Road signed Acaster Malbis. In approximately 1.8 miles site on left.

A very pleasant farm site with modernised facilities including a heated family/disabled shower room. A river boat pickup to York is 150 yards from the site entrance, and the village inn and restaurant are a short stroll away. A very convenient site for visiting York Racecourse.

Open: Easter or April to October **Last arrival:** 22.00 **Last departure:** noon

Pitches: from £20; from £20; from £20

Facilities: WiFi

Services:

Within 3 miles:

Additional site information: 1 acre site. Cars can be parked by caravans and tents. Awnings permitted. Fridge, freezer and microwave available.

ALLERSTON
Map 19 SE88

Places to visit

Scarborough Castle, SCARBOROUGH, YO11 1HY, 01723 372451
www.english-heritage.org.uk/daysout/properties/scarborough-castle

Pickering Castle, PICKERING, YO18 7AX, 01751 474989
www.english-heritage.org.uk/daysout/properties/pickering-castle

Great for kids: Flamingo Land Resort, KIRBY MISPERTON, YO17 6UX, 0800 408 8840, www.flamingoland.co.uk

Premier Park

Vale of Pickering Caravan Park
▶▶▶▶▶ 94%

tel: 01723 859280 **Carr House Farm YO18 7PQ**
email: info@valeofpickering.co.uk **web:** www.valeofpickering.co.uk
dir: On B1415, 1.75 miles from A170 (Pickering to Scarborough road).

A well-maintained, spacious family park with excellent facilities including a well-stocked shop, immaculate toilet facilities, and an interesting woodland walk. New for 2018 is a superb café that's open all day. A beautifully designed extension to the toilet block houses five family bathrooms and a wet room for less able visitors. Younger children will enjoy the attractive play area, while the large ball sports area will appeal to older ones. Three tastefully furnished and very well-equipped bell tents are also available for a glamping experience. The park is set in open countryside bounded by hedges, has manicured grassland and stunning seasonal floral displays, and is handy for the North Yorkshire Moors and the attractions of Scarborough.

Open: 6 March to 3 January **Last arrival:** 21.00 **Last departure:** 11.30

Pitches: from £19; from £19; from £15; 100 hardstanding pitches; 70 seasonal pitches

Leisure: **Facilities:** WiFi

Services: T

Within 3 miles:

Additional site information: 13 acre site. Cars can be parked by caravans and tents. Awnings permitted. No open fires or Chinese lanterns, no noise after 23.00. Microwave available.

Glamping available: Bell tents.

Additional glamping information: No pets. Cars can be parked by tents.

ALNE
Map 19 SE46

Places to visit

Beningbrough Hall, Gallery & Gardens, BENINGBROUGH, YO30 1DD, 01904 472027
www.nationaltrust.org.uk/beningbrough

Sutton Park, SUTTON-ON-THE-FOREST, YO61 1DP, 01347 810249
www.statelyhome.co.uk

Great for kids: National Railway Museum, YORK, YO26 4XJ, 03330 161010
www.nrm.org.uk

Premier Park

Alders Caravan Park

▶▶▶▶▶ 83%

tel: 01347 838722 **Home Farm YO61 1RY**
email: enquiries@homefarmalne.co.uk **web:** www.alderscaravanpark.co.uk
dir: *From A19 exit at Alne sign, in 1.5 miles left at T-junction, 0.5 mile site on left in village centre.*

A tastefully developed park on a working farm with screened pitches laid out in horseshoe-shaped areas. This well-designed park offers excellent toilet facilities including a bathroom and fully-serviced washing and toilet cubicles.
A woodland area and a water meadow are pleasant places to walk. Wooden pods are located in a separate landscaped area.

Open: March to October **Last arrival:** 21.00 **Last departure:** 14.00
Pitches: 🚐 from £22; 🚙 from £22; ▲ from £22; 🏠 see prices below;
6 hardstanding pitches; 71 seasonal pitches
Leisure:
Facilities: 🛁 ☉ 🖊 ✻ ⅙ 🛆 WiFi
Services: 🔌 🗑 🚽 ⚶ ⋒
Within 3 miles: ⌄ 🖊 🖺

Additional site information: 12 acre site. ⌃ Maximum 2 dogs per pitch. Cars can be parked by caravans and tents. Awnings permitted. Summer house. Farm produce for sale. Woodland walk, cricket club, Sustrans cycle track route 65. Car hire can be arranged.

Glamping available: Wooden pods from £41. **Changeover days:** Any day
Additional glamping information: No dogs in pods. Parking 20 metres from pods.

BISHOP MONKTON

Places to visit

Newby Hall & Gardens, RIPON, HG4 5AE, 01423 322583
www.newbyhall.com

Fountains Abbey & Studley Royal, RIPON, HG4 3DY, 01765 608888
www.nationaltrust.org.uk/fountains-abbey

Great for kids: Lightwater Valley Theme Park, NORTH STAINLEY, HG4 3HT, 01765 635321, www.lightwatervalley.co.uk

BISHOP MONKTON
Map 19 SE36

Church Farm Caravan Park

▶▶▶ 76%

tel: 01765 676578 & 07861 770164 **Knaresborough Road HG3 3QQ**
email: churchfarmcaravan@btinternet.com **web:** www.churchfarmcaravanpark.co.uk
dir: *From A61 at crossroads follow Bishop Monkton signs. 1.25 miles to village. At crossroads right into Knaresborough Road, site approximately 500 metres on right.*

A very pleasant rural site on a working farm, on the edge of the attractive village of Bishop Monkton with its well-stocked shop and pubs. Whilst very much a place to relax, there are many attractions close by, including Fountains Abbey, Newby Hall, Ripon and Harrogate.

Open: March to October **Last arrival:** 22.30 **Last departure:** noon
Pitches: * 🚐 from £17; 🚙 from £17; ▲ from £15; 1 hardstanding pitch
Facilities: 🛁 ☉ ✻ ⅙
Services: 🔌 🚽 ⚶
Within 3 miles: ⌄ 🖊 ∪ ◎ 🖽 🖺 🖺

Additional site information: 4 acre site. ⌃ 🚭 Cars can be parked by caravans and tents. Awnings permitted. No ball games.

BOLTON ABBEY
Map 19 SE05

Places to visit

Bolton Abbey, SKIPTON, BD23 6EX, 01756 718000
www.boltonabbey.com

Embsay and Bolton Abbey Steam Railway, BOLTON ABBEY, BD23 6AF, 01756 710614
www.embsayboltonabbeyrailway.org.uk

Great for kids: Hesketh Farm Park, SKIPTON, BD23 6HA, 01756 710444
www.heskethfarmpark.co.uk

Howgill Lodge

▶▶▶▶ 81%

tel: 01756 720655 **Barden BD23 6DJ**
email: info@howgill-lodge.co.uk **web:** www.howgill-lodge.co.uk
dir: *From Bolton Abbey take B6160 signed Burnsall. In 3 miles at Barden Tower right signed Appletreewick. 1.5 miles, at phone box right into lane to site.*

A beautifully-maintained and secluded site offering panoramic views of Wharfedale. The spacious hardstanding pitches are mainly terraced, and there is a separate tenting area with numerous picnic tables. There are three toilet facility blocks spread throughout the site, with the main block (including private, cubicled wash facilities) is appointed to a high standard. There is also a well-stocked shop.

Open: mid March to October **Last arrival:** 20.00 **Last departure:** noon
Pitches: 🚐 🚙 ▲; 20 hardstanding pitches
Leisure: ⚽
Facilities: ☉ 🖊 ✻ 🖺
Services: 🔌 🗑 🚽 🔒 ⌀ Ⓣ
Within 3 miles: 🖊

Additional site information: 4 acre site. ⌃ Cars can be parked by caravans and tents. Awnings permitted.

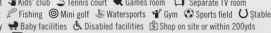

LEISURE: 🏊 Indoor swimming pool 🏊 Outdoor swimming pool 🛝 Children's playground 🖐 Kids' club 🎾 Tennis court 🎱 Games room 📺 Separate TV room 🏌 golf course 🏑 Pitch n putt 🛶 Boats for hire 🚲 Bikes for hire 🎬 Cinema 🎵 Entertainment 🎣 Fishing ◎ Mini golf 🤽 Watersports 🏋 Gym 🏏 Sports field ∪ Stables
FACILITIES: 🛁 Baths/Shower ☉ Electric shaver sockets 🖊 Hairdryer ✻ Ice Pack Facility 🚼 Baby facilities ⅙ Disabled facilities 🖺 Shop on site or within 200yds 🍖 BBQ area 🌲 Picnic area WiFi WiFi

CHOP GATE — Map 19 SE59

Places to visit

Mount Grace Priory, OSMOTHERLEY, DL6 3JG, 01609 883494
www.english-heritage.org.uk/daysout/properties/mount-grace-priory

Captain Cook Schoolroom Museum, GREAT AYTON, TS9 6NB
http://captaincookschoolroommuseum.co.uk

Lordstones Country Park

▶▶▶▶ 85%

tel: 01642 778482 **Carlton Bank TS9 7JH**
email: info@lordstones.com **web:** www.lordstones.com
dir: *From A172 between Stokesley and Osmotherley follow signs to Carlton-in-Cleveland. Through Carlton-in-Cleveland to Lordstones entrance.*

Situated in the North York Moors National Park and commanding one of the highest spots in the county, Lordstones has glorious views that extend over 40 miles. It is a privately-owned country park that has been developed to become a distinctive visitor venue. There is a first-class restaurant (The Belted Bull), a quality farm shop selling estate produce and a small camping-cum-glamping park. There are 20 pitches, some with electricity, enclosed by woodland, and two fully-equipped bell tents, yurts and five luxury Jumbo wooden pods, each with a wood-burning stove, kitchenette, toilet and outside decking with barbecue and seating. There is a purpose-built amenity building housing showers and toilet facilities. The Cleveland Way national trail and the coast-to-coast walk both pass close to the site.

Open: All year **Last arrival:** 17.00 **Last departure:** 11.00

Pitches: ▲; ⋔ see prices below

Facilities: ⊙ ♿ ⑤ ♨ 🥤 WiFi

Services: ⊕ 🍴 🍽 🏭

Additional site information: 150 acre site. 🐾 Cars can be parked by tents. Awnings permitted.

Glamping available: Bell tents from £55; wooden pods from £65; yurts from £70.
Changeover days: Monday, Friday

CONSTABLE BURTON

Places to visit

Middleham Castle, MIDDLEHAM, DL8 4QG, 01969 623899
www.english-heritage.org.uk/daysout/properties/middleham-castle

Great for kids: Bedale Museum, BEDALE, DL8 1AA, 01677 427516
www.bedalemuseum.org.uk

CONSTABLE BURTON — Map 19 SE19

Constable Burton Hall Caravan Park

▶▶▶▶ 83%

tel: 01677 450428 **DL8 5LJ**
email: caravanpark@constableburton.com **web:** www.cbcaravanpark.co.uk
dir: *From Leyburn on A684 towards Bedale, approximately 3 miles to site on left.*

A pretty site in the former deer park of the adjoining Constable Burton Hall, screened from the road by the park walls and surrounded by mature trees in a quiet rural location. The laundry is housed in a converted 18th-century deer barn and there is a pub and restaurant opposite; seasonal pitches are available. Please note that this site does not accept tents.

Open: April to October **Last arrival:** 20.00 **Last departure:** noon

Pitches: 🚐 from £21; 🚍 from £21

Facilities: 🛁 ⊙ 🅿 ✳ ♿ WiFi

Services: ⊕ 🖅 🔋 🔒

Within 3 miles: ⚓ ⑤

Additional site information: 10 acre site. 🐾 Cars can be parked by caravans. Awnings permitted. No commercial vehicles, no games. Family shower room.

EASINGWOLD — Map 19 SE56

Places to visit

Byland Abbey, COXWOLD, YO61 4BD, 0370 333 1181
www.english-heritage.org.uk/daysout/properties/byland-abbey

Folly Garth Caravan Park

▶▶ 75%

tel: 01347 821150 **Green Lane, Black Woods YO61 3ES**
dir: *From north: from A19 at roundabout follow Easingwold signs. In Easingwold follow Stillington signs. In approximately 3 miles turn right into Green Lane, site on right. From south: from A19 at roundabout follow Easingwold signs. In Easingwold turn right signed Helmsley (B1363) and Stillington. Right into Green Lane, site on right.*

A small country site tucked away at the end of a lane in a truly rural and tranquil setting, yet just 1.5 miles from the Georgian market town of Easingwold. Facilities include a well-equipped kitchen and a fully-carpeted lounge, with table and chairs, that opens onto a decking area. The toilets are appointed to a good standard.

Open: February to end December **Last arrival:** noon

Pitches: 🚐 🚍 ▲; 15 hardstanding pitches

Services: ⊕ 🖅 🍽

Within 3 miles: ⚓ ⑤

Additional site information: 3 acre site. 🐾 Dogs must be kept on leads at all times. 🚫 Cars can be parked by caravans and tents. Awnings permitted. No ball games.

PITCHES: 🚐 Caravans 🚍 Motorhomes ▲ Tents ⋔ Glamping accommodation **SERVICES:** ⊕ Electric hook-up 🖅 Launderette 🍴 Licensed bar 🔋 Calor Gas ⊘ Campingaz 🅣 Toilet fluid 🍽 Café/Restaurant 🏭 Fast Food/Takeaway 🔋 Battery charging ⚡ Motorhome service point * 2019 prices 🚫 No credit or debit cards 🐾 Dogs permitted 🚫 No dogs

FILEY
Map 17 TA18

Places to visit
Scarborough Castle, SCARBOROUGH, YO11 1HY, 01723 372451
www.english-heritage.org.uk/dayout/properties/scarborough-castle

Great for kids: Scarborough Sea Life Sanctuary, SCARBOROUGH, YO12 6RP
www.sealife.co.uk

Premier Park

Flower of May Holiday Park
►►►►► 91% HOLIDAY CENTRE

tel: 01723 584311 **Lebberston Cliff YO11 3NU**
email: info@flowerofmay.com **web:** www.flowerofmay.com
dir: *Take A165 from Scarborough towards Filey. Site signed.*

A well-run, high quality family holiday park with top class facilities. This large landscaped park offers a full range of recreational activities, with plenty to occupy everyone. Grass and hard pitches are available – all are on level ground, and arranged in avenues screened by shrubs. Enjoy the 'Scarborough Fair' museum, with its collection of restored fairground attractions, including rides, organs and vintage cars. There are 4-berth and 5-berth wooden camping pods, each with a decking area. Please note that prices for caravans, motorhomes and tent pitches are for a maximum of 4 people and 1 car (electricity not included).

Open: Easter to October (restricted service: early and late season – restricted opening hours in café, shop and bars) **Last arrival:** dusk **Last departure:** noon

Pitches: 🚐 from £24; 🚙 from £24; 🏕 from £24; 🏠 see prices below; 250 hardstanding pitches; 200 seasonal pitches
Leisure: 🏊 🎡 🔍 🎱 🎵 ⚽ ☺
Facilities: 🛁 ☺ 🚿 ❄ 🛁 💲 🛒 🍴 ♨ WiFi
Services: 🔌 🗑 🚮 🍴 🛒 🔒 🌿 T
Within 3 miles: 🎣 ♿ ∪ ◎ ⛵ ⛸ 🏇 🎯

Additional site information: 13 acre site. 🐕 1 dog per pitch by prior arrangement only. No noise after midnight. Squash, basketball court, skate park, table tennis.

Glamping available: Wooden pods 4 berth from £45; 5 berth from £55.

Changeover days: Any day

Additional glamping information: Wooden pods: (sleep 4 or 5) minimum stay 2 nights (3 nights at bank holidays and in school holidays). Microwave, kettle, beds with mattresses, sockets, lighting and decking area included. Cars can be parked by pods.

See advert opposite

Crows Nest Caravan Park
►►►► 91%

tel: 01723 582206 **Gristhorpe YO14 9PS**
email: enquiries@crowsnestcaravanpark.com **web:** www.crowsnestcaravanpark.com
dir: *5 miles south of Scarborough and 2 miles north of Filey. On seaward side of A165, signed from roundabout, near petrol station.*

A beautifully situated park on the coast between Scarborough and Filey, with excellent panoramic views. This large and mainly static park offers lively entertainment, and two bars. A small touring area is close to the attractions, and the main touring and camping section is at the top of the park overlooking the sea; this area is equipped with some excellent fully serviced pitches and a superb amenity block.

Open: March to October **Last departure:** noon
Pitches: 🚐 from £28; 🚙 from £28; 🏕 from £25; 50 hardstanding pitches
Leisure: 🏊 🎡 🔍 🎵 ⚽ ☺
Facilities: 🛁 ☺ 🚿 ❄ 🛁 💲 WiFi
Services: 🔌 🗑 🚮 🛒 ♨ 🌿 T
Within 3 miles: 🎣 ♿ ∪ ◎ ⛵

Additional site information: 20 acre site. 🐕 Dog park. Cars can be parked by caravans and tents. Awnings permitted. Prices based on 1 car and 4 adults.

Come touring or camping with us
and discover the gorgeous
Yorkshire coast and countryside...

FLOWER OF MAY
family holiday parks

Scarborough • York

Book: flowerofmay.com • 01723 584311

Picture of Goosewood Holiday Park

FILEY *continued*

Lebberston Touring Park

►►►► 91%

tel: 01723 585723 **Filey Road YO11 3PE**
email: info@lebberstontouring.co.uk **web:** www.lebberstontouring.co.uk
dir: *From A165 (Filey to Scarborough road) follow brown site signs.*

A peaceful family park in a gently-sloping rural area, where the quality facilities are maintained to a high standard of cleanliness. The keen owners are friendly and helpful, and create a relaxing atmosphere. A natural area offers views of the surrounding countryside through the shrubbery. Additional land offers 25 hardstandings and a stunning toilet block. Please note, this park does not accept tents.

Open: March to October **Last arrival:** 20.00 **Last departure:** 11.00

Pitches: 🚐 from £17; 🚌 from £17; 25 hardstanding pitches; 84 seasonal pitches

Leisure: ⚽

Facilities: 🛁 🔌 💨 ❄ ♿ [$] [WiFi]

Services: ⚡ 🧺 🛢 🍃 [T]

Within 3 miles: ⛳ 🎣 🐎 ◎ 🏄 🚣

Additional site information: 11 acre site. 🐕 Cars can be parked by caravans. Awnings permitted. No noise after 22.00.

Primrose Valley Holiday Park

►►►► 88% HOLIDAY CENTRE

tel: 01723 513771 **YO14 9RF**
email: primrosevalley@haven.com **web:** www.haven.com/primrosevalley
dir: *Signed from A165 (Scarborough to Bridlington road), 3 miles south of Filey.*

A large all-action holiday centre with a wide range of sports and leisure activities to suit everyone, from morning until late in the evening. The touring area is completely separate from the main park and has its own high quality amenity block. All touring pitches are fully serviced hardstandings with grassed awning strips. The lakeside development near the touring area provides a dine-in and takeaway bistro and watersport activities.

Open: mid March to end October **Last arrival:** anytime **Last departure:** 10.00

Pitches: 🚐 🚌; 34 hardstanding pitches

Leisure: 🏊 🌊 ✋ 🎾 🎱 🎵 🎣 ⚽

Facilities: 🛁 💨 ♿ [$] 🍖 🪑 [WiFi]

Services: ⚡ 🧺 🍷 🍽 🛒 🛢 🍃

Within 3 miles: ⛳ ◎ 🚣

Additional site information: 160 acre site. 🐕 Maximum 2 dogs per booking, certain dog breeds banned. No commercial vehicles, no bookings by persons under 21 years unless a family booking.

Blue Dolphin Holiday Park

►►►► 82% HOLIDAY CENTRE

tel: 01723 515155 **Gristhorpe Bay YO14 9PU**
email: bluedolphin@haven.com **web:** www.haven.com/bluedolphin
dir: *On A165, 2 miles north of Filey.*

There are great cliff-top views to be enjoyed from this fun-filled holiday centre with an extensive and separate touring area. The emphasis is on non-stop entertainment, with organised sports and clubs, all-weather leisure facilities, heated swimming pools (with multi-slide), and plenty of well-planned amusements. Pitches are mainly on level or gently-sloping grass plus there are some fully serviced hardstandings. The Galaxy Showbar was refurbished for the 2018 season. The beach is just two miles away.

Open: mid March to end October (restricted service: mid March to May and September to end October – outdoor pool closed and some facilities may be reduced) **Last arrival:** midnight **Last departure:** 10.00

Pitches: 🚐 🚌 ⛺; 33 hardstanding pitches; 20 seasonal pitches

Leisure: 🏊 🌊 🛝 ✋ 🎵 🎣 ⚽

Facilities: 🛁 🔌 ❄ ♿ [$] 🍖 🍼 [WiFi]

Services: ⚡ 🧺 🍷 🍽 🛒 🥡 🛢 🍃 [T]

Within 3 miles: ⛳ ◎

Additional site information: 85 acre site. 🐕 Maximum 2 dogs per booking, certain dog breeds banned. No commercial vehicles, no bookings by persons under 21 years unless a family booking.

Orchard Farm Holiday Village

►►►► 82%

tel: 01723 891582 **Stonegate, Hunmanby YO14 0PU**
email: info@orchardfarmholidayvillage.co.uk **web:** www.orchardfarmholidayvillage.co.uk
dir: *A165 from Scarborough towards Bridlington. Turn right signed Hunmanby, site on right just after rail bridge.*

Pitches are arranged around a large coarse fishing lake at this grassy park. The enthusiastic owners are friendly, and offer a wide range of amenities including an indoor heated swimming pool and a licensed bar.

Open: March to October (restricted service: off-peak season – some facilities reduced) **Last arrival:** 23.00 **Last departure:** 11.00

Pitches: 🚐 from £16; 🚌 from £16; ⛺ from £16; 48 hardstanding pitches

Leisure: 🏊 🛝 🎱 📺 🎵 🎣

Facilities: 🛁 🔌 💨 ❄ ♿ [$] 🪑 [WiFi]

Services: ⚡ 🧺 🍷 🛏 [T]

Within 3 miles: ⛳ ◎ 🏄

Additional site information: 14 acre site. 🐕 Cars can be parked by caravans and tents. Awnings permitted. No scooters, skateboards or similar. Miniature railway.

LEISURE: 🏊 Indoor swimming pool 🌊 Outdoor swimming pool 🛝 Children's playground ✋ Kids' club 🎾 Tennis court 🎱 Games room 📺 Separate TV room ⛳ golf course 🏌 Pitch n putt 🚣 Boats for hire 🚲 Bikes for hire 🎬 Cinema 🎵 Entertainment 🎣 Fishing ◎ Mini golf 🏄 Watersports 🏋 Gym ⚽ Sports field 🐎 Stables
FACILITIES: 🛁 Baths/Shower 🔌 Electric shaver sockets 💨 Hairdryer ❄ Ice Pack Facility 🍼 Baby facilities ♿ Disabled facilities [$] Shop on site or within 200yds 🍖 BBQ area 🪑 Picnic area [WiFi] WiFi

Reighton Sands Holiday Park

►►►► 80% HOLIDAY CENTRE

tel: 01723 890476 **Reighton Gap YO14 9SH**
email: reightonsands@haven.com **web:** www.haven.com/reightonsands
dir: *On A165, 5 miles south of Filey at Reighton Gap, signed.*

A large, lively holiday centre with a wide range of entertainment and all-weather leisure facilities (including an indoor play area), located just a 10-minute walk from a long sandy beach. There are good all-weather pitches and a large tenting field. The site is particularly geared towards families with young children.

Open: mid March to end October (restricted service: mid March to May and September to end October — some facilities may be reduced) **Last arrival:** 22.00 **Last departure:** 10.00

Pitches: 🚐 🚐 ▲; 47 hardstanding pitches

Leisure: 🏊 🏊 🎮 🛝 🎯 🎵 🎤

Facilities: 🏪 ☺ 🌳 ♿ 🛍️ 🚿 🎏 WiFi

Services: 🔌 🗄️ 🍺 🍽️ 🚮 ⚡

Within 3 miles: 🎣 ∪ ⊚ 🚲

Additional site information: 229 acre site. 🐕 Maximum 2 dogs per booking, certain dog breeds banned. No commercial vehicles, no bookings by persons under 21 years unless a family booking. Tents only accepted Early Spring bank holiday (school half term) and summer holidays.

Centenary Way Camping & Caravan Park

►►► 84%

tel: 01723 516415 **YO14 0HU**
dir: *From A165 onto A1039 signed Filey. 1st right to site.*

A friendly, owner managed family park with a direct link to the beach and close to town centre. The pretty landscaped grounds ensure a peaceful and relaxing stay, and a fairy garden with pop-up café is open during school holidays and at other peak periods. It is advisable to use sat nav rather than Google Earth when locating this park.

Open: March to October **Last arrival:** 21.00 **Last departure:** noon

Pitches: 🚐 from £16; 🚐 from £16; ▲ from £9; 25 hardstanding pitches

Leisure: 🎮

Facilities: 🏪 ☺ 🌳 ♿ 🛍️

Services: 🔌 🗄️ 🍽️ 🔋 ⚡

Within 3 miles: 🎣 🎣 ⊚ 🚲

Additional site information: 3 acre site. 🐕 Cars can be parked by caravans and tents. Awnings permitted. No group bookings in peak period, no 9-12 berth tents, no gazebos, no noise after 23.00.

Filey Brigg Touring Caravan & Country Park

►►► 83%

tel: 01723 513852 & 512512 **North Cliff YO14 9ET**
email: fileybrigg@scarborough.gov.uk **web:** www.fileybriggcaravanpark.com
dir: *A165 from Scarborough to Filey. Left onto A1039, at roundabout into Church Cliff Drive, to site.*

A municipal park overlooking Filey Brigg with splendid views along the coast, and set in a country park. The beach is just a short walk away, as is the resort of Filey.

There is a good quality amenity block, and 50 all-weather pitches are available. A well-stocked shop, café and an excellent children's playground are adjacent to the touring areas.

Open: end February to 2 January **Last arrival:** 18.00 **Last departure:** noon

Pitches: 🚐 from £16.50; 🚐 from £16.50; ▲ from £13.50; 82 hardstanding pitches

Leisure: 🎮 ⚽

Facilities: 🏪 ☺ 🌳 ♿ 🛍️ 🎏

Services: 🔌 🗄️ 🍽️ 🚮 🔋 T

Within 3 miles: 🎣 🎣 ∪ ⊚ 🚲

Additional site information: 9 acre site. 🐕 Cars can be parked by caravans and tents. Awnings permitted. No ball games.

HARROGATE   Map 19 SE35

Places to visit

RHS Garden Harlow Carr, HARROGATE, HG3 1QB, 01423 565418
www.rhs.org.uk/harlowcarr

The Royal Pump Room Museum, HARROGATE, HG1 2RY, 01423 556188
www.harrogate.gov.uk/museums

Great for kids: Brimham Rocks, BRIMHAM, HG3 4DW, 01423 780688
www.nationaltrust.org.uk/brimham-rocks

Premier Park

Ripley Caravan Park

►►►►► 87%

tel: 01423 770050 **Knaresborough Road, Ripley HG3 3AU**
email: info@ripleycaravanpark.com **web:** www.ripleycaravanpark.com
dir: *3 miles north of Harrogate on A61. Right at roundabout onto B6165 signed Knaresborough. Site 300 yards left.*

A well-run rural site in attractive meadowland which has been landscaped with mature tree plantings. The resident owners lovingly maintain the facilities, and there is a heated swimming pool and sauna, a games room, and a covered nursery playroom for small children. A bus calls every 15 minutes which gives easy access to Ripon and Leeds, and a cycleway and walkway leads from the site directly to Harrogate, a distance of approximately three miles. A former tractor shed has been tastefully converted in to a holiday home cottage, available for hire.

Open: 2nd week March to 31 October **Last arrival:** 21.00 **Last departure:** noon

Pitches: 🚐 from £18; 🚐 from £18; ▲ from £18; 60 hardstanding pitches; 75 seasonal pitches

Leisure: 🏊 🎮 🎣 ⚽

Facilities: 🏪 ☺ 🌳 🌳 ♿ 🛍️ WiFi

Services: 🔌 🗄️ 🔋 ⚡ 🛢️ 🔩 T

Within 3 miles: 🎣 🎣 ∪ ⊚ 🚲 🚲

Additional site information: 24 acre site. 🐕 Cars can be parked by caravans and tents. Awnings permitted. Family camping only. No open fires, off-ground BBQs only, no skateboards or rollerblades. No motorised scooters. No noise after 22.00. Football, volleyball, table tennis, pool table.

PITCHES: 🚐 Caravans 🚐 Motorhomes ▲ Tents 🏕 Glamping accommodation **SERVICES:** 🔌 Electric hook-up 🗄️ Launderette 🍺 Licensed bar
🔩 Calor Gas 🧷 Campingaz T Toilet fluid 🍽️ Café/Restaurant 🚮 Fast Food/Takeaway 🔋 Battery charging ⚡ Motorhome service point
*2019 prices 🚫 No credit or debit cards 🐕 Dogs permitted 🚫 No dogs

HARROGATE *continued*

Premier Park

Rudding Holiday Park
▶▶▶▶▶ 86%

tel: 01423 870439 **Follifoot HG3 1JH**
email: holiday-park@ruddingpark.com **web:** www.ruddingholidaypark.co.uk
dir: *From A1 take A59 to A658 signed Bradford. 4.5 miles, right and follow signs.*

A spacious park set in beautiful mature parkland of Rudding Park. The setting has been tastefully enhanced with terraced pitches and dry-stone walls. A separate area houses super pitches where all services are supplied, including picnic tables and excellent toilet facilities. An 18-hole golf course, 6-hole short course, driving range, golf academy, destination spa, heated outdoor swimming pool, the Deer House Family Pub and a children's play area complete the amenities.

Open: March to January (restricted service: November to January – reduced opening hours at shop and Deer House Pub. Outdoor swimming pool – only open in summer)
Last arrival: 22.00 **Last departure:** 11.00
Pitches: 🚐 from £20; 🚋 from £20; ⛺ from £20; 20 hardstanding pitches; 50 seasonal pitches
Leisure: 🏊 ⚔ 🎱 ⬇ 🎵 ⛳ ⚽ Spa
Facilities: 🛁 ⊙ 🗝 ❄ 🚿 🏪 🎇 🚻 🐕 WiFi
Services: 🔌 🔋 🚽 🍴 🍺 🧺 ⛽ 🔒 🌱 🚰
Within 3 miles: 🗝 ∪ ◎ 🐟 🏇

Additional site information: 50 acre site. 🐕 Cars can be parked by caravans and tents. Awnings permitted. Under 18s must be accompanied by an adult. Car hire can be arranged.

High Moor Farm Park
▶▶▶▶ 84%

tel: 01423 563637 **Skipton Road HG3 2LT**
email: highmoorfarmpark@btconnect.com **web:** www.highmoorfarmpark.co.uk
dir: *4 miles west of Harrogate on A59 towards Skipton.*

A family site with very good facilities, set beside a small wood and surrounded by thorn hedges. The numerous touring pitches are located in meadowland fields, each area with its own toilet block. A large heated indoor swimming pool, games room, 9-hole golf course, full-sized crown bowling green, and a bar serving meals and snacks are all popular. Please note that this park does not accept tents.

Open: Easter or April to October **Last arrival:** 23.30 **Last departure:** 15.00
Pitches: * 🚐 from £26; 🚋 from £26; 51 hardstanding pitches; 57 seasonal pitches
Leisure: 🏊 🎱 ⚽
Facilities: ⊙ 🗝 ❄ ♿ 🏪 🚻 WiFi
Services: 🔌 🔋 🚽 🍴 🧺 🛒 🔒 🌱 🚰
Within 3 miles: ⬇ 🗝 ∪ 🏇

Additional site information: 15 acre site. 🐕 Cars can be parked by caravans. Awnings permitted. No noise after midnight, no electric scooters.

LEISURE: 🏊 Indoor swimming pool 🏊 Outdoor swimming pool 🎢 Children's playground 👶 Kids' club 🎾 Tennis court 🎱 Games room 📺 Separate TV room ⬇ golf course ⛳ Pitch n putt 🚣 Boats for hire 🚲 Bikes for hire 🎬 Cinema 🎵 Entertainment 🎣 Fishing ◎ Mini golf 🏄 Watersports 💪 Gym ⚽ Sports field ∪ Stables
FACILITIES: 🛁 Baths/Shower ⊙ Electric shaver sockets 🗝 Hairdryer ❄ Ice Pack Facility 🚼 Baby facilities ♿ Disabled facilities 🏪 Shop on site or within 200yds 🎇 BBQ area 🌳 Picnic area WiFi WiFi

Harrogate Caravan Park
▶▶▶ 91%

tel: 01423 546145 **Great Yorkshire Showground HG2 8NZ**
email: info@harrogatecaravanpark.co.uk **web:** www.harrogatecaravanpark.co.uk
dir: *A1(M) junction 47, A59 to Harrogate. A658, then A661. At Sainsbury's lights turn left into Railway Road.*

Located on the perimeter of the Yorkshire Showground and owned by the Yorkshire Agricultural Society, this very peaceful park offers easy main road access and is popular at weekends and during the days of the shows. The site has a high standard amenity block (including a dog wash), extensive tree planting and smart, gravelled hardstanding pitches. This is a good base for visiting Harrogate and the Yorkshire Dales.

Open: early March to early November **Last arrival:** 20.00 **Last departure:** 11.00

Pitches: 🚐 from £22; 🚍 from £22; ▲ from £22; 52 hardstanding pitches

Leisure: ⚽

Facilities: 🏪 ⊙ 🅿 ⚷ 🖲 🚿 🎏 WiFi

Services: 🔌 🔲 🔋 ↯

Within 3 miles: ⌇ 🎣 ∪ ◎ ⛽ 🗓

Additional site information: 3.56 acre site. 🐕 Cars can be parked by caravans and tents. Awnings permitted. Shop and café adjacent, supermarket at end of road.

Shaws Trailer Park
▶▶ 69%

tel: 07921 761066 **Knaresborough Road HG2 7NE**
dir: *On A59, 1 mile from town centre. Site 0.5 mile southwest of Starbeck railway crossing.*

A long-established site just a mile from the centre of Harrogate. The all-weather pitches are arranged around a carefully kept grass area, and the toilets are basic but functional and clean. The entrance is on the bus route to Harrogate.

Open: All year **Last arrival:** 20.00 **Last departure:** 14.00

Pitches: 🚐 🚍 ▲; 29 hardstanding pitches

Facilities: 🏪 ⊙ ⚷

Services: 🔌 🔲 🍺

Within 3 miles: ⌇ 🎣 ⛽ 🗓 🖇

Additional site information: 11 acre site. Adults only. 🐕 🚫 Cars can be parked by caravans and tents. Awnings permitted.

HELMSLEY

Places to visit

Duncombe Park, HELMSLEY, YO62 5EB, 01439 770213
www.duncombepark.com

Helmsley Castle, HELMSLEY, YO62 5AB, 01439 770442
www.english-heritage.org.uk/daysout/properties/helmsley-castle

Great for kids: Flamingo Land Resort, KIRBY MISPERTON, YO17 6UX, 0800 408 8840, www.flamingoland.co.uk

HELMSLEY Map 19 SE68

Premier Park

Golden Square Caravan & Camping Park
▶▶▶▶ 88%

tel: 01439 788269 **Oswaldkirk YO62 5YQ**
email: reception@goldensquarecaravanpark.com
web: www.goldensquarecaravanpark.com
dir: *From York take B1363 to Oswaldkirk. Left onto B1257, 2nd left onto unclassified road signed Ampleforth, site 0.5 mile on right. Or A19 from Thirsk towards York. Left, follow 'Caravan Route avoiding Sutton Bank' signs, through Ampleforth to site in 1 mile.*

An excellent, popular and spacious site with very good facilities. This friendly, immaculately maintained park is set in a quiet rural situation with lovely views over the North York Moors. Terraced on three levels and surrounded by mature trees, it caters particularly for families, with excellent play areas and space for ball games. Country walks and mountain bike trails start here and an attractive holiday home area is also available. Please note that caravans are prohibited on the A170 at Sutton Bank between Thirsk and Helmsley.

Open: March to October (restricted service: November to 1 January statics only)
Last arrival: 21.00 **Last departure:** noon

Pitches: 🚐 from £19; 🚍 from £19; ▲ from £19; 30 hardstanding pitches; 50 seasonal pitches

Leisure: 🎢 🎣 🚴 ⚽

Facilities: 🏪 ⊙ 🅿 ✳ ⚷ 🖲 🎏 WiFi

Services: 🔌 🔲 🔋 ↯ 🍺 ⊘ T

Within 3 miles: ⌇ 🎣 ∪ ◎ 🗓

Additional site information: 12 acre site. 🐕 Cars can be parked by caravans and tents. Awnings permitted. No skateboards, fires, Chinese lanterns or hover boards. No noise after 23.00. Microwave available, storage compound, table tennis, pool table, woodland walks, cycle trails.

HELMSLEY *continued*

Foxholme Caravan Park

►►► 79%

tel: 01439 772336 **Gale Lane, Nawton YO62 7SD**
email: stay@foxholmecaravanpark.co.uk **web:** www.foxholmecaravanpark.co.uk
dir: *From Helmsley, east on A170, signed Scarborough. Continue to Beadlam, in centre of village turn right into Gale Lane.*

A quiet park set in beautiful northern Ryedale countryside, with a pleasant open aspect to all pitches and views toward both the Yorkshire Wolds and the Howardian Hills area of outstanding natural beauty. The facilities are well maintained, and the site is ideal as a touring base or a place to relax. Please note that caravans are prohibited on the A170 at Sutton Bank between Thirsk and Helmsley.

Open: Easter to October **Last arrival:** 23.00 **Last departure:** noon

Pitches: 🚐 from £25; 🚍 from £25; ▲ from £25; 30 seasonal pitches

Facilities: 🛁 ⊙ 🗗 ✳ ⅙

Services: 🔌 🗑 🧺 ⛽ 🔥 ⊘ Ⓣ

Within 3 miles: ⌸ ∪ ⑤

Additional site information: 6 acre site. Adults only. 🐾 😊 Cars can be parked by caravans and tents. Awnings permitted.

Premier Park

Riverside Caravan Park

►►►►► 90%

tel: 015242 61272 **LA2 7FJ**
email: info@riversidecaravanpark.co.uk **web:** www.riversidecaravanpark.co.uk
dir: *M6 junction 34, A683 towards Kirkby Lonsdale, right onto B6480 signed Bentham. Site signed from High Bentham town centre.*

A well-managed riverside park developed to a high standard, with level grass pitches set in avenues separated by trees, and there are excellent facilities for children, who are made to feel as important as the adults. It has an excellent, modern amenity block, including a family bathroom, and a well-stocked shop, laundry and information room. The superb games room and adventure playground are hugely popular, and the market town of High Bentham is close by. Please note that this site does not accept tents. Bentham Golf Club (within one mile) is also under same ownership with facilities available for Riverside customers.

Open: March to 2 January **Last arrival:** 20.00 **Last departure:** noon

Pitches: 🚐 from £22.50; 🚍; 27 hardstanding pitches; 50 seasonal pitches

Leisure: ⚲ 🎱 ✏

Facilities: 🛁 ⊙ 🗗 ⅙ ⑤ WiFi

Services: 🔌 🗑 ⛽ 🔥 Ⓣ

Within 3 miles: ⌸ ∪

Additional site information: 12 acre site. 🐾 Cars can be parked by caravans. Awnings permitted. Chargeable permits for private fishing, discounted green fees at Bentham Golf Club.

LEISURE: 🏊 Indoor swimming pool 🏊 Outdoor swimming pool ⚲ Children's playground 🧒 Kids' club 🎾 Tennis court 🎱 Games room 📺 Separate TV room
⌸ golf course 🏌 Pitch n putt 🚣 Boats for hire 🚲 Bikes for hire 🎬 Cinema 🎵 Entertainment 🎣 Fishing ◉ Mini golf 🏄 Watersports 🏋 Gym ⚽ Sports field ∪ Stables
FACILITIES: 🛁 Baths/Shower ⊙ Electric shaver sockets 🗗 Hairdryer ✳ Ice Pack Facility 🍼 Baby facilities ⅙ Disabled facilities ⑤ Shop on site or within 200yds
🍖 BBQ area 🍽 Picnic area WiFi WiFi

Lowther Hill Caravan Park

► 83%

tel: 015242 61657 **Clapham Road LA2 7FH**
web: www.caravancampingsites.co.uk/northyorkshire/lowtherhill/lowtherhill.html
dir: *A65 at Clapham onto B6480 signed Bentham. 3 miles to site on right. Or from M6 junction 34, A643 to Kirkby Lonsdale. In 6 miles turn right onto B6480 to Bentham. 9 miles, site on left between High Bentham and Clapham.*

A basic site with stunning panoramic views from every pitch. Peace reigns on this little park, though the tourist villages of Ingleton, Clapham and Settle are not far away. All pitches have electricity, and there is a heated toilet and washroom and dishwashing facilities.

Open: All year **Last arrival:** 21.00 **Last departure:** 14.00

Pitches: * 🚐 from £17.50; 🚐 from £17.50; ⛺ from £6; 4 hardstanding pitches; 7 seasonal pitches

Facilities: 🏠 ♿

Services: 🔌

Within 3 miles: ⚓ 🎣 💲 🔄

Additional site information: 1 acre site. 🐕 🚗 Cars can be parked by caravans and tents. Awnings permitted. Payment on arrival, no noise after midnight.

HUTTON-LE-HOLE
Map 19 SE79

Places to visit

Nunnington Hall, NUNNINGTON, YO62 5UY, 01439 748283
www.nationaltrust.org.uk/nunnington-hall

Rievaulx Abbey, RIEVAULX, YO62 5LB, 01439 798228
www.english-heritage.org.uk/daysout/properties/rievaulx-abbey

Great for kids: Pickering Castle, PICKERING, YO18 7AX, 01751 474989
www.english-heritage.org.uk/daysout/properties/pickering-castle

---

Hutton-le-Hole Caravan Park

►►►► 83%

tel: 01751 417261 **Westfield Lodge YO62 6UG**
email: info@huttonleholecaravanpark.co.uk **web:** www.huttonleholecaravanpark.co.uk
dir: *From A170 at Keldholme follow Hutton-le-Hole signs. Approximately 2 miles, over cattle grid, left in 500 yards into Park Drive, site signed.*

A small, high quality park on a working farm in the North York Moors National Park. The purpose-built toilet block offers en suite family rooms, and there is a choice of hardstanding or grass pitches within a well-tended area surrounded by hedges and shrubs. The pretty village with its facilities is a 10-minute walk away and the park is centrally located for visiting York, The Dales and other notable areas of interest. Please note, caravans are prohibited from the A170 at Sutton Bank between Thirsk and Helmsley.

Open: Easter to October **Last arrival:** 21.00 **Last departure:** noon

Pitches: 🚐 🚐 ⛺; 4 hardstanding pitches

Facilities: 🏠 ☺ 📧 ❄ ♿ ⊓ WiFi

Services: 🔌 🔋 T

Within 3 miles: ⚓ ∪ ◎ 💲

Additional site information: 5 acre site. 🐕 Cars can be parked by caravans and tents. Awnings permitted. Boot, bike and dog washing area, farm walks.

KETTLEWELL
Map 18 SD97

Places to visit

Grassington Folk Museum, GRASSINGTON, BD23 5AQ, 01756 753287
http://grassingtonfolkmuseum.org.uk

Great for kids: Kilnsey Park Estate, KILNSEY, BD23 5PS, 01756 752150
www.kilnseypark.co.uk

AA SMALL CAMPSITE OF THE YEAR 2019

Kettlewell Camping

►►►► 80%

tel: 07930 379079 & 01756 761684 **Conistone Lane BD23 5RE**
email: info@kettlewellcamping.co.uk **web:** www.kettlewellcamping.co.uk
dir: *From roundabout on A65 (north of Skipton) take B6265 signed Grassington. Through Threshfield (do not turn right for Grassington). Road becomes B6160. In Kettlewell, first signed Scargill. Follow brown tourist signs.*

Created from former farm fields, this superb camping site has stunning countryside views and is enclosed by well-maintained stone walls; it has the benefit of being just a few minutes' walk from Kettlewell with its craft shops, pubs, tea rooms and a village shop. A top-notch amenity block, fed by a bio-mass boiler, has underfloor heating and modern quality fixtures and fittings, and includes a family room with shower, toilet and washbasin. Free WiFi is available and a separate field, suitable for large families or groups, is also available in a more isolated location; it is enclosed by dry stone walling, is adjacent to a trickling stream and has a heated toilet and shower block, electric hook-ups and a picnic area. Please note, there is no laundry at this site.

Open: Easter to October half term (restricted service: only open from November to end March for special occasions) **Last arrival:** 20.30 **Last departure:** 11.00

Pitches: ⛺ from £21

Facilities: 🏠 ☺ 📧 ❄ ♿ 💲 🍴 ⊓ WiFi

Services: 🔌

Within 3 miles: 📧 ∪ 🔄

Additional site information: 0.6 acre site. 🐕 Dogs must be kept on leads at all times. Cars can be parked by tents. Awnings permitted. Quiet after 22.00. Fires permitted in raised fire pits only. Field available for exclusive hire with private facilities.

KIRKLINGTON
Map 16 SE38

Places to visit

Thirsk Birds of Prey Centre, THIRSK, YO7 4EU, 01845 587522
www.falconrycentre.co.uk

Great for kids: The Big Sheep and Little Cow Farm, BEDALE, DL8 1AW,
01677 422125, www.bigsheeplittlecow.co.uk

Camp Kátur

▶▶▶▶ 80% GLAMPING ONLY

tel: 01845 202100 **The Camphill Estate DL8 2LS**
email: info@campkatur.com **web:** www.campkatur.com
dir: A1(M) junction 50, A6055 towards Bedale. Left at 1st roundabout, 1st right to
Kirklington. Through Kirklington, approximately 1.5 miles to site on left.

Located within The Camp Estate, a popular centre for equestrian pursuits, quad
biking, orienteering and corporate team building, Camp Kátur is a unique glamping
destination with a choice of units set in meadowland or wooded areas that
comprise a wide variety of indigenous and imported trees. All the units are spaced
well apart ensuring optimum privacy, and all have the benefit of fire pits, barbecues
and outside seating areas. The safari tents and geo domes have en suite facilities
and other units are serviced by a communal shower, toilet and wash basin facility.
There is a great focus on upcycling materials here with fire pits created from
washing machine drums and galvanised buckets wash basins to name just two
ideas. There's a campers' kitchen, a barbecue pod seating 16 around a central
cooking area, and a rustic outdoor area ideal for gatherings such as a wedding
reception or an anniversary or birthday celebration. The eco spa has a sauna and
hot tub fuelled by wood-burning stoves.

Open: April to October **Last arrival:** 22.00 **Last departure:** 11.00

Leisure: ⚑ ♣ ☻ Spa

Facilities: 🖻 ✳ ♿ 🍴 🛋 WiFi

Within 3 miles: ⚓ ✐ ♺ ◎ 🛍

Accommodation available: Bell tents; safari tents; tipis; cabins; geo domes; wooden
unidomes; retro caravan; log cabin.

Changeover days: Monday, Wednesday, Friday, Sunday

Additional site information: 20 acre site. 🐾 Groups permitted only with management
permission. No noise after 22.00.

KNARESBOROUGH

Places to visit

RHS Garden Harlow Carr, HARROGATE, HG3 1QB, 01423 565418
www.rhs.org.uk/harlowcarr

Aldborough Roman Site, ALDBOROUGH, YO51 9ES, 01423 322768
www.english-heritage.org.uk/daysout/properties/aldborough-roman-site

KNARESBOROUGH
Map 19 SE35

Kingfisher Caravan Park

▶▶▶▶ 79%

tel: 01423 869411 **Low Moor Lane, Farnham HG5 9JB**
email: enquiries@kingfisher-caravanpark.co.uk **web:** www.kingfisher-caravanpark.co.uk
dir: From Knaresborough take A6055. Left in 1 mile towards Farnham, follow signs for
Kingfisher. Park entrance on left.

A large grassy site with open spaces set in a wooded area in rural countryside.
Whilst Harrogate, Fountains Abbey and York are within easy reach, visitors can if
they wish just relax and enjoy the grounds and lake, which are a magnet for an
increasing variety of wildlife. The park has a separate, flat tenting field with electric
hook-ups.

Open: March to October **Last arrival:** 20.00 **Last departure:** 14.00

Pitches: ⛺ 🚐 ▲; 30 seasonal pitches

Leisure: ⚑

Facilities: 🖻 ☉ 🍴 ✳ ♿ 🛍 🛋 🗮

Services: 🔌 🗄 🛢 🧹

Within 3 miles: ⚓ ♺ ✈ 目

Additional site information: 14 acre site. 🐾 ⊛ Cars can be parked by caravans and
tents. Awnings permitted. No football.

MASHAM
Map 19 SE28

Places to visit

Theakston Brewery & Visitor Centre, MASHAM, HG4 4YD, 01765 680000
www.theakstons.co.uk

Norton Conyers, RIPON, HG4 5EQ, 01765 640333
www.nortonconyers.org.uk

Great for kids: Lightwater Valley Theme Park, NORTH STAINLEY, HG4 3HT,
01765 635321, www.lightwatervalley.co.uk

Old Station Holiday Park

▶▶▶▶ 81%

tel: 01765 689569 **Old Station Yard, Low Burton HG4 4DF**
email: info@oldstation-masham.co.uk **web:** www.oldstation-masham.co.uk
dir: From south: A1(M) junction 50, B6267, left in 8 miles. From north: A1(M) junction 51,
A684 to Bedale, then B6268, 4 miles to site.

An interesting site at a former station that still retains a railway theme. The
enthusiastic and caring family owners have created a park with high quality
facilities. The reception and café are situated in a carefully restored wagon shed
and here a range of meals, using local produce, is offered. The small town of
Masham, with its Theakston and Black Sheep Breweries, is within easy walking
distance of the park. Holiday cottages and log cabins are also available for hire.

Open: March to November **Last arrival:** 20.00 **Last departure:** 11.00

Pitches: ⛺ from £20; 🚐 from £20; ▲ from £18; 🏠 see prices below;
12 hardstanding pitches; 16 seasonal pitches

Facilities: 🖻 ☉ 🍴 ✳ ♿ 🛍 🛋 🗮 WiFi

Services: 🔌 🗄 🍽 ♨ 🚮 ⊥ 🛢 T

Within 3 miles: ⚓ ♺ ♺

Additional site information: 3.75 acre site. 🐕 Cars can be parked by caravans. Awnings permitted. No cycling around site, no campfires. No ball games near caravans, motorhomes or tents.

Glamping available: BBQ cabins from £45.

Additional glamping information: BBQ cabins (sleep either 4 or 6) offer electricity, kettle and heater. Own bedding, crockery and cutlery required. Cars can be parked by cabins.

NABURN · Map 16 SE54

Places to visit

Clifford's Tower, YORK, YO1 9SA, 01904 646940
www.english-heritage.org.uk/daysout/properties/cliffords-tower-york

Fairfax House, YORK, YO1 9RN, 01904 655543
www.fairfaxhouse.co.uk

Great for kids: York's Chocolate Story, YORK, YO1 7LD, 01904 527765
http://yorkschocolatestory.com

Naburn Lock Caravan Park
▶▶▶▶ 91%

tel: 01904 728697 **YO19 4RU**
email: petercatherine@naburnlock.co.uk **web:** www.naburnlock.co.uk
dir: From A64 (York Designer Outlet) take A19 (north), left signed Naburn onto B1222, site on right in 0.5 mile.

A family park where the enthusiastic owners are steadily improving its quality. The mainly grass pitches are arranged in small groups separated by mature hedges. The park is close to the River Ouse, and the river towpath provides excellent walking and cycling opportunities. The river bus to nearby York leaves from a jetty beside the park.

Open: March to November **Last arrival:** 20.00 **Last departure:** 12.30

Pitches: 🚐 🚎 ▲; 50 hardstanding pitches

Leisure: ✎

Facilities: 🏠 ☉ 🦶 ⚒ ㄟ 🖐 ▥ **WiFi**

Services: 🔌 🗑 🔋 ⛽ 🛢 🗑 Ⓣ

Within 3 miles: ↺ ⚓

Additional site information: 7 acre site. 🐕 Cars can be parked by caravans and tents. Awnings permitted. Adults-only section available, quiet 23.00-07.00. Debit cards accepted (no credit cards). River fishing.

NORTH STAINLEY

Places to visit

Norton Conyers, RIPON, HG4 5EQ, 01765 640333
www.nortonconyers.org.uk

Theakston Brewery & Visitor Centre, MASHAM, HG4 4YD, 01765 680000
www.theakstons.co.uk

Great for kids: Lightwater Valley Theme Park, NORTH STAINLEY, HG4 3HT,
01765 635321, www.lightwatervalley.co.uk

NORTH STAINLEY · Map 19 SE27

Sleningford Watermill Caravan Camping Park
▶▶▶▶ 87%

tel: 01765 635201 **HG4 3HQ**
email: contact@sleningfordwatermill.co.uk **web:** www.sleningfordwatermill.co.uk
dir: Follow site sign on A6108 between North Stainley and West Tanfield.

The old watermill and the River Ure make an attractive setting for this touring park that is run by two enthusiastic managers. The site is laid out in two areas and the pitches are in meadowland close to mature woodland. Back-to-nature opportunities include a tree trail, bee garden, wild bird listings and river walks. Canoeing and fly fishing are also available.

Open: Easter and April to October **Last arrival:** 21.00 **Last departure:** 11.30

Pitches: * 🚐 from £23; 🚎 from £23; ▲ from £23; 8 hardstanding pitches;
49 seasonal pitches

Leisure: ✎ **Facilities:** 🏠 ☉ 🦶 ⚒ ㄟ 🖐 ▤

Services: 🔌 🗑 🔋 🛢 ⛽ Ⓣ **Within 3 miles:** ⚓ ⚓

Additional site information: 14 acre site. 🐕 Dogs must be on lead at all times. Cars can be parked by caravans and tents. Awnings permitted. No fires, no noise after 23.00. Newspapers can be ordered, table tennis, tree trail.

OSMOTHERLEY · Map 19 SE49

Places to visit

Mount Grace Priory, OSMOTHERLEY, DL6 3JG, 01609 883494
www.english-heritage.org.uk/daysout/properties/mount-grace-priory

Great for kids: Thirsk Birds of Prey Centre, THIRSK, YO7 4EU, 01845 587522
www.falconrycentre.co.uk

Premier Park

Cote Ghyll Caravan & Camping Park
▶▶▶▶▶ 89%

tel: 01609 883425 **DL6 3AH**
email: hills@coteghyll.com **web:** www.coteghyll.com
dir: Exit A19 (dual carriageway) at A684 (Northallerton junction). Follow signs to Osmotherley. Left in village centre. Site entrance 0.5 mile on right.

A quiet, peaceful site in a pleasant valley on the edge of moorland, close to the village. The park, which is served by two centrally located and well-equipped amenity blocks, is divided into terraces bordered by woodland, the only welcome distractions are the sounds of running water and birdsong. Mature trees, shrubs and an abundance of seasonal floral displays create a relaxing and peaceful atmosphere and the whole park is immaculately maintained. There are pubs and shops nearby and holiday statics for hire.

Open: March to October **Last arrival:** 20.00 **Last departure:** noon

Pitches: 🚐 🚎 ▲; 22 hardstanding pitches; 25 seasonal pitches

Leisure: ⚐ **Facilities:** 🏠 ☉ 🦶 ⚒ ㄟ 🖐 ▥ 🛒 **WiFi**

Services: 🔌 🗑 🍴 🏭 🔋 ⛽ 🛢 🗑 Ⓣ **Within 3 miles:** ⚓ ✎ ↺

Additional site information: 7 acre site. 🐕 Cars can be parked by caravans and tents. Awnings permitted. Quiet after 22.00, no camp fires. Freshly baked breakfast produce available. Nature trail, woodland walk to reservoir.

PITCHES: 🚐 Caravans 🚎 Motorhomes ▲ Tents 🏠 Glamping accommodation **SERVICES:** 🔌 Electric hook-up 🗑 Launderette 🍷 Licensed bar 🛢 Calor Gas 🌿 Campingaz Ⓣ Toilet fluid 🍴 Café/Restaurant 🏭 Fast Food/Takeaway 🔋 Battery charging ⚡ Motorhome service point * 2019 prices 🚫 No credit or debit cards 🐕 Dogs permitted 🚫 No dogs

PICKERING
Map 19 SE78

Places to visit

Pickering Castle, PICKERING, YO18 7AX, 01751 474989
www.english-heritage.org.uk/daysout/properties/pickering-castle

Great for kids: North Yorkshire Moors Railway, PICKERING, YO18 7AJ, 01751 472508, www.nymr.co.uk

Wayside Holiday Park
►►►► 81%

tel: 01751 472608 & 07940 938517 **Wrelton YO18 8PG**
email: wrelton@waysideholidaypark.co.uk **web:** www.waysideparks.co.uk
dir: 2.5 miles west of Pickering exit A170, follow signs at Wrelton.

Located in the village of Wrelton, this well-maintained seasonal touring and holiday home park is divided into small paddocks by mature hedging. The amenity block has smart, modern facilities. The village pub and restaurant are within a few minutes' walk of the park. Please note that this site has seasonal pitches only — caravans, motorhomes and tents are not accepted.

Open: March to October

Facilities: 🛁 ⊙ 🕭 🎄 WiFi

Services: 🔌 🗑

Within 3 miles: 🦌 🏌 ⟲ 🎣 🛒

Additional site information: 20 acre site. 🐕 😊 Awnings permitted.

POCKLINGTON
Map 17 SE84

Places to visit

Burnby Hall Gardens & Museum, POCKLINGTON, YO42 2QF, 01759 307125
www.burnbyhallgardens.com

South Lea Caravan Park
►►►► 84%

tel: 01759 303467 & 07989 616095 **The Balk YO42 2NX**
email: south.lea@btinternet.com **web:** www.south-lea.co.uk
dir: From A1079 (York to Hull road) between Barmby Moor and Hayton follow Pocklington (B1247) and brown tourist signs. Site 400 yards on left.

Located just off the main York road, South Lea Caravan Park is a tranquil, tidy and level site — its entrance opens up onto 15 secluded acres. The five touring areas — Sycamore, Birch, Ash, Oak and Willow — are serviced by a very well equipped and spotlessly clean facilities block surrounded by colourful flower troughs; the landscaping across the park is beautifully manicured. There's also a dog shower, lush grass tent pitches, a football field and playground, good local walks, and a bus service to local towns that stops at the front gate.

Open: March to October **Last arrival:** 20.00 **Last departure:** 16.00

Pitches: 🚐 from £17; 🚎 from £17; ⛺ from £17

Facilities: 🛁 ⊙ 🕭 ❄ 🎄

Services: 🔌 🔒 🍃

Within 3 miles: 🦌 🏌 ⟲ ◎ 🌊 🐟 🎣 🛒 🗑

Additional site information: 15 acre site. 🐕 😊 Cars can be parked by caravans and tents. Awnings permitted. Speed limit 5mph, no noise after 22.30, no kites or drones, children must be accompanied in toilet block.

RIPON
Map 19 SE37

See also North Stainley

Places to visit

Fountains Abbey & Studley Royal, RIPON, HG4 3DY, 01765 608888
www.nationaltrust.org.uk/fountains-abbey

Norton Conyers, RIPON, HG4 5EQ, 01765 640333
www.nortonconyers.org.uk

Great for kids: Thirsk Birds of Prey Centre, THIRSK, YO7 4EU, 01845 587522
www.falconrycentre.co.uk

Premier Park

Riverside Meadows Country Caravan Park
►►►►► 77%

tel: 01765 602964 **Ure Bank Top HG4 1JD**
email: info@flowerofmay.com **web:** www.flowerofmay.com
dir: From A61 roundabout (north of bridge) in Ripon follow A6108 Leyburn and Masham signs. At next roundabout, 2nd exit into Ure Bank. Road becomes Ure Bank Top. Site at end of road.

This pleasant, well-maintained site stands on high ground overlooking the River Ure, one mile from the town centre. The site has an excellent club with a family room and a quiet lounge. There are many walks to enjoy including those along the river, and free WiFi is available through the park. Please note that prices for caravans, motorhomes and tent pitches are for a maximum of 4 people and 1 car (electricity not included).

Open: Easter to October (restricted service: early and late season — bar open at weekends only) **Last arrival:** dusk **Last departure:** noon

Pitches: 🚐; 40 hardstanding pitches; 40 seasonal pitches

Leisure: 🎮 🎱 🖥 🎵

Facilities: 🛁 ⊙ 🕭 ❄ 🎄 🛒 🎄 WiFi

Services: 🔌 🗑 🍽 🍺 ⛽ 🔒 🪣

Within 3 miles: 🦌 🏌 ⟲ 🌊 🐟 🎣

Additional site information: 28 acre site. 🐕 Dogs accepted by prior arrangement only. Cars can be parked by caravans. Awnings permitted. No noise after midnight. Multi ball sports court, dog walking track.

LEISURE: 🛁 Indoor swimming pool 🏊 Outdoor swimming pool 🎢 Children's playground 👶 Kids' club ⚾ Tennis court 🎱 Games room 🖥 Separate TV room 🦌 golf course 🏌 Pitch n putt 🚣 Boats for hire 🚲 Bikes for hire 🎬 Cinema 🎵 Entertainment 🎣 Fishing ◎ Mini golf 🌊 Watersports 💪 Gym 🏐 Sports field ⟲ Stables
FACILITIES: 🛁 Baths/Shower ⊙ Electric shaver sockets 🕭 Hairdryer ❄ Ice Pack Facility 🍼 Baby facilities 🎄 Disabled facilities 🛒 Shop on site or within 200yds 🍖 BBQ area 🎄 Picnic area WiFi WiFi

ROBIN HOOD'S BAY Map 19 NZ90

See also Whitby

Places to visit

Whitby Abbey, WHITBY, YO22 4JT, 01947 603568
www.english-heritage.org.uk/daysout/properties/whitby-abbey

Scarborough Castle, SCARBOROUGH, YO11 1HY, 01723 372451
www.english-heritage.org.uk/daysout/properties/scarborough-castle

Great for kids: Scarborough Sea Life Sanctuary, SCARBOROUGH, YO12 6RP
www.sealife.co.uk

Grouse Hill Caravan Park

▶▶▶▶ 91%

tel: 01947 880543 & 881230 **Flask Bungalow Farm, Fylingdales YO22 4QH**
email: info@grousehill.co.uk web: www.grousehill.co.uk
dir: *From A171 (Whitby to Scarborough road), take loop road for Flask Inn (brown site sign).*

A spacious family park on a south-facing slope with attractive, mostly level, terraced pitches overlooking the North Yorkshire National Park. The site has quality, solar-heated toilet blocks, a treatment plant to ensure excellent drinking water, security barriers, play areas (including a woodland adventure play area), CCTV and WiFi. Heated wooden wigwams are available for hire. Please note that there are no hardstandings for tourers, only grass pitches, and this sloping site is not suitable for less able visitors (there are no disabled facilities). This is an ideal base for walking and touring.

Grouse Hill Caravan Park

Open: March to October (restricted service. Easter to May shop and reception reduced hours) **Last arrival:** 20.30 **Last departure:** noon

Pitches: 🚐 �"🏕 ⛺ 🛖; 30 hardstanding pitches; 20 seasonal pitches

Leisure: 🎣 **Facilities:** 🚿 ☺ 🏳 ✳ ♿ 💲 **WiFi**

Services: 🔌 🔲 🧺 ⚡ 🛒 🚿 T **Within 3 miles:** ⚓ ∪

Additional site information: 14 acre site. 🚗 Cars can be parked by caravans and tents. Awnings permitted. No noise after 22.30. 8 family washrooms available.

Glamping available: Wooden wigwams.

Additional glamping information: All wigwams offer fridge, microwave, kettle, toaster, heater and picnic bench. Running Water Wigwams also offer a toilet, TV, sink, table and four chairs. Cars can be parked by wigwams.

See advert below

PITCHES: 🚐 Caravans 🚍 Motorhomes ⛺ Tents 🛖 Glamping accommodation **SERVICES:** 🔌 Electric hook-up 🔲 Launderette 🍺 Licensed bar 🔋 Calor Gas 🔥 Campingaz T Toilet fluid 🍽 Café/Restaurant 🍔 Fast Food/Takeaway 🔋 Battery charging ⚡ Motorhome service point
∧ 2019 prices 🚫 No credit or debit cards 🐕 Dogs permitted 🚫 No dogs

ROBIN HOOD'S BAY *continued*

Middlewood Farm Holiday Park

►►►► 90%

tel: 01947 880414 **Middlewood Lane, Fylingthorpe YO22 4UF**
email: info@middlewoodfarm.com **web:** www.middlewoodfarm.com
dir: *From A171 towards Robin Hood's Bay, into Fylingthorpe. Site signed from A171.*

A peaceful, friendly family park enjoying panoramic views of Robin Hood's Bay in a picturesque fishing village. The park has two toilet blocks with private facilities. The village pub is a five-minute walk away, and the beach can be reached via a path leading directly from the site, which is also accessible for wheelchair users. There are 14 wooden pods called Gypsy Cabins available for hire.

Open: 7 February to 7 January (restricted service: November to Easter – tents not accepted) **Last arrival:** 20.00 **Last departure:** 11.00

Pitches: 🚐 from £19; 🚌 from £19; ⛺ from £19; 🛖 see prices below; 21 hardstanding pitches

Leisure: 🛝 **Facilities:** 🛁 🔌 💨 ❄ ♿ 🧺 [WiFi]

Services: 🚰 🌀 🧴 🔋 ⚓ 🔒 🍃 [T]

Within 3 miles: ⛳ 🎣 ⛵ 🏪

Additional site information: 7 acre site. 🐕 No dangerous dog breeds accepted. Cars can be parked by caravans and tents. Awnings permitted. No radios or noise after 23.00.
Glamping available: Wooden pods from £42. **Changeover days:** Any day

Additional glamping information: Wooden pods offer microwave, fridge, kettle, heater, sockets, beds and lighting. Cars can be parked by pods.

See advert opposite

ROSEDALE ABBEY Map 19 SE79

Places to visit

Pickering Castle, PICKERING, YO18 7AX, 01751 474989
www.english-heritage.org.uk/daysout/properties/pickering-castle

North Yorkshire Moors Railway, PICKERING, YO18 7AJ, 01751 472508
www.nymr.co.uk

Great for kids: Flamingo Land Resort, KIRBY MISPERTON, YO17 6UX, 0800 408 8840, www.flamingoland.co.uk

Rosedale Abbey Caravan Park

►►►► 88%

tel: 01751 417272 **YO18 8SA**
email: info@rosedaleabbeycaravanpark.co.uk **web:** www.rosedaleabbeycaravanpark.co.uk
dir: *From Pickering take A170 towards Sinnington for 2.25 miles. At Wrelton right onto unclassified road signed Cropton and Rosedale, 7 miles. Site on left in village.*

Set in a sheltered valley in the centre of the North Yorkshire Moors National Park, this popular park is close to the pretty village of Rosedale Abbey. It is divided into separate areas for tents, tourers and statics. It has well-tended grounds, and continues to be upgraded by the enthusiastic owners. Two toilet blocks offer private, combined facilities. There are six camping pods (with or without electricity) situated by the river. Please note that prices for caravans, motorhomes and tent pitches are for a maximum of 4 people and 1 car (electricity not included).

Open: March to October **Last arrival:** dusk **Last departure:** noon

Pitches: 🚐 from £24; 🚌 from £24; ⛺ from £24; 🛖 see prices below; 55 hardstanding pitches; 20 seasonal pitches

Leisure: 🛝

Facilities: 🛁 🔌 ❄ ♿ 🏪 🍖 🧺 👶 [WiFi]

Services: 🚰 🌀 🔋 🔒 🍃 [T]

Within 3 miles: ⛳ 🎣 🐴

Additional site information: 10 acre site. 🐕 Cars can be parked by caravans and tents. Awnings permitted. No noise after 23.00, dogs accepted by prior arrangement only. Freshly baked bread available.

Glamping available: Wooden pods from £40. **Changeover days:** Any day

Additional glamping information: Wooden pods; (sleep 5) maximum stay 2 nights (3 nights at bank holidays and in school holidays). Electricity, sockets, lighting, wooden decking included. 1 dog permitted per pod. Cars can be parked by pods.

SCARBOROUGH

See also Filey and Wykeham

Places to visit

Scarborough Castle, SCARBOROUGH, YO11 1HY, 01723 372451
www.english-heritage.org.uk/daysout/properties/scarborough-castle

Great for kids: Scarborough Sea Life Sanctuary, SCARBOROUGH, YO12 6RP
www.sealife.co.uk

SCARBOROUGH
Map 17 TA08

Scalby Close Park
▶▶▶▶ 79%

tel: 01723 365908 **Burniston Road YO13 0DA**
email: info@scalbyclosepark.co.uk **web:** www.scalbyclosepark.co.uk
dir: *2 miles north of Scarborough on A615 (coast road), 1 mile from junction with A171.*

An attractive, well-landscaped park that is run by enthusiastic owners. The site has a shower block, laundry, fully serviced pitches and a motorhome service point. Just two miles from Scarborough, this makes an ideal base from which to explore both the coast and lovely countryside.

Open: March to October **Last arrival:** 22.00 **Last departure:** noon

Pitches: 🚐 🚍; 42 hardstanding pitches

Facilities: ⊙ 🏳 ⚒ 🔥 ♿ 🛐 WiFi

Services: 🔌 🛅 📦 ⬆ ⊘ T

Within 3 miles: ⚓ 🏌 ∪ ⚓ 🎏

Additional site information: 3 acre site. 🐕 🚫 Cars can be parked by caravans. Awnings permitted.

Arosa Caravan & Camping Park
▶▶▶ 92%

tel: 01723 862166 & 07858 694077 **Ratten Row, Seamer YO12 4QB**
email: info@arosacamping.co.uk **web:** www.arosacamping.co.uk
dir: *A64 towards Scarborough onto B1261. On entering village 1st left at roundabout signed Seamer. From Pickering on A171 right at Seamer roundabout. Last right in village.*

A mature park in a secluded location, but with easy access to coastal attractions. The touring areas are hedge-screened to provide privacy. Excellent shower and toilet facilities are provided and a well-stocked bar serving food is also available. Barbecues and hog roasts are popular events during the warmer months.

Open: March to 4 January **Last arrival:** 21.00 **Last departure:** 11.00

Pitches: 🚐 🚍 🛖; 25 hardstanding pitches; 40 seasonal pitches

Leisure: 🎱 🎯 🎵

Facilities: 🏠 ⊙ 🏳 ⚒ ♿ 🛐 🍴 WiFi

Services: 🔌 🛅 📦 🍴 🍔 ⬆ 🔋 ⊘ T

Within 3 miles: ⚓ 🏌 ∪

Additional site information: 9 acre site. 🐕 Cars can be parked by caravans and tents. Awnings permitted. No noise after 23.00, no generators, no powered bikes or scooters.

Killerby Old Hall
▶▶▶ 81%

tel: 01723 583799 **Killerby YO11 3TW**
email: killerbyhall@btconnect.com **web:** www.killerbyoldhall.co.uk
dir: *From A165 between Scarborough and Filey, at Cayton Bay roundabout into Mill Lane towards Cayton. At T-junction left onto B1261 signed Filey. Site on left.*

A small secluded park, well sheltered by mature trees and shrubs, located at the rear of the old hall. All pitches are handstandings with electric hook-ups. Use of the small indoor swimming pool is shared by visitors to the hall's holiday accommodation. There is a children's play area.

Open: 14 February to 4 January **Last arrival:** 20.00 **Last departure:** noon

Pitches: 🚐 from £18.50; 🚍 from £18.50; 30 hardstanding pitches

Leisure: 🏊 🎱 🎯 ⚽

Facilities: 🏠 ⊙ 🏳 🍴 WiFi

Services: 🔌 🛅

Within 3 miles: ⚓ 🏌 ∪ ◎ 🎣 🛐

Additional site information: 2 acre site. 🐕 Cars can be parked by caravans. Awnings permitted.

PITCHES: 🚐 Caravans   🚍 Motorhomes   🛖 Tents   🏠 Glamping accommodation   **SERVICES:** 🔌 Electric hook-up   🛅 Launderette   🍴 Licensed bar
🏺 Calor Gas   ⊘ Campingaz   T Toilet fluid   🍴 Café/Restaurant   🍔 Fast Food/Takeaway   🔋 Battery charging   ⬆ Motorhome service point
* 2019 prices   🚫 No credit or debit cards   🐕 Dogs permitted   🚫 No dogs

SCOTCH CORNER
Map 19 NZ20

Places to visit

The Green Howards Museum, RICHMOND, DL10 4QN, 01748 826561
www.greenhowards.org.uk

Easby Abbey, EASBY, 0370 333 1181
www.english-heritage.org.uk/daysout/properties/easby-abbey

Scotch Corner Caravan Park
▶▶▶ 77%

tel: 01748 822530 & 07977 647722 **DL10 6NS**
email: marshallleisure@aol.com
dir: *From Scotch Corner junction of A1 and A66 take A6108/A6055 towards Richmond. At roundabout take 3rd exit, A6108/A6055, approximately 350 metres to site entrance.*

A well-maintained site with good facilities, ideally situated as a stopover, and an equally good location for touring. The Vintage Hotel, which serves food, can be accessed from the rear of the site.

Open: Easter or April to October **Last arrival:** 22.30 **Last departure:** noon

Pitches: 🚐 from £22; 🚏 from £22; ▲ from £16; 4 hardstanding pitches

Facilities: 🖼 ⊙ 🎇 ✳ ⅍ ⑤ 🎄 🏕

Services: 🔌 🗑 🍴 ⑩ 🛒 ⅄ 🔒 ⌀ ⊤

Within 3 miles: ⌁ ⌕ ∪ 🎿

Additional site information: 10 acre site. 🐾 Cars can be parked by caravans and tents. Awnings permitted. Recreation area for children, soft ball.

SHERIFF HUTTON
Map 19 SE66

Places to visit

Kirkham Priory, KIRKHAM, YO60 7JS, 01653 618768
www.english-heritage.org.uk/daysout/properties/kirkham-priory

Sutton Park, SUTTON-ON-THE-FOREST, YO61 1DP, 01347 810249
www.statelyhome.co.uk

Great for kids: Castle Howard, MALTON, YO60 7DA, 01653 648333
www.castlehoward.co.uk

York Meadows Caravan Park
▶▶▶▶ 85%

tel: 01347 878508 & 01439 788269 **York Road YO60 6QP**
email: reception@yorkmeadowscaravanpark.com
web: www.yorkmeadowscaravanpark.com
dir: *From York take A64 towards Scarborough. Left signed Flaxton and Sheriff Hutton. At West Lilling left signed Strensall. Site opposite junction.*

Peacefully located in open countryside and surrounded by mature trees, shrubs and wildlife areas, this park provides all level pitches and a modern, well-equipped

Robin Hood Caravan Park
Slingsby, York YO62 4AP
Tel: 01653 628391 Fax: 01653 628392
www.robinhoodcaravanpark.co.uk

Robin Hood Caravan & Camping Park is situated in the heart of picturesque Ryedale on the edge of the North Yorkshire village of Slingsby. Privately owned and operated by the Palmer family, this award-winning park is a perfect base for families and couples wishing to explore the stunning countryside of North Yorkshire.

Touring caravans, motorhomes and tents are always welcome. All weather pitches complete with electric hook-up and water and waste-disposal points are available. A small shop and off-licence serves your basic requirements. Calor Gas and Camping Gaz is stocked. A children's play area keeps the youngsters amused.

amenity block. Outdoor games such as draughts and snakes and ladders are available.

Open: March to October **Last arrival:** 21.00 **Last departure:** noon

Pitches: 🚐 from £19; 🚍 from £19; ▲ from £19; 45 hardstanding pitches; 20 seasonal pitches

Leisure: 🎯 ⚽

Facilities: 🏠 ⊙ ☂ ❄ ♿ ⑤ WiFi

Services: 🔌 ⑤ ⏚ 🛢 🥢 T

Within 3 miles: ⌖ 🎣 🎠

Additional site information: 12 acre site. 🐾 Cars can be parked by caravans and tents. Awnings permitted. No noise after 23.00, no skateboarding, hover boards, fires or Chinese lanterns. Fresh bread available. Outdoor table tennis.

SLINGSBY	Map 19 SE67

Places to visit

Nunnington Hall, NUNNINGTON, YO62 5UY, 01439 748283
www.nationaltrust.org.uk/nunnington-hall

Castle Howard, MALTON, YO60 7DA, 01653 648333
www.castlehoward.co.uk

Robin Hood Caravan & Camping Park
▶▶▶▶ 88%

tel: 01653 628391 **Green Dyke Lane YO62 4AP**
email: info@robinhoodcaravanpark.co.uk **web:** www.robinhoodcaravanpark.co.uk
dir: Access from B1257 (Malton to Helmsley road).

A pleasant, well-maintained, grassy park in a good location for touring North Yorkshire. Situated on the edge of the village of Slingsby, the park has

Robin Hood Caravan & Camping Park

Open: March to October **Last arrival:** 18.00 **Last departure:** noon

Pitches: 🚐 from £22; 🚍 from £22; ▲ from £16; 12 hardstanding pitches

Leisure: 🎯

Facilities: 🏠 ⊙ ☂ ❄ ♿ ⑤ 🍴 🛒 WiFi

Services: 🔌 ⑤ ⏚ 🛢 🥢 T

Within 3 miles: 🎣 ↺

Additional site information: 2 acre site. 🐾 Cars can be parked by caravans and tents. Awnings permitted. No noise after 23.00. Caravan hire, off licence, treasure trail.

See advert opposite

hardstandings and electricity for every pitch; 12 super pitches are available. The site has a centrally heated toilet block, and there is a treasure trail and play area for children.

PITCHES: 🚐 Caravans 🚍 Motorhomes ▲ Tents 🏕 Glamping accommodation **SERVICES:** 🔌 Electric hook-up ⑤ Launderette 🍺 Licensed bar
🛢 Calor Gas 🥢 Campingaz T Toilet fluid 🍴 Café/Restaurant 🍔 Fast Food/Takeaway 🔋 Battery charging ⚡ Motorhome service point
* 2019 prices 🚫 No credit or debit cards 🐾 Dogs permitted ⊗ No dogs

SNAINTON
Map 17 SE98

Places to visit

Scarborough Castle, SCARBOROUGH, YO11 1HY, 01723 372451
www.english-heritage.org.uk/daysout/properties/scarborough-castle

Pickering Castle, PICKERING, YO18 7AX, 01751 474989
www.english-heritage.org.uk/daysout/properties/pickering-castle

Great for kids: Scarborough Sea Life Sanctuary, SCARBOROUGH, YO12 6RP
www.sealife.co.uk

Premier Park

Jasmine Caravan Park
▶▶▶▶▶ 88%

tel: 01723 859240 **Cross Lane YO13 9BE**
email: enquiries@jasminepark.co.uk **web:** www.jasminepark.co.uk
dir: Take A170 from Pickering towards Scarborough. In Snainton, right into Barker's Lane (follow brown site sign). 0.5 mile, at crossroads left into Cross Lane. Site on left.

A peaceful and beautifully-presented park on the edge of a pretty village, and sheltered by high hedges. This picturesque park lies midway between Pickering and Scarborough on the southern edge of the North Yorkshire Moors. The toilet block with individual wash cubicles is maintained to a very high standard, and there is a licensed shop, a children's playground, and it is possible for larger units to be accommodated on hardstandings (please check when booking). Please note, there is no motorhome service point but super pitches for motorhomes are available.

Open: March to October **Last arrival:** 20.00 **Last departure:** noon
Pitches: 🚐 🚙 ▲; 68 hardstanding pitches; 42 seasonal pitches
Leisure: /🛝\ ❀
Facilities: 🛁 ⊙ ☂ ✳ 👤 🛒 🛒 WiFi
Services: 🚐 🛢 🔒 ⌀ T
Within 3 miles: ↧ ☂ ∪ ◉

Additional site information: 5 acre site. 🐕 Cars can be parked by caravans and tents. Awnings permitted. No noise after 23.00. Baby changing unit.

STAINFORTH
Map 18 SD86

Places to visit

Malham National Park Centre, MALHAM, BD23 4DA, 01729 833200
www.yorkshiredales.org.uk

Knight Stainforth Hall Caravan & Campsite
▶▶▶▶ 92%

tel: 01729 822200 **BD24 0DP**
email: info@knightstainforth.co.uk **web:** www.knightstainforth.co.uk
dir: From west: A65 onto B6480 towards Settle, left before swimming pool signed Little Stainforth. From east: through Settle on B6480, over bridge, 1st right.

Located near Settle and the River Ribble in the Yorkshire Dales National Park, this well-maintained family site is sheltered by mature woodland. It is an ideal base for walking or touring the beautiful surrounding area. The toilet block is appointed to a high standard and the lower part of the site benefits from the many trees that were planted a few years ago. A superb local stone building houses a smart reception, well-stocked shop, lounge and the Knights Table café and bistro, which features locally-sourced produce on the menus. Fishing and WiFi are also available.

Open: March to October **Last arrival:** 22.00 **Last departure:** noon
Pitches: 🚐 🚙 ▲; 30 hardstanding pitches
Leisure: /🛝\ ❀ ☂ ❀
Facilities: 🛁 ⊙ ☂ ✳ 👤 🛒 🛒 🛒 WiFi
Services: 🚐 🛢 🍴 🍽 🛒 🚚 ⚓ 🔒 ⌀ T
Within 3 miles: ↧

Additional site information: 6 acre site. 🐕 Cars can be parked by caravans and tents. Awnings permitted. No groups of unaccompanied minors.

STILLINGFLEET
Map 16 SE54

Places to visit

Merchant Adventurers' Hall, YORK, YO1 9XD, 01904 654818
www.theyorkcompany.co.uk

Mansion House, YORK, YO1 9QL, 01904 553663
www.mansionhouseyork.com

Great for kids: National Railway Museum, YORK, YO26 4XJ, 03330 161010
www.nrm.org.uk

Home Farm Caravan & Camping
▶▶ 77%

tel: 01904 728263 **Moreby YO19 6HN**
email: home_farm@hotmail.co.uk **web:** www.homefarmyork.co.uk
dir: 6 miles from York on B1222, 1.5 miles north of Stillingfleet.

A traditional meadowland site on a working farm bordered by parkland on one side and the River Ouse on another. Facilities are in converted farm buildings, and the family owners extend a friendly welcome to tourers. An excellent site for relaxing and unwinding, yet only a short distance from the attractions of York. There are four log cabins for holiday hire.

Open: February to December **Last arrival:** 22.00

Pitches: 🚐 from £16; 🚍 from £16; ⛺ from £14

Facilities: 🏪 ⊙ 🍴 ❄

Services: 🔌 🛒 🔋 🧴 T

Within 3 miles: 🎣 U ⛖

Additional site information: 5 acre site. 🐕 🚫 Cars can be parked by caravans and tents. Awnings permitted. Family washroom.

SUTTON-ON-THE-FOREST
Map 19 SE56

Places to visit

Sutton Park, SUTTON-ON-THE-FOREST, YO61 1DP, 01347 810249
www.statelyhome.co.uk

Treasurer's House, YORK, YO1 7JL, 01904 624247
www.nationaltrust.org.uk/treasurers-house-york

Great for kids: Jorvik Viking Centre, YORK, YO1 9WT, 01904 615505
www.jorvik-viking-centre.com

Premier Park

Goosewood Holiday Park
▶▶▶▶▶ 87%

tel: 01347 810829 **YO61 1ET**
email: info@flowerofmay.com **web:** www.flowerofmay.com
dir: *From A1237 take B1363. In 5 miles turn right. Right again in 0.5 mile, site on right.*

A relaxing and immaculately maintained park with its own lake and seasonal fishing. It is set in attractive woodland just six miles north of York. Mature shrubs and stunning seasonal floral displays at the entrance create an excellent first impression and the well-located toilet facilities are kept spotlessly clean. The generous patio pitches, providing optimum privacy, are randomly spaced throughout the site, and in addition to an excellent outdoor children's play area, you will find an indoor swimming pool, clubhouse, games room and bar and bistro. There are holiday homes for hire. Please note that prices shown are for a maximum of 4 people and 1 car (electricity not included).

Open: March to 2 January (restricted service: low season – shop, bar and pool reduced hours) **Last arrival:** dusk **Last departure:** noon

Pitches: 🚐 from £24; 🚍 from £24; 50 hardstanding pitches; 35 seasonal pitches

Leisure: 🏊 🎱 🎣

Facilities: 🏪 ⊙ 🍴 ❄ ♿ 🛁 🧺 🏬 WiFi

Services: 🔌 🛒 🛒 🍴 🛗 🔋 T

Within 3 miles: ♿ ⛖

Additional site information: 20 acre site. 🐕 Dogs accepted by prior arrangement only. Cars can be parked by caravans. Awnings permitted. No noise after midnight. Multi ball court.

THIRSK
Map 19 SE48

Places to visit

Monk Park Farm Visitor Centre, THIRSK, YO7 2AG, 01845 597730
www.monkparkfarm.co.uk

Byland Abbey, COXWOLD, YO61 4BD, 0370 333 1181
www.english-heritage.org.uk/daysout/properties/byland-abbey

Great for kids: Thirsk Birds of Prey Centre, THIRSK, YO7 4EU, 01845 587522
www.falconrycentre.co.uk

Premier Park

Hillside Caravan Park
▶▶▶▶▶ 86%

tel: 01845 537349 & 07711 643652 **Canvas Farm, Moor Road YO7 4BR**
email: info@hillsidecaravanpark.co.uk **web:** www.hillsidecaravanpark.co.uk
dir: *From Thirsk take A19 north, exit at Knayton sign. In 0.25 mile right (cross bridge over A19), through village. Site on left in approximately 1.5 miles.*

A high quality, spacious park with first-class facilities, set in open countryside. The striking sandstone amenity block houses the airy reception, shop and office, plus there's a kitchen and laundry, two excellent family rooms, a disabled room, a recreation room, two self-contained flats and four luxury camping pods for hire. This is an excellent base for walkers and for those wishing to explore the Thirsk area. Please note, the park does not accept tents.

Open: 4 February to 4 January **Last arrival:** 21.00 **Last departure:** noon

Pitches: * 🚐 from £25; 🚍 from £25; 🏠 see prices below; 50 hardstanding pitches

Leisure: 🎱 ✻

Facilities: 🏪 ⊙ 🍴 ❄ ♿ 🛁 🏬 WiFi

Services: 🔌 🛒 🛒 🔋 T

Within 3 miles: ♿ U

Additional site information: 9 acre site. 🐕 Cars can be parked by caravans. Awnings permitted. Self service coffee lounge.

Glamping available: Wooden pods ('mega pods') from £45. **Changeover days:** Any day

Additional glamping information: Mega pods are equipped with toilet, shower and hand basin. Cars can be parked by pods.

PITCHES: 🚐 Caravans 🚍 Motorhomes ⛺ Tents 🏠 Glamping accommodation **SERVICES:** 🔌 Electric hook-up 🛒 Launderette 🍴 Licensed bar
🔋 Calor Gas 🧴 Campingaz T Toilet fluid 🍴 Café/Restaurant 🛒 Fast Food/Takeaway 🔋 Battery charging 🛗 Motorhome service point
* 2019 prices 🚫 No credit or debit cards 🐕 Dogs permitted 🚫 No dogs

THIRSK *continued*

Thirkleby Hall Caravan Park
►►► 75%

tel: 01845 501360 & 07799 641815 **Thirkleby YO7 3AR**
email: greenwood.parks@virgin.net **web:** www.greenwoodparks.com
dir: *3 miles south of Thirsk on A19. Turn left through arched gatehouse into site.*

A long-established site in the grounds of the old hall, with statics in wooded areas around a fishing lake and tourers based on slightly sloping grassy pitches. There is a quality amenity block and laundry. This well-screened park has superb views of the Hambledon Hills.

Open: March to October **Last arrival:** 17.30 **Last departure:** 14.30

Pitches: ⊕ ⌂ Å; 3 hardstanding pitches; 20 seasonal pitches

Leisure: ⚽

Facilities: 🛁 ⊙ ☈ ✳ & ♨

Services: 🔌 🗓 🍽 🛒 ♨

Within 3 miles: ⌘ ✐ 🎱 🛒

Additional site information: 53 acre site. 🐕 🚗 Cars can be parked by caravans and tents. Awnings permitted. No noise after 23.00. Woodland walks.

TOLLERTON   Map 19 SE56

Places to visit

Beningbrough Hall, Gallery & Gardens, BENINGBROUGH, YO30 1DD, 01904 472027
www.nationaltrust.org.uk/beningbrough

Sutton Park, SUTTON-ON-THE-FOREST, YO61 1DP, 01347 810249
www.statelyhome.co.uk

Great for kids: Jorvik Viking Centre, YORK, YO1 9WT, 01904 615505
www.jorvik-viking-centre.com

Tollerton Holiday Park
►►►► 82%

tel: 01347 838313 & 07836 776704 **Station Rd YO61 1RD**
email: greenwood.parks@virgin.net **web:** www.greenwoodparks.com
dir: *From York take A19 towards Thirsk. At Cross Lanes left towards Tollerton. 1 mile to Chinese restaurant just before rail bridge. Site entrance through restaurant car park.*

Set in open countryside within a few minutes' walk of Tollerton and just a short drive from the Park & Ride for York, this is a small park. There's an amenity block of real quality, which includes a family bathroom and laundry. There is little disturbance from the East Coast mainline which passes nearby.

Open: March to October **Last arrival:** 20.00 **Last departure:** 15.00

Pitches: ⊕ ⌂ Å; 17 hardstanding pitches; 25 seasonal pitches

Leisure: ⚽

Facilities: 🛁 ⊙ ☈ ✳ & ♨

Services: 🔌 🗓 🍽 🛒 🛒 ♨

Within 3 miles: ⌘ ✐ 🛒

Additional site information: 5 acre site. 🐕 🚗 Cars can be parked by caravans and tents. Awnings permitted. No groups. Small fishing lake.

WEST KNAPTON   Map 19 SE87

Places to visit

Pickering Castle, PICKERING, YO18 7AX, 01751 474989
www.english-heritage.org.uk/daysout/properties/pickering-castle

North Yorkshire Moors Railway, PICKERING, YO18 7AJ, 01751 472508
www.nymr.co.uk

Great for kids: Eden Camp Modern History Theme Museum, MALTON, YO17 6RT, 01653 697777, www.edencamp.co.uk

Wolds Way Caravan and Camping
►►►► 83%

tel: 01944 728463 **West Farm YO17 8JE**
email: info@ryedalesbest.co.uk **web:** www.ryedalesbest.co.uk
dir: *Signed between Rillington and West Heslerton on A64 (Malton to Scarborough road). Site in 1.5 miles.*

A park on a working farm in a peaceful, high position on the Yorkshire Wolds, with magnificent views over the Vale of Pickering. This is an excellent walking area, with the Wolds Way passing the entrance to the site. A pleasant one and a half mile path leads to a lavender farm, with its first-class coffee shop.

Open: March to October **Last arrival:** 22.30 **Last departure:** 19.00

Pitches: ⊕ ⌂ Å; 5 hardstanding pitches

Facilities: ⊙ ✳ & 🛗 ♨ 🍴 WiFi

Services: 🔌 🗓 🛒 ♨ Ⓣ

Within 3 miles: ✐

Additional site information: 7.5 acre site. 🐕 Cars can be parked by caravans and tents. Awnings permitted. Free use of microwave, toaster and TV. Drinks machine, fridge and freezer.

WHITBY

See also Robin Hood's Bay

Places to visit

Whitby Abbey, WHITBY, YO22 4JT, 01947 603568
www.english-heritage.org.uk/daysout/properties/whitby-abbey

North Yorkshire Moors Railway, PICKERING, YO18 7AJ, 01751 472508
www.nymr.co.uk

LEISURE: 🏊 Indoor swimming pool 🏊 Outdoor swimming pool 🎢 Children's playground 🖐 Kids' club 🎾 Tennis court 🎱 Games room ⬜ Separate TV room ⛳ golf course ⛳ Pitch n putt ⛵ Boats for hire 🚲 Bikes for hire 🎬 Cinema 🎵 Entertainment 🎣 Fishing ⛳ Mini golf 🏄 Watersports 🏋 Gym 🏟 Sports field ♘ Stables
FACILITIES: 🛁 Baths/Shower ⊙ Electric shaver sockets ☈ Hairdryer ✳ Ice Pack Facility 🍼 Baby facilities & Disabled facilities 🛒 Shop on site or within 200yds 🍴 BBQ area 🧺 Picnic area WiFi WiFi

WHITBY
Map 19 NZ81

Ladycross Plantation Caravan Park
▶▶▶▶ 94%

tel: 01947 895502 **Egton YO21 1UA**
email: enquiries@ladycrossplantation.co.uk **web:** www.ladycrossplantation.co.uk
dir: *From A171 (Whitby to Teesside road) onto unclassified road (site signed).*

The unique forest setting creates an away-from-it-all feeling at this peaceful touring park set in 30 acres of woodland and run by enthusiastic owners. The pitches are sited in small groups in clearings around two smartly appointed amenity blocks which offer excellent facilities — underfloor heating, no-touch infra-red showers, cubicles, kitchen prep areas and laundry facilities. The site has 20 fully serviced pitches and tarmac access roads. It is well placed for visiting Whitby and the North York Moors. Children will enjoy exploring the one-mile woodland and nature walks. Oak lodges are available for hire or sale.

Open: March to November **Last arrival:** 20.00 **Last departure:** noon
Pitches: 🚐 🚐; 77 hardstanding pitches; 60 seasonal pitches
Facilities: ☉ 𝙁 ✳ ♿ ⑤ WiFi
Services: 🔌 ⑤ 🛒 ⬆ 🔋 ⌀ Ⓣ
Within 3 miles: ♨ 🏌 ◎ 🚣 ⛵ 🏇

Additional site information: 30 acre site. 🐕 Dogs must be kept on leads in all areas of the park. Cars can be parked by caravans. Awnings permitted. No noise after 22.00.

WYKEHAM
Map 17 SE98

Places to visit

Scarborough Castle, SCARBOROUGH, YO11 1HY, 01723 372451
www.english-heritage.org.uk/daysout/properties/scarborough-castle

Pickering Castle, PICKERING, YO18 7AX, 01751 474989
www.english-heritage.org.uk/daysout/properties/pickering-castle

Great for kids: Scarborough Sea Life Sanctuary, SCARBOROUGH, YO12 6RP
www.sealife.co.uk

Premier Park

St Helens in the Park
▶▶▶▶▶ 88%

tel: 01723 862771 **YO13 9QD**
email: caravans@wykeham.co.uk **web:** www.sthelenscaravanpark.co.uk
dir: *On A170 in village, 150 yards on left beyond Downe Arms Hotel towards Scarborough.*

Set on the edge of the North York Moors National Park, this delightfully landscaped park is immaculately maintained and thoughtfully laid out; the stunning floral displays around the park are noteworthy. There are top quality facilities, and a high level of customer care can be expected. The site is divided into terraces with tree-screening that creates smaller areas including an adults' zone. There are 10 camping pods for hire (eight have electricity). A cycle route leads through to the surrounding Wykeham Estate and there is a short pathway to the adjoining Downe Arms Country Inn. There is also a superb water activity area called AquaPark.

Open: 16 February to 15 January (restricted service: shop/café open from April to October only) **Last arrival:** 20.30 (arrivals from 13.30) **Last departure:** 11.00
Pitches: 🚐 from £19; 🚐 from £19; ⛺ from £12.50; 🏕 see prices below; 79 hardstanding pitches; 100 seasonal pitches
Leisure: 🏊 ⚽
Facilities: 🏢 ☉ 𝙁 ✳ ♿ ⑤ 🛒 🏧 WiFi
Services: 🔌 ⑤ 🍴 🍟 🔋 ⬆ ⌀ Ⓣ
Within 3 miles: ♨ 🏌 ∪ ◎ 🚣 🏇

Additional site information: 25 acre site. 🐕 Dogs must be kept on a lead at all times and never left unattended and exercised in designated area or off site only. Cars can be parked by caravans and tents. Awnings permitted. No noise after 22.00, no open fires. Family and adult-only super pitches available, caravan storage; 3-acre dog exercise field.

Glamping available: Wooden pods from £30.

Additional glamping information: Wooden pods equipped with wall-mounted heater, electric socket with USB ports, mirror, lights and black out curtains. Beds and bed linen not provided. Cars can be parked by pods.

PITCHES: 🚐 Caravans 🚐 Motorhomes ⛺ Tents 🏕 Glamping accommodation **SERVICES:** 🔌 Electric hook-up ⑤ Launderette 🍷 Licensed bar
🔋 Calor Gas ⌀ Campingaz Ⓣ Toilet fluid 🍴 Café/Restaurant 🏧 Fast Food/Takeaway ⬆ Battery charging ⬆ Motorhome service point
* 2019 prices ⊘ No credit or debit cards 🐕 Dogs permitted ⊗ No dogs

YORK
Map 16 SE65

See also Sheriff Hutton

Places to visit

The York Dungeon, YORK, YO1 9RD
www.thedungeons.com/york

York Brewery, YORK, YO1 6JT, 01904 621162
www.york-brewery.co.uk

Rawcliffe Manor Caravan Park
►►►► 81%

tel: 01904 640845 **Manor Lane, Shipton Road YO30 5TZ**
email: christine@lysanderarms.co.uk **web:** www.lysanderarms.co.uk
dir: *From roundabout junction of A1237 and A19, take A19 signed York, Clifton and Rawcliffe. 1st left into Manor Lane, follow brown camping signs.*

A lovely little adults-only site tucked away behind the Lysander Arms and located only minutes from the centre of York. Each of the 13 generously-sized pitches is fully serviced with an individual chemical disposal point, and the central toilet block is very airy, modern and spotlessly clean. The grounds have been imaginatively landscaped. The pub offers good food and the York Park & Ride facility is a 10-minute walk away.

Open: All year **Last arrival:** 18.00 **Last departure:** 11.00

Pitches: 🚐 🚌; 13 hardstanding pitches

Leisure: 🏊 🎱 🎵 ⛳ Spa

Facilities: 🚿 ☉ ✳ ♿ 🚽 🏺 **WiFi**

Services: 🔌 🗑 🛱 🍽 🏧 🛒 🔧 💧 🔒

Within 3 miles: ⌗ 🎣 ⛳ ◎ 🅿 $

Additional site information: 4.5 acre site. Adults only. 🐕 Cars can be parked by caravans. Awnings permitted. No noise after 23.00. Chemical disposal points on each pitch.

SOUTH YORKSHIRE

WORSBROUGH
Map 16 SE30

Places to visit

Monk Bretton Priory, BARNSLEY, S71 5QD, 0370 333 1181
www.english-heritage.org.uk/daysout/properties/monk-bretton-priory

Millennium Gallery, SHEFFIELD, S1 2PP, 0114 278 2600
www.museums-sheffield.org.uk

Great for kids: Magna Science Adventure Centre, ROTHERHAM, S60 1DX, 01709 720002
www.visitmagna.co.uk

Greensprings Touring Park
►►► 78%

tel: 01226 288298 **Rockley Abbey Farm, Rockley Lane S75 3DS**
email: greensprings_1@yahoo.co.uk
dir: *M1 junction 36, A61 to Barnsley. Left after 0.25 mile signed Pilley. Site in 1 mile at bottom of hill.*

A secluded and very peaceful farm site set amid woods and farmland, with access to the river and several good local walks. There are two touring areas, one gently sloping. Although not far from the M1, there is almost no traffic noise and this site is convenient for exploring the area's industrial heritage, as well as the Peak District. Improvements to amenities in 2018 have stepped up quality here with a newly built washroom block.

Open: April to 30 October **Last arrival:** 21.00 **Last departure:** noon

Pitches: 🚐 from £18; 🚌 from £18; ⛺ from £18; 30 hardstanding pitches; 22 seasonal pitches

Leisure: ⚽

Facilities: 🚿 ☉ ✳ ♿

Services: 🔌

Within 3 miles: ⌗ 🎣 ⛳ ◎ 🅿 $ 🗑

Additional site information: 4 acre site. 🐕 ⊜ Cars can be parked by caravans and tents. Awnings permitted.

WEST YORKSHIRE

BARDSEY
Map 16 SE34

Places to visit

Bramham Park, BRAMHAM, LS23 6ND, 01937 846000
www.bramhampark.co.uk

Thackray Medical Museum, LEEDS, LS9 7LN, 0113 244 4343
www.thackraymedicalmuseum.co.uk

Great for kids: Leeds Industrial Museum at Armley Mills, LEEDS, LS12 2QF,
0113 378 3173
www.leeds.gov.uk/museumsandgalleries/armleymills

Glenfield Caravan Park
►►►► 88%

tel: 01937 574657 & 07761 710862 **Blackmoor Lane LS17 9DZ**
email: glenfieldcp@aol.com **web:** www.glenfieldcaravanpark.co.uk
dir: *3 miles from A1 junction 45. From A58 at Bardsey into Church Lane, past church, up hill. 0.5 mile, site on right.*

A very friendly and quiet rural site in a well-screened, tree-lined meadow. This site has an excellent toilet block complete with family room and an increasing amount of hardstanding and fully serviced touring pitches. Discounted fees and food are both available at the local golf club. This is a convenient touring base for Leeds and the surrounding area.

Open: All year **Last arrival:** 21.00 **Last departure:** noon (late departures by prior arrangement)

Pitches: * 🚐 from £23; 🚐 from £23; ⛺ from £23; 30 hardstanding pitches; 10 seasonal pitches

Facilities: 🏠 ⊙ 🖉 ❄ ♿ 🛁 🚻 **WiFi**

Services: 🔌 🗑 🍺 🍴 🚽 🔋 🍃

Within 3 miles: 🎣 🖉 ∪ ◎ 🎖 💲

Additional site information: 4 acre site. 🐕 Cars can be parked by caravans and tents. Awnings permitted. Children must be supervised. Walking maps available.

LEEDS
Map 19 SE23

Places to visit

Temple Newsam Estate, LEEDS, LS15 0AE, 0113 336 7461
www.leeds.gov.uk/templenewsamhouse

Moor Lodge Park
►►►► 89%

tel: 01937 572424 **Blackmoor Lane, Bardsey LS17 9DZ**
email: moorlodgecp@aol.com **web:** www.moorlodgecaravanpark.co.uk
dir: *From A1(M) take A659 (south of Wetherby) signed Otley. Left onto A58 towards Leeds for 5 miles. Right after New Inn pub (Ling Lane), right at crossroads, 1 mile, site on right.*

A warm welcome is assured at this well-kept site set in a peaceful and beautiful setting, close to Harewood House and only 25 minutes' drive from York and the Dales; the centre of Leeds is just 15 minutes away. The touring area is for adults only. Please note, this site does not accept tents.

Open: All year **Last arrival:** 18.30 **Last departure:** noon

Pitches: 🚐 from £24; 🚐 from £24

Facilities: 🏠 ⊙ 🖉 ❄ 🚻 🚻 **WiFi**

Services: 🔌 🗑 🍴 🚽 🔋 🍃

Within 3 miles: 🎣 🖉 ∪ ◎ 🎖 💲

Additional site information: 7 acre site. Adults only. 🐕 Adjoining private dog walking field. Cars can be parked by caravans. Awnings permitted. No large groups.

Channel Islands

CHANNEL ISLANDS

GUERNSEY

CASTEL
Map 24

Places to visit

Sausmarez Manor, ST MARTIN, GY4 6SG, 01481 235571
www.sausmarezmanor.co.uk

Fort Grey Shipwreck Museum, ROCQUAINE BAY, GY7 9BY, 01481 265036
www.museums.gov.gg

Premier Park

Fauxquets Valley Campsite
▶▶▶▶▶ 86%

tel: 01481 255460 & 07781 413333 **GY5 7QL**
email: info@fauxquets.co.uk web: www.fauxquets.co.uk
dir: *From pier take 2nd exit at roundabout. At top of hill left into Queens Road.
2 miles. Right into Candie Road. Site opposite sign for German Occupation Museum.*

A beautiful, quiet farm site in a hidden valley close to the sea. The friendly and
helpful owners, who understand campers' needs, offer good quality facilities
and amenities, including spacious pitches and an outdoor swimming pool. There
are sports areas, a nature trail, pigs, sheep and chickens for the children to
visit, plus barbecue food and pizzas are available near the reception. There are
fully serviced pitches and also four self-contained lodges for hire. Motorhomes
are allowed on Guernsey — contact the site for details and a permit.

Open: May to 1 September Pitches: ⇌ Å
Leisure: ⚏ ▲ ⚲ ▯ ⚙ Facilities: ⊡ ⊙ ⅌ ✳ ⅋ ⑤ ㄓ WiFi
Services: ⊡ ⑤ 🍴 🎪 ⭐ 🔒 ⊘ ⊺
Within 3 miles: ⚓ ⌖ ∪ ◉ ⛷ ⚘ ⊟

Additional site information: 3 acre site. ⊣ Cars can be parked by tents. Awnings
permitted. Birdwatching.

ST SAMPSON
Map 24

Places to visit

Sausmarez Manor, ST MARTIN, GY4 6SG, 01481 235571
www.sausmarezmanor.co.uk

Castle Cornet, ST PETER PORT, GY1 1AU, 01481 721657
www.museums.gov.gg

Le Vaugrat Camp Site
▶▶▶ 90%

tel: 01481 257468 **Route de Vaugrat GY2 4TA**
email: enquiries@vaugratcampsite.com web: www.vaugratcampsite.com
dir: *From main coast road on northwest of island, site signed at Port Grat Bay into Route
de Vaugrat, near Peninsula Hotel.*

Overlooking the sea and set within the grounds of a lovely 17th-century house, this
level grassy park is backed by woodland, and is close to the lovely sandy beaches of
Port Grat and Grand Havre. It is run by a welcoming family who pride themselves on
creating magnificent floral displays. The facilities here are excellent and there are

18 electric hook-ups, plus several fully equipped tents for hire. A 'round the island'
bus stops very close to the site. Motorhomes are allowed on Guernsey — contact the
site for details and a permit.

Open: May to mid September

Pitches: ⇌ from £26; ⇌ from £26; Å from £26; ⋒ see prices below
Leisure: ▯ ⚙ Facilities: ⊡ ⊙ ⅌ ✳ ⅋ ⑤ ㄓ WiFi
Services: ⊡ ⑤ ⭐ 🔒 ⊘
Within 3 miles: ⚓ ⌖ ∪ ◉ ⛷ ⚘ ⊟

Additional site information: 6 acre site. Cars can be parked by caravans and tents.
Awnings permitted. No pets.

Glamping available: Ready-erected tents from £51.

Additional glamping information: Ready-erected tents: beds, bedding (not towels) and
cooking facilities are included. Electricity is not available. Cabanon Espace tents: sleep 6.
Bell tents: sleep 3 (adults only). Cars can be parked by tents.

VALE
Map 24

Places to visit

Guernsey Museum & Art Gallery, ST PETER PORT, GY1 1UG, 01481 726518
www.museums.gov.gg

Great for kids: Castle Cornet, ST PETER PORT, GY1 1AU, 01481 721657
www.museums.gov.gg

La Bailloterie Camping
▶▶▶▶ 86%

tel: 01481 243636 & 07781 103420 **GY3 5HA**
email: info@campinginguernsey.com web: www.campinginguernsey.com
dir: *3 miles north of St Peter Port into Vale Road to Crossways, at crossroads right into
Rue du Braye. Site 1st left at sign.*

A pretty rural site with one large touring field and a few small, well-screened
paddocks. This delightful site has been privately run for over 50 years and offers
good facilities in converted outbuildings and a woodland walk for visitors to enjoy.
There are two, two-bedroom, well-equipped camping lodges, four top quality and
very well-equipped safari tents (including a Cabanon tent) available
for hire. The beaches and a supermarket are a short walk away. Motorhomes are
allowed on Guernsey — contact the site for detailed instructions.

Open: 15 May to 15 September Last arrival: 23.00 Last departure: 11.00

Pitches: ⇌ from £8; Å from £8; ⋒ see prices below
Leisure: ▲ ⚙ ⚽ Facilities: ⊡ ⊙ ⅌ ✳ ⅋ ⑤ ㄓ ⛟ WiFi
Services: ⊡ ⑤ 🍴 🎪 ⭐ ⊘
Within 3 miles: ⚓ ⌖ ∪ ◉ ⛷ ⚘ ⊟

Additional site information: 10 acre site. ⊣ Dogs by prior arrangement only. Cars can be
parked by tents. Awnings permitted. Volleyball net, boules pitch, mini golf. Car hire can
be arranged.

Glamping available: Safari tents from £25; Pods from £20. Changeover days: Any day

Additional glamping information: Minimum stay 2 nights. Safari tents: prices per adult;
family packages available; no dogs. Pods: prices per adult, maximum 2 people, fully
equipped with bedding. Cars can be parked by pods and tents.

PITCHES: ⇌ Caravans ⇌ Motorhomes Å Tents ⋒ Glamping accommodation SERVICES: ⊡ Electric hook-up ⑤ Launderette 🍴 Licensed bar
⭐ Calor Gas ⊘ Campingaz ⊺ Toilet fluid 🍴 Café/Restaurant 🎪 Fast Food/Takeaway ⭐ Battery charging ⚘ Motorhome service point
* 2019 prices ⊗ No credit or debit cards ⊣ Dogs permitted ⊗ No dogs

JERSEY

ST MARTIN

Map 24

Places to visit

Mont Orgueil Castle, GOREY, JE3 6ET, 01534 853292
www.jerseyheritage.org

Maritime Museum, ST HELIER, JE2 3ND, 01534 811043
www.jerseyheritage.org

Great for kids: Elizabeth Castle, ST HELIER, JE2 3NU, 01534 723971
www.jerseyheritage.org

Premier Park

Rozel Camping Park

►►►►► 89%

tel: 01534 855200 **Summerville Farm JE3 6AX**
email: enquiries@rozelcamping.com **web:** www.rozelcamping.com
dir: *Take A6 from St Helier through Five Oaks to St Martins Church, turn right onto A38 towards Rozel, site on right.*

Customers can be sure of a warm welcome at this delightful family-run park. Set in the northeast of the island, it offers large spacious pitches (many with electricity) for tents, caravans and motorhomes. The heated swimming pool has a separate children's paddling pool, and there is an on-site shop selling groceries, wine, beer and some camping supplies. Smart amenity blocks and a laundry room are provided. The lovely Rozel Bay is just a short distance away and spectacular views of the French coast can be seen from one of the four fields on the park. Motorhomes and caravans will be met at the ferry and escorted to the park if requested when booking. Fully equipped, ready-erected tents available for hire.

Open: May to mid September **Last arrival:** 20.30 **Last departure:** noon

Pitches: 🚐 from £14; 🚗 from £14; ⚠ from £14; 🛖 see prices below

Leisure: 🏊 🎠 🔍 ⬜ ⚽

Facilities: 🛁 ☉ ⚗ ✳ ♿ 🅂 🛒 WiFi

Services: 🔌 🗑 🛒 ⬆ 🛢 🧺 Ⓣ

Within 3 miles: 🎣 🏌 ∪ ◎ ♨ ⚓

Additional site information: 4 acre site. 🐕 Cars can be parked by caravans and tents. Awnings permitted. No noise between 22.00–07.30. Free mini golf, table tennis. Freshly baked bread available.

Glamping available: Ready-erected tents from £60.

Additional glamping information: Ready-erected tents are fully equipped. Cars can be parked by tents.

ST OUEN

Map 24

Places to visit

Judith Quérée's Garden, ST OUEN, JE3 2FE, 01534 482191
www.judithqueree.com

Daisy Cottage Campsite

►►►► 88%

tel: 01534 481700 **Route de Vinchelez JE3 2DB**
email: hello@daisycottagecampsite.com **web:** www.daisycottagecampsite.com
dir: *From St Helier harbour, at 2nd roundabout, 1st exit onto A2 (Victoria Avenue) (becomes A1). At 'filter-in-turn' mini roundabout in Beaumont, right into La Route de Beaumont (signed St Ouen and A12). In St Ouen right into Route de Vinchelez. Site on right.*

The only campsite on the west side of the island. If you are looking for a peaceful site with spacious and well screened pitches and spotless facilities, Daisy Cottage would be the perfect choice. The whole emphasis is on having a peaceful and relaxing stay. The campsite also has a unique retreat offering a wide range of therapies, an on-site chiropractor and also a secluded decking area where you can just unwind or take part in yoga or relaxation classes. The campsite is also very close to Greve de Lecq with its delightful beach.

Open: April to October

Pitches: 🚐 🚗 ⚠ 🛖

Leisure: Spa

Facilities: 🛁 ✳ 🅂 🛒 🪑 WiFi

Services: 🔌 🗑 🛒

Within 3 miles: 🎣 ♨ 🎋

Additional site information: 2.5 acre site. 🐕 Cars can be parked by caravans and tents. Awnings permitted. No noise after 22.00.

Glamping available: 1 shepherd's hut.

Additional glamping information: Cars can be parked by shepherd's hut.

LEISURE: 🏊 Indoor swimming pool 🏊 Outdoor swimming pool 🎠 Children's playground 🖐 Kids' club 🎾 Tennis court 🔍 Games room ⬜ Separate TV room 🏌 golf course ⛳ Pitch n putt ⛵ Boats for hire 🚲 Bikes for hire 🎬 Cinema 🎵 Entertainment 🎣 Fishing ◎ Mini golf 🏄 Watersports 💪 Gym ⚽ Sports field ∪ Stables
FACILITIES: 🛁 Baths/Shower ☉ Electric shaver sockets ✂ Hairdryer ✳ Ice Pack Facility 🛒 Baby facilities ♿ Disabled facilities 🅂 Shop on site or within 200yds 🍖 BBQ area 🪑 Picnic area WiFi WiFi

TRINITY
Map 24

Places to visit

Hamptonne Country Life Museum, ST LAWRENCE, JE3 1HS, 01534 863955
www.jerseyheritage.org

Mont Orgueil Castle, GOREY, JE3 6ET, 01534 853292
www.jerseyheritage.org

Platinum Park

Durrell Wildlife Camp
▶▶▶▶▶ GLAMPING ONLY

tel: 01534 860097 & 07797 832534
Les Augres Manor, La Profonde Rue JE3 5BP
email: ashley.mullins@durrell.org **web:** www.durrell.org/camp
dir: *From St Helier take A8 to Trinity. At T-junction right signed Rozel and Durrell Wildlife. Site on right.*

Part of Jersey Zoo, the camp consists of 12 canvas geo domes set in a beautifully landscaped area. Each dome, named after different Lemur species, is sited in its own separate area offering good privacy. Inside is a king-size bed, two singles, a wood-burning stove and clothing storage space. Set on wooden decking, the domes have their own additional pod with high quality toilet, wash basin and shower plus a spacious fully-equipped kitchen. Table and chairs on the decking can be brought into the kitchen if the weather's not so good. Smaller tipis are available for extra children or guests. Guests have free, unlimited access to Jersey Zoo during its opening hours and can visit the excellent Café Firefly, which serves breakfasts, lunches and early evening meals, plus takeaway pizzas and Thai food. The whole holiday experience is quite magical.

Open: March to October **Last arrival:** 20.00 **Last departure:** 10.00

Facilities: 🚿 ✳ ♿ 🍴 ⤢ 📶

Within 3 miles: ⌴ ∪ ⤢ 🗓 💲 🗑

Accommodation available: Geo domes from £140.

Changeover days: Any day

Additional site information: No pets. No noise after 23.00. Free entry into Jersey Zoo. Cars can be parked by geo domes.

ISLE OF MAN

KIRK MICHAEL
Map 24 SC39

Places to visit

Peel Castle, PEEL, IM5 1TB, 01624 648000
www.manxnationalheritage.im

House of Manannan, PEEL, IM5 1TA, 01624 648000
www.manxnationalheritage.im

Great for kids: Curraghs Wildlife Park, BALLAUGH, IM7 5EA, 01624 897323
www.curraghswildlifepark.im

Glen Wyllin Campsite
▶▶▶ 80%

tel: 01624 878231 & 878836 **IM6 1AL**
email: tmdentith@manx.net **web:** www.glenwyllincampsite.co.uk
dir: *From Douglas take A1 to Ballacraine, right at lights onto A3 to Kirk Michael. Left onto A4 signed Peel. Site 100 yards on right.*

This site is set in a peaceful wooded glen with bridges over a babbling brook that divides the enclosed camping and touring areas, and where the only distractions are the welcome ones of running water and birdsong. A long gentle sloping tarmac road leads through the camping areas to a superb beach, a well stocked shop and hot food takeaway service are additional features. Ready-erected tents are available and future plans include secluded lodges.

Open: mid April to mid September **Last departure:** noon

Pitches: 🚐 🚍 🅰 🏠

Leisure: 🖵

Facilities: ⊙ 🅿 ✳ ♿ 🗓 🍴 ⤢ 📶

Services: 🔌 🗑 🍽 🛒 🔋

Within 3 miles: 🎣 ∪

Additional site information: 9 acre site. 🐕 Dogs must be kept under control. Cars can be parked by caravans and tents. Awnings permitted. No excess noise after midnight.

Glamping available: Ready erected tents.

Scotland

Scotland

With its remarkable, timeless beauty, jagged coastline and long and eventful history, Scotland is a country with something very special to offer. Around half the size of England, but with barely one fifth of its population and nearly 800 islands, the statistics alone are enough make you want to pack a suitcase and head north without hesitation.

The Scottish Borders region acts as a perfect introduction and is an obvious place to begin a tour of the country. The novelist and poet Sir Walter Scott was so moved by its remoteness and grandeur that he wrote: 'To my eye, these grey hills and all this wild border country have beauties peculiar to themselves. I like the very nakedness of the land; it has something bold and stern and solitary about it. If I did not see the heather at least once a year I think I should die.' Abbotsford, Scott's turreted mansion on the banks of the River Tweed near Melrose, was re-opened to the public in the summer of 2013 following a £12 million programme of major improvements.

Consisting of 1,800 square miles of dense forest, rolling green hills and the broad sweeps of heather that lifted Scott's spirits, this region is characterised by some of the country's most majestic landscapes. Adjacent to this region is Dumfries & Galloway, where, at Gretna Green on the border with England, eloping couples have tied the knot since Lord Hardwicke's Marriage Act came into force in 1754; it still can boast around 1,500 weddings a year. Travel north and you discover mile upon mile of open moorland and swathes of seemingly endless forest that stretch to the Ayrshire coast. At a crucial time in the country's history, it is fascinating to reflect on another momentous event in the story of Scotland when, following the signing of the Declaration of Arbroath in 1320, it became independent and was ruled by Robert the Bruce. Dumfries & Galloway is littered with the relics of his battles.

Not far from Dumfries is the cottage where Robert Burns, the Bard of Scotland, was born in 1759. This tiny white-washed dwelling, constructed of thatch and clay, was built by the poet's father two years earlier. In a 2009 poll, TV viewers voted Burns the 'Greatest ever Scot' and his song *Is there for Honest Poverty* opened the new Scottish Parliament in 1999. The cottage at Alloway is one of Scotland's most popular tourist attractions with a museum allowing the poet's collection of precious manuscripts, correspondence and artefacts to be housed in one building.

Scotland's two greatest cities, Glasgow and Edinburgh, include innumerable historic sites, popular landmarks and innovative visitor attractions. Edinburgh is home to the annual, internationally famous Military Tattoo; Glasgow, once the second city of the British Empire and yet synonymous with the dreadful slums and the grime of industry, has, in places, been transformed beyond recognition. The city hosted the Great Exhibitions of 1888 and 1901, was designated European City of Culture in 1990 and in 2014 became the setting for the highly successful Commonwealth Games.

To the north of Glasgow and Edinburgh lies a sublime landscape of tranquil lochs, fishing rivers, wooded glens and the fine cities of Perth and Dundee. There is also the superb scenery of The Trossachs, Loch Lomond and Stirling, which, with its handsome castle perched on a rocky crag, is Scotland's heritage capital. Sooner or later the might and majesty of the Cairngorms and the Grampians beckon, drawing you into a breathtakingly beautiful landscape of mountains and remote, rugged terrain. Scotland's isolated far north is further from many parts of England than a good many European destinations. Cape Wrath is Britain's most northerly outpost.

For many visitors, the Western Highlands is the place to go, evoking a truly unique and breathtaking sense of adventure. The list of island names seems endless – Skye, Mull, Iona, Jura, Islay – each with their own individual character and identity, and the reward of everlasting and treasured memories.

Rest and Be Thankful Pass near Arrochar ▷

ABERDEENSHIRE

ABOYNE
Map 23 NO59

Places to visit

Crathes Castle Garden & Estate, CRATHES, AB31 5QJ, 01330 844525
www.nts.org.uk/visit/places/crathes-castle

Great for kids: Craigievar Castle, ALFORD, AB33 8JF, 01339 883635
www.nts.org.uk/visit/places/craigievar

Aboyne Loch Caravan Park
►►► 76%

tel: 01339 886244 **AB34 5BR**
email: info@aboynelochcaravanpark.co.uk **web:** www.aboynelochcaravanpark.co.uk
dir: *On A93, 1 mile east of Aboyne.*

Located on the outskirts of Aboyne on a small outcrop which is almost surrounded by Loch Aboyne, this is a mature site within scenic Royal Deeside. The facilities are well maintained, and pitches are set amongst mature trees with most having views over the loch. Boat hire is offered and fishing (coarse and pike) is available. There is a regular bus service from the site entrance.

Open: 31 March to October **Last arrival:** 20.00 **Last departure:** noon

Pitches: 🚐 from £25; 🚚 from £25; ▲ from £15; 25 hardstanding pitches; 10 seasonal pitches

Leisure: 🎣 ⚲

Facilities: 🛁 ⊙ 🎦 ✳ 🕭 🍴 WiFi

Services: 🔌 🗑 🛒 ⛽ 🔒 🦮 🅃

Within 3 miles: ⚘ ∪ ◎ 🏊 🎿 ⓢ

Additional site information: 6 acre site. 🚗 Cars can be parked by caravans and tents. Awnings permitted. Car hire can be arranged.

ALFORD
Map 23 NJ51

Places to visit

Craigievar Castle, ALFORD, AB33 8JF, 01339 883635
www.nts.org.uk/visit/places/craigievar

Haughton House Holiday Park
►►► 78%

tel: 01975 562107 **Montgarrie Road AB33 8NA**
email: enquiries@haughtonhouse.co.uk **web:** www.haughtonhouse.co.uk
dir: *In Alford follow Haughton Country House signs.*

Located on the outskirts of Alford, this site is set within a large country park that has good countryside views. Under the same ownership as Huntly Castle Caravan Park (Huntly), this park receives the same attention to detail to ensure everything is of a high standard; the existing facilities are clean and well maintained. The pitches are set amid mature trees and the tenting area is in the old walled garden. There is plenty to do on site and within the country park which has various activities for children, including a narrow gauge railway that runs to the Grampian Transport Museum in nearby Alford.

Open: March to mid/end October **Last arrival:** 21.00 **Last departure:** noon

Pitches: 🚐 🚚 ▲; 71 hardstanding pitches; 20 seasonal pitches

Leisure: /🛝

Facilities: 🛁 ⊙ 🎦 ✳ 🕭 🍴 🍴 WiFi

Services: 🔌 🗑 🛒 ⛽ 🔒 🅃

Within 3 miles: ⚘ ⚲ ◎ ⓢ

Additional site information: 22 acre site. 🚗 Cars can be parked by caravans and tents. Awnings permitted. No noise after 22.30. Putting green, fishing permits.

BANFF
Map 23 NJ66

Places to visit

Duff House, BANFF, AB45 3SX, 01261 818181
www.historic-scotland.gov.uk

Banff Links Caravan Park
►►►► 86%

tel: 01261 812228 **Inverboyndie AB45 2JJ**
email: banfflinkscaravanpark@btconnect.com **web:** www.banfflinkscaravanpark.co.uk
dir: *From west: A98 onto B9038 signed Whitehills. 2nd right signed Inverboyndie. 4th left to site. From east (Banff): A98, right at brown 'Banff Links Beach' sign.*

This delightful small park, where the family owners are keen that their visitors enjoy their stay, is situated beside the award-winning sandy beach at Banff Links with magnificent views over the Moray coast. Set at sea level, there is direct access to the beach and also a large grass esplanade and play area for children. A pleasant walk on good level paths by the sea will take you to either Banff or the small village of Whitehill, which has a leisure boat harbour. It is ideally located for exploring this lovely coastline. Six static caravans are for hire.

Open: April to October **Last departure:** noon

Pitches: 🚐 🚚 ▲; 10 hardstanding pitches; 10 seasonal pitches

Facilities: 🎦 🕭 ⓢ 🍴 WiFi

Services: 🔌 🗑 🛒 ⛽ ∪ 🔒 🅃

Within 3 miles: ⚘ ⚲ ∪ ◎ 🏊

Additional site information: 5.78 acre site. 🚗 Cars can be parked by caravans and tents. Awnings permitted.

HUNTLY

Places to visit

Leith Hall, Garden & Estate, RHYNIE, AB54 4NQ, 01464 831216
www.nts.org.uk/visit/places/leith-hall

Glenfiddich Distillery, DUFFTOWN, AB55 4DH, 01340 820373
www.glenfiddich.com

LEISURE: 🏊 Indoor swimming pool 🏊 Outdoor swimming pool /🛝 Children's playground 🪁 Kids' club 🎾 Tennis court 🎱 Games room 📺 Separate TV room ⚘ golf course ⛳ Pitch n putt 🛥 Boats for hire 🚲 Bikes for hire 🎬 Cinema 🎵 Entertainment ⚲ Fishing ◎ Mini golf 🏊 Watersports 💪 Gym 🏐 Sports field ∪ Stables
FACILITIES: 🛁 Baths/Shower ⊙ Electric shaver sockets 🎦 Hairdryer ✳ Ice Pack Facility 🛒 Baby facilities 🕭 Disabled facilities ⓢ Shop on site or within 200yds 🍴 BBQ area 🍴 Picnic area WiFi WiFi

HUNTLY   Map 23 NJ53

Premier Park

Huntly Castle Caravan Park
▶▶▶▶▶   90%

tel: 01466 794999 **The Meadow AB54 4UJ**
email: enquiries@huntlycastle.co.uk **web:** www.huntlycastle.co.uk
dir: *From Aberdeen on A96 to Huntly. 0.75 mile after roundabout (on outskirts of Huntly) right towards town centre, left into Riverside Drive.*

A quality parkland site within striking distance of the Speyside Malt Whisky Trail, the beautiful Moray coast and the Cairngorm Mountains. The park provides exceptional toilet facilities, and there are some fully serviced pitches. The attractive town of Huntly is only a five-minute walk away, with its ruined castle plus a wide variety of restaurants and shops.

Open: April to October **Last arrival:** 20.00 **Last departure:** noon
Pitches: 🚐 🚍 ▲; 51 hardstanding pitches; 10 seasonal pitches
Leisure: ⚠
Facilities: 🏠 ⊙ 🏳 ⚙ ☆ 🔦 WiFi
Services: 🔌 🔟 🔋 ⚒ 🔒 Ⓣ
Within 3 miles: ⅃ 🏌 ⓢ

Additional site information: 15 acre site. 🐕 Cars can be parked by caravans and tents. Awnings permitted. No noise after 23.00.

KINTORE   Map 23 NJ71

Places to visit

Pitmedden Garden, PITMEDDEN, AB41 7PD, 01651 842352
www.nts.org.uk/visit/places/pitmedden-garden

Tolquhon Castle, PITMEDDEN, AB41 7LP, 01651 851286
www.historic-scotland.gov.uk

Great for kids: Castle Fraser, KEMNAY, AB51 7LD, 01330 833463
www.nts.org.uk/visit/places/castle-fraser

Hillhead Caravan Park
▶▶▶▶   77%

tel: 01467 632809 **AB51 0YX**
email: enquiries@hillheadcaravan.com **web:** www.hillheadcaravan.com
dir: *From south: A96 at Broomhill Roundabout follow Kintore (and brown camping sign) onto B987. At mini roundabout 1st left, immediately left signed Kemnay. Over A96, straight on at next roundabout, right signed Kintore. Site on right. From north: A96 at roundabout follow Kintore signs onto B987. 5th right into Forest Road. Over A96, 1st left to site on left.*

An attractive, nicely landscaped site, located on the outskirts of Kintore in the valley of the River Dee with excellent access to forest walks and within easy reach of the many attractions in rural Aberdeenshire. The toilet facilities are of a high standard. There are good play facilities for smaller children plus a small café with TV and internet access.

Open: All year **Last arrival:** 21.00 **Last departure:** 13.00
Pitches: 🚐 🚍 ▲; 17 hardstanding pitches; 10 seasonal pitches
Leisure: ⚓
Facilities: 🏠 ⊙ 🏳 ⚙ 🔦 ⓢ 🔋 🗑 WiFi
Services: 🔌 🔟 🔟 ⚒ 🔋 ⊘ Ⓣ
Within 3 miles: ⅃ 🏌

Additional site information: 1.5 acre site. 🐕 Cars can be parked by caravans and tents. Awnings permitted. Caravan storage, accessories shop.

MACDUFF   Map 23 NJ76

Places to visit

Duff House, BANFF, AB45 3SX, 01261 818181
www.historic-scotland.gov.uk

Great for kids: Macduff Marine Aquarium, MACDUFF, AB44 1SL, 01261 833369
www.macduff-aquarium.org.uk

Wester Bonnyton Farm Site
▶▶   68%

tel: 01261 832470 & 07813 443308 **Gamrie AB45 3EP**
email: westerbonnyton@gmail.com **web:** www.westerbonnyton.co.uk
dir: *From A98 (1 mile south of Macduff) take B9031 signed Rosehearty. Site 1.25 miles on right.*

A spacious farm site, with level touring pitches, overlooking the Moray Firth. The small, picturesque fishing villages of Gardenstown and Crovie and the larger town of Macduff, which has a marine aquarium, are all within easy reach. All the touring pitches have good views of the coastline. Families with children are welcome, and there is a play area and play barn.

Open: March to October
Pitches: 🚐 🚍 ▲; 5 hardstanding pitches; 1 seasonal pitch
Leisure: ⚠ ⚓
Facilities: 🏠 ⊙ 🏳 ⓢ 🗑 🗑 WiFi
Services: 🔌 🔟 🔋 🔒
Within 3 miles: ⅃ 🏌 ⚓ 🚶

Additional site information: 8 acre site. 🐕 Cars can be parked by caravans and tents. Awnings permitted.

MINTLAW
Map 23 NJ94

Places to visit

Aberdeenshire Farming Museum, MINTLAW, AB42 5FQ, 01771 624590
www.aberdeenshire.gov.uk/museums

Deer Abbey, OLD DEER
www.historic-scotland.gov.uk

Aden Caravan and Camping Park

►►► 85%

tel: 01771 623460 **Station Road AB42 5FQ**
email: info@adencaravanandcamping.co.uk web: www.adencaravanandcamping.co.uk
dir: *From Mintlaw take A950 signed New Pitsligo and Aden Country Park. Park on left.*

Situated adjacent to the 230-acre Aden Country Park, this is a small tranquil site offering excellent facilities. It is ideally located for visiting the many tourist attractions in this beautiful northeast coastal area. The site is only a short drive from the busy fishing towns of Fraserburgh and Peterhead, and as it is only an hour from Aberdeen's centre; this is an ideal spot for a short stay or a longer holiday, and there is one disabled-friendly static for hire. The adjacent country park plays host to numerous events throughout the year, including pipe band championships, horse events and various ranger-run activities.

Open: April to October **Last arrival:** 20.00 **Last departure:** noon

Pitches: 🚐 from £24; �caravan from £24; ▲ from £6.50; 🛖 see prices below; 31 hardstanding pitches; 14 seasonal pitches

Leisure: /▲\

Facilities: 🛁 ☉ 🝗 ৬ 🎇 WiFi

Services: 🔌 🖥 ↯ 🛒

Within 3 miles: ↳ 🔗 💲

Additional site information: 11.1 acre site. 🐾 Cars can be parked by caravans and tents. Awnings permitted.

Glamping available: 3 wooden pods from £50.

Additional glamping information: Wooden pods sleep up to 4 people. Cars can be parked by pods.

NORTH WATER BRIDGE

Places to visit

Edzell Castle and Garden, EDZELL, DD9 7UE, 01356 648631
www.historic-scotland.gov.uk

NORTH WATER BRIDGE
Map 23 NO66

Dovecot Caravan Park
►►► 77%

tel: 01674 840630 **AB30 1QL**
email: adele@dovecotcaravanpark.co.uk web: www.dovecotcaravanpark.co.uk
dir: *From Laurencekirk on A90, 5 miles, at Edzell Woods sign turn left. Site 500 yards on left.*

A level grassy site in a country area close to the A90, with mature trees screening one side and the River North Esk on the other. The immaculate toilet facilities make this a handy overnight stop in a good touring area.

Open: April to October **Last arrival:** 20.00 **Last departure:** noon

Pitches: 🚐 �caravan ▲; 8 hardstanding pitches; 8 seasonal pitches

Leisure: 🎱

Facilities: 🛁 ☉ 🝗 🎇 ৬ WiFi

Services: 🔌 ↯ 🛒 T

Additional site information: 6 acre site. 🐾 Cars can be parked by caravans and tents. Awnings permitted.

PETERHEAD
Map 23 NK14

Places to visit

Arbuthnot Museum, PETERHEAD, AB42 1QD, 01779 477778
www.aberdeenshire.gov.uk/museums

Lido Caravan Park
►►► 76%

tel: 01779 480205 **South Road AB42 2XX**
email: phd.lido@gmail.com web: www.peterheadlidocaravanpark.co.uk
dir: *From A90 (Aberdeen to Peterhead road) at Invernetty roundabout take A982.*

This small site is located on The Lido with direct access to a small sandy beach with a nice play area and sand dunes. The management team (new in 2018) have added neat hardstanding pitches, new static caravans and the older-style toilets are kept spotlessly clean. Each of the all-electric pitches has a view over Peterhead's busy harbour where there is always some boating activity taking place. The Martine Heritage Centre, a few minutes' walk from the site, has an excellent café.

Open: March to October

Pitches: 🚐 from £19; �caravan from £19; ▲ from £11; 15 hardstanding pitches; 16 seasonal pitches

Facilities: 🛁 ☉ 🝗 🎇 ৬ 💲 WiFi

Services: 🔌 🖥 ↯ 🛒 ⌀

Within 3 miles: ↳ 🔗 ∪ 🚣 🎣 🗓

Additional site information: 25 acre site. 🐾 Cars can be parked by caravans and tents. Awnings permitted.

LEISURE: 🏊 Indoor swimming pool 🏊 Outdoor swimming pool /▲\ Children's playground 👋 Kids' club 🎾 Tennis court 🎱 Games room 📺 Separate TV room ↳ golf course 🏌 Pitch n putt 🚣 Boats for hire 🚲 Bikes for hire 🎬 Cinema 🎭 Entertainment 🎣 Fishing ◎ Mini golf 🏄 Watersports 🏋 Gym 🏐 Sports field ∪ Stables **FACILITIES:** 🛁 Baths/Shower ☉ Electric shaver sockets 🝗 Hairdryer 🎇 Ice Pack Facility 🍼 Baby facilities ৬ Disabled facilities 💲 Shop on site or within 200yds 🍖 BBQ area 🎋 Picnic area WiFi WiFi

PORTSOY
Map 23 NJ56

Places to visit
Duff House, BANFF, AB45 3SX, 01261 818181
www.historic-scotland.gov.uk

Portsoy Links Caravan Park
►►► 76%

tel: 01261 842695 & 842222 **Links Road AB45 2RQ**
email: contact@portsoylinks.org **web:** www.portsoylinks.org
dir: *At Portsoy from A98 into Church Street. 2nd right into Institute Street (follow brown camping sign). At T-junction right, down slope to site.*

Taken into community ownership under the auspices of the Scottish Traditional Boats Festival, this is a lovely links-type site with stunning views across the bay. There is a large, safe, fenced play area for smaller children and the toilet facilities are kept clean and well maintained. Portsoy is a typical small fishing port and has various eateries and shops; it is very convenient for visiting the other small fishing villages on the North East Scotland's Coastal Trail.

Open: All year **Last arrival:** 20.00 **Last departure:** noon

Pitches: * 🚐 from £15; 🚌 from £15; ▲ from £15; 9 hardstanding pitches; 7 seasonal pitches

Leisure: ⚑

Facilities: 🏠 ☉ ⏇ 🕭 🎹 WiFi

Services: 🔌 🔲 🛢

Within 3 miles: 🎣 ⚲ 🛶 💲

Additional site information: 0.8 acre site. 🐕 Cars can be parked by caravans and tents. Awnings permitted. Coastal walks.

STRACHAN

Places to visit
Banchory Museum, BANCHORY, AB31 5SX, 01330 823367
www.aberdeenshire.gov.uk/museums

Crathes Castle Garden & Estate, CRATHES, AB31 5QJ, 01330 844525
www.nts.org.uk/visit/places/crathes-castle

Great for kids: Go Ape Crathes Castle, CRATHES, AB31 5QJ
www.goape.co.uk/crathes-castle

STRACHAN
Map 23 NO69

Feughside Caravan Park
►►►► 85%

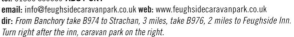

tel: 01330 850669 **AB31 6NT**
email: info@feughsidecaravanpark.co.uk **web:** www.feughsidecaravanpark.co.uk
dir: *From Banchory take B974 to Strachan, 3 miles, take B976, 2 miles to Feughside Inn. Turn right after the inn, caravan park on the right.*

A small, well maintained family-run site, set amongst mature trees and hedges and located five miles from Banchory and with stunning views of Clachnaben hill. The site is ideally suited to those wishing for a peaceful location that is within easy reach of scenic Royal Deeside.

Open: April to October **Last arrival:** 21.00 **Last departure:** noon

Pitches: 🚐 from £25; 🚌 from £25; ▲ from £17; 10 hardstanding pitches; 12 seasonal pitches

Leisure: ⚑

Facilities: 🏠 ☉ ⏇ ❆ 🕭 🎹 WiFi

Services: 🔌 🔲 🛒 🛢 ⊘

Within 3 miles: 🎣 ⚲ 🛶 💲

Additional site information: 5.5 acre site. 🐕 Dogs to be on lead at all times and exercised off park. Cars can be parked by caravans and tents. Awnings permitted. Quiet after 22.00, no open fires.

TURRIFF
Map 23 NJ75

Places to visit
Fyvie Castle, TURRIFF, AB53 8JS, 01651 891266
www.nts.org.uk/visit/places/fyvie-castle

Turriff Caravan Park
►►►► 79%

tel: 01888 562205 & 562943 **Station Road AB53 4ER**
email: info@turriffcaravanpark.com **web:** www.turriffcaravanpark.com
dir: *On A947, south of Turriff.*

Located on the outskirts of Turriff on the site of an old railway station, this site is owned by the local community. The pitches are level and the attractive landscaping is well maintained. The site also has a rally field. There is a large public park close to the site which has a boating pond and a large games park where the annual agricultural show is held. The town is only five minutes' walk through the park and has a good variety of shops. This is an ideal base for touring rural Aberdeenshire and the nearby Moray coastline with its traditional fishing villages.

Open: late March to end October **Last arrival:** 18.00 **Last departure:** 11.00

Pitches: 🚐 from £21.50; 🚌 from £21.50; ▲ from £13; 10 hardstanding pitches; 7 seasonal pitches

Leisure: ⚑ ⚽

Facilities: 🏠 ☉ ⏇ 🕭 🎹 WiFi

Services: 🔌 🔲 🛗 🛢

Within 3 miles: ↕ 🎣 ⚲ ◎ 🛶 💲

Additional site information: 5 acre site. 🐕 Cars can be parked by caravans and tents. Awnings permitted. No music or loud noise after 22.00.

ARGYLL & BUTE

CARRADALE — Map 20 NR83

Carradale Bay Caravan Park

►►► 90%

tel: 01583 431665 **PA28 6QG**
email: info@carradalebay.com **web:** www.carradalebay.com
dir: *A83 from Tarbert towards Campbeltown, left onto B842 (Carradale road), right onto B879. Site in 0.5 mile.*

A beautiful, natural site on the sea's edge with superb views over Kilbrannan Sound to the Isle of Arran. Pitches are landscaped into small bays broken up by shrubs and bushes, and backed by dunes close to the long sandy beach. The toilet facilities are appointed to a very high standard. An environmentally-aware site that requires the use of green toilet chemicals – available on the site. Lodges and static caravans for holiday hire.

Open: April to September **Last arrival:** 22.00 **Last departure:** noon

Pitches: 🚐 🚗 ⛺

Facilities: ⊙ 💇 ❄ ♿ [S] 🪑 [WiFi]

Services: ⚡ 🧺 [T] **Within 3 miles:** ⛳ 🎣 🐎 🏄 ⛵

Additional site information: 8 acre site. 🐕 Cars can be parked by caravans and tents. Awnings permitted.

GLENDARUEL — Map 20 NR98

Places to visit

Benmore Botanic Garden, BENMORE, PA23 8QU, 01369 706261
www.rbge.org.uk

Glendaruel Caravan Park

►►► 83%

tel: 01369 820267 **PA22 3AB**
email: mail@glendaruelcaravanpark.com **web:** www.glendaruelcaravanpark.com
dir: *A83 onto A815 to Strachur, 13 miles to site on A886. By ferry from Gourock to Dunoon take B836, then A886 for approximately 4 miles north. (Note: this route is not recommended for towing vehicles – 1:5 uphill gradient on B836).*

Glendaruel Gardens, with an arboretum, is the peaceful setting for this pleasant, well established wooded site in a valley surrounded by mountains. It is set back from the main road and screened by trees so that a peaceful stay is ensured. It has level grass and hardstanding pitches. A regular local bus service and a ferry at Portavadie (where there are retail outlets and eateries) make a day trip to the Mull of Kintyre a possibility. The Cowal Way, a long distance path, and a national cycle path pass the site. Static caravans and a 'little' camping lodge are for hire.

Open: April to October **Last arrival:** 22.00 **Last departure:** noon

Pitches: 🚐 🚗 ⛺; 15 hardstanding pitches; 12 seasonal pitches

Leisure: ⚽ **Facilities:** ⊙ 💇 ❄ [S] 🍖 🪑 [WiFi]

Services: ⚡ 🧺 🍴 🔒 🍃 [T] **Within 3 miles:** 🎣

Additional site information: 6 acre site. 🐕 Cars can be parked by caravans and tents. Awnings permitted. Sea trout and salmon fishing, woodland walks, 24-hour emergency phone.

OBAN — Map 20 NM82

Places to visit

Dunstaffnage Castle and Chapel, OBAN, PA37 1PZ, 01631 562465
www.historic-scotland.gov.uk

Bonawe Historic Iron Furnace, TAYNUILT, PA35 1JQ, 01866 822432
www.historic-scotland.gov.uk

Great for kids: Scottish Sea Life Sanctuary, BARCALDINE, PA37 1SE, 01631 720386
www.visitsealife.com/oban

Oban Caravan & Camping Park

►►► 84%

tel: 01631 562425 **Gallanachmore Farm, Gallanach Road PA34 4QH**
email: info@obancaravanpark.com **web:** www.obancaravanpark.com
dir: *From Oban centre follow signs for Mull Ferry. After terminal follow Gallanach signs. 2 miles to site.*

Situated two miles from Oban, this lovely site has pleasant terraced areas that are separated by large swathes of well maintained grass and natural landscaping. Many pitches overlook the busy ferry route between Oban and the Isle of Colonsay. The site is convenient for the ferry terminal in Oban, as well as the train and bus stations, making this an ideal site for both main holidays or for shorter stays. The owners have plans to install family rooms together with a new washroom block in the future. Well-equipped camping pods are located in an area that offers privacy.

Open: Easter, April to October (restricted service: Easter to end May and September to October – shop closed) **Last arrival:** 20.00 (later arrivals by prior arrangement) **Last departure:** noon

Pitches: 🚐 from £21; 🚗 from £21; ⛺ from £18; 🛖 see prices below; 40 hardstanding pitches; 10 seasonal pitches

Leisure: 🛝 🎱 📺

Facilities: 🛁 ⊙ 💇 ❄ [S] 🍖 🪑 [WiFi]

Services: ⚡ 🧺 🍴 🚰 🔒 🍃 [T]

Within 3 miles: ⛳ 🎣 🐎 🏄 ⛵ 🎬

Additional site information: 15 acre site. 🐕 Cars can be parked by caravans and tents. Awnings permitted. No commercial vehicles, no noise after 23.00. Indoor kitchen for tent campers, fresh bread available each morning.

Glamping available: Wooden pods from £45. **Changeover days:** Any day

Additional glamping information: Wooden pods (sleep 4) offer electricity, heating, fridge, kettle, microwave, toaster and electric hob. Cars can be parked by pods.

LEISURE: 🏊 Indoor swimming pool 🌊 Outdoor swimming pool 🛝 Children's playground 👋 Kids' club 🎾 Tennis court 🎱 Games room 📺 Separate TV room ⛳ golf course ⛳ Pitch n putt ⛵ Boats for hire 🚲 Bikes for hire 🎬 Cinema 🎵 Entertainment 🎣 Fishing ◎ Mini golf 🏄 Watersports 🏋 Gym ⚽ Sports field 🐎 Stables
FACILITIES: 🛁 Baths/Shower ⊙ Electric shaver sockets 💇 Hairdryer ❄ Ice Pack Facility 👶 Baby facilities ♿ Disabled facilities [S] Shop on site or within 200yds 🍖 BBQ area 🪑 Picnic area [WiFi] WiFi

SOUTH AYRSHIRE

AYR
Map 20 NS32

Places to visit

Robert Burns Birthplace Museum, ALLOWAY, KA7 4PQ, 01292 443700
www.burnsmuseum.org.uk

Great for kids: Heads of Ayr Farm Park, ALLOWAY, KA7 4LD, 01292 441210
www.headsofayrfarmpark.co.uk

Premier Park

Craig Tara Holiday Park
▶▶▶▶▶ 87% HOLIDAY CENTRE

tel: 0800 975 7579 & 01292 265141 **KA7 4LB**
email: craigtara@haven.com **web:** www.haven.com/craigtara
dir: A77 towards Stranraer, 2nd right after Bankfield roundabout. Follow signs for
A719 and park.

This lovely holiday centre on the outskirts of Ayr is set in a sheltered spot on the
coast, with direct access to a small beach. The park has a great family
atmosphere with welcoming staff and entertainment for all ages. The touring
area is in a secluded area, with an amenity block and 40 fully serviced
hardstanding pitches. At the heart of the holiday centre are various large
complexes with show bars, restaurants, takeaways, computer games and slot
machines. There are also good shops, a supermarket with a bakery, and a large
soft play area. The pool complex facilities are excellent with flumes, slides,
splash zones and overhead viewing walkways. There is a regular service bus
to Ayr.

Open: mid March to end October (restricted service: mid March to May and September
to end October – some facilities may be reduced) **Last arrival:** anytime (must be
pre-booked) **Last departure:** 10.00

Pitches: 🚐 🚛, 44 hardstanding pitches

Leisure: 🏊 🎱 🎣 🎵 🎯

Facilities: 🏪 ☺ ♿ 🏧 🌲 WiFi

Services: 🔌 🎫 🍽 🍴 🏪 🔒

Within 3 miles: ✏ ⛳ ⊚ 🎢

Additional site information: 213 acre site. 🐕 Maximum 2 dogs per booking, certain
dog breeds banned. No commercial vehicles, no bookings by persons under 21 years
unless a family booking. Fresh produce from bakery. Nature walks (as part of Nature
Rockz), table tennis, racket sports.

BARRHILL

Places to visit

Bargany Gardens, OLD DAILLY, KA26 9QL, 01465 871249
www.bargany.com

BARRHILL
Map 20 NX28

Barrhill Holiday Park
▶▶▶▶ 82%

tel: 01465 821355 & 07718 389144 **KA26 0PZ**
email: relax@barrhillholidaypark@.com **web:** www.barrhillholidaypark.com
dir: On A714 (Newton Stewart to Girvan road). 1 mile north of Barrhill.

A small, friendly park in a tranquil rural location, screened from the A714 by trees.
The park is terraced and well landscaped, and a high quality amenity block
includes disabled facilities. The local bus to Girvan stops at the site entrance.

Open: March to January **Last arrival:** 22.00 **Last departure:** 10.00

Pitches: * 🚐 from £20; 🚛 from £20; 🏕 from £7; 🏠 see prices below;
30 hardstanding pitches

Leisure: 🎱

Facilities: 🏪 ☺ 🏧 ❄ ♿ 🌲 WiFi

Services: 🔌 🎫 🚰 🔒 T

Within 3 miles: ✏ 🏧

Additional site information: 6 acre site. 🐕 Cars can be parked by caravans and tents.
Awnings permitted. No noise after 23.00.

Glamping available: Wooden pods from £90 with hot tub; £153 for a 2 night stay.

Additional glamping information: Wooden pods (sleeps 5). 5 have hot tubs, 2 have
showers. Communal kitchen. Each pod has toilet, basin, microwave, TV, mini fridge,
kettle, picnic table and fire pit. No glassware permitted in or around hot tubs. Hot tubs
may not be used after 23.00. Minimum stay 2 nights. Cars can be parked by pods.

DUMFRIES & GALLOWAY

ANNAN
Map 21 NY16

Places to visit

Ruthwell Cross, RUTHWELL, 0131 558 9326
www.historic-scotland.gov.uk

Great for kids: Caerlaverock Castle, CAERLAVEROCK, DG1 4RU, 01387 770244
www.historic-scotland.gov.uk

Galabank Caravan & Camping
▶▶ 74%

tel: 01461 203539 & 07999 344520 **North Street DG12 5DQ**
email: margaret.ramage@hotmail.com
dir: Site access via North Street.

A tidy, well-maintained grassy little park with spotless facilities close to the centre
of town but with pleasant rural views, and skirted by the River Annan.

Open: March to October **Last departure:** noon

Pitches: 🚐 from £12.50; 🚛 from £12.50; 🏕 from £9

Facilities: 🏪 ☺ 🏧 🌲

Services: 🔌

Within 3 miles: ♪ ✏ ⛳ 🎢 🏧

Additional site information: 1 acre site. 🐕 🚭 Cars can be parked by caravans and
tents. Awnings permitted. No commercial vehicles. Social club adjacent. Washing
machine and tumble dryer in ladies' block.

PITCHES: 🚐 Caravans 🚛 Motorhomes 🏕 Tents 🏠 Glamping accommodation **SERVICES:** 🔌 Electric hook-up 🎫 Launderette 🍽 Licensed bar
🔒 Calor Gas 🌿 Campingaz T Toilet fluid 🍴 Café/Restaurant 🚰 Fast Food/Takeaway 🔋 Battery charging ⛟ Motorhome service point
* 2019 prices 🚫 No credit or debit cards 🐕 Dogs permitted ⊗ No dogs

BRIGHOUSE BAY — Map 20 NX64

Places to visit

MacLellan's Castle, KIRKCUDBRIGHT, DG6 4JD, 01557 331856
www.historic-scotland.gov.uk

Broughton House & Garden, KIRKCUDBRIGHT, DG6 4JX, 01557 330437
www.nts.org.uk/visit/places/broughton-house

Premier Park

Brighouse Bay Holiday Park
► ► ► ► ► 90%

tel: 01557 870267 **DG6 4TS**
email: info@gillespie-leisure.co.uk **web:** www.gillespie-leisure.co.uk
dir: *From Gatehouse of Fleet take A755 towards Kirkcudbright, onto B727 (signed Borgue). Or from Kirkcudbright take A755 onto B727. Site signed in 3 miles.*

This top class park has a country club feel and enjoys a marvellous coastal setting adjacent to the beach and has superb views. Pitches have been imaginatively sculpted into the meadowland, where stone walls and hedges blend in with the site's mature trees. These features, together with the large range of leisure activities, make this an excellent park for families who enjoy an active holiday. The site has an 18-hole golf course with its own PGA professional. Many of the facilities are at an extra charge. Wooden pods and self-catering units are available for hire.

Open: All year (restricted service: 1 November to 31 December and 1 February to 31 March reduced hours at leisure club (closed throughout January)) **Last arrival:** 20.00 **Last departure:** 11.00

Pitches: * ⬜ from £23.50; ⬜ from £23.50; ⛺ from £12; ⛺ see prices below; 100 hardstanding pitches; 50 seasonal pitches

Leisure: 🏊 ⛰ ⚽ ⛳ 🎣 🏓 ⛹

Facilities: 🛁 ☉ ⬦ ✳ ♿ 🛒 🅿 ⬤ WiFi

Services: ⬤ 🔵 🍴 🍽 ⬛ ⬥ 🔒 ⬦ Ⓣ

Within 3 miles: ∪ ◎

Additional site information: 120 acre site. 🐕 Dogs must be kept on leads. Cars can be parked by caravans and tents. Awnings permitted. No noise after 22.30, no jet skis, 10mph speed limit on site. No open fires or fire pits. Mini golf, outdoor bowling green, jacuzzi, slipway, coarse fishing, sea angling, pony trekking (seasonal), mountain bike trails.

Glamping available: Wooden pods from £47.

Additional glamping information: Wooden pods: own camping equipment required but kettle, microwave and fridge provided. Minimum stay 2 nights. Cars can be parked by pods.

DALBEATTIE — Map 21 NX86

Places to visit

Threave Garden & Estate, CASTLE DOUGLAS, DG7 1RX, 01556 502575
www.nts.org.uk/visit/places/threave-garden

Orchardton Tower, PALNACKIE
www.historic-scotland.gov.uk

Glenearly Caravan Park
► ► ► ► 86%

tel: 01556 611393 **DG5 4NE**
email: glenearlycaravan@btconnect.com **web:** www.glenearlycaravanpark.co.uk
dir: *From Dumfries take A711 towards Dalbeattie. Site entrance after Edingham Farm on right (200 yards before boundary sign).*

An excellent small park set in open countryside with good views of Long Fell, Maidenpap and Dalbeattie Forest. The park is located in 84 acres of farmland which has been carefully managed over the years to provide a peaceful and secluded location for a tranquil holiday. The attention to detail is excellent with neatly kept grass, well tended borders and an excellent amenity block. There's a fishing lochan and woodland plus a wildlife walk. Dalbeattie is a leisurely 10-minute walk away and the local bus passes the end of the farm road. The beautiful Solway coast is just five minutes away by car with Rockcliffe, Colvend and Kippford interesting places to explore. For the more adventurous, the mountain bike trails are numerous.

Open: All year **Last arrival:** 19.00 **Last departure:** noon

Pitches: ⬜ from £20; ⬜ from £20; ⛺ from £20; 33 hardstanding pitches; 10 seasonal pitches

Leisure: ⛰ ⚽ 🎣

Facilities: 🛁 ☉ ⬦ ✳ ♿ WiFi

Services: ⬤ 🔵 ⬛ ⬥ 🔒

Within 3 miles: 🎣 ∪ ◎ ⬤ ⬤ 🛒

Additional site information: 10 acre site. 🐕 Cars can be parked by caravans and tents. Awnings permitted. No commercial vehicles. Table tennis, pool table.

LEISURE: 🏊 Indoor swimming pool ⬤ Outdoor swimming pool ⛰ Children's playground 🛝 Kids' club ⬤ Tennis court ⚽ Games room ⬜ Separate TV room ⛳ golf course 🏌 Pitch n putt ⬤ Boats for hire 🚲 Bikes for hire 🎬 Cinema 🎵 Entertainment 🎣 Fishing ◎ Mini golf ⬤ Watersports 🏋 Gym ⬤ Sports field ∪ Stables
FACILITIES: 🛁 Baths/Shower ☉ Electric shaver sockets ⬦ Hairdryer ✳ Ice Pack Facility ⬤ Baby facilities ♿ Disabled facilities 🛒 Shop on site or within 200yds ⬛ BBQ area 🅿 Picnic area WiFi WiFi

ECCLEFECHAN — Map 21 NY17

Places to visit

Robert Burns House, DUMFRIES, DG1 2PS, 01387 255297
www.dumgal.gov.uk

Old Bridge House Museum, DUMFRIES, DG2 7BE, 01387 256904
www.dumgal.gov.uk

Great for kids: Dumfries Museum & Camera Obscura, DUMFRIES, DG2 7SW, 01387 253374, www.dumgal.gov.uk

Premier Park

Hoddom Castle Caravan Park 🛖

►►►►► 84%

tel: 01576 300251 **Hoddom DG11 1AS**
email: enquiries@hoddomcastle.co.uk **web:** www.hoddomcastle.co.uk
dir: *M74 junction 19, B725 signed Ecclefechan. At next roundabout left onto B7076. Right at crossroads in Ecclefechan, follow site signs. Left at T-junction onto B723. Right onto B725 to site. Or from Annan on B721 take B723 signed Lockerbie and follow site signs.*

A lovely, peaceful family park located close to Annan, with its large range of shops and eateries. There are three amenity blocks, one is adjacent to the reception in part of the old castle buildings. There are extensive grounds, with many walks including the Annan Way which borders the River Annan. The park is neatly divided into statics, seasonal tourers and touring pitches with a large area for tents, plus seven attractive wooden 'chill' pods and four Kelo huts for hire. Fishing, a 9-hole golf course and a large children's play area are available; the small restaurant and café are open daily.

Open: Easter or April to October **Last arrival:** 20.00 **Last departure:** 13.00

Pitches: 🚐 from £20; 🚌 from £20; ⛺ from £15; 🛖 see prices below; 63 hardstanding pitches; 94 seasonal pitches

Leisure: 🛝 🏓 🎣 🎭 🪶

Facilities: 🛁 😊 💨 ❄ ♿ [$] 🍖 ⛱

Services: 🔌 🧺 🍷 🍴 🍔 ⤓ 🛢 [T]

Within 3 miles: 🎯

Additional site information: 28 acre site. 🐕 Cars can be parked by caravans and tents. Awnings permitted. No electric scooters, no gazebos, no fires, no noise after midnight.

Glamping available: Wooden pods from £47; Kelo huts from £62.

Additional glamping information: Dogs permitted in some pods and Kelo huts only. Cars can be parked by pods and huts.

GATEHOUSE OF FLEET — Map 20 NX55

Places to visit

MacLellan's Castle, KIRKCUDBRIGHT, DG6 4JD, 01557 331856
www.historic-scotland.gov.uk

Cairnsmore of Fleet National Nature Reserve, GATEHOUSE OF FLEET, DG7 2BP, 01557 814435
www.nnr-scotland.org.uk/cairnsmore-of-fleet

Premier Park

Auchenlarie Holiday Park 🛖

►►►►► 90% HOLIDAY CENTRE

tel: 01556 506200 **DG7 2EX**
email: enquiries@auchenlarie.co.uk **web:** www.swalwellholidaygroup.co.uk
dir: *Direct access from A75, 5 miles west of Gatehouse of Fleet.*

A well-organised family park set on cliffs overlooking Wigtown Bay, with its own sandy beach. The tenting area, on sloping grassland surrounded by mature trees, has its own sanitary facilities, while the marked caravan pitches are in paddocks, with open views and the provision of high quality toilets. The leisure centre includes a swimming pool, gym, solarium and sports hall; there's an entertainment suite with live cabaret acts, and the Lavender Room offers beauty treatments and massages. There are static caravans and lodges to rent – five have hot tubs.

Open: mid February to October **Last arrival:** 20.00 **Last departure:** noon

Pitches: 🚐 from £22; 🚌 from £22; ⛺ from £22; 🛖 see prices below; 52 hardstanding pitches

Leisure: 🏊 🛝 ✋ 🏓 🎭 🪶 🏋 ⚽

Facilities: 🛁 😊 💨 ❄ ♿ [$] 🍖 ⛱ 🚼 [WiFi]

Services: 🔌 🧺 🍷 🍴 🍔 🔋 ⤓ 🛢 🔥 [T]

Within 3 miles: 🎣 🐎 🎯

Additional site information: 32 acre site. 🐕 Crazy golf, children's entertainment.

Glamping available: Swift S-pods from £45. **Changeover days:** Any day

Additional glamping information: Cars can be parked by pods.

Anwoth Caravan Site

►►►► 85%

tel: 01557 814333 & 01556 506200 **DG7 2JU**
email: enquiries@auchenlarie.co.uk **web:** www.swalwellholidaygroup.co.uk
dir: *From A75 into Gatehouse of Fleet, site on right towards Stranraer. Signed from town centre.*

A very high quality park in a peaceful sheltered setting within easy walking distance of the village, ideally placed for exploring the scenic hills, valleys and coastline. Grass, hardstanding and fully serviced pitches are available and guests may use the leisure facilities at the sister site, Auchenlarie Holiday Park.

Open: March to October **Last arrival:** 20.00 **Last departure:** noon

Pitches: 🚐 from £22; 🚌 from £22; ⛺ from £22; 13 hardstanding pitches

Facilities: 🛁 😊 💨 ❄ ♿ ⛱ [WiFi]

Services: 🔌 🧺 🛢 🔥 **Within 3 miles:** 🎣 🪶 [$]

Additional site information: 2 acre site. 🐕 Cars can be parked by caravans and tents. Awnings permitted.

PITCHES: 🚐 Caravans 🚌 Motorhomes ⛺ Tents 🛖 Glamping accommodation **SERVICES:** 🔌 Electric hook-up 🧺 Launderette 🍷 Licensed bar 🛢 Calor Gas 🔥 Campingaz [T] Toilet fluid 🍴 Café/Restaurant 🍔 Fast Food/Takeaway 🔋 Battery charging ⤓ Motorhome service point
* 2019 prices 💳 No credit or debit cards 🐕 Dogs permitted 🚫 No dogs

GRETNA   Map 21 NY36

Places to visit

Carlisle Cathedral, CARLISLE, CA3 8TZ, 01228 548151
www.carlislecathedral.org.uk

Tullie House Museum & Art Gallery Trust, CARLISLE, CA3 8TP, 01228 618718
www.tulliehouse.co.uk

Great for kids: Carlisle Castle, CARLISLE, CA3 8UR, 01228 591922
www.english-heritage.org.uk/daysout/properties/carlisle-castle

Braids Caravan Park
▶▶▶▶ 78%

tel: 01461 337409 **Annan Road DG16 5DQ**
email: enquiries@thebraidscaravanpark.co.uk **web:** www.thebraidscaravanpark.co.uk
dir: *On B721, 0.5 mile from village on right, towards Annan.*

A very well-maintained park conveniently located on the outskirts of Gretna village. Within walking distance is Gretna Gateway Outlet Village, and nearby is Gretna Green with the World Famous Old Blacksmith's Shop. It proves a convenient stop-over for anyone travelling to and from the north of Scotland or Northern Ireland (via the ferry at Stranraer). The park has first-class toilet facilities and generously-sized all-weather pitches. Please note that tents are not accepted. A rally field and a meeting room are available.

Open: All year **Last arrival:** 20.00 (19.00 in winter) **Last departure:** noon

Pitches: * 🚐 from £20; 🚃 from £20; 42 hardstanding pitches

Facilities: 🏠 ⊙ 🇫 ✳ 🔥 WiFi

Services: 🔌 🗓 ⬆ 🔒 T

Within 3 miles: Ⓢ

Additional site information: 5 acre site. 🐕 Cars can be parked by caravans. Awnings permitted.

King Robert the Bruce's Cave Caravan & Camping Park
▶▶▶▶ 78%

tel: 01461 800285 & 07779 138694 **Cove Estate, Kirkpatrick Fleming DG11 3AT**
email: enquiries@brucescave.co.uk **web:** www.brucescave.co.uk
dir: *Exit A74(M) junction 21, follow Kirkpatrick Fleming signs, north through village, pass Station Inn, left at Bruce's Court. Over rail crossing to site.*

The lovely wooded grounds of an old castle and mansion are the setting for this pleasant park. The mature woodland is a haven for wildlife; there is a riverside walk to Robert the Bruce's Cave and on-site coarse fishing is available. A toilet block with en suite facilities is especially useful to families. The site is convenient for the A74(M) and there is a good local bus service available nearby; the site is on a National Cycle Route.

Open: April to November (restricted service: November – shop closed, water restrictions)
Last arrival: 22.00 **Last departure:** 16.00

Pitches: * 🚐 from £17; 🚃 from £17; ⛺ from £13; 10 hardstanding pitches; 60 seasonal pitches

Leisure: 🎡 🔍 ⚽ ✿

Facilities: 🏠 ⊙ 🇫 ✳ 🔥 Ⓢ 🍖 🪑 WiFi

Services: 🔌 🗓 ⬆ ⬆ 🔒 🧹 T

Within 3 miles: Ⓤ ≋

Additional site information: 80 acre site. 🐕 Dogs must be kept on leads at all times. Cars can be parked by caravans and tents. Awnings permitted. No noise after 23.00. First aid available.

KIRKCUDBRIGHT   Map 20 NX65

Places to visit

The Stewartry Museum, KIRKCUDBRIGHT, DG6 4AQ, 01557 331643
www.dumgal.gov.uk

Tolbooth Art Centre, KIRKCUDBRIGHT, DG6 4JL, 01557 331556
www.dumgal.gov.uk

Great for kids: Broughton House & Garden, KIRKCUDBRIGHT, DG6 4JX, 01557 330437
www.nts.org.uk/visit/places/broughton-house

Premier Park

Seaward Holiday Park
▶▶▶▶▶ 85%

tel: 01557 870267 **Dhoon Bay DG6 4TJ**
email: info@gillespie-leisure.co.uk **web:** www.gillespie-leisure.co.uk
dir: *A711 to Kirkcudbright. In Kirkcudbright right onto A755 signed Borgue and Gatehouse of Fleet. Left onto B727 signed Borgue. Through Borgue to The Dhoon, site on left.*

An attractive park with outstanding views over Kirkcudbright Bay which forms part of the Dee Estuary. Access to a sandy cove with rock pools is just across the road. Facilities are well organised and neatly kept, and the park offers a very peaceful atmosphere. The leisure facilities at the other Gillespie Parks are available to visitors at Seaward Holiday Park. There are five static homes and two mini lodges for hire.

Open: March to October (restricted service: March to Spring bank holiday and September to October – swimming pool closed) **Last arrival:** 20.00
Last departure: 11.00

Pitches: * 🚐 from £22; 🚃 from £22; ⛺ from £18.50; 🏠 see prices below; 20 hardstanding pitches; 6 seasonal pitches

Leisure: ≋ 🎡 🔍

Facilities: 🏠 ⊙ 🇫 ✳ 🔥 Ⓢ 🛒 WiFi

Services: 🔌 🗓 ⬆ 🔒 🧹 T

Within 3 miles: ↓ 🎣 Ⓤ ◎

Additional site information: 23 acre site. 🐕 Cars can be parked by caravans and tents. Awnings permitted. No noise after 22.30, 10mph speed limit on site. No open fires or fire pits. No children in play area after 22.30. Sea angling.

Glamping available: Mini lodges from £49.

Additional glamping information: Mini lodges: own camping equipment required. Minimum stay 2 nights. No pets allowed. Cars can be parked by lodges.

LANGHOLM   Map 21 NY38

Places to visit

Hermitage Castle, HERMITAGE, TD9 0LU, 01387 376222
www.historic-scotland.gov.uk

Ewes Water Caravan & Camping Park
▶▶ 67%

tel: 013873 80386 **Milntown DG13 0BG**
dir: *Accessed directly from A7, approximately 0.5 mile north of Langholm. Site in Langholm Rugby Club.*

Situated in a very convenient location on the A7 and on the banks of the River Esk, this small, attractive park lies in a sheltered wooded valley close to an unspoilt Borders' town. There is a large play area for games.

Open: April to September **Last departure:** noon

Pitches: 🚐 🚍 ▲

Facilities: ☺ ✳ ও ☷ ⊓

Services: 🔌 🔋 🔒 🗑

Within 3 miles: ⚲ ◢ ⑤

Additional site information: 2 acre site. 🐕 ⊗ Cars can be parked by caravans and tents. Awnings permitted. Large play area.

LOCKERBIE

See Ecclefechan

PALNACKIE   Map 21 NX85

Places to visit

Orchardton Tower, PALNACKIE,
www.historic-scotland.gov.uk

Threave Garden & Estate, CASTLE DOUGLAS, DG7 1RX, 01556 502575
www.nts.org.uk/visit/places/threave-garden

Barlochan Caravan Park
▶▶▶ 80%

tel: 01557 870267 **DG7 1PF**
email: info@gillespie-leisure.co.uk **web:** www.gillespie-leisure.co.uk
dir: *On A711 (Dalbeattie to Auchencairn road). Site signed before Palnackie.*

This is a lovely small caravan site situated within a short drive of the county town of Dalbeattie. It is ideally situated for exploring this particularly attractive area. The

site has a number of static homes set on level terraces, with mature planting, whilst the caravan and camping pitches are located on the lower area, near the outdoor heated pool. There are hardstanding pitches, grass pitches with electricty for tents and two wooden pods. The site is part of the Gillespie Group and customers can use the facilities at their other sites.

Open: April to October (restricted service: April to Spring bank holiday and September to October – swimming pool closed) **Last arrival:** 20.00 **Last departure:** 11.30

Pitches: 🚐 from £20.50; 🚍 from £20.50; ▲ from £17; 🛖 see prices below; 16 hardstanding pitches; 2 seasonal pitches

Leisure: 🏊 🎠 🎣 ☐ 🎱 ⚽

Facilities: 🚿 🅿 ✳ ও ⑤ 🚿 🛒 WiFi

Services: 🔌 🔋 🔋 🔒 🗑 T

Within 3 miles: ⚲ ◎

Additional site information: 9 acre site. 🐕 Cars can be parked by caravans and tents. Awnings permitted. No noise afrer 23.00. Family games and TV room.

Glamping available: 2 wooden pods from £42 (children over 5 £5, dogs £3).

Additional glamping information: Cars can be parked by pods.

PARTON   Map 20 NX67

Places to visit

Throave Garden & Estate, CASTLE DOUGLAS, DG7 1RX, 01556 502575
www.nts.org.uk/visit/places/threave-garden

Threave Castle, CASTLE DOUGLAS, DG7 1TJ, 07711 223101
www.historic-scotland.gov.uk

Loch Ken Holiday Park
▶▶▶▶ 87%

tel: 01644 470282 **DG7 3NE**
email: office@lochkenholidaypark.co.uk **web:** www.lochkenholidaypark.co.uk
dir: *On A713, north of Parton. Site on main road (Note: it is advisable not to use sat nav).*

Run with energy, enthusiasm and commitment by the hands-on Bryson family, this busy and popular park, with a natural emphasis on water activities, is set on the eastern shores of Loch Ken. With superb views, it is in a peaceful and beautiful spot adjacent to the RSPB Ken Dee Marshes reserve, with direct access to the loch for fishing and boat launching. It is also on the Galloway Red Kite Trail. The park offers a variety of watersports (canoeing, sailing, water skiing) as well as farm visits and nature trails.

Open: February to mid November (restricted service: February to March (except Easter) and November – reduced shop hours) **Last departure:** noon

Pitches: 🚐 🚍 ▲; 20 hardstanding pitches; 15 seasonal pitches

Leisure: 🖐 🎣 🎵 ⚽

Facilities: ☺ 🅿 ✳ ও ⑤ 🛒 ⊓ WiFi

Services: 🔌 🔋 🔋 🔒 🗑 T

Within 3 miles: ◢ 🚣 🎣

Additional site information: 15 acre site. 🐕 Cars can be parked by caravans and tents. Awnings permitted. No noise after 22.00. Boat and canoe hire.

PORT WILLIAM Map 20 NX34

Places to visit

Glenluce Abbey, GLENLUCE, DG8 0AF, 01581 300541
www.historic-scotland.gov.uk

Whithorn Priory and Museum, WHITHORN, DG8 8PY, 01988 500700
www.historic-scotland.gov.uk

Kings Green Caravan Site

►►► 81%

tel: 01988 700489 & 700711 **South Street DG8 9SG**
web: www.kingsgreencaravanpark.com
dir: *Direct access from A747 at junction with B7085 towards Whithorn.*

Located on the edge of Port William, with beautiful views across Luce Bay as far as the Isle of Man, this is a community-run site which offers good facilities and large grass pitches, with direct access to the pebble shore where otters have been seen. The road which runs along the coast is relatively traffic free so does not detract from the tranquillity of this small site. Two public boat launches are available. There are several good shops in the village and a local bus, with links to Whithorn, Garlieston and Newton Stewart, runs past the site.

Open: mid March to October **Last arrival:** 20.00 **Last departure:** noon

Pitches: 🚐 from £15; 🚌 from £15; ⛺ from £12

Facilities: 🛁 🔌 💨 ♿ $ 🍖 🧺 [WiFi]

Services: 🔧 🧼

Within 3 miles: ⛳ 🎣 🌊

Additional site information: 3 acre site. 🐕 Cars can be parked by caravans and tents. Awnings permitted. No golf, no fireworks. Free book lending.

SANDHEAD Map 20 NX04

Places to visit

Glenwhan Gardens, STRANRAER, DG9 8PH, 01581 400222
www.glenwhangardens.co.uk

Great for kids: Castle Kennedy Gardens, STRANRAER, DG9 8SL, 01776 702024
www.castlekennedygardens.com

Sands of Luce Holiday Park

►►►► 90%

tel: 01776 830456 **Sands of Luce DG9 9JN**
email: info@sandsofluceholidaypark.co.uk **web:** www.sandsofluceholidaypark.co.uk
dir: *From south and east: left from A75 onto B7084 signed Drummore. Site signed at junction with A716. From north: A77 through Stranraer towards Portpatrick, 2 miles, follow A716 signed Drummore, site signed in 5 miles.*

This is a large, well-managed holiday park overlooking Luce Bay. It has a private boat launch and direct access to a wide sandy beach, which proves popular with kite surfers. The Lighthouse is a truly upmarket restaurant and bar with space for live entertainment. Attached to the Lighthouse is the reception, and the staff at the bar can also handle arrivals and other enquiries; this arrangement significantly extends the checking in times. A wide range of entertainment, listed on daily planners, is on offer and includes kite flying, kite surfing, foraging and cooking, and entertainers for both adults and children. There is a regular bus that passes the park entrance, and Stranraer, the Mull of Galloway or Port Logan Botanical Gardens are not far away by car.

Open: March to January (restricted service: November to January – toilet block and shower closed) **Last arrival:** 20.00 **Last departure:** noon

Pitches: 🚐 from £20; 🚌 from £20; ⛺ from £10; 20 hardstanding pitches

Leisure: 🛝 🎱 🎭 ⚽

Facilities: 🛁 🔌 💨 ❄ ♿ $ 🍖 🧺 [WiFi]

Services: 🔧 🧼 🍷 🍽 🔥 🔋 🚽

Within 3 miles: ⛳ 🎣 🌊 ⛵

Additional site information: 30 acre site. 🐕 Owners must clear up after their dogs. Cars can be parked by caravans and tents. Awnings permitted. No quad bikes. Boat launching and storage.

SANDYHILLS Map 21 NX85

Places to visit

Threave Garden & Estate, CASTLE DOUGLAS, DG7 1RX, 01556 502575
www.nts.org.uk/visit/places/threave-garden

Orchardton Tower, PALNACKIE
www.historic-scotland.gov.uk

Great for kids: Threave Castle, CASTLE DOUGLAS, DG7 1TJ, 07711 223101
www.historic-scotland.gov.uk

Sandyhills Bay Holiday Park

►►►► 80%

tel: 01557 870267 **DG5 4NY**
email: info@gillespie-leisure.co.uk **web:** www.gillespie-leisure.co.uk
dir: *On A710, 7 miles from Dalbeattie, 6.5 miles from Kirkbean.*

A well maintained park in a superb location beside a beach, and close to many attractive villages. The level, grassy site is sheltered by woodland, and the south-facing Sandyhills Bay and beach, with their caves and rock pools provide endless entertainment for all the family. The leisure facilities at Brighouse Bay are available to visitors to Sandyhills Bay. Two wooden pods and two wooden wigwams are on offer.

Open: April to October **Last arrival:** 20.00 **Last departure:** 11.30

Pitches: 🚐 from £21; 🚌 from £21; ⛺ from £17.50; 🛖 see prices below; 5 hardstanding pitches

Leisure: 🛝

Facilities: 🛁 🔌 💨 ❄ $ 🍖 🧺 [WiFi]

Services: 🔧 🧼 🔥 🔋 🛒 🍃 [T]

Within 3 miles: ⛳ 🎣

Additional site information: 15 acre site. 🐕 Cars can be parked by caravans and tents. Awnings permitted. No motorised scooters, jet skis or own quad bikes. No noise after midnight, no open fires.

Glamping available: Wooden pods from £47; wooden wigwams from £45.

Additional glamping information: Wooden pods and wooden wigwams offer kettle, microwave, fridge with freezer compartment, toaster. Wooden wigwams also offer TV and are dog friendly (£3 a night). Cars can be parked by pods and wigwams.

LEISURE: 🏊 Indoor swimming pool 🏖 Outdoor swimming pool 🛝 Children's playground ✋ Kids' club 🎾 Tennis court 🎱 Games room 📺 Separate TV room ⛳ golf course 🏌 Pitch n putt ⛵ Boats for hire 🚲 Bikes for hire 🎬 Cinema 🎭 Entertainment 🎣 Fishing ◎ Mini golf 🌊 Watersports 🏋 Gym ⚽ Sports field 🐎 Stables
FACILITIES: 🛁 Baths/Shower 🔌 Electric shaver sockets 💨 Hairdryer ❄ Ice Pack Facility 🍼 Baby facilities ♿ Disabled facilities $ Shop on site or within 200yds 🍖 BBQ area 🧺 Picnic area [WiFi] WiFi

STRANRAER — Map 20 NX06

Places to visit

Glenwhan Gardens, STRANRAER, DG9 8PH, 01581 400222
www.glenwhangardens.co.uk

Great for kids: Castle Kennedy Gardens, STRANRAER, DG9 8SL, 01776 702024
www.castlekennedygardens.com

Aird Donald Caravan Park

►►►► 82%

tel: 01776 702025 **London Road DG9 8RN**
email: enquiries@aird-donald.co.uk **web:** www.aird-donald.co.uk
dir: *From A75 left on entering Stranraer (signed). Opposite school, site 300 yards.*

A spacious touring site set behind mature trees and within a five-minute walk of Stranraer town centre at the head of Loch Ryan. It is an ideal base to tour the 'Rhins of Galloway', to visit Port Logan Botanic Gardens (half an hour's drive) or the Mull of Galloway Lighthouse (a 45-minute drive). It provides a very convenient stopover for the Cairnryan ferry to Ireland, but there's plenty to do in the area if staying longer. A 25-pitch rally field is available.

Open: All year except 2 weeks at Christmas and New Year (restricted service: October to March – tents not accepted) **Last arrival:** 22.00 **Last departure:** 11.00

Pitches: * 🚐 from £17; 🚌 from £17; ⛺ from £8; 24 hardstanding pitches

Facilities: 🛁 ☺ 💨 ♿ [WiFi]

Services: 🔌 🧺 🔋 🚰 🛢 🔥

Within 3 miles: ⛳ 🎣 🐴 🌊 🏄 🎦 🛍

Additional site information: 12 acre site. 🐕 🚫💳 Cars can be parked by caravans and tents. Awnings permitted. No commercial vehicles.

WIGTOWN — Map 20 NX45

Places to visit

Whithorn Priory and Museum, WHITHORN, DG8 8PY, 01988 500700
www.historic-scotland.gov.uk

Drumroamin Farm Camping & Touring Site

►►► 91%

tel: 01988 840613 & 07752 471456 **1 South Balfern DG8 9DB**
email: enquiry@drumroamin.co.uk **web:** www.drumroamin.co.uk
dir: *A75 towards Newton Stewart, onto A714 for Wigtown. Left on B7005 through Bladnock, A746 through Kirkinner. Take B7004 signed Garlieston, 2nd left opposite Kilsture Forest, site 0.75 mile at end of lane.*

Located near Wigtown and Newton Stewart, this is an easily accessible site for those wishing to stay in a rural location; it is an open and spacious site overlooking Wigtown Bay and the Galloway Hills. There is a large and separate tent field with a well-equipped day room, while the touring pitches can easily accommodate rally events. The toilet and other facilities are maintained in an exemplary manner. The sheltered camp kitchen proves very popular especially in adverse weather; a drive-through motorhome service point is also available. The RSPB Crook of Baldoon reserve is a 10-minute walk away. There is a good bus service at the top of the road which goes to Newton Stewart, Wigtown and Whithorn. Two of the three statics on site are for hire.

Open: All year **Last arrival:** 21.00 **Last departure:** noon

Pitches: * 🚐 from £20; 🚌 from £20; ⛺ from £17

Leisure: 🛝 🎾

Facilities: 🛁 ☺ 💨 ❄ ♿ 🍖 🪑 [WiFi]

Services: 🔌 🧺 🔋 🚰

Within 3 miles: ⛳ 🎣 🛍

Additional site information: 5 acre site. 🐕 Dogs must be on leads at all times. Cars can be parked by caravans and tents. Awnings permitted. No fires, no noise after 22.00. Ball games area.

WEST DUNBARTONSHIRE

BALLOCH — Map 20 NS38

Places to visit

Loch Lomond Bird of Prey Centre, BALLOCH, G83 8QL, 01389 729239
www.llbopc.co.uk

The Tall Ship at Riverside, GLASGOW, G3 8RS, 0141 357 3699
www.thetallship.com

Great for kids: Loch Lomond Sea Life Aquarium, BALLOCH, G83 8QL, 01389 721500
www.visitsealife.com/loch-lomond

Premier Park

Lomond Woods Holiday Park 🛖

►►►►► 84%

tel: 01389 755000 **Old Luss Road G83 8QP**
email: lomondwoods@woodleisure.co.uk **web:** www.woodleisure.co.uk
dir: *From A82, 17 miles north of Glasgow, take A811 (Stirling to Balloch road). Left at 1st roundabout, follow holiday park signs, 150 yards on left.*

This site is ideally placed on the southern end of Loch Lomond, the UK's largest inland water and a designated National Park. This site has something to suit all tastes from the most energetic visitor to those who just wish to relax. Fully serviced pitches are available and there are three family rooms. There are loch cruises and boats to hire, plus retail outlets, superstores and eateries within easy walking distance. A drive or cycle ride along Loch Lomond reveals breathtaking views. There are two large boat storage areas. Please note that this site does not accept tents. Holiday caravans and lodges and three camping pods are available to let.

Open: All year **Last arrival:** 20.00 **Last departure:** noon

Pitches: 🚐 🚌 🛖; 115 hardstanding pitches; 55 seasonal pitches

Leisure: 🛝 🎾 🎮

Facilities: 🛁 ☺ 💨 ❄ ♿ 🛍 🪑 [WiFi]

Services: 🔌 🧺 🔋 🚰 🛢 [T]

Within 3 miles: ⛳ 🎣 🐴 🎯 🌊 🏄

Additional site information: 13 acre site. 🐕 Cars can be parked by caravans. Awnings permitted. No jet skis, no commercial vehicles, no boats. Table tennis.

Glamping available: Wooden pods; en suite pods. **Changeover days:** Any day

Additional glamping information: Cars can be parked by pods.

PITCHES: 🚐 Caravans 🚌 Motorhomes ⛺ Tents 🛖 Glamping accommodation **SERVICES:** 🔌 Electric hook-up 🧺 Launderette 🍷 Licensed bar 🛢 Calor Gas 🔥 Campingaz [T] Toilet fluid 🍽 Café/Restaurant 🍔 Fast Food/Takeaway 🔋 Battery charging 🚰 Motorhome service point
* 2019 prices 🚫💳 No credit or debit cards 🐕 Dogs permitted 🚫🐕 No dogs

FIFE

ST ANDREWS
Map 21 NO51

Places to visit

St Andrews Castle, ST ANDREWS, KY16 9AR, 01334 477196
www.historic-scotland.gov.uk

British Golf Museum, ST ANDREWS, KY16 9AB, 01334 460046
www.britishgolfmuseum.co.uk

Great for kids: St Andrews Aquarium, ST ANDREWS, KY16 9AS, 01334 474786
www.standrewsaquarium.co.uk

Platinum Park

Cairnsmill Holiday Park
▶▶▶▶▶

tel: 01334 473604 **Largo Road KY16 8NN**
email: cairnsmill@aol.com **web:** www.cairnsmill.co.uk
dir: *A915 from St Andrews towards Lathones. In approximately 2 miles, site on right.*

Hidden behind mature trees and hedging in open countryside on the outskirts of the historic university town of St Andrews, this top quality holiday park is ideally placed for visiting the nearby town and to explore further afield in Fife or across the Tay Bridge to the city of Dundee and beyond. The facilities on offer at this park are simply excellent and include a swimming pool complex, bar and café, games room and a soft play area, in addition to the various play areas located throughout the park. There is a small fishing lochan with a walkway leading towards the town and the botanical gardens. The toilet facilities are first class with two blocks for the touring area and a separate block for the tent field. The six rooms in a bunkhouse means that extended family and friends can holiday together. The local bus service stops at the park entrance.

Open: All year (restricted service: winter – prior bookings only) **Last arrival:** flexible
Last departure: 11.00

Pitches: * 🚐 from £28; 🚐 from £26; ▲ from £9 🏠; 33 hardstanding pitches; 24 seasonal pitches

---

Leisure: 🏊 🎣 🔨 ▭ 🎵 ⛳ Spa **Facilities:** ☺ ☂ ✳ ♿ 🏠 🚾 🏖 🚮 WiFi
Services: 🔌 🗑 🕳 🍴 🛋 🔼 💼 🌿 T
Within 3 miles: ⚓ ∪ ◎ 🚤 ⚓ 🎯

Additional site information: 27 acre site. 🐕 Cars can be parked by caravans and tents. Awnings permitted. No noise after midnight. 1 car per pitch. Electric car hire (seasonal). Car hire can be arranged.

Glamping available: 2 wooden pods. **Changeover days:** Any day

Additional glamping information: Wooden pods (sleep 4) offer fridge, TV, microwave, toaster and kettle.

Platinum Park

Craigtoun Meadows Holiday Park
▶▶▶▶▶

tel: 01334 475959 **Mount Melville KY16 8PQ**
email: info@craigtounmeadows.co.uk **web:** www.craigtounmeadows.co.uk
dir: *M90 junction 8, A91 to St Andrews. Just after Guardbridge right for Strathkinness. At 2nd crossroads left for Craigtoun.*

Craigtoun Meadows is only a short drive from the centre of St Andrews which has numerous tourist attractions, from historic buildings, harbour aquarium and

---

LEISURE: 🏊 Indoor swimming pool 🏊 Outdoor swimming pool 🛝 Children's playground 🎣 Kids' club 🎾 Tennis court 🔨 Games room ▭ Separate TV room
⛳ golf course ⛳ Pitch n putt 🚣 Boats for hire 🚲 Bikes for hire 🎬 Cinema 🎵 Entertainment 🎣 Fishing ◎ Mini golf 🏄 Watersports 🏋 Gym ⚽ Sports field ∪ Stables
FACILITIES: 🛁 Baths/Shower ☺ Electric shaver sockets ✂ Hairdryer ✳ Ice Pack Facility 👶 Baby facilities ♿ Disabled facilities 🏪 Shop on site or within 200yds
🍖 BBQ area 🏕 Picnic area WiFi WiFi

the wide, sandy beach where the running scene from *Chariots of Fire* was filmed. The site is set in part of the Craigtoun Estate and the holiday homes and touring area are separated by mature woodland and shrubs. The grounds are very well maintained and a large area of woodland has been set aside as a natural habitat for wildlife, and deer and red squirrels are seen regularly. The well maintained amenity block is centrally located and provides private facilities, including spacious showers and baths. The pitches are very large, fully serviced and are exceptionally well spaced. Two wooden pods, in a lovely setting, are available for hire. St Andrews is 'the home of golf' so the numerous courses in the area are a challenge for any golfer.

Craigtoun Meadows Holiday Park

Open: 15 March to October (restricted service: March to Easter and September to October – shop closed, reduced opening hours at restaurant) **Last arrival:** 21.00 **Last departure:** 11.00

Pitches: 🚐 from £24.50; 🚙 from £24.50; ▲ from £20; 🏠 see prices below; 56 hardstanding pitches; 12 seasonal pitches

Leisure: 🎱 ⚽ 🎮

Facilities: 🚿 ⊙ 🅿 ⚿ 🚽 🛁 WiFi

Services: 🔌 🗑 🍽 🚮 🔋 ⚡

Within 3 miles: 🚣 ⚲ ∪ ⚘ 🎯 🚴 🎣 🎱 💲

Additional site information: 32 acre site. Cars can be parked by caravans and tents. Awnings permitted. No groups of unaccompanied minors, no pets. Putting green, zip wire, all-weather football pitch.

Glamping available: Wooden pods from £50. **Changeover days:** Any day

Additional glamping information: Wooden pods: stays from 1 night to 2 weeks. Fridge, freezer, microwave, kettle, toaster and TV provided. Bring own bedding and cutlery. Amenity building within 50 metres. Cars can be parked by pods.

See advert opposite

HIGHLAND

ACHARACLE

Places to visit

RSPB Glenborrodale, GLENBORRODALE, PH36 4JP, 01463 715000
www.rspb.org.uk/reserves-and-events/reserves-a-z/glenborrodale

Ariundle Oakwood National Nature Reserve, FORT WILLIAM, PH33 6SW, 01397 704716
www.nnr-scotland.org.uk/ariundle-oakwood

ACHARACLE

Map 22 NM66

Resipole Farm Holiday Park
▶▶▶▶ 83%

tel: 01967 431235 **Resipole Farm PH36 4HX**
email: accounts@resipole.co.uk **web:** www.resipole.co.uk
dir: *From A82 between North Ballachulish and Fort William take ferry from Corran to Ardgour. Left onto A861 signed Strontian. Through Strontian towards Salen. Site approximately 8 miles on right.*

Set within one of the most beautiful areas of Scotland, the views directly from the site over Loch Sunart to the remote West Highland mountains are truly stunning. The site is a perfect location for anyone who enjoys exploring mountains and lochs, seeing the amazing Scottish wildlife or just wants to relax and unwind in a truly tranquil place. The site has WiFi and a good mobile signal, a well-stocked shop and a slipway onto Loch Sunart. An art gallery adjoins the site.

Open: Easter to October **Last arrival:** 21.00 **Last departure:** noon

Pitches: * 🚐 from £23; 🚙 from £23; ▲ from £23; 🏠 see prices below; 20 hardstanding pitches; 20 seasonal pitches

Leisure: 🎱 ⚲ **Facilities:** 🚿 ⊙ 🅿 ✳ ⚿ 🗑 🚽 🔋 WiFi

Services: 🔌 🗑 🛒 ⚡ 🔋 🔋 🚿 T **Within 3 miles:** 🚴 🎣

Additional site information: 8 acre site. 🐕 Cars can be parked by caravans and tents. Awnings permitted.

Glamping available: Wooden pods from £55.

Additional glamping information: Wooden pods offer 2 single beds (can convert to 3 beds), kettle, electric sockets, USB charge sockets, picnic bench and decking. Cars can be parked by pods.

See advert on page 346

PITCHES: 🚐 Caravans 🚙 Motorhomes ▲ Tents 🏠 Glamping accommodation **SERVICES:** 🔌 Electric hook-up 🗑 Launderette 🍺 Licensed bar
🔋 Calor Gas ⊘ Campingaz T Toilet fluid 🍽 Café/Restaurant 🚮 Fast Food/Takeaway 🔋 Battery charging ⚡ Motorhome service point
* 2019 prices 🚫 No credit or debit cards 🐕 Dogs permitted 🚫 No dogs

AVIEMORE
Map 23 NH81

Places to visit

The Strathspey Railway, AVIEMORE, PH22 1PY, 01479 810725
www.strathspeyrailway.co.uk

Great for kids: Landmark Forest Adventure Park, CARRBRIDGE, PH23 3AJ,
01479 841613
www.landmarkpark.co.uk

Aviemore Glamping
 ▶▶▶▶ 90% GLAMPING ONLY

tel: 01479 810717 **Eriskay, Craig Na Gower Avenue PH22 1RW**
email: aviemoreglamping@outlook.com **web:** www.aviemoreglamping.com
dir: *From south: exit A9 onto B9152 signed Aviemore. Take 2nd exit at roundabout signed town centre. 2nd exit at next roundabout. 5th left into Craig Na Gower Avenue (signed dental surgery). Site at end of lane.*

Aviemore is a well known outdoor enthusiasts' hotspot attracting tourists throughout the year for hillwalking and climbing in the Cairngorms, watersports at Loch Morlich and Loch Insch and skiing in the winter. Aviemore Glamping is a bit of a hidden secret, located in the landscaped grounds of the owner's home yet is only a short walk from the town centre. The four wooden eco-pods are beautifully built and luxuriously equipped with quality fittings and excellent en suite shower rooms; ideal for couples who are looking for something unique at a sensible price. The eco-pods are available all year and are heated to counter the chilly Scottish climate.

Open: All year **Last arrival:** 18.00 **Last departure:** 10.00

Facilities: 🖨 ℙ ☀ 🛒 🪑 **WiFi**

Within 3 miles: ↨ ℘ ∪ 🎱 ⑤ ☉

Accommodation available: Wooden pods.

Additional site information: 0.33 acre site. ⊗ Breakfasts available. Minimum stay 2 nights.

DUROR
Map 22 NM95

Places to visit

Glencoe Folk Museum, GLENCOE, PH49 4HS
www.glencoemuseum.com

Achindarroch Touring Park
▶▶▶ 80%

tel: 01631 740329 **PA38 4BS**
email: stay@achindarrochtp.co.uk **web:** www.achindarrochtp.co.uk
dir: *A82 onto A828 at Ballachulish Bridge then towards Oban for 5.2 miles. In Duror, site on left, signed.*

A long established, well-laid out park which continues to be maintained to a high standard by an enthusiastic and friendly family team. There is a well-appointed heated toilet block and spacious all-weather pitches plus 2- and 4-person wooden camping pods for hire. The park is well placed for visits to Oban, Fort William and Glencoe. A wide variety of outdoor sports is available in the area.

Open: 24 January to 16 January **Last departure:** 11.00

Pitches: 🚐 🚎 ▲ 🏠; 21 hardstanding pitches; 10 seasonal pitches

Facilities: 🖨 ☉ ℙ ☀ 🛒 🪑 🛒 **WiFi**

Services: 🔌 ⑤ 🚽 ⬇ 🛒

Within 3 miles: ℘ ∪

Additional site information: 5 acre site. 🐕 Cars can be parked by caravans and tents. Awnings permitted. Groups by prior arrangement only. Campers' kitchen with freezer, toaster, kettle, microwave and boot dryer.

Glamping available: Wooden pods.

EVANTON	Map 23 NH66

Places to visit

Highland Museum of Childhood, STRATHPEFFER, IV14 9DH, 01997 421031
www.highlandmuseumofchildhood.org.uk

Black Rock Caravan Park
►►►► 80%

tel: 01349 830917 **Balconie Street IV16 9UN**
email: blackrockholidays@gmail.com **web:** www.blackrockscotland.com
dir: *Just off A9, 1 mile from the Cromarty Bridge.*

The River Glass flows along the side of this lovely park which is located in a small, almost secret valley near Black Rock Gorge, just a mile from the A9 and on the beautiful 'North Coast 500' route. There is a range of possibilities to suit all tastes including touring pitches, which include hardstandings and 34 fully serviced pitches, two wooden wigwams, an S-pod and a bunkhouse. It's an easy drive into Inverness, and the Black Isle provides a dolphin-watching experience at Channory Point; there's also great walking in nearby Glen Glass and Ben Wyvis. A regular bus service passes the site entrance and there's a railway station in nearby Alness.

Open: April to October **Last arrival:** 19.00 **Last departure:** noon

Pitches: ⛟ from £22; ⛟ from £22; ⛺ from £9.50; ⛺ see prices below; 20 hardstanding pitches; 10 seasonal pitches

Leisure: ⛫

Facilities: 🏠 ☺ 🐾 ⚒ ♿ 🎌 WiFi

Services: 🔌 🎰 🛗 ⚡ 🔋 🚰 T

Within 3 miles: 🚶 ✏ 💲

Additional site information: 4.5 acre site. 🐕 Cars can be parked by caravans. Awnings permitted. No open fires, no noise after 23.00.

Glamping available: 2 wooden wigwams from £15; 1 S-pod from £40; 1 family luxury pod £60.

Additional glamping information: Cars can be parked by pods and wigwams.

FORT WILLIAM	Map 22 NN17

Places to visit

West Highland Museum, FORT WILLIAM, PH33 6AJ, 01397 702169
www.westhighlandmuseum.org.uk

Ariundle Oakwood National Nature Reserve, FORT WILLIAM, PH33 6SW,
01397 704716
www.nnr-scotland.org.uk/ariundle-oakwood

AA CAMPSITE OF THE YEAR
FOR SCOTLAND 2019

Glen Nevis Caravan & Camping Park
►►►► 92%

tel: 01397 702191 **Glen Nevis PH33 6SX**
email: holidays@glen-nevis.co.uk **web:** www.glen-nevis.co.uk
dir: *From A82 (northern outskirts of Fort William) follow Glen Nevis signs at mini roundabout. Site 2.5 miles on right.*

This is a large and very well maintained park, situated in Glen Nevis with easy access to the main footpath leading to Ben Nevis. Located a few miles from Fort William, the site is near Neptune's Staircase on the Caledonian Canal and the Great Glen. The site is divided into areas by beech hedges to give a sense of seclusion for caravan and motorhome users who have their own amenity blocks; tent campers have their own specific areas and large well-kept amenity blocks. To cater for those who are seeking a glamping experience, five luxury, wooden camping pods are available – all have unrivalled views towards Ben Nevis. The park has a restaurant and café.

Open: 15 March to October (restricted service: March and October – limited restaurant facilities) **Last arrival:** 22.00 **Last departure:** noon

Pitches: ⛟ ⛟ ⛺; ⛺ see prices below; 150 hardstanding pitches

Leisure: ⛫ ✏

Facilities: 🏠 ☺ 🐾 ⚒ ♿ 💲 🚰 🎌 WiFi

Services: 🔌 🎰 🍴 🍽 🚚 🛗 ⚡ 🔋 🚰 T

Within 3 miles: 🚶

Additional site information: 30 acre site. 🐕 Cars can be parked by caravans and tents Awnings permitted Quiet from 23.00–08.00.

Glamping available: Wooden pods from £60.

Additional glamping information: Wooden pods: dogs by prior arrangement only. Cars can be parked by pods.

GAIRLOCH   Map 22 NG87

Places to visit

Gairloch Heritage Museum, GAIRLOCH, IV21 2BP, 01445 712287
www.gairlochheritagemuseum.org

Inverewe Garden, POOLEWE, IV22 2LG, 01445 781229
www.nts.org.uk/visit/places/inverewe

Gairloch Caravan Park
▶▶▶ 79%

tel: 01445 712373 **Strath IV21 2BX**
email: info@gairlochcaravanpark.com **web:** www.gairlochcaravanpark.com
dir: *From A832 take B8021 signed Melvaig towards Strath. In 0.5 mile turn right, just
after Millcroft Hotel. Immediately right again.*

A clean, well-maintained site on flat, coastal grassland close to Loch Gairloch. The
owners and managers are hard working and well organised. The park offers
hardstandings, good shrub and flower planting and a bunkhouse that provides
accommodation for families.

Open: April to October **Last arrival:** 20.00 **Last departure:** noon

Pitches: 🚐 🚕 ▲; 13 hardstanding pitches; 8 seasonal pitches

Facilities: 🛁 ☺ 🗝 ✳ $ WiFi

Services: 🔌 🗑 🚽 ⬇ 🛒 🗑 T

Within 3 miles: ♨ 🎣 ◎ 🚣 🏊

Additional site information: 6 acre site. 🐎 Cars can be parked by caravans and tents.
Awnings permitted. No noise after 23.00.

GLENCOE   Map 22 NN15

Places to visit

Glencoe Folk Museum, GLENCOE, PH49 4HS
www.glencoemuseum.com

Invercoe Caravan & Camping Park
▶▶▶▶ 87%

tel: 01855 811210 **PH49 4HP**
email: holidays@invercoe.co.uk **web:** www.invercoe.co.uk
dir: *Exit A82 at Glencoe Hotel onto B863 for 0.25 mile.*

A level grass site set on the shore of Loch Leven, with excellent mountain views. The
area is ideal for both walking and climbing, and also offers a choice of several
freshwater and saltwater lochs. Convenient for the good shopping in Fort William.
There are two 'micro lodge' wooden pods for hire.

Open: All year **Last departure:** noon

Pitches: 🚐 🚕 ▲ 🏠

Facilities: ☺ 🗝 ✳ ♿ $ 🎪 WiFi

Services: 🔌 🗑 🚽 ⬇ 🗑 T

Within 3 miles: ♨ 🎣 🏊

Additional site information: 5 acre site. 🐎 Cars can be parked by caravans and tents.
Awnings permitted. No large group bookings.

Glamping available: Wooden pods.

Additional glamping information: Cars can be parked by pods.

LEISURE: 🏊 Indoor swimming pool 🏊 Outdoor swimming pool 🎢 Children's playground 🪁 Kids' club 🎾 Tennis court 🎱 Games room 📺 Separate TV room
♨ golf course 🏌 Pitch n putt 🚣 Boats for hire 🚲 Bikes for hire 🎬 Cinema 🎵 Entertainment 🎣 Fishing ◎ Mini golf 🏄 Watersports 🏋 Gym ⚽ Sports field ♘ Stables
FACILITIES: 🛁 Baths/Shower ☺ Electric shaver sockets 🗝 Hairdryer ✳ Ice Pack Facility ♨ Baby facilities ♿ Disabled facilities $ Shop on site or within 200yds
🍖 BBQ area 🎪 Picnic area WiFi WiFi

JOHN O'GROATS
Map 23 ND37

Places to visit
The Castle & Gardens of Mey, THURSO, KW14 8XH, 01847 851473
www.castleofmey.org.uk

RSPB Dunnet Head, DUNNET, KW14 8XS, 01463 715000
www.rspb.org.uk/reserves-and-events/reserves-a-z/dunnet-head

John O'Groats Caravan Site
►►► 85%

tel: 01955 611329 & 07762 336359 **KW1 4YR**
email: info@johnogroatscampsite.co.uk **web:** www.johnogroatscampsite.co.uk
dir: At end of A99.

An attractive site in an open position above the seashore and looking out towards the Orkney Islands. Nearby is the passenger ferry that makes day trips to the Orkneys, and there are grey seals to watch, and sea angling can be organised by the site owners.

Open: April to September **Last arrival:** 22.00 **Last departure:** 11.00

Pitches: 🚐 from £18; 🚍 from £18; ▲ from £16; 30 hardstanding pitches

Facilities: 🏠 ☺ 🅿 ✳ ♿ **WiFi** **Services:** 🔌 🌀 🔋 ↯ 🔧 **Within 3 miles:** 🏃 🗓

Additional site information: 4 acre site. 🐾 Cars can be parked by caravans and tents. Awnings permitted. No noise after 22.00.

LAIDE
Map 22 NG89

Places to visit
Inverewe Garden, POOLEWE, IV22 2LG, 01445 781229
www.nts.org.uk/visit/places/inverewe

Gruinard Bay Caravan Park
►►► 73%

tel: 01445 731556 **IV22 2ND**
email: stay@gruinardbay.co.uk **web:** www.gruinardbay.co.uk
dir: From Inverness or Ullapool take A832 to Gairloch, follow signs to Laide. (Note: on Inverness to Gairloch road – short stretch of single-track road with passing places just prior to Gairloch).

With views across Gruinard Bay to the Summer Isles and the mountains, this is a lovely, small, beach-front park in a particularly peaceful location with views across to the Summer Isles and is located on the North Coast 500 route. There is direct access to a small sandy beach from where you can see fish from the beach or rocks, and the site has free WiFi access. The small post office provides basic groceries, while larger shops can be found in Aultbea, Poolewe, Gairloch and Ullapool, where there are ferries to the Outer Hebrides. Being beside a beach, the site has no hardstandings but the grass pitches are on well-compacted shingle. The park and surrounding area abounds with wildlife – you may catch a glimpse of the occasional otter or seal.

Open: April to October **Last arrival:** 22.00

Pitches: 🚐 from £11; 🚍 from £11; ▲ from £11; 5 hardstanding pitches

Leisure: 🏊 **Facilities:** 🏠 ☺ 🅿 **WiFi**

Services: 🔌 🌀 ↯ 🔒 **Within 3 miles:** 🛒

Additional site information: 3.5 acre site. 🐾 Cars can be parked by caravans and tents. Awnings permitted. No noise after 22.00.

LAIRG
Map 23 NC50

Woodend Caravan & Camping Site
►►► 70%

tel: 01549 402248 **Achnairn IV27 4DN**
dir: 4 miles north of Lairg exit A836 onto A838, signed at Achnairn.

A clean, simple site set in hilly moors and woodland with access to Loch Shin. The area is popular with fishing and boating enthusiasts, and there is a choice of golf courses within a 30-mile radius. A spacious campers' kitchen is a useful amenity. There's also a holiday cottage to hire.

Open: April to September **Last arrival:** 23.00

Pitches: 🚐 🚍 ▲; 5 hardstanding pitches **Facilities:** ☺ 🅿 ✳

Services: 🔌 🌀 **Within 3 miles:** 🏃 🎣

Additional site information: 4 acre site. 🐾 Cars can be parked by caravans and tents. Awnings permitted.

ULLAPOOL
Map 22 NH19

Places to visit
Corrieshalloch Gorge National Nature Reserve, BRAEMORE, IV23 2PJ, 01445 781229
www.nts.org.uk/visit/places/corrieshalloch-gorge

Broomfield Holiday Park
►►► 80%

tel: 01854 612020 & 612664 **West Shore Street IV26 2UT**
email: sross@broomfieldhp.com **web:** www.broomfieldhp.com
dir: Into Ullapool on A893, 2nd right after harbour.

Set right on the water's edge of Loch Broom and the open sea, with lovely views of the Summer Isles. This clean, well maintained and managed park is close to the harbour and town centre with restaurants, bars and shops. The Ullapool ferry allows easy access to the Hebridian Islands for day trips or longer visits.

Open: Easter or April to September **Last arrival:** 22.30 **Last departure:** noon

Pitches: 🚐 from £21; 🚍 from £20; ▲ from £19; 72 hardstanding pitches

Leisure: 🎱 **Facilities:** ☺ ✳ ♿ 🛒 🍴 **WiFi** **Services:** 🔌 🌀 🔋 ↯

Within 3 miles: ♨ 🏃 🎯

Additional site information: 12 acre site. 🐾 Dogs must be on a lead at all times. Cars can be parked by caravans and tents. Awnings permitted. No noise at night.

SOUTH LANARKSHIRE

ABINGTON — Map 21 NS92

Places to visit

Museum of Lead Mining, WANLOCKHEAD, ML12 6UT, 01659 74387
www.leadminingmuseum.co.uk

Mount View Caravan Park

▶▶▶ 79%

tel: 01864 502808 **ML12 6RW**
email: info@mountviewcaravanpark.co.uk **web:** www.mountviewcaravanpark.co.uk
dir: M74 junction 13, A702 south into Abington. Left into Station Road, over river and railway. Site on right.

A delightfully maturing family park, surrounded by the Southern Uplands and handily located between Carlisle and Glasgow. It is an excellent stopover site for those travelling between Scotland and the south, and the West Coast Railway passes beside the park.

Open: March to October **Last arrival:** 20.45 **Last departure:** 11.30

Pitches: 🚐 🚌 🛆; 42 hardstanding pitches; 18 seasonal pitches

Leisure: 🛝

Facilities: 🛁 ☉ 🗲 🕭 🛒

Services: 🚱 🗑 🔒

Within 3 miles: ⚓ 🎣 ⑤

Additional site information: 5.5 acre site. 🐾 Dogs must be exercised off site. Cars can be parked by caravans and tents. Awnings permitted. 5mph speed limit. Debit cards accepted (no credit cards). Emergency phone.

EAST LOTHIAN

DUNBAR — Map 21 NT67

Places to visit

Preston Mill & Phantassie Doocot, EAST LINTON, EH40 3DS, 01620 860426
www.nts.org.uk/visit/places/preston-mill

Great for kids: Tantallon Castle, NORTH BERWICK, EH39 5PN, 01620 892727
www.historic-scotland.gov.uk

Premier Park

Thurston Manor Leisure Park

▶▶▶▶▶ 90%

tel: 01368 840643 **Innerwick EH42 1SA**
email: holidays@verdantleisure.co.uk **web:** www.thurstonmanor.co.uk
dir: 4 miles south of Dunbar, follow site signs from A1.

A pleasant park set in 250 acres of unspoilt countryside. The touring (no tents) and static areas of this large park are in separate areas. The main touring area occupies an open, level position, and the toilet facilities are modern and exceptionally well maintained. There is a superb family toilet block. The park boasts a well-stocked fishing loch, a heated indoor swimming pool, steam room, sauna, jacuzzi, mini-gym and fitness room plus seasonal entertainment. Fly fishing is available.

Open: 13 February to January **Last arrival:** 23.00 **Last departure:** 10.00

Pitches: 🚐 from £17; 🚌 from £17; 68 hardstanding pitches; 60 seasonal pitches

Leisure: 🏊 🛝 👪 🔍 ▭ 🎵 🎣 🎯 🏟 Spa

Facilities: 🛁 ☉ 🗲 🕭 🛒 ⑤ 🛒 🐾 WiFi

Services: 🚱 🗑 🗑 🍽 ⚒ 🛒 🔒 🛒 🗑 T

Additional site information: 175 acre site. 🐾 Cars can be parked by caravans. Awnings permitted. Quiet after 23.00.

Belhaven Bay Caravan & Camping Park

▶▶▶▶ 85%

tel: 01368 865956 **Belhaven Bay EH42 1TS**
email: belhaven@meadowhead.co.uk **web:** www.meadowhead.co.uk
dir: A1 onto A1087 towards Dunbar. 1 mile to site in John Muir Park.

Located on the outskirts of Dunbar, this is a sheltered park within walking distance of the beach. There is a regular bus service to Dunbar where there is an East Coast Main Line railway station. The site is also convenient for the A1 and well placed for visiting the area's many seaside towns and various visitor attractions. There is a large children's play area. Six static caravans and three wooden wigwam pods are available for hire.

Open: March to October **Last arrival:** 20.00 **Last departure:** noon

Pitches: 🚐 from £17.75; 🚌 from £17.75; 🛆 from £17.75; 🏠 see prices below; 11 hardstanding pitches

Leisure: 🛝

Facilities: 🛁 ☉ 🗲 🕭 🛒 ⑤ 🛒 🛒 WiFi

Services: 🚱 🗑 🛒 T

Within 3 miles: ⚓ 🎣 U ◎ 🛥

Additional site information: 40 acre site. 🐾 Cars can be parked by caravans and tents. Awnings permitted. No rollerblades or skateboards, no open fires, no noise 23.00–07.00.

Glamping available: Wooden wigwams from £55.

LONGNIDDRY — Map 21 NT47

Places to visit

Prestongrange Museum, PRESTONPANS, EH32 9RX, 0131 653 2904
www.prestongrange.org

Great for kids: Myreton Motor Museum, ABERLADY, EH32 0PZ, 07585 356931
www.myretonmotormuseum.co.uk

Premier Park

Seton Sands Holiday Village

▶▶▶▶▶ 87% HOLIDAY CENTRE

tel: 01875 813333 **EH32 0QF**
email: setonsands@haven.com **web:** www.haven.com/setonsands
dir: A1 to A198 exit, take B6371 to Cockenzie. Right onto B1348. Site 1 mile on right.

A well-equipped holiday centre facing onto the Firth of Forth with mature landscaping. A dedicated entertainment team offers plenty of organised activities for children and there are pleasant bars, a show bar and a modern restaurant. It offers good sports and leisure facilities, including a multi-sports court, swimming pool, 9-hole golf course and a variety of play areas, so there's always plenty to do without leaving the park. The touring area offers fully-serviced pitches set in lovely landscaping with a dedicated on-site warden. There is a regular bus from the site entrance, which makes day trips to Edinburgh easy. 150 holiday homes are available for hire. Please note, this site does not accept tents.

Open: mid March to end October (restricted service: mid March to May and September to end October – facilities may be reduced) **Last arrival:** 22.00 **Last departure:** 10.00

Pitches: 🚐 🚍; 40 hardstanding pitches

Leisure: 🏊 🎣 🛝 🎵 🏸

Facilities: 🚿 🅿 ♿ 🛁 🏧 WiFi

Services: 🔌 🧺 🕯️ 🍴 🍟 🔒

Within 3 miles: ∪

Additional site information: 1.75 acre site. 🐕 Maximum 2 dogs per booking, certain dog breeds banned. No commercial vehicles, no bookings by persons under 21 years unless a family booking.

WEST LOTHIAN

EAST CALDER   Map 21 NT06

Places to visit

Almond Valley Heritage Trust, LIVINGSTON, EH54 7AR, 01506 414957
www.almondvalley.co.uk

Malleny Garden, BALERNO, EH14 7AF, 0131 665 1546
www.nts.org.uk/visit/places/malleny-garden

Linwater Caravan Park
▶▶▶▶ 87%

tel: 0131 333 3326 **West Clifton FH53 0HT**
email: admin@linwater.co.uk **web:** www.linwater.co.uk
dir: *M9 junction 1, follow B7030 and Newbridge signs. Left after petrol station and Macdonalds onto B7030. 2 miles, turn right after Edinburgh International Climbing Arena (EICA), follow site signs.*

This is a farmland park in a peaceful rural area with access to good motorway and rail links enabling exploration of the heart of Scotland. The family who own the park are excellent hosts and offer a friendly service which is borne out by the many customers who return year after year. The grounds are very pleasant and the toilets are kept in an exemplary manner. It is a particularly popular park, especially with those wishing to visit the Royal Highland Show, the Edinburgh Festival and Military Tattoo. There are four wooden wigwams (known as timber tents), and a self-catering lodge in a half acre, for hire.

Open: All year **Last arrival:** 21.00 **Last departure:** noon

Pitches: 🚐 from £22; 🚍 from £22; ⛺ from £17 🛖; 22 hardstanding pitches

Leisure: 🛝 🏸

Facilities: 🚿 ☉ 🅿 ⚟ ♿ 🛁 WiFi

Services: 🔌 🧺 🕯️ 🔋 🛠️ 🔒 ⊘ T

Additional site information: 5 acre site. 🐕 Maximum 2 dogs per booking. Cars can be parked by caravans and tents. Awnings permitted. No noise after 23.00, no entry to main site after 21.00 (late arrivals area available). Takeaway food can be ordered for delivery, small shop sells basics only, woodland dog walk.

Glamping available: Wooden wigwams. **Changeover days:** Any day

Additional glamping information: Cars can be parked by wigwams.

LINLITHGOW   Map 21 NS97

Places to visit

Linlithgow Palace, LINLITHGOW, EH49 7AL, 01506 842896
www.historic-scotland.gov.uk

House of The Binns, LINLITHGOW, EH49 7NA
www.nts.org.uk/visit/places/house-of-binns

Great for kids: Blackness Castle, LINLITHGOW, EH49 7NH, 01506 834807
www.historic-scotland.gov.uk

Beecraigs Caravan & Camping Site
▶▶▶▶ 92%

tel: 01506 284516 & 284510 **Beecraigs Country Park, The Visitor Centre EH49 6PL**
email: mail@beecraigs.com **web:** www.beecraigs.com
dir: *M9 junction 3 (from east) or junction 4 (from west), A803 to Linlithgow. From A803 into Preston Road signed Beecraigs Country Park. Reception in visitor centre. (Note: Preston Road route is steep and winding).*

Located on the hills above Linlithgow with unrivalled views towards the Forth Bridges, Beecraigs Country Park has an excellent caravan and camping site, with two modern washrooms, large hardstanding pitches and a secluded tenting area, together with 6- and 4-person cabins. Two 'little lodges' are also available for hire. There are extensive walks and cycle trails, a fishing loch, deer park, farm and a very large play area for children. There is a lovely visitor centre, shop and café at the site entrance and there are good road and train links nearby, making trips into Edinburgh an easy affair; for those who wish for something more relaxing, boat trips are available.

Open: All year (restricted service: 25 to 26 December and 1 to 2 January – no new arrivals) **Last arrival:** 19.00 **Last departure:** noon

Pitches: 🚐 from £20.70; 🚍 from £20.70; ⛺ from £17.10; 🛖 see prices below; 23 hardstanding pitches

Leisure: 🛝 🏸 **Facilities:** 🚿 ☉ 🅿 ⚟ ♿ 🚻 🛁 WiFi

Services: 🔌 🧺 🍴 🔋 🛠️ T **Within 3 miles:** 🛝 ∪ ⛵ 🛁

Additional site information: 6 acre site. 🐕 Cars can be parked by caravans. Awnings permitted. Site standards apply. Country park facilities, WiFi only available in visitor centre.

Glamping available: Cabins (Little Lodges) from £41.40.

Additional glamping information: Little Lodges sleep 4 or 6. Maximum 1 dog per cabin. Use of shower block on site. Cars can be parked by cabins.

MORAY

ABERLOUR
Map 23 NJ24

Places to visit

Balvenie Castle, DUFFTOWN, AB55 4DH, 01340 820121
www.historic-scotland.gov.uk

Glenfiddich Distillery, DUFFTOWN, AB55 4DH, 01340 820373
www.glenfiddich.com

Speyside Gardens Caravan Park
▶▶▶▶ 82%

tel: 01340 871586 **AB38 9LD**
email: info@speysidegardens.com **web:** www.speysidegardens.com
dir: *Midway between Aberlour and Craigellachie on A95 turn onto unclassified road. Site signed. (Note: vehicles over 10' 6" should use A941 (Dufftown to Craigellachie road).*

This attractive parkland site is set in the five-acre walled garden of the Victorian Aberlour House, surrounded by the spectacular scenery of the Cairngorm National Park, through pine tree glens, to the famous Moray coastline; the park is also well placed for taking the world renowned Speyside Malt Whisky Trail. It offers a small, well-appointed toilet block, laundry and small licensed shop.

Open: March to October **Last arrival:** 19.00 **Last departure:** noon

Pitches: 🚐 from £21; 🚙 from £21; ▲ from £16; 24 hardstanding pitches; 10 seasonal pitches

Leisure: 🎢

Facilities: 🛁 ⊙ 🅿 ✳ & 🏪 🎪

Services: 🔌 🗑 🍽 🚽 🛢 🧺 🇹

Within 3 miles: 🕳 🖉

Additional site information: 5 acre site. 🔄 Cars can be parked by caravans and tents. Awnings permitted. Maximum 5mph speed limit on site, no noise after 23.00.

ELGIN
Map 23 NJ26

Places to visit

Elgin Museum, ELGIN, IV30 1EQ, 01343 543675
www.elginmuseum.org.uk

Elgin Cathedral, ELGIN, IV30 1HU, 01343 547171
www.historic-scotland.gov.uk

Woodlands Rest
▶▶▶▶ 85% GLAMPING ONLY

tel: 0784 389 8930 **Aldroughty Woods**
email: reservations@aldroughtywoods.co.uk **web:** www.aldroughtywoods.co.uk
dir: *Phone for directions (Note: this site does not have a post code).*

The traditional yurt and shepherd's hut at this glamping site blend seemingly into the private 25 acres of mature natural woodland, which forms part of Aldroughty Woods; both provide an ideal retreat for those looking for a peaceful and relaxing holiday. The units are far enough apart to ensure privacy but can be hired together; each has its own individual hut with cooking and toilet facilities. This site is totally off-grid and the owner has been very inventive in providing the power and water. The units are meticulously maintained and provide excellent facilities; the yurt has a large double bed and a set of bunk beds, table and seating, whilst the shepherd's hut has a double bed. Each has a wood-burner (wood and charcoal is provided), outdoor seating and fire pits. The customer service is excellent and the owner provides a friendly but unobtrusive daily service that includes making meals to your own requirements, from breakfast to full dinners. Woodlands Rest is a place to sit back and listen to birdsong, watch the red squirrels and spot roe deer as you walk through the beech woods.

Open: All year **Last arrival:** 22.00 **Last departure:** 11.00

Accommodation available: 1 yurt, 1 shepherd's hut.

Additional site information: 25 acre site. 🔄 Site only closes due to bad weather and snow.

LOSSIEMOUTH
Map 23 NJ27

Places to visit

Elgin Cathedral, ELGIN, IV30 1HU, 01343 547171
www.historic-scotland.gov.uk

Duffus Castle, DUFFUS, IV30 5RH
www.historic-scotland.gov.uk

Premier Park

Silver Sands Holiday Park
▶▶▶▶▶ 84%

tel: 01343 813262 **Covesea, West Beach IV31 6SP**
email: holidays@silver-sands.co.uk **web:** www.silver-sands.co.uk
dir: *Take B9040 from Lossiemouth, 2 miles to site.*

This is an ideal family park located on the Moray coast two miles from the busy seaside town of Lossiemouth. There is direct access to a sandy beach and the entertainment complex caters for both children and adults, with a pool, sauna, steam room and a large gym. There is a well-stocked shop, takeaway food and a small bistro-style café on site. With a golf course adjacent to the park and several others within easy driving distance (including the world famous Nairn Golf Course), this site makes a perfect base for golfers and those touring the area. There are fully serviced hardstandings and 15 static caravans for hire.

Open: 24 March to end October **Last arrival:** 22.00 **Last departure:** noon

Pitches: 🚐 from £25; 🚙 from £30; ▲ from £17; 94 hardstanding pitches; 17 seasonal pitches

Leisure: 🏊 🎢 🤚 🎱 🎵 🏌

Facilities: 🛁 ⊙ 🅿 ✳ & 🏪 🍴 🎪 🐾 📶

Services: 🔌 🗑 🍴 🍽 🏧 🧳 🛢 🧺 🇹

Within 3 miles: 🕳 🖉 ∪ ◎ 🛥 ⛵

Additional site information: 60 acre site. 🔄 Cars can be parked by caravans and tents. Awnings permitted. Crazy golf.

PERTH & KINROSS

BLAIR ATHOLL
Map 23 NN86

Places to visit

Blair Castle, BLAIR ATHOLL, PH18 5TL, 01796 481207
www.blair-castle.co.uk

Killiecrankie Visitor Centre, KILLIECRANKIE, PH16 5LG, 01796 473233
www.nts.org.uk/visit/places/killiecrankie

Premier Park

Blair Castle Caravan Park
▶▶▶▶▶ 91%

tel: 01796 481263 **PH18 5SR**
email: mail@blaircastlecaravanpark.co.uk **web:** www.blaircastlecaravanpark.co.uk
dir: From A9 onto B8079 at Aldclune, follow to Blair Atholl. Site on right after crossing bridge in village.

An attractive site set in impressive seclusion within the Atholl Estate, surrounded by mature woodland and the River Tilt. Although a large park, the various groups of pitches are located throughout the extensive grounds, and each has its own sanitary block with all-cubicled facilities of a very high standard. There is a choice of grass pitches, hardstandings and fully serviced pitches. This park is particularly suitable for the larger type of motorhome. There are wooden pods that each sleep two adults.

Open: March to November **Last arrival:** 21.30 **Last departure:** noon

Pitches: 🚐 from £20; 🚐 from £30; ▲ from £18; 🏕 see prices below; 155 hardstanding pitches; 68 seasonal pitches

Leisure: ⚑ 🔍 🎣 ⚽

Facilities: 🚿 ⊙ 🍳 ❄ ♿ Ⓢ 🔥 WiFi

Services: 🔌 🧺 🍺 ♨ 🔋 🐕 🕤 Ⓣ

Within 3 miles: 🚴 ♻ ◎

Additional site information: 32 acre site. 🐕 Cars can be parked by caravans and tents. Awnings permitted. Family park, no noise after 23.00.

Glamping available: Wooden pods from £35. **Changeover days:** Any day

See advert on page 354

Premier Park

River Tilt Caravan Park
▶▶▶▶▶ 85%

tel: 01796 481467 **Invertilt Road, Bridge of Tilt PH18 5TE**
email: stuart@rivertilt.co.uk **web:** www.rivertiltpark.co.uk
dir: 7 miles north of Pitlochry on A9, take B8079 to Blair Atholl. Site at rear of Tilt Hotel.

An attractive park with magnificent views of the surrounding mountains, idyllically set in hilly woodland country on the banks of the River Tilt, adjacent to the golf course. There is also a leisure complex with heated indoor swimming pool, sun lounge area, spa pool and multi-gym, all available for an extra charge; outdoors there is a short tennis court. The toilet facilities are very good.

Open: 16 March to 12 November **Last arrival:** 21.00 **Last departure:** noon

Pitches: 🚐 from £24; 🚐 from £22; ▲ from £10; 15 hardstanding pitches; 10 seasonal pitches

Leisure: 🏊 🎣 🎾 Spa

Facilities: 🚿 ⊙ 🍳 ❄ Ⓢ 🔥 WiFi

Services: 🔌 🧺 🍺 🍽 🔋 ♨ 🐕 🐕

Within 3 miles: 🚴 ♻ ◎ 🎣

Additional site information: 2 acre site. 🐕 Cars can be parked by caravans and tents. Awnings permitted. Sauna, solarium, steam room.

COMRIE   Map 21 NN72

Places to visit

Caithness Glass Visitor Centre, CRIEFF, PH7 4HQ, 01764 654014
www.caithnessglass.co.uk

Drummond Castle Gardens, MUTHILL, PH7 4HN, 01764 681433
www.drummondcastlegardens.co.uk

Twenty Shilling Wood Caravan Park

▶▶▶ 77%

tel: 01764 670411 **PH6 2JY**
email: alowe20@aol.com **web:** www.twentyshillingwoodcaravanpark.co.uk
dir: *On A85, 0.5 mile west of Comrie towards St Fillans. Site opposite Tullybannocher café.*

Situated on the outskirts of Comrie, this is a tranquil and mature site that offers terraced pitches in a well-maintained woodland setting which screens the site from the road. The site facilities are clean and well maintained and the family owners are very helpful. It is ideally located for exploring the Perthshire countryside – there are stunning drives to beautiful lochs and charming rural villages such as Comrie, which is a short walk away. There are various hiking and cycling trails, for all levels of ability, that can be accessed from the site. Please note, tents are not accepted.

Open: 18 March to 20 October **Last arrival:** 21.00 **Last departure:** 18.00
Pitches: * 🚐 from £25; 🚐 from £25; 14 hardstanding pitches; 32 seasonal pitches
Leisure: 🛝 🎣
Facilities: 🛁 ☉ 🎣 ✳ 🛒 WiFi
Services: 🔌 🗑 🖊 ⛽ 🚽 T
Within 3 miles: 🎣 ⛳ 🛒

Additional site information: 10.5 acre site. 🐕 Maximum of 2 dogs per pitch. Cars can be parked by caravans. Awnings permitted. Booking advisable at all times, no noise after 23.00. Woodland walk.

DUNKELD

Places to visit

The Ell Shop & Little Houses, DUNKELD, PH8 0AN, 01350 728641
www.nts.org.uk/visit/places/dunkeld

Loch of the Lowes Visitor Centre, DUNKELD, PH8 0HH, 01350 727337
www.swt.org.uk

LEISURE: 🏊 Indoor swimming pool 🏊 Outdoor swimming pool 🛝 Children's playground 🤾 Kids' club 🎾 Tennis court 🎱 Games room 📺 Separate TV room ⛳ golf course ⛳ Pitch n putt 🚣 Boats for hire 🚴 Bikes for hire 🎬 Cinema 🎵 Entertainment 🎣 Fishing ⛳ Mini golf 🏄 Watersports 🏋 Gym 🏟 Sports field 🐴 Stables
FACILITIES: 🛁 Baths/Shower ☉ Electric shaver sockets 🎣 Hairdryer ✳ Ice Pack Facility 🛒 Baby facilities ♿ Disabled facilities 🏪 Shop on site or within 200yds 🍖 BBQ area 🧺 Picnic area WiFi WiFi

DUNKELD
Map 21 NO04

Inver Mill Farm Caravan Park
►►►► 80%

tel: 01350 727477 **Inver PH8 0JR**
email: invermill@talk21.com **web:** www.invermillfarm.com
dir: *A9 onto A822 then immediately right to Inver.*

A peaceful park on level former farmland, located on the banks of the River Braan and surrounded by mature trees and hills. The active resident owners keep the park in very good condition.

Open: mid March to October **Last arrival:** 22.00 **Last departure:** noon

Pitches: * 🚐 from £22; 🚌 from £22; ▲ from £19; 3 hardstanding pitches

Facilities: 🛁 ⊙ 🅿 ⚫ ⚪ WiFi

Services: 🔌 ⭕ 🔋 ⚰ ⚱ ⚗

Within 3 miles: ⚲ ⚲ ⓢ

Additional site information: 5 acre site. 🐕 Cars can be parked by caravans and tents. Awnings permitted.

KINLOCH RANNOCH
Map 23 NN65

Places to visit

The Scottish Crannog Centre, KENMORE, PH15 2HY, 01887 830503
www.crannog.co.uk

Kilvrecht Campsite
► 76%

tel: 0300 0676380 **PH16 5QA**
email: tay.fd@forestry.gsi.gov.uk **web:** www.forestry.gov.uk
dir: *From north shore: on B846 to Kinloch Rannoch. Follow South Loch Rannoch sign. Over river bridge, 1st right signed Kilvrecht. Approach via unclassified road along loch, with Forestry Commission signs.*

Set within a large forest clearing, approximately half a mile from the road to Kinloch Rannoch which runs along the loch. This is a beautifully maintained site, with good clean facilities, for those who wish for a peaceful break. It also makes an ideal base for those who prefer the more active outdoor activities of hill walking (Schiehallion is within easy reach) or mountain biking; it is a great spot to observe the multitude of birds and wildlife in the area. Please note, the site has no electricity.

Open: April to October **Last arrival:** 22.00 **Last departure:** 10.00

Pitches: 🚐 🚌 ▲

Facilities: ⚫ 🍴

Within 3 miles: ⚲ ⚲ ⓢ

Additional site information: 17 acre site. 🐕 ⊘ Cars can be parked by caravans and tents. Awnings permitted. No fires.

PITLOCHRY

Places to visit

Edradour Distillery, PITLOCHRY, PH16 5JP, 01796 472095
www.edradour.com

PITLOCHRY
Map 23 NN95

Milton of Fonab Caravan Park
►►►► 90%

tel: 01796 472882 **Bridge Road PH16 5NA**
email: info@fonab.co.uk **web:** www.fonab.co.uk
dir: *From south: on A924, pass petrol station on left, next left opposite Bell's Distillery into Bridge Road. Cross river, site on left. From north (and Pitlochry centre): on A924, under rail bridge, turn right opposite Bell's Distillery into Bridge Road.*

This is a lovely, peaceful site set on the banks of the River Tummel on the outskirts of Pitlochry. Getting here is easy as the A9 is nearby and there is a good bus service and a mainline rail station in the town. The site is exceptionally well maintained, with large pitches, good washrooms and a well-stocked shop, and it is an ideal base for exploring this scenic part of Perthshire. The area is famous for the whisky industry, and Bell's Distillery is a short walk from the site entrance as is the Pitlochry Festival Theatre.

Open: mid March to 5 November **Last arrival:** 21.00 **Last departure:** 13.00
Pitches: 🚐 from £21; 🚌 from £21; ▲ from £21; 74 hardstanding pitches
Leisure: 🅿 **Facilities:** 🛁 ⊙ 🅿 ⚫ ⚪ ⓢ WiFi
Services: 🔌 ⭕ ⚰ ⚗ ⚱ T **Within 3 miles:** ⚲ ◎ ⚲ ⚲
Additional site information: 15 acre site. 🐕 Cars can be parked by caravans and tents. Awnings permitted. Couples and families only. No motor cycles.

Faskally Caravan Park
►►►► 88%

tel: 01796 472007 **PH16 5LA**
email: info@faskally.co.uk **web:** www.faskally.co.uk
dir: *1.5 miles north of Pitlochry on B8019.*

A large park near Pitlochry, which is divided into smaller areas by mature trees and set within well-tended grounds. This family-owned site has two large amenity blocks and an entertainment complex with a heated swimming pool, bar, restaurant and indoor games area. There are numerous walks from the site and it is ideal for either a longer stay to explore the area or as a convenient stopover. A regular bus service is available at the site entrance.

Open: 15 March to October **Last arrival:** 23.00 **Last departure:** 11.00
Pitches: 🚐 🚌 ▲; 45 hardstanding pitches **Leisure:** 🏊 ⚫ 🎵 Spa
Facilities: ⊙ 🅿 ⚫ ⚪ ⓢ WiFi **Services:** 🔌 ⭕ ⚱ 🍴 ⚰ ⚗ T
Within 3 miles: ⚲ ⚲ ∪ ⚲
Additional site information: 27 acre site. 🐕 Cars can be parked by caravans and tents. Awnings permitted.

SCOTTISH BORDERS

LAUDER
Map 21 NT54

Thirlestane Castle Caravan & Camping Site
▶▶▶ 86%

tel: 01578 718884 & 07976 231032 **Thirlestane Castle TD2 6RU**
email: info@thirlestanecastlepark.co.uk **web:** www.thirlestanecastlepark.co.uk
dir: *Signed from A68 and A697, just south of Lauder.*

Located on the outskirts of Lauder, close to the A68 and within the grounds of Thirlestane Castle, this is an ideal site from which to explore the many attractions in the Scottish Borders. The amenity block is immaculately maintained and the pitches are behind the estate boundary wall that provides a secluded and peaceful location. There is a regular bus service near the site entrance.

Open: April to October **Last arrival:** 20.00 **Last departure:** noon

Pitches: 🚐 �'🏕 Ａ; 30 hardstanding pitches; 55 seasonal pitches

Leisure: ⚲ 🎣

Facilities: 🚿 ⊙ & 🛒 WiFi

Services: 🔌 🗑 ⏚

Within 3 miles: ⛳ 🛍

Additional site information: 5 acre site. 🚗 Cars can be parked by caravans and tents. Awnings permitted. Tourer storage facilities, discounted access to castle and grounds during opening hours.

PAXTON
Map 21 NT95

Paxton House Caravan Park
▶ 77%

tel: 01289 386291 & 07803 352706 **Paxton House TD15 1SZ**
email: info@paxtonhouse.com **web:** www.paxtonhousecaravanpark.co.uk
dir: *From A1 (west of Berwick-upon-Tweed) take B6461 signed Paxton. In approximately 5 miles Paxton House entrance on left.*

This site is situated within the walled garden of the glorious 18th-century, John Adams' designed Paxton House, just three miles from Berwick-upon-Tweed. Tourers who stay in the quaint caravan park are able to enjoy access to the extensive grounds of the house – with stunning herbaceous borders, wild woodlands, riverside walks and a fantastic playground, there is plenty to keep the whole family entertained. Guests can take advantage of a discount in the shop and tearoom, and take a tour of Paxton House for a small fee. There are plenty of interesting activities on the doorstep, including seaside and historic walks, theatres and sports centres.

Open: All year **Last arrival:** 18.00 **Last departure:** 10.30

Pitches: * 🚐 from £15; �'🏕 from £15 🏠; 15 hardstanding pitches

Services: 🔌 🍽

Additional site information: 🚗 Cars can be parked by caravans. Awnings permitted. Internet access available.

Glamping available: 4 canvas cottages. **Changeover days:** Any day

Additional glamping information: Canvas cottages offer hardwood floor, wooden furniture, wood-burning stove, cooking facilities and en suite bathroom. Children and dogs welcome.

PEEBLES
Map 21 NT24

Places to visit
Kailzie Gardens, PEEBLES, EH45 9HT, 01721 720007
www.kailziegardens.com

Robert Smail's Printing Works, INNERLEITHEN, EH44 6HA, 01896 830206
www.nts.org.uk/visit/places/robert-smails

Great for kids: Go Ape Glentress Forest, PEEBLES, EH45 8NB
www.goape.co.uk/peebles

Crossburn Caravan Park
▶▶▶▶ 84%

tel: 01721 720501 **Edinburgh Road EH45 8ED**
email: info@crossburncaravans.co.uk **web:** www.crossburn-caravans.com
dir: *0.5 mile north of Peebles on A703.*

A peaceful park, on the edge of Peebles and within easy driving distance for Edinburgh and the Scottish Borders. The park is divided by well-maintained landscaping and mature trees, and has good views over the countryside. There is a regular bus service at the site entrance and Peebles has a wide range of shops and attractions. The facilities are maintained to a high standard. Four-person wooden pods are available for hire. There is also a main caravan dealership on site, and a large stock of spares and accessories are available.

Open: March to November **Last arrival:** 21.00 **Last departure:** noon (later by arrangement)

Pitches: 🚐 from £28; 🚐 from £28; Ａ from £12; 🏠 see prices below; 28 hardstanding pitches; 16 seasonal pitches

Leisure: ⚲

Facilities: 🚿 ⊙ 🗡 ✳ & 🛍 WiFi

Services: 🔌 🗑 🚰 ⏚ 🛢 🧴 🅣

Within 3 miles: ⛳ 🎣 ⛺

Additional site information: 6 acre site. 🚗 Cars can be parked by caravans and tents. Awnings permitted. No noise after 23.00.

Glamping available: Wooden pods from £45.

Additional glamping information: Wooden pods: last time of departure 11.00. Cars can be parked by pods.

STIRLING

ABERFOYLE

Places to visit
Inchmahome Priory, PORT OF MENTEITH, FK8 3RA, 01877 385294
www.historic-scotland.gov.uk

Great for kids: Go Ape Aberfoyle, ABERFOYLE, FK8 3SY
www.goape.co.uk/aberfoyle

ABERFOYLE
Map 20 NN50

Premier Park

Trossachs Holiday Park
▶▶▶▶▶ 91%

tel: 01877 382614 **FK8 3SA**
email: info@trossachsholidays.co.uk **web:** www.trossachsholidays.co.uk
dir: *Access on east side of A81, 1 mile south of junction A821 and 3 miles south of Aberfoyle.*

An attractively landscaped and peaceful park with outstanding views towards the hills, including the Munro of Ben Lomond. Set within the Loch Lomond National Park, boating, walking, cycling and beautiful drives over the Dukes Pass through the Trossachs are just some of the attractions within easy reach. Bikes can be hired from the reception and there is an internet café that sells home-baked items. There are lodges for hire.

Open: March to October **Last arrival:** 21.00 **Last departure:** noon

Pitches: 🚐 from £20; 🚐 from £20; ▲ from £17.50; 46 hardstanding pitches; 24 seasonal pitches

Leisure: 🄰 🔍 ▢

Facilities: 🛁 ☉ 🄿 ☀ 🛒 🔥 **WiFi**

Services: 🔌 🛗 🧺 🚐 🔋 🆛

Within 3 miles: 🛝 🖋 ♻ 🛒 ⛷

Additional site information: 40 acre site. 🐾 Cars can be parked by caravans and tents. Awnings permitted. Groups by prior arrangement only.

See advert on page 358

BLAIRLOGIE
Map 21 NS89

Places to visit
Alloa Tower, ALLOA, FK10 1PP, 01259 211701
www.nts.org.uk/visit/places/alloa-tower

The National Wallace Monument, STIRLING, FK9 5LF, 01786 472140
www.nationalwallacemonument.com

Great for kids: Blair Drummond Safari & Adventure Park, BLAIR DRUMMOND, FK9 4UR, 01786 841456
www.blairdrummond.com

Witches Craig Caravan & Camping Park
▶▶▶▶ 90%

tel: 01786 474947 **FK9 5PX**
email: info@witchescraig.co.uk **web:** www.witchescraig.co.uk
dir: *3 miles northeast of Stirling on A91 (Hillfoots to St Andrews road).*

In an attractive setting with direct access to the lower slopes of the dramatic Ochil Hills, this is a well-maintained family-run park. It is in the centre of 'Braveheart' country, with easy access to historical sites and many popular attractions.

Open: April to October **Last arrival:** 20.00 **Last departure:** noon

Pitches: 🚐 from £22.60, 🚐 from £22.50; ▲ from £17.50; 60 hardstanding pitches, 6 seasonal pitches

Leisure: 🄰 **Facilities:** 🛁 ☉ 🄿 ☀ 🛒 🔥 **WiFi**

Services: 🔌 🛗 🧺 🚐 🔋 🛒 ♻ 🆛 **Within 3 miles:** 🛝 🖋 ♻ 🛒 ⛳ 🏇 🚲

Additional site information: 5 acre site. 🐾 Cars can be parked by caravans and tents. Awnings permitted. Food preparation area, cooking shelters, baby bath and changing area.

LUIB
Map 20 NN42

Places to visit
Ben Lawers National Nature Reserve, KILLIN, FK21 8TY, 01567 820988
www.nnr-scotland.org.uk/ben-lawers

Glendochart Holiday Park
▶▶▶▶ 74%

tel: 01567 820637 **FK20 8QT**
email: info@glendochart-caravanpark.co.uk **web:** www.glendochart-caravanpark.co.uk
dir: *On A85 (Oban to Stirling road) midway between Killin and Crianlarich.*

A small site located on the A85 some eight miles from Killin, with boating and fishing available on Loch Tay. It is also convenient for Oban, Fort William and Loch Lomond. Hill walkers have direct access to numerous walks to suit all levels of ability, including the nearby Munro of Ben More. There is a regular bus service at the site entrance, and nearby Crianlarich provides access to the West Highland Railway known as Britain's most scenic rail route, and also the West Highland Way. An ideal site as a stopover to the west coast or for a longer holiday.

Open: March to November **Last arrival:** 21.00 **Last departure:** noon

Pitches: 🚐 from £18.50; 🚐 from £18.50; ▲ from £15; 28 hardstanding pitches

Facilities: ☉ 🄿 ☀ 🛒 🔥 **Services:** 🔌 🛗 🧺 🔋 ♻ **Within 3 miles:** 🖋

Additional site information: 15 acre site. 🐾 Cars can be parked by caravans and tents. Awnings permitted.

PITCHES: 🚐 Caravans 🚐 Motorhomes ▲ Tents 🏕 Glamping accommodation **SERVICES:** 🔌 Electric hook-up 🛗 Launderette 🍷 Licensed bar
🛒 Calor Gas 🌿 Campingaz 🆛 Toilet fluid 🍴 Café/Restaurant 🍔 Fast Food/Takeaway 🔋 Battery charging 🛠 Motorhome service point
* 2019 prices 🚫 No credit or debit cards 🐾 Dogs permitted 🚫 No dogs

STIRLING

See Blairlogie

TYNDRUM
Map 20 NN33

Premier Park

Strathfillan Wigwam Village

►►►►► 80% GLAMPING ONLY

tel: 01838 400251 & 07817 483126 **Auchtertyre Farm FK20 8RU**
email: enquiries@wigwamholidays.com **web:** www.wigwamholidays.com
dir: *From A82 (3 miles north of Crianlarich) site on right. Follow signs for Strathfillan Wigwams and farm shop.*

The hand-crafted wooden wigwams provide good accommodation, especially for walkers as this site is on the West Highland Way. Available all year, each unit is well insulated, has electric panel heaters and an external wood-burner (wood is available at the Trading Post shop). They are spotlessly clean and well maintained. The wigwams have been grouped in small clusters, some have outstanding mountain views and others benefit from the seclusion of a woodland setting. The 'upper' toilet facilities were fully refurbished in 2018. The lodges, with kitchen, shower and toilet, cater for up to eight, and a small yurt is also available for hire. The surrounding area offers many walking and mountain bike opportunities (bike hire available), and various eateries can be found in Tyndrum, not far away. There is a local bus service at the end of the farm road. The site offers touring pitches as well.

Open: All year **Last arrival:** 20.00 (or by prior arrangement) **Last departure:** 10.30

Leisure: ⬜ ⛳

Facilities: 🛁 🦱 ⑤ 🍳 🍴 WiFi

Within 3 miles: 🚴

Accommodation available: Yurt; wooden wigwams.

Additional site information: 6 acre site. 🐾 No noise or music after 23.00. En suite wigwams have own kitchens. Cars can be parked by units.

SCOTTISH ISLANDS

ISLE OF ARRAN

KILDONAN
Map 20 NS02

Places to visit
Isle of Arran Heritage Museum, BRODICK, KA27 8DP, 01770 302636
www.arranmuseum.co.uk

Seal Shore Camping and Touring Site

►►►► 86%

tel: 01770 820320 **KA27 8SE**
email: enquiries@campingarran.com **web:** www.campingarran.com
dir: *From ferry terminal in Brodick turn left, 12 miles, through Lamlash and Whiting Bay. Left to Kildonan, site on left.*

On the south coast of Arran and only 12 miles from the ferry at Brodick, this is a peaceful, family-run site with direct access to a sandy beach. There are fabulous views across the water to Pladda Island and Ailsa Craig, and an abundance of wildlife. The site is suited for all types of touring vehicles but caters very well for non-motorised campers. The resident owner, also a registered fisherman, sells fresh lobsters and crabs, and on request will give fishing lessons on a small, privately owned lochan. There is an undercover barbecue, campers' kitchen and day room with TV. A bus, which stops on request, travels around the island. There are two wooden pods and one gypsy caravan for hire.

Open: March to October **Last arrival:** 21.00 **Last departure:** noon

Pitches: 🚐 from £23; 🚍 from £23; ▲ from £18; 🏠 see prices below; 8 hardstanding pitches

Leisure: 🎯 🎣 ⬜

Facilities: 🛁 ⊙ 🦱 ✳ ⚿ ⑤ 🍳 🍴 WiFi

Services: 🔌 🔄 🍽 🧺 ⛽ 🧼 🔟

Within 3 miles: ⚓ 🚴

Trossachs Holiday Park

ABERFOYLE

David Bellamy Gold Conservation Award

46 Hard-standing serviced and fully serviced Touring Pitches

20 Serviced Tent Pitches

Luxury Timber Lodges for Hire

ABERFOYLE, STIRLINGSHIRE
FK8 3SA

01877 382614

www.trossachsholidays.co.uk

Scottish TOURIST BOARD ★★★★★ HOLIDAY PARK

AA ►►►►► Campsite 2019 Gold Award

LEISURE: 🏊 Indoor swimming pool 🏊 Outdoor swimming pool 🎢 Children's playground ✋ Kids' club 🎾 Tennis court 🎱 Games room 📺 Separate TV room
⛳ golf course 🏌 Pitch n putt 🚣 Boats for hire 🚲 Bikes for hire 🎬 Cinema 🎵 Entertainment 🎣 Fishing ⛳ Mini golf 🏄 Watersports 🏋 Gym ⚽ Sports field 🐴 Stables
FACILITIES: 🛁 Baths/Shower ⊙ Electric shaver sockets 🦱 Hairdryer ✳ Ice Pack Facility 🍼 Baby facilities ♿ Disabled facilities ⑤ Shop on site or within 200yds
🍳 BBQ area 🍴 Picnic area WiFi WiFi

Additional site information: 3 acre site. 🐕 Dogs £1 per day. Cars can be parked by caravans. Awnings permitted. No fires, no gazebos, no noise after 22.00. Car parking not available on all caravan pitches. Small shop sells basic essentials. Car hire can be arranged.

Glamping available: 1 gypsy caravan from £35; 2 wooden pods from £35.

Changeover days: Any day

Additional glamping information: No cooking or smoking in pods or gypsy caravan. Departure time 10.00

KILMORY | Map 20 NR92

Premier Park

Runach Arainn

▶▶▶▶▶ 92% GLAMPING ONLY

tel: 01770 870515 **The Old Manse KA27 8PH**
email: runacharainn@gmail.com **web:** www.runacharainn.com
dir: *From ferry at Brodick, turn left onto A481 signed South and Lamlash. Through Lamlash and Whiting Bay. Approximately 9 miles to Kilmory. In Kilmory, 1st right, pass church to site.*

Runach Arainn, Gaelic for 'Secret Arran', lives up to its name – hidden away in a quiet and beautiful part of the Isle of Arran, just a 15-minute walk from a lovely beach on the southern shore of the island. It offers superb 20ft-diameter yurts that were made in Scotland. The style of the interiors together with private bathrooms for each yurt (in an amenity building), create a charming camping experience that includes many creature comforts for a truly exceptional stay. Fire pits and outdoor cooking facilities are also available.

Open: February to November **Last arrival:** 22.00 **Last departure:** 10.00

Facilities: 🏪 ♿ 🚿 🚐 WiFi

Accommodation available: 3 yurts from £70.

Changeover days: Any day

Additional site information: 2 acre site. No pets, no stag or hen parties. Two yurts sleep 6; 1 yurt sleeps 4. Each has wood-burning stove (including oven and hob). Firewood. Dedicated private bathroom. Towels and bedding provided.

ISLE OF MULL

CRAIGNURE | Map 20 NM73

Places to visit

Duart Castle, CRAIGNURE, PA64 6AP, 01680 812309
www.duartcastle.com

Shieling Holidays Mull

▶▶▶▶ 86%

tel: 01680 812496 **PA65 6AY**
email: sales@shielingholidays.co.uk **web:** www.shielingholidays.co.uk
dir: *From ferry left onto A849 to Iona. 400 metres, left at church, follow site signs towards sea.*

A lovely site on the water's edge with spectacular views, and less than one mile from the ferry landing. Hardstandings and service points are provided for motorhomes, and there are astro-turf pitches for tents. The park also offers cottages and unique, en suite Shielings (cottage tents) for hire and bunkhouse accommodation for families. There is also a wildlife trail on site.

Open: 2 March to 5 November **Last arrival:** 22.00 **Last departure:** noon

Pitches: 🚐 🚐 ⛺ 🏠; 30 hardstanding pitches

Leisure: 🎣 🍳 🎱

Facilities: 🏪 ☺ 🅿 ✳ ♿ 🚿 🚐 WiFi

Services: 🔌 🅾 🔋 ⬇ 🛢 🧺 🚾

Within 3 miles: 🎿 ⛳ ⓢ

Additional site information: 7 acre site. 🐕 Cars can be parked by caravans and tents. Awnings permitted. Wildlife trail.

Glamping available: Shielings (cottage tents). **Changeover days:** Any day

PITCHES: 🚐 Caravans 🚐 Motorhomes ⛺ Tents 🏠 Glamping accommodation **SERVICES:** 🔌 Electric hook-up 🅾 Launderette 🍺 Licensed bar
🔥 Calor Gas 🔥 Campingaz Ⓣ Toilet fluid 🍽 Café/Restaurant 🍔 Fast Food/Takeaway 🔋 Battery charging 🛠 Motorhome service point
* 2019 prices 🚫 No credit or debit cards 🐕 Dogs permitted 🚫 No dogs

ISLE OF SKYE

EDINBANE
Map 22 NG35

Places to visit

Dunvegan Castle and Gardens, DUNVEGAN, IV55 8WF, 01470 521206
www.dunvegancastle.com

Skye Camping & Caravanning Club Site
►►►► 95%

tel: 01470 582230 & 024 7647 5426 **Loch Greshornish, Borve IV51 9PS**
email: skye.site@campingandcaravanningclub.co.uk
web: www.campingandcaravanningclub.co.uk/skye
dir: *Approximately 12 miles from Portree on A850 (Dunvegan road). Site by loch shore.*

This campsite is memorable for its stunning waterside location and glorious views, the generous pitch density, the overall range of its facilities, and the impressive ongoing improvements made by the enthusiastic franchisee owners. The layout maximises the beauty of the scenery, and genuine customer care is very evident – an excellent tourist information room and campers' shelter being just two examples. The amenity block has smart, modern fittings, including excellent showers, a generously proportioned disabled room and a family bathroom. This is a 'green' site that uses only eco-friendly toilet fluids, which are available on site. There is a shop, two yurts and two camping pods for hire. Non-club members are very welcome too.

Open: April to October **Last arrival:** 20.00 (earliest arrival 13.00) **Last departure:** noon

Pitches: 🚐 from £7.85; 🚚 from £7.85; ▲ from £7.85; ⛺ see prices below; 44 hardstanding pitches

Leisure: 🎣

Facilities: 🛁 ☉ 🪒 ✳ ♿ 🏪 ⊓ WiFi

Services: 🔌 🗑 🔋 🚽 🛢 🌿 Ⓣ

Within 3 miles: 🏌 ↻

Additional site information: 7.5 acre site. 🐕 Cars can be parked by caravans and tents. Awnings permitted. Barrier locked 23.00–07.00. Car hire can be arranged.

Glamping available: 2 wooden pods from £43; 2 yurts from £80.

Changeover days: Any day

Additional glamping information: Wooden pods: 2 nights minimum stay. Yurts: 3 nights minimum stay. Cars can be parked by pods and yurts.

STAFFIN
Map 22 NG46

Staffin Camping & Caravanning
►►► 82%

tel: 01470 562213 **IV51 9JX**
email: staffincampsite@btinternet.com **web:** www.staffincampsite.co.uk
dir: *On A855, 16 miles north of Portree. Turn right before 40mph signs.*

This site provides an ideal base to rest and appreciate the peace and tranquillity of the north of Skye. It is a large sloping grassy site with level hardstandings for motorhomes and caravans. The site has older but good amenities. Nearby Staffin has a village store and a number of cafés. Sea and loch fishing are available nearby and the Totternish Ridge and surrounding area offer ample hill walking opportunities. It is a relatively short drive over The Quirang to reach the ferry terminal at Uig.

Open: April to October **Last arrival:** 20.00 **Last departure:** 11.00

Pitches: 🚐 from £17; 🚚 from £17; ▲ from £16; 18 hardstanding pitches

Leisure: 🎣

Facilities: ☉ 🪒 ✳ ♿ 🛁 ⊓ WiFi

Services: 🔌 🗑 🔋 🛢 🌿

Within 3 miles: 🎣 🏌 🛒

Additional site information: 2.5 acre site. 🐕 ⊛ Cars can be parked by caravans and tents. Awnings permitted. No music after 22.00. In wet weather may not be possible to park cars by caravans and tents. Picnic tables, kitchen area, campers' bothy.

Wales

Wales

Wales — a place of myth and legend, a country loved passionately by actors and poets and male voice choirs, a land of rugged mountain grandeur and craggy, meandering coastline. Crossing the Severn Bridge, you sense at once you are entering a completely different country. The culture is different, so are the traditions and so are the physical characteristics. With its lush hills and dramatic headlands, it has echoes of other Celtic lands — most notably, Ireland and Scotland.

Wales's legacy of famous names from the world of the arts is truly impressive. Richard Burton hailed from the valleys in South Wales, Anthony Hopkins originates from Port Talbot and Dylan Thomas was born over a century ago in a house on a hilltop street in Swansea. His birthplace in Cwmdonkin Drive can be hired for self-catering breaks and holidays and there is even the chance to sleep in the poet's tiny bedroom. Thomas described the house as 'a provincial villa…a small, not very well painted gateless house…very nice, very respective.'

Further west is the house where he lived in his final years. Thomas and his wife Caitlin moved to the Boat House at Laugharne, 40 miles from Swansea, in the spring of 1949. With its magnificent views across an expansive estuary, this was Dylan Thomas's perfect retreat and much of his creative writing was completed in the modest wooden shed on a bluff above the house. The Boat House is open to visitors and nearby Brown's Hotel, his favourite watering hole, offers the chance to relax and enjoy something to eat and drink.

On the Pembrokeshire coast, renowned for its beautiful beaches, is another, less familiar link with Dylan Thomas. The old fishing village of Lower Fishguard was home to a film unit of almost 100 people in the early months of 1971. Presided over by the film director Andrew Sinclair, filming of Thomas's classic play *Under Milk Wood* began, with Richard Burton and Peter O'Toole among the many film stars seen around the village. A young, virtually unknown David Jason, also appeared in the film. Sinclair and his team built false fronts on the dock cottages and created an undertaker's parlour – among other work. The National Eisteddfod in Llangollen is one of the most important events in the Welsh cultural calendar, celebrating the country's long heritage of storytelling, music and poetry.

Think of Wales and you often think of castles. The formidable Caernarfon Castle, the setting for the investure of the Prince of Wales in 1969, stands in the northwest corner of the country. Harlech Castle was built around 1283 by Edward I and from it are seen the peaks of Snowdonia. This glorious region of towering summits and crags, which has the highest range of mountains in England and Wales and is now a National Park, has long attracted walkers and climbers. Edmund Hillary and his team rehearsed here for the first successful assault on Everest in 1953. However, Snowdonia is not just about mountain peaks. There are plenty of gentler alternatives, including an extensive network of lowland routes, forest trails and waymarked walks. Below Snowdon lies the historic village of Llanberis, one of the region's most popular attractions and ideally placed for touring Snowdonia. Betws-y-Coed is another mountain resort with a range of delightful walks exploring picturesque river scenery and pretty, pastoral uplands.

For the buzz and vibrancy of the city, Swansea and Cardiff cannot be beaten, the latter boasting a lively café culture, docklands-style apartments, a science discovery centre that's fun for all the family, and the internationally renowned Wales Millennium Centre (Canolfan Mileniwm Cymru). However, in terms of Welsh scenery, there is so much waiting to be discovered and explored; the grand, immensely varied landscape of the Brecon Beacons, and the gentler, pastoral acres of the Welsh Borders – among a host of famed beauty spots throughout Wales.

◁ The Preseli Hills

ISLE OF ANGLESEY

BEAUMARIS — Map 14 SH67

Places to visit

Beaumaris Castle, BEAUMARIS, LL58 8AP, 01248 810361
http://cadw.gov.wales/daysout/beaumaris-castle/?lang=en

Kingsbridge Caravan Park

▶▶▶▶ 83%

tel: 01248 490636 & 07774 842199 **Camp Road, Llanfaes LL58 8LR**
email: info@kingsbridgecaravanpark.co.uk **web:** www.kingsbridgecaravanpark.co.uk
dir: *From either Menai Bridge or Britannia Bridge follow signs for Beaumaris and A545. In Beaumaris (castle on left) take B5109 towards Llangoed, 2 miles to crossroads, turn left signed Kingsbridge.*

Peacefully located two miles from historic Beaumaris, this long-established park has been transformed by its caring owners into a must-stay destination for lovers of walking and wildlife. The generously sized pitches are located in two separate touring areas – one for families and one for adults only – each has its own modern, well-equipped amenity block that are smartly presented with quality decor and fittings. Please note that a laundry is not provided but modern facilities are available in nearby Beaumaris.

Open: March to October **Last arrival:** 21.00 **Last departure:** noon
Pitches: * 🚐 from £19; 🚏 from £19; ▲ from £19; 21 hardstanding pitches; 25 seasonal pitches
Leisure: ⚙ ⚽
Facilities: 🛁 ☺ 🏳 ✻ 💲 WiFi
Services: 🔌 🚰 ⚱ 🛢 🌱 T
Within 3 miles: 🎣 🦯 ∪ 🛶 🗒

Additional site information: 14 acre site. 🐾 Cars can be parked by caravans and tents. Awnings permitted. No noise after 23.00, no camp fires.

DULAS — Map 14 SH48

Places to visit

Din Lligwy Hut Group, LLANALLGO, 0300 0256000
http://cadw.gov.wales/daysout/dinlligwyhutgroup/?lang=en

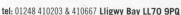

Premier Park

Tyddyn Isaf Caravan Park

▶▶▶▶▶ 93%

tel: 01248 410203 & 410667 **Lligwy Bay LL70 9PQ**
email: mail@tyddynisaf.co.uk **web:** www.tyddynisaf.co.uk
dir: *Take A5025 through Benllech to Moelfre roundabout, left towards Amlwch to Brynrefail. Turn right to Lligwy at phone box. Site 0.5 mile down lane on right.*

A beautifully situated, and very spacious family park on rising ground adjacent to a sandy beach, with magnificent views overlooking Lligwy Bay. A private footpath leads directly to the beach and there is an excellent nature trail around the park. The site has very good toilet facilities, including a block with underfloor heating and excellent unisex privacy cubicles, a well-stocked shop, and bar/restaurant serving meals, which are best enjoyed on the terrace with its magnificent coast and sea views. A new toilet and shower block for campers, a fully-equipped gym and business centre will be on stream for the summer of 2019. Dogs are welcome in the two superb sea-view Mediterranean beach huts, located beside the terrace at the bar.

Open: March to October (restricted service: March to July and September to October – opening times in bar and shop reduced) **Last arrival:** 21.30 **Last departure:** 11.00
Pitches: 🚐 🚏 ▲; 60 hardstanding pitches; 50 seasonal pitches
Leisure: 🖵
Facilities: 🛁 ☺ 🏳 ✻ ⚿ 💲 🍴 WiFi
Services: 🔌 🗒 🍴 🍽 🍺 🚰 ⚱ 🛢 🌱 T
Within 3 miles: 🎣 🦯 ∪ 🛶 🏌

Additional site information: 16 acre site. 🐾 Cars can be parked by caravans and tents. Awnings permitted. No groups, loud music or open fires, maximum 3 units can be booked together. Baby changing unit. Woodland walk.

DWYRAN
Map 14 SH46

Places to visit
Great for kids: Anglesey Sea Zoo, BRYNSIENCYN, LL61 6TQ, 01248 430411
www.angleseyseazoo.co.uk

Premier Park

LLanfair Hall

▶▶▶▶▶ 89% GLAMPING ONLY

tel: 01248 440031 & 07946 388869 **LL61 6AX**
email: stay@llanfairhall.com **web:** www.llanfairhall.com
dir: *Cross Menai Strait on A55. Immediately left, then left onto A4080. After 8 miles right onto B4419, then 2nd left. Keep right at fork, 1st house on right.*

Located within a peaceful, small rural estate and convenient for Newborough Beach and many of Anglesey's attractions, this must-do holiday destination is perfect for that 'away from it all' experience whether wishing for an activity or relaxing break. Five large pods, created from seasoned wood and lined with sheep wool for extra insulation, are carefully equipped with specially designed furnishings, and all benefit from quality en suite wet rooms with shower, washbasin and toilet. In addition to some cooking and food storage facilities, a communal, well-equipped campers' kitchen, drying room and outdoor covered barbecue are also provided. The larger log cabin is ideal for families and a light-limiting policy ensures breathtaking views of the night sky.

Open: All year **Last arrival:** anytime **Last departure:** 10.15

Facilities: ⌂ ✴ ☷ ⊓

Within 3 miles: ✐ ⋃ 🖫

Accommodation available: 5 wooden pods from £70; 1 log cabin from £50 per person per night (minimum stay 2 nights).

Changeover days: Any day

Additional site information: 5 acre site. ⌖ 🅰 Table tennis, giant chess, outdoor pizza ovens, geodome. Pods: personal BBQ/fire pit, fridge, bathroom, Freeview TV, double and sofa bed. Shared access to communal field kitchen, drying room, and covered BBQ building.

MARIAN-GLAS
Map 14 SH58

Places to visit
Din Lligwy Hut Group, LLANALLGO, 0300 0256000
http://cadw.gov.wales/daysout/dinlligwyhutgroup/?lang=en

Capel Lligwy, LLANALLGO, LL72 8LS, 03000 256000
http://cadw.gov.wales/daysout/capellligwy/?lang=en

Platinum Park

Home Farm Caravan Park
▶▶▶▶▶

tel: 01248 410614 **LL73 8PH**
email: enq@homefarm-anglesey.co.uk **web:** www.homefarm-anglesey.co.uk
dir: *On A5025, 2 miles north of Benllech. Site 300 metres beyond church.*

A first-class park run with passion and enthusiasm, set in an elevated and secluded position sheltered by trees, and with good planting and landscaping. The peaceful rural setting affords views of farmland, the sea and the mountains of Snowdonia. The modern toilet blocks are spotlessly clean and well maintained, and there are excellent play facilities for children both indoors and out. Facilities also include a visitors' parking area and a smart reception and shop. The area is blessed with sandy beaches, and the local pubs and shops cater for everyday needs.

Open: April to October **Last arrival:** 21.00 **Last departure:** noon

Pitches: ⌂ ⌂ 🅰; 65 hardstanding pitches

Leisure: ⌂ ♒ ◉ ⊐ ⚽

Facilities: ⌂ ☉ ✐ ✴ ⚒ 🖫 ☷ WiFi

Services: ⚡ 🖫 ⌂ ⋁ ⌂ ⊘ ⊤

Within 3 miles: ⌂ ✐ ⋃ ♒

Additional site information: 12 acre site. ⌖ Cars can be parked by caravans and tents. Awnings permitted. No roller blades, skateboards or scooters.

RHOS LLIGWY
Map 14 SH48

Places to visit

Din Lligwy Hut Group, LLANALLGO, 0300 0256000
http://cadw.gov.wales/daysout/dinlligwyhutgroup/?lang=en

Capel Lligwy, LLANALLGO, LL72 8LS, 03000 256000
http://cadw.gov.wales/daysout/capellligwy/?lang=en

Ty'n Rhos Caravan Park
►►► 78%

tel: 01248 852417 **Lligwy Bay, Moelfre LL72 8NL**
email: robert@bodafonpark.co.uk **web:** www.bodafonpark.co.uk
dir: *Take A5025 from Benllech to Moelfre roundabout, right to T-junction in Moelfre. Left, approximately 2 miles, pass crossroads leading to beach, site 50 metres on right.*

A family park close to the beautiful beach at Lligwy Bay, and cliff walks along the Heritage Coast. Historic Din Lligwy and the shops at picturesque Moelfre are nearby. All the touring pitches have water, electric hook-up and TV connection. Amenities, including toilets, showers and a laundry, are equipped with stylish fixtures and fittings. Please note that guests should register at Bodafon Caravan Park in Benllech where detailed directions will be given and pitches allocated.

Open: March to October **Last arrival:** 20.00 **Last departure:** 11.00
Pitches: 🚐 from £28; 🚌 from £28; ▲ from £24; 4 hardstanding pitches; 48 seasonal pitches
Facilities: 🏠 ☉ ❄ 🅰 🍴 WiFi
Services: 🔌 🔄 🔒
Within 3 miles: ♨ ⚷ ∪ 🏊 🅢

Additional site information: 10 acre site. 🐕 Cars can be parked by caravans and tents. Awnings permitted. No campfires, no noise after 23.00. Boat park.

BRIDGEND

PORTHCAWL
Map 9 SS87

Places to visit

Newcastle, BRIDGEND, 0300 0256000
http://cadw.gov.wales/daysout/newcastle/?lang=en

Coity Castle, COITY, CF35 6BG, 03000 256000
http://cadw.gov.wales/daysout/coitycastle/?lang=en

Great for kids: Margam Country Park, PORT TALBOT, SA13 2TJ, 01639 881635
www.margamcountrypark.co.uk

Brodawel Camping & Caravan Park
►►►► 84%

tel: 01656 783231 **Moor Lane, Nottage CF36 3EJ**
email: info@brodawelcamping.co.uk **web:** www.brodawelcamping.co.uk
dir: *M4 junction 37, A4229 towards Porthcawl. After Grove Golf Club right into Moor Lane, follow site signs.*

A lovely family park close to sea and other attractions, with a lush grass touring field that provides generously sized pitches; most have electric hook-up. There is a

smart amenity block appointed to a high standard, with good privacy options, and a well-stocked shop and WiFi.

Open: April to mid October **Last arrival:** 19.00 **Last departure:** 11.00
Pitches: ✱ 🚐 from £17; 🚌 from £17; ▲ from £17; 4 hardstanding pitches; 40 seasonal pitches
Leisure: 🅰 🎱
Facilities: 🏠 ☉ 🖊 ❄ 🅰 🅢 🍴 🪑 WiFi
Services: 🔌 🔄 🔼 🔒 🧽 🆃
Within 3 miles: ♨ ⚷ ∪ ◎ 🏊 ⛵ 🏁

Additional site information: 4 acre site. 🐕 Cars can be parked by caravans and tents. Awnings permitted. No noise between 22.30–8.00. Free electrical sockets, undercover picnic area.

CARMARTHENSHIRE

LLANDDAROG
Map 8 SN51

Places to visit

The National Botanic Garden of Wales, LLANARTHNE, SA32 8HG, 01558 667149
www.botanicgarden.wales

Carmarthen Caravan Park
►►► 80%

tel: 01267 275666 & 07484 711340 **Coedhirion SA32 8BQ**
email: welshfarmhouse@hotmail.com **web:** www.welshfarm.co.uk
dir: *M4 junction 49, A48 towards Carmarthen. Straight on at Cross Hands roundabout. Left at Fferm Coedhirian sign. Site entrance 1st right.*

Ideally located between the end of M4 and Carmarthen, this rural farm park provides a relaxing and peaceful environment for touring the many attractions in the area. All the gently sloping touring pitches have electric hook-ups and there are some hardstandings for larger units and motorhomes. The amenity block provides three unisex shower, washbasin and toilet rooms. The small lake adjacent to the park is a magnet for wildlife.

Open: All year **Last arrival:** 22.00 (later if pre-arranged) **Last departure:** 14.00
Pitches: 🚐 🚌 ▲; 10 hardstanding pitches; 5 seasonal pitches
Leisure: ⚙
Facilities: 🏠 ☉ 🖊 🍴 🪑
Services: 🔌 🔄 🆃
Within 3 miles: ♨ ⚷ 🅢

Additional site information: 5 acre site. 🐕 ⚑ Cars can be parked by caravans and tents. Awnings permitted. No noise after midnight, no Chinese lanterns. Woodland walk. Car hire can be arranged. Internet access available.

LLANDOVERY

Places to visit

Dolaucothi Gold Mines, PUMSAINT, SA19 8US, 01558 650177
www.nationaltrust.org.uk/dolaucothi-gold-mines

LEISURE: 🏊 Indoor swimming pool 🏊 Outdoor swimming pool 🅰 Children's playground 🎣 Kids' club ᘛ Tennis court 🎱 Games room 🖵 Separate TV room ♨ golf course ⛳ Pitch n putt ⛵ Boats for hire 🚲 Bikes for hire 🎬 Cinema 🎵 Entertainment ⚷ Fishing ◎ Mini golf 🏄 Watersports 🏋 Gym ⚙ Sports field ∪ Stables
FACILITIES: 🏠 Baths/Shower ☉ Electric shaver sockets 🖊 Hairdryer ❄ Ice Pack Facility 🍼 Baby facilities 🅰 Disabled facilities 🅢 Shop on site or within 200yds 🍴 BBQ area 🪑 Picnic area WiFi WiFi

LLANDOVERY
Map 9 SN73

Llandovery Caravan Park
▶▶▶ 80%

tel: 01550 721065 **Church Bank SA20 ODT**
email: llandoverycaravanpark@gmail.com
web: www.llandovery-caravan-camping-park.co.uk
dir: *A40 from Carmarthen, over rail crossing, past junction with A483 (Builth Wells). Turn right for Llangadog, past church, 1st right signed Rugby Club and Camping.*

Within easy walking distance of the town centre and adjacent to the notable Llandovery Dragons Rugby Club, this constantly improving park is an ideal base for touring the Brecon Beacons and many local attractions. Most pitches have both water and a hardstanding, and guests are welcome to use the popular on-site rugby club lounge bar. Please note, a laundry is not provided but there is one in the town.

Open: All year **Last arrival:** 20.00 **Last departure:** 20.00

Pitches: 🚐 🚍 🛖; 60 seasonal pitches

Leisure: 🎱 ⚽ **Facilities:** 🚿 ⊙ ♿ WiFi

Services: 🔌 🍺 🍴 **Within 3 miles:** ⌕ 🏇 🖰 🎣 🏧 🛒 🗑

Additional site information: 8 acre site. 🐕 🚫 Cars can be parked by caravans and tents. Awnings permitted.

NEWCASTLE EMLYN
Map 8 SN34

Places to visit
Cilgerran Castle, CILGERRAN, SA43 2SF, 01239 621339
http://cadw.gov.wales/daysout/cilgerran-castle/?lang=en

Castell Henllys Iron Age Fort, CRYMYCH, SA41 3UT, 01239 891319
www.castellhenllys.com

Premier Park

Cenarth Falls Holiday Park
▶▶▶▶▶ 88%

Best of British

tel: 01239 710345 **Cenarth SA38 9JS**
email: enquiries@cenarth-holipark.co.uk **web:** www.cenarth-holipark.co.uk
dir: *From Newcastle Emlyn on A484 towards Cardigan. Through Cenarth, site on right.*

Located close to the village of Cenarth where the River Teifi, famous for its salmon and trout fishing, cascades through the Cenarth Falls Gorge. With beautifully landscaped grounds and spotless amenities, the park also benefits from an indoor heated swimming pool, sauna, fitness suite and a restaurant with bar.

Open: March to November (restricted service: off-peak season – bar and meals available at weekends only) **Last arrival:** 20.00 **Last departure:** 11.00

Pitches: 🚐 from £18; 🚍 from £18; 🛖 from £18; 27 hardstanding pitches

Leisure: 🏊 🏊 🎱 🎣 🎵 🏌

Facilities: 🚿 ⊙ 🌡 ❄ ♿ WiFi

Services: 🔌 🗑 🍺 🍴 🏧 ⬆ 🖰

Within 3 miles: 🏇 🎣 🛒

Additional site information: 2 acre site. 🐕 Cars can be parked by caravans and tents. Awnings permitted. No skateboards or hover boards. Pool table.

Moelfryn Caravan & Camping Park
▶▶▶▶ 86%

tel: 01559 371231 **Ty-Cefn, Pant-y-Bwlch SA38 9JE**
email: info@moelfryncaravanpark.co.uk **web:** www.moelfryncaravanpark.co.uk
dir: *A484 from Carmarthen towards Cynwyl Elfed. Pass the shops on right, 200 yards take left fork onto B4333 towards Hermon. In 7 miles follow brown sign on left. Turn left, site on right.*

A small, beautifully maintained, family-run park in a glorious elevated location overlooking the valley of the River Teifi. Pitches are level and spacious, and well screened by hedging and mature trees. The centrally located amenity block has stylish decor, smart cladding, provision of good privacy options and excellent fixtures and fittings.

Open: March to 10 January **Last arrival:** 22.00 **Last departure:** noon

Pitches: 🚐 from £14.50; 🚍 from £14.50; 🛖 from £14.50; 18 hardstanding pitches; 12 seasonal pitches

Facilities: 🚿 ⊙ 🌡 ❄ WiFi

Services: 🔌 🗑 🏧 🔋 🚫 **Within 3 miles:** ⌕ 🏇 🖰 🏌 🎣 🛒

Additional site information: 3 acre site. 🐕 Dogs must be kept on leads at all times and owners must clear up after their dogs. Cars can be parked by caravans and tents. Awnings permitted. Games to be played in designated area only. Caravan storage, seasonal pitches.

Argoed Meadow Caravan and Camping Site
▶▶▶▶ 82%

tel: 01239 710690 **Argoed Farm SA38 9JL**
email: argoedfarm@btinternet.com **web:** www.cenarthcampsite.co.uk
dir: *From Newcastle Emlyn on A484 towards Cenarth, take B4332. Site 300 yards on right.*

A warm welcome is assured at this attractive and immaculately maintained site, situated on the banks of the River Teifi and close to Cenarth Falls Gorge. The spotlessly clean amenity block provides very good privacy options for the less able visitors.

Open: All year **Last arrival:** anytime **Last departure:** noon

Pitches: * 🚐 from £22; 🚍 from £22; 🛖 from £20; 5 hardstanding pitches; 10 seasonal pitches

Leisure: 🎣 **Facilities:** 🚿 ⊙ 🌡 ❄ ♿ 🗑 🍴

Services: 🔌 🗑 🏧 🔋 🚫 **Within 3 miles:** 🖰 🏌

Additional site information: 3 acre site. 🐕 🚫 Cars can be parked by caravans and tents. Awnings permitted. No bikes or skateboards.

NEWCASTLE EMLYN *continued*

Afon Teifi Caravan & Camping Park
▶▶▶▶ 81%

tel: 01559 370532 **Pentrecagal SA38 9HT**
email: afonteifi@btinternet.com **web:** www.afonteifi.co.uk
dir: *Signed from A484, 2 miles east of Newcastle Emlyn.*

Set on the banks of the River Teifi, a famous salmon and sea trout river, this secluded, family-owned and run park has good views. It is only two miles from the market town of Newcastle Emlyn. The large amenity block is equipped with modern fixtures and fittings, and free WiFi is available throughout the park. Dog owners will especially appreciate the 12 acres of land, including a river walk – here there are also benches to relax on and enjoy the sounds of the river and the birdsong.

Open: April to October **Last arrival:** 23.00

Pitches: * 🚐 from £24; 🚙 from £24; 🏕 from £12; 22 hardstanding pitches; 25 seasonal pitches

Leisure: ⚠ 🔍 ⚽ ⚽

Facilities: 🛁 ⊙ 🌡 ✳ 👤 🚽 🎪 🛒 WiFi

Services: 🔌 🛢 🍴 ⛽ 💧 🛢 🍾 T Within 3 miles: ⚓ U ◎

Additional site information: 6 acre site. 🐾 Cars can be parked by caravans and tents. Awnings permitted. No noise after midnight, no bikes or scooters to be ridden after dark. Riverside and woodland walks.

CEREDIGION

ABERAERON
Map 8 SN46

Places to visit
Llanerchaeron, ABERAERON, SA48 8DG, 01545 570200
www.nationaltrust.org.uk/llanerchaeron

Cae Hir Gardens, CRIBYN, SA48 7NG, 01570 471116
www.caehirgardens.com

Aeron Coast Caravan Park
▶▶▶ 93%

tel: 01545 570349 **North Road SA46 OJF**
email: enquiries@aeroncoast.co.uk **web:** www.aeroncoast.co.uk
dir: *From Aberaeron on A487 (coast road) towards Aberystwyth. Filling station on left at entrance.*

A well-managed family holiday park on the edge of the attractive resort of Aberaeron, with direct access to the beach. All the spacious pitches are level. On-site facilities include an extensive outdoor pool complex, a multi-activity outdoor sports area, an indoor children's play area, a games room and an entertainment suite.

Open: March to October **Last arrival:** 23.00 **Last departure:** 11.00

Pitches: 🚐 from £17; 🚙 from £17; 🏕 from £17; 30 hardstanding pitches

Leisure: 🏊 ⚠ 🎣 🔍 ⬜ 🎵 🎯 **Facilities:** 🛁 ⊙ 🌡 ✳ 👤 WiFi

Services: 🔌 🛢 🍴 ⛽ 💧 🛢 🍾 T

Within 3 miles: 🎣 U 🏊 ⑤

Additional site information: 22 acre site. 🐾 Cars can be parked by caravans and tents. Awnings permitted. Families only. No motorcycles.

NEW QUAY
Map 8 SN35

Places to visit
Llanerchaeron, ABERAERON, SA48 8DG, 01545 570200
www.nationaltrust.org.uk/llanerchaeron

Premier Park

Quay West Holiday Park
▶▶▶▶▶ 87% HOLIDAY HOME PARK

tel: 01545 560477 **SA45 9SE**
email: quaywest@haven.com **web:** www.haven.com/quaywest
dir: *From Cardigan on A487 left onto A486 into New Quay. Or from Aberystwyth on A487 right onto B4342 into New Quay.*

This holiday park enjoys a stunning clifftop position overlooking picturesque New Quay and Cardigan Bay. It's an easy walk to a glorious sandy beach, and the all-action on-site activities include heated swimming pools, SplashZone, football, archery and fencing (with professional tuition), the Aqua Bar and terrace and a kiddies' Pic 'n' Paint room. There is a good range of holiday caravans.

Open: mid March to October

Holiday Homes: Sleep 8 Bedrooms 2 Bathrooms 1 Toilets 1 Microwave Freezer TV Sky/Freeview

Leisure: 🏊 🏊 ⚠ 👤 🎯

Additional site information: 🐾 Most dog breeds accepted (please check when booking). Dogs must be kept on leads at all times. The facilities provided in the holiday homes may differ depending on the grade.

CONWY

BETWS-YN-RHOS
Map 14 SH97

Places to visit
Bodelwyddan Castle and Park, BODELWYDDAN, LL18 5YA, 01745 584060
www.bodelwyddan-castle.co.uk

Bodnant Garden, TAL-Y-CAFN, LL28 5RE, 01492 650460
www.nationaltrust.org.uk/bodnantgarden

Plas Farm Caravan & Lodge Park
▶▶▶▶ 87%

tel: 01492 680254 & 07831 482176 **LL22 8AU**
email: info@plasfarmcaravanpark.co.uk **web:** www.plasfarmcaravanpark.co.uk
dir: *A55 junction 24, A547 through Abergele, straight on at 2 mini roundabouts, follow Rhyd-Y-Foel signs, 3 miles. Left, follow signs.*

Ideally located for exploring the many attractions of north Wales and within easy travelling distance of historic Chester, this beautifully landscaped park, adjacent to a 16th-century farmhouse, is certainly a popular choice. There are superb pitches, many fully serviced and on a terraced area; the camping area, sited in woodland, ensures tranquillity and relaxation, with only birdsong to disturb the peace. There are two modern amenity blocks, a good laundry and a well-equipped campers' kitchen.

Open: March to October **Last arrival:** 19.00 **Last departure:** 11.00

Pitches: * 🚐 from £21; 🚙 from £21; 54 hardstanding pitches

LEISURE: 🏊 Indoor swimming pool 🏊 Outdoor swimming pool ⚠ Children's playground 👤 Kids' club 🎾 Tennis court 🔍 Games room ⬜ Separate TV room
⚓ golf course 🎯 Pitch n putt 🚣 Boats for hire 🚲 Bikes for hire 🎬 Cinema 🎵 Entertainment 🎣 Fishing ◎ Mini golf 🏊 Watersports 🏋 Gym 🎪 Sports field U Stables
FACILITIES: 🛁 Baths/Shower ⊙ Electric shaver sockets 🌡 Hairdryer ✳ Ice Pack Facility 🍼 Baby facilities 👤 Disabled facilities ⑤ Shop on site or within 200yds
🍖 BBQ area 🍴 Picnic area WiFi WiFi

Leisure: ⚙ Facilities: 🚿 ⊙ 🅿 ⚒ ♿ 🛏 WiFi
Services: 🔌 🔄 🍴 🔋 ⚡ 🚰 T Within 3 miles: ⚽ 🎣 ⛳ 🚴 ♨ 🛒

Additional site information: 10 acre site. 🐾 Cars can be parked by caravans. Awnings permitted. No large groups, no campfires. Quiet after 23.00. Woodland walk, shopping service. Car hire can be arranged.

Hunters Hamlet Caravan Park
▶▶▶▶ 85%

tel: 01745 832237 & 07721 552105 **Sirior Goch Farm LL22 8PL**
email: huntershamlet@aol.com **web:** www.huntershamlet.co.uk
dir: *From A55 (westbound), A547 junction 24 into Abergele. At 2nd lights turn left by George and Dragon pub, onto A548. 2.75 miles, right at crossroads onto B5381. Site 0.5 mile on left.*

A warm welcome is assured at this long established, family-run working farm park adjacent to the owners' Georgian farmhouse. Well-spaced pitches, including 15 with water, electricity and TV hook-up, are within two attractive hedge-screened grassy paddocks. The well-maintained amenity block includes unisex bathrooms. Please note, this site does not accept tents.

Open: March to October **Last arrival:** 22.00 **Last departure:** noon
Pitches: * 🚐 from £18; 🚍 from £18; 30 hardstanding pitches
Leisure: ⚙ Facilities: 🚿 ⊙ 🅿 ⚒ ♿ 🛏 WiFi
Services: 🔌 🔄 🍴 ⚡ Within 3 miles: ⚽ 🎣 🛒

Additional site information: 2.5 acre site. 🐾 Dogs must not be left unattended. Cars can be parked by caravans. Awnings permitted. No football. Family bathroom.

LLANDDULAS   Map 14 SH97

Places to visit

Rhuddlan Castle, RHUDDLAN, LL18 5AD, 01745 590777
http://cadw.gov.wales/daysout/rhuddlancastle/?lang=en

Bodelwyddan Castle and Park, BODELWYDDAN, LL18 5YA, 01745 584060
www.bodelwyddan-castle.co.uk

Premier Park

Bron-Y-Wendon Caravan Park
▶▶▶▶▶ 88%

tel: 01492 512903 **Wern Road LL22 8HG**
email: stay@bronywendon.co.uk **web:** www.bronywendon.co.uk
dir: *From A55 towards Llandudno turn right at Llanddulas and A547 junction 23 sign, sharp right. 200 yards, under A55 bridge. Park on left.*

A top quality site in a stunning location, with panoramic sea views from every pitch and excellent purpose-built toilet facilities including heated shower blocks. Pitch density is excellent, offering a high degree of privacy, and the grounds are beautifully landscaped and immaculately maintained. Super pitches are available. The staff are helpful and friendly, and everything from landscaping to maintenance has a stamp of excellence. An ideal seaside base for touring Snowdonia and visiting Colwyn Bay, Llandudno and Conwy.

Open: All year **Last arrival:** 19.00 summer/17.00 winter **Last departure:** 11.00
Pitches: * 🚐 from £23; 🚍 from £23; 110 hardstanding pitches
Leisure: ⚙ Facilities: 🚿 ⊙ 🅿 ♿ WiFi

Services: 🔌 🔄 🚰 🔋 ⚡ T
Within 3 miles: ⚽ 🎣 ♨ 🚴 🛒

Additional site information: 8 acre site. 🐾 Dogs must be kept on a lead at all times. Cars can be parked by caravans. Awnings permitted. No loose ball games, kites or frisbees. Late arrival bays, 4 holiday cottages.

LLANRWST   Map 14 SH86

Places to visit

Gwydir Uchaf Chapel, LLANRWST, 0300 0256000
http://cadw.gov.wales/daysout/gwydiruchafchapel/?lang=en

Trefriw Woollen Mills, TREFRIW, LL27 0NQ, 01492 640462
www.t-w-m.co.uk

Great for kids: Conwy Valley Railway Museum, BETWS-Y-COED, LL24 0AL, 01690 710568
www.conwyrailwaymuseum.co.uk

Premier Park

Bron Derw Touring Caravan Park
▶▶▶▶▶ 88%

tel: 01492 640494 **LL26 0YT**
email: bronderw@aol.com **web:** www.bronderw-wales.co.uk
dir: *A55 onto A470 for Betws-y-Coed and Llanrwst. In Llanrwst left into Parry Road signed Llanddoged. Left at T-junction, site signed at 1st farm entrance on right.*

Bron Derw, once a dairy farm, is beautifully landscaped with stunning floral displays and surrounded by hills. The park has been built to a very high standard and is fully matured. All pitches are fully serviced, and there is a heated, stone-built toilet block with excellent and immaculately maintained facilities. The Parc Derwen adults-only field has 28 fully serviced pitches and its own designated amenity block. CCTV security cameras cover the whole park.

Open: March to October **Last arrival:** 21.00 **Last departure:** 11.00
Pitches: * 🚐 from £25; 🚍 from £25; 48 hardstanding pitches; 17 seasonal pitches
Facilities: 🚿 ⊙ 🅿 ♿ 🛏 WiFi
Services: 🔌 🔄 🚰 ⚡ T Within 3 miles: 🎣 🛒

Additional site information: 4.5 acre site. 🐾 Cars can be parked by caravans. Awnings permitted. Children must be supervised, no bikes, scooters or skateboards, no noise after 23.00.

LLANRWST *continued*

Bodnant Caravan Park

▶▶▶▶ 86%

tel: 01492 640248 **Nebo Road LL26 OSD**
email: ermin@bodnant-caravan-park.co.uk **web:** www.bodnant-caravan-park.co.uk
dir: *From A470 in Llanrwst at lights take B5427 signed Nebo (opposite garage). Immediately right signed Nebo. Site 300 yards on right, opposite leisure centre.*

This well maintained and stunningly attractive park is filled with flower beds, and the landscape includes shrubberies and trees. The statics are unobtrusively sited and the quality, spotlessly clean toilet blocks have fully serviced private cubicles. All caravan pitches are multi-service, and the tent pitches serviced. There is a separate playing field and rally field, and there are lots of farm animals on the park to keep children entertained. Victorian farming implements are on display around the touring fields.

Open: March to end October **Last arrival:** 21.00 **Last departure:** 11.00
Pitches: 🚐 🚛 🛖; 20 hardstanding pitches
Facilities: 🛁 ☺ 𝒫 ♿ WiFi
Services: 🔌 🔒 ⌀
Within 3 miles: ⌕ 𝒫 ≋ ≋ 🛒 🔒

Additional site information: 5 acre site. 🐾 Cars can be parked by caravans and tents. Awnings permitted. No bikes, skateboards or camp fires, main gates locked 23.00 to 08.00, no noise after 23.00.

DENBIGHSHIRE

PRESTATYN   Map 15 SJ08

Places to visit

Basingwerk Abbey, HOLYWELL, CH8 7GH, 0300 0256000
http://cadw.gov.wales/daysout/basingwerk-abbey/?lang=en

Rhuddlan Castle, RHUDDLAN, LL18 5AD, 01745 590777
http://cadw.gov.wales/daysout/rhuddlancastle/?lang=en

Premier Park

Presthaven Sands Holiday Park

▶▶▶▶▶ 85% HOLIDAY CENTRE

tel: 01745 856471 **Gronant LL19 9TT**
email: presthavensands@haven.com **web:** www.haven.com/presthavensands
dir: *A548 from Prestatyn towards Gronant. Site signed (Note: for sat nav use LL19 9ST).*

Set beside two miles of superb sandy beaches and dunes (with donkeys on site at weekends), this constantly improving holiday park provides a wide range of both indoor and outdoor attractions. The small touring field at the park entrance offers all-electric and mostly hardstanding pitches. The small touring field at the park entrance offers good electric pitches – the majority are hardstanding and include five super pitches. The centrally located entertainment area includes two indoor swimming pools, excellent children's activities and a choice of eating outlets.

Open: mid March to end October (restricted service: mid March to May and September to end October – facilities may be reduced) **Last arrival:** 20.00 **Last departure:** 10.00
Pitches: 🚐 🚛; 39 hardstanding pitches
Leisure: ≋ ≋ 🖐 🎵
Facilities: 🛁 ☺ ♿ 🔒 WiFi
Services: 🔌 🔒 🍴 🍽 🛒 🔩
Within 3 miles: ⌕ 𝒫 ♺ ◎ 🎵

Additional site information: 21 acre site. 🐾 Maximum 2 dogs per booking, certain dog breeds banned. No commercial vehicles, no bookings by persons under 21 years unless a family booking.

RHUALLT   Map 15 SJ07

Places to visit

Rhuddlan Castle, RHUDDLAN, LL18 5AD, 01745 590777
http://cadw.gov.wales/daysout/rhuddlancastle/?lang=en

Bodelwyddan Castle and Park, BODELWYDDAN, LL18 5YA, 01745 584060
www.bodelwyddan-castle.co.uk

Penisar Mynydd Caravan Park

▶▶▶▶ 90%

tel: 01745 582227 & 07831 408017 **Caerwys Road LL17 0TY**
email: contact@penisarmynydd.co.uk **web:** www.penisarmynydd.co.uk
dir: *From A55 junction 29 follow Dyserth and brown caravan signs. Site 500 yards on right.*

A very tranquil, attractively laid-out park set in three grassy paddocks with a superb facilities block including a disabled room and dishwashing area. The majority of pitches are super pitches. Immaculately maintained throughout, the park is within easy reach of historic Chester and the seaside resort of Rhyl.

Open: March to 15 January **Last arrival:** 21.00 **Last departure:** 21.00
Pitches: 🚐 from £16; 🚛 from £16; 🛖 from £14; 71 hardstanding pitches; 30 seasonal pitches
Leisure: ✪
Facilities: ☺ ✳ ♿ 🪑 WiFi
Services: 🔌 🔒 🛒 🔩 🔒
Within 3 miles: ⌕ 𝒫 ♺ ◎ ≋ 🎵 🔒

Additional site information: 6.6 acre site. 🐾 Cars can be parked by caravans and tents. Awnings permitted. No cycling, no fires. Rally area.

GWYNEDD

ABERSOCH
Map 14 SH32

Places to visit

Plas-yn-Rhiw, PLAS YN RHIW, LL53 8AB, 01758 780219
www.nationaltrust.org.uk/plas-yn-rhiw

Beach View Caravan Park
▶▶▶▶ 85%

tel: 01758 712956 **Bwlchtocyn LL53 7BT**
email: beachviewabersoch4@gmail.com
dir: A499 to Abersoch. Through Abersoch and Sarn Bach. Straight on at crossroads, next left signed Porth Tocyn Hotel. Pass chapel. Left at next Porth Tocyn Hotel sign. Site on left.

A long established clifftop park with stunning views of both the sea and the countryside. The grounds are immaculately maintained, and pitches are mainly hardstanding with good electric hook-ups. Just a six-minute walk from the beach.

Open: mid March to mid October **Last arrival:** 21.00 **Last departure:** noon

Pitches: 🚐 🚍 ▲; 47 hardstanding pitches; 40 seasonal pitches

Facilities: 🏠 ☺ 🏳 ✳

Services: 🔌 🗑 ⚡ 🛢 ⌀

Within 3 miles: ↓ 🎣 ∪ ⛷ ⌖ 🔲

Additional site information: 4 acre site. 🐾 🚫 Cars can be parked by caravans and tents. Awnings permitted. Families only.

Deucoch Touring & Camping Park
▶▶▶▶ 85%

tel: 01758 713293 & 07740 281770 **Sarn Bach LL53 7LD**
email: info@deucoch.com **web:** www.deucoch.com
dir: From Abersoch take Sarn Bach road, at crossroads turn right, site on right in 800 yards.

This is a colourful, sheltered site with stunning views of Cardigan Bay and the mountains that is situated just a mile from Abersoch and a long sandy beach. The friendly, enthusiastic, hands-on proprietors make year-on-year improvements to enhance their visitors' experience. Facilities include a superb chalet for dishwashing, outdoor hot showers for wetsuits, caravan sales and repairs, and a farmer's produce van delivers at weekends.

Open: March to October **Last arrival:** 18.00 **Last departure:** 11.00

Pitches: 🚐 🚍 ▲; 10 hardstanding pitches

Leisure: ⌂

Facilities: 🏠 ☺ 🏳 ✳ 🚿 🛗 WiFi

Services: 🔌 🗑 ⌄

Within 3 miles: ↓ 🎣 ∪ ⛷ ⌖ 🔲

Additional site information: 5 acre site. 🐾 🚫 Cars can be parked by caravans and tents. Awnings permitted. Families only.

Tyn-y-Mur Touring & Camping
▶▶▶▶ 83%

tel: 01758 712328 & 07732 677073 **Lon Garmon LL53 7UL**
email: info@tyn-y-mur.co.uk **web:** www.tyn-y-mur.co.uk
dir: From Pwllheli into Abersoch on A499, sharp right at Land and Sea Garage. Site approximately 0.5 mile on left.

A family-only park in a glorious hill-top location overlooking a lush valley and with views extending across Abersoch to the mountains beyond Cardigan Bay. Good, clean, modern toilet facilities and spacious tent pitches on a level grassy field are on offer. A pretty shrub and flower display at the entrance surrounds a ship's anchor recovered from a Royal Navy frigate which was lost in the bay in 1948. There is a pathway from the site to private river fishing, and the beach at Abersoch is just a short walk away. The amenity block was refurbished to a high standard for the 2018 season, and free WiFi is available throughout the park.

Open: April to October (opens mid March, weather permitting) **Last arrival:** 21.00 (earliest 13.00) **Last departure:** 11.00

Pitches: 🚐 🚍 ▲; 54 hardstanding pitches; 49 seasonal pitches

Leisure: ⌂ 🎣 ⚽

Facilities: 🏠 ☺ ✳ 🚿 🛗 WiFi

Services: 🔌 🗑 🛒 🛢 🗑 ⌀ 🔲

Within 3 miles: ↓ ∪ ⛷ ⌖ 🏇

Additional site information: 22 acre site. 🐾 1 dog per unit. Cars can be parked by caravans and tents. Awnings permitted. Couples and families only. No open fires, no motorcycles, no noise after 23.00. Boat park.

Bryn Bach Caravan & Camping Site
▶▶▶▶ 80%

tel: 07391 561160 & 07899 061737 **Tyddyn Talgoch Uchaf, Bwlchtocyn LL53 7BT**
email: brynbach@abersochcaravanandcamping.co.uk **web:** www.abersochcamping.co.uk
dir: From Abersoch take Sarn Bach road for approximately 1 mile, left at sign for Bwlchtocyn. Site approximately 1 mile on left.

Stunning views towards the beach and across the bay to the Snowdonia mountains and a warm welcome are assured at this very well-maintained park on the outskirts of Abersoch. Pitch sizes are generous and a smart chalet houses the reception, a well-stocked shop and a cycle-hire facility. Quality family rooms are available in amenity blocks and two glamping bell tents on spacious decking with stunning views are also for hire.

Open: March to October **Last arrival:** 19.00 **Last departure:** 11.00

Pitches: 🚐 from £24; 🚍 from £24; ▲ from £19; 🏠 see prices below; 28 hardstanding pitches; 28 seasonal pitches

Leisure: 🚴

Facilities: 🏠 ☺ 🏳 ✳ 🚿 🛗 🛗 WiFi

Services: 🔌 🗑 ⌄ 🛢 🔲

Within 3 miles: ↓ 🎣 ∪ ⛷ ⌖

Additional site information: 3.5 acre site. 🐾 Cars can be parked by caravans and tents. Awnings permitted. No campfires, only breathable ground sheets permitted, children must return to pitch by 21.00. Boat/jet ski park.

Glamping available: Bell tents from £85.

Additional glamping information: Bell tents: Family and couples only, no dogs allowed in tents. Cars can be parked by tents.

PITCHES: 🚐 Caravans 🚍 Motorhomes ▲ Tents 🏠 Glamping accommodation **SERVICES:** 🔌 Electric hook-up 🗑 Launderette 🍺 Licensed bar 🛢 Calor Gas ⌀ Campingaz 🔲 Toilet fluid 🍽 Café/Restaurant 🛒 Fast Food/Takeaway 🛗 Battery charging ⌄ Motorhome service point
* 2019 prices 🚫 No credit or debit cards 🐾 Dogs permitted 🚫 No dogs

ABERSOCH *continued*

Rhydolion
▶▶▶ 73%

tel: 01758 712342 **Llangian LL53 7LR**
email: enquiries@rhydolion.co.uk **web:** www.rhydolion.co.uk/caravan_camping.htm
dir: *From A499 take unclassified road to Llangian for 1 mile, left, through Llangian. Site 1.5 miles after road forks towards Hell's Mouth and Porth Neigwl.*

A peaceful, small site with good views, on a working farm close to the long sandy surfers beach at Hell's Mouth. The simple toilet facilities are kept to a high standard by the friendly owners, and nearby Abersoch is a mecca for boat owners and water sports enthusiasts.

Open: March to October **Last arrival:** 22.00 **Last departure:** noon

Pitches: 🚐 from £20; 🚚 from £20; ⛺ from £16

Leisure: ⊛ **Facilities:** ☺ ❄

Services: 🔌 🗑 🧺

Within 3 miles: ⚓ 🎣 ∪ ◎ 🛶 ⛷ 🛍

Additional site information: 1.5 acre site. 🐕 Dogs only accepted by prior arrangement. ⊘ Cars can be parked by caravans and tents. Awnings permitted. Families and couples only. Fridge freezers and microwave available.

BANGOR — Map 14 SH57

Places to visit

Penrhyn Castle, BANGOR, LL57 4HN, 01248 353084
www.nationaltrust.org.uk/penrhyncastle

Storiel, BANGOR, LL57 1DT, 01248 353368
www.gwynedd.gov.uk/museums

Great for kids: GreenWood Forest Park, Y FELINHELI, LL56 4QN, 01248 671493
www.greenwoodforestpark.co.uk

Treborth Hall Farm Caravan Park
▶▶▶ 74%

tel: 01248 364399 **The Old Barn, Treborth Hall Farm LL57 2RX**
email: enquiries@treborthleisure.co.uk **web:** www.treborthleisure.co.uk
dir: *A55 junction 9, 1st left at roundabout, straight over at 2nd roundabout, site approximately 800 yards on left.*

Set in eight acres of beautiful parkland with its own trout fishing lake and golf course, this park offers serviced pitches in a sheltered, walled orchard. Tents have a separate grass area, and there is a good clean toilet block. A static holiday caravan, with access for the less able, is available for hire. This is a useful base for families, with easy access to the Menai Straits, Anglesey beaches, Snowdon and the Lleyn peninsula.

Open: Easter to end October **Last arrival:** 22.30 **Last departure:** 10.30

Pitches: 🚐 from £27; 🚚 from £23; ⛺ from £10; 34 hardstanding pitches

Leisure: 🛝 ⚓ 🎣

Facilities: 🛁 🪵 WiFi

Services: 🔌 **Within 3 miles:** ◎ 🛶 🎱 🛍 🗑

Additional site information: 8 acre site. 🐕 Cars can be parked by caravans and tents. Awnings permitted.

BARMOUTH — Map 14 SH61

Places to visit

Harlech Castle, HARLECH, LL46 2YH, 01766 780552
http://cadw.gov.wales/daysout/harlechcastle/?lang=en

Cymer Abbey, PENRHYNDEUDRAETH, LL40 2HE, 0300 0256000
http://cadw.gov.wales/daysout/cymer-abbey/?lang=en

AA CAMPSITE OF THE YEAR FOR WALES 2019

Premier Park

Trawsdir Touring Caravans & Camping Park

▶▶▶▶▶ 93%

tel: 01341 280999 & 07798 520888 **Llanaber LL42 1RR**
email: enquiries@trawsdir.co.uk **web:** www.barmouthholidays.co.uk
dir: *3 miles north of Barmouth on A496, just past Nor Bar on right.*

Well run by the owners, this quality park enjoys spectacular views to the sea and hills, and is very accessible for motor traffic. The facilities are appointed to a very high standard, and include spacious cubicles containing showers and washbasins, individual showers, smart toilets with sensor-operated flush and underfloor heating. Tents and caravans have their own designated areas divided by dry-stone walls (both have spacious fully serviced pitches). The site is very suitable for large recreational vehicles, and there are camping pods for hire. There is an excellent children's play area and an illuminated concrete dog walk that leads directly to the nearby pub which offers takeaway pizza and fish suppers, in addition to restaurant meals. Fast WiFi connection is available throughout the park.

Open: March to January **Last arrival:** 17.00 **Last departure:** 11.00

Pitches: 🚐 from £20; 🚚 from £20; ⛺ from £13; 🛖 see prices below; 70 hardstanding pitches; 30 seasonal pitches

Leisure: 🛝

Facilities: 🛁 ☺ 🎣 ❄ ♿ 🛍 🍴 🪵 🐕 WiFi

Services: 🔌 🗑 🧺 ⛽ 🔒 🚿 T

Within 3 miles: 🎣 🛶

Additional site information: 15 acre site. 🐕 Cars can be parked by caravans and tents. Awnings permitted. Families and couples only. Milk, bread etc available from reception, camping equipment available.

Glamping available: Wooden pods from £35.

Additional glamping information: Minimum stay 2 nights. Pet-friendly and no-pets-allowed pods available. Pods offer balcony area, BBQ, sea views and TV. Cars can be parked by pods.

Premier Park

Hendre Mynach Touring Caravan & Camping Park

►►►►► 87%

tel: 01341 280262 **Llanaber Road LL42 1YR**
email: info@hendremynach.co.uk **web:** www.hendremynach.co.uk
dir: *0.75 mile north of Barmouth on A496.*

A constantly improving site where the enthusiastic owners invest year on year to enhance the customer experience. Although there is a steep decent to the arrivals' area, staff are always on hand to assist. The beautifully maintained touring areas benefit from attractive hedge screening around the large well-spaced pitches that are equipped with water and TV hook-ups. Three camping pods, two static caravans with dog friendly options and a holiday home on site are also availabe to rent. There is direct access to the seafront which leads to the town centre and its many attractions.

Open: 1 March to 9 January (restricted service: winter months – shop closed)
Last arrival: 22.00 **Last departure:** 11.30

Pitches: 🚐 🚌 ⛺; 85 hardstanding pitches; 10 seasonal pitches

Leisure: 🛝

Facilities: 🛁 ⊙ 💨 ✲ ♿ 🛍 [WiFi]

Services: 🔌 🧺 🚰 🛢 🔥 [T]

Within 3 miles: 🎣 🐎 ⛵ 🏬

Additional site information: 10 acre site. 🐕 Cars can be parked by caravans and tents. Awnings permitted. No open fires.

BETWS GARMON Map 14 SH55

Places to visit

Snowdon Mountain Railway, LLANBERIS, LL55 4TY, 01286 870223
www.snowdonrailway.co.uk

Great for kids: Dolbadarn Castle, LLANBERIS, LL55 4UD, 0300 0256000
http://cadw.gov.wales/daysout/dolbadarncastle/?lang=en

Premier Park

Bryn Gloch Caravan & Camping Park

►►►►► 84%

tel: 01286 650216 **LL54 7YY**
email: eurig@bryngloch.co.uk **web:** www.campwales.co.uk
dir: *On A4085, 5 miles southeast of Caernarfon.*

An excellent family-run site with immaculate modern facilities, and all level pitches in beautiful surroundings. The park offers the best of two worlds, with its bustling holiday atmosphere and the peaceful natural surroundings; there are plenty of walks in the area. The 28 acres of level fields are separated by mature hedges and trees, guaranteeing sufficient space for families wishing to spread themselves out. There are some excellent fully serviced camping pitches and static holiday caravans for hire.

Open: All year (restricted service: November to February – shop and games room closed) **Last arrival:** 23.00 **Last departure:** 17.00

Pitches: 🚐 from £20; 🚌 from £20; ⛺ from £20; 80 hardstanding pitches; 80 seasonal pitches

Leisure: 🛝 🔍 📺 🎣

Facilities: 🛁 ⊙ 💨 ✲ ♿ 🛍 🍖 ⛩ [WiFi]

Services: 🔌 🧺 🍟 🔋 🚰 🛢 🔥 [T]

Within 3 miles: ⛳ 🐎 🎯 ⛵

Additional site information: 28 acre site. 🐕 Cars can be parked by caravans and tents. Awnings permitted. No noise after 23.00. Heated family bathroom, mother and baby room, table tennis.

CAERNARFON
Map 14 SH46

See also Dinas Dinlle and Llandwrog

Places to visit

Welsh Highland Railway, CAERNARFON, LL55 2YD, 01766 516024
www.festrail.co.uk

Great for kids: Caernarfon Castle, CAERNARFON, LL55 2AY, 01286 677617
http://cadw.gov.wales/daysout/caernarfon-castle/?skip=1&lang=en

Riverside Camping
▶▶▶▶ 89%

tel: 01286 678781 **Seiont Nurseries, Pont Rug LL55 2BB**
email: info@riversidecamping.co.uk **web:** www.riversidecamping.co.uk
dir: *2 miles from Caernarfon on right of A4086 towards Llanberis, follow signs at entrance.*

Set in the grounds of a former garden centre and enjoying a superb location along the River Seiont, this park is approached by an impressive tree-lined drive. Immaculately maintained by the owners, there is a mixture of riverside grassy pitches and fully serviced pitches for caravans and motorhomes. Hardstanding pitches have electric hook-up, water, drainage and TV connection (particularly suitable for motorhomes). In addition to the smart amenity block, other facilities include an excellent café/restaurant, a volleyball court and boules pitch; river fishing permits are also available. The three superb chalets, each for six people, have wood-burning stoves, picnic gardens and Japanese hot tubs. This is a haven of peace close to Caernarfon, Snowdonia and offers some great walking opportunities.

Open: 14 March to October **Last arrival:** anytime **Last departure:** noon

Pitches: 🚐 from £25; 🚙 from £27; ▲ from £19 🏠; 16 hardstanding pitches; 10 seasonal pitches

Leisure: 🎠 🔍 🎣 ⚽

Facilities: 🛁 ☉ 🏻 ❄ 🚿 🚼 ♿ 🚻 🛒 WiFi

Services: 🔌 🔄 🍺 🍴 🏪 🛒 🛆

Within 3 miles: ⚓ ∪ ⊚ ⛵ ⌖ 🏪

Additional site information: 5 acre site. 🐕 Awnings permitted. No fires, no loud music. Debit cards accepted (no credit cards). Family shower room, undercover picnic area, table tennis, volleyball. Woodland dog walk.

Glamping available: Tented lodges. **Changeover days:** Monday and Friday

Additional glamping information: Beds, linen and towels provided, fully equipped. Wood burner, no electricity. Dogs accepted in 2 units only. No stag or hen groups.

Llys Derwen Caravan & Camping Site
▶▶▶▶ 86%

tel: 01286 673322 **Ffordd Bryngwyn, Llanrug LL55 4RD**
email: llysderwen@aol.com **web:** www.llysderwen.co.uk
dir: *A55 junction 11 (follow Bangor (A5) and Llanberis signs). At roundabout left signed Betws-y-Coed (A5) and Llanberis (A4244). At next roundabout right signed Llanberis. Right at T-junction signed Caernarfon onto A4086. Through Llanrug, left at Y Glyntwrog pub, site 500 metres on right.*

On the outskirts of the village of Llanrug, three miles from Caernarfon on the way to Llanberis and Snowdon. A beautifully maintained site with enthusiastic owners who are constantly investing to improve the facilities. The amenity block is appointed to a high standard and the immaculately maintained grounds are planted with an abundance of colourful shrubs and seasonal flowers.

Open: March to October **Last arrival:** 22.00 **Last departure:** noon

Pitches: 🚐 🚙 ▲

Facilities: 🛁 ☉ 🏻 ❄ ♿

Services: 🔌 🔄 🛒 🛆

Within 3 miles: ⚓ 🎣 ∪ ⛵ ⌖ 🏪

Additional site information: 4 acre site. 🐕 ⊛ Cars can be parked by caravans and tents. Awnings permitted. No open fires, no ball games, no noise after 22.00.

Plas Gwyn Caravan & Camping Park
▶▶▶▶ 82%

tel: 01286 672619 **Llanrug LL55 2AQ**
email: info@plasgwyn.co.uk **web:** www.plasgwyn.co.uk
dir: *A4086, 3 miles east of Caernarfon, site on right. Between River Seiont and Llanrug.*

A secluded park in an ideal location for visiting the glorious nearby beaches, historic Caernarfon, the attractions of Snowdonia and for walking opportunities. The site is set within the grounds of Plas Gwyn House, a Georgian property with colonial additions; the friendly owners constantly improve the facilities. There is a 'breakfast butty' service and fresh tea and coffee is available for delivery to individual pitches. The all-electric pitches include hardstandings and five that are fully serviced. Three 'timber tents' (wooden pods) and five statics are available for hire.

Open: March to October **Last arrival:** 22.00 **Last departure:** 11.30

Pitches: 🚐 🚙 ▲ 🏠; 8 hardstanding pitches; 8 seasonal pitches

Facilities: 🛁 ☉ 🏻 ❄ ♿ 🏪 🛒 WiFi

Services: 🔌 🔄 🛒 🛆 🔒 🍃 T

Within 3 miles: ⚓ 🎣 ∪ ⛵ ⌖

Additional site information: 3 acre site. 🐕 Cars can be parked by caravans and tents. Awnings permitted. Minimum noise 22.00 to midnight, complete quiet midnight to 08.00.

Glamping available: Wooden pods.

Additional glamping information: Wooden pods: maximum of 4 people per unit. Cars can be parked by pods.

LEISURE: 🏊 Indoor swimming pool 🏊 Outdoor swimming pool 🎠 Children's playground ✋ Kids' club 🎾 Tennis court 🎱 Games room 📺 Separate TV room
⛳ golf course 🏏 Pitch n putt 🚣 Boats for hire 🚲 Bikes for hire 🎬 Cinema 🎭 Entertainment 🎣 Fishing ⛳ Mini golf 🏄 Watersports 🏋 Gym 🌀 Sports field ∪ Stables
FACILITIES: 🛁 Baths/Shower ☉ Electric shaver sockets 🏻 Hairdryer ❄ Ice Pack Facility 🚼 Baby facilities ♿ Disabled facilities 🏪 Shop on site or within 200yds
🍴 BBQ area 🛒 Picnic area WiFi WiFi

CRICCIETH
Map 14 SH43

Places to visit

Criccieth Castle, CRICCIETH, LL52 0DP, 01766 522227
http://cadw.gov.wales/daysout/criccieth-castle/?lang=en

Portmeirion, PORTMEIRION, LL48 6ER, 01766 770000
www.portmeirion-village.com

Great for kids: Ffestiniog Railway, PORTHMADOG, LL49 9NF, 01766 516024
www.festrail.co.uk

Eisteddfa

▶▶▶▶ 91%

tel: 01766 522696 **Eisteddfa Lodge, Pentrefelin LL52 0PT**
email: info@eisteddfapark.co.uk **web:** www.eisteddfapark.co.uk
dir: *From Porthmadog take A497 towards Criccieth. Approximately 3.5 miles, through Pentrefelin, site signed 1st right after Plas Gwyn Nursing Home.*

A quiet, secluded park on elevated ground, sheltered by the Snowdonia Mountains and with lovely views of Cardigan Bay; Criccieth is nearby. The enthusiastic owners have carried out major investment in recent years to provide top-notch amenity blocks with good privacy options, especially for families. There's a field and play area, woodland walks, six superb slate-based hardstandings, a 'cocoon pod', two tipis and three static holiday caravans for hire, plus a three acre coarse fishing lake adjacent to the park.

Open: March to October **Last arrival:** 22.30 **Last departure:** 11.00

Pitches: 🚐 🚍 ⛺, 🛖 see prices below; 17 hardstanding pitches; 20 seasonal pitches

Leisure: 🎣 ⚽ **Facilities:** ⊙ ℗ ✳ ♿ 🏺 🎋

Services: 🔌 🔋 🍽 ♨ 🛢 ⊘ **Within 3 miles:** ⚓ 🏌 ∪ ◎ 🚴 ✈ 🗓 🏪

Additional site information: 24 acre site. 🐕 Cars can be parked by caravans and tents. Awnings permitted. No noise after 22.30. Baby bath available.

Glamping available: 2 tipis from £55; 1 cabin (cocoon pod) from £22.50.

Additional glamping information: Cars can be parked by glamping units.

Llwyn-Bugeilydd Caravan & Camping Site
▶▶▶ 85%

tel: 01766 522235 & 07752 784358 **LL52 0PN**
email: post@snowdoniacaravanpark.co.uk **web:** www.snowdoniacaravanpark.co.uk
dir: *From Porthmadog on A497, 1 mile north of Criccieth on B4411. Site 2nd on right. From A55 take A487 through Caernarfon. After Bryncir right onto B4411, site on left in 3.5 miles.*

This is a peaceful rural site, close to the coast and Snowdonia attractions, that has been greatly improved in recent years and offers well-spaced, mostly grass pitches and a stylish amenity block. Winter caravan storage and free WiFi are also available.

Open: March to October **Last arrival:** anytime **Last departure:** 11.00

Pitches: 🚐 🚍 ⛺; 1 hardstanding pitch; 40 seasonal pitches

Leisure: 🎱 ⚽ **Facilities:** 🏺 ⊙ ℗ ✳ 🏺 🎋 WiFi

Services: 🔌 🔋 🍽 **Within 3 miles:** ⚓ 🏌 ∪ ◎ 🚴 ✈ 🏪

Additional site information: 6 acre site. 🐕 Cars can be parked by caravans and tents. Awnings permitted. No skateboards, no noise between 22.30 to 08.00, caravan storage until evening of departure available if required (no charge).

DINAS DINLLE
Map 14 SH45

Places to visit

Inigo Jones Slateworks, GROESLON, LL54 7UE, 01286 830242
www.inigojones.co.uk

Caernarfon Castle, CAERNARFON, LL55 2AY, 01286 677617
http://cadw.gov.wales/daysout/caernarfon-castle/?skip=1&lang=en

Great for kids: Welsh Highland Railway, CAERNARFON, LL55 2YD, 01766 516024
www.festrail.co.uk

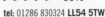
Premier Park

Dinlle Caravan Park
▶▶▶▶▶ 85%

tel: 01286 830324 **LL54 5TW**
email: enquiries@dinllecaravanpark.co.uk **web:** www.thornleyleisure.co.uk
dir: *From A487 at roundabout take A499 signed Pwllheli. Right at Caernarfon Airport and brown camping signs.*

A very accessible, well-kept, grassy site adjacent to a sandy beach and with good views towards Snowdonia. The park, with a superb landscaped entrance, is situated on flat grassland that provides plenty of space for large groups. The man-made dunes offer campers additional protection from sea breezes. The lounge bar and family room are comfortable places in which to relax, and children will enjoy the exciting adventure playground. There are camping pods, with decking and barbecue areas, for hire. A golf club, a nature reserve and the Caernarfon Airworld Museum at the airport can all be accessed from the beach road.

Open: March to November **Last arrival:** 22.00 **Last departure:** noon

Pitches: 🚐 from £20; 🚍 from £20; ⛺ from £20; 🛖 see prices below; 83 hardstanding pitches; 80 seasonal pitches

Leisure: ⚓ 🎿 🎣 🎵

Facilities: 📺 ⊙ ℗ ✳ ♿ 🏪 WiFi

Services: 🔌 🔋 🍽 ♨ 🛢 ⊘

Within 3 miles: 🏌 ∪ 🚴

Additional site information: 20 acre site. 🐕 Cars can be parked by caravans and tents. Awnings permitted. No skateboards, scooters, hoverboards, boats or jet skis.

Glamping available: Wooden pods from £30. **Changeover days:** Any day

Additional glamping information: Wooden pods sleep 4. 1 double bed, 2 single beds. Minimum stay 2 nights. Cars can be parked by pods.

DYFFRYN ARDUDWY Map 14 SH52

Places to visit

Harlech Castle, HARLECH, LL46 2YH, 01766 780552
http://cadw.gov.wales/daysout/harlechcastle/?lang=en

Murmur-yr-Afon Touring Park

►►► 83%

tel: 01341 247353 **LL44 2BE**
email: murmuryrafon1@btinternet.com **web:** www.murmuryrafon.co.uk
dir: *On A496, north of Dyffryn Ardudwy.*

A pleasant park alongside a wooded stream on the edge of the village, with an adjoining pub and handy for large sandy beaches. Expect good, clean facilities, and lovely views of rolling hills and mountains.

Open: March to October **Last arrival:** 22.00 **Last departure:** 11.00

Pitches: 🚐 🚌 ⛺; 37 hardstanding pitches; 30 seasonal pitches

Leisure: 🛝

Facilities: 🛁 🔌 💨 ❄ ♿ 🍖

Services: 🔧 🧺 ♻

Within 3 miles: ⛳ 🎣 🌊 🏪

Additional site information: 7.5 acre site. 🐕 Cars can be parked by caravans and tents. Awnings permitted.

LLANDWROG

Places to visit

Welsh Highland Railway, CAERNARFON, LL55 2YD, 01766 516024
www.festrail.co.uk

Great for kids: Caernarfon Castle, CAERNARFON, LL55 2AY, 01286 677617
http://cadw.gov.wales/daysout/caernarfon-castle/?skip=1&lang=en

LLANDWROG Map 14 SH45

White Tower Caravan Park

►►►► 89%

tel: 01286 830649 & 07802 562785 **LL54 5UH**
email: whitetower@supanet.com **web:** www.whitetowerpark.co.uk
dir: *From Caernarfon take A487 Porthmadog road. 1st right into Pant Road signed Llanfaglan and Saron. Site 3 miles on right.*

There are lovely views of Snowdonia from this park that is located just two miles from the beach at Dinas Dinlle. A well-maintained toilet block offers a wide range of facilities and most of the hardstanding pitches are fully serviced. Popular amenities include an outdoor heated swimming pool, a lounge bar with family room, and a games and TV room.

Open: March to 10 January (restricted service: March to mid May and September to November – bar closed weekdays) **Last arrival:** 23.00 **Last departure:** noon

Pitches: * 🚐 from £25; 🚌 from £25; 50 hardstanding pitches; 50 seasonal pitches

Leisure: 🏊 🛝 ♟ 📺 🎵

Facilities: 🛁 🔌 💨 ♿ 📶

Services: 🔧 🧺 🍷 ♻ 🔒

Within 3 miles: ⛳ 🎣 🐴 🌊 🚤 🏪

Additional site information: 6 acre site. 🐕 Cars can be parked by caravans. Awnings permitted.

PONT-RUG

See Caernarfon

PORTHMADOG

Places to visit

Portmeirion, PORTMEIRION, LL48 6ER, 01766 770000
www.portmeirion-village.com

Great for kids: Ffestiniog Railway, PORTHMADOG, LL49 9NF, 01766 516024
www.festrail.co.uk

Premier Park

Greenacres Holiday Park
▶▶▶▶▶ 87% HOLIDAY CENTRE

tel: 01766 512781 **Black Rock Sands, Morfa Bychan LL49 9YF**
email: greenacres@haven.com **web:** www.haven.com/greenacres
dir: *From Porthmadog High Street follow Black Rock Sands signs between The Factory Shop and Post Office. Park 2 miles on left at end of Morfa Bychan.*

A quality holiday park on level ground just a short walk from Black Rock Sands, and set against a backdrop of Snowdonia National Park. All touring pitches are on hardstandings surrounded by closely-mown grass, and are near the entertainment complex. A full programme of entertainment, organised clubs, indoor and outdoor sports and leisure, pubs, shows and cabarets all add to a holiday experience here. The bowling alley and a large shop with a bakery are useful amenities. The superb touring field has excellent fully serviced Euro pitches, extensive, colourful planting and a smart, well-equipped amenity block.

Open: mid March to end October (restricted service: mid March to May and September to October – some facilities may be reduced) **Last arrival:** 22.00 **Last departure:** 10.00

Pitches: 🚐 🚐; 40 hardstanding pitches

Leisure: 🏊 🎢 💆 🎣 ♫ ⚽ ☺

Facilities: 🏪 ☺ ♿ 🅂 🚻 🚮 WiFi

Services: 🔌 🗄 🍺 🍽 🛒 🔋 🧴

Within 3 miles: ↓ 🎣 ∪ ◎

Additional site information: 121 acre site. 🐾 Maximum 2 dogs per booking, certain dog breeds banned. No commercial vehicles, no bookings by persons under 21 years unless a family booking, no open fires.

Places to visit

Lloyd George Museum, LLANYSTUMDWY, LL52 0SH, 01766 522071
www.gwynedd.gov.uk/museums

Great for kids: Criccieth Castle, CRICCIETH, LL52 0DP, 01766 522227
http://cadw.gov.wales/daysout/criccieth-castle/?lang=en

Premier Park

Hafan y Môr Holiday Park
▶▶▶▶▶ 90% HOLIDAY CENTRE

tel: 01758 612112 **LL53 6HJ**
email: hafanymor@haven.com **web:** www.haven.com/hafanymor
dir: *From Caernarfon take A499 to Pwllheli. A497 to Porthmadog. Park on right, approximately 3 miles from Pwllheli. Or from Telford, A5, A494 to Bala. Right for Porthmadog. Left at roundabout in Porthmadog signed Criccieth and Pwllheli. Park on left, 3 miles from Criccieth.*

Located between Pwllheli and Criccieth, and surrounded by mature trees that attract wildlife, this popular holiday centre provides a wide range of all-weather attractions. Activities include a sports hall, an ornamental boating lake, a large indoor swimming pool, a show bar and a high-ropes activity, plus Segways are available. The indoor Splash Zone was completely upgraded for 2018 season. There are also great eating options – the Mash and Barrel bar and bistro, Traditional Fish and Chips, Burger King, Papa John's and a Starbucks coffeehouse. The touring area includes 75 fully serviced all-weather pitches and a top notch, air-conditioned amenity block.

Open: mid March to end October (restricted service: mid March to May and September to end October – reduced facilities) **Last arrival:** 21.00 **Last departure:** 10.00

Pitches: 🚐 🚐; 75 hardstanding pitches

Leisure: 🏊 💆 ⛳ ♫

Facilities: 🏪 🅟 ♿ 🅂 🚮 WiFi

Services: 🔌 🗄 🍺 🍽 🚮 🛍

Within 3 miles: ↓ 🎣 ∪ ◎ 🚴 ⛵

Additional site information: 500 acre site. 🐾 Maximum 2 dogs per booking, certain dog breeds banned. No commercial vehicles, no bookings by persons under 21 years unless a family booking.

Abererch Sands Holiday Centre
▶▶▶ 75%

tel: 01758 612327 **LL53 6PJ**
email: enquiries@abererch-sands.co.uk **web:** www.abererch-sands.co.uk
dir: *On A497 (Porthmadog to Pwllheli road), 1 mile from Pwllheli.*

Glorious views of Snowdonia and Cardigan Bay can be enjoyed from this very secure, family-run site adjacent to a railway station and a four-mile stretch of sandy beach. During the past two years, the amenity block has been completely refurbished to have stylish decor and modern, efficient fixtures and fittings. A large, heated indoor swimming pool, snooker room, pool room, fitness centre and children's play area make this an ideal holiday venue.

Open: March to October **Last arrival:** 21.00 **Last departure:** noon

Pitches: 🚐 🚐 🏕; 70 hardstanding pitches

Leisure: 🏊 🎢 🔍 💆

Facilities: 🏪 ☺ ❄ ♿ 🅂 WiFi

Services: 🔌 🗄 🔋 ⛟ 🛍 🧴 🚾

Within 3 miles: ↓ 🎣 ∪ 🚴 ⛵ ⛳ 🎯

Additional site information: 85 acre site. 🐾 Cars can be parked by caravans and tents. Awnings permitted.

TAL-Y-BONT
Map 14 SH52

Places to visit

Cymer Abbey, PENRHYNDEUDRAETH, LL40 2HE, 0300 0256000
http://cadw.gov.wales/daysout/cymer-abbey/?lang=en

Harlech Castle, HARLECH, LL46 2YH, 01766 780552
http://cadw.gov.wales/daysout/harlechcastle/?lang=en

Premier Park

Islawrffordd Caravan Park
▶▶▶▶▶ 92%

tel: 01341 247269 **LL43 2AQ**
email: info@islawrffordd.co.uk **web:** www.islawrffordd.co.uk
dir: From A496 into Ffordd Glan-Mor towards sea, follow brown campsite sign. Over rail line, site on left.

Situated on the coast between Barmouth and Harlech and within the Snowdonia National Park, this site has clear views of Cardigan Bay, the Lleyn Peninsula and the Snowdonia and Cader Idris mountain ranges. This is an excellent, family-run and family-friendly park that has seen considerable investment over recent years. Fully matured, the touring area boasts fully-serviced pitches, a superb toilet block with underfloor heating and top-quality fittings; there is private access to miles of sandy beach, adjacent to which is an outdoor activity park suitable for children of all ages, opening for 2019. A superb restaurant and bar, 'Nineteen57', offers both formal and relaxed areas for enjoying locally-sourced food.

Open: 14 February to 3 January **Last arrival:** 20.00 **Last departure:** noon
Pitches: 🚐 from £39; 🚎 from £39; 75 hardstanding pitches; 50 seasonal pitches
Leisure: 🏊 🎠 🖵
Facilities: 🛁 ☉ 🗲 ✳ ♿ WiFi
Services: 🔌 🗑 🚽 🍽 🎰 🛒 ⛽ 🛢 🖾 🗂
Within 3 miles: 🎣 🛶 🖹
Additional site information: 25 acre site. 🐕 Cars can be parked by caravans and tents. Awnings permitted. Strictly for families and couples only.

TYWYN

Places to visit

Talyllyn Railway, TYWYN, LL36 9EY, 01654 710472
www.talyllyn.co.uk

Castell-y-Bere, LLANFIHANGEL-Y-PENNANT, 0300 0256000
http://cadw.gov.wales/daysout/castell-y-bere/?lang=en

Great for kids: King Arthur's Labyrinth, CORRIS, SY20 9RF, 01654 761584
www.kingarthurslabyrinth.co.uk

TYWYN
Map 14 SH50

Ynysymaengwyn Caravan Park
▶▶▶▶ 81%

tel: 01654 710684 **LL36 9RY**
email: rita@ynysy.co.uk **web:** www.ynysy.co.uk
dir: On A493, 1 mile north of Tywyn, towards Dolgellau.

A lovely park set in the wooded grounds of a former manor house, with designated nature trails through 13 acres of wildlife-rich woodland, scenic river walks, fishing and a sandy beach nearby. The attractive stone amenity block is clean and well kept, and this smart municipal park is ideal for families.

Open: March to November **Last arrival:** 23.00 **Last departure:** noon
Pitches: 🚐 from £20; 🚎 from £20; ⛺ from £14; 10 hardstanding pitches; 5 seasonal pitches
Leisure: 🎠 🎣
Facilities: 🛁 ☉ 🗲 ✳ ♿ 🖵 WiFi
Services: 🔌 🗑 🛒 ⛽ 🛢 🖾
Within 3 miles: 🎣 🛶 ◎ 🎣 🖹 🗂
Additional site information: 4 acre site. 🐕 Cars can be parked by caravans and tents. Awnings permitted. Woodland walk.

MONMOUTHSHIRE

ABERGAVENNY
Map 9 SO21

Places to visit

Big Pit National Coal Museum, BLAENAVON, NP4 9XP, 029 2057 3650
www.museumwales.ac.uk

Hen Gwrt, LLANTILIO CROSSENNY, 0300 0256000
http://cadw.gov.wales/daysout/hengwrtmoatedsite/?lang=en

Great for kids: Raglan Castle, RAGLAN, NP15 2BT, 01291 690228
http://cadw.gov.wales/daysout/raglancastle/?lang=en

Wernddu Caravan Park
▶▶▶▶ 84%

tel: 01873 856223 **Old Ross Road NP7 8NG**
email: info@wernddu-golf-club.co.uk **web:** www.wernddu-golf-club.co.uk
dir: From A465, north of Abergavenny, take B4521 signed Skenfrith. Site on right in 0.25 mile.

Located north of the town centre, this former fruit farm, adjacent to a golf club and driving range, is managed by three generations of the same family, and has been transformed into an ideal base for those visiting the many nearby attractions. The well-spaced touring pitches have water, electricity and waste water disposal, and the smart modern amenity block provides very good privacy options. Site guests are welcome to use the golf club bar which also serves meals during the busy months; they are also eligible for half-price green fees. There is no shop on site but a daily newspaper service is provided, and a mini-market is less than a mile away.

Open: March to October **Last arrival:** 21.00 **Last departure:** noon
Pitches: 🚐 from £20; 🚎 from £20; ⛺ from £20; 30 seasonal pitches
Leisure: 🏌 🎣

LEISURE: 🏊 Indoor swimming pool 🏊 Outdoor swimming pool 🎠 Children's playground 🖐 Kids' club 🎾 Tennis court 🎱 Games room 🖵 Separate TV room 🏌 golf course ⛳ Pitch n putt 🚣 Boats for hire 🚲 Bikes for hire 🎬 Cinema 🎵 Entertainment 🎣 Fishing ◎ Mini golf 🏄 Watersports 🏋 Gym 🏐 Sports field 🐴 Stables
FACILITIES: 🛁 Baths/Shower ☉ Electric shaver sockets 🗲 Hairdryer ✳ Ice Pack Facility 🍼 Baby facilities ♿ Disabled facilities 🗂 Shop on site or within 200yds 🍖 BBQ area 🪑 Picnic area WiFi WiFi

Facilities: 🏠 ⚊ ⚕ 🚿 🍴 WiFi
Services: 🔌 🗄 🍽 🍴 🚮 🚻
Within 3 miles: ∪ ◎ 🎯 🛒

Additional site information: 6 acre site. Adults only. 🐕 Cars can be parked by caravans and tents. Awnings permitted. No fires. No noise after 23.00. 20 touring grass pitches. Driving range, bar with sports TV.

Pyscodlyn Farm Caravan & Camping Site
▶▶▶▶ 82%

tel: 01873 853271 & 07816 447942 **Llanwenarth Citra NP7 7ER**
email: info@pyscodlyncaravanpark.com **web:** www.pyscodlyncaravanpark.com
dir: *From Abergavenny take A40 (Brecon road), site 1.5 miles from entrance of Nevill Hall Hospital, on left 50 yards past phone box.*

With its outstanding views of the mountains, this quiet park in the Brecon Beacons National Park makes a pleasant holiday venue for country lovers. The Sugarloaf Mountain and the River Usk are within easy walking distance and, despite being a working farm, dogs are welcome but must be under strict control of course. The separate ladies' and gents' amenity blocks are appointed to a high standard. Please note that credit and debit cards are not accepted at this site.

Open: April to October
Pitches: 🚐 from £16; 🚍 from £16; 🛖 from £15
Leisure: ⚲
Facilities: 🏠 ☉ 🅿 ⚊ ⚕
Services: 🔌 🗄 🚮 🔋 ⊘
Within 3 miles: 🎯 ∪ ◎ 🛒 ⑆

Additional site information: 4.5 acre site. 🐕 🐾 Cars can be parked by caravans and tents. Awnings permitted. No noise after 23.00, no open fires. Car hire can be arranged.

DINGESTOW   Map 9 SO41
Places to visit
Raglan Castle, RAGLAN, NP15 2BT, 01291 690228
http://cadw.gov.wales/daysout/raglancastle/?lang=en

Tintern Abbey, TINTERN PARVA, NP16 6SE, 01291 689251
http://cadw.gov.wales/daysout/tinternabbey/?lang=en

Bridge Caravan Park & Camping Site
▶▶▶ 86%

tel: 01600 740241 **Bridge Farm NP25 4DY**
email: info@bridgecaravanpark.co.uk
dir: *M4 junction 24, A449 towards Monmouth. Left onto A40 towards Abergavenny. Turn right (across dual carriageway) signed Dingestow (and brown caravan sign).*

The River Trothy runs along the edge of this quiet village park, which has been owned by the same family for many years. The touring pitches are both grass and hardstanding, and have a woodland backdrop. The quality facilities are enhanced by good laundry equipment. River fishing is available on site, and there is a dog walking area. The village shop is within 100 yards and a playing field within 200 yards.

Open: Easter to October **Last arrival:** 22.00 **Last departure:** 16.00
Pitches: 🚐 🚍 🛖; 15 hardstanding pitches; 50 seasonal pitches

Leisure: ⚲
Facilities: 🏠 ☉ 🅿 ⚊ ⚕ ⑆
Services: 🔌 🗄 🚛 🚮 🔋 ⊘ T
Within 3 miles: 🎯 ∪ ⚞ 🛒

Additional site information: 4 acre site. 🐕 🐾 Cars can be parked by caravans and tents. Awnings permitted.

LLANVAIR DISCOED   Map 9 ST49
Places to visit
Chepstow Castle, CHEPSTOW, NP16 5EY, 01291 624065
http://cadw.gov.wales/daysout/chepstow-castle/?lang=en

AA GLAMPING SITE OF THE YEAR 2019

Premier Park

Penhein Glamping
▶▶▶▶▶ 91% GLAMPING ONLY

tel: 01633 400581 **Penhein NP16 6RB**
email: enquiries@penhein.co.uk **web:** www.penhein.co.uk
dir: *M48 junction 2, A446 towards Chepstow. 1st exit at roundabout onto A48 signed Caerwent. Approximately 8 miles, through Caerwent, right signed Llanvair Discoed. 1st right at village sign, immediately left into private drive. Site 1.5 miles.*

Tucked away in secluded woodland surrounded by peaceful countryside, the six beautiful Alachigh tents are cosy and warm and kitted out with everything you need to feel at home. The sumptuous interiors have comfortable beds (a double, two truckle beds and a sofa bed for children), quality dining furniture, lanterns, a cold water sink, a large cool box and a wood-burning stove (wood provided), plus an en suite modern, low-level flushing toilet. Outside each tent there is a fire pit for barbecues and carved tree-trunk seating. There are level bark pathways between the tents, and a 'cheat's kitchen' in the centre of the site, with microwave, cooking hobs and a freezer as there is no electricity in the tents themselves. The separate shower block has a drying room, underfloor heating, monsoon showers and a Victorian-style roll-top bath. In addition, there's a communal tent with a wood-burning stove and a wildflower meadow for games.

Open: March to November **Last arrival:** 19.00 **Last departure:** 11.00
Leisure: ⚙
Facilities: 🏠 ⚊ 🚿 🍴
Within 3 miles: 🎯 ⑆ 🗄

Accommodation available: Alachigh tents.
Changeover days: Monday, Wednesday, Friday
Additional site information: 11 acre site. No pets. 8-acre private wildflower and hay meadow, walks on 400-acre farm (woodlands and fields). Christmas and New Year bookings possible.

USK
Map 9 SO30

Places to visit

Caerleon Roman Fortress and Baths, CAERLEON, NP18 1AE, 01663 422518
http://cadw.gov.wales/daysout/Caerleon-roman-fortress-baths/?lang=en

Big Pit National Coal Museum, BLAENAVON, NP4 9XP, 029 2057 3650
www.museumwales.ac.uk

Great for kids: Greenmeadow Community Farm, CWMBRAN, NP44 5AJ,
01633 647662
www.greenmeadowcommunityfarm.org.uk

Premier Park

Pont Kemys Caravan & Camping Park
▶▶▶▶▶ 87%

tel: 01873 880688 & 07976 960832 **Chainbridge NP7 9DS**
email: info@pontkemys.com **web:** www.pontkemys.com
dir: *From Usk take B4598 towards Abergavenny. Approximately 4 miles, over river bridge, bear right, 300 yards to site. For other routes contact site for detailed directions.*

A peaceful park next to the River Usk, offering an excellent standard of toilet facilities with family rooms. The adults-only field benefits from large fully serviced pitches with wide divisions for additional privacy, and a section of the park has fully serviced pitches. The park is in a rural area with mature trees and country views, and attracts quiet visitors who enjoy the many attractions of this area.

Open: March to October **Last arrival:** 21.00 **Last departure:** noon
Pitches: ⌖ ⌖ ▲; 29 hardstanding pitches; 25 seasonal pitches
Leisure: ☐ ⊛
Facilities: ☺ ⊙ ℙ ✳ ⅋ ⊟ WiFi
Services: ⊕ ⊡ ⬛ ⬚ ⚿ ⊘ T
Within 3 miles: ℗ ⚲ ⑤

Additional site information: 8 acre site. 🐾 Cars can be parked by caravans and tents. Awnings permitted. No music. Mother and baby room, kitchen facilities for groups.

PEMBROKESHIRE

BROAD HAVEN
Map 8 SM81

Places to visit

Llawhaden Castle, LLAWHADEN, 0300 0256000
http://cadw.gov.wales/daysout/llawhadencastle/?lang=en

Great for kids: Scolton Manor Museum & Country Park, SCOLTONS, A62 5QL
01437 731328
www.pembrokeshirevirtualmuseum.co.uk

Creampots Touring Caravan & Camping Park
▶▶▶▶ 86%

tel: 01437 781776 **Broadway SA62 3TU**
email: creampots@btconnect.com **web:** www.creampots.co.uk
dir: *From Haverfordwest take B4341 to Broadway. Turn left, follow brown tourist signs to site.*

Set just outside the Pembrokeshire National Park, this quiet site is just one and a half miles from a safe sandy beach at Broad Haven, and the coastal footpath. Most of the well spaced pitches in the beautifully landscaped touring areas have hardstandings and a new amenity block was opened in 2018.

Open: March to October **Last arrival:** 20.00 **Last departure:** 11.00
Pitches: ⌖ ⌖ ▲; 47 hardstanding pitches
Facilities: ☺ ⊙ ℙ ✳ ⅋ ⊟ WiFi
Services: ⊕ ⊡ ⬛ ⬚ ⊘
Within 3 miles: ⚲ ℗ ∪ ⚲ ⚲ ⊞ ⑤

Additional site information: 8 acre site. 🐾 Cars can be parked by caravans and tents. Awnings permitted.

South Cockett Caravan & Camping Park
▶▶▶ 78%

tel: 07774 782572 and 01437 781296 **South Cockett SA62 3TU**
email: esmejames@hotmail.co.uk **web:** www.southcockett.co.uk
dir: *From Haverfordwest take B4341 to Broad Haven, at Broadway turn left, site in 300 yards.*

A warm welcome is assured at this small site on a working farm. The touring areas are divided into neat paddocks by high, well-trimmed hedges, and there are good toilet facilities. The lovely beach at Broad Haven is only about two miles away.

Open: Easter to October **Last arrival:** 22.30
Pitches: ⌖ from £18.00; ⌖ from £18.00 ▲ from £15.00; 25 seasonal pitches
Leisure: ⊛
Facilities: ☺ ⊙ ✳ ⅋ WiFi
Services: ⊕ ⊡ ⬛ ⚿ ⊘
Within 3 miles: ℗ ∪ ⚲ ⚲ ⑤

Additional site information: 6 acre site. 🐾 ⊛ Cars can be parked by caravans and tents. Awnings permitted. No noise after dark.

LEISURE: 🏊 Indoor swimming pool 🏊 Outdoor swimming pool Ⓐ Children's playground 👍 Kids' club 🎾 Tennis court 🎱 Games room 📺 Separate TV room ⛳ golf course 🏌 Pitch n putt 🚣 Boats for hire 🚲 Bikes for hire 🎬 Cinema 🎵 Entertainment 🎣 Fishing ⛳ Mini golf 🏄 Watersports 🏋 Gym ⊛ Sports field ∪ Stables
FACILITIES: ☺ Baths/Shower ⊙ Electric shaver sockets ℙ Hairdryer ✳ Ice Pack Facility 👶 Baby facilities ♿ Disabled facilities ⑤ Shop on site or within 200yds 🍖 BBQ area ⊟ Picnic area WiFi WiFi

FISHGUARD
Map 8 SM93

Places to visit

Pentre Ifan Burial Chamber, NEWPORT, 0300 0256000
http://cadw.gov.wales/daysout/pentreifanburialchamber/?lang=en

Great for kids: OceanLab, FISHGUARDS, A64 0DE, 01348 874737
www.oceanlab.co.uk

Fishguard Bay Resort
▶▶▶▶ 90%

tel: 01348 811415 **Garn Gelli SA65 9ET**
email: enquiries@fishguardbay.com **web:** www.fishguardbay.com
dir: *Accessed from A487. Turn at park sign onto single track road. (Note: if approaching Fishguard from Cardigan on A487 ignore sat nav to turn right).*

Set high up on cliffs with outstanding views of Fishguard Bay, this site has the Pembrokeshire Coastal Path running right through its centre, so affording many opportunities for wonderful walks. The park is extremely well maintained, with a good toilet block, a common room with TV, a lounge with library, laundry and a well-stocked shop. There are family safari tents in addition to two camping pods with superb sea views; a 'pamper pod' is a available for relaxing spa treatments.

Open: March to 9 January **Last arrival:** anytime **Last departure:** noon

Pitches: 🚐 🚎 🛖 🏕; 10 hardstanding pitches

Leisure: ⚲ 🎣 🖵

Facilities: 🛍 ⊙ 🌢 ✳ 🛐 🎏 WiFi

Services: 🔌 🖭 🛒 🧺 🔋 ⌀ T

Within 3 miles: 🅿 ∪ ⩾ ⤧ 🗓

Additional site information: 7 acre site. 🐕 Cars can be parked by caravans and tents. Awnings permitted. No commercial vehicles. Spa treatments. Freshly baked bread and pastries available.

Glamping available: 2 wooden pods; safari tents. **Changeover days:** Any day

Additional glamping information: Wooden pods offer TV, fridge, BBQ, double sofa bed, 2 small bunk beds. Bedding is not included. Cars can be parked by pods.

HASGUARD CROSS
Map 8 SM80

Places to visit

Marloes Sands, MARLOES, 01437 720385
www.nationaltrust.org.uk/marloes-sands-and-mere

Hasguard Cross Caravan Park
▶▶▶ 88%

tel: 01437 781443 **SA62 3SL**
email: hasguard@aol.com **web:** www.hasguardcross.co.uk
dir: *From Haverfordwest take B4327 towards Dale. In 7 miles right at crossroads. Site 1st right.*

A very clean, efficient and well-run site in the Pembrokeshire National Park, just one and a half miles from the sea and beach at Little Haven, and with views of the surrounding hills. The very well-equipped amenity block has quality decor, fixtures and fittings, and a licensed bar (evenings only) serves a range of popular dishes.

Open: All year **Last arrival:** 21.00 **Last departure:** 10.00

Pitches: 🚐 🚎 🛖; 3 hardstanding pitches

Leisure: ⊛

Facilities: ⊙ 🌢 ✳ & 🎏 WiFi

Services: 🔌 🖭 🛒 🍽 🧺 🛒 ⌵ 🔋

Within 3 miles: ↨ 🅿 ∪ ⩾ ⤧ 🛐

Additional site information: 4.5 acre site. 🐕 Cars can be parked by caravans and tents. Awnings permitted. No noise after 22.30, no fires or open BBQs. August – tent field available for 28 days.

PITCHES: 🚐 Caravans 🚎 Motorhomes 🛖 Tents 🏠 Glamping accommodation **SERVICES:** 🔌 Electric hook-up 🖭 Launderette 🍺 Licensed bar
🛢 Calor Gas ⌀ Campingaz T Toilet fluid 🍽 Café/Restaurant 🍟 Fast Food/Takeaway 🔋 Battery charging ⚙ Motorhome service point
* 2019 prices 🚫 No credit or debit cards 🐕 Dogs permitted ⊗ No dogs

HAVERFORDWEST — Map 8 SM91

Places to visit

Llawhaden Castle, LLAWHADEN, 0300 0256000
http://cadw.gov.wales/daysout/llawhadencastle/?lang=en

Great for kids: Oakwood Theme Park, NARBERTH, SA67 8DE, 01834 815170
www.oakwoodthemepark.co.uk

Nolton Cross Caravan Park

🛖

►►► 81%

tel: 01437 710701 & 07814 779020 **Nolton SA62 3NP**
email: info@noltoncross-holidays.co.uk **web:** www.noltoncross-holidays.co.uk
dir: *1 mile from A487 (Haverfordwest to St Davids road) at Simpson Cross, towards Nolton and Broadhaven.*

High grassy banks surround the touring area of this park adjacent to the owners' working farm. It is located on open ground above the sea and St Bride's Bay (within one and a half miles), and there is a coarse fishing lake close by – equipment for hire and reduced permit rates for campers are available. There are shepherd's huts for hire and WiFi is available.

Open: March to December **Last arrival:** 22.00 **Last departure:** noon

Pitches: 🚐 from £12.50; 🚌 from £12.50; ⛺ from £12.50; 🛖 see prices below; 5 hardstanding pitches

Leisure: 🛝 🎣

Facilities: 🛁 🔌 ❄ [S] 🧺 [WiFi]

Services: 🔧 ⚙ 🛏 ⛽ 🍃 [T]

Within 3 miles: 🐴 🏄

Additional site information: 4 acre site. 🐕 Dogs must be kept on leads. Cars can be parked by caravans and tents. Awnings permitted. No youth groups. Site shop open high season only.

Glamping available: 2 shepherd's huts from £40. **Changeover days:** Any day

Additional glamping information: Cars can be parked by shepherd's huts.

LITTLE HAVEN

See Hasguard Cross

ST DAVIDS

Places to visit

St Davids Cathedral, ST DAVIDS, SA62 6PE, 01437 720202
www.stdavidscathedral.org.uk

St Davids Bishop's Palace, ST DAVIDS, SA62 6PE, 01437 720517
http://cadw.gov.wales/daysout/stdavidsbishopspalace/?lang=en

ST DAVIDS — Map 8 SM72

Premier Park

Caerfai Bay Caravan & Tent Park

►►►►► 92%

tel: 01437 720274 **Caerfai Bay SA62 6QT**
email: info@caerfaibay.co.uk **web:** www.caerfaibay.co.uk
dir: *From Haverfordwest on A487 towards St Davids, left at roundabout into Caerfai Road (Ffordd Caerfai) signed Caerfai Bay. Or from Fishguard take A487 to St Davids. At roundabout left into Glasfryn Road. At roundabout, second exit into Caerfai Road (Ffordd Caerfai). Site on right at end of road, before beach car park.*

Magnificent coastal scenery and an outlook over St Bride's Bay can be enjoyed from this delightful site, located just 300 yards from a bathing beach. The park offers good roadways, modern water points, solar-heated wet suit shower rooms and excellent toilet facilities, which include four family rooms. There is a very good farm shop just across the road.

Open: March to early November **Last arrival:** 21.00 **Last departure:** 11.00

Pitches: 🚐 from £21; 🚌 from £14; ⛺ from £14; 26 hardstanding pitches

Facilities: 🛁 🔌 💨 ❄ ♿ [WiFi]

Services: 🔧 ⚙ 🛏 ⛽ 🔒 🍃 [T]

Within 3 miles: ⛳ 🎣 🏄 ⛵ [S]

Additional site information: 10 acre site. 🐕 No dogs in tent field mid July to August. Cars can be parked by caravans and tents. Awnings permitted. No skateboards or rollerblades, no audible devices after 22.00, quiet after 23.00. Local farm shop nearby is open from end May to end August.

Tretio Caravan & Camping Park

►►► 82%

tel: 01437 781600 & 07814 588289 **SA62 6DE**
email: info@tretio.com **web:** www.tretio.com
dir: *From St Davids take A487 towards Fishguard, left at Rugby Football Club, straight on for 3 miles. Site signed, right to site.*

A warm welcome is assured at this long established family-oriented holiday destination that's in a rural location with superb country views and close to beautiful beaches. On-site facilities include an attractive well-equipped amenity block and a small shop selling essentials. The small cathedral city of St Davids is only three miles away.

Open: March to October **Last arrival:** 20.00 **Last departure:** 10.00

Pitches: * 🚐 from £16; 🚌 from £16; ⛺ from £16; 1 hardstanding pitch; 8 seasonal pitches

Leisure: 🛝 🎣 ⚽

Facilities: 🏪 👶 🚿 ✳ ♿ 🍖 ⛩ [WiFi]

Services: 🔌 🧺 🔋

Within 3 miles: ⛳ 🎯 🚣 🌲 🛍

Additional site information: 6.5 acre site. 🐕 Cars can be parked by caravans and tents. Awnings permitted. Quiet after 22.00. Climbing wall, play area.

TENBY

Map 8 SN10

Places to visit

Tudor Merchant's House, TENBY, SA70 7BX, 01834 842279
www.nationaltrust.org.uk/tudormerchantshouse

Tenby Museum & Art Gallery, TENBY, SA70 7BP, 01834 842809
www.tenbymuseum.org.uk

Great for kids: Colby Woodland Garden, AMROTH, SA67 8PP, 01834 811885
www.nationaltrust.org.uk/colby-woodland-garden

Premier Park

Kiln Park Holiday Centre

►►►►► 86% HOLIDAY CENTRE

🛖 2017 2018

tel: 01834 844121 **Marsh Road SA70 8RB**
email: kilnpark@haven.com **web:** www.haven.com/kilnpark
dir: *Follow A477, A478 to Tenby for 6 miles. Then follow signs to Penally, site 0.5 mile on left.*

A large holiday complex complete with leisure and sports facilities and lots of entertainment for all the family. There are bars and cafés, including the stylish Harbwr Lights Bistro, and plenty of security. This touring, camping and static site is on the outskirts of town, and it's only a short walk through dunes to the sandy beach. The modern amenity block provides a stylish interior with underfloor heating and superb fixtures and fittings.

Open: mid March to end October (restricted service: mid March to May and September to end October – some facilities may be reduced) **Last arrival:** dusk **Last departure:** 10.00

Pitches: 🚐 🚌 ⛺; 🛖 see prices below; 60 hardstanding pitches

Leisure: 🏊 🏊 🛝 👋 🎭 ♫ ⚽

Facilities: 🏪 🚿 ♿ 🛍 🍖 ⛩ [WiFi]

Services: 🔌 🧺 🍷 🍴 🍔 🛢 🔥

Within 3 miles: 🎣 ⛳ 🐴 🎯 🚣 🌲 🎬

Additional site information: 103 acre site. 🐕 Maximum 2 dogs per booking, certain dog breeds banned. No commercial vehicles, no bookings by persons under 21 years unless a family booking. Entertainment complex, bowling and putting green.

Glamping available: Safari tents from £129. **Changeover days:** Mondays and Fridays

Additional glamping information: Safari tents: minimum stay 3 nights. Cars can be parked by tents.

Trefalun Park

►►►► 88%

tel: 01646 651514 **Devonshire Drive, St Florence SA70 8RD**
email: trefalun@aol.com **web:** www.trefalunpark.co.uk
dir: *1.5 miles northwest of St Florence and 0.5 mile north of B4318.*

Set within 12 acres of sheltered, well-kept grounds, this quiet country park offers well-maintained, level, grass pitches separated by bushes and trees, with plenty of space to relax in. Children can feed the park's friendly pets. Plenty of activities are available at the nearby Heatherton Country Sports Park, including go-karting, indoor bowls, golf and bumper boating.

Open: Easter to October **Last arrival:** 19.00 **Last departure:** noon

Pitches: 🚐 from £20; 🚌 from £20; ⛺ from £20; 90 hardstanding pitches; 55 seasonal pitches

Leisure: 🛝

Facilities: 🏪 👶 🚿 ✳ ♿ [WiFi]

Services: 🔌 🧺 🔋 ⚓ 🛢 🔥 [T]

Within 3 miles: 🎣 ⛳ 🎯 🚣 🌲 🛍

Additional site information: 12 acre site. 🐕 Cars can be parked by caravans and tents. Awnings permitted. No motorised scooters, no gazebos.

See advert on page 386

TENBY *continued*

Well Park Caravan & Camping Site
►►►► 83%

tel: 01834 842179 **SA70 8TL**
email: enquiries@wellparkcaravans.co.uk **web:** www.wellparkcaravans.co.uk
dir: *A478 towards Tenby. At roundabout at Kilgetty follow Tenby and A478 signs. 3 miles to next roundabout, take 2nd exit, site 2nd right.*

An attractive, well-maintained park with good landscaping from trees, ornamental shrubs and flower borders. The amenities include a launderette and indoor dishwashing area, games room with table tennis, and an enclosed play area. The park is ideally situated between Tenby and Saundersfoot; Tenby just a 15-minute walk away, or the town can be reached via a traffic-free cycle track.

Open: March to October (restricted service: March to mid June and mid September to October – bar may be closed) **Last arrival:** 22.00 **Last departure:** 11.00

Pitches: ⊞ from £20; ⊞ from £20; ▲ from £18; 16 hardstanding pitches

Leisure: ⚞ 🔍 ▢

Facilities: 🛁 ☉ 🇫 ⚒ ⚐ 🎋 WiFi

Services: 🔌 🗊 🍽 🛄 🔧 🔒 ⊘

Within 3 miles: ⌘ ⚓ ∪ ◎ 🌊 🎣 💲

Additional site information: 10 acre site. 🐾 Cars can be parked by caravans and tents. Awnings permitted. Family groups only. TV hook-ups.

Wood Park Caravans
►►► 80%

tel: 01834 843414 **New Hedges SA70 8TL**
email: info@woodpark.co.uk **web:** www.woodpark.co.uk
dir: *A477 from Carmarthen to St Clears. At roundabout onto A477 signed Pembroke Dock. At Kilgetty roundabout left onto A478 signed Tenby. At next roundabout take 2nd exit signed Tenby (ignore 1st exit signs for New Hedges and Saundersfoot). 2nd right to site (signed).*

Situated in beautiful countryside between the popular seaside resorts of Tenby and Saundersfoot, and with Waterwynch Bay just a 15-minute walk away, this peaceful site provides a spacious and relaxing atmosphere for holidays. The slightly sloping touring area is divided by shrubs and hedge-screened paddocks, and a licensed bar and games room are also available.

Open: Spring bank holiday to September (restricted service: September – bar may be closed) **Last arrival:** 22.00 **Last departure:** 10.00

Pitches: ⊞ ⊞ ▲; 40 hardstanding pitches; 10 seasonal pitches

Leisure: ⚞ 🔍

Facilities: 🛁 ☉ 🇫 ⚒ WiFi

Services: 🔌 🗊 🍽 🛄 🔒 ⊘

Within 3 miles: ⌘ ⚓ ◎ 🌊 🎣 💲

Additional site information: 10 acre site. 🚫 🐾 Cars can be parked by caravans and tents. Awnings permitted. No groups, 1 car per unit only.

LEISURE: 🏊 Indoor swimming pool 🏊 Outdoor swimming pool ⚞ Children's playground 👋 Kids' club 🎾 Tennis court 🔍 Games room ▢ Separate TV room ⌘ golf course ⚲ Pitch n putt ⛵ Boats for hire 🚲 Bikes for hire 🎬 Cinema 🎵 Entertainment ⚓ Fishing ◎ Mini golf 🌊 Watersports 🏋 Gym 🏐 Sports field ∪ Stables
FACILITIES: 🛁 Baths/Shower ☉ Electric shaver sockets 🇫 Hairdryer ⚒ Ice Pack Facility 🛄 Baby facilities 👤 Disabled facilities 💲 Shop on site or within 200yds 🍖 BBQ area 🎋 Picnic area WiFi WiFi

POWYS

BRECON
Map 9 SO02

Places to visit

Regimental Museum of The Royal Welsh, BRECON, LD3 7EB, 01874 613310
www.royalwelsh.org.uk

Tretower Court & Castle, TRETOWER, NP8 1RD, 01874 730279
http://cadw.gov.wales/daysout/tretowercourtandcastle/?lang=en

Premier Park

Pencelli Castle Caravan & Camping Park
▶▶▶▶▶ 91%

tel: 01874 665451 **Pencelli LD3 7LX**
email: pencelli@tiscali.co.uk **web:** www.pencelli-castle.com
dir: *A40 onto B4588 (2 miles east of Brecon), follow signs to Pencelli.*

Lying in the heart of the Brecon Beacons National Park, this charming park offers peace, beautiful scenery and high quality facilities. It is bordered by the Brecon and Monmouth Canal. The attention to detail is superb, and the well-equipped, heated toilets with en suite cubicles are matched by a drying room for clothes and boots, full laundry and a shop. Regular buses stop just outside the gate and go to Brecon, Abergavenny and Swansea.

Open: 15 February to November (restricted service: mid February to Easter and 30 October to November – shop closed) **Last arrival:** 22.00 **Last departure:** noon

Pitches: 🚐 �", Å; 40 hardstanding pitches

Leisure: 🎣 ⛳ ☺

Facilities: 🛁 ⊙ 🚻 ✗ & 🖐 🎫 WiFi

Services: 🔌 🗑 🔋 ⚗ 🔒 🞠 T

Within 3 miles: 🎣 ∪ ⚓ 🏇

Additional site information: 10 acre site. ⊗ Only assistance dogs permitted. Cars can be parked by caravans and tents. Awnings permitted. No radios, music or camp fires.

BRONLLYS
Map 9 SO13

Places to visit

Regimental Museum of The Royal Welsh, BRECON, LD3 7EB, 01874 613310
www.royalwelsh.org.uk

Anchorage Caravan Park
▶▶▶▶ 84%

tel: 01874 711246 **LD3 0LD**
email: info@anchoragecp.co.uk **web:** www.anchoragecp.co.uk
dir: *A40 to Brecon. At roundabout take A470 signed Hereford (this road becomes A438). Approximately 8 miles, at roundabout follow Bronllys signs. In Bronllys follow brown campsite signs.*

A well-maintained site with a choice of south-facing, sloping grass pitches and superb views of the Black Mountains, or a more sheltered lower area with a number of excellent super pitches. The site is a short distance from the water sports centre at Llangorse Lake.

Open: All year (restricted service: November to March – TV room closed)
Last arrival: 23.00 **Last departure:** 18.00

Pitches: * 🚐 from £14; 🚐 from £14; Å from £14; 🔌 hardstanding pitches, 60 seasonal pitches

Leisure: 🎣 ▢

Facilities: 🛁 ⊙ 🚻 ✗ & 🖐 🞠 WiFi

Services: 🔌 🗑 🔋 🔒 ⚗ T

Within 3 miles: 🎣 ∪

Additional site information: 8 acre site. 🐕 Cars can be parked by caravans and tents. Awnings permitted. Hairdresser.

BUILTH WELLS | Map 9 SO05

Places to visit

RSPB Carngafallt, RHAYADER, LD6 5HP, 01654 700222
www.rspb.org.uk/reserves-and-events/reserves-a-z/carngafallt

Premier Park

Fforest Fields Caravan & Camping Park
►►►►► 86%

tel: 01982 570406 **Hundred House LD1 5RT**
email: office@fforestfields.co.uk **web:** www.fforestfields.co.uk
dir: *From town centre follow New Radnor signs on A481. 4 miles to signed entrance on right, 0.5 mile before Hundred House village. (Note: if using sat nav, entrance is not centred on postcode).*

This is a constantly improving, sheltered park surrounded by magnificent scenery and an abundance of wildlife. The spacious pitches are well laid out to create optimum privacy, and the superb eco-friendly amenity block is fuelled by a bio-mass boiler and solar panels. The glamping field with superb lake and country views, contains four yurts that have adjacent pod kitchens and a centrally located toilet; this all adds up to a genuine 'away from it all' experience, and the Fforest Café specialises in local produce. The historic town of Builth Wells and The Royal Welsh Showground are just four miles away.

Open: All year **Last arrival:** 21.00 **Last departure:** 18.00
Pitches: 🚐 🚃 ▲ 🏠; 30 hardstanding pitches
Leisure: ⚽

Facilities: 🛁 ☉ 🍽 ✳ 🛗 🖕 🍴 🛒 WiFi
Services: 🔌 🔃 🍽 📧 🔒 🧺 🅣
Within 3 miles: 🦮 🎣 🛶 🚴 🎡

Additional site information: 15 acre site. 🐕 Dogs must be kept on leads at all times. Cars can be parked by caravans and tents. Awnings permitted. No loud music. Quiet after 22.30. Fridges, microwave, electric kettle and phone-charging available.

Glamping available: 4 yurts. **Changeover days:** Monday, Friday

Additional glamping information: Yurts sleep 4. Minimum stay 2 nights. Double bed (two single beds optional), wood-burning stove, wooden floors, decking area, fully-equipped kitchen pod. Off-grid – solar power only. 2 dogs permitted (additional deposit required).

CHURCHSTOKE | Map 15 SO29

Places to visit

Montgomery Castle, MONTGOMERY, 0300 0256000
http://cadw.gov.wales/daysout/montgomerycastle/?lang=en

Premier Park

Daisy Bank Caravan Park
►►►►► 85%

tel: 01588 620471 **Snead SY15 6EB**
email: enquiries@daisy-bank.co.uk **web:** www.daisy-bank.co.uk
dir: *On A489, 2 miles east of Churchstoke.*

Peacefully located between Craven Arms and Churchstoke and surrounded by rolling hills, this idyllic, adults-only park offers generously sized, fully serviced pitches; some with superb country views – all are situated in attractive hedged areas. The immaculately maintained amenity blocks provide smart, modern fittings and excellent privacy options. Camping pods, a pitch and putt course and free WiFi are also available.

Open: All year **Last arrival:** 20.00 **Last departure:** noon

Pitches: * 🚐 from £21; 🚃 from £21; ▲ from £21; 🏠 see prices below; 45 hardstanding pitches; 40 seasonal pitches

Facilities: ☉ 🍴 ✳ 🛗 🛒 🍴 WiFi
Services: 🔌 🔃 🔒 🧺 🅣
Within 3 miles: ◎

Additional site information: 7 acre site. Adults only. 🐕 Cars can be parked by caravans and tents. Awnings permitted. Caravan storage.

Glamping available: Wooden pods from £34. **Changeover days:** Any day

Additional glamping information: Cars can be parked by pods.

CRICKHOWELL

Places to visit

Tretower Court & Castle, TRETOWER, NP8 1RD, 01874 730279
http://cadw.gov.wales/daysout/tretowercourtandcastle/?lang=en

Big Pit National Coal Museum, BLAENAVON, NP4 9XP, 029 2057 3650
www.museumwales.ac.uk

CRICKHOWELL
Map 9 SO21

Riverside Caravan & Camping Park
▶▶▶▶ 84%

tel: 01873 810397 & 07827 625405 **New Road NP8 1AY**
email: riversidecaravanpark@outlook.com web: www.riversidecaravanscrickhowell.co.uk
dir: *On A4077, well signed from A40.*

Within a few minutes' walk from the river and town centre with its excellent shopping and eating choices, is this all-level park. It is surrounded by mature hedges and trees to create privacy and has an excellent amenity block with stylish decor, modern fixtures and fittings and very good privacy options.

Open: March to October **Last arrival:** 21.00

Pitches: 🚐 from £22; 🚌 from £22; ⛺ from £20

Facilities: 🛁 ☺ ℉ ※ ♿ 🖫 WiFi

Services: 🔌 🖫 ☷ ⬆ 🔒

Within 3 miles: ⅃ ⌗ ∪ ≈

Additional site information: 3.5 acre site. Adults only. 🐾 ⊗ Cars can be parked by caravans and tents. Awnings permitted. No fires, no noise after 22.00. Large canopied area for cooking, drying clothes, etc.

LLANDRINDOD WELLS
Map 9 SO06

Places to visit
RSPB Carngafallt, RHAYADER, LD6 5HP, 01654 700222
www.rspb.org.uk/reserves-and-events/reserves-a-z/carngafallt

Disserth Caravan & Camping Park
▶▶▶▶ 84%

tel: 01597 860277 **Disserth, Howey LD1 6NL**
email: disserthcaravan@btconnect.com web: www.disserth.biz
dir: *1 mile from A483, between Newbridge-on-Wye and Howey, by church. Follow brown signs from A483 or A470.*

By a 13th-century church, this is a delightfully secluded and predominantly adult park that sits in a beautiful valley on the banks of the River Ithon, a tributary of the River Wye. It has a small bar which is open at weekends and during busy periods. The amenity block and laundry are appointed to a high standard and provide good privacy options. The site offers a shepherd's hut and a wooden 'morphPod' for hire.

Open: March to October **Last arrival:** sunset **Last departure:** noon

Pitches: * 🚐 from £15; 🚌 from £15; ⛺ from £12; 🏠 see prices below; 6 hardstanding pitches

Leisure: ⌗

Facilities: 🛁 ☺ ℉ ※ ♿ ▦ WiFi

Services: 🔌 🖫 🍴 🛒 ☷ 🔒 🍃 T

Within 3 miles: ⅃ ∪ 🅗 🖫

Additional site information: 4 acre site. 🐾 Maximum 2 pets. Cars can be parked by caravans and tents. Awnings permitted. Quiet after 22.30. Private trout fishing.

Glamping available: Wooden pod from £40; shepherd's hut from £30.

Changeover days: Any day

Additional glamping information: Wooden pod offers twin beds; Shepherd's hut offers microwave, fridge, kettle, heating, pull-down double bed and private shower and toilet. Cars can be parked by pods and huts.

Dalmore Camping & Caravanning Park
▶▶ 82%

tel: 01597 822483 **Howey LD1 5RG**
dir: *From A483 between Llandrindod Wells and Builth Wells follow site signs at hill top. 3 miles from Llandrindod Wells and 4 miles from Builth Wells.*

An intimate and well laid out adults-only park. Pitches are attractively terraced to ensure that all enjoy the wonderful views from this splendidly landscaped little park.

Open: March to October **Last arrival:** 22.00 **Last departure:** noon

Pitches: 🚐 from £11; 🚌 from £11; ⛺ from £11; 12 hardstanding pitches; 6 seasonal pitches

Facilities: 🛁 ☺ ℉ ※ 🍴

Services: 🔌 ☷ ⬆ 🔒 🍃

Within 3 miles: ⅃ ⌗ ◎ 🅗 🖫 🖫

Additional site information: 3 acre site. Adults only. No pets. ⊗ Cars can be parked by caravans and tents. Awnings permitted. Gates closed 23.00–07.00, no ball games. Separate male and female washing areas, no cubicles.

LLANGORS
Map 9 SO12

Places to visit
Regimental Museum of The Royal Welsh, BRECON, LD3 7EB, 01874 613310
www.royalwelsh.org.uk

Great for kids: Tretower Court & Castle, TRETOWER, NP8 1RD, 01874 730279
http://cadw.gov.wales/daysout/tretowercourtandcastle/?lang=en

Lakeside Caravan Park
▶▶▶ 83%

tel: 01874 658226 **LD3 7TR**
email: reception@llangorselake.co.uk web: www.llangorselake.co.uk
dir: *Exit A40 at Bwlch onto B4560 towards Llangorse. Site signed towards lake in Llangorse village.*

Surrounded by spectacular mountains and set close to Llangorse Lake, with mooring and launching facilities, this is a must do holiday destination for lovers of outdoor pursuits, from walking to watersports, and even pike fishing for which the lake is renowned. The hedge- or tree-screened touring areas provide generously-sized pitches. There's a well-stocked shop, bar and café, with a takeaway, under the same ownership.

Open: Easter or April to October (restricted service: March to May and September to October – reduced opening hours in clubhouse and restaurant) **Last arrival:** 21.30 **Last departure:** 10.00

Pitches: 🚐 from £18.25; 🚌 from £18.25; ⛺ from £14; 16 hardstanding pitches

Leisure: 🅐 🎣 ⌗

Facilities: 🛁 ☺ ℉ ※ ♿ 🖫 ▦ 🍴 WiFi

Services: 🔌 🖫 🍴 🍽 🛒 🔒 🍃 T

Within 3 miles: ∪ ≈ ≈

Additional site information: 2 acre site. 🐾 No dogs permitted in hire caravans. Cars can be parked by caravans and tents. Awnings permitted. No open fires, noise to be kept to a minimum after 23.00. Boat hire in summer.

PITCHES: 🚐 Caravans 🚌 Motorhomes ⛺ Tents 🏠 Glamping accommodation **SERVICES:** 🔌 Electric hook-up 🖫 Launderette 🍴 Licensed bar 🔒 Calor Gas 🍃 Campingaz T Toilet fluid 🍽 Café/Restaurant 🛒 Fast Food/Takeaway ☷ Battery charging ⬆ Motorhome service point * 2019 prices ⊗ No credit or debit cards 🐾 Dogs permitted ⊗ No dogs

LLANIDLOES
Map 9 SN98

Places to visit
Bryntail Lead Mine Buildings, LLANIDLOES, 0300 0256000
http://cadw.gov.wales/daysout/bryntail-lead-mine-buildings/?lang=en

Gilfach Nature Reserve & Visitor Centre, RHAYADER, LD6 5LF, 01597 823298
www.rwtwales.org

Premier Park

Red Kite Touring Park
►►►►► 86%

tel: 01686 412122 **Van Road SY18 6NG**
email: info@redkitetouringpark.co.uk **web:** www.redkitetouringpark.co.uk
dir: *From roundabout on A470 at Llanidloes take B4518 signed Penffordd-las Staylittle. At next roundabout take 3rd exit signed Machynlleth. Over river. 1st left (B4518) signed Penffordd-las Staylittle. Pass Clywedog Riverside Holiday Home Park on left, site in approximately 100 yards.*

Within a few minutes' walk from the historic town centre, this stunningly located park has been created on undulating hills and fields, which include two lakes, one being a habitat for newts. All pitches are fully serviced to include a green chemical disposal point and TV hook-up, and the superb amenity block with underfloor heating provides excellent fixtures and fittings coupled with privacy options for both men and women. Please note, this is an adults-only park.

Open: March to January **Last arrival:** 19.00 **Last departure:** noon
Pitches: ⏚ from £27; ⛺ from £27; 66 hardstanding pitches; 10 seasonal pitches
Leisure: ⚲
Facilities: ⬛ ⊙ ⌇ ✳ ⟐ ⅀ WiFi
Services: ⏚ ⓢ ⥮ ⬛ Ⓣ
Within 3 miles: ⚲ ⑤

Additional site information: 20 acre site. Adults only. ⌁ Enclosed dog run, dog wash. Cars can be parked by caravans. Awnings permitted. Fresh milk available. Car hire can be arranged.

MIDDLETOWN
Map 15 SJ31

Places to visit
Powis Castle & Garden, WELSHPOOL, SY21 8RF, 01938 551944
www.nationaltrust.org.uk/powis-castle-and-garden

Bank Farm Caravan Park
►►► 81%

tel: 01938 570526 & 07753 685260 **SY21 8EJ**
email: bankfarmcaravans@yahoo.co.uk **web:** www.bankfarmcaravans.co.uk
dir: *13 miles west of Shrewsbury, 5 miles east of Welshpool on A458.*

This is an attractive park on a small farm that's maintained to a high standard. There are two touring areas located on both sides of the A458; each has its own amenity block and direct access to the hills, mountains and woodland. The site has an excellent display of topiary, trimmed hedges, trees and colourful shrubs. WiFi is available throughout the park, and both a pub serving good food and a large play area are nearby.

Open: March to October **Last arrival:** 20.00
Pitches: ⏚ ⛺ ⚕
Leisure: ⅍ ⚲ ⚲
Facilities: ⬛ ⊙ ✳ ⟐ ⅀ WiFi
Services: ⏚ ⓢ ⥮ ⬛

Additional site information: 2 acre site. ⌁ Cars can be parked by caravans and tents. Awnings permitted. Coarse fishing, jacuzzi, snooker room.

SWANSEA

PONTARDDULAIS
Map 8 SN50

Places to visit
RSPB Cwm Clydach, CLYDACH, SA6 5SU, 029 2035 3000
www.rspb.org.uk/reserves-and-events/reserves-a-z/cwm-clydach

Premier Park

River View Touring Park
►►►►► 86%

tel: 01269 844876 **The Dingle, Llanedi SA4 0FH**
email: info@riverviewtp.com
dir: *M4 junction 49, A483 signed Llandeilo and Ammanford. 1st left after layby. Site in 300 yards on left. (Note: if approaching from north or west on A48 and using sat nav do not exit A48 before Port Abraham roundabout).*

Located in a peaceful valley surrounded by mature trees and with a river meandering through the lower touring areas, this long established holiday destination is constantly being improved by enthusiastic owners and wardens. A well-equipped amenity block is centrally located between upper and lower touring fields which are designated as 'family' and 'adults-only' respectively. Adjacent to the family field, a mini farm has been created – here there are chickens, lambs and a variety of small pig breeds.

Open: March to November **Last arrival:** 20.30 **Last departure:** noon
Pitches: ⏚ ⛺ ⚕ ⅏; 46 hardstanding pitches; 16 seasonal pitches
Leisure: ⅍ ⚲ ⚽
Facilities: ⬛ ⊙ ⌇ ✳ ⟐ ⅀ ⟐ ⅀ WiFi
Services: ⏚ ⓢ ⥮ ⬛ ⚲ Ⓣ
Within 3 miles: ⚲ ⟲ ◎ ≋

Additional site information: 6 acre site. ⌁ Cars can be parked by caravans and tents. Awnings permitted. No commercial vehicles.

Glamping available: Wooden pod.

Additional glamping information: Cars can be parked by pod.

LEISURE: 🏊 Indoor swimming pool ⚊ Outdoor swimming pool ⅍ Children's playground 👋 Kids' club ⚲ Tennis court ⚲ Games room ▭ Separate TV room ⚲ golf course ⚐ Pitch n putt ⚓ Boats for hire ⚲ Bikes for hire 🎬 Cinema ♫ Entertainment ⚲ Fishing ◎ Mini golf ≋ Watersports 🏋 Gym ⚽ Sports field ⟲ Stables
FACILITIES: ⬛ Baths/Shower ⊙ Electric shaver sockets ⌇ Hairdryer ✳ Ice Pack Facility ⚲ Baby facilities ⟐ Disabled facilities ⅀ Shop on site or within 200yds ⚲ BBQ area ⟐ Picnic area WiFi WiFi

PORT EYNON
Map 8 SS48

Places to visit

Weobley Castle, LLANRHIDIAN, SA3 1HB, 01792 390012
http://cadw.gov.wales/daysout/weobleycastle/?lang=en

Gower Heritage Centre, PARKMILL, SA3 2EH, 01792 371206
www.gowerheritagecentre.co.uk

Great for kids: Oxwich Castle, OXWICH, SA3 1ND, 01792 390359
http://cadw.gov.wales/daysout/oxwichcastle/?lang=en

Skysea Camping & Caravan Park
▶▶▶▶ 83%

tel: 01792 390795 **SA3 1NL**
email: booking@porteynon.com
dir: *A4118 to Port Eynon, site adjacent to beach.*

Set in an unrivalled location alongside the safe sandy beach of Port Eynon on the Gower Peninsula, this popular park is an ideal family holiday spot; it is also close to an attractive village with pubs and shops. The sloping ground has been partly terraced and most pitches have sea views; the excellent toilet facilities include three superb family bathrooms.

Open: All year **Last arrival:** 22.00 **Last departure:** 15.00

Pitches: 🚐 🚐 ▲

Facilities: ☺ ♿ 🛅 WiFi

Services: 🔌 🗐 ⚓ 🔋 🧴 T

Within 3 miles: ✐ ∪ ⅏

Additional site information: 12 acre site. 🐕 Cars can be parked by caravans and tents. Awnings permitted.

RHOSSILI
Map 8 SS48

Places to visit

Weobley Castle, LLANRHIDIAN, SA3 1HB, 01792 390012
http://cadw.gov.wales/daysout/weobleycastle/?lang=en

Gower Heritage Centre, PARKMILL, SA3 2EH, 01792 371206
www.gowerheritagecentre.co.uk

Great for kids: Oxwich Castle, OXWICH, SA3 1ND, 01792 390359
http://cadw.gov.wales/daysout/oxwichcastle/?lang=en

Pitton Cross Caravan & Camping Park

▶▶▶ 91%

tel: 01792 390593 **SA3 1PT**
email: admin@pittoncross.co.uk **web:** www.pittoncross.co.uk
dir: *2 miles west of Scurlage on B4247, site on left.*

Surrounded by farmland close to sandy Mewslade Bay, which is within walking distance across fields, this grassy park is divided by hedging into paddocks, with hardstandings for motorhomes available; there are also shepherd's hut-style cabins for hire. Some areas are deliberately left uncultivated, resulting in colourful displays of wild flowers including roses and orchids. Rhossili Beach, which is popular with surfers, and the Welsh Coastal Path are nearby. WiFi is available in the touring caravan areas of park. Both children's kites and power kites are sold on site, and instruction is available; Geocaching and paragliding are possible too.

Open: All year (restricted service: November to March – no bread, milk or newspapers) **Last arrival:** 21.00 **Last departure:** 11.00

Pitches: 🚐 from £24; 🚐 from £24; ▲ from £12; 🏠 see prices below; 27 hardstanding pitches

Leisure: ⌂

Facilities: 🏪 ☺ 🅿 ✳ ♿ 🛅 WiFi

Services: 🔌 🗐 ⚓ 🧴 T

Within 3 miles: ✐ ⅏

Additional site information: 6 acre site. 🐕 Dogs must be kept on leads at all times. Cars can be parked by caravans and tents. Awnings permitted. Quiet at all times. Charcoal BBQs must be off ground, no fire pits or log burning.

Glamping available: Shepherd's hut-style cabins from £100.

Additional glamping information: Cars can be parked by cabins.

SWANSEA
Map 9 SS69

Places to visit
Swansea Museum, SWANSEA, SA1 1SN, 01792 653763
www.swanseamuseum.co.uk

Great for kids: Plantasia, SWANSEA, SA1 2AL, 01792 474555
www.swansea.gov.uk/plantasia

Riverside Caravan Park
▶▶▶▶ 80% HOLIDAY CENTRE

tel: 01792 775587 **Ynys Forgan Farm, Morriston SA6 6QL**
email: reception@riversideswansea.com **web:** www.riversideswansea.com
dir: *M4 junction 45 follow Swansea signs. Before joining A4067 turn left into private road signed to site.*

A large and busy park close to the M4 but in a quiet location beside the River Taw. This friendly, family orientated site has a licensed club and bar with a full high-season entertainment programme. There is a choice of eating outlets – the clubhouse restaurant, takeaway and chip shop. The park has a good indoor pool.

Open: All year (restricted service: in winter months – pool and club closed)
Last arrival: midnight **Last departure:** noon

Pitches: 🚐 🚌 ⛺

Leisure: 🏊 🎠 🎯 🖥 🎵 🎣

Facilities: 🛁 ⊙ 🎀 ✳ ⚕ ⑤ 🎪 WiFi

Services: 🔌 🗄 🚰 ⚱ 🛒 🏧 🍃 Ⓣ

Within 3 miles: 🎣 ⛳ 🚴 🏇

Additional site information: 5 acre site. 🐕 Dogs by prior arrangement only, no aggressive breeds permitted. Fishing on site by arrangement.

WREXHAM

BRONINGTON
Map 15 SJ43

Places to visit
Erddig, WREXHAM, LL13 0YT, 01978 355314
www.nationaltrust.org.uk/erddig

The Little Yurt Meadow
▶▶▶▶ 87% GLAMPING ONLY

tel: 01948 780136 & 07984 400134 **Bay Tree Barns, Mill Road SY13 3HJ**
email: sharon@thelittleyurtmeadow.co.uk **web:** www.thelittleyurtmeadow.co.uk
dir: *A525 from Whitchurch to Redbrook. In Redbrook left onto A495 (Oswestry). Right to Bronington. At staggered crossroads right into Mill Road.*

Located in a former meadow on the Shropshire–Welsh border, this site has become a luxury glamping destination for those wishing to escape from the pressures of everyday life. Three spacious yurts with stylishly furnished interiors are equipped with sumptuous beds, two settees (one converts to a sofa bed), a wood-burning stove, mini-cooker and lots of quality extras. Each yurt has its own allocated luxury shower room and there are areas for communal indoor and outdoor relaxation.

Open: All year **Last arrival:** 23.00 **Last departure:** 11.00

Leisure: 🎯 🎾 ⚽ Spa

Facilities: 🛁 🎀 ✳ ⚕ ⑤ 🎪 🎪

Within 3 miles: 🎣 ⛳ ◎ 🚣 🏊

Accommodation available: Yurts from £180 (up to 4 people). Dogs permitted if whole site rented together.

Additional site information: 3 acre site. 🐾 No noise after 23.00. Self-catering kitchen area, wet rooms, table tennis, darts, pool, hot tub. Minimum stay 2 nights from Thursday, Friday, Saturday or Sunday. Noise level to be kept to a minimum. Cars can be parked by units.

LEISURE: 🏊 Indoor swimming pool 🏊 Outdoor swimming pool 🎠 Children's playground 👶 Kids' club 🎾 Tennis court 🎯 Games room 🖥 Separate TV room ⛳ golf course 🏌 Pitch n putt ⛵ Boats for hire 🚴 Bikes for hire 🎬 Cinema 🎵 Entertainment 🎣 Fishing ◎ Mini golf 🚣 Watersports 🏋 Gym 🏟 Sports field ⛲ Stables **FACILITIES:** 🛁 Baths/Shower ⊙ Electric shaver sockets 🎀 Hairdryer ✳ Ice Pack Facility 🚼 Baby facilities ⚕ Disabled facilities ⑤ Shop on site or within 200yds 🎪 BBQ area 🎪 Picnic area WiFi WiFi

EYTON	Map 15 SJ34

Places to visit

Erddig, WREXHAM, LL13 0YT, 01978 355314
www.nationaltrust.org.uk/erddig

Chirk Castle, CHIRK, LL14 5AF, 01691 777701
www.nationaltrust.org.uk/chirk-castle

Platinum Park

Plassey Holiday Park
►►►►►

tel: 01978 780277 **The Plassey LL13 0SP**
email: enquiries@plassey.com **web:** www.plassey.com
dir: *From A483 at Bangor-on-Dee exit onto B5426 for 2.5 miles. Site entrance signed on left.*

A lovely park set in several hundred acres of quiet farm and meadowland in the Dee Valley. The superb toilet facilities include individual cubicles for total privacy and security, while the Edwardian farm buildings have been converted into a super restaurant, coffee shop, beauty studio and various craft outlets. There is plenty here to entertain the whole family, from scenic walks and a swimming pool to free fishing and use of the 9-hole golf course. For that memorable glamping experience, new cabins with en suite facilities and outside hot tubs were introduced in 2018.

Open: February to November **Last arrival:** 20.30 **Last departure:** noon
Pitches: 🚐 🚌 ▲ 🏠; 85 hardstanding pitches; 60 seasonal pitches
Leisure: 🏊 ♨ 🎯 🎣 🏃 🎾
Facilities: 🏠 ☺ 🦶 ❄ 🚿 🛁 🎏 🧺 WiFi
Services: 🔌 🔄 🍺 🍽 🚮 🔋 🔧 🛢 🚿 ⊤
Within 3 miles: 🏌 ◎ 🎯

Additional site information: 10 acre site. 🐾 Cars can be parked by caravans and tents. Awnings permitted. No footballs or skateboards. No noise after 23.00. Sauna, badminton, table tennis, driving range.
Glamping available: 10 wooden pods (plodges); 4 safari tents.
Changeover days: Friday and Saturday
Additional glamping information: Wooden pods (plodges) and safari tents: minimum stay 3 nights. Pods fully furnished and equipped with hot tubs.

OVERTON	Map 15 SJ34

Premier Park

The Trotting Mare Caravan Park
►►►►► 87%

tel: 01978 711963 **LL13 0LE**
email: info@thetrottingmare.co.uk **web:** www.thetrottingmare.co.uk
dir: *From Oswestry towards Whitchurch take A495. In Ellesmere take A528 towards Overton. Site on left. Or from Wrexham take A525 signed Whitchurch. In Marchwiel turn right onto A528 towards Overton. Through Overton to Ellesmere A528, site on right.*

Located between Overton-on-Dee and Ellesmere, this adults-only touring park is quietly located behind The Trotting Mare pub. The majority of pitches are fully serviced, and creative landscaping and a free coarse-fishing lake are additional benefits. A superb amenity block is served by a bio-mass boiler and equipped with stylish decor and top-notch fixtures and fittings.

Open: All year **Last arrival:** 20.00 **Last departure:** noon
Pitches: 🚐 🚌 ▲; 43 hardstanding pitches
Leisure: 🎣
Facilities: 🏠 ☺ 🦶 ❄ 🚿 WiFi
Services: 🔌 🔄 🍺 🍽 🔋 🔧
Within 3 miles: 🏌 🏌 ◎ ⓢ

Additional site information: 4.2 acre site. Adults only. 🐾 Cars can be parked by caravans and tents. Awnings permitted. No commercial vehicles, no open fires, no gas bottles outside caravan or awning, no bikes, no ball games, no noise after 23.00. Car hire can be arranged.

PITCHES: 🚐 Caravans 🚌 Motorhomes ▲ Tents 🏠 Glamping accommodation **SERVICES:** 🔌 Electric hook-up 🔄 Launderette 🍺 Licensed bar 🛢 Calor Gas ⊘ Campingaz ⊤ Toilet fluid 🍽 Café/Restaurant 🚮 Fast Food/Takeaway 🔋 Battery charging 🔧 Motorhome service point * 2019 prices 🚫 No credit or debit cards 🐾 Dogs permitted 🚫 No dogs

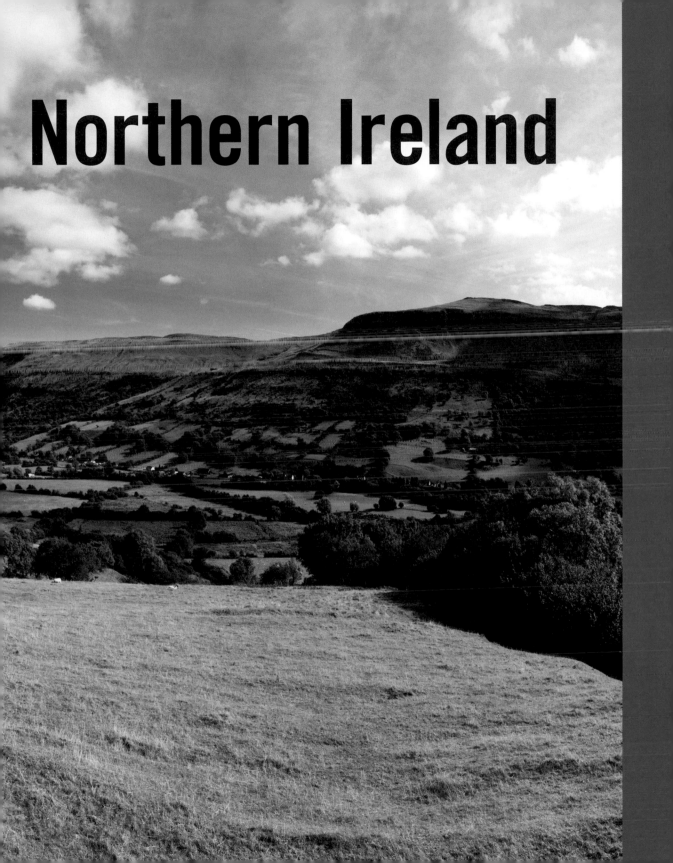

Northern Ireland

COUNTY ANTRIM

ANTRIM · Map 1 D5

Places to visit

Antrim Round Tower, ANTRIM, BT41 1BJ, 028 9082 3207
www.discovernorthernireland.com/Antrim-Round-Tower-Antrim-P2813

Great for kids: Belfast Zoological Gardens, BELFAST, BT36 7PN, 028 9077 6277
www.belfastzoo.co.uk

Six Mile Water Caravan Park

►►►► 83%

tel: 028 9446 4963 **Lough Road BT41 4DG**
email: sixmilewater@antrimandnewtownabbey.gov.uk
web: www.antrimandnewtownabbey.gov.uk/caravanpark
dir: *From A6 (Dublin road) into Lough Road signed Antrim Forum and Loughshore Park. Site at end of road on right.*

This is a peaceful touring site, surrounded by trees and mature hedges, that is part of a large municipal park with boating and outdoor sports opportunities; it is also adjacent to a golf club and within easy walking distance of Antrim and The Forum Leisure Complex. All the generously spaced pitches have hardstandings and electric hook-ups and in addition to a well-equipped amenity block, a lounge is also available.

Open: March to October (restricted service: February and November – open at weekends only) **Last arrival:** 21.00 **Last departure:** noon

Pitches: 🚐 🚏 Å; 37 hardstanding pitches

Leisure: 🔍 ▢

Facilities: 🏠 ☺ 🅿 & 🛗 🛱 WiFi

Services: 🔌 🗑 🍽 🛒 ⬇

Within 3 miles: ⌗ 🖉 ◎ 🎿 🎣 🛍

Additional site information: 9.61 acre site. 🐾 Cars can be parked by caravans and tents. Awnings permitted. Maximum stay 7 nights. No noise between 22.00–08.00. Watersports, angling stands.

BALLYCASTLE · Map 1 D6

Places to visit

Carrick-a-Rede Rope Bridge and Larrybane Visitor Centre, CARRICK-A-REDE, BT54 6LS, 028 2073 3335
www.nationaltrust.org.uk/carrick-a-rede

Old Bushmills Distillery, BUSHMILLS, BT57 8XH, 028 2073 3218
www.bushmills.com

Causeway Coast Holiday Park

►►►► 86% HOLIDAY CENTRE

tel: 028 2076 2550 & 07720 464465 **21 Clare Road BT54 5DB**
email: causewaycoast@hagansleisure.co.uk **web:** www.hagansleisure.co.uk
dir: *From A44 in Ballycastle follow Portrush sign (A2). 1st right into Moyle Road. At T-junction right into Clare Road.*

In an elevated location close to the seafront with views of Ballycastle Bay and Rathlin Island, this bustling holiday park is ideally located for visiting the many attractions along this unspoilt coastline including the Giant's Causeway just 15 minutes away. Facilities include a pub, a well-equipped indoor swimming pool with slide and an outdoor play area. Most of the grassed touring pitches have an electric supply. Tents are not accepted.

Open: March to October **Last arrival:** 23.00 **Last departure:** 10.00

Pitches: 🚐 🚏; 20 hardstanding pitches

Leisure: 🏊 ⁄ℕ 🔍

Facilities: 🏠 🅿 & 🛱 WiFi

Services: 🔌 🗑 🍽 🛒 🛍 T

Within 3 miles: ⌗ 🖉 U ◎ 🎿 🎿 🛍

Additional site information: 28 acre site. 🐾 Quiet time 22.00–07.00, no children out after 23.00.

Watertop Farm

►►►► 83%

tel: 028 2076 2576 **188 Cushendall Road BT54 6RN**
email: watertopfarm@aol.com **web:** www.watertopfarm.co.uk
dir: *From Ballycastle left at Margee bridge onto Cushendall Road (A2). Through Ballyvoy. Site on left just before Ballypatrick Forest. Or from Cushendall take A2, pass Ballypatrick forest, site on right.*

In an idyllic and peaceful location that's within easy reach of major attractions, this unique holiday destination provides very good standards for caravan, motorhome and camping customers. There are three strategically located areas that take full advantage of the surroundings – the lake, the farmland and woodlands. During holiday periods on-site attractions include lake boating, pony trekking, karting, and for indoor amusement there's a large multi-function games room and an animal barn with many domesticated breeds. There is also a superb two-bedroom chalet, with great views, that offers a wood-burner, fully-equipped kitchen and great outdoor furniture.

Open: Easter to October (restricted service: off-peak season – some activities restricted) **Last arrival:** anytime **Last departure:** 14.00

Pitches: 🚐 from £25; 🚏 from £25; Å from £15; 8 hardstanding pitches

Leisure: ⁄ℕ 🔍 ▢

Facilities: 🏠 ☺ ✳ & 🛗 🛱

Services: 🔌 🗑 🍽 🛒 🛒 ⬇

Within 3 miles: ⌗ 🖉 U 🎿 🛍

Additional site information: 1 acre site. 🐾 Cars can be parked by caravans and tents. Awnings permitted. No noise after 23.00, no camp fires.

BUSHMILLS

Places to visit

Old Bushmills Distillery, BUSHMILLS, BT57 8XH, 028 2073 3218
www.bushmills.com

LEISURE: 🏊 Indoor swimming pool 🏊 Outdoor swimming pool ⁄ℕ Children's playground 👋 Kids' club 🎾 Tennis court 🔍 Games room ▢ Separate TV room ⌗ golf course 🚩 Pitch n putt 🚣 Boats for hire 🚲 Bikes for hire ▢ Cinema 🎵 Entertainment 🖉 Fishing ◎ Mini golf 🎿 Watersports 💪 Gym ✿ Sports field U Stables
FACILITIES: 🏠 Baths/Shower ☺ Electric shaver sockets 🅿 Hairdryer ✳ Ice Pack Facility 🛒 Baby facilities & Disabled facilities 🛍 Shop on site or within 200yds 🛗 BBQ area 🛱 Picnic area WiFi WiFi

BUSHMILLS	Map 1 D6

AA CAMPSITE OF THE YEAR FOR NORTHERN IRELAND 2019

Premier Park

Ballyness Caravan Park
▶▶▶▶▶ 93%

tel: 028 2073 2393 **40 Castlecatt Road BT57 8TN**
email: info@ballynesscaravanpark.com web: www.ballynesscaravanpark.com
dir: 0.5 mile south of Bushmills on B66, follow signs.

A peacefully located, quality park with superb toilet and other facilities, on farmland beside St Columb's Rill, the stream that supplies the famous nearby Bushmills Distillery which is close by. The friendly owners created this park with the discerning camper in mind and continue to invest year-on-year to enhance the customer experience. The site has fully serviced, hardstanding pitches and an indoor games barn, play park and football field, free WiFi, a centrally heated amenity building, an 8-acre dog walk and wildlife ponds. It is close to the Giant's Causeway, shops, pubs and restaurants; the Causeway Rambler bus stops at the site on route to the north coast attractions (April to September).

Open: 17 March to October **Last arrival:** 21.00 **Last departure:** noon
Pitches: * 🚐 from £26; 🚍 from £26; 49 hardstanding pitches
Leisure: 🎡 🎱 🖥 ⚽ **Facilities:** 📷 ☺ 🌂 ⚒ ⚙ 🛒 WiFi
Services: 🔌 🗑 🧺 🔧 🏴 🥖 T **Within 3 miles:** 🎣 🏌
Additional site information: 23 acre site. 🐕 Cars can be parked by caravans. Awnings permitted. Library, accessories shop.

BELFAST

DUNDONALD

Places to visit

Mount Stewart, NEWTOWNARDS, BT22 2AD, 028 4278 8387
www.nationaltrust.org.uk/mount-stewart

Giant's Ring, BELFAST, 028 9082 3207
www.discovernorthernireland.com/Giants-Ring-Belfast-P2791

Great for kids: Belfast Zoological Gardens, BELFAST, BT36 7PN, 028 9077 6277
www.belfastzoo.co.uk

DUNDONALD	Map 1 D5

Dundonald Touring Caravan Park
▶▶▶▶ 81%

tel: 028 9080 9123 & 028 9080 9129 **111 Old Dundonald Road BT16 1XT**
email: dundonaldcaravanpark@lisburncastlereagh.gov.uk
web: www.dundonaldcaravanpark.com
dir: From Belfast city centre follow M3 and A20 to City Airport. Then A20 to Newtownards, follow signs to Dundonald and Ulster Hospital. At hospital turn right at sign for Dundonald International Ice Bowl. Follow to end, turn right, Ice Bowl on left.

A purpose-built site in a quiet corner of Dundonald Leisure Park on the outskirts of Belfast. This peaceful park provides excellent, well-spaced, fully serviced pitches and is ideally located for touring County Down and exploring the capital city of Belfast. In the winter it offers an 'Aire de Service' for motorhomes and caravans with hygiene facilities.

Open: mid March to October (restricted service: November to March – Aire de Service restricted to motorhomes and caravans with own bathroom facilities)
Last departure: noon
Pitches: * 🚐 from £24; 🚍 from £24; ⛺ from £16.50; 22 hardstanding pitches
Facilities: 📷 ☺ ⚒ ⚙ 🍴 🪑 WiFi **Services:** 🔌 🗑
Within 3 miles: 🎣 🏌 🎳 ◎ 🚌 💲
Additional site information: 1.5 acre site. 🐕 Cars can be parked by caravans and tents. Awnings permitted. No commercial vehicles or vans permitted (including any on tow). Dundonald International Ice Bowl, adjacent to the park, offers bowling, indoor play area, Olympic-size ice rink (additional charges apply).

See advert on page 398

PITCHES: 🚐 Caravans 🚍 Motorhomes ⛺ Tents 🏕 Glamping accommodation SERVICES: 🔌 Electric hook-up 🗑 Launderette 🍺 Licensed bar
🔥 Calor Gas 🌿 Campingaz T Toilet fluid 🍴 Café/Restaurant 🍔 Fast Food/Takeaway 🔋 Battery charging 🏴 Motorhome service point
* 2019 prices 🚫 No credit or debit cards 🐕 Dogs permitted 🚫 No dogs

COUNTY FERMANAGH

BELCOO — Map 1 C5

Places to visit

Florence Court, ENNISKILLEN, BT92 1DB, 028 6634 8249
www.nationaltrust.org.uk/florence-court

Premier Park

Rushin House Caravan Park
▶▶▶▶▶ 86%

tel: 028 6638 6519 **Holywell BT93 5DU**
email: enquiries@rushinhouse.com **web:** www.rushinhousecaravanpark.com
dir: *From Enniskillen take A4 west for 13 miles to Belcoo. Right onto B52 towards Garrison for 1 mile. Site signed.*

This park occupies a scenic location overlooking Lough MacNean, close to the picturesque village of Belcoo, and is the product of meticulous planning and execution. There are 24 very generous, fully serviced pitches standing on a terrace overlooking the lough, with additional tenting pitches below; all are accessed via well-kept, wide tarmac roads. Facilities include a lovely, well-equipped play area and a hard surface, fenced five-a-side football pitch. There is a slipway providing boat access to the lough and, of course, fishing; there is an access path to the lake that is suitable for less able visitors to use. The excellent toilet facilities are purpose-built and include family rooms.

Open: mid March to October (November to March - Aire de Service facilities available)
Last arrival: 21.00 **Last departure:** 13.00

Pitches: 🚐 🚙 Å; 38 hardstanding pitches

Leisure: 🏊 🖵 ⚽

Facilities: ⊙ ℙ ✳ ⅙ 🪑 📶

Services: 🔌 🗑 🧺 ⬆ 🛢 🧹

Within 3 miles: 🎣 🛶 🐟 💲

Additional site information: 5 acre site. 🐕 Cars can be parked by caravans. Awnings permitted. Lakeside walk.

IRVINESTOWN — Map 1 C5

Places to visit

Castle Coole, ENNISKILLEN, BT74 6JY, 028 6632 2690
www.nationaltrust.org.uk/castle-coole

Castle Balfour, LISNASKEA, 028 9082 3207
www.discovernorthernireland.com/Castle-Balfour-Lisnaskea-Enniskillen-P2901

Castle Archdale Caravan Park & Camping Site
▶▶▶▶ 85%

tel: 028 6862 1333 **Lisnarick BT94 1PP**
email: info@castlearchdale.com **web:** www.castlearchdale.com
dir: *From Irvinestown take B534 signed Lisnarick. Left onto B82 signed Enniskillen. In approximately 1 mile right by church, site signed.*

This park is located within the grounds of Castle Archdale Country Park on the shores of Lough Erne which boasts stunning scenery, forest walks and also war and wildlife museums. The site is ideal for watersport enthusiasts with its marina and launching facilities. Also on site there's a shop, licensed restaurant, takeaway and play park. There are fully serviced, hardstanding pitches.

LEISURE: 🏊 Indoor swimming pool 🌊 Outdoor swimming pool 🛝 Children's playground 🧒 Kids' club 🎾 Tennis court 🎱 Games room 🖵 Separate TV room 🏌 golf course 🚩 Pitch n putt 🚣 Boats for hire 🚲 Bikes for hire 🎬 Cinema 🎵 Entertainment 🎣 Fishing 🔵 Mini golf 🏄 Watersports 🏋 Gym 🏟 Sports field ♘ Stables
FACILITIES: 🛁 Baths/Shower ⊙ Electric shaver sockets ℙ Hairdryer ✳ Ice Pack Facility 🍼 Baby facilities 🦽 Disabled facilities 💲 Shop on site or within 200yds 🍖 BBQ area 🧺 Picnic area 📶 WiFi

Open: April to October (restricted service: April to June and September to October – shop and bar closed on weekdays) **Last departure:** noon

Pitches: 🚐 from £25; 🚍 from £25; 🏕 from £10; 150 hardstanding pitches

Leisure: ♟ ⚲

Facilities: 🛁 ⊙ ✳ ♿ 🅂 🍴 ⊓ WiFi

Services: 🔌 🗑 ♨ 🍽 🚮 ⛽ ⬆ 🔋 🗝 Ⓣ

Within 3 miles: ↳ ∪ ☇ ✈

Additional site information: 11 acre site. 🐕 Cars can be parked by caravans and tents. Awnings permitted. No open fires, no noise after 23.00. Car hire can be arranged.

COUNTY TYRONE

DUNGANNON   Map 1 C5

Dungannon Park
▶▶▶▶ 87%

tel: 028 8772 8690 & 03000 132132 **Moy Road BT71 6DY**
email: parks@midulstercouncil.org **web:** www.midulstercouncil.org
dir: *M1 junction 15, A29 towards Dungannon, left at 2nd lights.*

Set within the magnificent public Dungannon Park, with a fishing lake, cricket ground and regular concerts during the summer months, this family-friendly caravan park provides excellent fully serviced pitches and a stylish well-equipped amenity block. Another benefit is the attractive coffee shop.

Open: March to October **Last arrival:** 20.00 **Last departure:** noon

Pitches: * 🚐 from £24.50; 🚍 from £24.50; 🏕 from £14.50; 24 hardstanding pitches

Leisure: 🎣 ⚲ ⚽

Facilities: 🛁 ⊙ ⚑ ✳ ♿ 🍴 ⊓ WiFi

Services: 🔌 🗑 🍽

Within 3 miles: ↳ ∪ 🗓 🅂

Additional site information: 4 acre site. 🐕 Dogs must be on leads at all times. Cars can be parked by caravans and tents. Awnings permitted. No noise between 22.00–08.00, no generators, no commercial vehicles, speed limit 10mph, no dish washing in toilet block.

PITCHES: 🚐 Caravans   🚍 Motorhomes   🏕 Tents   ⛺ Glamping accommodation   **SERVICES:** 🔌 Electric hook-up   🗑 Launderette   🍸 Licensed bar
🔋 Calor Gas   🗝 Campingaz   Ⓣ Toilet fluid   🍽 Café/Restaurant   🍟 Fast Food/Takeaway   🔋 Battery charging   ⬆ Motorhome service point
* 2019 prices   🚫 No credit or debit cards   🐕 Dogs permitted   🚫 No dogs

COUNTY MAPS

England

1 Bedfordshire
2 Berkshire
3 Bristol
4 Buckinghamshire
5 Cambridgeshire
6 Greater Manchester
7 Herefordshire
8 Hertfordshire
9 Leicestershire
10 Northamptonshire
11 Nottinghamshire
12 Rutland
13 Staffordshire
14 Warwickshire
15 West Midlands
16 Worcestershire

Scotland

17 City of Glasgow
18 Clackmannanshire
19 East Ayrshire
20 East Dunbartonshire
21 East Renfrewshire
22 Perth & Kinross
23 Renfrewshire
24 South Lanarkshire
25 West Dunbartonshire

Wales

26 Blaenau Gwent
27 Bridgend
28 Caerphilly
29 Denbighshire
30 Flintshire
31 Merthyr Tydfil
32 Monmouthshire
33 Neath Port Talbot
34 Newport
35 Rhondda Cynon Taf
36 Torfaen
37 Vale of Glamorgan
38 Wrexham

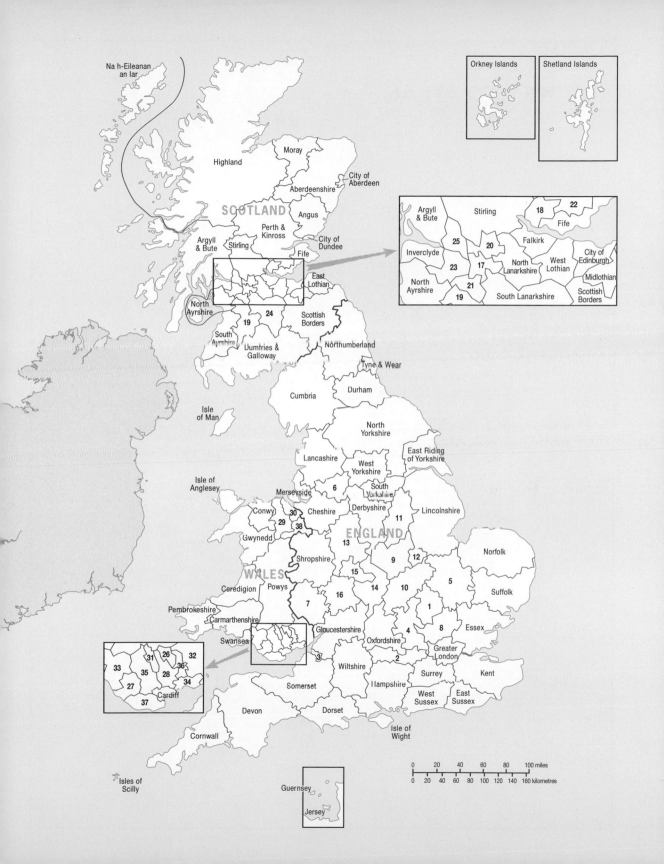

Na h-Eileanan
an Iar

Orkney Islands

Shetland Islands

Highland

Moray

City of
Aberdeen

Aberdeenshire

SCOTLAND

Angus

Perth &
Kinross

City of
Dundee

Argyll
& Bute

Stirling

Fife

| Argyll & Bute | Stirling | 18 | 22 |

| | | Fife | |

| 25 | 20 | Falkirk | |

Inverclyde

| 23 | 17 | North Lanarkshire | West Lothian | City of Edinburgh |

North
Ayrshire

| 21 | | South Lanarkshire | | Midlothian |

19

East
Lothian

North
Ayrshire

19   24

Scottish
Borders

South
Ayrshire

Dumfries &
Galloway

Northumberland

Tyne & Wear

Isle
of Man

Cumbria

Durham

North
Yorkshire

Lancashire

West
Yorkshire

East Riding
of Yorkshire

Isle of
Anglesey

Merseyside

6

South
Yorkshire

Conwy

30

Cheshire

Derbyshire

Lincolnshire

29

38

Gwynedd

11

ENGLAND

13

Shropshire

Norfolk

9   12

Ceredigion

Powys

15

Suffolk

14   10   5

WALES

16

7

1

Pembrokeshire

Carmarthenshire

Gloucestershire

4   8   Essex

Swansea

3

Oxfordshire

Greater
London

| 31 | 26 | 32 |

| 33 | | 36 | |

| | 35 | 28 | 34 |

| 27 | Cardiff | |

37

Wiltshire

2

Surrey

Kent

Somerset

Hampshire

West
Sussex

East
Sussex

Devon

Dorset

Isle of
Wight

Cornwall

Isles of
Scilly

Guernsey

Jersey

0   20   40   60   80   100 miles

0 20 40 60 80 100 120 140 160 kilometres

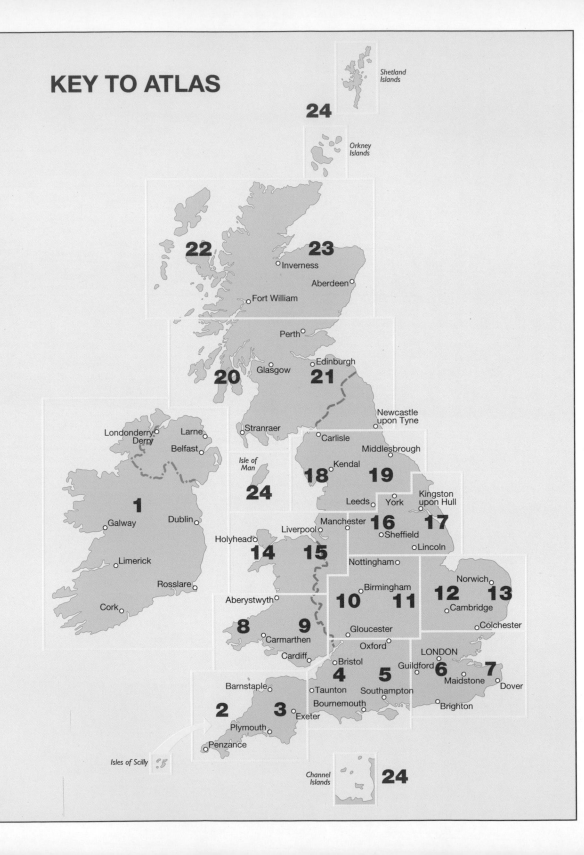

KEY TO ATLAS

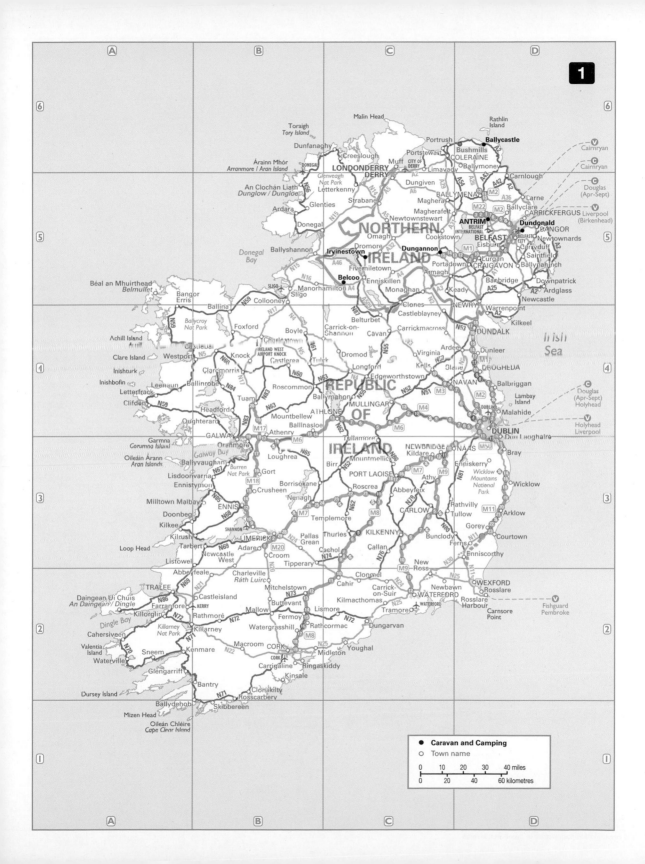

Legend:

- Motorway/toll motorway — M6
- Motorway junction full/restricted. Service area
- Primary route single/dual carriageway — A33
- Other A road single/dual carriageway — A34
- B road — B3400
- Unclassified road
- Vehicle ferry — V
- Fast vehicle ferry or catamaran — C
- ● Polruan — Caravan and Camping
- ● Barmouth — AA Campsite Award Winner
- ○ Oundle — Town/Village name
- National boundary
- **ESSEX** — English county name & boundary
- **CONWY** — Welsh county name & boundary
- **MORAY** — Scottish county name & boundary
- National Park

Lundy

Hartland Point
Hartland

Morwenstow

Kilkhampton

Bude
Bude
Bay
Stratto
Widemouth Bay
Bridgeru
Week
St Mary

Crackington
Haven

Boscastle
A30

Tintagel

Delabole
Camelford
La

Port Isaac
Pendoggett
Bolventor
BODMIN MOOR
A30

Polzeath

Harlyn
Rock
St Tudy
St Merryn
Padstow
Blisland

Porthcothan
A389
Wadebridge

Mawgan
Porth
Rumford
St Mawgan
C O R N W A L L
St Cleer

Watergate Bay
CORNWALL NEWQUAY
Ruthernbridge
Bodmin
Dobwalls

St Columb Major
Lanivet
A38
Liskeard

Newquay
White Cross
Roche
Bugle
St Keyne

West Pentire
A392
A391
Luxulyan
Lostwithiel

Holywell Bay
Cubert
Indian Queens
Summercourt
St Blazey Gate
St Blazey
Pelynt

Rose
Rejerrah
St Austell
Fowey
Loo

Perranporth
Goonhavern
Carlyon Bay
Polruan
Polperro

St Agnes
A30
Ladock
St Stephen
A390
A3061

Porthtowan
A39
Grampound
Pentewan

Portreath
Blackwater
Tregony
Mevagissey

St Ives Bay
Chacewater
Truro
Gorran
Gorran Haven

Zennor
Gwithian
St Day
Carnon Downs
Portloe

St Ives
Redruth
A393
Portscatho

Lelant
Camborne
St Just-in-Roseland
St Mawes

Carnhell Green
A30
Penryn
Falmouth

Hayle
Leedstown
A394

St Just
Penzance
Ashton
Helston
Constantine
Mawnan Smith

Land's End
Marazion
Rosudgeon
Gweek
Manaccan

Newlyn
Praa Sands
Porthleven
St Keverne

Sennen
Mousehole
Mount's Bay

Porthcurno
Treen

Mullion
Coverack

Kennack Sands
Cadgwith

Lizard
Lizard Point

Isles of Scilly inset:

Bryher
St Martin's
Higher Town
New Grimsby
Tresco
ISLES OF SCILLY
Hugh Town
St Mary's
Middle Town
Old Town
ISLES OF SCILLY (ST MARY'S)
St Agnes
SV

SW

For continuation pages refer to numbered arrows

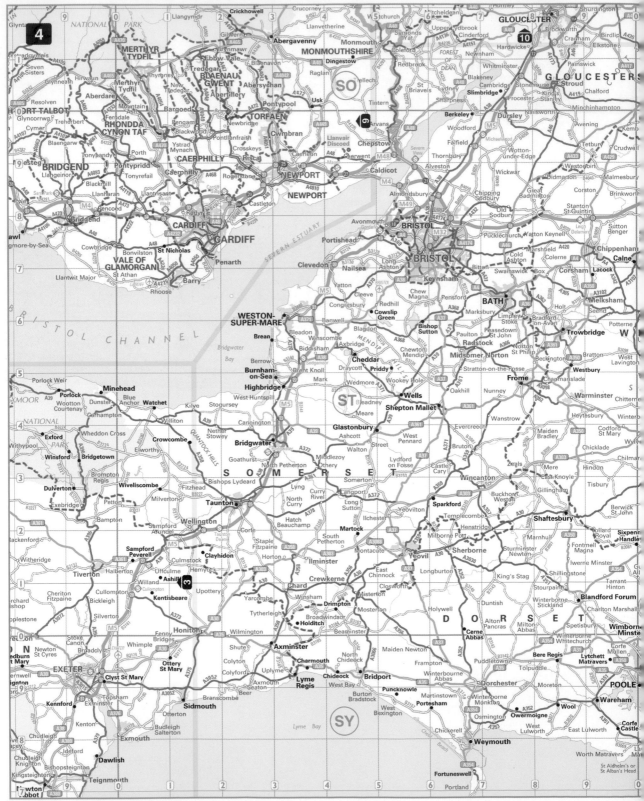

For continuation pages refer to numbered arrows

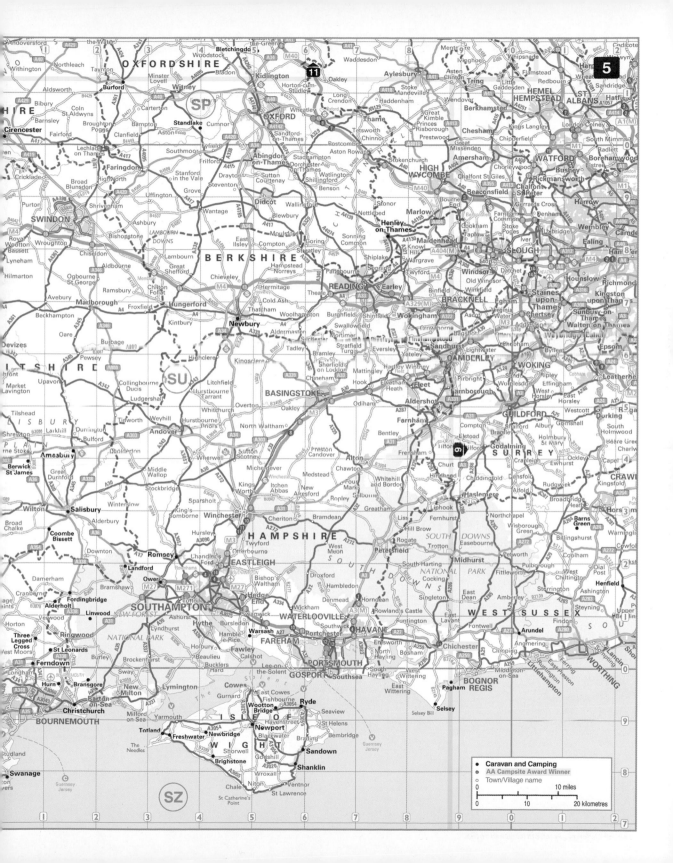

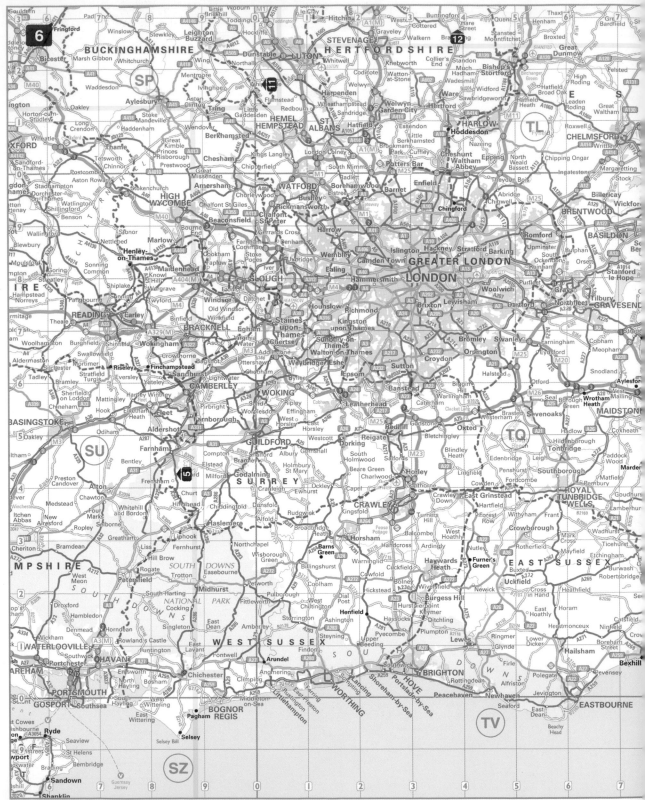

For continuation pages refer to numbered arrows

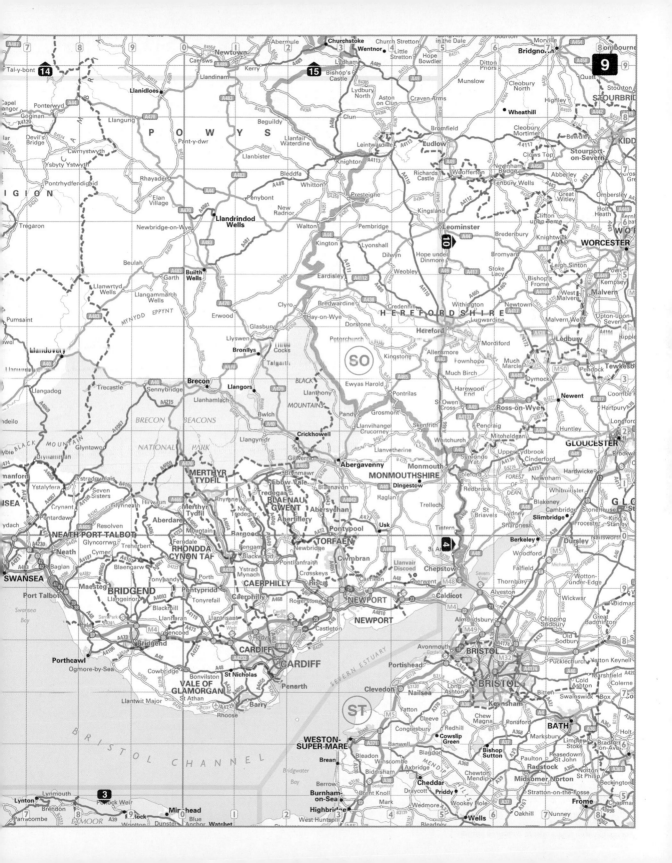

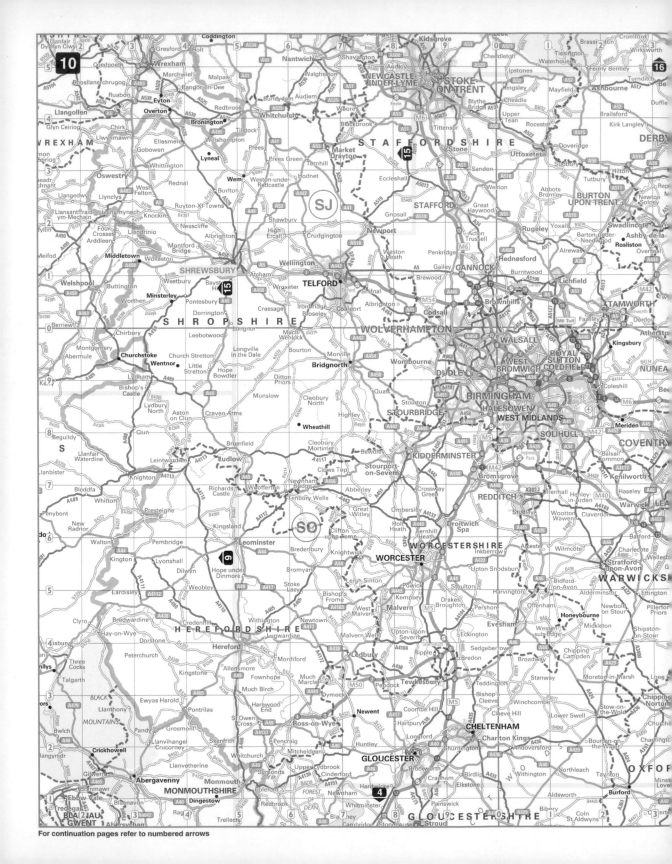

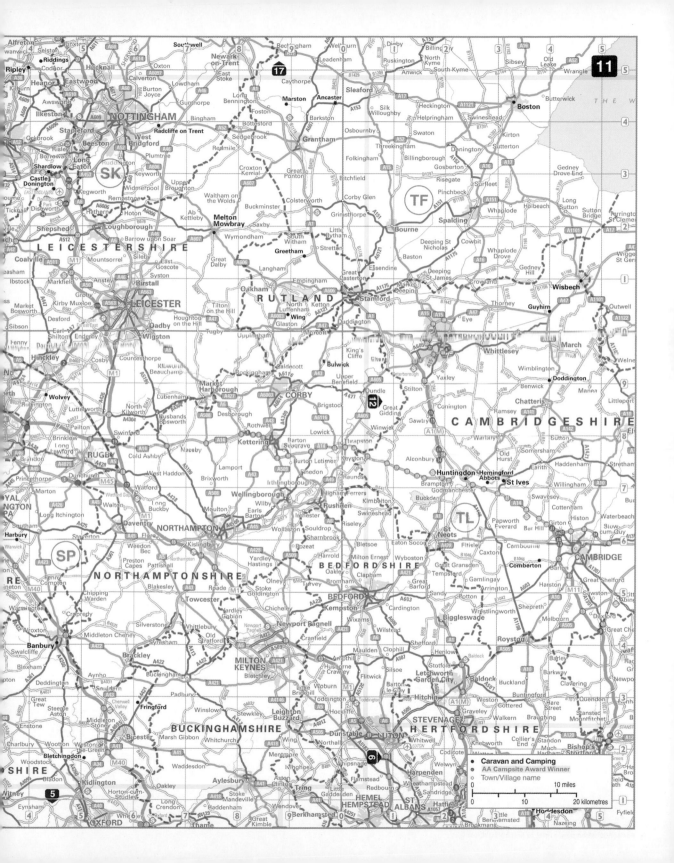

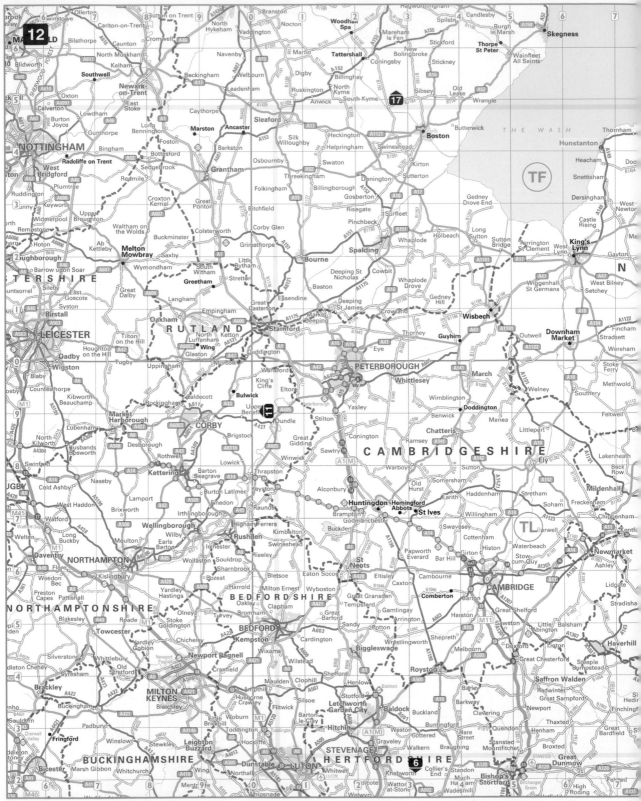

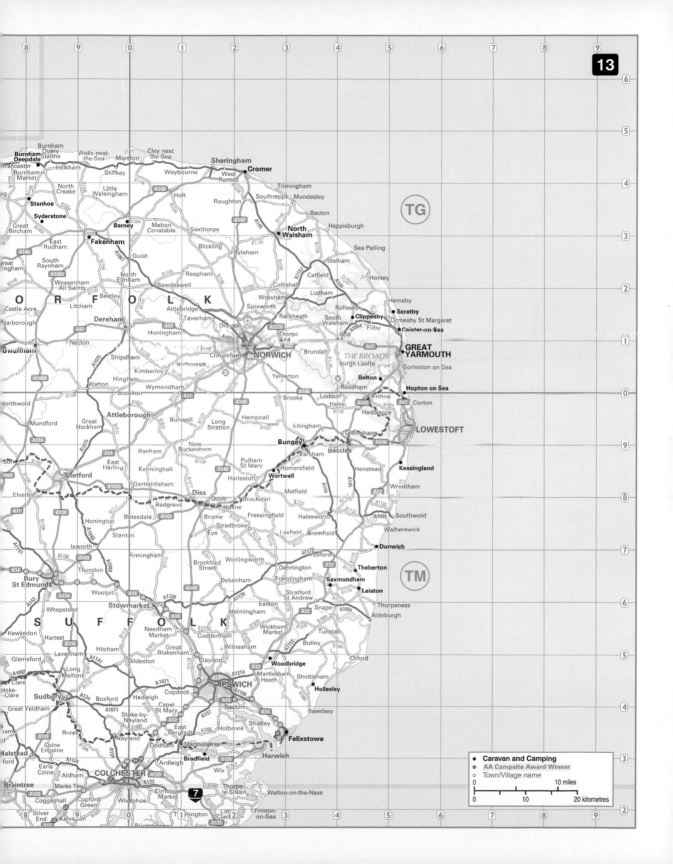

14

IRISH

SEA

Dublin

Dublin

Cemaes
Amlwch
Dulas
ISLE OF
ANGLESEY
Rhôs Lligwy
Llanerchymedd
Marian-Glas
Red Wharf
Benllech Bay
Holyhead
Llanfachraeth
Llangoed
Trearddur Bay
Pentraeth
Holy
Island
Rhosneigr
Llangefni
Beaumaris
Menai
Bridge
Bangor
Llanfairfechan
Aberffraw
Llanfair
P.G.
Y Felinheli
Llanllechid
Dwyran
Bethesda
Newborough
Caernarfon
Llanrug
Bontnewydd
Llanberis
Llanwnda
Betws
Dinas Dinlle
Garmon
Llandwrog
Penygroes
Rhyd Ddu
Clynnog-fawr

Llandudno
Rhôs-
on-Sea
Deganwy
Colwyn Bay
Llanddulas
Abergele
Conwy
Penmaenmawr
Llansanffraid
Glan Conwy
Betws-yn-Rhos
Tal-y-Cafn
Llanfairfe...
Llanfair
Talhaiarn
Llansannan
Tal-y-Bont
Llangernyw
Trefriw
Llanrwst
Bylchau
CONWY
Capel Curig
Betws-y-Coed
Dolwyddelan
Penmachno
Pentrefoelas
Cerrigydrudion
Y Mae...

Llanaelhaearn
PENINSULA
Morfa Nefyn
Nefyn
Bodfuan
Llanystumdwy
Sarn
Pwllheli
Criccieth
Borth-y-Gest
Aberdaron
Y Rhiw
Llanbedrog
Abersoch
Bardsey
Island

Prenteg
Tremadog
Porthmadog
Maentwrog
Penrhyndeudraeth
Penrhyn
Talsarnau
Trawsfynydd
Harlech
Llanbedr
Ganllwyd
Dyffryn Ardudwy
Tal-y-bont
Barmouth
Fairbourne
Llwyngwril
Bryncrug
Tywyn
Pennal
Aberdyfi
Borth
Tal-y-bont
Llandre
Aberystwyth
Capel
Bangor

Beddgelert
Blaenau Ffestiniog
Ffestiniog

SNOWDONIA
NATIONAL
GWYNEDD
PARK
Llanuwchllyn
Bala
Dolgellau
Dinas-Mawddwy
Mallwyd
Corris
Cemmaes
Road
Machynlleth
Carno
Ponterwyd
Llanidloes
Llangadfa...
Llanbrynmair
Llanfyllin

(SH)
(SN)

9

• Caravan and Camping
• AA Campsite Award Winner
○ Town/Village name

0   10 miles
0   10   20 kilometres

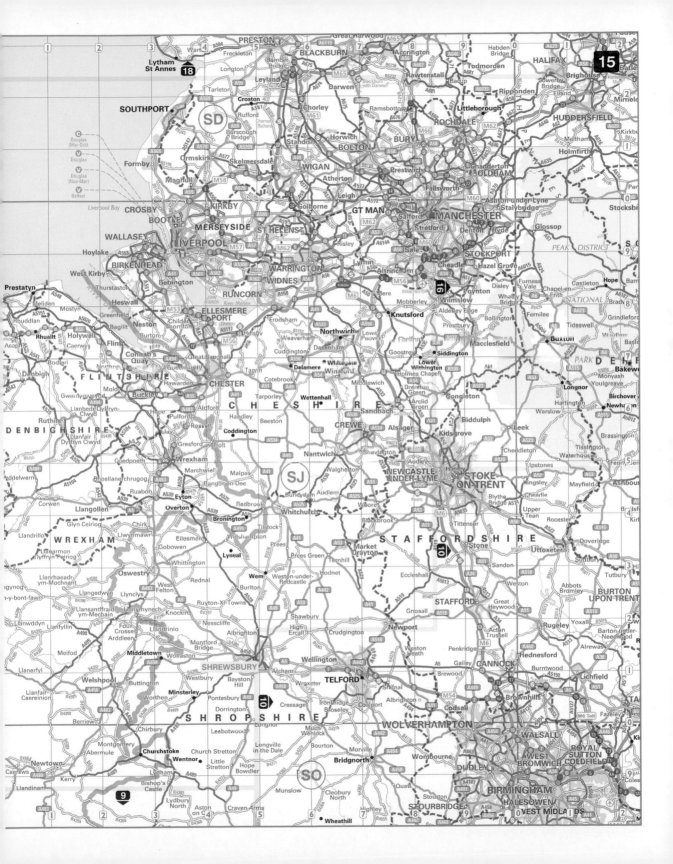

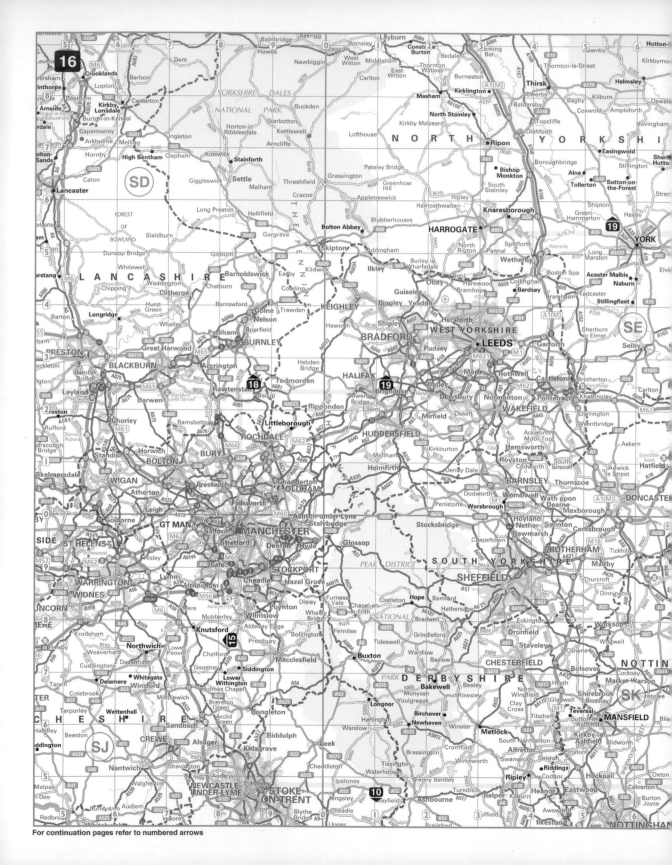

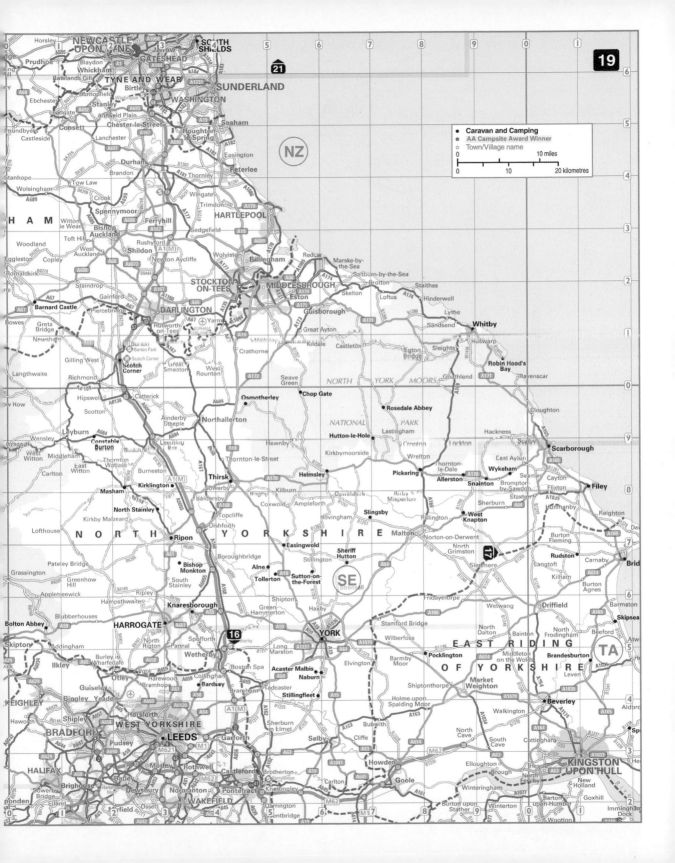

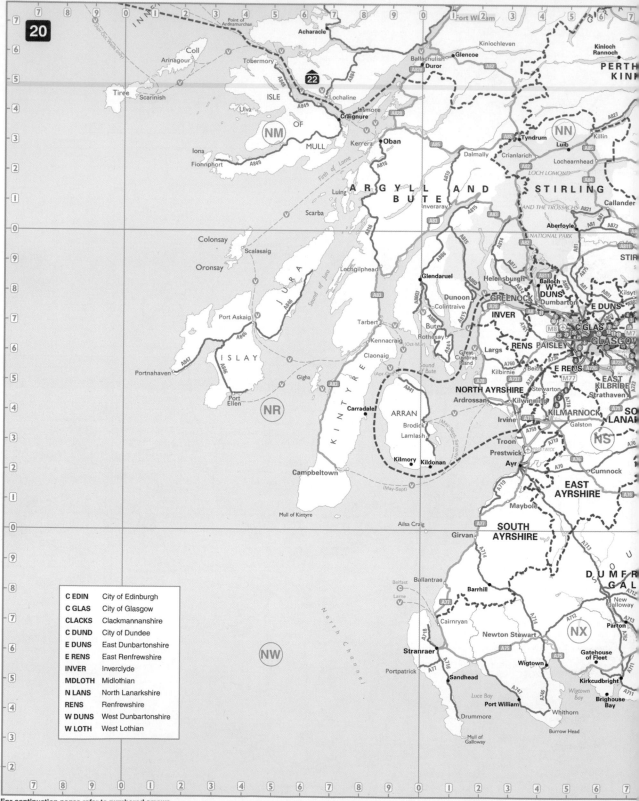

22

NM

NN

NR

NS

NW

NX

PERTH
KIN

ARGYLL AND
BUTE

STIRLING

ISLE
OF
MULL

JURA

ISLAY

KINTYRE

ARRAN

NORTH AYRSHIRE

EAST
KILBRIDE

SO
LANA

EAST
AYRSHIRE

SOUTH
AYRSHIRE

DUMFR
GAL

C GLAS
RENS PAISLEY
GLASGO
GREENOCK
INVER
W
DUNS
Dumbarton
E DUNS
E RENS

Fort Wi   am
Kinlochleven
Glencoe
Kinloch
Rannoch
Ballachulish
Duror
Acharacle
Tobermory
Coll
Arinagour
Tiree
Scarinish
Lochaline
Inshore
Craignure
Kerrera
Oban
Iona
Fionnphort
Ulva
Luing
Scarba
Colonsay
Scalasaig
Oronsay
Lochgilphead
Glendaruel
Dunoon
Colintraive
Bute
Rothesay
Tarbert
Kennacraig
Claonaig
Gigha
Port Askaig
Portnahaven
Port
Ellen
Carradale
Brodick
Lamlash
Kilmory
Kildonan
Campbeltown
Mull of Kintyre
Ailsa Craig
Girvan
Point of
Ardnamurchan
Kinloch
Rannoch
Killin
Tyndrum
Luib
Lochearnhead
Dalmally
Crianlarich
Callander
Aberfoyle
Balloch
Kilsyt
Helensburgh
Largs
Kilbirnie
Beith
Stewarton
Kilwinning
Ardrossan
Irvine
KILMARNOCK
Galston
Troon
Prestwick
Ayr
Cumnock
Maybole
Belfast
Larne
Ballantrae
Barrhill
Cairnryan
Newton Stewart
Stranraer
Portpatrick
Sandhead
Port William
Drummore
Mull of
Galloway
Burrow Head
Whithorn
Wigtown
Gatehouse
of Fleet
Kirkcudbright
Brighouse
Bay
Parton
New
Galloway
Inveraray
Strathaven
Hamilton
Kilmarnock

LOCH LOMOND
AND THE TROSSACHS
NATIONAL PARK

Firth of Lorne
Sound of Jura
Sound of Bute
North Channel
Luce Bay
Wigtown
Bay

C EDIN	City of Edinburgh
C GLAS	City of Glasgow
CLACKS	Clackmannanshire
C DUND	City of Dundee
E DUNS	East Dunbartonshire
E RENS	East Renfrewshire
INVER	Inverclyde
MDLOTH	Midlothian
N LANS	North Lanarkshire
RENS	Renfrewshire
W DUNS	West Dunbartonshire
W LOTH	West Lothian

Cape Wrath

Rudha Rhobhanais
(Butt of Lewis)
Port Nis
(Port of Ness)

NA

Great
Bernera

Cellar
Head

A857

ISLE

A858

LEWIS

Carlabhagh
(Carloway)

A857

NB

Scourie

A894

OF

Steornabhagh
(Stornoway)

Tiumpan
Head

STORNOWAY

A837

Lochinver

Inchnadamph

A835

NA H–EILEANAN
AN IAR

A859

A866

A859

A855

A859

Scarp

THE MINCH

Taransay

A831

Lochinver

Taransay

A859

Tairbeart
(Tarbert)

Scalpay

Granord
Bay

Laide

Ullapool

HARRIS

A832

A835

A859

Pabbay

THE LITTLE MINCH

Gairloch

Boreray

Berneray

A832

Uig

A855

Kinlochewe

A832

NORTH UIST

A865

Loch nam Madadh
(Lochmaddy)

NG

Achnasheen

A832

A867

A865

Ronay

Benbecula

Dunvegan

Edinbane

A850

Portree

A896

A890

Cannich

NF

Wiay

ISLE

A87

Raasay

A890

SOUTH
UIST

A865

OF

A863

Drynoch

Scalpay

Kyle of
Lochalsh

A87

NORTH

WEST

HIGHLANDS

SKYE

(Apr-Oct)

Loch Baghasdail
(Lochboisdale)

A865

Soay

A87

Eriskay

Canna

Ardvasar

A851

A887

A87

A82

BARRA

A888

Rùm

Mallaig

Invergarry

Bàgh a Chaisteil
(Castlebay)

Eigg

Arisaig

A830

Sandray

A861

Spean
Bridge

A82

Mingulay

Muck

A830

A861

INNER HEBRIDES

Point of
Ardnamurchan

NM

Acharacle

Fort William

NL

Coll

Arinagour

Tobermory

A884

A861

Kinlochleven

Ballachulish

Glencoe

A82

Duror

A828

Tiree

Scarinish

20

ISLE

A848

Lochaline

Lismore

A828

Ulva

OF

A849

Craignure

Kerrera

Oban

A85

Iona

MULL

Tyn

Fionnphort

A849

Lorne

A816

Dalmally

A85

Crianlarich

For continuation pages refer to numbered arrows

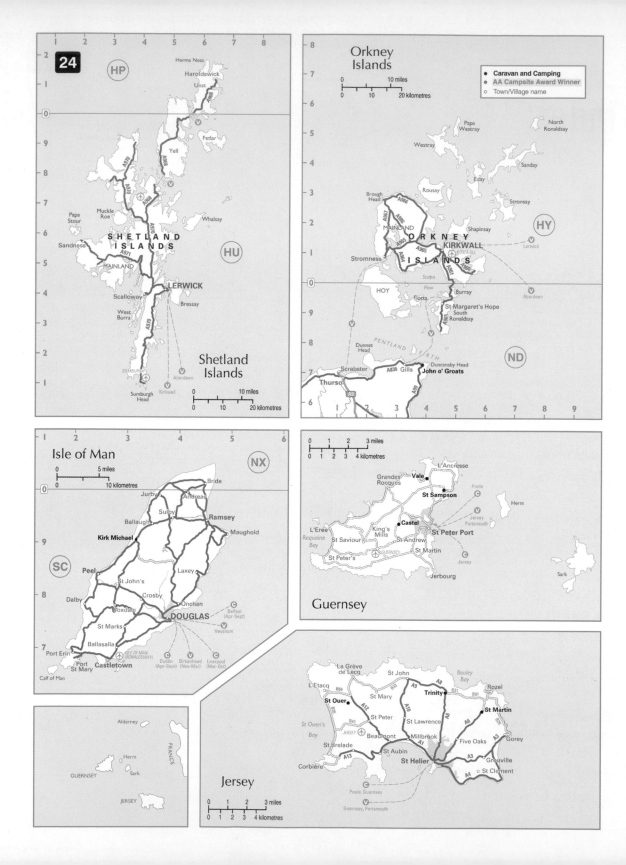

Index

A

B

C

D

E

G

I

J

K

M

R

S

T

Readers' Report Form

Please send this form to:
The Editor, AA Caravan & Camping Guide,
AA Lifestyle Guides,
AA Publishing,
Fanum House,
Basingstoke RG21 4EA

email: lifestyleguides@theAA.com

Please use this form to tell us about any site that you have visited, whether it is in the guide or not currently listed. Feedback from readers helps us to keep our guide accurate and up to date. However, if you have a complaint during your visit, we recommend that you discuss the matter with the management there and then, so that they have a chance to put things right.

Please note that the AA does not undertake to arbitrate between you and the establishment, or to obtain compensation or engage in protracted correspondence.

The information you supply below may form personal data. We only use the personal data provided in this form to acknowledge and answer your comments.

Date _____

Your name (block capitals) _____

Your address (block capitals) _____

_____

_____

Postcode _____

E-mail address _____

Name of site/park _____

Location _____

Comments

_____

_____

_____

_____

_____

_____

(please attach a separate sheet if necessary)   PTO

Readers' Report Form *continued*

Have you bought this guide before? ☐ YES ☐ NO

How often do you visit a caravan park or camp site? (tick one choice)
Once a year ☐   Twice a year ☐   Three times a year ☐
More than three times a year ☐

How long do you generally stay at a park or site? (tick one choice)
One night ☐   Up to a week ☐   1 week ☐
2 weeks ☐   Over 2 weeks ☐

Do you have a: (tick all that apply)
Tent ☐   Caravan ☐   Motorhome ☐

Please answer these questions to help us make improvements to the guide:
Which of these factors are the most important when choosing a site? (tick one choice)
Location ☐   Toilet/washing facilities ☐   Personal Recommendation ☐
Leisure facilities ☐
Other (please state)
_____

Do you read the editorial features in the guide? ☐ YES ☐ NO

Do you use the location atlas? ☐ YES ☐ NO

What elements of the guide do you find most useful when choosing a site/park? (tick all that apply)
Descriptions ☐   Photos ☐   Advertisements ☐

Is there any other information you would like to see added to this guide?

_____
_____
_____
_____
_____
_____
_____

Readers' Report Form

Please send this form to:
The Editor, AA Caravan & Camping Guide,
AA Lifestyle Guides,
AA Publishing,
Fanum House,
Basingstoke RG21 4EA

email: lifestyleguides@theAA.com

Please use this form to tell us about any site that you have visited, whether it is in the guide or not currently listed. Feedback from readers helps us to keep our guide accurate and up to date. However, if you have a complaint during your visit, we recommend that you discuss the matter with the management there and then, so that they have a chance to put things right

Please note that the AA does not undertake to arbitrate between you and the establishment, or to obtain compensation or engage in protracted correspondence.

The information you supply below may form personal data. We only use the personal data provided in this form to acknowledge and answer your comments.

Date

Your name (block capitals)

Your address (block capitals)

Postcode

E-mail address

Name of site/park

Location

Comments

(please attach a separate sheet if necessary)   PTO

Readers' Report Form *continued*

Have you bought this guide before? ☐ YES ☐ NO

How often do you visit a caravan park or camp site? (tick one choice)
Once a year ☐   Twice a year ☐   Three times a year ☐
More than three times a year ☐

How long do you generally stay at a park or site? (tick one choice)
One night ☐   Up to a week ☐   1 week ☐
2 weeks ☐   Over 2 weeks ☐

Do you have a: (tick all that apply)
Tent ☐   Caravan ☐   Motorhome ☐

Please answer these questions to help us make improvements to the guide:
Which of these factors are the most important when choosing a site? (tick one choice)
Location ☐   Toilet/washing facilities ☐   Personal Recommendation ☐
Leisure facilities ☐
Other (please state)
_____

Do you read the editorial features in the guide? ☐ YES ☐ NO

Do you use the location atlas? ☐ YES ☐ NO

What elements of the guide do you find most useful when choosing a site/park? (tick all that apply)
Descriptions ☐   Photos ☐   Advertisements ☐

Is there any other information you would like to see added to this guide?
_____
_____
_____
_____
_____
_____
_____

Readers' Report Form

Please send this form to:
The Editor, AA Caravan & Camping Guide,
AA Lifestyle Guides,
AA Publishing,
Fanum House,
Basingstoke RG21 4EA

email: lifestyleguides@theAA.com

Please use this form to tell us about any site that you have visited, whether it is in the guide or not currently listed. Feedback from readers helps us to keep our guide accurate and up to date. However, if you have a complaint during your visit, we recommend that you discuss the matter with the management there and then, so that they have a chance to put things right.

Please note that the AA does not undertake to arbitrate between you and the establishment, or to obtain compensation or engage in protracted correspondence.

The information you supply below may form personal data. We only use the personal data provided in this form to acknowledge and answer your comments.

Date ....

Your name (block capitals) ....

Your address (block capitals) ....

....

....

....   Postcode ....

E-mail address ....

Name of site/park ....

Location ....

Comments

....

....

....

....

....

....

(please attach a separate sheet if necessary)   PTO

Readers' Report Form *continued*

Have you bought this guide before? ☐ YES ☐ NO

How often do you visit a caravan park or camp site? (tick one choice)
Once a year ☐   Twice a year ☐   Three times a year ☐
More than three times a year ☐

How long do you generally stay at a park or site? (tick one choice)
One night ☐   Up to a week ☐   1 week ☐
2 weeks ☐   Over 2 weeks ☐

Do you have a: (tick all that apply)
Tent ☐   Caravan ☐   Motorhome ☐

Please answer these questions to help us make improvements to the guide:
Which of these factors are the most important when choosing a site? (tick one choice)
Location ☐   Toilet/washing facilities ☐   Personal Recommendation ☐
Leisure facilities ☐
Other (please state)
_____
_____

Do you read the editorial features in the guide? ☐ YES ☐ NO

Do you use the location atlas?   ☐ YES ☐ NO

What elements of the guide do you find most useful when choosing a site/park? (tick all that apply)
Descriptions ☐   Photos ☐   Advertisements ☐

Is there any other information you would like to see added to this guide?

_____
_____
_____
_____
_____
_____
_____
_____

Image credits:
The Automobile Association wishes to thank the following photographers and organisations for their assistance in the preparation of this book.

Abbreviations for the picture credits are as follows – (t) top; (b) bottom; (l) left; (r) right; (c) centre; (AA) AA World Travel Library.

3 Courtesy of Harford Bridge Holiday Park; 4 courtesy of Trevedra Farm Caravan & Camping Site; 5b courtesy of The Old Oaks Touring Park; 8 Jim Holden/Alamy Stock Photo; 14–19 (background) AA/A Burton; 14l courtesy of Concierge Camping; 14r courtesy of Glen Nevis Caravan & Camping Park; 15l courtesy of Trawsdir Touring Caravans & Camping Park; 15r courtesy of Trethem Mill Touring Park; 16l courtesy of Broadhembury Caravan & Camping Park; 16r courtesy of Oxon Hall Touring Park; 17l courtesy of Old Hall Caravan Park; 17r courtesy of Ord House Country Park; 18l courtesy of Searles Leisure Resort; 18r courtesy of Penhein Glamping; 19l courtesy of Kettlewell Camping; 19r courtesy of Summer Valley Touring Park; 20–26 site images courtesy of The Old Oaks Touring Park; 28 AA/J Tims; 29 courtesy of Tristram Caravan & Camping Park; 31 AA/J Tims; 33 courtesy of Treloy Touring Park; 35 courtesy of Bron Derw Touring Caravan Park; 37 courtesy of River Valley Holiday Park; 42 Vincent Lowe/Alamy Stock; 47 courtesy of Woodhall Country Park; 50–51 AA/J Tims; 59 Andrew Kearton/Alamy Stock Photo; 60 AA/A Burton; 81 AA/A Burton; 95 AA/J Tims; 112 AA/S Day; 123 AA/J Tims; 131 AA/J Tims; 132 AA/A Burton; 162 AA/ G Edwardes; 164 AA/A Newey; 199 AA/M/Moody; 200 AA/A Newey; 229l AA/J Tims; 229r AA/S Day; 230 AA/A Baker; 253 AA/M Morris; 254 AA/A Burton; 272 AA/T Mackie; 279 AA/T Mackie; 280 AA/L Noble; 294 AA/J Tims; 324 AA/W Voysey; 317 AA/J Tims; 328-329 AA/J Henderson; 331 AA/D Henderson; 361 AA/J Henderson; 362-363 AA/M Bauer; 364 AA/C Warren; 383 AA/I Tims; 394–395 AA/ C Hill; 399 AA/C Hill; 463 AA/J Tims.

Every effort has been made to trace the copyright holders, and we apologise in advance for any unintentional omissions or errors. We would be pleased to apply any corrections in a following edition of this publication.

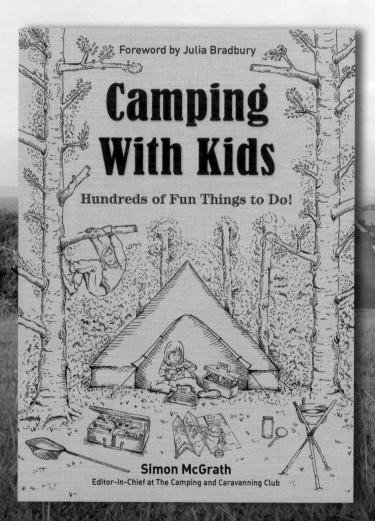